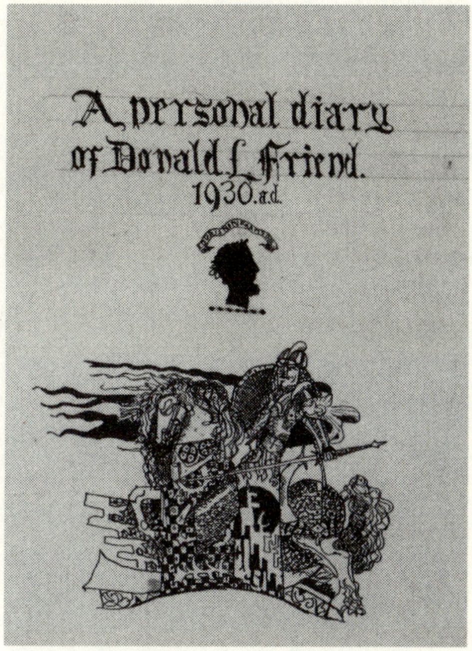
A personal diary
of Donald L Friend.
1930.a.d.

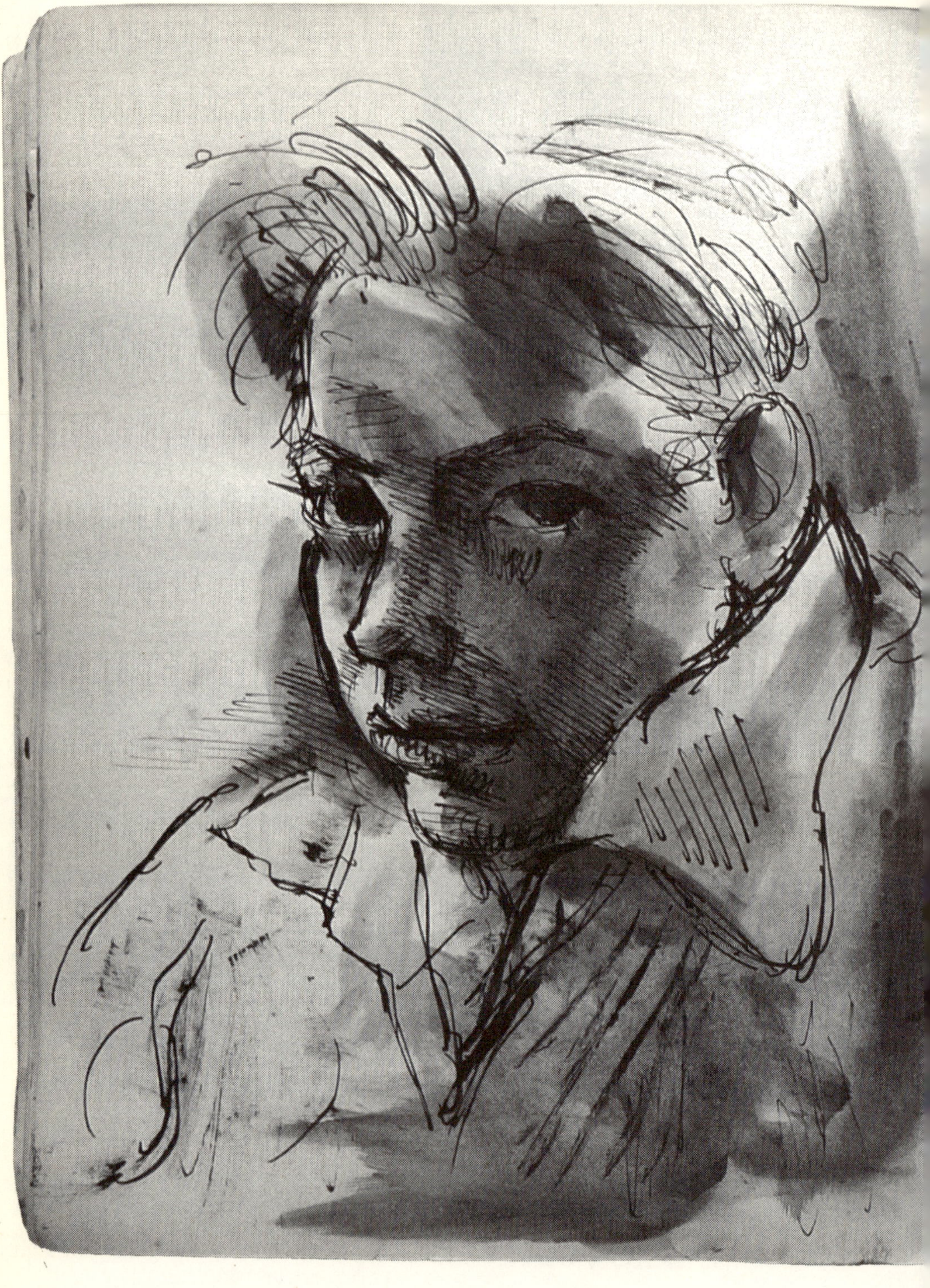

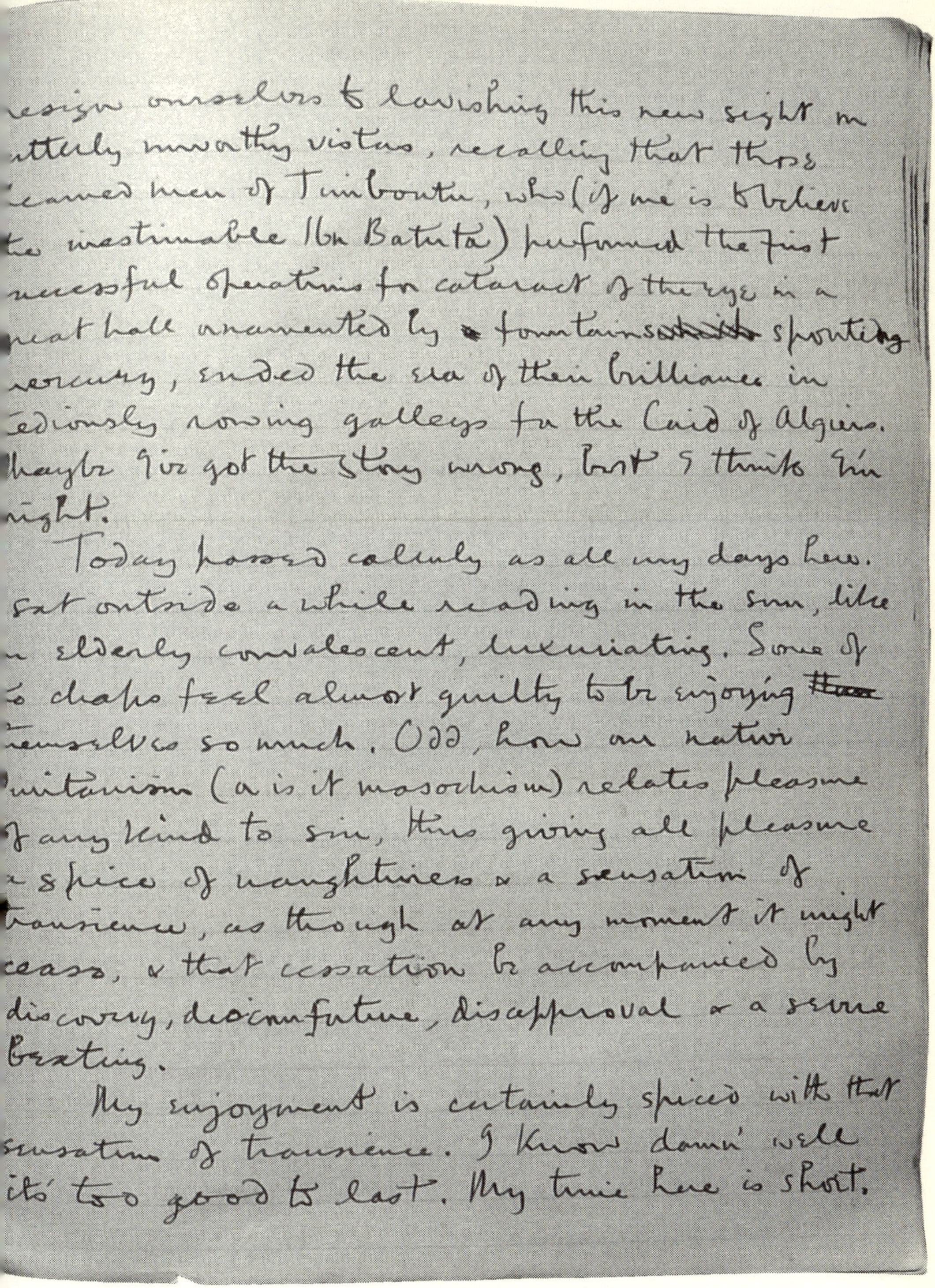

resign ourselves to lavishing this new sight on utterly unworthy vistas, recalling that those learned men of Timbuctu, who (if one is to believe the inestimable Ibn Batuta) performed the first successful operations for cataract of the eye in a great hall ornamented by fountains spouting mercury, ended the era of their brilliance in tediously rowing galleys for the Caid of Algiers. Maybe I've got the story wrong, but I think I'm right.

Today passed calmly as all my days here. I sat outside a while reading in the sun, like an elderly convalescent, luxuriating. Some of the chaps feel almost guilty to be enjoying themselves so much. Odd, how our native puritanism (or is it masochism) relates pleasure of any kind to sin, thus giving all pleasure a spice of naughtiness & a sensation of transience, as though at any moment it might cease, & that cessation be accompanied by discovery, discomfiture, disapproval & a severe beating.

My enjoyment is certainly spiced with that sensation of transience. I know damn well it's too good to last. My time here is short.

1. *Self-portrait (1943).*

Donald Friend (1915–1989) is one of Australia's most significant artists. Many of his works are held in the collections of the National Gallery of Australia, Canberra, and the Art Gallery of New South Wales, and four volumes of his diaries have been published by the National Library of Australia.

Ian Britain is a former editor of *Meanjin*, the author of *Once an Australian* and the co-editor, with Brenda Niall, of *The Oxford Book of Australian Schooldays*. He lives in Melbourne and is writing Donald Friend's biography.

THE DONALD FRIEND DIARIES

Chronicles & confessions of an Australian artist

EDITED BY IAN BRITAIN

FOREWORD BY BARRY HUMPHRIES

TEXT PUBLISHING MELBOURNE AUSTRALIA

Text Publishing acknowledges the support of the National Library of Australia and the Trustees of the Trusts of the Will of the late Donald Friend

The paper used in this book is manufactured only
from wood grown in sustainable regrowth forests.

The Text Publishing Company
Swann House
22 William Street
Melbourne Victoria 3000
Australia
textpublishing.com.au

This edition first published by The Text Publishing Company, 2010

Cover and text design by W.H. Chong
Typeset in Goudy Old Style by J&M Typesetting
Printed in Australia by Griffin Press

National Library of Australia
Cataloguing-in-Publication entry:
Friend, Donald, 1915-1989.
The Donald Friend diaries : chronicles & confessions of an Australian artist / Donald Friend ; edited by Ian Britain.
ISBN 9781921656705
Friend, Donald, 1915-1989--Biography. Artists--Australia--Biography.
Britain, Ian, 1948-
709.2

This project has been assisted by the Australian Government through the Australia Council for the Arts, its arts funding and advisory body.

To those who were in at the chase, USA, 2009:

Philip in Boston and on the road

Bob in New York and Woodstock

Claire and Nick at Harvard

David and Bob in Philadelphia

CONTENTS

FOREWORD

Not seldom, draughtsmen make vivid writers. It is something about their ability to transmit ideas, impressions and observations directly from the eye to the pen. The diaries of a great draughtsman like Augustus John testify to this, but there are many others, from da Vinci to Delacroix to van Gogh. I first came across Donald Friend's work when I was a member of the Argonauts Club, the children's radio program on the ABC. I won a prize which happened to be the Ure Smith edition of *Present Day Art in Australia*, in which some of Friend's drawings and paintings were reproduced. They were vivid and original, if a little too genitocentric for my young and puritanical tastes. Much later I got to know the artist through our mutual friend Russell Drysdale and I even paid him a visit when he was living in some style on the island of Bali.

This was a time when Bali still retained some of its pre-war magic, which exists to this day in the remoter regions, and long before it was invaded by the worst type of Australians. Donald's house, in which he painted and wrote surrounded by an army of adoring houseboys, was on the beach, and Donald was sorely vexed by tourists who kept trooping through the gate and peeking through his windows. 'It's terrible!' he complained. 'They just ignore the sign I put on the gate.' 'Show me the sign,' I said, and he led me down to the low fence that separated his property from the intruding world. There was indeed a large sign on the gate, which read NO ADMISSION. 'I think,' I ventured cautiously, 'that the public just think they can enter your estate without charge. It might be better if the sign said NO ADMITTANCE.' He pondered this for a minute and we laughed.

He resembled a mischievous satyr by Norman Lindsay (another good writer) and was very happy in his idyllic island setting, but ill health finally brought him back to Australia, where he had fallen out of fashion and his benevolent form of paedophilia was less favourably regarded by the authorities.

Robert Hughes had excoriated Friend and some of his contemporaries as members of what he called 'the Australian Charm School', and the new taste for abstract expressionism had made Donald a back number. He became difficult, alcoholic and worst of all poor, but helped by a few devoted friends like Drysdale's daughter Lynne,

Margaret Olley and Elizabeth Summons he lived on, wretchedly, in a motel at Bondi.

Subsequently his voluminous writings have been published and his diaries—witty, learned and scabrous—are among the most evocative and amusing writings in all of Australian literature. Hitherto they have only been available in an *edition deluxe*, and this publisher is to be thanked for giving us a popular edition of the art and speculations of a brilliant and unique man.

Barry Humphries
June 2010

THE DONALD FRIEND DIARIES

NOTE ON THE EDITION

Donald Friend (1915–89) is known principally as an Australian landscape and figurative artist but he also wrote and talked unceasingly about art, and about his life and the world around him. These pronouncements are to be found in their richest concentration in the near-to-fifty volumes of diaries and notebooks that he kept fairly regularly over sixty years, from age thirteen until near his death. The only substantial gaps in the record are his childhood years, up to the late 1920s; the period 1932–37, for part of which he claimed to have kept a diary (the so-called 'Amatory Curiosa') but then to have lost it; and the years 1940–41, when he was resettling in Australia after spending four years abroad. Some of these gaps are filled in by retrospective observations in his diaries on the periods concerned, by letters he wrote at the time and by reminiscences in interviews he gave in later life. This edition of his autobiographical records represents a selection from the full range of sources, synthesised into a seamless narrative.

It is not a scholarly edition, like the magisterial four-volume set of Friend's diaries published by the National Library of Australia between 2001 and 2006, edited by Anne Gray (volume 1) and Paul Hetherington (volumes 2–4). It is designed to be read for pleasure and stimulation, in the hope that readers will graduate to the larger edition and may even be inspired to seek out the original manuscript, printed or audio sources in various public and private collections around Australia. A page-by-page guide to these sources, as deployed here, is available on a CD from Text Publishing.

My brief, from Text, was to make an abridgement of the four-volume edition of the diaries that would draw on its text and illustrations, and inherit its compilers' apparatus of notes, glossaries and acknowledgements to those consulted in the process of its publication. But from the start I was also given a free hand to embellish and adapt that edition in various ways, so as to make mine a distinctive, if not entirely new, publication. This process involved numerous additions (indicated in the key to sources), as well as much compression, conflation and cutting.

Together with extracts from letters and interviews covering those periods that the diaries don't record, I have reproduced some material from the manuscript diaries that previous editors chose not to include.

I have also introduced material that was buried or lost for many years in Australian and American collections but which my recent researches have managed to uncover. These include a notebook from Friend's Nigerian years that is held by the Mitchell Library, Sydney, and two volumes of his wartime diaries (for August–September 1943 and January 1944) that were purchased by an American collector and have only just been returned to Australia to join their companion volumes at the National Library. The illustrations are mainly reproduced from those in the National Library's edition, but I have supplemented these occasionally with hitherto-unpublished images from the manuscript diaries or drawings in public and private collections. Full citations are in the List of Illustrations at the end of the book.

The note numbers in the text refer to the endnotes for each corresponding year of Friend's diary. The endnotes are grouped under the relevant decade at the end of each chapter. They contain brief information about individuals, institutions, places, terms and titles referred to in the text, but they are provided for the first reference only in each instance. Readers seeking guidance on subsequent references may do so by locating the initial reference, and its corresponding endnote, through the index. Abbreviations used in the endnotes are listed below. I have added many new entries and details to the notes provided in the National Library's edition.

There are various other innovations in the present volume. In accord with its 'chronicle' format, I have rearranged sections of some of the text as it appears in the original or already published versions, and I have also re-dated many entries and inserted locations. These locations are italicised in the text, and they are specified not in every entry but only when they change. The date given refers to the day or week or month in which the activities described took place, rather than to when Friend got around to recording them. The idea is to show Friend's whereabouts, and to chart his movements, as precisely as his (and occasionally other) evidence allows. Although in most cases these dates will be very close—if not identical—to those in the original manuscript, in a few instances they may be years apart.

This procedure sometimes necessitated changes to Friend's original tenses, and there have been other occasional substitutions (definite for indefinite articles, or vice versa) and insertions (mainly of single words such as 'and' and 'I'). I have not scrupled to correct his punctuation on the rare occasions he lapses, nor to standardise his spelling and readjust his paragraphing here and there. The intention of these changes is to facilitate clarity and coherence as well as precision, and nowhere have I knowingly distorted the substance or intended meaning of his words.

Ian Britain
July 2010

ABBREVIATIONS IN CHAPTER ENDNOTES AND LIST OF ILLUSTRATIONS

AGNSW Art Gallery of New South Wales

DFD 1 *The Diaries of Donald Friend*, volume 1, edited by Anne Gray (National Library of Australia, Canberra; 2001)

DFD 2; ***DFD 3***; ***DFD 4*** *The Diaries of Donald Friend*, volumes 2–4, edited by Paul Hetherington (National Library of Australia, Canberra; 2003, 2005, 2006)

NLA MS 5959 National Library of Australia, illustrated manuscripts and diaries of Donald Friend

All geographical distances given in the notes are approximate.

INTRODUCTION

'Of course this diary is fatal reading to anyone who would wish to respect my character,' Donald Friend noted in an entry for August 1943. While these words may invite us to take a peek inside this intimate document, their author nowhere invites us to like him. Not shamelessly but brazenly, he can label himself a user, a liar, a money-grubber, a snob, a cynic, a coward, a narcissist, an alcoholic, a pederast, and a hedonist; his intellect 'precocious' and 'frivolous'; his artistic work 'lightweight', 'mediocre' and 'unimportant'. In almost the same breath, he might be found declaring the genius of his painting and drawing, the elitism of his taste, the promiscuity of his sexual appetites, and the puritanism of his morals regarding other people's sexual or social behaviour.

Contradictory, if not hypocritical, none of these self-representations will endear him to many of us. Taken together, though, they should make us wary of readily fixing labels to him, or of accepting without question or qualification his own. 'I am many me's,' he averred in one of his earliest diary entries, when just fourteen; and as the diary unfolds over the next sixty years, we catch glimpses of a more generous, truth-respecting, unmaterialistic, democratic, compassionate, emotionally committed, sexually polymorphous, even chastely self-restrained Friend.

We should be just as wary of making too much of these redeeming moments. Friend was alert to the way in which 'one records such a thing as a small virtue, in defending a reprehensible character'. He would also have been the first to resist the application to himself of what he divined in the pages of his much-admired fellow diarist Samuel Pepys, three centuries earlier: 'the picture of humanity unadorned, its daily round laid bare with its daily thoughts and little sins and vices, the nobility that does not recognise itself.'

It was not just that Friend suspected his own sins of being rather greater; he also had—or at least professed to—recurring doubts about the significance, integrity and literary quality of his diary, compared with Pepys' or other classic models of the genre. He could dismiss an individual entry he'd just written, or the whole enterprise, as 'pointless', 'rude', 'immoral', 'idiotic ebullience', 'folios of bilge', 'rum-lubricated pen scrawls', 'volumes of nonsense', 'bullshit as usual, and badly expressed', a 'catalogue of weaknesses, sins and cynicisms and sentimentalities', 'Vapid

Thoughts, Vacuous Opinions, Vain Desires and Vacant Doings'. Other people's more positive appreciation didn't always allay these doubts. The first selections from his diary were published in book form only a year after he'd resumed keeping it, following his enlistment in the Australian Army in 1942, and this edition, *Gunner's Diary*, became a bestseller. He was just twenty-eight. While his publisher promptly commissioned a sequel (*Painter's Journal*, which came out in 1946), Friend became depressed when he spied a copy of the first volume in a second-hand bookshop in Sydney in October 1945: 'It reads now like extracts from a gushing gossip column. Very shallow and silly and only occasionally witty...A slipshod trifle.'

Allowing for an element of irony as well as of depression in such self-lacerations, there is plenty in the diary to justify them: maudlin longeurs, arch cadenzas, drunken ramblings, and even a few passages in scrambled Asian and European languages that may be 'nonsense' or a studious code but in either case are a reader's nightmare. (Pepys used code, or shorthand, throughout his diaries, which took generations of patient scholarship to decipher.) If such features were really all there was to Friend's chronicles, we might well wonder why he bothered to go on keeping them for so long—and why we should bother looking at them.

In Friend's case, as he put it a few months into his army career, he was 'obsessed by this compulsion to make a record. It is so easy to forget things.' Such an imperative stemmed partly from the extraordinary external pressures of the day that had persuaded him to enlist in the first place. Having returned home to Sydney from long forays in Europe, Africa and northern Australia, he had been brought up against the graveness of the international situation by the entry of some Japanese submarines into the city's harbour on 31 May 1942. Nowhere near as dramatic or disastrous as the fall of Singapore to the same enemy, three months earlier, this was nonetheless a disturbing portent of Australia's vulnerability.

Not everyone in those scary circumstances rushed to keep a diary; and Friend was only returning—if more concertedly—to a habit he'd picked up much earlier. There were clearly longer-standing internal pressures, deep-seated personal needs, to which he was also responding in taking up the habit again. He had first been prompted to 'make a record' when his mother gave him an exquisitely bound and printed 'Diary for 1929' as a present. A precocious and imaginative schoolboy, he had eagerly filled its blank spaces with fanciful drawings of historical characters in faraway places, as well as with notations (sometimes no less fanciful) of his daily thoughts and activities at home or at school in Sydney, or on holidays at the family's grazing property. The same internal pressure was at work when he started his soldier's diary in a series of sketchbooks and exercise books, more than a decade later: 'its essential function is an escape from reality,' he reflected in an entry of June 1943. What a diary offered him, even in these more modest formats, was a readily accessible private space into which he could disappear daily, away from the demands and conventions of politics, society and bureaucratic institutions.

There was no contradiction between its functions as an *aide-memoir* and an escape hatch from reality. Its pages offered him the chance to record his fantasies, dreams and ideals but also to confront, in a reflective mood and a creative form, the very things he was escaping from in the real world. In addition, as he grew into adulthood, the diary enabled him to monitor those inner demons of sexual yearning, material ambition and alcoholic excess that had started to creep up on him. It was never just escapist.

The mood was never just monotonous, either. Whether we catch him reflecting on public or on private matters, we find a great deal more buoyancy and optimism to balance the angst than we do in the diaries of similarly self-lacerating artists of the same period, such as Tennessee Williams or John Cheever. For Friend, the discipline of regular record-keeping could in itself provide a balancing mechanism, a corrective to melancholia. 'It seems this diary is nothing but a record of degeneracy and torment,' he began his entry for 27 August 1950. 'Well,' he proceeds to write, 'let's get on with it, first some successes.'

In its joint capacities, as chronicle and confessional, Friend's diary was not separate from but a complement to his practice as a painter and draughtsman. The drawings with which he embellished the text are only the most obvious sign of this. At least implicitly, Friend was adverting to the connections between his visual and verbal 'record-making', their shared imperatives, when he wrote in his diary for 1943: 'all forms of art are ultimately expressions of psychological entanglements—a symptom of discontent with what exists, and therefore a desire to make concrete one's wishful thought.'

To win wider appeal, art has to be more than just the working-out or working-through of the artist's private compulsions; and Friend's diary-writing, for all the deficiencies in it that he identified, shares many of the most attractive qualities of his drawing. Fluency and fluidity, precision and concision, passion and poignancy, drama and charm: these are not all-pervasive features of his prose but they are sufficiently to the fore to counter the waves of self-pity and the facetious froth.

'The diary was never written for publication,' Friend told a colleague in 1943, 'so all the writing is completely unrevised and uncorrected… scribbled in those hasty moments between one dreary activity and another.' This remained true of his recording method over the next half-century, when there was often much more of excitement to report, and as he became increasingly aware of the diary's potential to attract an external audience. The continuous sense of spontaneity about his words is something else that is shared with his drawings, lending vivacity to each medium and—if not complete veracity—an arresting candour.

Even in a filleted form, such as represented by my selection here, there remains much gossip and navel-gazing. It would be to misrepresent his chronicles to slice away those features entirely—not to say impossible. It would also be to strip them of much of their wider significance. Over the course of his seventy-four years Friend lived in various parts of eastern and northern Australia, and in a number of foreign countries, directly witnessing, where not participating in, key events and long-term shifts in their political and social development. He also met, and often befriended, many fellow artists, writers and cultural figures in other fields. Beyond its relevance to our understanding of his art and sensibility, his compulsive self-documenting is full of interest for the picture it conveys of the engagement of a not-so-ordinary Australian with the ordinary as well as extraordinary worlds in which he moved.

Not despite but often because of its idiosyncratic perspectives, this record of a cosmopolitan, highly erudite as well as highly artistic, mainly—and openly—homosexual patrician provides a succession of crisply rendered observations that would enrich any social or cultural history of the twentieth century. These observations are often incidental rather than sustained or thought-through; and they are nearly always debatable. But there's scarcely a major subject—love, art, nature, religion, war, race, migration, travel, social class, politics, the economy and the law, even sport (which he loathed)—that they don't somewhere, somehow, illuminate.

In an entry of his diary at the end of 1946, Friend records coming across 'a huge bundle of ancient letters...dating from the time I was in London. Wonderful letters: humorous, delightful, dramatic, affectionate, loving, annoyed, gossiping letters...So many of them were so good, and written reflecting the history of the time, that carefully selected and published they would make an admirable commentary on the state of mind of people up until, and during the first year of, the war.' Friend could have as confidently applied these words to his diary—and it was to run on for several decades longer. This document reflects only his own 'state of mind', but its vivid and astute characterisations of other people lend it something of the quality of good fiction as well as of good history. And the bonus—unusual even in artists' diaries—is that so many of these pen portraits are visual as well as verbal.

The broad appeal of Friend's diary had already been established by 1946, not only by the publication and reception of those two selections from it, *Gunner's Diary* and *Painter's Journal*, but also by the passionate enthusiasm it had aroused in an outsider to Australia. In 1943, an American lieutenant posted to Sydney, Edgar Kaufmann, had been shown some volumes of the diary by Friend's fellow artist Russell Drysdale. Kaufmann had yet to be introduced to Friend but, Drysdale reported, he had already 'fallen' for his work 'in a big way'. Kaufmann came from a family of distinguished connoisseurs and collectors; in the 1930s he and his father had commissioned America's most famous architect, Frank Lloyd Wright, to build them a country retreat, Fallingwater, near Pittsburgh. Kaufmann ended up purchasing two of the volumes from Friend and taking them back home at the end of World War II. He went on to become a curator at the Museum of Modern Art in New York.

One of the great thrills for me in preparing this edition was to rediscover and retrieve those volumes. They had been lost for decades. They were the missing parts of a cultural treasure, however flawed its maker. The original thrill that Kaufmann felt in beholding them was as sure a testimony as any to the diary's special status. He instinctively recognised a unique work of art.

The diary may also be accounted a great work of literature. It ranks among the most capacious and compelling of autobiographical enterprises in any language.

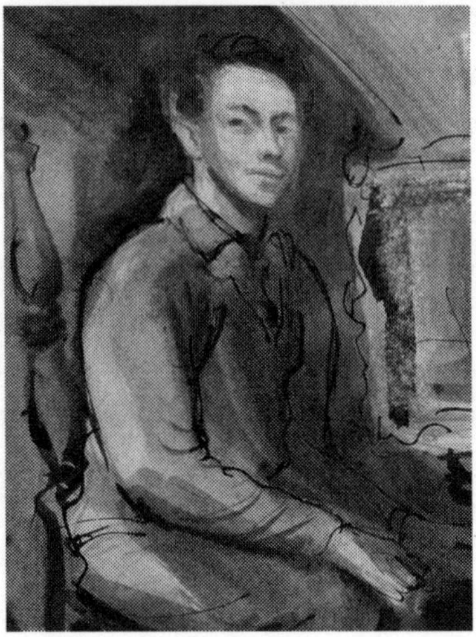

CHRONOLOGY OF DONALD FRIEND'S LIFE

1915 Born on 6 February in Sydney, at home (Murdoch Street, Cremorne).

1915–26 Moves between Sydney and properties in rural New South Wales, including Glendon, near Warialda, acquired as a family trust in 1923 when his sister, GWEN FRIEND, is born. His parents separate, and he goes to live in Bowral with his mother and siblings while attending preparatory school at Tudor House in Moss Vale.

1927–29 The family moves to Sydney while he attends school at Cranbrook. He starts drawing classes with SYDNEY LONG. Holidays spent at Glendon.

1930 Attends Sydney Grammar School.

1931 Leaves school permanently to return to Glendon.

1932 Gravitates between Glendon and Sydney, where he enrols at the Royal Art Society School.

1933 Travels in Queensland and the Torres Strait Islands. Meets CHARLIE and UMMA SAILOR and their children, who become a second family to him.

1934–35 Enrols in ANTONIO DATTILO-RUBBO's art classes in Sydney.

Visits the Blue Mountains (with PETER FINCH), and Melbourne and Brisbane (with DONALD MURRAY).

1936–38 Travels to England, where he is enrolled as a student at the Westminster School of Art. First public exhibition of his work, at R. E. A. WILSON's gallery in London. Travels to Nigeria via France, and the north and west coasts of Africa.

1939 Based in Nigeria, where he gravitates between Lagos and various regional centres, notably Ikerre, where he becomes adviser to the Ogoga (king). Learns that a daughter has been born to him in London.

1940 Returns to Australia. Begins exhibiting with the Contemporary Art Society, the Society of Artists and the Macquarie Galleries in Sydney. Meets RUSSELL (TAS) DRYSDALE.

1941 Travels to Cairns, revisiting the Sailors, and to Green Island.

1942 Returns to Sydney and holds his first Australian solo show at Macquarie Galleries. Enlists as a gunner in the Australian Infantry Forces and is posted to Hume Camp, near Albury.

1943 Posted to Greta, near Maitland. Volunteers for an anti-malarial experimental program stationed on the Atherton Tableland, in northern Queensland. Extracts from his war diaries are published, as *Gunner's Diary*.

1944 Returns to Greta and is then posted to Chermside Camp, near Brisbane. Meets EDGAR J. KAUFMANN, JR., and JUSTIN O'BRIEN.

1945 Appointed official war artist and dispatched to Borneo. At the end of the war, returns to Sydney.

1946 Lives at Merioola, the artist's community in Sydney, while awaiting demobilisation, before travelling again to Cairns and Torres Strait in the wake of a thwarted romantic attachment. Further extracts of his war diaries are published, as *Painter's Journal*.

1947 Moves back to Merioola, before settling in Hill End, near Bathurst, with Donald Murray. His father dies.

1948 Gravitates between Hill End and Sydney, where his work is featured in various exhibitions.

1949 Travels to Italy and England.

1950 In Ischia, develops an attachment to a local fisherman,

ATTILIO GUARRACINO, whom he has met through JEFFREY SMART. Exhibits drawings in London at the Redfern Gallery before returning to Australia with Guarracino.

1951 Based at Hill End, while exhibiting in Sydney and Brisbane, and visiting Melbourne, where Guarracino has gone to live. Wins the Flotta Lauro Travelling Art Prize.

1952 Returns to Italy on the proceeds of the Flotta Lauro prize, and travels also to Greece, Corfu, Spain. Based in London, where the Redfern Gallery exhibits his work again.

1953 Continues to live in London, where he witnesses and draws the coronation of Queen Elizabeth II. Returns to Australia via Italy and Sri Lanka, and settles again at Hill End.

1954 Travels to Queensland with MARGARET OLLEY, revisiting the Sailor family in Cairns.

1955 Wins the Blake Prize for religious art. Researches and writes a history of Hill End, *Hillendiana*. Makes another trip to Queensland.

1956 Gravitates between Hill End and Sydney, where he stays with the Drysdale family. *Hillendiana* published.

1957–61 Travels to Sri Lanka. Stays with BEVIS BAWA and subsequently meets Bevis's brother, architect GEOFFREY BAWA. Holds exhibitions in Colombo while continuing to have his work shown in Australia and London.

1962 Returns to Australia, to live in Sydney. Exhibits there and in Western Australia. Meets ROBERT HUGHES, MITTY LEE-BROWN and JOHN BELL. Befriends JAMES FAIRFAX.

1963 Travels to Queensland and visits IAN FAIRWEATHER on Bribie Island.

1964 Exhibits his sculpture with Mitty Lee-Brown's in Sydney, and stays often with her and her husband at their rural property in NSW.

1965 Robert Hughes's monograph, *Donald Friend*, is published. Friend develops another frustrated passion—for his current model, STEWART HOLMAN.

1966 Visits, and exhibits in, Melbourne and Brisbane. Meets BARRY HUMPHRIES and BRETT WHITELEY. Leaves for Bali. Meets WIJA WAWO-RUNTU.

1967 Travels in Bali, India, Iran, Turkey, Greece, Italy, and back to Bali. Returns to Sydney to await his resident's visa for Indonesia.

1968–70 Settles in Bali. Commissioned to buy Balinese and Javanese art for Australian collections by the Commonwealth Art Advisory Board. Starts to suffer from various illnesses, including tuberculosis, and returns to Sydney briefly for hospitalisation.

1971–72 Based in Bali, where a film crew visits to make a documentary about his life there, *Tamu—the Guest*. Brief trips to France (for exhibitions of his work), Sri Lanka, and Sydney (to arrange hospital treatment there for his most trusted household servant, MADJA).

1973–74 Based in Bali, with a brief trip to Sri Lanka and India to consult Geoffrey Bawa about plans for a museum to be attached to his house in Batujimbar. Exhibitions of his work held in Sydney, Newcastle and Melbourne.

1975 In Bali, starts writing and illustrating *Bumbooziana*. Visits Sydney and Melbourne for retrospective exhibitions of his work. Death of his mother.

1976–78 Continues to write and paint in Bali, with a trip to Italy and visits to Melbourne for exhibitions, a launch of his book *The Cosmic Turtle*, consultations with publisher RICHARD GRIFFIN and a spell in hospital.

1979 Gravitates between Bali and Melbourne, while continuing with writing and book-illustration projects for Griffin.

1980 Based in Melbourne, staying with Guarracino and his wife. Returns to Bali briefly to arrange for the sale of his house there and pack up his possessions.

1981 Exhibits in Brisbane. Following a quarrel with Guarracino, he leaves Melbourne for Sydney.

1982–88 Permanently resettles in Sydney, with occasional expeditions to Melbourne and Queensland. Despite increasingly frequent bouts of illness, he continues to write and publish, paint, draw and etch, and he participates in the making of another film about him (directed by DON BENNETTS).

1989 Dies in his sleep on 16 August at his house in Sydney (Holdsworth Street, Woollahra).

1920s

23rd May.

A mackerel sky. I've been waiting for months
for the large and variable sky seen from my
window to present me with this one. As a child
I used think of skies like this as being flocks
of sheep. I'd seen sheep; I didn't know what
'mackerel' were. I knew very early that one of
the amazing and very satisfactory things about
anything one noticed was like something
else. Sheep I'd never had a high
opinion of, but their having a
mirror-image grazing on blue, open
paddocks of sky endowed, alienated
them with an altogether strangely
different value. Upside-down skysheep!
It's strange to wander into that terra incognita
to find oneself clearly revealed, as a person with
a subconscious mind still operating. A surprise
to be,

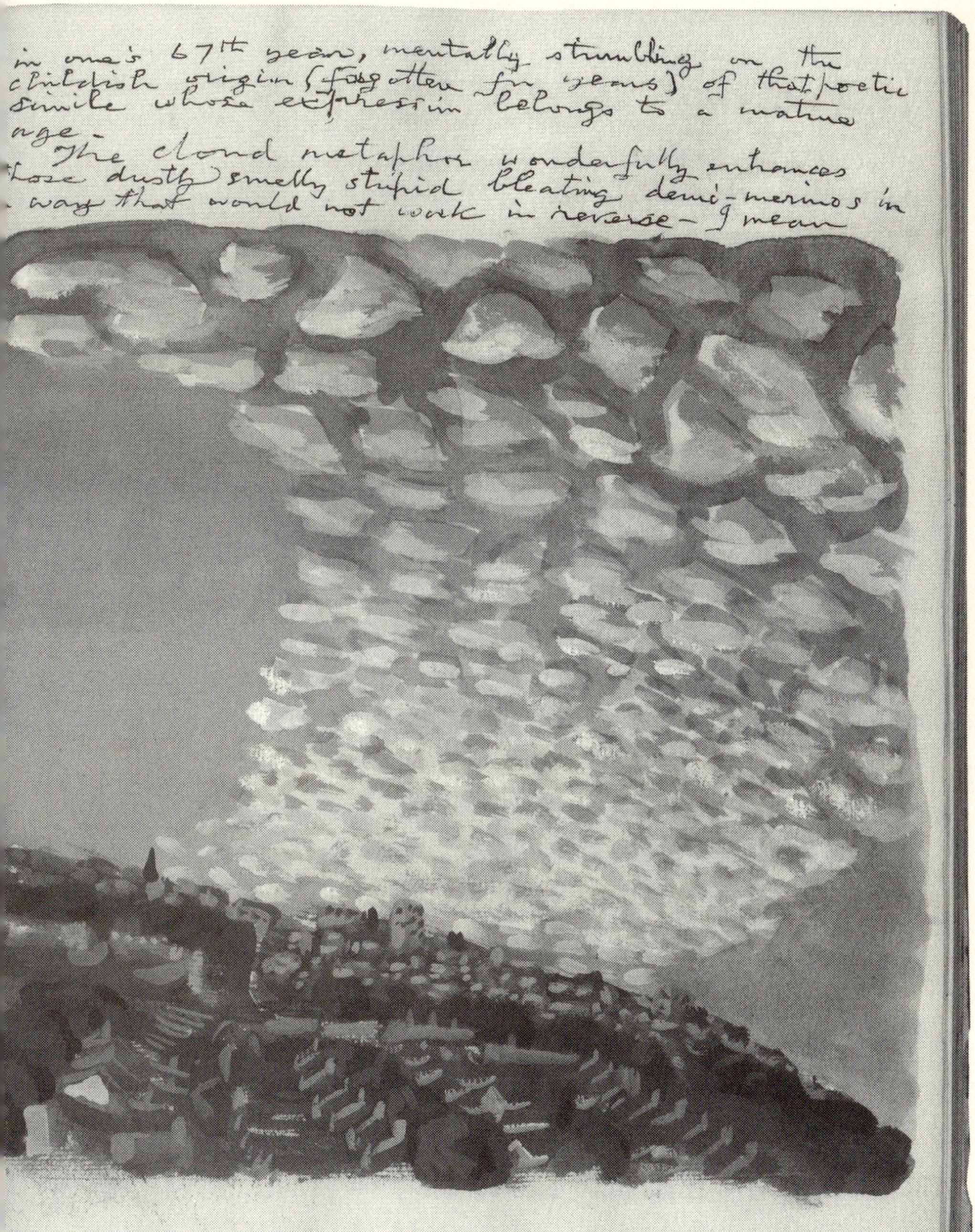

2. *Upside-down-sky-sheep* (1982).

Early to mid-1920s

Woorang Downs.[1] Skies like flocks of sheep. Sheep I'd never had a high opinion of, but their having a mirror-image grazing on blue open paddocks of sky endowed them with an altogether strangely different value. Upside-down sky-sheep!

Bowral.[2] The porridgy smell of the nursery. The crackly white starchiness of the abominable Nanny. Constant washings and tidyings. Tricycles and toys. Honey in the comb: the greatest relish of my brothers[3] and myself. Honeycombs appeared on the nursery table in a little pinewood box, and the portioning out, because of our savage rivalries aimed at getting more than a fair share, was overseen by one of those nannies.

My mother[4] in a sort of beehive hat with a motoring veil, or slim and pretty in jodhpurs as she dismounted her big bay horse in the drive, and other such sights gave me my real pleasure.

Moss Vale.[5] At school in a Great Stately Home of Australia called Tudor House.[6] A heavenly spot. There was a little church put up by Governor Macquarie[7]—with convicts' graves and very awful windows, and a great Brass Eagle. The Headmaster devised a baby-blue velvet bag sewn with the Tudor rose so that the collection money made no clink, and thus break the holy silence, or the sanctity of our beastly little minds. A lady in a chiffon picture-hat used to play the organ, which was one with a hand-bellows pumped laboriously by a sweaty red, but I believe devout, yokel. The churchyard with great pine trees, and the holy little boys, a classic spot. Also a river where we swam near the weir, looking with longing eyes towards Bowral, which was home.

Sydney. Chasecote, Granny's[8] house at Kuringai Chase[9]—Ming[10] bowls & Satsuma[11], the big brass Buddha with celadon bowls of flowers, the Jade Teapot & the tiny Kuan Yin[12] & a general scent of roses & lavender & potpourri, and fine books & rare prints & paintings. Interminable tennis and tea afternoons.

My grandfather's auction rooms, James R. Lawson's[13]—its gloomy, cluttered grandeurs.

1926–28

Sydney. Cranbrook.[1] When I first went to boarding school, I became infatuated with the Arabs through reading a thriller in a comic paper. It was called 'Omar the Avenger', and intrigued me so much that I identified completely with the hero of the tale. I told all the other little boys I was really an Arab, and that my real name was Sheikh Omar, a Bedouin chief in exile from the machinations of a villainous Wagir by the name of Hassan the Dreadful. They didn't believe it of course (nasty little cynics), but that made me all the more stubborn, until I invented a brilliantly adventurous background which convinced quite a few.

I had my first art lessons at Cranbrook. A very simple business of painting an apple and a book.

1929

5 January Far Hills, at Gladswood Gardens, Double Bay.[1] Spend a very useless day, as lazy as everybody else. The heat is at its highest and the birds forget to sing and the best thing for men to do is swim. The garden droops and the water runs dry, while men and women alike eat lettuce and drink iced drinks. Bushfires ravage the country and houseflies ravage the city.

7 January Buy a most wonderful brass box, made in the fourteenth or fifteenth century, depicting the life of a man and his wife with two children, and the fighting of dragons and bears on the ends and the three stages of their lives together on one side: Spring, Motherhood and Old Age. I am greatly pleased with this purchase, as I am a lover of antiques.

11 January Bushfires—excessive heat—flies by day and mosquitoes by night till everyone is nearly bursting with peevishness, and verily, the whole city and country alike are waiting for rain.

We went down to Bondi this evening and the sky was a brazen colour, being neither pink nor grey nor blue, the sea rolled in a sluggish fashion and the air changed its heat many times.

20 January This must be considered as a special day, as many things of import have happened and the most important of these is my appearance in the papers. Therein described as 'the artistic son of Mrs Leslie Friend'.[2]

26 January I have painted a fantasy which I immodestly make an avowal that it is a wonder in colour. It illustrates a mythical moon, casting into sepia silhouette a tree, making it more weird is a bat, flying across the face of the moon.

5 February Should go to school, but don't. A terrible storm that does much damage, but doesn't damage our abode. Have done quite a lot of painting lately, and have made up my mind that I shall be an artist. And I shall be famous!

6 February My fourteenth birthday. Spend a happy day and don't go to school. Mother has given me the most wonderful and valuable book of famous paintings. Among them is a rare print of Corot's *Bent Tree*.[3] In the book are biographies of many famous artists.

8 February This night go to school, having come four days late. Inky Radford, one delightful *amigo* of mine, has not arrived back from Goulbourn, where his father is Bishop, and I have not even one of the 'Wits' (consisting of Peter Sharland, Pip Maclay[4], Cox and myself) to keep me from complete boredom. Imprisoned as a boarder at Cranbrook.

1 March *En route to Goulburn.* Inky and I pack in the afternoon and leave the school at 4 o'clock. Mum sent me a monocle. Inky called me a count and I called him Baron in the train and we behaved in a very Baronial manner amusing all the passengers, who were by then in an embarrassed state.

8 March *Sydney*. Sharland met me this morning and doled out to me some awful news—namely that I have twenty more days to spend with him, after which he is leaving for England with his mother. We vowed to go like anything and give the school a hot time in our last little hour. I am truly angry concerning his going as we were blood-chums.

10 March Just a typical Sunday and do nothing but loaf. Church has plenty of room for improvement. Why on earth are there not a few robes and jewels, and candles. I long for delicious chants and invocations in Latin and French.

16 March Far Hills. I did deign most graciously to get up and promenade my manorial hall. The luxury and romantic softness of this place are a delightful contrast with the cold, hard facts of school.

24 March Do go home today, and make two artistic wooden glasses for the 'hooch' party that is to be between us four Lords in the ancient catacombs, a hidden place on the school bounds. The Lords being: Earl Donald of Rochester, Baron John of Radford, Earl Peter of Harland and Grand Duke Paul of Russia.

April Peter Sharland shall leave soon. I shall be dreadfully lonely without him. I like him so much: too much, I think.

Radford and I go down to the catacombs and there build a secret suite of rooms under the ample floor of the old stables, with wooden walls. Across the roof of this room are great oak beams. Start a collection of 'old pewter'. We found most of the 'pieces' (really Governor Chelmsford's[5] discarded saucepans) in and around the catacombs. We also have a fine pair of armchairs. Furniture was a near approach of the Flemish style.

Manage to get home and go with mother to see Pavlova[6] the Russian dancer, whom I consider immortal.

Am confirmed by the Archbishop of Sydney.[7] Am horribly impressed and reformed to a monstrous degree.

Go to party, Arthur Benjamin's[8] (a great pianist whom I heard and met at the Town Hall), and hear the Sonata which he has just composed. Have a good time and a cocktail, which went rather to my head.

May Go down to the catacombs and install a library, with a bookcase full of books. This night, there with Radford, dress in armour, adventure much in the garden and just miss getting caught.

The boys left home for the station, and the whole house is in a state of peace. Mother and I have quite rightly resolved to have a good time these holidays, and we'll poke round all sorts of places.

Did go this night to see again the Mlle Pavlova, who dances in *Autumn Leaves*[9] and *Chopiniana*[10]. Really, methinks that she is supernatural. So light. So much rhythm yet one is simply lost in a dream. I was charmed to the marrow.

Go to Granny Lawson's, have a lovely day among her beautiful antiques. She has a set of genuine Sheraton chairs, and we together discussed art in general. Do a portrait, after the style of the immortal Joshua Reynolds[11], which so far as it is done promises well for my reputation as an artist.

June The weather is calm and sombre. All around the red and brown-tinted leaves are fluttering to the ground. Rose leaves look marvellous in their tints of dark ruby, yellow, light green and even black. Now and then a wind comes and shakes them, and cruelly bundles the fragile things about. It is a philosopher's harvest indeed, so beautifully sad and calm.

Go to the catacombs and read. We have there the most refined atmosphere, with the pewter on the blackened beams, and the bookcase that looks colonial Dutch, so well have we fashioned it out of boxes. The catacombs have prints of Rembrandt's[12] and Vermeer's[13] pictures hung on the mighty beams that cross the roof. The flowers are kept in test tube vases. Thus sheltered, John and I wrote plays, books or poems as our moods decreed. We even gave an afternoon tea party to our friendly masters.

It is a paradise haven. Wish that my Peter were here to enjoy the place. I am quite happy, but for an intense longing that I have for Peter. I am glad none know of this. I adore not telling anyone, it gives me confidence.

I read a simply wondrous book entitled *The Great Roxhythe*.[14] Entirely enchanted thereby.

July Go home to find mother is most seriously ill. I shall never forget entering her room. There she lay, her eyes a most wonderful brown, her skin taut over her cheekbones, without a wrinkle. I talked to her all the afternoon.

Horrible crisis. The masters have found the catacombs. Return to pull down the catacombs, as decreed. With the dawn comes light. Have secretly determined to build it again some day.

Have an amusing conversation with masters concerning my immorality, and from whom it is inherited (John Wilmot, Earl of Rochester[15]).

Look at some famous pictures, and admire Corot's *Bent Tree*. Really, one of my present ambitions is to be able to paint like Corot. I wonder if I ever shall.

August Am in such a mood that I could write much about Nothing (indeed, a dangerous mood!) as Mr Palmer, at school, remarked that he sincerely enjoyed my exam papers, as they were captivatingly, eloquently about nothing! Of course, I thanked him for his flattering compliment.

Caned for not having my hair brushed. Have decided that Cranbrook is most certainly deteriorating. Some dreadful Australian boys are creating discords all around me, especially a mad friend who is both a snob and bourgeois, a horrible and queer mixture. I hate these Australians more and more every day. Wish to God that I was out of Australia. I long for the day that I shall set sail for England.

Radford and I went down to the catacombs. We put up one wall (because it looked bare), we put up the bookcase (because I needed it), we put up curtains (they looked so bright), we tidied the place up, we also put some flowers in. At night the catacombs put on a most Bohemian aspect, with candlelight etc. Very delightful. We lit our clay oven and made a weird concoction from potatoes, fried in liquorice, as we had no fat. It was impossible to eat.

Go to Windsor with mother where we look for the old Moses graves.[16] Have afternoon tea and the woman calls mother 'deary' while the man calls her 'my lady'.

See my brothers off to Dad's station. (I, of course, do not go.) And after which I go to the State Theatre[17] with mother. They had a simply disgusting 'Talky' program.[18] I am interested to see that Russia wars with China. Even if they do not win the Bolshevists will be quietened a little.[19] Thank goodness!

September I have lately studied myself. The reward of my studies is this—I am a very incarnation of John Wilmot. At times gay, longing to leave this horrible political tangle of Australia. I long to travel on the Continent, and meet the gaiety in Paris, of great and talented persons. At other times I am greatly impressed by pure beauty alone, by philosophy, the fatality of Omar Khayam[20], the beautiful thoughts in poetry.

So many things have drawn my imagination. Siam, Tonking, Annam and so on have exercised such a fascination for me that they rival Timbuktu. The Spice Islands, ancient Portuguese forts, the seventeenth-century Dutch trading posts, the exotic sultanates. The lands of Conrad[21] and Somerset Maugham[22], abounding in magical names—Tarakan, Sandakan, Labuan. Engraved on stamps, a little square of paper with native heads and strange palm trees, Labuan[23] represented the last word in enchanted Arabian Nights islands.

I draw many things. I am oblivious to all others, I do not hear when I am spoken to—I don't see—but then I am entirely happy. At the end of drawing I am nervy and temperamental. The soul within me is soon cured when I put on Beethoven's Concerto.[24] I rejoice and change to the time of the music. This is the *real* me. Changing, stepping to the music. Percy Grainger[25] I've always *loathed.* O God—the 'Country Garden', the abominable 'Gumsucker's March' etc., etc. And the terrible tinkling yet athletic recordings of his playing, so pyrotechnically, the music of real masters. Most of his own compositions sound to my ears like a musician's interpretation of Kipling's 'If'[26]—or that once-popular recitation, 'The Green Eye of the Little Yellow God'[27].

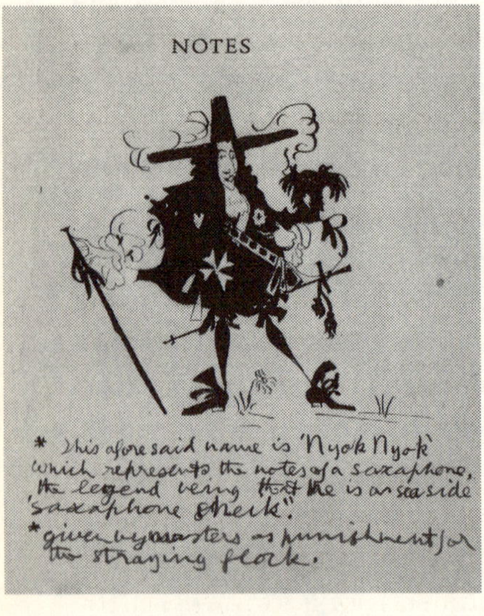

3. *Ancestor at the Stuart court (1929).*

I greatly admire the Stuart Kings.[28] They were gay, but they were clever and witty. I am dreadfully proud that they are my ancestors. But I am many me's and only two me's ever show: the Great Roxhythy me and the extremely artistic and pleasure-loving me.

Arthur Benjamin visited us. He was very charming as usual. When he, mother and I were alone he proposed that I should journey to England with him! He shall introduce me, and I shall seriously take up painting and drawing, of which I am so fond. My father, of course, may step in, but mother shall talk the affair over with him.

Through Benjamin's patronage I

was interviewed by the press for the *Daily Telegraph*, whose reporter took some of my 'creations' for reproduction. I shall become famous. Anyhow I shall make an attempt. I hope that my art shall soon be perfect.

October A large notice and photograph appeared in the *Telegraph* Pictorial of me.[29] All school has seen the Pictorial. I do not mind in the slightest. They shall never be great. They are the bourgeois of Australia; the common rich, not aristocrats.

I went to dancing and had an excellent time in spite of excessive heat (oh, what heat!) and the future promises a little *affaire de coeur*. Heaven knows that I need one.

My art is greatly improving, and I do much painting. Hope soon to be great. The collection of miniatures above the fireplace is growing rapidly in size and beauty. They are nearly all on old coins.

Go to the afternoon art classes at Syd Long's[30], a celebrated artist, for drawing. There I met two very attractive people (female)! Both young, one a real 'cutie'. The mercury rises quickly! She is young, and fresh: she wears Parisian clothes, and has a sweet foreign manner, and a lovely ethereal Russian face. She is very shy, and we have not even exchanged frivolous words yet. Still, the affair is amusing. The work I do there (that which is not amorous) deals mostly with plaster of Paris heads of Dead Caesars.

I hate night classes. There is a large attendance, and mostly by office duds and shop-girls with a taste for drawing.

At present, school is to me not such an educational centre as it is one social. I go there mostly to write and talk and entertain with wits of my own age and development—amuse myself in the accustomed lazy manner. Masters cannot realise this, and thus they act foolishly and weakly. Mr Flooke sent me to the Head for doing a caricature of him as Caesar. The Head appeared in a simply towering and absurd rage and caned me immediately without letting me get a word in edgeways. What an idiot! There is a spirit abroad of hostility towards the Head. He is a narrow-minded old coot! Parents are continually complaining of his rotten management.

My latest craze as far as my art is concerned is a flair for the beautiful colonial buildings in the vicinity of Macquarie Street, Sydney. All are buildings that are entwined with the history of Australia. Burdekin

House[31] is a marvel, with the most marvellous furniture, antique, and worth many thousand pounds. Spent a wonderful Sunday at the ancient Wentworth House[32] at Vaucluse. They have restored all the old historic furniture and pictures. I noted the old Venetian glass wine set, and Dresden vases. Also some marvellous four-post beds. Indeed I should greatly treasure a four-poster myself.

November Mr Flooke told us that it was the Roman practice to have more than one wife. I said to him, 'Plenty of practice, eh Sir?' and I have never seen him blush before!

School holds very few charms at present. I am disgustingly bored, and treat all work with a nasty, cold indifference.

Go to the Drawing Class. My affair has already become part of the gossip of our form at school. A ghastly crisis reached: my Russian Countess's name is WHITE! I felt aghast when I heard the news. Of course, the name makes no difference to her. My Miss White is as lovely as ever, and my absurd caprice is getting on visibly.

Mother offered me a cigarette, and henceforward I shall smoke, though very seldom, and under the eye of my adorable mother.

It is a queer thing, that when I have been drawing and painting all day, I grow brain-weary and temperamental, I hate all interruption or the senseless insistent clatter of my sister.[33]

Early December I realise now, quite fully, that no one but myself sees in my pictures that which is but a glimpse of my ideal. They applaud the picture that I have disliked. Still, I have my own ideal and, as I shall rely on the artistic public, why not paint pictures that please their ideal? Even though it soils the pure light of my own particular line of beauty, which their eyes do not see?

I dreamed a Great Dream—as I watched, from my balcony, the great blue expanse, a marvellous galleon appeared. The sides of it were hung with crimson and gold brocades, and on the scented summer breeze came the strains of marvellous triumphal music, magnificent. I turned and many exquisite people greeted me. They were dressed in sapphires and diamonds and glorious cloths and brocades. But I was grandest of all, arrayed in cloth of gold, and amethysts, pearls and rubies. And they all bowed to me. I was their ideal—the talented magnificent.

Mid-December School breaks up. My mistake at Cranbrook was that I brought too much of the 'personality' to school and, though amusing to the broadminded circle of my own class and friends, that was not appreciated by the general public—and though the Classic masters were tolerant enough, the satyr of my compositions and flippant conversations were the causes of an enmity with those masters. Thus I have decided that my school life shall be the 'common or garden' life that I should lead, and my home life shall be the life of artistic ease and loving of the quaint and beautiful which help so much to inspire and uphold my writing and drawing: which latter I propose to take as a profession in later life—if the Land, that Ogre with clutching claws of deadly dry labour-life, does not claim me.

I leave for Glendon, a squat country homestead 600 miles from mother.[34] I shall be away from all decent civilisation in a far land of strangers. A place of smelling sheep and cattle, and of men with filthy stubby fingers! Ach! The dread of leaving this city adored for the swarms of flies and mosquitoes.

Rather enjoy journey, the countryside was extremely lovely, but lacks the colour that I much love. Having spent a good night's sleep en train, I awoke and at 10 o'clock the train pulled in at Moree, where the coffee was nice but the meat was bad. Got into another branch train and journeyed on to Glendon Siding. The homestead is very ordinary.

Last week of December *Glendon*. Go out and muster sheep. Most amusing operation, all performed on horseback. It was in such a performance that the far-famed Australasian dialect was formed, also many new words were invented.

Receive a letter from mother. So full of news and love, written on notepaper of rapturous beauty. How I adore mother's letters!

Dad[35] arrived, and Beauty, my pony, was in a frivolous mood. I galloped dangerously down to meet the paternal parent and pulled the horse up onto its haunches. Dad, who has no character, and dresses in plain suit, brown shoes, country man's hat, white shirt, black tie, greeted me, not having seen me for over six years, with 'Hallo Don, how are yer?' For a moment I sat dazed, then realising, I offered my hand. Was ever a greeting less dramatic!

NOTES: 1920s

Early to mid-1920s

1. One of the Friend family's grazing properties in northwestern New South Wales, near Moree, 640 kilometres from Sydney.
2. Town, and prosperous rural retreat, in the Southern Highlands of NSW, 115 kilometres southwest of Sydney.
3. Harley Friend (1912–78); Terence (Ten) Friend (1918–2002).
4. Gwendolyn Friend, née Lawson (1887–1975).
5. Town in the Southern Highlands, 130 kilometres southwest of Sydney.
6. A private day and boarding preparatory school for boys, established in Sydney in 1897. It moved to its present rural site in 1902.
7. Lachlan Macquarie (1762–1824), Governor of NSW, 1810–21.
8. Marie Lawson, née Rossiter (1860–1947), Friend's maternal grandmother.
9. Area of the North Shore of Sydney, 20 kilometres from the city. Includes the suburb of Turramurra, which in some sources is given as Friend's maternal grandmother's address. North Turramurra borders on Kuringai Chase National Park.
10. The ruling dynasty of China, 1368–1644.
11. A region in the southern island of Japan that gave its name to a type of pottery.
12. Ancient Chinese goddess of mercy and compassion, and a popular subject of statuary.
13. James Robert Lawson (1860–1926), Donald Friend's maternal grandfather, founder of a succession of furniture and fine arts auctioneering firms in Sydney from the end of the nineteenth century.

1926–28

1. A boarding and day school for boys in Bellevue Hill, established in 1918 on the site and in the buildings of the former NSW Government House.

1929

1. The Friend family's flat in Sydney from the later 1920s to mid-1931.
2. None of the major Sydney newspapers of this date—the *Sunday Pictorial*, the *Sunday Sun* or the *Sunday News*—carried any such item.
3. Jean-Baptiste-Camille Corot (1796–1875), French painter. *The Bent Tree*, or *The Leaning Tree-trunk*, dates from the 1860s and is held by the National Gallery, London.
4. Paul Maclay (1916–2002). He became a regular announcer on ABC national radio from 1947.

5. Frederic Thesiger, 3rd Baron Chelmsford (1868–1933), Governor of NSW, 1909–12.
6. Anna Pavlova (1881–1931), Russian ballerina, who toured Australia in 1929.
7. The Most Rev. John Charles Wright (1861–1933), Archbishop of Sydney, 1909–33.
8. Australian-born composer, conductor and pianist (1893–1960). In 1911 he went to England to further his career but revisited Australia for extended periods over the following two decades.
9. The original Russian title (1907) of the ballet that became better known as *Les Sylphides*, with choreography by Michel Fokine and music by Frédéric Chopin (see **1938**, note 17).
10. Ballet, with choreography by Pavlova and music by Chopin, that premiered in 1918.
11. English portrait painter (1723–92).
12. Rembrandt van Rijn (1606–69), Dutch painter.
13. Jan Vermeer (1632–75), Dutch painter.
14. A novel (1923) by Georgette Heyer concerning a fictional spy in later seventeenth-century England.
15. English satirical poet and libertine (1647–80), from whom Friend's family on his mother's side (the Rossiters) claimed descent.
16. Moses was the old family name of Donald's paternal line. This was changed to Friend (the maiden name of Donald's paternal grandmother) around 1920, following a quarrel between Donald's father and uncle with their father. (For further details of these family members, see **1929**, note 35; **1931**, notes 9, 10.) The Moses family's connection with Windsor, on the Hawkesbury River 55 kilometres northwest of Sydney, dates to soon after the town's foundation in 1810. Donald's great-great-grandfather Uriah Moses (1778–1847), transported to Australia as a convict in 1800, was granted a ticket of leave in 1812 while living in the Hawkesbury district. In the 1828 Census he was listed as a baker in Windsor. Cf diary entries for 11–14 October 1977, and 2 August 1985.
17. In Market Street, Sydney, opened in 1929.
18. 'Talkies' started to take over from silent movies by the end of the 1920s. The program at the State Theatre consisted of 'The First All-Talking Comedy Drama', *The Home Towners*, plus the 'all-talking drama' *The Carnival Man*, together with a stage review, *The Blue Idea*, featuring the State Beauty Ballet.
19. Fighting between China and the Soviet Union, under Stalin, continued along the Manchurian border from August till December 1929, when a truce was reached.

20. Persian poet (1048–1131), author of the *Rubáiyát*, famously translated into English by Edward Fitzgerald in 1859.
21. Joseph Conrad (1857–1924), Polish-born English novelist, who set many of his works in Africa, Asia, the Pacific Islands and South America.
22. French-born English novelist and short-story writer (1874–1965), who set many of his works in Asian outposts of the British Empire.
23. In reality, the main island of a small archipelago a few kilometres off the coast of Borneo. Friend was to serve there as a war artist in the Australian forces in June 1945 (see diary entries for 1945).
24. Ludwig van Beethoven (1770–1827), German composer. It is not clear which concerto Friend is referring to here. In two diary entries for 1931 (31 October of this edition and *DFD 1*, p. 61) he specifically comments on the Violin Concerto in D but the mood he says this induces is not unambiguously one of rejoicing.
25. Australian-born composer (1882–1961), who became an American citizen in 1918.
26. Poem of 1896 by Rudyard Kipling (1865–1936), Indian-born British author (cf **1939**, note 27).
27. A dramatic monologue (1911) by English poet and actor J. Milton Hayes (1884–1940).
28. James I, who ruled England from 1603 to 1625; Charles I, 1625–49; Charles II, 1660–85; James II, 1685–88.
29. 'Imaginative Boy', in the column 'Gossip of the Town', *Sunday Pictorial* (Sydney), 6 October 1929, p. 7.
30. Sydney Long (1871–1955), Australian painter, printmaker and teacher. Friend started taking lessons from him possibly at Cranbrook (see his entry for 22 July 1929 in *DFD 1*, p. 6), then at Long's studio in central Sydney (see diary entry for 19 March 1931 and **1931**, note 3) and at the Royal Art Society of NSW (see **1932**, note 1).
31. In Macquarie Street, Sydney, built in 1841 for shopkeeper Thomas Burdekin.
32. Better known as Vaucluse House, in Wentworth Street, Vaucluse, an eastern suburb of Sydney, 8 kilometres from the centre. Built in 1802, it became the family home of leading NSW politician William Charles Wentworth from 1827 to 1853.
33. Gwenyth (Gwen) Friend (born 1923).
34. Another of the Friends' grazing properties in northwestern NSW, actually just over 600 kilometres—not miles—from Sydney, and situated between the towns of Warialda and Gravesend.
35. Les Friend (1885–1947), born Leslie Moses (cf **1929**, note 16, on the change of the family name).

1930s

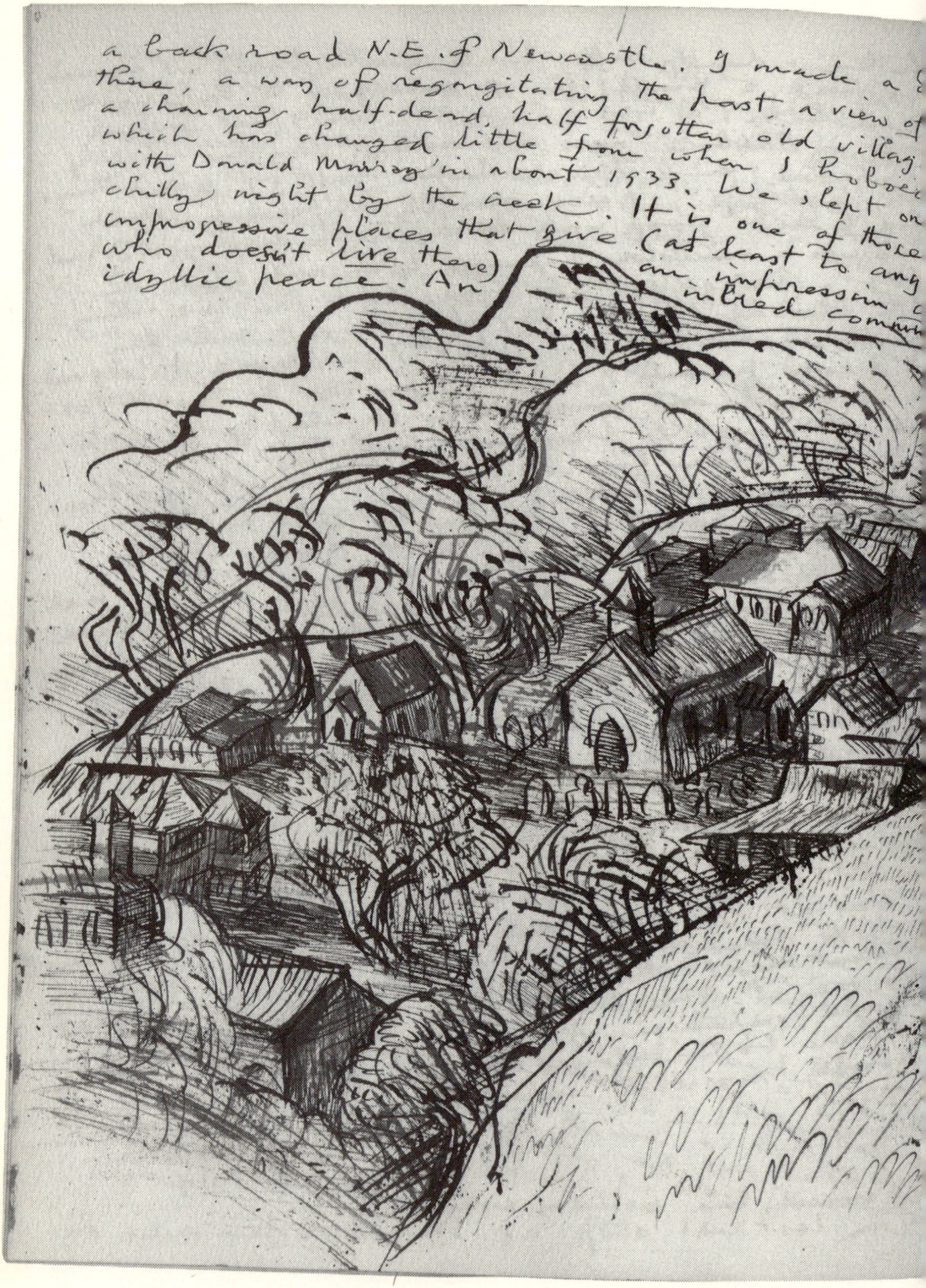
a back road N.E. of Newcastle. I made a
there, a way of regurgitating the past, a view of
a charming half-dead, half forgotten old villag
which has changed little from when I hoboe
with Donald Murray in about 1933. We slept on
chilly night by the creek. It is one of those
unprogressive places that give (at least to any
who doesn't live there) an impression
idyllic peace. An inbred commun

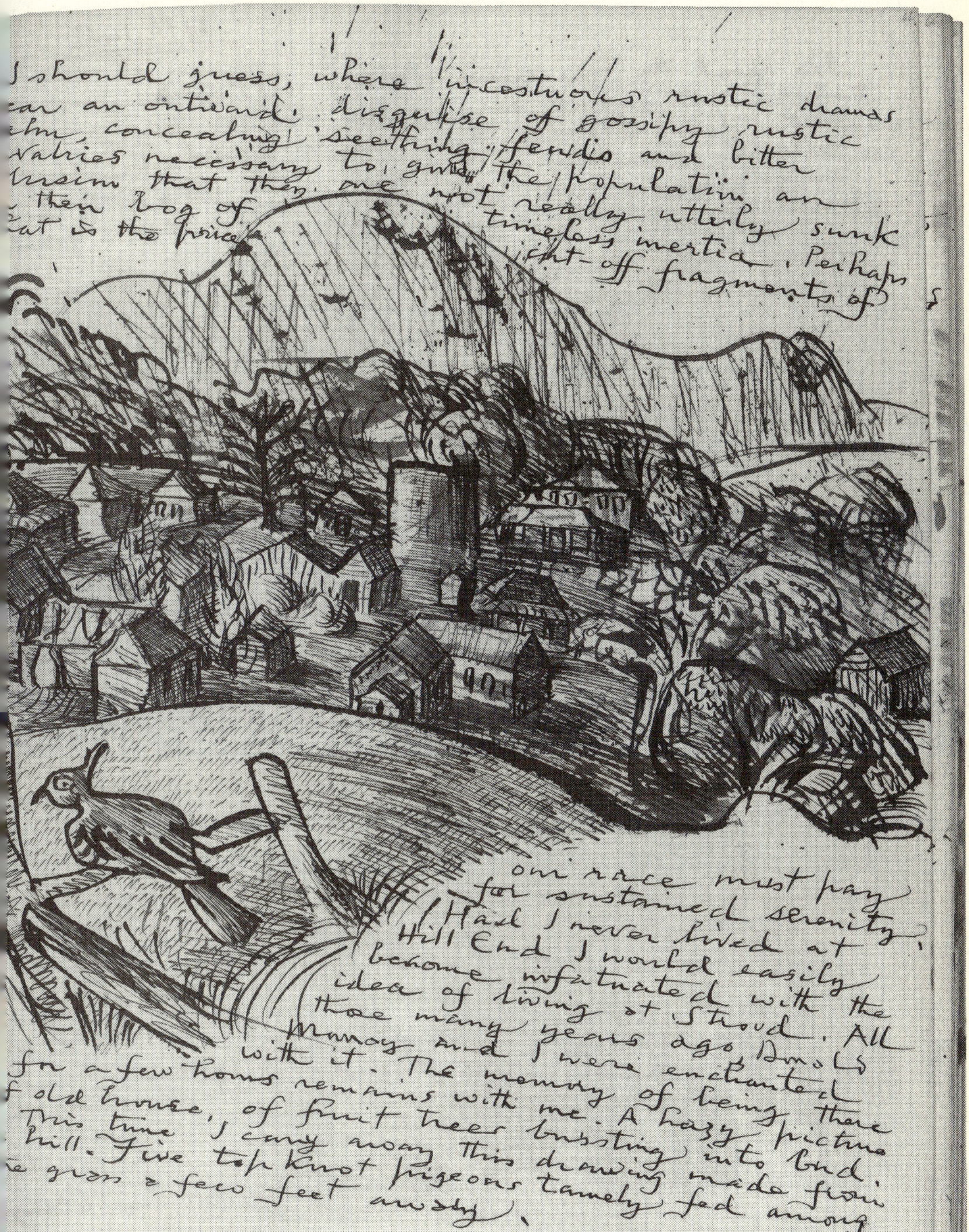

4. *Memory of Stroud* (1982).

1930

February *Sydney*. I willingly plunge once again into the comfortable artistry that constitutes civilisation. Every moment an inspiration is, and every hour a novelty, every day a new delight. Just to see the gorgeous brocade on the lovely table, and the works of Art on the walls, to hear the immortal music (the Greig piano concerto[1]) and to see my lovely Mother, and her delightful friends, is the joy of life.

I have the most fascinating mother in Australia. She is beautiful to look at, has perfect taste in clothes and everything else. Her conversation and repartee are famous in many circles. I thank the Gods and destinies that gave me such a mother as mine.

Before I left Cranbrook last term I mentioned to one or two masters that I intended to go to Europe. Since then, however, I have been seen, intact with all the emblems of Sydney Grammar School.[2] I was greatly impressed by the manner with which I was received—no taunting or other uncomfortable liabilities. I have discovered ever so many Cranbrook boys at Grammar.

June This hell-purged place is on the edge of a financial breakdown[3], and I hope that the beastly working class goes with it. The traditionally 'Sunny Sydney' has lately lost her dawn-radiant reputation, as the weather is wet and there has lately been a terrific crime-wave, making it dangerous to go out at night for fear of robbers or vitriol-squirters. In fact, Australia has spent, gone broke, become crook, and has reached a climax. Banks closed and businesses bankrupt. Dole queues, hoboing and all that.

Winter is a time of long, long nights by the roaring fire, and cigarette smoke, and mulled port, and the intimate talk of the most amusing of friends. It was decided that my state of health was discovered in wine, that my morals had been purged in cigarettes, and that my soul was soaked with dissipation. We spent a gorgeous evening in the dark, the room being illumined only by the hell-blood red of the fire—and the room was permeated by the scent of pure camaraderie.

What romance there is in these winter nights, the wind outside shrieks hopeless curses, and the trees like despairing lovers moan answers of tortured passion, and bend in will to the cruel Lady Wind. The rain lashes furiously against the windows and the thunder rolls great threats and curses.

I have studied hard all the faiths and beliefs possible, I have gazed deep into crystals, attempted without success to breach the Depth between dead and living, studied legends and the stories of heroes and vast idiocies impossible to credit. I have attempted Russian charms, Nordic and French, studied Andersen's[4] and Grimm's[5] witchcraft and all, but nothing seems to act. But the moon permeates the Dark with some improving Something—perhaps a perfume—a colour—an essence. There is magic in the moon. Wading knee-deep in elusive inspirations and producing pictures showing some mixture of effect—some unrestful doubtfulness of style—suddenly, with no warning, I crashed on a delightful and magnificent theme to weave my pictures about—moon magic!—dark mysterious realms of enchanted blackness—abounding in black witches with lovely faces—a great cauldron of moonlighted wishes; something new and barbarically old to weave and bind with imagination and ink.

I finished the picture *The Enchanted Castle* which, executed in black ink, represents a jewelled and carven coach, drawn by four white horses rushing through space, or rather clattering over a bank of black clouds, from a radiant chateau lit by the rays of the dawn sun. Mother likes the picture.

I'm simply bursting with happiness! I've escaped from the disturbed realms of the house, and am languishing in the most wicked manner by the beach. I'm enveloped in a lovely, ethereal fog, which is embroidered with the sun,

5. *Title page to 1930 manuscript diary.*

and all the symbols of happiness. There is the harbour, stretching misty realms of gold and light blue, and the far shore is a fairy paradise, woven of jewel-spangled delight. Such misty and languorous mornings, when Vaucluse and Potts Point[6] appeared as gentle green islands, with flashing white houses with red roofs, emerging from a sea of clouds, and the great Bridge, still unfinished, lost its steely modern appearance, and became a great, grey rainbow, standing over the dreamy harbour, as a kind and fatherly guardian.[7] And as the Sun rises—shedding his rosy dawn-radiance around, and making the mists grey and abstract, I know there is Magic in the Sun.

July The town had few attractions at this time and the only shows worth seeing were the lovely Greta Garbo[8] in *Anna Christie*[9] and Taliaferro[10] in the lead of *Let Us Be Gay!*[11] Much strengthened by various and delightful reports concerning the sophisticated charms of the adorable Norma Shearer[12], Mother and I made bold to sally forth to the Plaza Theatre[13]. Upon our arrival we were overwhelmed by the voluptuous Spanish air of the place. Spanish maidens hither'd and thither'd midst much fluttering of fans and swaying of mantillas (or vanillas: whatever one calls those lengthy lace-curtains that drop so invitingly from tortoise-shell hairpins!). There was nothing (except, perhaps, a slight aroma of Spanish onions permeating the dusky air with many a romantic and suggestive whiff) needed to complete the atmosphere of the theatre. Norma Shearer did not disappoint: she was just simply devastatingly beautiful.

At mother's last delightful party a violinist promised to send me a folio of wonderful reproductions of the French moderns. Aye, there is the rub—the reproductions could not be detected with a magnifying glass—but the *moderne* pictures they upheld were so obscenely childish that I have fled before the folio. Since I saw them I have not drawn a line—and even my writing has suffered horribly. I can write of nothing personal, lest I grow too rude, and the public would censure the book. Can't I do anything? No, I can't. I am disapproved of. In certain scribal meanderings at school I have been accused of long-windedness. It's about time that someone installed a new all-electric me. I am rebelliously writing this because I am writing for myself. No one else has enough subtlety to understand it.

How much I long for the days when I am famous. Ah, to see the book magnate, clothed in a check suit, and with a scarlet and blue tie, stride towards me with a confident visage: 'I want you to illustrate a book!' he says. 'Oh,' I answer, lighting a cigarette in an irritating manner (forgetting to offer him one), 'how much?' 'About £100,' he says, dropping his eyes. I stare very deep and amusedly at the diamond pin in his tie. 'Is that all?' 'Well, of course, there's royalties.' 'Yes, I suppose there are!' 'We'll make it £170.' I woke up.

I visited the Art Gallery[14] and I gazed fascinated at the fairy-like consistency of Norman Lindsay's[15] etchings—I rejoiced.

December My mother asked me what I wanted for Christmas, and I said, 'There's a wonderful book with a hundred pen drawing illustrations, of Norman Lindsay, and it's called *The Satyricon of Petronius*, and I'd love to have that.' A limited edition and wonderfully bound in vellum.[16]

Lindsay was an absolute god as far as I was concerned. I admire his pen drawings and the drawings influenced me a lot. I did get the discipline of pen drawing from him, and I owe that to him.

1931

29–30 January *En route to Glendon.* I left Sydney—bound for the arid northwest. I lit a cigarette and made a lengthy tour of the train—which to my boredom and disgust, rendered naught but a few odd old fogies, odiously smoking their pipes, with their expensive, pink-tipped nasal organs closely embracing the racing news. I reflected bitterly on eternity as I munched an ancient meat pie at Newcastle.

I watched the sun dawn magnificently over the brown, dull plains. Wide open spaces. The train puffed despairingly along—stopping now and then at a tiny siding with nothing else in sight for miles around, except a tanned and grimy station hand, leaning on the rails of the siding. Eventually, we reached Moree. I got out and boarded the ancient branch line which went to Glendon Siding. The date of the engine was 1878, and it took four hours to puff itself to my destination.

Glendon—Hell—My brother Ten was there, and the cook; everyone else was out on the run, so I changed into riding breeches and strolled disconsolately about.

31 January This day blazoned forth in dry, thirsty heat. Ten and I mounted our horses and rode over to the river Gwydir, where it flows through Glendon. Near the river is a pine-clad hill, rich in topaz and carnelian—glowing transparent and rosy: we collected some beautiful specimens. Later, we swam in the olive depths of the Gwydir.

That evening we had mutton: boiled mutton that was lukewarm—ugh! And melting butter on slabs of half-hearted toast.

6 February My birthday today. I am 16 years of age, being blessed with a genius for art and a talent for writing. My mother, known as Adorable, is a lady of extreme beauty, wit and sophistication, it is from this gracious lady that I inherit all talents—she is the descendant of John Wilmot, Earl of Rochester, who was reputedly an illegitimate son of Charles I. This explains Adorable's eyes—so magnetic and brown are they that an aged servant, unknowing of the descent, said they were the laughing, lovely eyes of Charles Stuart himself. The elder brother, Harley, monstrous grim of appearance and most unbelievably grown-up for 18. Ten is younger, fair-haired and good-looking.

I am by nature extremely generous, and I have always been used generously except by my father and his family. They are my sworn enemies. It was at his order that I am to be given 10/- per week wages for work as hard as that of Harley.

On my return from a ride to the remote corners of the estate I found a telegram from L'adorable awaiting me. It was such a pleasant and darling communication from what seems another world—the world of fine china—crisp linen and heavy brocades—lovely light voices, and intelligence—art, civilisation, rather a remote world from this hell which could be a paradise. My father disapproved of this art business. He thought artists were just one grade worse than parsons, actually.

News has arrived that we are to expect the odious paternal parent soon. Damn! Skeleton at the feast—fly in the ointment! I shall keep out of his way as much as possible.

9–10 February Dad, that most base reptile, really must be feeling the Depression to arrive in his Packard[1]. At dinner he was pretty unbearable, being so utterly ordinary that horses and cricket comprised the main line of his conversation. This man's very ordinariness chokes outspoken hate—those fishy eyes—that black tie, with its common gold clasp. God, how I hate him!

It seems that it was expected that I would be coming up to this prison for good these holidays! I vigorously replied that I should more likely be going to England than chasing unintelligent sheep about on a hopeless spot in the obscurity that is Australia.

12 February *En route to Sydney*. The straining and wheezing engine stopped at the siding, and picked up our traps and ourselves, and continued its weary way to the plains and Moree. The journey was terribly dull—mile after mile of unalterable country—here and there a station or a windmill relieved the tension of the flat landscape. Presently more hilly country was reached and the sun sank. Sleep came easily—lulled by the monotonous click of the rails, and the windy roar of the train—a strange melody, a potent lullaby.

Mid-February *Sydney*. None can conjecture my utter gladness on arriving home to Gladswood Gardens. Thin cups, with glowing patterns, and marvellous tea that contrasted vividly with the station brew. Brocades—beautiful pictures.

Met Bobby Helpmann[2], wit, wistful dancer, choreographer and marvellous mime. I liked him. One of those rare personalities who flowed like a stream rushing down rapids—leaping, chuckling, throwing out spray like cascades of diamonds, flashing over rocks: mingling confidently with calm river stretches, allying itself always to its own essence, the great ocean.

21 February This education is really rather useless—except as a foundation on which to embroider truths in conversation. Were I left stranded today, I could not earn money honestly by all the many wiles I've learnt. Who cares to buy even the most lovely pictures nowadays? I'll have to take to bushranging or blackmailing methinks. I cannot work on the land—my aesthetic sense forbids; if driven, perhaps I could. But who would take an inexperienced hand at my age?

10 March I am at a turning point in my career. My education is almost complete, as much as I shall need in life that is taught by school I know, and my outside knowledge is informed by watching other people's tragedies and joys—their charming comedies. It is highly likely that I shall leave Sydney Grammar School as suddenly and dramatically as I've left many schools—an unpremeditated leaving. I almost feel that I am rushing forever to an unknown destination—what shall happen there? Will I like it? I adore leaving schools.

18 March It seems so hard to describe days at school—they are very same. I long constantly for the friendships and gaiety of Cranbrook—where one knew everyone. At Sydney Grammar I know so few—having no really amusing and intimate friends except Pip, Bert and Bill. Bill—being dark and handsome in a gypsy sort of way—is an extremely attractive young man. The maths are the only things I don't understand—it's so dashed involved.

19 March I was working on my first etching—tremendously thrilling—at Sydney Long's studio at the top of Callaghan House.[3]

20 March The science master (hatchet-faced scoundrel) has told us—licking his thin lips in fanatic ecstasy—in religious unction—that the whole chlorine and hydrochloric acid question will be brought before our eyes next Tuesday. Our geography master is a scream—he talks anti-Lang[4] for most of the lesson—the other half he raves about getting jobs in such impossible times. Strange as it may seem, however, I do know a little geography.

24 March Back to the everlasting sameness that always happens in a different way—I suppose it's like love—only I haven't tasted that yet. I felt cooped up in the evening—and went for a long solitary walk in the dark—ending it by wandering—rather depressed—around the twisting paths and little stairways of Cranbrook gardens. I often long to be there again—I know not why, because my Cranbrook days, though gay, were not all so pleasant. One never remembers the bad times.

26 March In the evening I went out for a walk—and entered Cranbrook gardens by the little-used gate on the tennis courts.

The garden is gorgeous—a really old place, relic of the days when Cranbrook was Government House. The jasmine was out on the little tree, and filled the night with a burden of exotic scent.

27 March This was a day that many uneducated waifs who are serving at Sydney Grammar have waited and longed for. It was announced that a half-holiday would be given for the swimming sports. About halfway through the program we became bored, and left the baths and went to the Art Gallery, situated nearby. Our main object there was to inspect the marvellous Norman Lindsay watercolours and the Syd Longs and Hilder's[5] colourful pictures, most beautiful of which was a study of a sailing ship, executed in green. Long's *Mill*[6] was wonderful. As for Lindsay's work, it was too gorgeous for words—too colourful and thrilling for music to describe! I saw Lloyd Rees's[7] delightful pencil drawings.

31 March Owing to a swollen lip, I stayed at home today. Seeing nothing else to do, I took out my inks and paper and drew a picture. The subject was a rather over-merry banquet, taking place in a huge arras-hung hall—the central figure is a merry prince flirting with a duchess.

5 April Harley and Ten went out to visit that ghastly den of hypocrisy, the Moses home at Ashfield.[8] So L'adorable and I went out for a walk. My august grandmother on the paternal side[9] is the most dreadful woman—having pitted all her influence against L'adorable. A mercilessly righteous woman, utterly devoid of humanity, whose character is but a cardhouse of the rigid, soulless conventions of her class & time. Well—I hope her bed falls in—and all her fowls die.

The family is rather peculiar about money. They place a huge importance on it, & yet are incapable of that grand inspired extravagance without which cash is only a sterile principle. They are always quarrelling about it, intriguing for it. I think money is as great an eccentricity with them as painting is with me. My grandmother spends about £200 per annum. Her wealth is a thing of legends. She counts the apples in the pantry, so that the maids cannot steal them. She has a garden full of lovely flowers, but has never in her life sent any to anyone.

It would seem that horticulture tends to distil black humours & furious passions. My grandfather[10], a man noted for wealth, meanness, violence & intolerance, devoted his later life to growing dahlias & breeding fox-terriers: his father before him, noted for the same furious temperament & a fanatic interest in cricket (he cut off two of his children without a penny because they declared that there had been cricketers greater than W. G. Grace[11]) openly avowed a fondness for carnations.

7 April After dinner we ventured forth to see Gloria Swanson[12] in *What a Widow!*[13] It was a marvellous show—Gloria Swanson being too fascinating for words—scintillating and rich (thank the Lord for a' that[14]—I can't stand sordid stories).

10 April Rain and wind howled—furies danced among the trees—and I felt groggy; so school was not visited. I think that nothing is more pleasant than sitting smoking on the sofa before a blazing fire—with a good book—or just thoughts. So few people possess the power of liking loneliness. I painted and did pen work in the afternoon—one successful result being a bookplate for L'adorable which I shall etch after I have finished the first plate, on which I am working.

30 April My art master, Syd Long, and I talked on various subjects—he pictured me striving to create bigger and better sheep in my coming visit to the station. I told him of my intention of having etching implements on the station, and of sending the plates down to be printed. I began blacking my new plate. After it was bitten and printed—with which process Syd Long helped me—he seemed rather pleased with the result, a bookplate for L'adorable.

1 May This was to be the future Australian New Year—the first day of the Glorious Revolution, whose main aim was to be equity and freedom etc., etc. Riots and all sorts of thrilling things were expected—so I sharpened up my ancient crusading sword. Nothing has happened. The town went about its usual ways—and the square was full of unemployed people discussing ways and means of enlightening the world.

4 May During the course of a leisurely moment in science, I drew the triangular teacher—who methinks, hath a soft spot in a stony heart for me—with a satanically ironic expression on his comely countenance, with two little horns protruding from his dome. The drawing was passed round the class, and finally into the hands of Bill, who showed it to the teacher—a dangerous psychological experiment. Glory be! The soft spot in the stony teacher made him smile benevolently.

11 May I was inspired to draw an idea that I have hitherto been unable to express—a modernistic semi-Lindsay type of thing—with laughing—hating—fearing faces in a whirl—all swept into cogs and immense spinning wheels—irresistible and eternal machinery.

13 May The school at large is enraptured with the illusion that I was off to Paris! I was charged with unspeakable messages to the chorus girls of the Folies Bergères.[15] The end of the rich pampered life. We were to leave school and Sydney, and I to leave forever that old style of being.

20 May *Glendon*. A new character has been added to our choice menagerie—a cook. She is indeed an extraordinary character—weareth very short red plain dresses edged with lace of a frivolous character. She has a strange voice. Her cooking, may it be said, is a distinct improvement.

This day has been entirely spent in the shady and picturesque precincts of Tea-Tree Mill, about a mile from the homestead. We decided to build a cubby in the centre of one of the lovely trees; the tree of our choice is the joining of five trees in one common root, which is the floor of the main room. The walls of the house are thatched with leaves and branches. We shall bury the balance of carnelians, agates and topaz that we have collected during our various adventurings, in the vicinity of this house.

27 May This has been the happiest day—spent by the rushing river—now half-flooded by heavy rains—a thing of rippling, casual strength—no longer olive green as usual, but a muddy brown. Ten shot a brace of tiny grey woodpigeons which we roasted on a stick in the coals of an open fire for lunch. Tea was boiled in an enamel cup, a billy not being available. Later, we went hunting for precious stones in one of the numerous pine-covered hills in the district, and by a sheer fluke, I found the most magnificent topaz yet discovered on the station. The sun shone and everything was too perfect. I shall remember this day through many a hazardous moon. As soon as we were home, and before the fire, down came torrents of rain—the sound of rain drumming on the roof thrills me—makes one feel secure, out of the wind.

3 June Il papa approached and, as he mended a puncture in his luxurious Packard, he spoke to me the first speech that I have yet had addressed to me from him. He expects to go broke during the next fortnight—he owes on Carrington[16], the other station, and people may close on him any day, sending him bankrupt. He went on accusing L'adorable of incomprehensible extravagance, and of half a dozen utterly untrue things. As far as I can see, he's forgotten what she is like—and wreaks bitter curses on a wraith of imagination.

8 June Harley, whose fishing score in the last many moons is an unbroken nil, asked us to go fishing with him this afternoon, and during a chase from tree to tree on the riverbank, I fell into the river. So I stood, high and almost dry, in a conspicuous place on the bank, unadorned by the various pruderies of civilisation, until my garments dried on the fence.

13 June Only the pale grey and yellow light preceded the sun. After a hasty breakfast in the icy, misty frigidity, the most enjoyable ride I've had—and presently the frosty mauve grass bent under sheep, hurrying and startled. Luscious dawn—golden and red, and a cloudless sky, the sun casting yellow on the grass and purple shadows a haze of mist rose above the flock. After we'd yarded them, the ghastly business of tailing the lambs began. I emerged covered in gore—my hands a dripping with the warm hateful blood—that sticky scarlet. I hate it less now.

24 June I created the Bacchanal[17]—a picture à la Lindsay, with flying limbs and hilarious laughter and Bacchus—giant, and his bushy face alight with surprising benevolence—and the light of gods and miracles shining on and bathing his limbs—and the women, the wild nude sirens dancing and laughing, their limbs burden'd with sunny shadow, and wine spilling in warm red scarletness from the heavy, full chalices: leopards, and satyrs piping amusedly.

9–10 July Ah—the Heaven of gorgeous joy at seeing Adorable. At last is civilisation arrived! At last the symbol and wheel upon which my destiny turns. I long for an unknown quality—I know not what—but it is not to be found here—she shall bring it—perhaps it's glamour—an unmistakeable, indefinable essence.

Van loads of crates and boxes and all the dear furniture arrived. I unpacked boxes of china and brass—and silver and green glass and glittering crystal.

Luscious warm sleep—full of rich dreams, full of such luxurious imagery that I have missed and yearned for many a day. Adorable is the bringer of the most marvellous joys.

Last week of July I have a thousand things to write about really and a million subjects to draw, but I am mostly engrossed in thinking the language of Michael Arlen.[18] His phraseology fascinates me, and I spend many hours of spare time reading his stories. I have started to write a book in the style of Arlen—the subject is to be some amusing incidents of the life at Gladswood Gardens—nothing in the world gives me greater joy than slinging off at the eminently respectable pillars of the society.

All predict a brilliant artistic career for me. I have been told by sages and seers that in June or July I shall leave for England. July is almost over, and I have been disappointed for the last three years. Australia is a very beautiful country, and full of adventure. But it is not the land of an artist, no, not this uneducated and new land for me. Except for an hereditary hatred for the Labor Party[19], my instincts for the nation are utterly undeveloped.

There is such a regrettable lack of subject in one's life—so few people have exciting things happen to them.

7 September On the trellis at the back of the house, there grow two vines: one is the grape, and the other, a tortured tangle of wisteria. The ashy pale clumps that covered the former have just begun to amass into a gorgeously scented wonder of mauve—exquisite. Reminding me even of the vine that strangles the Georgian pillars at Cranbrook—and also of that exquisite and famous vine that hangs heavily on the pillars supporting the flagged verandah of Wentworth House.

10 September Papa made arrangements to inspect Highland Plain sheep and cattle. We met at the yards adjoining Highland. His Majesty, who, despite his sneering at ordinary cleanliness, let alone effeminacy, wore a woven wool waistcoat of a delicate fawn shade, and an apricot silk shirt. He was as ordinary as ever—that awful, swamping ordinariness.

22 September I lazed this day away swimming in the Gwidyr. The willow trees down by the river are simply gorgeous. Now is the time to admire them—not yet fully decked, with trailers of narrow fresh leaves sometimes twenty feet in length: despite which the shapely trees seem surprisingly nude, reminding one of some lovely nymph, standing in a pool from whose depths she emerges, clothed only in astonishing lengths of wet hair, clinging as though caressing to the perfection of her form.

Large golden carp, black mottled like leopards, laze gleaming in the rippling shallows, so drowsy one could catch them in the hand. We build a crazy raft and spend days down there fishing. We cook the fish in mud, blackfella fashion.

2 October I painted and read unsuccessfully by turns, and the evening was deep ere I had completed the one success in an exasperating day—a self-portrait in pencil—rather effeminate, I think, but remarkably like me.

Then Adorable and I talked for some time, until the persisting shouts of thunder from without ended an interesting talk on delicious past indiscretions. I went to my room, lit all the way along the verandah in vivid lightning—terrifying and glorious silhouettes of the mountains and trees and grotesque flashes of intense blue light spread like spider webs across the sky. Awful crashes and roars and brittle sound vibrate the furniture around my bed, whence I now write by shaky candlelight.

18 October Adorable came down to the Gwidyr in the sulky with Gwen. We swam the ponies, and bathed, and showed her all the delightful places—including the black rocks that jut out with the rapids, forming a peaceful pool of deepest green, edged with massive sand banks on the shore side, and by the grotesque base of black rock on the other. And on the river side of the rocks the water foams and roars in white and effervescent fury, banked by grotesque ti-trees, gesturing and posturing fantastically with coiling and awkward limbs in the savage shapes of humans and ghouls.

Adorable hates the river somehow—flies, etc., I suppose. I don't enjoy it half as much with the civilised accessories of afternoon tea, bathers and whatnot. They seem to cramp one's enjoyment of everything *au naturel.*

31 October Today went by quickly and hotly—spent by myself in the modelling and gilding and painting of a little Spanish galleon, about four and a half inches in length. The hull is perfect, being hollowed out absolutely, leaving the sides about a tenth of an inch thick, pierced by gunports. The sails are golden parchment, emblazoned in crimson and black with heraldic gargoyles and eagles. The masts are gilt and crimson-striped. I wrote a letter to Sydney Long, which I shall post along with a folio of my latest drawings for his criticism. I am going to attempt to find a market for them.

I had quite an enthralling talk with Adorable—long into the night, to the gloomy ecstasies of Beethoven's Violin Concerto—the intense waiting for that divine orchestra to stumble upon the inevitable theme—and the wonderful full tones of Kreisler's[20] violin.

12 November Dad relieved the tension of these past few days' expectancy by arriving in a luxurious and new grey Packard; donated by his mother, it turned out. He was closeted in deep and earnest conference with Adorable for some time, and later she confided to me the result of their talk. To my great relief it was a divorce. Dad has gone and fallen hard for a 25-year-old, whom he wishes to marry.

19 November The chez-vous at the Smiths of Warialda[21] this evening proved excessively boring with flashes of genuine entertainment. At dark we reached the deserted town—lightless—soundless, death. Mr Penrose directed us to the scene of the orgy. We were the first to arrive, it happened: we supplied card tables, cards and bridge scores, portable gramophone and a lot of dance records.

Presently people arrived—they were an awful crowd—flash young men in insufferable clothes—coatless and coarse. Women—ugh!—creatures in cotton stockings and shapeless dresses far above the knees. Many grouped themselves around the piano and played awful dirges of waltzes, and sang lustily.

Adorable and Mrs Dunn and a charming girl accompanying her were the only people dressed in long dresses—she was in a taffeta confection of pinks, they in black lace. Talking to them was the most enjoyable part of the whole evening.

1932

Sydney. The Royal Art Society School[1] under Dattilo-Rubbo[2] and Syd Long. Dear old Cavaliere Dattilo-Rubbo shone with an air of *grande manière* connoisseurship. A tremendous interest in art, and an ability to spot talent in his students. A wonderful personality and very amusing. A very human contact with his students. Very short and bulky, and a bit eccentric, but really an extremely attractive man. A marvellous speaking voice. He spoke broken English but I think he simply decided not to speak Australian English because he could be much more amusing and effective using it as a medium. He was so funny and on the ball.

Some of the very early works I've seen of his were very interesting, but they were never great paintings. He was not a good painter, but he was an absolutely wonderful teacher. A real artist in his whole approach to things. A thing had to be good but he didn't give a damn if it was ultra modern or not. If it was good it was good and that was that. He'd talk about the Old Masters. Of course, Michelangelo[3] and Raphael[4]. And he had prints of Italian master drawings. He didn't really champion Australian artists on the whole. He wasn't really very interested in people like Streeton[5], Norman Lindsay. But he wasn't intolerant about them. He didn't have any objection to Modigliani.[6] Just the abstract of abstract. It was the Bovril[7] without any beef in it.

Out here Impressionism was wildly avant-garde. Van Goghs[8] and Gauguins[9] were a revolution. That sort of thing was regarded as absolutely outrageous. Van Gogh et cetera shocked and horrified Sydney Long. He even thought of Margaret Preston[10] as being a dangerous revolutionary.

Glendon. I had to go and learn to run the property that my father had settled on myself and my brothers. Castrating lambs and all that sort of thing.

Charlie Sanderson, a young, well-educated half-Siamese who came out here to study agriculture, went broke in the middle of his studies and became a hobo. He came to Glendon on the track, walking the country in search of work. We gave him a job. He was my first real friend. He was an enchanting person. My friendship with Charlie led me into contact with a world I would never otherwise have known. Though my interest had lain in that direction since childhood, he had much to do with that interest in orientals and orientalism. So I've much to be grateful for to Charlie.

He didn't get such a good bargain out of it: the unwelcome pestering of an infatuated adolescent. Hard cheese on the Siamese.

1933

When Charlie left I was at loggerheads with the family, loathed Glendon, and ran away and became a hobo. Somehow anything to do with blood gives me the horrors. That's really why I didn't stay on the land—cutting off the intimate parts of lambs' anatomies was really too much to stand for. Beside that horror, the endless blague about the price of wool paled to insignificance. Regular meals nicely cooked and the deadly certainty of tomorrow—the delicious cool sheets and soft mattresses—unblemished by Sin—all the joys, with their balancing drawbacks, of that sort of life can only do for me for a rest between acts. Flower arrangements, fabrics and Orrefors glass[1] all go with an inane cackle of talk and equally inane state of mind. Very amusing, very nice, but you need to go hoboing after a dose of it to purge the brain of nonsense.

I heard Charlie had gone to Queensland, and it was there I went, searching for him, immersed in the backwash of emotion of one of those painful calf-loves. I didn't find him, but I learnt an enormous lot about people and independence and myself, becoming part of the world of vagabonds, carrying my swag, tramping, and begging my food. One would be caught jumping the rattlers[2], and the police would beat you up a bit, and put you in the cells for a week. Queensland was pretty rough and tough.

Magnetic Island.[3] A tropical paradise. Meaning, I suppose, that it wasn't full of tin roofs and mosquitoes, and it was warm. I lived in a cave on a rocky point. It had once been an Abos' camp, and there were weird indistinct scrawls in ochre and white on rough walls, and just at the entrance, a sort of platform of rock, and the ancient inhabitants had cut there a well in the rock. It was full of the leaves and debris of fifty years, but I cleaned it out, and soon the rain filled it with sweet water. I built a small roof of thatched grass above it, to shade and cool it.

The natives who made the cave and the well had all been killed. The young bucks from Townsville used to come over with shooting parties to hunt them. In those days—even now—Aborigines weren't considered quite human. The Church made a declaration that they hadn't any immortal souls. That *was* convenient. People could murder and massacre as much as they pleased without qualms of conscience. Gawd, what a racket! What a belief!

From the rock ledge there was a sheer drop of about thirty feet to the sea, which ever pounded and surged there, making a lullaby or any sort of song you were in the mood for. It was a calm place, and warm, and I would lie naked in the sun, and brown my skin to mahogany.

I had a supply of flour and salt, sugar, fat and tea. There was fruit in plenty growing on the fertile lower reaches of the island, such things as pawpaw, mangoes and mandarins. There were plenty of fish. I could sit all day on a rock, with a line, or go down at night when the tide was low, with a torch of pine and a pronged spear, and walk waist-deep in the quiet dark waters of the bay, spearing the barramundi that rose to look at the flame.

My cave looked over the blue to Townsville, and the mountain there, all very fine and purple and gold. It was very pleasing to the eye. To the right of the cave the coast curved back into a little bay, with a sickle moon of gold sand, and a fringe of coconut palms. I used to wonder about the rocky paths, and climb the hills. It was so sunbathed and quiet, and from nearly every point you could look out to the sea. On one side, the ocean side, I could see where the disturbed waters foamed over the Great Barrier Reef, and on the other, there were the mountains and the land. Sometimes down on the wave-washed rocks I'd see a great sea-turtle come blowing and puffing by, oaring the boisterous waves with his paddles like a trireme.

The days were placid, but full of curious events that seemed idyllic. There was a natural amphitheatre of rock on one of the hills. It was like a Stonehenge.[4]

Cairns. The Mecca of all 'travellers' in the winter months. About three hundred of us hoboes were camped in the Showground there. (This was at the worst of the Depression, when we were a numerous tribe.) Now all the big towns of the North except Cairns had erected big regular camps, with bunks, shower rooms & so on for the hoboes, so when we were given notice to get out so they could hold the annual agricultural show in the grounds, we sent a spokesman to parley. He demanded for us a shelter. The mayor refused to hear any of it, & sent another notice to quit. We refused.

Then the show got up in arms. They would come in numbers & chase us out, they said. We prepared our defences. The grounds were surrounded by an eight-foot fence. We put piles of stones at strategic spots, the more desperate characters armed themselves with clubs and bicycle chains.

Then came the day of the great battle. The townee rabble approached our walls headed by the Salvation Army band playing 'Onward Christian Soldiers'[5], very bravely, until a gibber from our defences silenced the big drum & robbed the tune of guts. Then, as the battle joined, it began to pour with rain. We were hopelessly outnumbered & fled in the wet dusk. It was a comic riot, & like all efforts by underdogs to assert their rights by violence, futile & inglorious. But we enjoyed it.

I found the Sailor family[6] in Malaytown[7], and through them another fascinating world. I was on the dole, a very thorough waster and vagabond. Charlie Sailor took me in and announced to Umma, his wife, that I was from then on his son, and he told the rest of his children I was their elder brother. After that I lived with them in Malaytown.

Torres Strait Islands. Those islands are really lovely. Picked up three island lingos in six months. Mer[8] was my special island. One of those symbolic places that one must somehow get to one day, like Timbuktu and Byzantium.

Went and stayed with the Kanakas.[9] The hard-driven boys sang when forced to dive on a dangerous reef where strong currents churned the water to milk. Those island songs are wine in my blood. Long lines of lithe Kanakas rhythmically singing, their strong grace mocking the seas they sing of, with undulating movements entranced in the jungle rhyme of the drums, and dark faces gleaming fitfully in lantern light, deep-throated voices harmonising in the poetic chants of ancient times.

Black Melanesian youths sprawled on the lugger decks at night like wreaths of glinting ebony. They sang such curious sad cadences to this star or that—or maybe it was a paean to the ungodly mountain, Gelam, that rises and frown over the palms of Mer.

Sydney. Came back from being on the track. I wasn't very well received by relations, but I was given an allowance of £50 a year. I was living in a cellar of a house up in The Rocks[10], the old dungeon at Buggery Barn.

1934

Dattilo-Rubbo wasn't with the Royal Art Society School any longer. He had a proper old-fashioned studio in Bligh Street. And so I went along to see him. I had no money, so he took me on there as a student.

Dattilo-Rubbo's wasn't a big school but there were enough students to keep it interesting. He was a very thorough teacher. He wasn't harsh at all but his criticism was outright and strong and helpful. You'd spend five days on the one drawing, from the nude, and you'd think you had it absolutely perfect, a great masterpiece. Rubbo used to call me 'Donaltello'[1], and he'd come along and say: 'Ah, Donaltello, rub it-it out. Rub it-it out.' Your heart was breaking, and you'd rub it out, and start the whole bloody thing again.

He'd do his teacher's duty by the ones who had no talent. And that was that. But the ones who really had talent, he took some trouble over. If you were asked to his house, and I was on three or four occasions, it was a very, very great honour. Lunch. Italian food.

One or two students annoyed him deliberately. They thought he was hopelessly old-fashioned. Our revolt was expressed in forms and styles (cubist, abstract, etc.) from a revolt inaugurated by French artists twenty years before we took it up in our own country. The Sydney modern art movement started off with Roy de Maistre[2], who was painting cubist pictures before he went to Europe. Such people weren't popular here. There were very very few people buying paintings—I suppose not more than twenty in the whole of Sydney. They were highly sophisticated in their taste and they bought early Margaret Prestons and that sort of thing.

Sydney art was lively. Sydney artists enjoyed themselves in their attics, drinking plonk and eating crusts of bread. And we all lived that sort of life up here, in attics round Kings Cross.[3] We had a marvellous bloody time, and we did all sorts of interesting things. Plenty of laughter—and plenty of laughter in the paintings. Inevitably a lot of us detested one another's work, but that didn't stop us from all being together and having parties. A sort of Sydney bohemia.

What saved me from becoming the type of a dozen creatures I know, was meeting Donald Murray[4]. Murray and I shared a mad attic up at the Cross, at ten shillings and sixpence a week. From the window we could look into the garden of a convent. There we used to watch some wildly gay nuns who played tennis. On the court, in their great black robes that flapped crazily in the wind, they looked like a concourse of crows dancing at a Sabbath. People in impossible hats. Sundry wicked ones, in elegant silk dressing gowns, trip down the boulevards with a blue and white jug to get the morning milk. The racket of trams, music from cafés.

For a short time in Kings Cross, Peter Finch[5] and I were lovers. Peter and I had met at a mad sleazy Bohemian party, where there was a lot of unemployed actors. We had the same sense of humour, great rapport. He became absolutely fascinated by my stories of 'jumping the rattler' up in Queensland as a hobo and, as things were so bad in Sydney—poor Peter was broke beyond belief—I pawned the Norman Lindsay *Satyricon* and we went off hoboing together, riding free on those goods trains. I showed him the ropes.

Katoomba.[6] Peter's concept of a vagabond's life had about it something of a strolling player. For a while we camped outside Katoomba in an empty cottage in the Blue Mountains—bitterly cold. We lived on a terrible diet: oatmeal porridge, dates and vegetables pinched from a paddock. Peter and I pretended to be Russian Cossack horse dancers, and invented a complete horse-dancing Kultur for the spoofing of the citizens. Going into the village, Peter was a White Russian polo player, a sort of orphan of the Revolution. He had a pair of boots which by some sleight of imagination became a complete Cossack costume, and he spoke no more than six words of English. My own part allowed me a few words more. I was a faithful serf who had helped him escape the Bolsheviks—so that as hoboes we had a certain outlandish chic which served better than a knock at the door to ask a kind lady for a hand-out.

Sydney. It's irresistible. Suddenly I just can't help it, I must masquerade. At the instigation of a romantic hostess, I arrived at a party in a landau (one of those that used to ply at Manly) drawn by two white horses. I was dressed as a Malay princeling, with pearls, silver kris, sarong and all, and a terrifically grand manner, which broke down towards the end when I got a bit plastered.

I sold peanuts at the Sydney show[7], dressed up as an Indian. It was very funny, because part of the time I had to be inside a sort of imitation elephant, shooting the packets of peanuts down its hollow trunk to the waiting customers. I saw lots of people I knew—country people mostly—but they didn't know me.

I delivered a lecture on Brahma[8], impersonating Krishnamurti[9]. Two of us with an interpreter pretended we were Sumatran polo players in a pub at Narrabeen.[10] But why do it? That's what's really interesting. I really can't define any reason at all. The masquerade (and the oriental angle) are obviously symptoms of something or other.

Melbourne. Christmas with Donald Murray. The City of Patronage—I hate Melbourne. I don't like those houses, and those Rich and Powerful dowagers—and the general air of all painters: all the beastly affectations of their cults and isms. People bubbling babyishly about complexes and homosexuality and symbolism and all the half-cooked misunderstood esoterica of creeds and labels. I prefer the vulgarities of Sydney. It's an extroverted town, and it's never gone in much for dignity. Melbourne, of course—dignity's headquarters, so long as it's got a good blue suit. It was Sydney that was doing the exciting things. I don't know whether it's the Sydney climate, or the sort of social history behind Sydney going right back.

1935

Sydney. Dattilo-Rubbo's class four or five days a week, and sometimes two or three nights a week.

En route to Queensland. I hoboed with Donald Murray. Crazy journey. Murray and I were enchanted with Stroud, a charming half-dead, half-forgotten old village a few miles on a back road northeast of Newcastle. Old houses, fruit trees bursting into bud. There for a few hours.

Brisbane. Murray and I were here for a week or two. The War Memorial[1] by the Sacred Flame when I boiled my billy on that same eternal light; the palm tree near our lodging whose fruits I ate experimentally to Murray's cries of '*poison!*'; the bright lollipop-pink walls of the room; listening to Handel.[2]

Murray I have counted my dearest friend: I have known so well the extremely fine side of his nature. He did nothing but good to me, and taught me enough to go through a pretty hectic and dangerous life without getting hurt overmuch. All of philosophy, and of understanding, I have from him.

Sydney. Towards the end of 1935 Murray and I lived in a large stable with a loft and flagged courtyard at Edgecliff.[3]

Ian Lang[4] was an incredible rococo interior decorator with red hair & heart attacks, inextricably interwoven into our life in Sydney. A peculiarly inspired salesman, he once sold a watercolour of mine to a blind man. He was responsible for some of the most fabulous contemporary legends of Potts Point of that time.

1936

January to 10 October Working very hard and doing night classes as well as day classes at Rubbo's studio, until my grandmother gave me £100 and I went to England on that. When I left I discarded my books, and belongings, a load of Chinese porcelain, glass, furniture: the bright rugs on the floor, and precious gods of bronze and brass from Tibet and India and China; the folios of reproductions of lovely paintings, my own works, my clothes and debts.

Second week of October to third week of November *En route to England.* I travelled with two small suitcases. In Perth I bought a New Guinea fetish smeared in white and ochre.

Ceylon. Aden. A Mediterranean isle glimpsed from a ship bound for Italy.[1]

1937

January to August *London*. A London that takes most people a long lifetime of SIN to find. All the really wild and picturesque unspoilt places. I was liked, courted and even loved by an astonishing variety of interesting, *fantastic* people. I have some marvellous friends, and my *affaires de coeur* have usually been most happy.

My figure is slim and my hair is long and my eyes are wild like a poet's. My mouth expresses the insatiably erotic desire for insatiability, and my brows have lost none of their fine curve. I don't wear woollies, I sleep without pyjamas and I live alone most of the time, because I hate seeing other people's clothes messing up the place.

At the L.C.C. Westminster Art School.[1] They didn't teach in the same way that Rubbo used to, but when they did come to your easel you really paid attention to them, because they were pretty good. A lot of the teaching at Rubbo's was based on the George Lambert[2] line: drawing with a very crisp pencil outline, and then the form you expressed with pencil shading with reflected light. When I went to London I gave away all of that idea and I had to work to express the entire form in the varying strengths and weaknesses of this contour line, the outside line. I don't think I worked in oil till I got to London. The accent was on painters like Cézanne[3] and Braque[4] and Picasso[5].

Bernard Meninski[6] was my master; Mark Gertler[7], the other master. Mervyn Peake[8] was teaching there also. He was a good draughtsman. Gertler was a very fine painter, very considered, admired. He was a fairly melancholic type. He had a dim, subdued personality, but I didn't know him personally very well, simply as a teacher. Meninski was a brilliant draughtsman, not much of a painter.

John Passmore[9] valued Meninski (who taught both of us in London) for his passion for the philosophy of Spinoza[10]. One found a lot of—well, four or five—students that I'd known in Sydney, who'd been Dattilo-Rubbo students, were already there. An amusing girl called Anne Penelope Ross[11]—very pretty, and funny in her dramatic fainting-away, whisper voice; Jean Appleton[12], a good, stupid, cow-like woman.

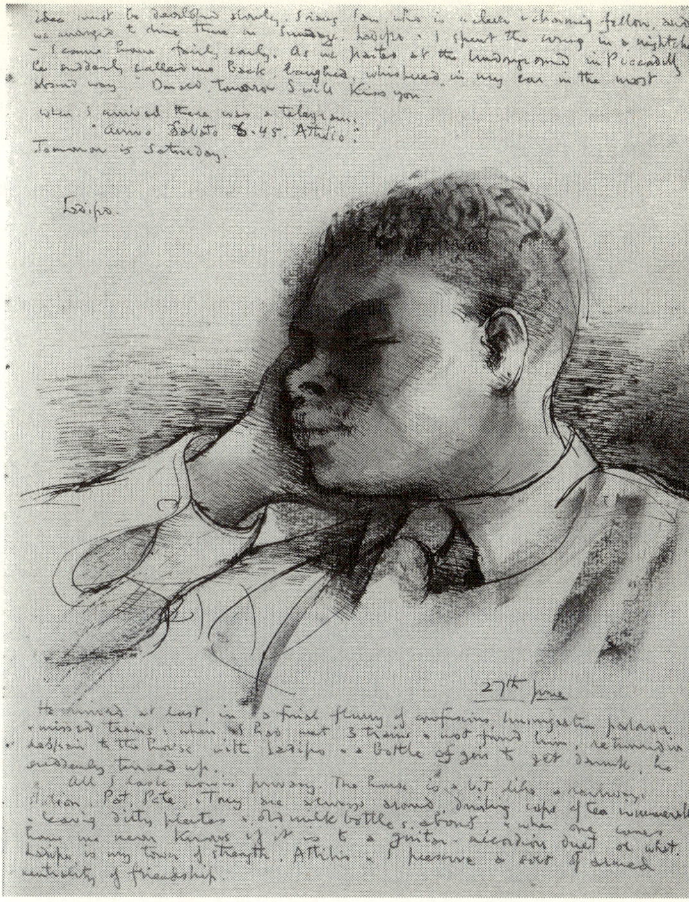

6. *'Ladipo'* (1950).

I first met William Dobell[13] when a student in London. There seemed something infantile to me—lower-middle-class in all his judgements on people, and his shyness. He was probably happiest with very ordinary people. He liked very sordid situations in which he found founts of sentiment. Bill was, in the proper sense of the word, vulgar: his strength lay in that vulgarity, the common touch, cocking a snook at pretensions, yet very sensitive to a feeling of social inferiority. He was not intelligent, had appalling taste. In his company one felt easy: his wit had a touch of irony, a touch of knife-sharp bitchiness, and I'm sure he regarded us all with an easygoing indifference.

I have painted and painted, and sold some. I left the Westminster, and R. E. A. Wilson[14], the agent-millionaire, put on a little show for me, with four or five other draughtsmen. Walter Sickert[15] was one of them. Augustus John[16] was another. My work didn't look shameful amongst them.

My drawings sold two guineas, three guineas, even four guineas for one or two of them.

The first mature oil painting I did, on emerging from the cocoon of studentism, Arthur Benjamin bought. The model was my young African companion, the wonderful, delightful Ladipo[17], whose companionship was certainly the most profound of my European experiences. I kicked so many dull whites out of bed in London.

People over here envy me rather, because they see someone who apparently is a raw colonial coming in and finding the things they have searched a dreary lifetime for. Also, they can only see things from the outside, and watch me indulging in round after round of the new and strange. All these highlights of culture.

One great advantage the Sydney artists did have, from the thirties onwards, was that they did go abroad and they knew from constantly looking at them great works of all kinds in the galleries of Europe and England.

I frequent Coffee-Ann's and meet the set I go round with in Soho.[18] Club Colonial. A very low homosexual nightclub called Pansy Jack's Sailors Dance Bar: more Greek than the Greeks, my dear! An underdone steak with mushrooms, or crisp Soho bread, or a chicken pilau at the Delhi restaurant, or the highfalutin talk that comes through the beards at Bertorelli's.[19]

Amid the mad hot rhythms of swing and the dusky crowd that danced, jazzed and suzi-q'ed to Happy Blake's[20] music at the Shim-Sham club, I heard Ladipo saying: 'My forefathers are stones in Ife.' I also heard: 'The King in Lagos has the keys of the sea, and he can let the flood in, if he likes.' And then the clarinets flowed on in their loud variations, crowning in the blood of their wild fleshy cries the narration of Olokun[21], who commands the sea, and the drums that shocked and rumbled in Happy's hands shouted the storied fame of gods and goddesses.

I met an anthropologist at the British Museum. He wanted to go to Nigeria and find out something about the Owo[22] people. So I took him to a dive and introduced him to Akintaro, the son of the King of Owo. I speak Yoruba (Owo language) quite well. The fellow was astounded, because he is considered quite an authority, but I speak the language far better than he, and probably know a deal more.

There was Appleton Aiken, an American historian. I illustrated a book on the Restoration rakes for him.[23] A most entertaining bloke. I'd take him one drawing per week to his flat in Ebury Street, then we'd go up town and have a terrific meal, drink till mellow and then discuss the work in hand. He entertained me magnificently with a series of huge parties in my honour—Arabian Nights effects. Odennino's, the Barcelona, Isola Bella and other havens du chef gourmet.

The Café Royal[24]—plush seats and young men in brocade dressing gowns. Bourgeois afternoon teas accompanied by trivial and uninformed chatter. Dowagers in tea gowns, dowagers with sculpted mauve hair, for art shows. The company of untalented students. Gossipy old men of the mauve decade.

The Fitzroy Tavern. The sight of drunken Nina Hamnett[25], drunken Betty May[26], Sylvia Gosse[27] or Duncan Grant[28]. The bogus—the glamorous cadging bogus: a happy inspiring sight, a good show, as though they were real genius.[29]

The wild days of Count Potocki's heyday (Vladislav III, pretender to the throne of Poland).[30] His wardrobe consisted solely of long monk-like velvet robes & cloaks & a sort of velvet beret with ostrich plumes. His hair reached down to his waist. His palace at that time consisted of a couple of rooms in Lamb's Conduit Street[31], with a great banner of the Potocki arms waving from a window over the street. One room contained the great Potocki bed that had bounced many a wanton beneath the heraldic canopy. There were bookshelves crammed with pamphlets on astrology (which he practised), necromancy, Polish history, amatory curiosa, naughty novels and fascism, of which he was very fond. The walls were covered with an extraordinary variety of decorations, mostly bad: there were astrological charts, engravings of eminent Potockis, of Pilsudski[32], rather amateurish woodcuts of obscene subjects, photographs of statues of Apollo, and some of his own poems. In the other room there was a little printing machine—a handpress, the gift of Aldous Huxley[33], benches covered with inky type, piles of paper that went to the creating of his quarterly *Right Review*[34], devoted to the further glory of 'Kings, princes, poets, genius and fascism'. There was also a little tin tub in which his Highness took his bath.

Aleister Crowley[35]: the unholy rituals of black mass, whereby we raised the foul fiend in Mecklenburgh Square[36]. I wondered if all the lurid stories of his strangling babies, orgiac occult rites, were the result of his own boasting. The Baroness von der Feldt[37] was a black magicianess of the Aleister Crowley group, but confided in all & sundry that she lived by worming blueprints of new armaments out of elderly gentlemen at the War Office. I met her at Count Potocki's. She was a dreadful woman: dark and very handsome, whose harping voice bore the burden of an accent that vacillated with cosmopolitan eccentricity between the Bowery, Billingsgate & Buenos Aires. She claimed to be descended from 'the old Aztec aristocracy' with shameless mendacity.

Patrick Carleton's[38] rooms in Maida Vale[39]: a lot of books, and shelves with several figurines, and shards of figured pottery, fragments of statuary he'd dug up in Chaldea, blue tiles brought back from Persia. Ladipo was there, listening with patent boredom to the classics, becoming wildly alive to jazz. A negro called Ambrose brought us some gramophone records from America. Ambrose was a dancer: he wore a heavy gold bracelet, dressed 'hep', smoked marijuana and was well educated. He played the records—a sort of piano playing new to my ears. 'We call that "boogie",' he said.

Cambridge. Lovely, dreamy days in company with the shades of Newton[40] and a score of Rural Deans. I float in a punt down the Cam, or pole up towards Grantchester with Paddy Carleton and a few poets for company. Towers blue with mist and nostalgia, yellow with pallid sun, trees eternally budding, a lazy river with bright fresh crocuses on the bank. One leisurely afternoon, after winning an argument on the existence of God hands down (there were six of us in a punt near Grantchester) Ladipo turned to me and said—'anyway, God is where my bread is. You are my God.'

September *Paris*. Arthur Benjamin and I went with Lorne Munroe[41]. O Seine, Notre Dame, *café au lait*, Dubonnet, Louvre, songs, the beguine by a sextet of Cubans, bistros. Café loungers who were my friends in Montparnasse[42]. Affairs that began and never ended.

France was absolute heaven—so much better than England—God! The food and drinks alone make life worthwhile, let alone the dancing and sunlight and incredibly lovely towns, alive and ancient. England is dead and ancient. The French are lovely lovers of life and places and people. The English are clumsy lovers of a smug and outworn code of respectability. I would choke the English with the whole of their Empire for one province of France.

The Riviera. Bread & cheese & honey & wine, & the landscapes of an idyll. There is life and sunshine—chateaux standing in glades of green trees, and brooks, and soft-spoken peasants—and the olive groves above the blue Mediterranean, and fields of vine with people working—bright-coloured hills. Wherever one stops—in the most remote parts, there is an auberge with amazing dishes to serve, and cool phantastic drinks to stimulate your hunger.

It is a pity that Australia is not only anti-intellectual, but anti-traditional as well. The culture imported by the first settlers did not outlive the fourth decade of the nineteenth century. I loved in Europe that strong bond between present & past. Every day's affairs intimately mingled with the life of ancients, even in the most trivial ways. I recall how, sunbaking on the beach at Le Lavandou[43], we bought roasted peanuts from the wrinkled old Provençale vendor, with his odd song of 'cacouettes'. Arthur Benjamin told the tale of the word and its derivation. 'It was during the period of Roman decadence. The word celebrates the Emperor's first-born. All sorts of things were named after the child. So with the peanuts imported from North Africa. It meant the wretched infant's excrement—hence the French "cacouette".'

Early December *London*. I didn't give a damn for Australia. I sometimes used to think how lovely it would be to have an Australian summer. But that was simply because I was cold and uncomfortable. I'd much have preferred summer in the Greek Isles, or Antibes, or Trinidad, or Algiers or Spain. I just wanted warm weather and blue skies and the sea.

London is a lousy place and very big. Its lousiness is compensated by the British Museum, the things in the Victoria and Albert[44], the National Gallery and about five or six quite amusing people who live in Bloomsbury[45] and Soho. Its size is not compensated by anything. Its climate is a direct sign of disapproval from heaven. Its social life is organised with many thousand uppity little cliques, each of which is an ingrowing sore unaware of the existence of other sores. The members of these cliques know the significance of life when they are all gathered together. When they part to become individuals they are lonely and miserable, going their many foolish ways in sadness without wisdom.

Pat de Maré[46], a medical student, looked after me through a terribly broke period. I lived in his studio in Fitzroy Street while he went to

Sweden. He returned in the hour of my greatest misery, to find me with one potato between me and destitution. I was so deep in misery, it was as though half my mind and half my body had gone away. Patrick got me drunk for three days. After that, things began to improve and I got some money from Australia.

I played melancholy and romantic music on the gramophone I bought for a few shillings at the Caledonian market. Liszt—*Consolation 3*[47]; Purcell—a trumpet voluntary[48] that always struck one as being inexpressibly funny.

13 December Perfect hell here—the most ghastly cold, the most ghastly population (English are unutterably awful people) and no money. My success is a bit past tense at the moment—I've spent all the cash and can't get any more. My sole finance an awful overdraft, lots of debts and two farthings.

I know a terrific lot about London life now from the inside—and the more I know the more I despise and hate. This country is about five hundred years behind Australia in governmental principles (absolutely feudal) and sixty behind in ordinary cleanliness. The people are as cold as fish, and their minds as narrow and dirty as the mean dogshitten alleys of this execrable city.

My model, alas, has just returned to Nigeria. I have suffered the most ghastly shattering to my heart and I have been absolutely numb and bewildered. I was in such a bad way that I considered suicide. However, thinking the thing over seriously before committing myself, I decided that a compromise could be effected by joining the army for six years. In my opinion military service was an equation of self-inflicted death, with the advantage that one might emerge alive again, & be able to rebuild a new life. Ultimately, of course I found that even my despair was not great enough to merit so drastic a cure, & took the far pleasanter course of drowning the bitterness of old love in a dozen new ones.

I am not always unhappy. But God I am sick of myself.

Last week of December I got ill before with bronchial 'flu, pneumonia—I thought I'd die. I nearly did. So Christmas was spent ill in bed by me—Arthur Benjamin heard I was ill and brought me eggs and three bottles of brandy, so I sat in bed all day boozing brandy and milk. I got drunk, alone and cold as hell.

Everyone seems to have been ill at Christmas; but people were frightfully sweet to me, and thousands came in pilgrimage to make flower and fruit offerings.

1938

1 January Thousands bicker at breakfast—repressed and reserved, struck badly by the sudden tristesses of reality. New Year, the hysterical happiness of Piccadilly at midnight, was illusion: the intolerable repetition of bacon and eggs is reality eternal, stretching from youth to old age.

It is foully cold. The gaunt drab houses frown at the sooty little black-green square called a garden. Curtains are drawn to hide the unhappy dreary pot plants and the grey sky beyond them, and the succession of terraced houses that stretch in weary sameness away—away. God! The loneliness of those little rooms: the frigid silence of

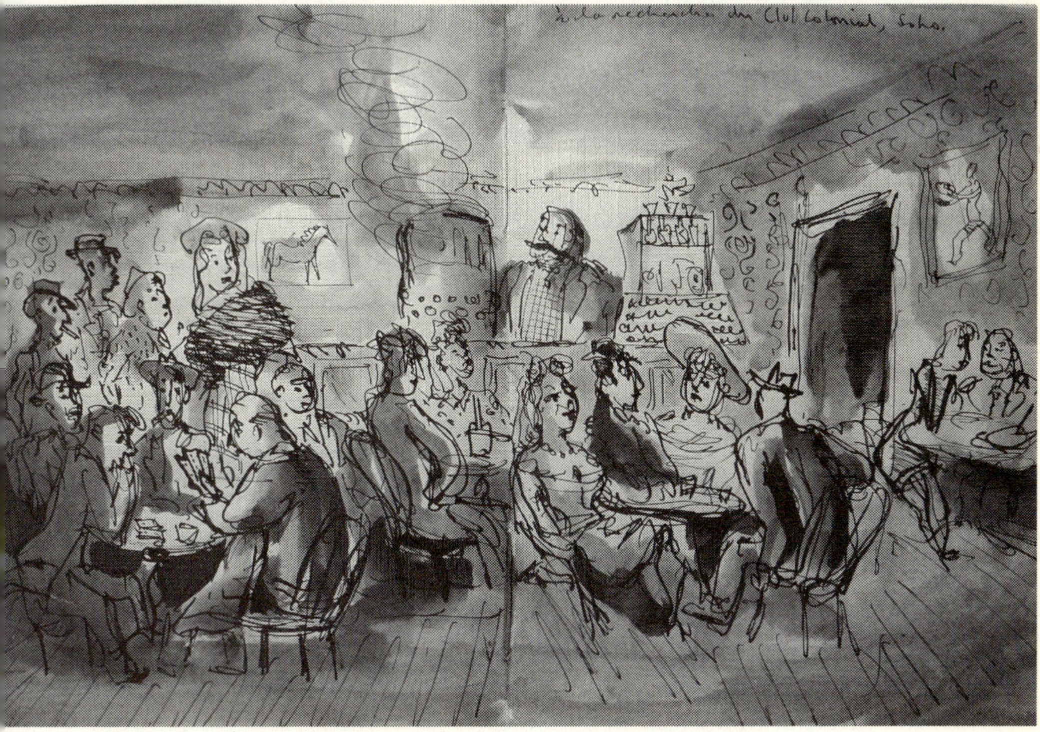

7. *'À la recherche du Club Colonial, Soho'* (1943).

them, while outside on the stairs a charwoman hums and clanks a bucket.

Few books, no music and no money. And long, long hours waiting for it to be a reasonable time to call on someone, just sitting thinking with a ghastly feeling of loss and loneliness in the heart. The tiring flagstones of the street, walked in weariness that makes near seem so far, and far seem an ultimate of pain and aching legs merging into an infinity of boredom and indifference.

I could not get up until today. I'm well again now. Oh boy! I went to a very wild party, and later on to the clubs.

9 January Everything in London is improving—I have got a very good job now that will last about two or three months, and have been offered another one: I have to see a man who wants to buy a picture. By summertime I should have about £200, if I save.

May *Glasgow.* A good journey—we were driving for sixteen hours before we got here. It's a rotten city—all black and dull—no life. We—Bill Dobell, Arthur Murch[1], Lelia Suleau[2], who said so many marvellous things, and did so many crazy ones—made the design and constructions for the wool mural for the Australian Wool Pavilion, Glasgow Exhibition.[3]

June to August *London and Wales.* An amazing intrigue to crack up my affair with Ladipo. That old Edwardian rake, Wilson, is a really competent sinner—a sort of arch-sensualist. Infinitely attractive, clever, understanding and wicked; the most pleasant and extraordinary mixture, but dangerous—more so than anyone I have known; for as far as I can see, his mind, his motives, actions and morals have absolutely no boundaries, and like the devil, he is benevolent.

The filthy old art dealer had a flat in London and a large old place in a loathsome village called Penmaenmawr. The two Warburton girls kept house for him. Jenny Warburton was the younger of two sisters, both of them Wilson's mistresses. They took it in turns to look after the London place—the one whose turn it was to stay in Wales had to look after the children (there were four little ones).[4]

In those evenings in London, as often as not, he'd propose either that we all three went to bed together, or he'd ring up a couple of pliant young guardsmen, a policeman and a few whores, and, standing pinkly nude, spindle-legged and drunk by the gramophone, playing over and over again Ravel's *Boléro*[5], would jovially burlesque the character of a Master of Ceremonies conducting the obscenities of an orgy. 'How I love to see you young people enjoying yourselves,' he would say, to the squirming mass of well-paid copulators. And next evening, there would be Jenny, sitting as usual demurely by the fireside, darning socks.

Jenny is a nice fresh country girl, not at all sophisticated, not very good-looking, not very clever. I liked Jenny from the start, as I have liked so many women, because they make me feel at home, and don't ask foolish questions. I did not feel the antagonism that 'smart' females arouse in me. Wilson thought that 'it would be *nice* for me' to have an affair with her. I did not want it. The situation was arranged by him, and I could not back out. I went to stay in Wales with Jenny, on Wilson's insistence. I was imprisoned by Wilson, and made to rape his mistress while he sold my favourite negro to his hideous lustful bourgeois other mistress, Jenny's sister.

Early to mid-September O dear, the things that do happen in the twentieth century make one furious. I quarrelled with Wilson, and after that I didn't see them again, and left England. The life of poverty I sometimes led here—so cheap, so bare, so chilly—was something to escape from. This bohemian knocking about sickened me. Soho is a bit like the moth-eaten memoirs of a worn-out model. Away from the gross over-rich and the pallid under-rich, from the heavy galleon-like dowagers with their unappreciative patronage of art and tea parties and bridge parties unending, from babble of English tongues and stink of London smoke, from absurd manners and absurd beliefs—the escapist escaped again, this time from the irritating sizzling of the Nordic frying pan to the all-consuming fire equatorial.

Things were beginning to blow up in Europe. I thought I'd prefer not to be an eyewitness. In London and Paris, of all things except the paintings in the art galleries, I loved most the negro nightclubs. I thought of the provincial lack of true culture of my own country, and quickly decided I couldn't bear to face the Bradman, Harbour Bridge versus Collins Street and Yarra controversy[6], and other such futilities of my own tribe. I thought, that if those dark people could find so much carefree enjoyment in Europe, where they lived under every disadvantage of colonial prejudice and poverty—what a whale of a good time they'd have in their own place!

Tired of England: tired of my life, I wanted to find a new place and a new nation. To travel again! And soon I dreamed recurrently of the South Seas and the Torres Straits, of my hoboing adventures in north Queensland, of a glimpse of Ceylon. Africa! My feet itched to be on the move again. The wherewithal—I left it to the god that takes care of my overdraft. I deserted my canvases and folios. Gladly. I was bound to a far land to hear the throb of the distant drum and a hint of eerier singing on the wind.

'So you are going to Nigeria,' Aleister Crowley said. The great Mystic, Grand Master, slowly sipped his draught as though it were the blood of a Mende[7] slave.

Last fortnight of September *Marseilles*. It was lonely and I was aimlessly waiting a few days for the boat, sitting for hours drinking aperitifs and thinking. Rich dizzy contrasts of riches and poverty. The women talked in bright brittle squeaks: the men all looked as though they'd been painted by Monet[8]: the streets were in the manner of Pissaro[9]. By the harbour in little cafés festooned with mirrors, dreadful big fat women sprawl on your knees as soon as you sit down. In the dark hilly narrow streets harlots unseen hiss loudly from the casements to solicit your attention. Then out from the stews into a broad glorious boulevard massed with trees among glowing lights, the wide pavement checkered with red wicker chairs and leisurely folk—coffee, cognac, vermouth, cassis.

With friends I made, mostly young Dahomian students returning home, we sailed from Marseilles aboard the *SS Banfora*—a ghastly Massageries Maritimes[10] hell-ship. I travelled Third Class.

The Munich crisis[11] started when we were still in the Mediterranean.

First fortnight of October *En route to Nigeria*. The Barbary Coast. Morocco, Algiers. The boat is becoming really interesting. Since we left Dakkar[12] we have had a batch of young African university students on board—a superb crowd of happy intelligent young men with most searchingly enquiring minds. At Freetown[13], the Christianised African dandies are quite revolting, mannerless and stupid. At Accra[14], I did not go ashore—it was far too rough.

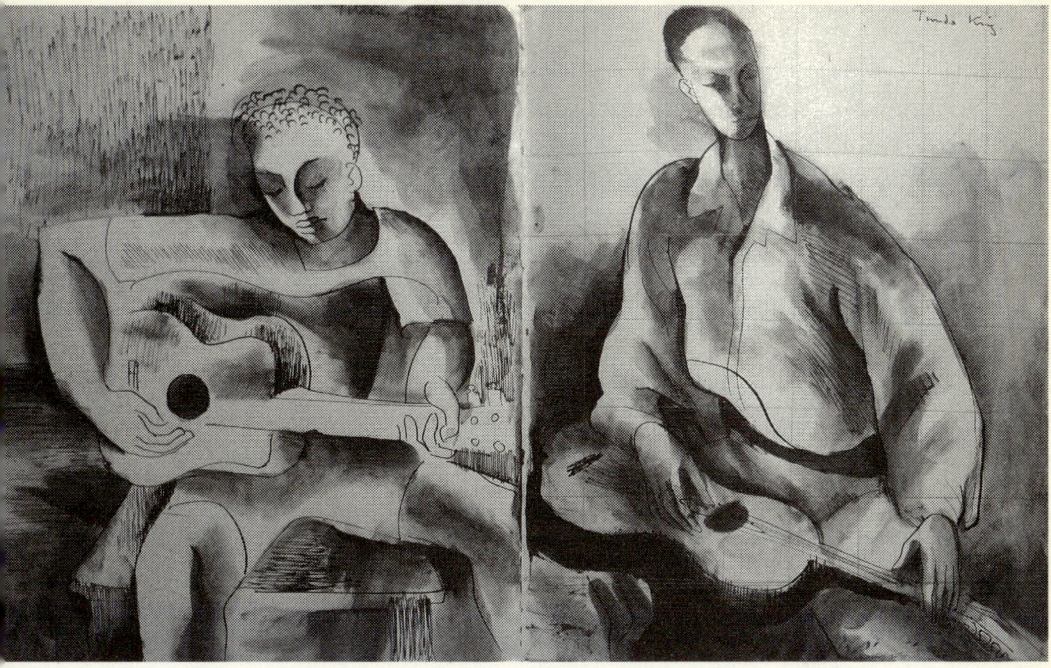

8. *'Tundé King' (1944).*

Sassandra, Abidjan, Whydah, Cotonou, Porto-Novo—white and rose towns[15] set in palms by the frothing surf. Green and gold coast—the heat, the flies, the swirl of black humanity strutting in floral velvet trousers, in plum-velvet 'Bourdillon' hats[16], the frantic dusky children, shouting, weeping.

In some port in the Gulf of Guinea or the Bight of Benin—I can never tell which—I lay under a canvas awning watching the glistening black boys load cargo to barbaric chanting, whilst in the First Class saloon someone played Chopin[17], and in the Third Class a smoking-room gramophone broadcasted the William Tell Overture[18], a curious and tumultuous imitation storm made by a Wurlitzer organ which permeates the whole boat; an overcrowded canvas of sound. All under a pitiless sun.

I parted with a shirt to the winning flirtation of a naughty deck boy, whose cajolery utterly broke my resistance: half an hour later he made an even more impassioned declaration of affection which was followed by the expression of an irresistible desire for my pants, since they had sheathed so much that was precious to his impressionable African heart. But I am firm on this point. However, it is yet twelve or fourteen hours to Lagos, and, as somebody once very sagely said, almost anything except the construction of Rome can be accomplished within this time.

Mid- to end of October *Lagos*. I arrived in the middle of the rainy season. I stayed a few weeks with a kindly family at Yaba[19] until I secured two rooms in a house. It is a native house with a compound, slaves and squalling, bawling women with ditto black kids and a sinister patriarch and enormous matriarch to keep all in order.

I engaged a jewel-like black servant, Sam Aruleiba, about 25, who does cooking, marketing, laundry and housework. He was a bright lad, and for the first few days rather terrified of me, looking at me as if I'd suddenly blow up at any moment, or change into an aeroplane. But he soon got used to me. Sam's wage is 30/- per month. My rent about the same. Of course I supply all his food and clothes and lodgings.

The days passed quickly. The first strangeness wore off. I wandered about the town a lot. It's an odd place, built on a low island in a lagoon, connected with the mainland by Carter Bridge. A great deal of the town is built on land reclaimed from the swamp. When there's a storm, many of the high houses rock like ships. Most of the streets are pretty squalid, and there is much noise, and filth, and a general richly foetid atmosphere of birth-death-germination. Bright clothes abound—scarlet and green and multicoloured trousers and all that sort of thing. During the day sunglare drains the colour out of everything. But round about sundown, that is the time to see Lagos. Then the trees are richly green and lush, and the water laps coolly along the marina, and a breeze sweeps the town from the sea. Then it is a pleasure to stroll through the angled alleys chocked with noisy life, and dodge the shrilling scampering children.

Three sailors carousing at the bar, and one of them, a poet, inditing odes. Dark lovely harlots swayed into vision, with the drumming of drums and arpeggios of guitars, into a vision distorted by drink. I gazed into the ages of life, my ignorant infancy, vicious adolescence, my whorey old youth, and the juvenile senescence yet to come, that looms as a threat of dyed beard and senile fumblings: how long, O lord, ere I lapse into the darks of mine antiquity?

In Lagos one is never out of hearing of music, night or day. Through the windows pour in the clicking and booming of instruments, supplemented by nostalgic bursts of song, melancholy cadences sung in chorus. Scandalous calypsos of Tundé King[20], that gay wicked young Yoruba[21] of Lagos.

Early to mid-December I am spending the days recovering from fever and painting and writing—all very depressing. I am writing a book. It began as a really fine ethnological study of West Africa and much has been done.[22]

The natives are the most profound realists in existence. Perhaps I should say surrealists, as their conception of realism puts dear old Marx and his feeble devils of materialism to shame. Spiritual matter here is an obvious form of matter, only a little less crude than physical matter.

Last week of December Xmas here utterly incredible—devil dances, tom-toms and god knows what for days and nights on end. Roaring rhythmic deep chanting, punctuated by staccato clinks of little bells. And so on, all day and all night and for two days and two nights after.

A smart flagellation of sound: expectant, prophetic. Xmas sacrifice is near: the denial, the justification. Christmas dinner. Blood and meat!

It's hot and steamy, and the air is charged with the weird strength of a sort of climactic restless charge of jet-black hysteria.

Lagos provides an aesthetic aperitif for any gourmand with Titanic enough guts for such a cocktail—foretaste as it is of a gargantuan rich bellyful that the rest of Africa provides.

1939

January *Ifan.*[1] I have now flown from the noise and wildness of Lagos to a little country village. An absolutely heavenly spot—very secluded and most interesting and beautiful—no sanitation, no Europeans, and little mud huts with palm-thatch roofs—picturesque and full of scorpions. I am very happy just now, writing and painting and going on long deliciously dangerous walks in the jungle—the wildest tangle imaginable, ropes of scented white flowers, palms of exquisite elegance and great handsome florid trees choked with orchids that have obviously been filched from a millionaire's hothouse. These are decorated with splendidly patterned pythons, as the red narrow paths are with leopards. I adore Africa. I can't think why people ever leave it by any road but death.

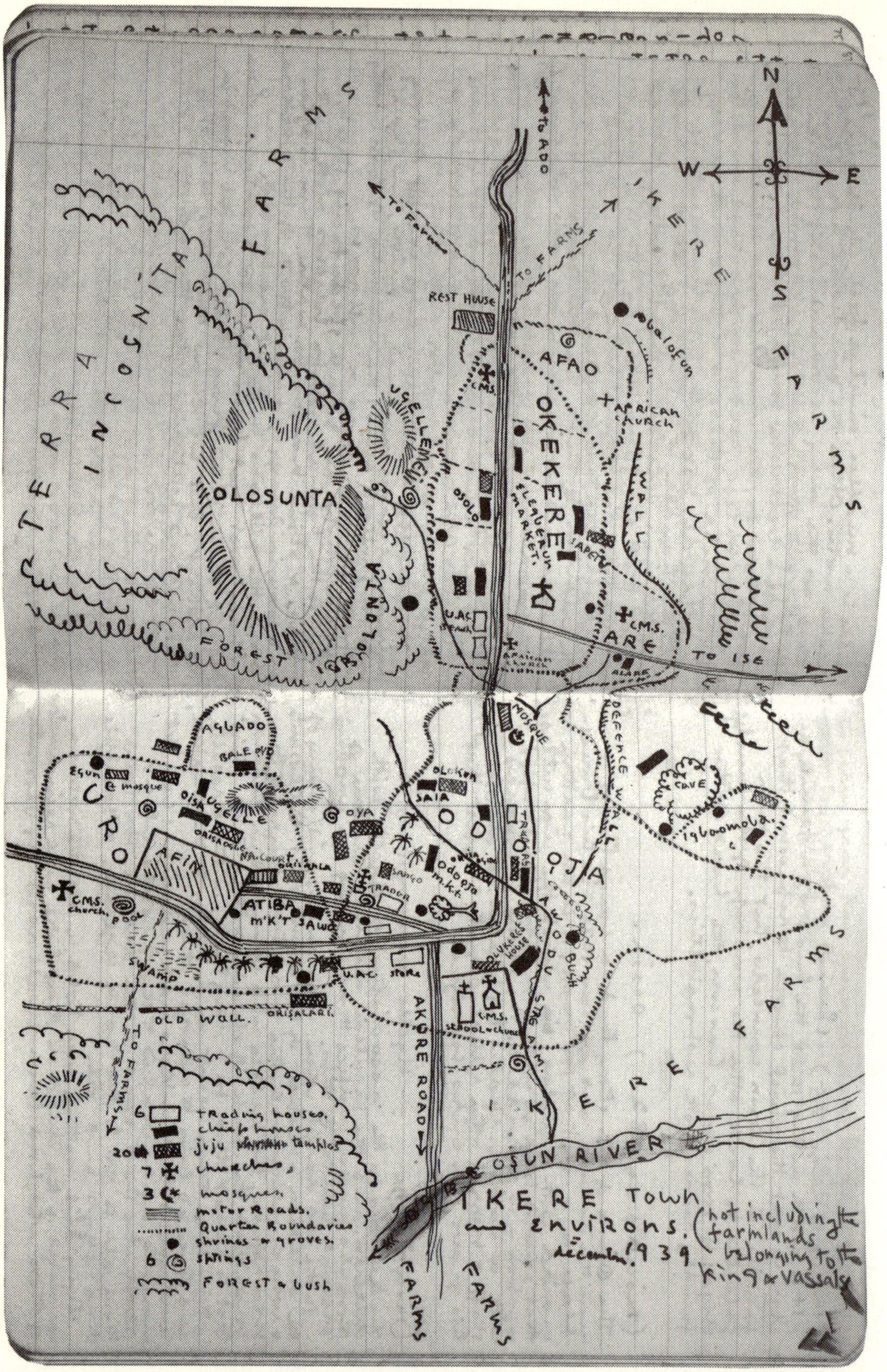

9. 'Ikere [sic] town and environs' (1939).

February to mid-March *Ikerre*.[2] Wonderful Boy's Own Annual[3] time amongst the splendours of the Oba's[4] palace and the mysteries of glorious shrines and the singing and drumming that never ceases there.

I like Africa more and more. The country has absolutely unlimited scope for enjoyment—when you get coral-clad obas who ride through their despotic states in Mercedes-Benz cars, and who drink one bottle of Cointreau a day, and who have in constant attendance drums and slaves, and to whom no man may speak unless he is prostrated flat on the ground and who wear their crowns with a jaunty air (even in bed, I'm told)—so much grander than our silly social monarchs in lounge suits being polite and opening flower shows, kings of a 'democratic' state. I have an admiration for these baroque black despots, with their terrific way of making justice—of the direct contact between king and people—the people are very moral and honest too, through a curious communistic principle. The compound is responsible for each man it contains, and should one trespass, the whole lot suffer, so that the majority find it in their interest to enforce law and order. Better by far than the liquid anarchism of each man for himself—I mean, as a means of keeping a community intact—that is the base of English law.

I have lived in my 24 years more than most people of 60 have done. I am successful in that I have attained more of love, and of adventure, and have tasted the emotions and senses both sweet and bitter at their full strength. I have created work that has made my name already respected amongst the intellectuals wherever I have been. Luckily I am very popular with the savage ones—I like them better than the semi-Europeanised sort—they are more honest and more wise.

Where I am is the ultimate land of illusion and mystery and romance, and I love it—it has all the glamour of a film and all the humanity of real life, with an odd section set aside for living gods and magic and a mad music that sets your soul free from the body to lounge unharnessed through the long crooked roads of eternity.

Here I am the mastermind, the philosopher, savant, teacher and artist. In Australia I am some of these, but above all a sort of cheated romanticist and black sheep with a slight reputation for insanity.

24 March *Lagos*. I've become the father of a daughter in Britain.[5] The Wicked Wilson says he will be delighted to care for the kid which he thinks will be a solace for his old age. It all adds up all right. I lost Ladipo, and the villain of the piece is saddled with my infant for life. This sounds more bitter than I feel. In fact I am happy to have immortalised myself in the flesh.

I went into this thing because it was easier to do so than not to: because whatever my own feelings in the matter were, it gave a great deal of pleasure to Wilson (somehow one puts him first instinctively) and to Jenny. She does not love me: rather she likes me. I don't suppose she wants to marry me. It was understood from the beginning that the affair was entirely Wilson's responsibility. The outcome of it, the child, made me happy. It seems more important than all the rest of it. I have had little share in it but the begetting—'the hurly-burly of the chaise longue', as Cynthia Asquith[6] says.

14 June War propaganda is being pumped out in every issue of the newspapers. Eight months ago the attitude of the entire public was 'We don't want War'—now they're yelling 'Why don't we squash Germany, Japan and Italy'.

The next war will do more harm and less good than the last one. The people of course deserve to get it in the neck all the time because they're always prepared to be made mugs with stupid drivel about Bolshies, Huns or Hitler. If there is a war, I'd suffer gaol rather than attend it. Why should I suffer in a combat whose only tangible outcome is to stabilise trade for Big Trade combines. For they are the real rulers of the world, who make wars or declare peace. Neither war nor peace are any good under the present condition for the majority of mankind.

I prefer my ex-cannibals; at least they're sane and polite, and know what's what in their world. I feel a deal safer here among the 'savages' than if I were left to the tender mercies of warmongers and dowagers with white feathers in the 'civilised' world. The bush natives here are far more cultured and intelligent than the half-baked bourgeois gossips in Sydney with the intellectual standards of baboons and the morals of monks dosed with cantharides[7].

Let them all yell 'Hurrah!' or 'Heil' or 'God Save the King' or 'Hang the Kaiser'—I'm going to sit in my hut and suck a mango. I like the arts of peace.

18–19 June I've got to dislike Lagos very much in some ways. It seems to be such a centre of all that's lousy that we've introduced: the ghastly ignorant outlook of the educated Africans who have entirely lost their own culture and never managed to pick up more than the worst forms of European glitter.

The town is full of extraordinary societies—which exist to thieve and cheat, yet are motivated by romantic notions inspired by cowboy films. Brothels, though illegal, are fairly frankly labelled with a notice—such as 'big men 6d Small men 3d'. Big men etc., in this context, refers to social standing, not penitic dimensions. The young men in clubs are goodtime charlies from all over Africa, and are easily seduced but hardly worthwhile.

Yet half an hour's paddling in a canoe over the lagoon will get you to primitive villages made of thatch and bamboos, set among the palms. It's as though one has retrogressed a thousand years into Arcadia in thirty minutes' journey. A miracle!—the people are honest and simple (easily duped, says the Marxist) and leave their wares for days—piles of produce and so on—safely protected by a little charm from all theft.

I deplore the 'progress' that I see, when it costs happiness, integrity and all the ideals worth fighting for. I cannot admire the unlovely world of enlightenment, and would like to see the Yorubas skip this century by continuing their life of primitive communism. At heart I am a retrogressionist longing to live in the past, and when not ignoring the present, castigating it. Of course all those I knew and liked have gone their ways now I suppose and got jobs, and inherited money, and any of those things that make bogus bohemians into respectable little bourgeoises. I have a feeling that the things I knew so very few years ago are passing or have passed, and that no one will be, as Murray and I were, symbols of a certain rather crazy, but very exalted, state of mind. I still feel a bit like Little Lord Fauntleroy[8] in long pants, and with a sort of horror realise I'm no longer 19: and that all that will never be the same again. But I'll yet be a greybeard.

The rainy season has arrived, so it pours for hours every day, and mosquitoes are bad. All the local Europeans wear mosquito boots which look most exotic—as though they were a sort of surrealist Russian *corps de ballet* resting in between acts with solar topies on—perhaps a ballet on the theme of 'Mad Dogs and Englishmen'[9]—though god knows they're terrified of 'the midday sun' out here, and wouldn't dream of going out in it.

10–11 July Trek to Ikerre with the faithful Sam. The King of Ikerre, the Ogoga[10], offered me a house and servants. The journey up was ghastly. There is nothing I know so exasperating as lorry travel in Nigeria. One is absolutely helpless in the hands of the driver and his underling, and they are the most contrary people on god's earth. It's no good giving any order or making any arrangement. With awe inspiring politeness and terrible deliberation they do exactly as they like. After some hours of it I sank into the perfect passivity of an ancient Tibetan monk.

Third week of July The festival of Oloba, a yam god, was celebrated. The populace performed a very odd ritual, which indicates the yam as a phallic affair. They spent the morning most lewdly and ribaldly cursing, insulting and degrading one another's sexual organs, with an imagination of obscenity worthy of Rabelais[11].

From the top of the great rock—it must be over a hundred feet high—called Ugelle, one can see far out over wildly mountainous landscape. From here Olosunta, the great granite mountain that was a god, seems intimately near yet sacredly remote.

On this steep rock, near parts that are either torn away by ages of rainwater or deliberately hollowed out (like the native wells in certain Aboriginal camps I have seen in Australia) there are grooves, evidently man-made, in the rock surface. Possibly these are relics of early cavemen.

Looking down from Ugelle on the town, which in all covers about four square miles and contains some 12,000 souls, I realised how well planned it was—the compounds uncrowded, the long buildings of the ruler's harem with its broad streets, and groves of palms that every now and then break the massing deep green of jungle trees on the outskirts of the town, or form a sighing oasis around the emerald ponds where ducks waddle comically.

At the Orisa Ogbe shrine, a perfect specimen beautifully kept and decorated, there are two doors by the carver, Chief Olowe[12] of Ise[13], now dead. These are stamped with his extremely individual style. Olowe manages to convey a great deal of lively variety into the postures and expressions of his figures. It is evident that the carver was a creative artist who was not satisfied with the hackneyed range of subjects left him by his forebears, but who went about and observed life around him, incorporating it with humorous observations into his work.

A grave procession marched into the palace yard set apart for ritual occasions. I hurried to take my place beside the Ogoga, who was wearing a white robe and a particularly gorgeous crown, ornamented with nine yellow, blue, orange and vermilion birds with tasselled white tails. These crowns, like all Yoruba royal insignia, are amazingly skilfully made of beadwork. It's very different from the usual African stuff, this Yoruba work. It has something intellectual and worked out about it, quite unlike the sensual, emotional and instinctively good work of Congo[14] and Cameroons[15] and Gold Coast[16].

I feel a vague irritability and for no reason life seems empty. Probably it's because there are only three or four people in the town who speak English, and there is absolutely no one I can communicate ideas with. It's our attitude of mind, not our mental capacity, that's so different from the negroes. It's having been brought up in surroundings, among books and traditions that make us marshal and discipline our ideas along certain lines. The negro mind seems at first to be horribly confused. Its discipline is different, not its scope. They are realists. They want everything said and nothing taken for granted. A series of definite statements and questions in Basic English, with no detail neglected, is the only possible for a White–Black conversation. This is a terrible effort. Our wit, and most things that are pleasant and facile, are dependent on what is left unsaid. Here I can leave nothing unsaid, and the result is an extraordinary uneasiness and feeling of treading on thin ice.

3 August I have often eaten native food, but my constitution has never adapted to it. The pepper content not only burns one's mouth cruelly, but acts as a strong aphrodisiac—or the rest of it has never failed to give me diarrhoea. I could not afford the crates of tinned food that most Europeans cart around with them, and the Ikerre products, though lavish in quantity, had little variety. After a time everything tasted the same. There was an abundance of chicken and 'bush meat'—little deer and so on. It is very tasty, game and tender. Porcupines (very delicate and succulent), goat, sheep and dog. The latter reminded me fondly of those fat expensive ladies in Bond Street[17]. Usual vegetables were yams, plantains, okra and corn, and of fruit, pineapples and pawpaws. That, with palm wine and tea, comprises my present diet.

7 August Moved into the house the Ogoga had given me. A two-storey erection in the big court of the Afin[18]. Made of mud faced with concrete, and an original, quaint piece of architecture, the brainchild of a former monarch. Grand views from its many windows. Its upper verandah an excellent vantage point from which to watch the picturesque occasions which punctuate the Ikerran day.

9 August I don't, and can't, pretend to be an elegant writer, for if I were endowed with elegance, as well as with qualities of mind and wealth, I would spend my time, not in writing of events in African life, but in recording the delicate, sensitive and interesting reactions to polite, possible and romantic occasions, of beautiful people with large incomes. These works would be dedicated to the great joy and satisfaction of people not so well blessed with material benefits of this dreary vale of tears. People who need continual reminders of other and more elevated things than poverty, to enable them to be reconciled to a lot devoid of dinners at Claridges[19], gowns by Chanel[20] and perfumes by Coty[21].

In this barbaric retreat I have been reading some of this sort of literature, and have found it an immense blessing. The popularity of this sweet soporific literature, of course, is with the poor. The poor? Who wants to read about the poor? Poverty makes people unpleasant.

Therefore, while I write about the 'savages', I read about the rich: the fat, beautiful, sated rich: the glamorous, lovely rich: the rich who can afford Mercedes-Benz cars: the rich who can afford to be virtuous.

11 August It would puzzle a great many English (who prefer, when criticising another race, to forget the fact that most people use Christmas as an excuse for boozing and gorging), to see the general atmosphere of jollity that prevails, even in the most sacred of these occasions. They might come to the conclusion that they are used as an excuse for carnival. Yet this is not the case. The dancing and singing, though thoroughly and frankly enjoyed by all and sundry, rather in contrast to the sanctimonious gloom of gothic sacred feasts, is definitely deeply sacramental.

These African gods, profoundly believed in, often terrible, are so much life itself, that our *dim* attitude, our canting *church voices* and general decadent paraphernalia of pseudo-mystery used to whip up a belief only half-sincere, would be shockingly out of place. To hear a professional cleric say 'Let us rejoice in the Lord' is one of the saddest things I know. But to hear the archaic 'Ire wo wo wo' rise from the lips of that enchanted, rapt congregation, immersed in a rite that is really living and actual, is an extremely opposite experience.

First half of September Heigh-ho—it sounds like war hysteria. A messenger arrived here the other day and said it had started.[22] I'm thoroughly disillusioned with European culture—that can do no better with its great geniuses than use their brains to devise machines for the annihilation of mankind. Maybe it means the end of all this that we've taken 2,000 years to build: maybe it'll be the end of capitalism and private property, and I'll never enjoy my looked-forward-to dividend from Glendon. Maybe the time is coming when we will have to live by our merits rather than by inherited position. Oh Hell! I hope not. My merits are few enough.

There'll be talk of Goodies and Baddies as though the nations are playing cowboys and Indians: just great big grown-up kids! What good can come out of this cataclysm?—it's not the destruction of people that I deplore, but the destruction of the genius and knowledge they contain, and the annihilation, inevitable, of works of art and libraries and all the inanimate things that proclaim the real glory of mankind: not men but their works. I don't regret the wiping out of a lot of shrill greasy intellectuals, but their unborn poems and paintings and books, and the ideas to which they have not yet given voice. I do hate it so, and despise it, and fear it, this war. What will happen to all the friends and lovers with whom I have wasted hours and months and years of youth? Are all the things we thought and said to terminate with a bullet?

Second half of September My house filled with treasures of carved wood. I heard new songs, noted strange customs, and the general calm of life soon put Europe's troubles out of my head. I used to enjoy those nights when we told stories. The laughter and singing and lamplight on the flash of ivory teeth and dusky faces, and gleaming on the white walls and

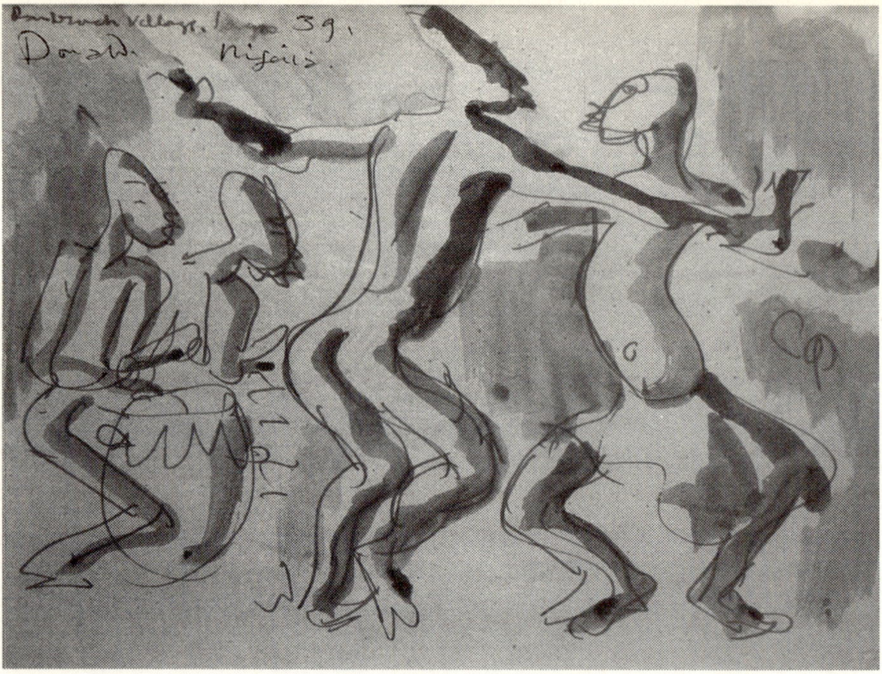

10. Yoruba: pulsing rhythms (1939).

the barbaric shapes and colours of the idols, and the boldly patterned cloths. Outside, the dark night and cool wind and sound of distant drums. Within, the group around the table, and a jar of white chrysanthemums. Sam and his wife Olonite kept me roaring with mirth with very lewd stories. One could write a Yoruba *Decameron*[23] or *1001 Nights*[24] with this material.

One thing to the good is, out here the children have no bogies or secrets about sex—they know as soon as they can talk, so they grow up without the usual complexes. What an odd sentiment ours is—keeping the facts wrapped up in voodoo as a grand surprise—a ghastly shock—for the Bridal night. The Africans are realists—they have none of our ridiculous falsifications about things. When they appear to be superstitious and so on, one can usually find that the superstition or custom is used simply to enforce a reasonable law. I like their defiant, cynical song pregnant with Yoruba realisms—a sort of disillusioned shameless facing the facts that is rarely found in Aryan races ('Britons never never will be slaves'[25] —despite the lifelong bondage of the majority).

When I drink a lot, my brain reels with their songs, their wild, soft Yoruba words, their insatiable bloody pulsing rhythms, and the whole hot fascination of their silken black forms, sensuously subtle, walking as though walking were an untranslatably exquisite dark rite, dancing, sobbing. Those people knew the complete answer to everything in physical life.

The Yorubas in the up-country kingdoms never fall in love, nor know what it means: they marry, are fond of their wives much as a man is of his friends. But they do not fall in love. Yet the sons of the chiefs and wealthy men who are sent to Kings College[26] in Lagos do. There they are given a very good college training of the English sort. But in place of their own system of natural sex education they get all our taboos, pruderies and what the bee does to the blossom reticences. That, in conjunction with segregation of the sexes, completes the set-up. The new literate class, immensely influenced by novels and magazines, have found, and begun to practise, Romantic Love. The inevitable claptrap of education—especially mission education, which is inseparable from sex-voodoos and segregation, lays the foundation. It is surely true that romantic love exists only in nations whose laws of behaviour enforce a certain segregation of sexes. I have seen frankly erotic carvings exhibited publicly in the unsophisticated towns of the interior. No one there takes much notice of the subject matter. Yet when some rude drawings and paintings were shown in a crafts exhibition in Lagos, several educated natives complained that such obscenities should be shown. Already, you see, education had sown in them the seeds of European prudishness and body taboos. Among such natives, there exists a very specialised attitude toward women and sex in general, whereas the illiterates of the interior have no more an especial attitude toward sex than they have toward farming, or any other general occupation.

Last week of September The dreary vacuum of the Methodist Sabbath is felt even here—the bells of the mission church and all the young educated men looking godly. On Sunday they all visit and enquire about the war. I'm so indifferent I just dish out a few Kiplingesque[27] sentiments to get rid of them. Of course I can't wholly approve of my own flippancy—Germany has outraged all laws, sentimental or legal, of human relationship and decency, but there are so many people ranting on that harp string at the moment that my voice is hardly necessary. Germany, we heard, had done this and that; had here advanced and there retreated. A submarine had—but who could visualise a submarine here in Ikerre? Who knew where Poland was, or could describe a commissar? Who had seen a machine gun? So we continued our peace, as though, like the last Lemurians[28] meditating on the Himalayan slopes, we were walled about with an invisible barrier, impregnable to men and gunfire.

Second and third weeks of October My feet got poisoned. I had scarce recovered from that when a violent fever laid me low. I thought I'd peg out. I've decided to leave Africa and return home. I am depressed, rather unhappy and not pleased with myself, and rather afraid at the moment. I wish to God I could do something constantly, happily and intelligently—it would be too much to ask that the activity were in any degree useful. Why now I don't really know, this place has overnight become sinister. My very faithful Sam has told me that it's not very safe here much longer, and he is frankly scared out of his wits and said if I didn't leave he would in any case—so I go.

What I dearly want is to hear some precious music—Prokofiev[29] would do well; hear some precious talk—the refined tea babble of a dowager would do. I'd like to escape into a more comfortable style of unreality than that from which I suffer now.

My habits are all awful ones. I smoke twenty-five cigarettes a day. I don't drink often. I still paint well without genius. My amorous inclinations are only slightly altered—the modification being the exclusion of mariners. My career in Africa infinitely more virtuous and subdued than in Europe. None of those orgies. Trimalchio[30] would have settled down to monogamist heterosexual domesticity had he lived on the Equator.

How sick I am of Africa now. I'll go batty if I can't get out. I've come to the conclusion that Africa ought to be entirely suppressed, and confined to literature. The same with Europe, or at least the part of it that engages in futile wars.

First half of November A great missionary has come to town and we had a real Harvest Festival. He is an Archdeacon and quite archaic. I had a glorious conversation over tea on the Possibility of the Grecian Love of Youth being Revived under the Auspices of Mother Church. It was all incredibly amusing, and I was a Good Boy and went to church for the first time since I left Australia.

The Harvest service was a great do. In the middle of the Lord's Prayer the Ogoga turned up with about 200 of his wives and family, an orchestra of drums with a heavenly clarinet and some fifes, and a number of slaves with orange and vermilion beach umbrellas. He wore a crown two feet high of superb beadwork, and a cloak of silver sequins lined with scarlet taffeta. He processed with drums and attendants and all into the church, smiling benignly at the congregation, the entire of which prostrated as flat to the floor as pews would allow, crying protestations of allegiance. He reached the unhappy deacon, wrung his hand and motioned to two slaves who stepped forward, pressing into the reverend gentleman's hands a tightly bound but very angry duck. The Ogoga sat down, his wives around him, and slaves busy with fans, and he graciously signalled 'On with the Show'. The duck squawked on the floor of the pulpit. I nearly died. Afterwards we had tea at my house, and managed to soothe the deacon's shattered soul. His cry was that one couldn't *do* anything, it had all been so amiably intended.

The Ogoga—though I like him well—is indisputably a self-deluding, amiable, courteous, occasionally generous and incredibly selfish person. He is growing more and more despotic. He often uses the native court as a means to gain his own personal revenges and punishes often imaginary slights with punishments quite out of proportion to the offences. He is surrounded by fools and flatterers. The amount of favour-currying and bum-kissing that goes on in the Palace make Versailles[31] look like a Communist Heaven. The network of compliments and gifts and praise they indulge in to bring about the downfall of one for whom they profess friendship would shock Machiavelli[32]. The Ogoga is unpopular at the moment, and there are rumbles of discontent and rebellion all over the town. He is a clever man—crafty, that is in his own interests—or immediate gain, but vain to such a degree that he has entirely forgotten other and stronger powers above him. He lives and thinks more like an African despot of the eighteenth century than one living in 1939.

End of November A great native exhibition at Ikare[33], some distance from Ikerre. A Jamaican negro—nice man—asked me to be Hon. Sec. for the Arts section. I stayed with the Jamaican and also an 80-year-old Bishop.

A number of the carved doors were obscene. One showed a row of very great men indulging in Greek Games[34], the head man of the law was performing a more nominal rite with a woman. It just shows the unreceptivity of the Christian mentality—the bishop has been out here fifty years. They can't see what's before their eyes, even when examining it, their minds are so castrated.

Of course, the World, flesh and devil are also well represented in the form of District Officers and traders and various Europeans, their minds softened by Cambridge, and their wits made flexible with gin and bitters. English humour is still in very virile flower in West Africa. *Punch*[35] is read ritually, and every club and private house resounds to red-cheeked mirth resultant from jests of the funny-ha-ha as opposed to the funny-peculiar or funny-superior varieties. Thus I, who am after all basically derived from this Saxon stock, quickly learned to entertain my peers with funny-ha-has; nevertheless within me an acid rebellion lurked.

Last half of December *Ikerre*. I am so remote here that I am remote from myself. I've been beguiling my many idle hours making models in beeswax, and casting them in bronze, at the local smithy. My mind has become quite immersed in the local beliefs and traditions. No one before, and probably again, will know them as I do.

I am writing two books now. One an absurd satire, and the other, an ethnological study mixed up with biography. It's my personal solution, my escape from all horror. I wonder if this war is the last of capitalism and private property. It'd be a bit of a blow to see communism in my own time—and not have the fat joys of a rich man's son—that sweetest of all balms to the soul, an unearned increment—and to find that my forebears were rather ruthless and grasping and piratic, building up a fortune and tending land only for the common people to come and take it all.

I'm writing to Papa. I think it's fair to let him know my attitude about war. He can't kick much. He didn't fight in the last one—and anyway, whatever the innumerable demerits of my life have been, I have not been a coward. He writes sometimes, quite friendly cheerful, noncommittal sorts of letters, I really think he wants to keep the peace with me, and realises that I can't be such a cissy as he used to think.

I'm coming home. I leave if all goes well in February. I'm most frightfully excited about it. Things here are much the same—that is, in turmoil—more mad intrigues. I'll probably want to come back here again. I adore this country, and the life here could be so perfect if only one wasn't so mentally isolated. The sort of people—except missionaries, who are ordained by God and aren't really people at all, but fairies—who come out here are either technicians, Scotch slumboys who have by dint of incredible tenacity educated themselves and got the job, or governors, people who by incredible tenacity cling on to *all* their illusions, both of heredity and environment. My trouble is I'm not sufficiently self-contained. I get a curious longing to talk with white people and read their books, when after all they're not much different from the Africans, except in colour, and they speak English better.

Now the trees have shed their leaves, and instead the grey branches are loaded with huge scarlet flowers. The skies are very pale these days, and everything misted with blue. The little garden is parched. Chickens lie about languidly. They are too lazy to get into the shade. They don't sit down like respectable birds, but sprawl, legs outstretched, reclining like debauched Romans. A goat absentmindedly chews the tail feathers of one. The chicken is too vitiated to protest. Several cows have been sacrificed this morning, whether to the juju Santa Claus or to a local god I don't know.

The Yorubas, surrounded as they are by the most glorious landscapes and natural gardens, see no beauty in fine vistas, and use no flowers as ornament. One can hardly be surprised. Were the Balinese or Tahitians transported to the Guinea Coast they'd soon perforce leave weaving leis and wearing hibiscus and frangipani. Nature in those happy Polynesian isles is a generous gentle entity. On our coast, a cruel and cunning, powerful constant enemy. Man's existence is a never-ending struggle against encroaching forests, and the very flowers threaten and poison, and witches dwell in all their blooms. In Yoruba land we don't love the forest and its flowers—we propitiate them, fearing.

NOTES: 1930s

1930

1. Piano Concerto in A minor, Opus 16, by Edvard Grieg (1843–1907), Norwegian composer.
2. An independent school for boys in Darlinghurst, officially opened in 1857.
3. The New York stock-market crash on 29 October 1929 signalled the beginnings of the worldwide Great Depression, the effects of which were felt in Australia well into the 1930s.
4. Hans Christian Andersen (1805–75), Danish writer of fairy tales.
5. The brothers Grimm, Jacob (1785–1863) and Wilhelm (1786–1859), German-born collectors of folk and fairy tales.
6. An inner suburb of Sydney, 3 kilometres from the centre.
7. The Sydney Harbour Bridge, on which preliminary construction began in 1925, was opened in 1932.
8. Swedish-born actress (1905–90), who had moved to Hollywood.
9. A play (1920) by American dramatist Eugene O'Neill, adapted into a film starring Garbo in 1930. The film screened in Sydney at the Plaza Theatre (see **1930**, note 13), 6 June – 3 July.
10. Edith Taliaferro (1894–1958), American actress touring Australia at the time.
11. A play (1929) by American dramatist Rachel Crothers, staged at the Criterion Theatre, Sydney, with Taliaferro, 24 May – 19 June.
12. Canadian-born Hollywood film actress (1902–83), starring in the film *The Divorcee* (1930).
13. Decorated in the style of a 'Castilian castle', the Plaza Theatre at 600 George Street, Sydney, had opened its doors on 11 April 1930. *The Divorcee* screened there 4–30 July.
14. The AGNSW, known in Friend's youth as the National Art Gallery, has been situated in The Domain, Sydney, since the first decade of the twentieth century, and is the leading public gallery in the state.
15. Australian painter, writer, illustrator and cartoonist (1879–1969).
16. *The complete works of Gaius Petronius / done into English by Jack Lindsay; with one hundred illustrations by Norman Lindsay*, Fanfrolico Press edition (London, 1927). Gaius Petronius Arbiter (c. 27–66) was a Roman courtier during the reign of Nero. The authorship of the *Satyricon*, a satirical novel contained in this edition together with some poems, is not certain but is most commonly attributed to Petronius. Jack Lindsay (1900–90) was Norman Lindsay's eldest son. Born and educated in Australia, he lived in England from 1927. Cf **1937**, note 26.

1931

1. American luxury car, produced from 1899.
2. Robert Helpmann (1909–86), Australian-born dancer, choreographer, actor and director. In January 1931, he was appearing in Sydney as a 'specialty dancer' in a revival of the American musical comedy *The Belle of New York* at Her Majesty's Theatre.
3. A building at 393 George Street, Sydney.
4. John Thomas (Jack) Lang (1876–1975), Labor Premier of NSW, 1925–27, 1930–32.
5. Jesse Jewhurst Hilder (1881–1916), Australian painter.
6. Probably *The Old Mill* (1916) or *Mill by the River* (1913), acquired by the AGNSW in 1919 and 1931 respectively.
7. Australian painter (1895–1988). Cf diary entry for last week of September 1985.
8. Suburb of Sydney, 10 kilometres west of the centre.
9. Alice Moses, née Friend (1858–1943).
10. Henry (Harry) Moses (1858–1938), a former Australian test cricketer.
11. English cricketer (1848–1915).
12. American film actress (1899–1983).
13. Hollywood film (1930).
14. An echo of Robert Burns's poem 'A Man's a Man for A' That' (1795).
15. The most famous music hall in Paris, established in the early 1870s.
16. A grazing property owned and run by Friend's father at Jerries Plains, near Singleton, NSW, 200 kilometres north of Sydney.
17. A scene of revelry in the classicist tradition of seventeenth-century European painting. Most renderings included the figure of the Roman wine god, Bacchus. Cf diary entries for 13 December 1948 and 8 November 1951.
18. Bulgarian-born novelist, dramatist and scriptwriter (1895–1956), whose original name was Dikran Kouyoumdjian. He was educated in England, where he published his greatest success as a novelist, *The Green Hat* (1924), set in fashionable London society.
19. The Australian Labor Party was founded in 1891. It was in government in NSW between 1930 and 1932 under Premier Lang—see **1931**, note 4. It had contested seats in the federal parliament since Federation.
20. Fritz Kreisler (1875–1962), Austrian-born violinist, recorded the Beethoven Violin Concerto with the Berlin State Opera Orchestra in 1926.
21. See **1929**, note 34.

1932

1. The Royal Art Society of NSW came into existence in 1903 as the successor to the Art Society of NSW, founded in Sydney in 1880. The art school attached to these organisations dated to 1885.
2. Antonio Dattilo-Rubbo (1870–1955), Italian-born painter and teacher, who emigrated to Australia in 1897. In 1932 he was appointed cavaliere of the Order of the Crown of Italy.
3. Michelangelo Buonarroti (1475–1564), Italian painter and sculptor.
4. Raffaello Sanzio (1483–1520), Italian painter.
5. Sir Arthur Streeton (1867–1943), Australian painter, who lived mainly in England between 1897 and 1923.
6. Amedeo Modigliani (1884–1920), Italian-born painter, who moved to Paris in 1906.
7. A commercial beverage made from meat extract and developed in the 1870s.
8. Vincent van Gogh (1853–1890), Dutch painter.
9. Paul Gauguin (1851–1903), French-born painter, who spent the last twelve years of his life in Tahiti and Polynesia.
10. Australian painter (1875–1963).

1933

1. Fine glassware produced by a company based in the Swedish village of Orrefors from 1898.
2. Australian slang for boarding a train illegally.
3. Off the coast of northern Queensland, on the Great Barrier Reef, near Townsville.
4. A circular setting of large standing stones located in Wiltshire, England, and dating to 2200–3100 BC.
5. English hymn, with words by Sabine Baring-Gould (1865) and music by Arthur Sullivan (1871).
6. The paterfamilias was Charlie Sailor (c. 1890–1944), also known as Tifé Watea, born on Darnley Island, Torres Strait, the son of Sailor (Sela) Lifu from New Caledonia and Gimai of Darnley. In 1916 he had married Louisa, also known as Umma, the daughter of Douglas Pitt from Jamaica and Sopa from New Caledonia. There were nine children in the family, five from a previous marriage of Umma's.
7. The unofficial name of a fringe village above the banks of Alligator Creek in Cairns, north Queensland. It became home to a diverse group of non-white labour communities from Malaya, India, Ceylon and the Torres Strait.
8. Also known as Murray Island.
9. The unofficial name for indentured labourers from the Pacific Islands,

first brought to Queensland in the 1860s.

10. The oldest neighbourhood of Sydney, on the harbour foreshore, near Circular Quay.

1934

1. Presumably a play on Donatello, the familiar name of Donato di Niccolò di Betto Bardi (c. 1386–1466), Florentine artist and sculptor.
2. Australian-born painter (1894–1968), who studied under Dattilo-Rubbo at the Royal Art Society of NSW, and went to live permanently in London in 1930.
3. Familiarly known as 'the Cross', Kings Cross is an inner-city locality of Sydney that acquired a reputation as a bohemian quarter from the early decades of the twentieth century.
4. English-born bon viveur (1908–88), and part-time model at Dattilo-Rubbo's school, who became one of Friend's closest friends, and possibly an early lover.
5. English-born actor (1916–77), who lived in Australia between 1926 and 1948, where he became a prominent stage and radio performer, before returning to England and carving out an international film career. He married three times and had relationships with a number of leading actresses.
6. Town and popular resort, 118 kilometres west of Sydney.
7. The Sydney Royal Easter Show, an agriculture and livestock show, and fun fair, first held in 1823. In 1934 it was located at Moore Park.
8. The Hindu god of creation.
9. Jiddu Krishnamurti (1895–1986), Indian writer, speaker and teacher on philosophical and spiritual subjects.
10. A northern beachside suburb of Sydney, 25 kilometres from the city centre.

1935

1. The Shrine of Remembrance, located in Anzac Square between Ann and Adelaide streets, Brisbane, and built shortly after the end of World War I. With its 'Eternal Flame', the Shrine was dedicated on Armistice Day, 11 November 1930.
2. George Friedrich Handel (1685–1759), German-born composer, who spent most of his mature years in England.
3. An eastern suburb of Sydney, 3 kilometres from the city centre.
4. English-born ballet dancer and furniture dealer, who ran an interiors shop in Kings Cross with Donald Murray. He returned to Europe before the onset of World War II.

1936

1. Friend's ship, the *Ormonde* (of the Orient Steam Navigation Line), left Sydney on 10 October. After travelling via the eastern and southern coasts of Australia to Perth (or its port, Fremantle), the ship proceeded across the Indian Ocean to Ceylon (the name of Sri Lanka till 1972), where Friend would later return to live for a few years—see diary entries for 1957–62. The *Ormonde* then crossed to the Red Sea, where it passed Aden, before travelling through the Suez Canal and into the Mediterranean, where some of the passengers disembarked at Naples, in Italy. It is possible that the 'Mediterranean isle' to which Friend refers is Ischia, on the western edge of the Gulf of Naples, where he was also to live at various times in the future—see diary entries for 1949–50 and 1952. On this voyage he continued with the *Ormonde* to London, where it docked at Tilbury on 19 November 1936.

1937

1. Operated by the London County Council, attached to the Westminster Technical Institute and located from 1904 in Vincent Square, Westminster. From the time of its foundation in the mid-Victorian era, it had made a name for its progressive styles and teaching methods, in reaction against those of the Royal Academy Schools founded a century earlier (cf **1949**, note 20).
2. Russian-born painter (1873–1930), who emigrated to Australia with his family in 1887, lived mainly in England between 1901 and 1921, then returned to Australia.
3. Paul Cézanne (1839–1906), French painter.
4. Georges Braque (1882–1962), French painter.
5. Pablo Picasso (1881–1973), Spanish painter and sculptor.
6. Russian-born painter (1891–1950), who taught life drawing at the Westminster School of Art between 1920 and 1940.
7. English painter (1891–1939), who became associated with the Bloomsbury Group. He taught part-time at the Westminster School of Art from the early 1930s.
8. Chinese-born English painter, illustrator and author (1911–68), best known for the surreal Gormenghast trilogy of novels. He took up his position at the Westminster School of Art in 1936, teaching life drawing.
9. Australian painter and teacher (1904–84), who spent from 1933 to 1950 in England and Europe.
10. Baruch Spinoza (1632–77), Dutch philosopher.
11. Painter and sculptor from a prosperous Brisbane family, who in 1952 resettled in England and married a teacher from her and Friend's days at the Westminster School of Art, Blair Hughes-Stanton.
12. Painter and art teacher (1911–2003).

13. Australian painter (1899–1970), who in 1929 went to London to study at the Slade School, where he won prizes for draughtsmanship and painting. He returned to Australia in 1939.
14. London-based art dealer (c. 1884 – early 1960s), whose present gallery was at 32 Cork Street, Mayfair.
15. German-born English painter (1860–1942).
16. Welsh-born painter (1878–1962). There is no available catalogue or other record of any such show featuring John along with Friend, Sickert and 'four or five other draughtsmen'. Friend and Sickert, but not John, were represented with some fourteen other artists in a show and catalogue of Wilson's the following year: *Figure Drawings by English Artists of the Nineteenth & Twentieth Centuries* (June–July 1938). Two of Friend's works appeared in this catalogue: items 8 and 9, p. 4.

    Another work by Friend, 'from the exhibition of his drawings held at Mr. R.E.A. Wilson's gallery', is reproduced in the *London Mercury*, vol. 38, no. 225, July 1938, facing p. 25. No reference is made here to any accompanying works by Sickert, John or others; it was probably Friend's first solo exhibition.
17. A Nigerian living in London in the 1930s and later.
18. The bohemian quarter in central London, off Charing Cross Road.
19. Restaurant in Charlotte Street, Fitzrovia, London, opened in 1913 by the four Bertorelli brothers from Italy.
20. Trinidad-born jazz drummer who played in various bands in London in the 1930s.
21. A West African deity that personifies patience, endurance, sternness, the ocean and royalty.
22. A town in southwestern Nigeria, at the southern edge of the Yoruba Hills.
23. William Appleton Aiken (1907–57), who became Professor of English and European history at Lehigh University, Pennsylvania, from 1940. The book on Regency rakes never appears to have been published, perhaps running into the same censorship problems that prevented publication in the same decade of Graham Greene's book on a related subject, *Lord Rochester's Monkey* (eventually published in 1974).
24. Established in 1845 in Regent Street, London.
25. Welsh-born artist and writer (1890–1956), who lived in London and became known as the Queen of Bohemia.
26. London-born artist's model and memoirist, who moved in bohemian and occult circles between the world wars. In the late 1920s she had briefly been the lover of Jack Lindsay (see **1930**, note 16).
27. English painter and engraver (1881–1968), born Laura Gosse. She was the daughter of English novelist, memoirist and critic Sir Edmund Gosse.
28. Scottish-born painter (1885–1978), who became a core member of the Bloomsbury Group—cf **1937**, note 45.

29. What was 'bogus' and what constituted 'genius' had deeply exercised Wyndham Lewis in his satirical novel on the English art scene, *The Apes of God* (1930).
30. Geoffrey Wladyslaw Vaile Potocki de Montalk, New Zealand-born poet and eccentric (1903–96), who moved in London artistic circles in the 1930s before settling in France.
31. In Bloomsbury—see **1937**, note 45.
32. Józef Klemens Pilsudski (1867–1935), Polish political and military leader.
33. English novelist (1894–1963).
34. Right-wing literary magazine that appeared intermittently between 1936 and 1973.
35. English occultist and writer (1875–1947), born Edward Alexander Crowley.
36. In Bloomsbury—see **1937**, note 45.
37. Pseudonym for Mrs Barry Field.
38. London-based novelist and archaeologist, whose books include *Under the Hog: A Novel of Richard III* (1937) and *Buried Empires: The Earliest Civilizations of the Middle East* (1939).
39. Suburb in West London.
40. Sir Isaac Newton (1643–1727), English mathematician and physicist, based at Trinity College, Cambridge.
41. Canadian cellist Munroe (born 1924) was a protégé of Arthur Benjamin's. He studied at the Royal College of Music in 1937–39. He then settled in the USA and in 1964 became principal cellist of the New York Philharmonic Orchestra.
42. Paris's main artistic and bohemian quarter, on the Left Bank of the river Seine.
43. Seaside resort on the French Riviera.
44. The museum of decorative arts and design, founded in 1852, named after Queen Victoria and Prince Albert, and located in South Kensington.
45. An area of central London in the south of the borough of Camden, where the British Museum is situated, and where many intellectuals and artists congregated, most notably the Bloomsbury Group from the early years of the twentieth century.
46. Patrick Baltzar de Maré (1916–2008), English-born musician and medico, of Swedish origin, who became consultant psychotherapist at St George's Hospital, London following World War II.
47. Piano composition in D Flat Major by Hungarian composer and pianist Franz Liszt (1811–86).
48. *Trumpet Tune in D*, by English composer Jeremiah Clarke (c. 1674–1707), misattributed to his compatriot Henry Purcell (1659–95).

1938

1. Australian painter and sculptor (1902–89), who travelled to Europe in 1936 and returned to Australia during World War II.
2. Australian painter who travelled to Europe in 1936 with Arthur Murch.
3. The 'Empire Exhibition, Scotland 1938' was an international exposition held at Bellahouston Park in Glasgow, from May to December 1938.
4. Penmaenmawr is a coastal town in North Wales. Jenny's sister, Winifred, went on to marry Wilson and, in an obituary for her (*Independent*, London, 14 June 1996), her maiden name is given as Walford.
5. A one-movement orchestral piece with a sensually repetitive theme, written by French composer Maurice Ravel (1875–1937) and premiered in 1928.
6. An allusion to the rivalry in Australia between its two largest cities, Sydney and Melbourne. The Test cricketer Don Bradman (1908–2001), born and raised in rural NSW, had based himself in Sydney from the end of the 1920s. Collins Street is one of inner-city Melbourne's main thoroughfares and the Yarra is the river that runs through the city.
7. An ethnic group in Sierra Leone, hundreds of thousands of whom were transported to the Americas as slaves between the sixteenth and eighteenth centuries.
8. Claude Monet (1840–1926) was a founder of French impressionist painting.
9. Camille Pissarro (1830–1903), born in St Thomas in the Caribbean, became a leading impressionist painter in France and England.
10. A French maritime company in Marseilles, trading under that name from 1871.
11. An agreement between Germany, the UK, France and Italy, providing for the cession to Germany of certain territories in Czechoslovakia, signed at Munich and dated 29 September 1938. This was intended to appease Germany's leader, Adolf Hitler, and secure peace in Europe.
12. Capital of Senegal.
13. Capital of Sierra Leone.
14. Capital of Gold Coast—cf **1939**, note 14.
15. In what was then French West Africa (Côte d'Ivoire and Dahomey).
16. A wide-brimmed hat, possibly like the one featured in the 1887 painting *Jubilee Hat* by English painter Frank Wright Bourdillon (1851–1924).
17. Frédéric Chopin (1810–49), Polish composer.
18. The best known part of the opera *Giuillaume Tell* (1827), by Italian composer Gioachini Rossini.
19. A suburb of Lagos.
20. Nigerian musician (1910 – late 1980s), credited as the founder of Jùjú music.

21. Dominant ethnic group in the southern states of Nigeria.
22. This work was never published, but substantial parts of the text exist in notebooks held by the National Library of Australia, Canberra, and the Mitchell Library, Sydney.

1939

1. In southern Nigeria.
2. A town in Ekiti state, southwestern Nigeria.
3. The annual collection of adventure stories and other features published in the periodical the *Boy's Own Paper* between 1879 and 1967.
4. A local title equivalent to king, also known in Ikerre as the Ogoga—cf diary entry for 10–11 July 1939.
5. Named Jennifer, after her mother—cf diary entry for June to August 1938 on the circumstances of the conception.
6. English fiction-writer and diarist (1887–1960).
7. An aphrodisiac prepared from dried beetles (or the 'Spanish fly').
8. The eponymous young hero of the novel (1886) by English-American author Frances Hodgson Burnett.
9. Title of 1932 song by English dramatist and songwriter Noël Coward, containing the refrain 'Mad dogs and Englishmen go out in the midday sun'.
10. Alowolodu II, who had become Ogoga of Ikerre-Ekiti in 1928.
11. François Rabelais (c. 1494–1553), French satirist and writer of bawdy tales.
12. Nigerian artist (c. 1873–1938).
13. City in Ekiti region, Nigeria.
14. Belgian colony in West Africa, 1908–60.
15. Former German colony in West Africa, divided between Britain and France in 1919.
16. British colony in West Africa, 1821–1957. Now Ghana.
17. Fashionable shopping street in central London.
18. The Ogoga's palace in Ikerre.
19. The fashionable London hotel in Brook Street, Mayfair.
20. The Parisian fashion house of French couturier Coco Chanel.
21. The Parisian perfume house founded in 1904 by François Coty.
22. The start of World War II is generally dated to Hitler's invasion of Poland on 1 September, which prompted France and England to declare war on Germany a couple of days later.
23. A collection of tales (c. 1350–53) by Italian poet Giovanni Boccaccio (1313–75).

24. A collection of medieval Persian and Arabic folk tales, also known as the *Arabian Nights*, from the title of the first English-language edition (1706).
25. A line from the song 'Rule Britannia' (1740), with words by James Thomson and music by Thomas Arne.
26. A secondary school for boys, established in 1909.
27. The writings of Kipling (see **1929**, note 26) were noted for their militaristic and jingoistic sentiments.
28. The legendary ancient race of a lost land sometimes located in the Indian Ocean.
29. Sergei Prokofiev (1891–1953), Russian composer.
30. A character in Petronius's *Satyricon*—cf **1930**, note 16.
31. The major French royal palace between 1682 and 1789, near Paris.
32. Niccolò Machiavelli (1469–1527), Italian political philosopher, best known for his treatise on canny diplomacy, *The Prince* (1513).
33. Town in Ondo state, southwestern Nigeria.
34. An allusion to the homosexual practices of athletes and others in ancient Greece, sometimes depicted on classical pottery.
35. A satirical magazine published in England from 1841 to 1992 and 1996 to 2002.

1940s

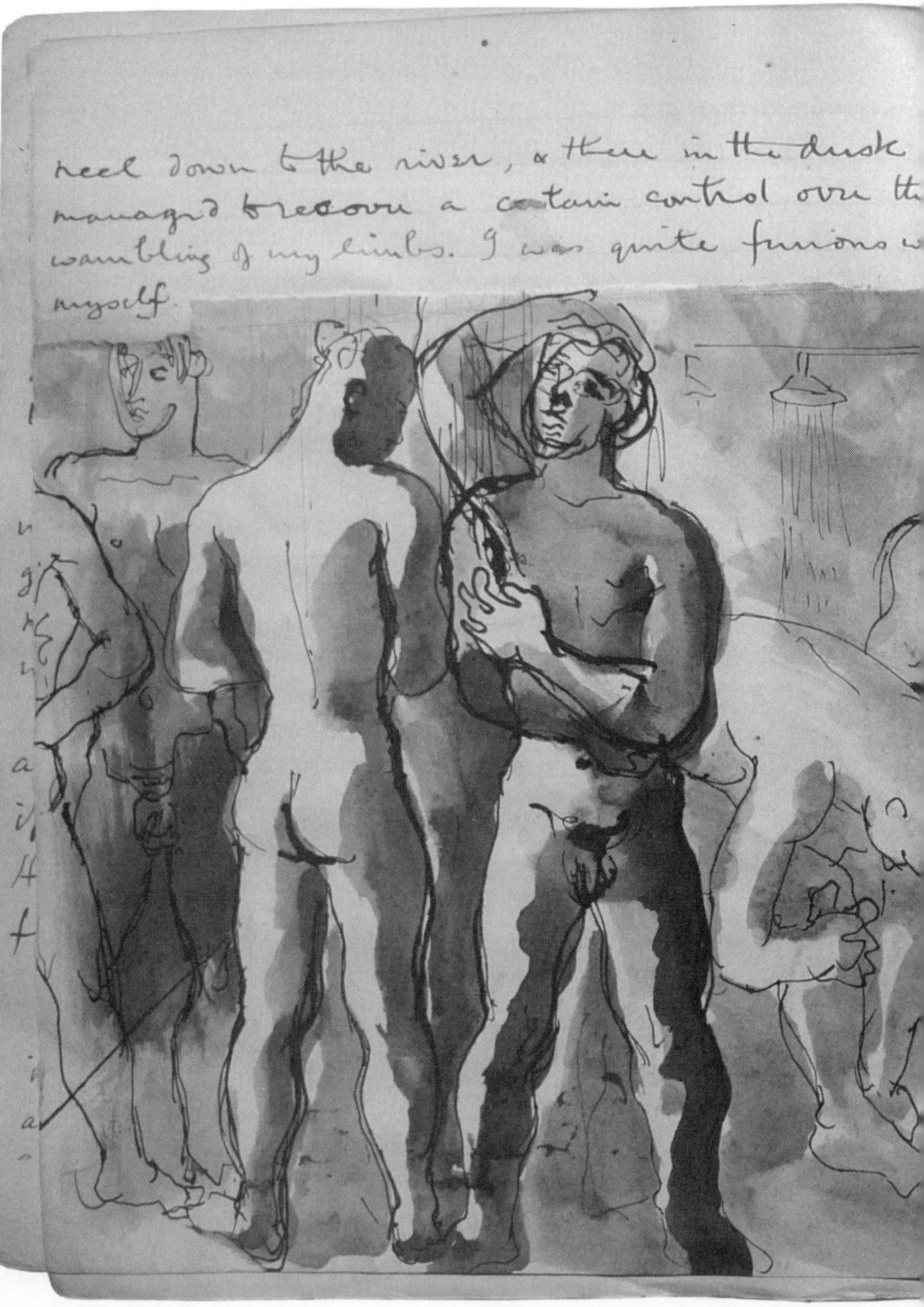
reel down to the river, & there in the dusk
managed to recover a certain control over th
wambling of my limbs. I was quite furious w
myself.

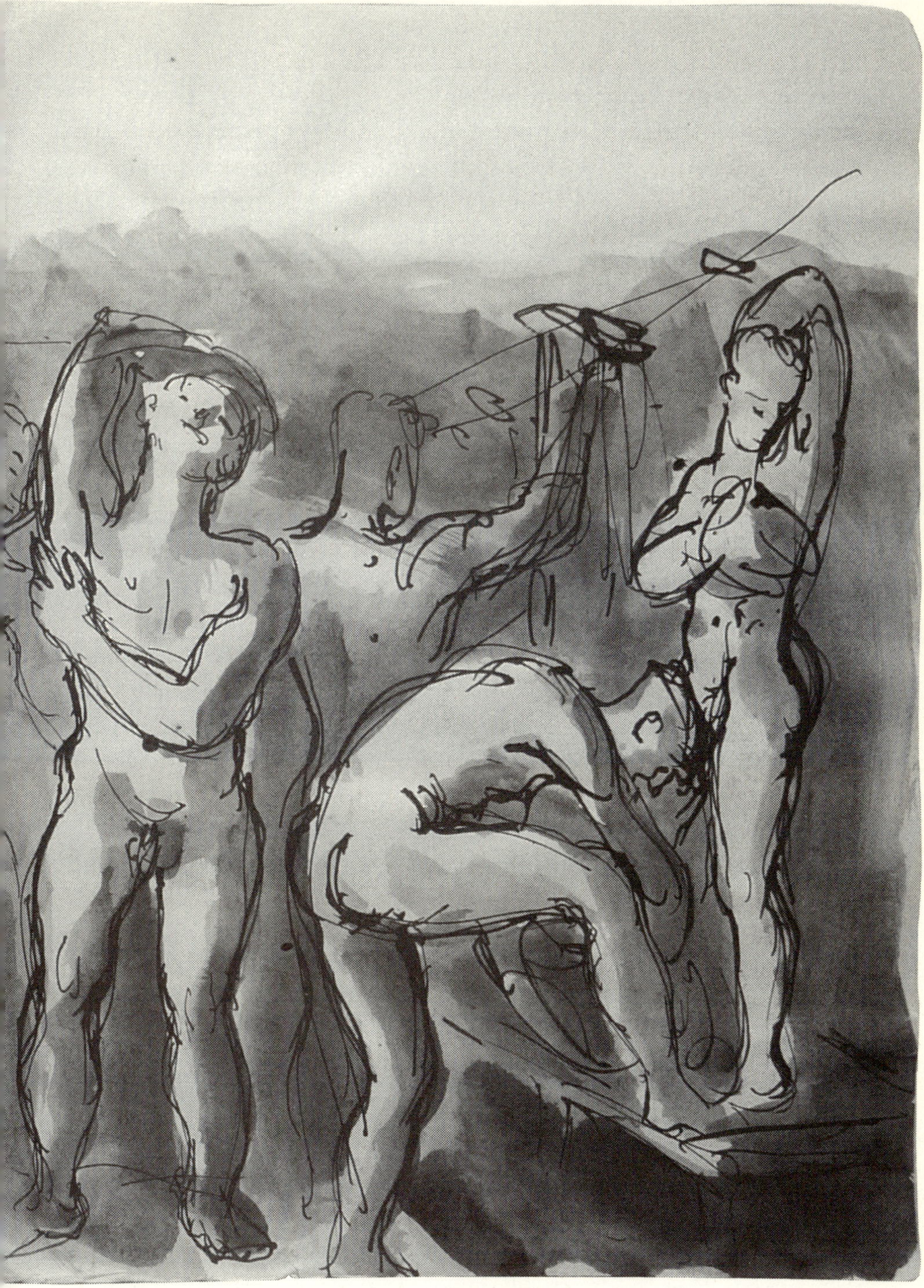

11. Soldiers showering (1943).

1940

January Lagos is its usual mixture of irreconcilable opposites—black and white—the green gardens of the European reservation and the squalid stink of the town. Shifting, restless, without standards, like a chronic sore on the body of Yorubaland. What shall cure it? For some reason Nigerians admire it. 'There is life in Lagos,' they say. 'Life' means the pubs and whores and picture shows and the peculiar irresponsible fecklessness which is the peculiar character of Lagos. Neither fascism nor communism will do it any good. It is, I think, a self-existing entity.

When I hear a man is Lagosian, I am careful before I trust him. He's charming, and talks amusingly, and makes jokes: like as not he'll borrow money from you in five minutes, and he'd sell his grandmother's skin. And I do not speak as an official living in isolated grandeur in the reservation. I lived in the native town, among natives. The country people are pleasanter to deal with, and far more honest.

Nowadays, one can find men from every race in Africa in Lagos. To understand the peculiarities of such 'civilised' places, one must understand fully the culture of Africa as well as Europe, and know just as intimately the history of their impact. From these two have grown a third state, which, though yet not stable, is extremely different from those from which it sprung, and may be called a culture, though it is infinitely inferior to its parent cultures. O my poor old Yoruba—all the favours you've suffered from the disinterested philanthropy of the whites! Christianity is the herald and cause of disruption and decay of all security, sanity and moral systems which, indivisible from fetish, express the needs of the people.

The worst flaw in the Yoruba character is an acute individualism. About 99 per cent of Yoruba don't give a damn for anybody or anything but no. 1. It is quite evident that this philosophy is of fairly recent development. Much of their history tends to show that the people as a rule had quite an excellent sense of social responsibility. The more I have learnt of them, the more I have realised what an appalling comedown the Yorubas have suffered, in both the destruction of the state, and even more drastic, in the degeneration of character. These characteristics make it almost impossible in many parts to introduce measures for the public good. They are invariably opposed by the majority for the most naively selfish reasons.

20 February I am coming home. There is a great boat—the *Nestor*—Blue Funnel line[1]—only First Class. I'm so excited. I sit dreaming of home—of work—writing, painting, and people, and darling Kings Cross.

I have many cases full of gorgeous cloth and carvings—ebony, ivory, and the spoils of the dark continent.

Last week of February At Lagos a whole delegation of Black Men came to see me off.

My last night in West Africa by the beach at Sekondi-Takoradi[2]. A whitish-grey building of vaguely disreputable appearance looks on to the sea and sand and serried rows of canoes, palms and fishing nets. This is the Grand Hotel Akropolis. The walls are yellow and vermilion, and outside the doors and wide windows, the sun glares whitely on the world, like an immense arc-light bleaching the colour from all things. Yet the room is cool. And the 'boy'—a veritable black Ganymede[3] with the nicest smile on the West Coast—brings you the local beer, which is good and cold. The sight of the heat, one's own coolness, the rushing of the breakers on the shore—oh it's a real paradise is the Akropolis!

That night we danced, drinking cool crème de menthe frappés. Then we bathed on the beach outside, and young Ganymede brought us drinks and watched us amusedly, the while playing a guitar softly and inconsequently, murmuring amusing obscene songs, quiet, rhythmic, that abound on the Coast. We went back to the ship in a canoe, and took him with us to sing on the way. He gave me two red parrot feathers such as the medicine man sell in the market: the last gift I received on African soil. Next morning West Africa was a blue blur on the horizon.

March Shipboard life—suspended animation: deck quoits, novels, meals. At night we lounged on the blacked-out deck, looking dumbly at the black sea and sky. Or in the airtight fug of the lounge, we grow garrulous over drinks and cards. All our absurd little activities and pleasures, vastly unimportant in the black ship on a black sea, under a black sky.

Our old familiar selves are dead: our homelands changed. No one who goes to the Guinea Coast emerges unchanged. Most of us leave our souls there, to travel the world as 'dead men walking', or only live again when we return to the beloved heat and humidity and horrors that we curse at, grumble at, escape from. So stranger beware when you see that low coastline with its surf and palms. It's a land of subtle demons. It's the land of frustrations, when the eye is dazed with beauty and colours, enchanting, dirty, luring, sordid, madly exciting and magical: but untouchable, incomprehensible, and once you land there you will return there again and again, but you will not fathom its indefinable enchantment.

At the vile cities of Capetown and Durban, I found myself rather uncomfortable and out of sympathy with civilised life—or maybe it was that I was oppressed all the time by the insinuating presence of a Slave race of negroes—so different from the Coast. Anyway I hated it. The South Africans who got off there were most horribly scandalised at my views and opinions.

April to May *Sydney*. Kings Cross has a genuine Berlin air. *Everybody* is wicked. Wolfgang Cardamatis[4] welcomed me royally, and now we are in the process of living happily in a state of mad sin in no. 10 Rockwall Crescent, Potts Point. Mama oddly much approves of my Wolf ménage. We are really doing an incredible amount of work. We are both painting all day and most of the night. I have done three oils—two very bad, one work of genius, and four very good drawings—one 'Bust of Dietrich's hands'[5]—nice—and a lovely wild Kings X scene, 'La Vie au chez côté de Cardamatis'[6]. We cook our own meals here—so good. Wolf is being so lovely and sweet and virtuous.

July Domestic life in no. 10 continues like a Symphonie Fantastique[7], with the usual obligato of 10,000 harps, punctuated by drunken sobbing cries from Wolf and from me. Love sits enthroned. But Wolf explains that when he lives with one person he yearns for another 'on principle'—principle indeed!

Are there any Normal People? And what does normality consist of? Mad Bohemia of my younger days has gone forever, and its inhabitants married or become commercial and successful—*seducta ad suburbam.*[8] But we work, are Happy, Sober and Good. Life is quite nice. I have blue corduroys and expensive shirts.

I wrote a letter to W. Ashton[9], Director of the Art Gallery of NSW. He has hidden 44 modern paintings in the cellars. I feel that those with power should be among the first to fight against the stupid escapist anachronistic tendency to condemn and mock and hide away the cultural products of our century. Gum trees or pretty ladies with convenient swathes of tulle may be pretty in themselves, and have attractive sentimental or politely (ah—so politely!) sensual associations. But it does not follow that paintings of them are good. The quality of a painting is in itself not in its subject. Let us see something of the art of the twentieth century: the fine things it has produced might help us to be less discouraged at the evil.

August Karoon[10], Orwell St, Kings X: we go up in the world, yet reverting to our first address—this is the place I had years ago, and it's really lovely and Wolf says full of fragrant memories. We've got a whole roof and two balconies and dozens of windows with Parisian views, and a magnificent golden wall-bed which is quite terrifying and turns into a Jacobean wardrobe by day, and we have shower rooms and bathrooms in great numbers and hot water laid on, and it's all very lovely. We work a lot, and most of our days are spent (tra la la la![11]) cooking, dusting and washing up and everyone is incredibly envious.

I showed with the Contemporary Art Society[12] but really I wasn't much of a member, I was simply a painter.

September The Society of Artists[13] gave me an exhibition. The Contemporaries of course thought the Society was all very well but terribly old world and old-fashioned, Gum Tree painters and so on, but I couldn't be bothered with the passionate art politics and that sort of thing which didn't much interest me. The Society of Artists was a much more solid sort of thing. I showed with them, but I could never get myself involved in selection committees and hanging committees and all the rest of it, and all that is good for an artist who is ambitious to get along; and I liked a lot of the artists, but I don't like that sort of organisation to do with art. They are necessary, but it's not really my thing at all. I'm just interested in painting and always was. I have now sold four paintings in the Exhibition.

I am very good and virtuous these days. Almost priggish: I feel old and reasonable and mature, and somehow I hate mad gaiety and the superficial people who affect it. I fear life and people more than I ever did before: paranoia perhaps. All these absurd unreal values upset me—sentiment and horror, the falsity of the motives that any moment may drag me into some hell of harshness and death and cruelty—the search for glory, or victory, or power, or any number of peculiar abstractions.

I paint and draw hours every day, and till late into the night. Briefness of all that now exists flows into my work: a terrible haste to express it. I work and work but am really quite muddled and unhappy and do wish that Wolf was less of a detribalised Bulgarian. I'm just as bad but dully. There is much emotional stress. Wolf is sick of my complacency and I tire of his irresponsibility. Wolf's insight into the bogusness of humanity is bitter and corrosive. There is nothing but turmoil. Wolf got bored and just disappeared in a most urgent time of work—haven't seen him for days—*such* a trustworthy lad—has let me down very badly on another thing too so I really am furious.

Peter Finch is a bright spot. I have so few friends or acquaintances even. Here I sit among guitars, le journal and artificial ruins—desolate.

November to December Ercildoune, 91 Elizabeth Bay Road: I am enchanted with my new place—it is a jewel—Macarthur-Onslows'[14] ex-town-house—a magnificent colonial house, utterly lovely. It's really gorgeous and spacious—doors with porcelain bouquet-painted knobs, and a great garden with a marvellous view of Rushcutters Bay[15], and a jacaranda and numerous flowers—the room is huge and high, with French windows (three of them) on to a balcony over the Bay. Mabel[16], Wolf, Wallace Thornton[17] and I have the upstairs flat, so besides our own rooms, each with a different and wonderful verandah, we have kitchen, bathroom and breakfast room, so it's all very palatial. I have a huge marble fireplace and over it the drawings of the Ikerre doors which make an interesting tapestry pattern.

The Macquarie Galleries[18] opened its portrait show and I have had good notices. Met Russell Drysdale.[19] He came up from Melbourne. I am terribly happy just now and working hard.

I have become Australian art correspondent for the *Christian Science Monitor*, Boston, USA.[20] An editor asked me for an article on the convict-primitive painters. I wrote it without exaggerations or lies. But he insisted on at least *one* illustration. Then stirred in my mind plans for a hoax. The Mitchell Library[21] had offered no suitable illustration of the primitive. I must make one myself. The real inspiration occurred in Jim Tyrell's bookshop in George Street, when I found a pile of old photographs of

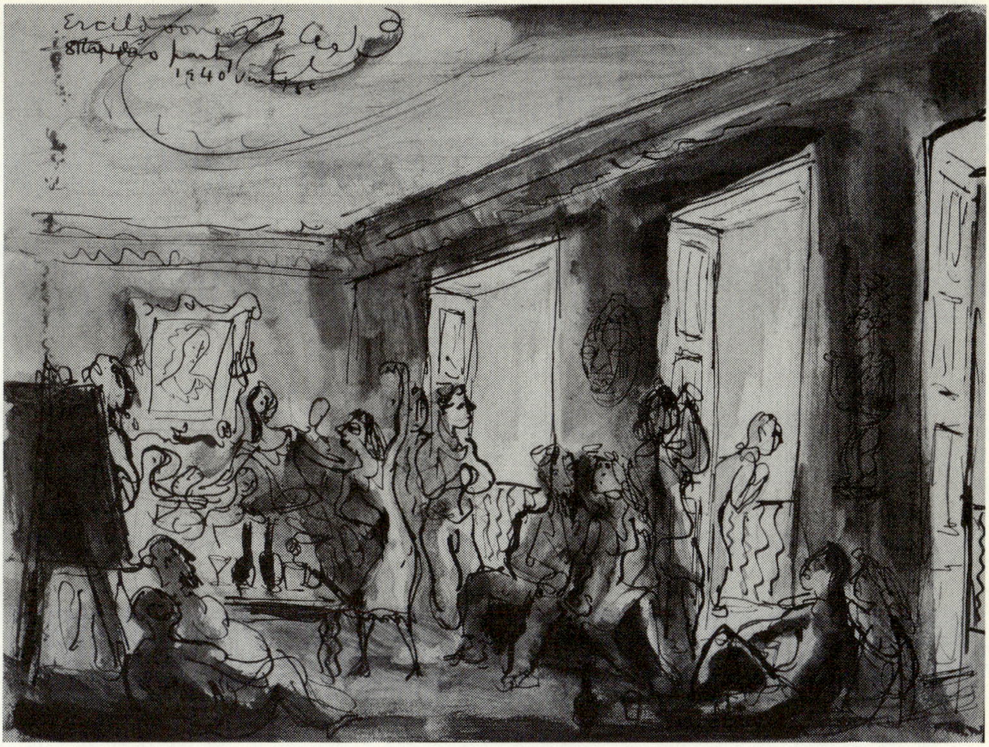

12. 'Ercildoune studio party' (1940).

colonial prints and views. I bought some of these and made a careful collage depicting Sydney Cove in about 1810. In the middle distance I glued a little group of Aborigines around a campfire, from another early print. I had it photographed. Probably the most intriguing, lovable, naive little primitive ever produced in Australia. Of course, I had to provide a history for it. It was in the form of a miniature learned biography, quoting copiously from bogus contemporary diaries.[22]

I paint a tremendous lot. But restless. What can I do about this coming conscription? I have had malaria.

1941

January I realised, in the heat, yet in a mood of most zero Siberian frigidity and depression, the truly tragic essence of my silly life—which is that whilst I have a painful and urgent inclination toward the most stupid, dangerous and exotic forms of promiscuity I have really no talent for it; and the lack of realisation makes me paint and be terribly lonely and unhappy—maybe it's worth it for the colours on the canvas, I don't know. I wish I were dead.

Early March Our wonderful grandeur of Ercildoune. The old house is surely worthier of a more dignified crowd than we. God, what a mob! That huge room with French windows onto a balcony over the bay, the rich coloured masks I brought from Africa, gramophone playing the Rachmaninov Piano Concerto[1] on quiet evenings, playing madly rowdy boogie on noisy ones. Mabel dancing a sort of heathenish fandango around a four-gallon tin of Tahitian rum punch. Someone left a burning cigarette on the feather bed and the whole caboose went up in smoke. When at last the thing was subdued the whole place was a swamp of ash, soot and dirty water.

It was really too much. I went into town and got a ticket to Cairns. Ercildoune is now a perfect House of Usher[2]. The pace and style of life must constantly change, and I outworked my Sydney inspiration. Soon I shall be a tough bear again, with a check shirt and all, and a scandalous vocabulary of Northern words. The North will give me new impetus, and new motives in painting.

12–15 March *En route to Cairns.* My cabin on the train is early 1880 workmanship with wonderful red plush, mahogany panels and curious surreal chandeliers.

I have taken a great ceremonial hot bath at the Brisbane railway station to sober me after several hours' solid drinking with bums and soldiers in an unbelievable pub—where the most incredible old whores gathered in a bevy round the men's lavatory in the yard—in a word, the True Northern flavour.

Rockhampton and Mackay passed in a glory of reminiscence. On the railway stations check shirts abound, and those tight-bummed northern trousers, and Italians boldly speaking their own language.

We reach Townsville. It's incredibly hot and steamy, and the horribly green fields and hills are blue with moist haze. The air is positively West African, and my body has responded with that curious lightness and emptiness, the slightly sick feeling that was with me most of the time in Nigeria.

16 March *Cairns*. Here I am at last, back at my own haunts and accorded a marvellous Melanesian welcome. We all lie about all day and night playing guitars and singing the most lovely native songs in a sort of eternity of indolence. The Sailors are utterly amazing—old Charlie an immense bulky strong sort of giant, jet black, and with an utterly terrifying face—and a personality equal to appearance—subtle, childish—kindly, cunning—everything, and incredibly likeable and loves me as a son. Umma, his wife, when one knows her really well, turns out to be a complete pagan. The children of my last visit are young men—make me feel quite old. The daughters are amusing and a delight—one is austere, like a black Emily Brontë[3] in a mauve hairnet.

Malaytown—among the mangroves, tumbled shacks on the edge of turgid Alligator Creek—much the same as ever, and a little more fantastic. Every one, besides their own island language, speaks the most peculiar Malay pidgin. We talk a good deal of Malay in the house—mine of course is based on a great deal of guesswork, but still manages to preserve a reputation for fluency.

I do a little drawing, but most of the time, nothing. The mosquitoes and sandflies are hell—but what a lovely escape!

4 April Cairns is more incredible than ever—I wandered in to the ritziest pub on the strand to have a drink—it was wooden, and in that beloved tradition of yore, except that the walls had been Cecil Beatonised[4], but swing doors prevailed: a modern onyx bar, circular, enshrined the most unbelievable ice-chest machine, immense, elaborate and very mechanical, painted that green which houseflies adore, and stained with rust and scratched, so that, except for little nickel rails and knobs supporting bottle openers, various glasses and several orchids and ferns, it looked quite like an old fishing-boat engine—the barmaid was In the Tradition, and also the other drinkers: I myself was a sort of Somerset Maugham stage property, with my white clothes and famous one-day Queensland Green Beard.

The whole damn place up to the far north was extremely homosexual really, but it wasn't just lah di dah-ing about the place and wearing daffodil trousers and so on, it was all very butch and tough and whatever went on, well it was just fun and games between mates.

6–7 April *Pine Creek.* A stay with one of Umma's sons, at a most remote place. He has a farm there. One goes by dinghy through a twelve-mile maze of mangrove creeks and swamps full of most incredible carnivorous alligators and such, and finally arrives at this gorgeous place—a fruit farm with oranges and bananas, granadillas and what-not, and very wild mountains and a river with a waterfall—all Melanesians on the farm—we worked—digging, ploughing—picking fruit, and swimming, guitar playing and island songs, and spearing fish—I adored it.

End of April to mid-September *Green Island.*[5] Mabel White caught me up, and the fun began all over again. Really, rather an ugly woman, with a cracked voice. But such an insane zest, such a really generous, wildly romantic nature and deeply warm of heart.

I have been in a sort of trance, sometimes very happy and sometimes miserable. The real trouble is celibacy—most unwilling—that combines with a rarefied love of people and this sort of life. One's own desires are so foolish and then of course People—Mabel mostly—crash in with loud storms of tactless stupidity mixed with zany kindness and a complete inability to see what is occurring inside one. Then I get quite mad and hysterical inside but have to remain very nice and agreeable externally (one can't hide away). Then at other times this place is so gloriously tranquil—a sort of Robinson Crusoe[6] paradise. I wander out on the reef, or solitary on the beaches, and in glades of palms—it's really terribly disturbing and lovely. But there is an awful lack of the right person. Hundreds of dreadful tourists came over, but among them a lovely and primitive boy of about seventeen who with an extraordinary self possession sat down and talked with me—very naive and sweet—I was quite infatuated—but inconsequently and stupidly I refrained. How one regrets virtuous impulses!

I have painted the small, darkly jewel-coloured Kanaka, the reclining subject that has always tempted and delighted me. I've never come to the end of that subject. It's no use looking at the thing and saying 'Gauguin' simply because of that master's superb *Manao Tupapau*[7]. This has nothing to do with it. It's my own, and for all my admiration for Gauguin's amazing picture, I resent the comparison. After all, were I to paint a Madonna and child, would it be fair to infer a plagiarism from 500 masters of the Renaissance?

20 September *Cairns.* Dance. The band of guitars struck up a sort of Asiatic polka. Three or four couples of Malay girls, dressed in their favourite lolly pink, sauntered on to the floor and danced to this amusing sort of beguine—opposite one another, the while vaguely waving handkerchiefs as they traipsed about, negligently, graceful. To this we all chanted. Charlie sat like an Epstein[8] statue in ebony for the whole evening. At intervals roaring a command to all and sundry to take partners for a one-step—or a mazurka or whatever it might be.

27 September *Pine Creek.* Down in the creek, where the soil changes to salty mud and the gums and palms and exotic trees cease and the menacing monotonous mangroves commence, spreading flatly for miles, alligators cough and bark at night, and swirl in the water, suddenly. Innumerable little beetles and creatures creak and croak like the percussion section of a rumba orchestra, and flying foxes chatter and quarrel in nervy spasms. It is quite terrifying.

First week of December *Cairns.* Discussing the war very learnedly in Pidgin English with the Torres Straits lugger boys. I showed how we need never fear Japan's coming in the war. I made a rough map, showing Japan, a tiny group of islands, neighboured by warring China, hostile Russia, and then surrounded entirely by American and British coasts, islands and naval bases, and an armed Australia and New Zealand in the south.

The lugger boys were very impressed. So was I when the Japs attacked Pearl Harbor[9] a week later.

1942

Mid-February The wet season has arrived. Hot winds blow all the time and I'm sick of it all. The desires of the flesh are present a hundredfold, the symbols that arouse them are all scattered about in a glorious debauch of nearness. As far as I am concerned, boats are a great symbol. In themselves they don't mean anything at all to me: I know nothing about them and have never bothered to find out. I should much rather travel in a liner than any lugger, yet the very sight of these luggers breeds a mad excitement and hunger—a damned inconvenient hunger, as the only means of obtaining that satisfaction lures me from

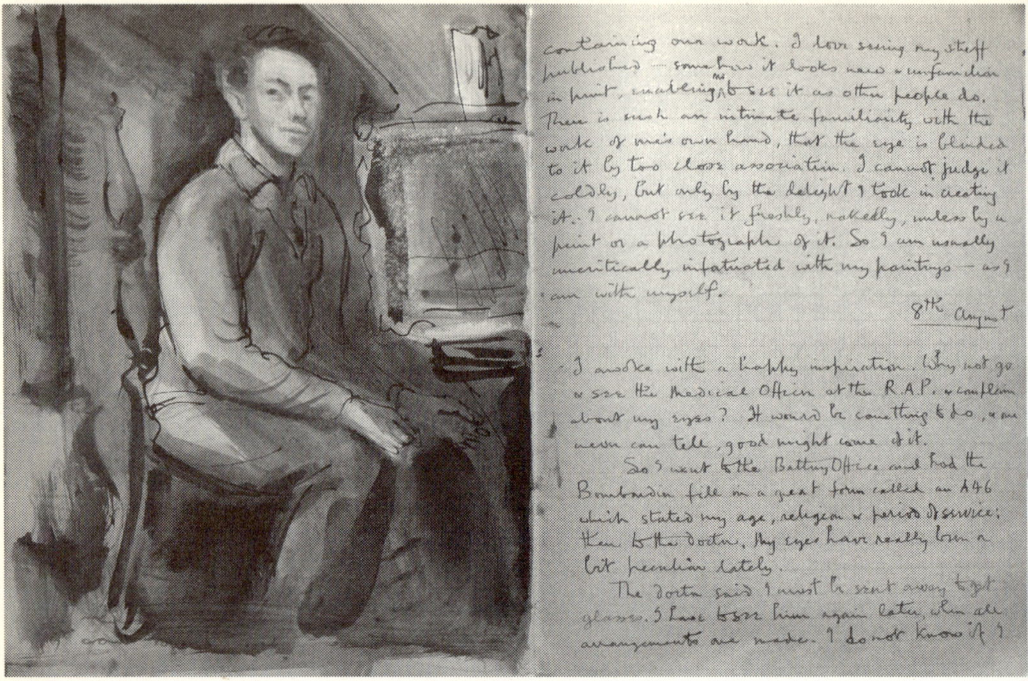

13. *Self-portrait with easel (1943).*

my proper environment into fields which are exceptionally barren.

I'm utterly fed up with all these people, and go through the agonies of exasperation at the charm they hold for me. They are much more irritating than the Africans at their worst. I suppose it's because their true culture is so warped or watered down with Protestant Christianity: that they talk English all the time, yet it conveys to me nothing of what I desire from that language.

There is no wit in the North—or none for the non-hoboes. I have not one friend I can go to, and sit down for a while and chat. There is not one place I can go and sit reading undisturbed. The army can't be worse than this. If I don't go south I'll go mad.

The wireless has just announced the fall of Singapore.[1]

Late February to May *Sydney*. I returned from the North and took a shivering draughty shed in Billyard Avenue[2] to camp in until the Elizabeth Bay House[3] was ready. It rained and rained there for days. Ah those spacious, gracious palmy days that followed! The wild parties. Conversations, jokes, ideas.

22 June I joined the AIF.[4] I went to a sort of log cabin erected in the middle of Martin Place.[5] A lot of the chaps are very young. I think the most common incentive is this—that if they did not join the AIF they'd be yanked into the militia anyway, and as a secondary consideration, civilian life nowadays is becoming so strained and hectic that army life can hardly be much more uncomfortable. Illusions of heroism, death-with-honour and the like are extremely rare motives. Why?—because after all, in the last war those motives were the chief incentives to volunteers. Firstly, our propaganda is hopelessly inadequate, and is as often as not greeted with derisive disbelief; secondly, this generation is politically disillusioned and has practically no faith in the actions and promises of its leaders.

29–30 June *Hume Camp, Albury.*[6] If you want some haven remote from the worries of war, where you will not be constantly wrought-up by news of attacks and defeats, where the sound of battle is dim and distant—then join the army. At once you are in a peculiar backwater; you read no newspapers, hear no radio bulletins. The dreadful wrangle with all its tales of horror, dishonour, torture and bloodshed becomes as a mirage. You drill all day and sleep dead weary at night. To the soldier, I assure you, the sergeant major's bellowing is far more terrible than all the tales of battle yet to come, or the roar of distant guns. And all the marching, the rifle drill and gun practice seem to be less a dress rehearsal to mortal struggle than the choreography of a very lengthy and stupid ballet, sans audience and sans applause.

Well, in a way I *do* enjoy being in it. Of course a lot of the time it's just plain bloody awful, then some of the time it's just nothing at all—indifferent—a sort of physical and mental vacuum in which neither pleasurable nor objectionable sensations are recorded. Then there are moments of happiness. Quite a lot of the time I am much diverted by the most amazing absurdities. The physical hardness of the life does not worry me at all. After all, in Africa and in the North, as well as in England, I have undergone much tougher ordeals. What upsets me most of all is the complete absence of intellectual companionship. So far I have not met one person with whom I can talk straightforwardly, nor anyone who has moved in the same world as myself, so I am really isolated. Actually, communicating with one's comrades can only be done on a very limited scale because it is only possible for them to digest the most simple and primitive ideas, which must be expressed in an extreme form of the Australian dialect, which is composed mainly of swear words and expletives. Really, I might just as well be living amongst a rabble of Hottentots[7]. They're not so bad though, in the bush-potato-eating-peasant way—warm, stupid, kindly—these are their virtues.

There are a few bourgeois in the camp. They are quite detestable, far more so than the peasants. They are businessmen and very jolly, and really they are atrocious. But I am like an envious cripple squinting with venomous malice at those who possess talents that I do not. Just the same, they are talents I would despise to possess.

When I was a civilian I could go anywhere and do anything at all, and I was an equal with the lowest and the highest in the land, whomever I chose as my companions. But now I am a gunner, I am in every way the social inferior of some people whom I did not choose to mix with: and there are others—casual acquaintances and friends who are officers—who once esteemed it quite a thing to know me. Now I feel too damned diffident even to greet them, whilst they do not recognise me, seeing only the uniform and not the man inside of it. It is hard to recognise a former acquaintance in uniform. He has lost all those traits, the gestures, the walk whereby one knew him: there remains only a face and hands emerging from a swamp of khaki cloth. I think his mind is often lost too. After all one has only about an hour's freedom a day, and in that hour, no privacy.

In here I must obey the most trivial word, do things without rhyme or reason for people who, for all the world would have lost, need never have existed at all. I do not resent it, though I do not think it strictly necessary. The war itself is necessary only as the necessary outcome of people's unbounded stupidity. In this war, I am not a man: I am a potential soldier. Outside the war I am an artist, which is more than a man. Without artists you would be an even more useless pack of barbarians than you are now.

First week of July I went into hospital with a wretched skin infection. It was really rather heavenly—hot baths and decent food, and a great deal of lazing around. The place was rather overcrowded, so I slept in a tent—but with a bed. The tent lines were camouflaged—pleasantly absurd mural designs of donkeys, emus and such creatures in the primitive manner that gave the infectious ward a sort of gay abandoned air: like frivolous wigwams.

Last half of July Every night buses go from Hume Camp into Albury. I go in about twice a week. First, I eat an enormous underdone rump steak, which makes me feel very happy. Then I go to the Albury Club and have a few drinks. After that I get a taxi and go to see Tas and Bonny[8] Drysdale. Tas is a very good painter. Then we just talk, sitting by the fire, drinking. The talk is quite the most glorious thing. It is like being in heaven finding that you still have a mind that works sharply and easily, and that all the things you value are enjoyed and valued by other people. For the time I am there I am once more moving among realities. You find again a world with solid foundations. Because in the army all these good things are not considered to have any existence at all. There, the entire universe is based on axioms and suppositions that I cannot conceive as having the faintest relation to truth.

28 August I have been going through all the forms and ceremonies without realising their true significance. Today I awoke quite suddenly from my acceptance of it all. During a lecture on Tommy guns a sergeant was explaining that the bullet on entering a man's body made only a small hole, but on its exit a 'great bloody mess of a hole big enough to put your fist in'. They have been teaching me a number of incredible ways of killing men.

No, I don't mind very much. You see, I know myself so well. I shall be very revolted and disgusted at first, as much at the actual physical spilling of blood as at the much more important principles that are involved in the spilling of it. Then I shall quickly get used to it, as in the past I have become accustomed to seemingly impossible situations.

September Death is not silent now, but a screaming rowdy thing. Shining machines shall loudly dive from those azure skies, kin to hopping croaking crows, madmen that grind and tear. I once thought it would come to me quietly, after a long time, and take me swiftly to some clean solitude of white bones on white sand, without song or ceremony. My prophecy has changed. Havoc surrounds it. I won't like it at all.

Aeroplanes I cannot help continue to regard as unnatural, new-fangled

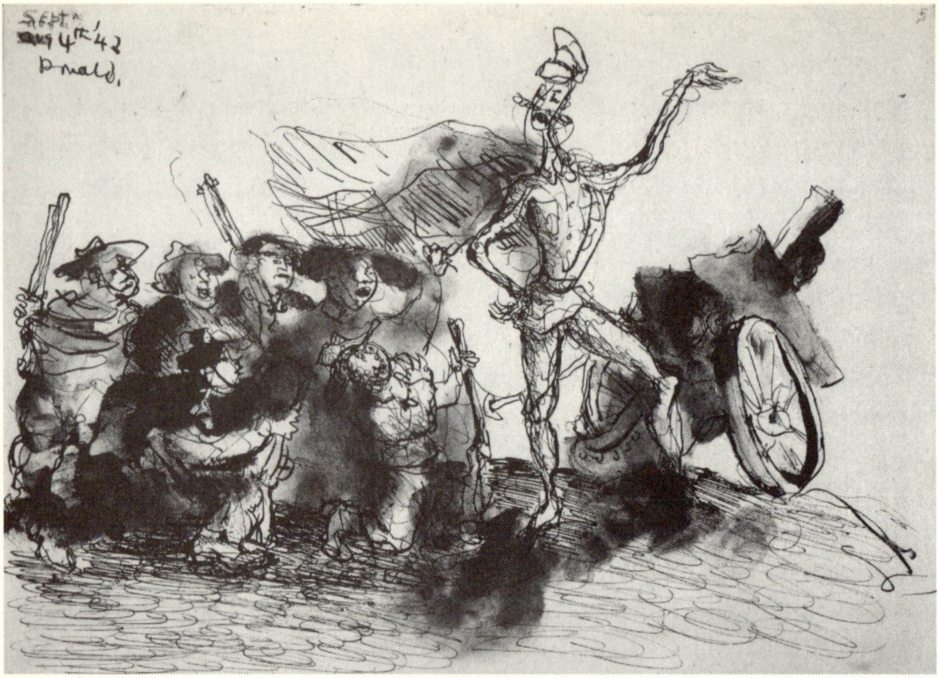

14. Study for 'Mars and Venus' (1942).

affairs, harbingers of trouble and discontent, in no way carrying out the purposes for which they were designed, but perverting inevitably by their very nature all peaceful and dignified emprises into expeditions of graceless scurrying speed, guided by hasty and savage decisions of war, or by the greedy raiding and grubbing after money and exploitation. No. Give me the gracious days of my own generation, with its ambling motorcars and locomotives, its gently old-style gramophones, the soft beat of *le jazzhot* and the accompanying rattle of the cocaine syringes: these are means of gentlemanly leisure, the serene habits of a tribe who yet dare to express contempt for your beastly flying machines. Brand me Tory if you will. I will have none of them.

Would that I were taking *déjeuner* with Verlaine[9], Honoré de Balzac[10], Cézanne, Braque, Modigliani, George Moore[11], Lady Asquith, Monet, Manet[12] and the whole mad merry crew, *les artistes ravissantes*! Every now and then these bouts of nostalgia creep on me, as a mist over bog country. Then fain I retire from the jolly round of military occasions, strike my zither, and devise a day *à la recherche du temps perdu*.

I have sold a painting to Daryl Lindsay[13], furthermore, I have commenced on the panel *Mars and Venus*. It is going well. There is a tavern in this town frequented by myself and an Evelyn Waugh (*Vile Bodies*)[14] Drunken Major. In drink—or in the ultra-sensitive perception of humanity inspired by the right amount of it—one's entire existence becomes exciting.

2–5 October *Sydney*. Ah the harbour! Ah Macleay Street, even Ah the Central Railway Station on my arrival in a state of wayward ecstasy. The lovely and the ghastly alike have by miracles survived cigarette rationing, milk zoning and austerity. It's heaven to be in Sydney again.

Strawberries and cream for breakfast. No, I can't believe it. It isn't true, it can't be. I count the hours, and waste them, lying in complete idleness. Swimming occasionally, drinking, lying in the sun on the sand. Gwen's place at Newport[15] is like Gauguin's hut in Tahiti, set among trees, and there are vines with red flowers. The roof is bright yellow and blue, with a balcony of palm thatch. Inside, the walls are lined with fine Tongan tapa cloth, beautifully patterned in fawn, white and black, with curious words or signs written in the design.

7 October I have returned to camp today from leave. I am very glad to be back; I am being very surprised at myself for thinking this. I found that such fragments as I could assemble of my past life were most unsatisfactory—jumpy, nervous, febrile, silly and discontented. I only realised what that was when I returned here, once more remote and cut off from the emotions, ambitions and intricacies of the past. Whilst here I toil through the long clear day, work without motive on clearly reasonless tasks, unperturbed by all absurdities, untouched by ambitions, emotions and intrigues; unattached as a Hindu holy man, at peace with the war. And in the evenings in my tent, candlelit, writing and listening to the desultory burblings of the men, I find my calm. The army feeds me, clothes me, tends me hand and foot in my simple wants, procures me castor oil for my uncomplicated ailments, works me, pays me, and leaves me yet with time and leisure to think my private thoughts: even in the moments of most frantic activity deigns not to break the web of my inward meditations.

15 October The route march was perfect, with all circumstances harmonious. We climbed a range of hills with much sweat and labour and stood on the crest looking down on the River Murray[16] and the great lagoon formed by the weir at Bonegilla[17]. From the lagoon rises a surprising forest of dead trees, gesturing through the water. After descending from the hills we marched along close to the river's edge. Then the path took us through a field of deep-purple flowers, and in passing the soldiers plucked them and thrust them in their hats, as garlands. Beyond the field we reached the road, and crossed over the seven-spanned bridge into Victoria.

This tale of garlanded soldiers sounds like a lie, but actually it is a sort of miracle. Just consider these unlikely men—mostly toughs or peasants and those few who were neither are former businessmen, shopkeepers and lawyers. Anyway, all of them would have regarded the idea of wearing garlands of flowers in their hats with almost fanatical aversion. Yet here in the army the thing is merely a natural gesture to express *joie de vivre*, although the life and environment is generally lowering, coarser, harder, there is in some curious sense a return to medieval feeling, caused paradoxically by these toughening circumstances. We have been forced together, and must take refuge in one another as an escape from life, and have become a community in such a sense as our race has not known for several centuries, except in a few brief periods of extreme disquiet.

21 October Drinking tonight at the canteen I met a chap (a journalist) who said, when I claimed a non-personal attitude about the more bloody side of the war, 'show me a Nazi bastard, and I'll kill him!' I just can't accept it. How can one kill personally and passionately a creature who is so much the victim of calculated, aggressive conditioning? As I see it, these enemies must be exterminated, but not as human creatures knowingly possessed of an evil will, but as a horde deluded with an antisocial creed, and therefore dangerous. But to talk that passionate unthinking way about it—or worse, to believe that way, is to deny all our claim to civilisation. I am willing to kill—but with regret. I am not willing to hate, since there is no person to hate, but only a force of mad belief behind those millions of persons whom we fight. I can only hate the idea that drives them, not deluded humanity.

27 October The training is becoming more concentrated, the days really strenuous. Bayonet drill is most exhausting, but relieved by pep talks on the technique of slaughter, in an odd way killingly funny—those sudden flashes of grisly realism ('Go for his guts: the throat is very vulnerable, but a difficult target; don't attempt the eyes!') suddenly crashing on to the sweet blue afternoon air, in macabre variance with the pastoral scene and the young sunburnt chaps, so innocent and silly and unprepared for horror. The magpies carol in the trees and the grass is thick with little blue flowers and dandelions, and the saxophonist in the army division practises 'Ave Maria'[18] with many gluey cadences, the notes cutting through the gory commands. 'Get that look in your eyes,' he shouts. It is very warm. These are the calmest, loveliest days I have ever seen in Australia. That's really what makes this rehearsal so weird.

A hectic beer and swing party with Tas and Bon Drysdale. That beloved zoom of clarinets, and the young negress's voice like black honey, and all those mad zombies, the smoke, the drink, the terrific clamour of talk, and as a consistent threat running through the dazed hours of drunken release, Bon and I stepping the sweet deliberate boogie-woogie beat that evenly breaks in bass and drums and piano, so balanced and logical, like Bach[19] or Euclid[20], a divinely even contrapuntal sort of Socratic dialogue[21], an inevitable fascinating follow-through of question and answer in music. It was a lovely party; very rowdy.

December I continued my nonsensical mural decorations in the sergeants' mess. The designs are rather the sort you get in American barbecue stands. One never knows with oneself how low one is capable of sinking on the mental plane. These murals are almost a map of my tunnellings into the primitive but oddly likeable backwardness of the twentieth-century military mind. People do not realise there is a subtle difference between an artist and a third-rate signwriter.

1943

First week of January *Sydney*. Tas's new house[1] is lovely. I find it hard to believe I have so much peace. As soon as I am out of the protective sphere of the Drysdales, I am as alone as I was at first in London. The city is full of a foreign rowdy rabble, mostly American. Until very recently I never suffered from race prejudice. But I can't stand all these Yanks about the place, corrupting everything like mad. I distrust their awful pink toothbrush outlook on life. And they think that if a man believes in God, Kellogg's Cornflakes and the President they are brothers of all mankind, loving and loveable, and Democrats are quite entitled to lynch niggers.

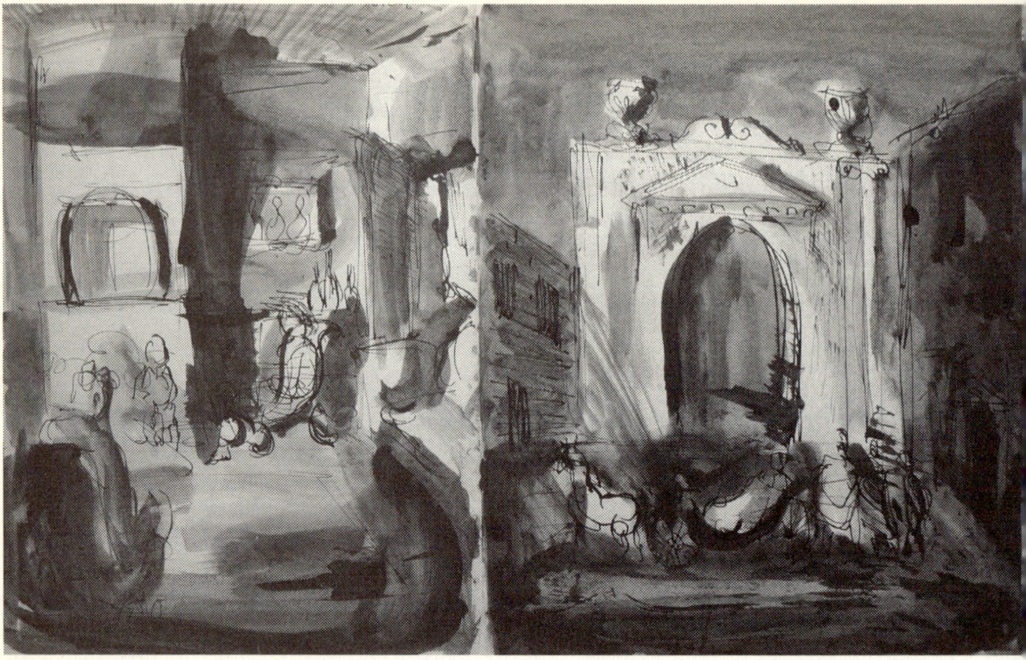

15. Tas's new house (1944).

1–4 March *School of Military Intelligence, Seabrae, near Brisbane.* I was amused to find the place to be just exactly as I had envisioned it during the awful journey—one of those wood and cardboard Queensland boarding houses, set in steamy heat among mosquito-ridden mango groves by the shore, immersed in the peculiar damp rich green lushness that is an essential quality of Queensland.

The work is definitely difficult—the instructors very good. We go out into the country making maps, hear lectures on dozens of subjects—army organisation, arms, tactics, and so on. There is no parade ground mucking about at all.

6 March *Brisbane.* The stained-glass windows in one of the churches gave me quite a shock—especially considering the crude lustiness of the people. The whole design was weirdly decadent—Beardsleyesque[2]. The Madonna, emaciated but madly fashionable, smiles strangely with lips like rare scarlet flowers and ogles the congregation from her deep-hued glassy height with positively opium sodden eyes—distended and dilated. Her halo is monstrous, poised with the infinite chic of one of Schiaparelli's[3] wildest creations. One pale hand, taloned with long nails, blood-coloured, nonchalantly balances the superbly sophisticated infant Jesus, the other droops with languor from the intricate patterns of her rich strange swathings, jewelled with almost unbearably heavy rings. The angels and saints that hover about in fabulous raiment look like a crowd of jaded aristocratic degenerates. Cherubs, bewinged seraphs, speed them all on their way.

9 March *Seabrea*. During Sergeants Formal Mess this bloke who was talking about the Japs held that they were horribly near to animal, citing their many really ghastly atrocities, the results of which he had actually seen. My argument was that they were super-civilised—a thousand times more than we are. And that whilst capable of amazing subtleties of refinement, they are also capable of depths of bestiality which even the most degraded of our race would not dare to realise in physical fact. Now I hold that not only are the subtleties infinitely advanced from our level, but that the bestialities are equally removed, not towards the animal (since even the most fierce animals are merely *animal*, *not* consciously sadistically vicious), but instead are approaches to an almost divine status of ecstatic perversion, such as yet we have not had the imagination to aspire to.

This is very sophisticated maybe: and perhaps one should not think these things in wartime. I wonder whether my valuation, lacking so much of actual experience, and certainly lacking all the emotional attitude that *must* come from witnessing such horrors as the Japs have perpetrated, can be the surer.

12 April I've failed. I missed passing by a couple of points. My abysmal inexperience of course. I was the only student in the school without any previous experience of Intelligence work. But it's no use trying to make excuses for myself. I'm stupid at these things, and that's all there is to it. They said some very nice things about me in the personal report. But what's the use of being liked if you're not a soldier? I have not the right kind of mind. I can only function properly as a completely free individual.

15 April *Sydney*. Breakfasting at Usher's Hotel. Mr Menzies[4] (the Prime Minister or something) sat at the next table, solemnly shovelling down the eggs and bacon that later in the day would emerge from his lips, transmuted by the wondrous alchemy of gastric juices, as political speeches.

Early to mid-May *Greta.* A long-established camp about six hours' journey from Sydney, near Maitland[5]. The officers here seem to me to be a pretty disgusting crew. They squabble and jibber, and in the mess behave quite revoltingly. Their basic make-up consists of a mixture of the mentality of a suburban shopkeeper, the snobbishness of the nouveau riche, the morals of apes and the inhibitions of an 'Englishman'.

19 May God, how I'd love a few weeks to myself in a studio with tubes and tubes of paint. My head is full of paintings. I remember saying, when I joined the army, that an artist should experience everything possible of the life of his times, since it is his job to express his world. That included the war. I still believe that. But I have experienced too much war without having been in at the kill. The great common experience that I sought, that in experiencing it I might be able to express it, seems to have missed me out. I'm only competent to express the effect of army routine on human beings. I have not pierced the deeper mysteries—reaction to bloodshed, exhaustion, attack, bombardment, inaction, retreat, or the situations and emotional bonds between men who have shared these violences together. I can see it in others—but so many are inarticulate. I regret that it doesn't exist in myself.

I am *not* a soldier. I am an artist.

19 June It is accepted that all forms of art are ultimately expressions of psychological entanglements—a symptom of discontent with what exists, and therefore a desire to make concrete one's wishful thought. The work of art, say, is the successful sidestepping of unsocial behaviour. Maybe I'm getting a bit too deep into this. Art is the expression of desire in indirect abstract terms.

14 July The working of the mind is a thing in itself, and the truths revealed in mental flights have often no relation in physical truth (as physical-truth-in-itself). So we love an original liar who shows a bright mind in the most flagrant untruths: so also we love an honest man in the trueness and directness of his actions.

I would rather read Homer's account of the Trojan Wars[6] than a military report compiled by General Blamey[7]. Or a toothpaste advertisement than a chemical analysis of the commodity. Which only goes to show that my intellectual tastes are a bit frivolous—or are they? The fable is usually in better taste, and a discerning man can read beneath the elegances of grammatical construction a truth (though it is framed as a lie) more solid & whole than that which indigestibly dull but accurate catalogues can possibly furnish.

As usual in writing this, I finish up contradicting what I set out to prove in the first place. No one knows the Ultimate Truth, thank goodness. But what does that matter? It is probably a jewel of many facets, cut in such a cunning manner that each of the manifold planes of its surface shines the more brilliantly by taking light from opposing planes.

However faulty my arguments, however tedious my wranglings, they are just as likely to hit the mark as anyone else's. My 'is' and your 'is not' both fall short of the same target or both strike it, in different places.

When I get to babbling like this, it's time to go to bed.

17 July I have always valued idleness, & esteemed only a limited sphere of activity—painting, writing, dancing, drinking and talking. For the rest, those estimable labours that create sweat and pride from most men, I value them only in other people.

Thus one of the posters in the office—'Develop the Aggressive Spirit'—merely makes me wonder why I am so incapable of aggression, or sympathy for it. I suppose it is the monopoly of uneasy extroverts. It somehow disgusts me as a quality, even in these times and circumstances when it is a sort of virtue. That there is a necessity to develop aggressiveness implies that a spineless man should cloak himself in a prickly camouflage to frighten away bogeys. And that is what most aggressive people do.

I do not like to force my will on people. I think most of them are too inferior to understand *why* I think certain things should be done—and I think it is useless to act without knowing the motive. So I prefer to keep most of my ideas to myself (though it must be hard for you to believe after reading so much babble). In any case I doubt if anyone can benefit from them besides myself.

21 July There was a time, as everyone knows, when we were civilised enough to bestow even on machines of destruction proportions & ornaments that made them acceptable objects to men of taste. The correct attitudes toward such things was that of the gentle superstitious natives of Java, who regarded a baroque ornamented bronze cannon, that had been brought to their island by the spice-greedy Portuguese, as a fertility fetish, and to this day their women deck it with wreaths of flowers in the belief that their sacrifices will bring them sons. But who among the thousands in Greta would have either the imagination, inclination, opportunity, desire or moral courage to conceal the jagged unloveliness of the sawn-off new type of 25-pounder mountain gun under garlands of hibiscus?

We have created nations built on machines, have given more power to the machines than we can control, have made our engines for greed. And in all this, we are tied to the machines and the meanings we have endowed them with. So there is no more harmony with the natural world: nature has become a hothouse thing. The forests we lose ourselves in are labyrinths of pistons & cylinders & gears & steam whistles.

22 July It seems odd that I, the chronicler of the fortunes of this band, am with but definitely not of them. I am identifying myself more & more with the troop itself, & less & less with the men in it. The thing as a whole is often quite comprehensible, & at odd ridiculous moments, even sympathetic. Yet the individual members of it, with so few exceptions, strike me as repulsive, as do those crotchety Olympian individuals higher up whose post-alcoholic headaches are visited on us, miraculously transmuted by alchemic-martial processes into new & difficult steps in the military pavane.

26 July Tas Drysdale wrote. He described the evening at Mrs McEacharn's.[8] The details make me sick with nostalgia. 'Cocktails before dinner, Hock with chicken à la Loo' (the brilliant Chinese steward; how that man gives me the *grand seigneur* feeling!). Reading this, puny, probably prohibitionist Posterity, you may get some idea of what enjoyment was like—how witty, beautiful and wise people relaxed, in those days before Our Deliverers organised everything so well that nothing was possible anymore.

1 August The talk turned to abnormal sex. Judging by the frequency of buggery as a subject for small talk, one would gather that gunners as a tribe were anal-eroticists. But here again I find no wisdom in what they say. After all, when some poor wretch makes a spectacle of himself dressing as a woman, or unsuccessfully attempting to seduce somebody's chauffeur, few people have sympathy to discern tragedy beneath the farce. And the tragedy as well as the farce are creatures of society's injustice. Yet the history of European culture is largely a list of the triumphs of 'peculiar' people. Abnormality is often the behaviour of genius. Normality is the legendary ideal of morons.

7 August There is such an intimate familiarity with the work of one's own hand that the eye is blinded to it by too close association. I cannot judge it coldly, but only by the delight I took in creating it. I cannot see it freshly, nakedly, unless by a print or a photograph of it. So I am usually uncritically infatuated with my paintings—as I am with myself.

Second week of August *Tamworth Hospital.* My eyes have really been a bit peculiar lately. The doctor said I must be sent away to get glasses.

I like this place. The food is very good, the nurses & sisters agreeable. There is one called Gallopin' Rose.

One of the men said, watching me draw—'Well, you put the lines down anywhere, & it comes out human.' He seemed surprised. Gallopin' Rose visited us for a while, & posed while I drew her. Looking extra demure. It is not a good likeness—mine seldom are. I particularly wanted to make a note of how these uniforms are: I can never remember such details. I like the medieval coifs, reminiscent of van Eyck[9] & Roger van der Weyden[10].

The Society of Artists exhibition opened, but I didn't see the newspapers, & so don't know what the critics said. No doubt I'll hear soon enough. I can imagine what Paul Haefliger[11] will say of my 'frivolity' & 'superficial humour' & 'brilliant facility that seems worthy of a better cause' & all the rest of it. He demands a sort of stolid solemnity in painting, much the same as that attitude which makes people whisper & refrain from laughter in church. He allows no humanity in art. He is the sort of man who could never appreciate Aristophanes[12], since he sees laughter as a sort of ignoble, unintellectual accident, the profession of clowns but the downfall of serious men.

God, how I wish I'd been there. I adore these gaudy crushes with toothy dowagers bubbling at the brim, and all those mad people pretending to be what they're not. The delightfully exhilarating atmosphere of social & intellectual snobbism acts on me like a drug.

14 August Why the devil do people regard the whole sum of modern art as Surrealist?—I suppose it's because they only contact art by means of the daily press, just as the hoi polloi used to denounce it all as 'Futuristic'—another journalist term.

Anyway, since they have never bothered to find out anything about it, they are not entitled to criticise. It is not our fault that art is none of their business.

18 August I sat outside awhile reading in the sun, like an elderly convalescent, luxuriating. Some of the chaps feel almost guilty to be enjoying themselves so much. Odd, how our native puritanism (or is it masochism) relates pleasure of any kind to sin, thus giving all pleasure a spice of naughtiness & a sensation of transience, as though at any moment it might cease, & that cessation be accompanied by discovery, discomfiture, disapproval & a severe beating.

21 August Election Day. We voted at a sort of Methodist-chapel-cum-Recreation-room. It was not really what I had expected: I was ready for Hogarthian[13] scenes of mad gaiety & corruption, with perfidious Lt Colonels plying the troops with rum in order to coerce the peasants into voting for the Wicked Capitalists.

But no—it was a sober affair. One hearty-looking soldier tried to persuade me to vote for labour, & scowled furiously when I marked the Wicked Capitalists with the tokens of my favour.

I don't think it as much use though: Curtin[14] is pretty certain to return to power. But one must make some sort of gesture of defiance towards the fast-encroaching oppressiveness of the merciless Proletariat, who are more actively anti-cultural than Menzies' dullard intellectual sluggishness has energy to be.

By casting such a vote, one may by a minute fraction stem the tide, delay annihilation for an hour or two. Not that I have any illusions of a

Renaissance resulting if they do get in. They are all dull Business Men with no culture at all. But their ideal of life is a sort of pleasant easygoing corrupt Democracy which finds leisure for such bourgeois frivolities as art for snobbism's sake.

22 August The group around the fire were discussing nudism with disapproval: for my benefit one pointed out that painting from nude models was probably responsible for the notorious moral depravity of artists. I find it strange that a race so taken up with physical aspects of life that their intelligences are practically null is so goddamned prudish.

'Wouldn't you be shocked if you saw someone walking down the street naked?'—what a bloody absurd question! I think the shockingness of nudity lies entirely in the depravity of those who regard it as such. It is curious that from any natural standards, the average attitude to this and a variety of other subjects is quite abnormal. None of these people can tell one wherein exactly lies the moral differences between an unclothed ape & horse & a man.

First half of September *En route to Queensland.* Three months of malaria experiments. Here we are in the country of lush cane fields and Douanier Rousseau[15] jungles. The whole land and sky drips moisture. It is all fruitily wet and green and purple clouds hang low to shroud the hills. Then we came to the Gordonvale mountain[16], the pyramid, rising up very grandly, clad in thick white mists like a view of Fuji by Hokusai[17].

The air in these cane towns is warmly laden with the mingled scents of molasses and frangipani—an exotic mixture. We travelled through a fertile valley hemmed by huge mountains, and presently began to climb a very wild and twisty pass. The scenery grew grander and grander, until it became a series of vistas more wildly romantic than any I have ever seen. Finally we reached the Tableland and ended our journey at a sprawling huge convalescent camp beyond Atherton[18].

As far as you could see in the straggling bush there were tents and sheds. These northern camps are completely different from anything we have in the south. They all share an oddly ragtime, decayed untidiness. They look like gold-rush camps. I relish the subtle atmosphere of laziness. Here I think, one might manage to exist in reasonable idleness without forever having some wretchedly conscientious

NCO[19] poking about the tents on the lookout for malingerers and bludgers.

Third week of September A sister took me down to see a cage full of guinea pigs that I needed for a drawing, *Los Medicos*[20]. These guinea pigs were outside the pathology laboratory. One of the doctors poked his head out to ask us in for a drink. They had ice-cream and fruit drinks in the laboratory ice chest. I was suddenly in the centre of a crowd of amusing, civilised people. It was one of those odd magical transitions. The talk at the moment was of Bach.

I like the sister in charge, and yarned for quite a while with her. She was talking of the strange instinctive revolt against all authority, which is almost peculiar to Australians. In her view, this characteristic is an inherited tradition from the convict period. I'm inclined to agree. It doesn't exist to any extent with the Europeans or Americans. She also spoke of the positive distaste that soldiers in hospital have towards making any use of the army educational service. She linked this with the authority-hatred motif, on the grounds that since education is usually associated with the top dogs, most of the underdogs regard it as something to be avoided, lest they too become bosses and thus objects of dislike. Also, I think Australians have always interested themselves in purely physical perfection to the complete exclusion of mental attainments. Animals! But in all these things, they are abnormally sensitive to criticism and get positively ferocious if any outsider

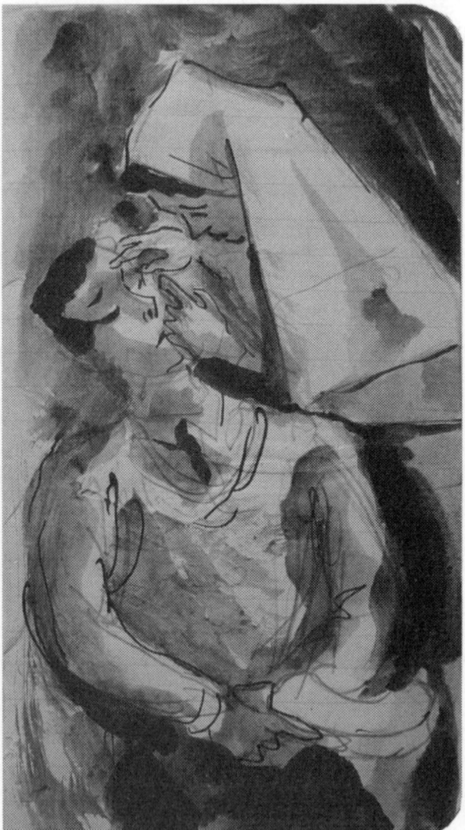

16. Sister in charge (1944).

dare suggest that all that is Australian is not the best in the world. Even the notorious accent—that ill-begotten polyglot of cockney, war pidgin and bad tonsils—is defended as being virile in contrast to the effeminacy of English.

22 September After much parading, we were transferred over to Ward 6 to begin the malarial experiment. The sister packed us off to a hall of horrors called the blood bank—as though one could be overdrawn, or have a credit of so many port-wine-like pints. And there the ghouls and vampires gather in the semblance of fair women, speaking deceptive sweet words, and then, when least expected, they jab a thirsty hypodermic into a vein.

5 October I have been tranquil now for some weeks and my only real discontent is that discontent which is one of the first themes of my character—it finds here no object on which to vent itself. What I really need is somebody with a strong will, an alert mind, whose knowledge is equal to mine, yet whose views are opposite. Someone I can argue with, be scathingly rude to, and receive the same treatment back. But here, the people of quality are people I admire, whose views are harmonious. They are valuable people to know, since I admire them, and at the same time they confirm me in my beliefs. But also I need to quarrel with my equals. Nothing so much as intellectual strife sharpens the mind, wakes and develops one's views and promotes creativeness.

9 October If only these world planners did not offer us so immense and vague a new world after the war. It is as though they promised us infinity or immortality, or any such vast abstraction too huge and undefined for the mind to grasp. Everyone with a voice is doing it—generals, bank directors, politicians, and the Sunday ranters in the Domain[21]. They build huge cathedrals, universities, hospitals of words.

Mid- to end of October Paint obsesses me. It is a much worse madness than drawing. My evening meal was a still life that I regretfully devoured. My shower became momentous because just when I had decided that it is foolish puritanism to ruin the sensation of warmth by turning on the cold at the end, I suddenly realised that I could put in a group of half-naked soldiers in the foreground, in tropical-green trousers, their skins a rich coral red. The thing needs some such note of sudden colour to relieve the general scheme of fluctuating greys, browns and greens, which are all subdued.

The difficulties are these, that I am attempting to combine decoration with satire, movement and a strong abstract pattern. Now I have never before tried to combine, or to discipline, a picture full of movement to decorative abstraction. The latter is usually the main theme in which subject is static, quiescent. But in my new picture, subject is quite as important. I want to load it with colour, with conceits of satire. I want to form a greater fusion between the actual physical shapes of bodies with the abstract design of the figure in art.

But I have got back the feel of paint now; the thick gluey, creamy tactile delight of it, the sensitiveness to its texture; so that now each loaded brush stroke caresses the board surface and clings, fusing richly with the paint already set down. Or it spreads luminously thin as a glaze giving brilliance to the under-painting, and glows more lovely than flowers. I love the sensation of it as nothing else. Love, food, writing, money or music, nor flattery nor sincere admiration nor the company of friends (all the things I am most partial to) could not seduce me from my painting.

6 November In Parliament, Dame Enid Lyons[22] made an impassioned plea for sex taboos. She vigorously opposed measures to teach sex education in schools. Such a delicate subject, she felt, should be left to the parents. Dear old Enid! The appalling ignorance and reticence of our forebears must be perpetrated as a sacred heritage. The kids must be lied to and muddled up with ridiculous evasions, resulting in complexes, fixations and what have you, and incorrect knowledge being smuttily bandied about (how I recall the schoolboys' ideas and interest in sex!). These people! The 'innocence' of children that they goo over is at its best a sublime naturalism unwarped by any of the intricate lies we are later taught to live.

It is the parents who, with their old indecent pruderies and totems, first smirch the child's mind with obscene evasions. By putting the value of obscenity on sex they sow the seeds of shame and stupidity. Adulthood, with a reasonable and natural approach to knowledge of the ordinary functions of the body, could be quite as 'innocent' as childhood (is eating, drinking, sleeping a sin against the Holy Ghost? Sanctimonious spook!).

13 November On the land, the crops go unharvested for lack of labour, resulting in artificial minor famines in a land of plenty. The land starves for men, whilst the militia and half the AIF idles about in camps, wasting years in drill and oft-repeated instructions, growing more and more bored and disillusioned, and eating their heads off. We, the soldiers, are as ravenous as the greasy profiteers, and nearly as expensive.

2 December Queensland has that salty, brutal flavour, raucous, bawdy and utterly physical. It seems to sum up that sweaty, loud, hot animality that exudes from the very hills around here, that utter lack of fineness, delicacy. There is no art in its people, no brain, nothing but raw instinct and primal urges; they debauch sexually with perspiring zest, *sans affection*. Maybe they're healthier than we decadent southerners, with our finicky connoisseurship, of love of comfort. Watching their ways, one feels that the south is soft and civilised and somehow exotically degenerate. But much preferable.

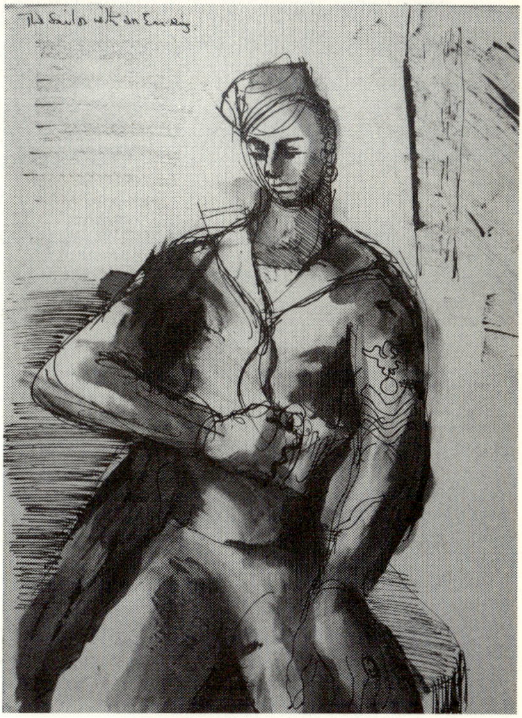

17. *'The sailor with an ear-ring'* (1944).

8 December The tail end of the malarial experiment. Now that we are leaving here, I see that in some way this place, for all that I have cursed it, has a light flavour of the Mediterranean isles—just a tinge, since where there should be a broken alabaster limb of Dionysus[23], one finds a granite outcrop. There are no mountains with snow caps, nor wine to be cooled with the snow, and in the people, no softness nor the jaded grace of a remembered civilisation. No olives, pines, cedars, honey, nor nightingales to hymn the moon. Only a reminiscent clarity of sparkling air. But even that is too bloody hot.

12 December *Brisbane*. They call this place now 'the American village'—and the name is justified. Yanks—millions of them, soldiers, sailors and marines. And the girls! One has read so much about juveniles going on the streets, being found in brothels with sailors, but it took the females at the Town Hall to make me realise how widespread it is. I really think the majority of them were under 18 years old, and some—quite a few, were no more than 12 to 14 and 15: painted up in the reckless Queensland style.

The dancing was another innovation. I remember how Queensland danced a little while ago; waltzes, two-steps, the Pride of Erin[24] and all those Victorian affairs. Now they jitterbug at a terrific speed. That huge hall crowded with Yankees and the infant harlots gyrating, kicking, wriggling, belly-wobbling, bum-popping, tapping, whirling insanely like people possessed of a devil. All the time during these chaotic activities, the girls' faces were expressionless, mesmerised, their shallow eyes glazed, their lips—which seemed to express at the same time the softness of childhood and the viciousness of accomplished whoredom—set and straight. They seemed drugged, while their bodies (bed-wracked, easy) pulsed erotic contortions to the rhythm.

The few Australian soldiers were pathetic. The girls wouldn't dance with them. They huddled together in a little bunch, staring pop-eyed at the mad witches' Sabbath, and swearing furiously.

1944

Second week of January *Sydney*. In between lunching, parties and boozing, I've been painting. How shall I ever be able to go back to the army?—these last months, culminating in long leave in Sydney, have quite unfitted me, not that I was at any time what you might call an enthusiast for military buggering about. On leave I am myself, I am a man: I do the things I please to do. Now I feel bloody lousy, seeing the end in sight.

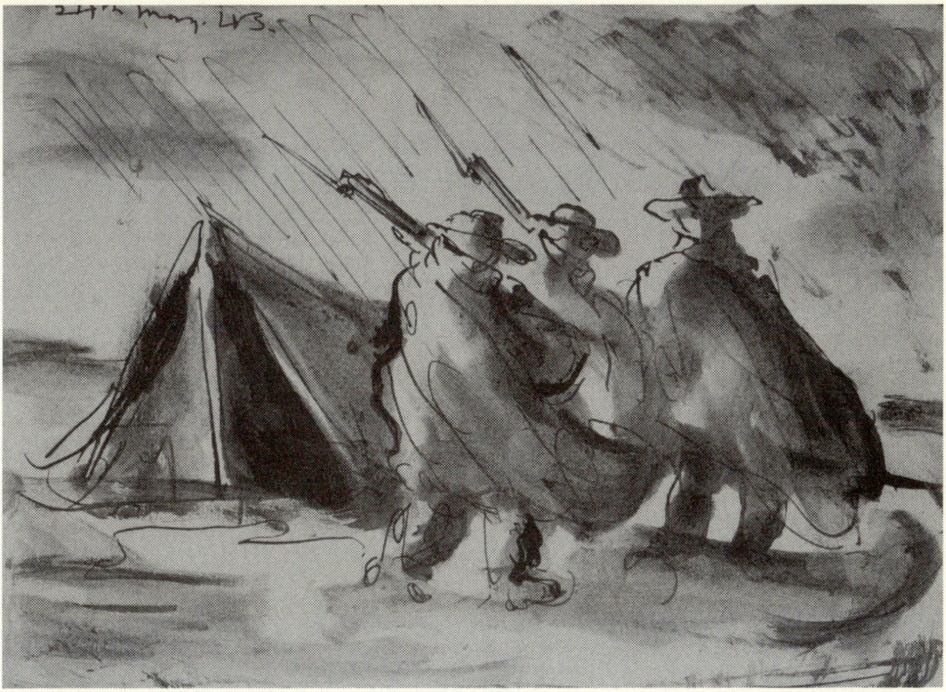

18. Three soldiers in rain (1943).

25 January *Burleigh.*[1] The routine of life here is pleasant enough. We surf and laze about in the sun a lot. I spent some time desperately avoiding ball games, the *bête noir* and plague of my life. It really is time I got out of Australia. I've been hanging around the bloody country for four years now.

I avoided all camp activities today, simply by walking off. I spent most of the day on the hot sand in the dunes, reading, thinking and watching the breakers. And all that disturbed my peace was an aeroplane towing a target, at which the ack-ack guns were firing, their exploding shells making little solid white scones of smoke against the blue.

28 January Tonight I am on guard duty, and it is raining miserably, with occasional downpours rushing over the leaden skies in the shape of empurpled columns. For me, there is a perverse enchantment about guard duties. I spent my shift in a telephone box, looking out through its dim spattered windows on to a vista of rushing black shadows, a vermilion lamppost, a sourish yellow electric light, and occasional soldiers walking braced against the wind and rain. It was warm in there, and dry. I was snug with the storm around me.

I never seem to take any path but the paths of escape on my own accord these days. I float with the tide. Why should I do anything else anyway?—it's not as though my heart was in the thing. It's odd, this drifting. In my own life I had quite a bit of initiative. I got in and out of my own trouble: I went my own way, usually alone. Really, in a way, apart from my artistic endeavours, I was a sort of cross between the black sheep type and the Empire-builder. The tastes of a savant and the morals of a louse. Very restless, yet wanting to attach myself to things, places, people long enough to make them my own and explore their sincerities as well as enjoy their superficialities. In some ways I was a sort of puritan: I still am. I have a sort of anger in me about many things that seem reckless and cheap.

Promiscuity always irritated me; yet I was often promiscuous. But with me the affairs of a day or a night or a week were enjoyed deeply and genuinely until boredom set in. But when I saw the same thing in other people, I was uneasy.

Guard seems to make me muddleheadedly introspective.

1 February We were encouraged to take on correspondence courses. But the men themselves are not the faintest bit interested. Mental activity, they feel, is difficult and boring. They prefer unthinking action—sweating, fighting, eating, boozing, whoring. These things coupled with a mental attitude might lose their juicy flavour. Maybe they're right, anyway. To be animal is natural, to think, obscene. Lust is a happy thing that only becomes bestial once you begin bothering your head about it.

Bill Dobell won the Archibald Prize with his portrait of Joshua Smith.[2] I saw the painting before he sent it in—a superb piece of work. The newspapers have gone to town on it—they are all full of photographs and quotations from horrified art-Tories. The academicians are very, very angry. And of course, Pro bono publico and Mother of Nine are shooting off their mouths. The Archibald is not to be awarded for art, an indignant public opines, it is to be given for an Official Type of portrait—nothing to do with art at all. The great powerful mass of morons have a preconceived idea on what a portrait is. Tawdry, sentimental realism, that's what the bastards want. For them, the likeness 'So real you feel you could go and shake the old bugger by the hand'—

the still life, 'You know, it was so life-like that a bee came in the window and tried to settle on one of the flowers.' The distortions of Rembrandt, El Greco[3] and all the rest are beside the point.

17 February An army is a homosexual institution. One would think that it were better to arrange unnatural liaisons and comradeship amongst the men with whom one was compelled to live, fight, suffer and perhaps die. Remember the Greek Legion of Lovers that died to the last man against the Persians[4]—or Napoleon's revision of the French law intended to encourage 'Greek love' among his armies because he believed that such bonds were good for morale.[5] Doesn't that apply to us also?

Since those days, one cannot believe that human nature has changed. But society and taboos have become more complicated, honesty as regards sex (and who's to say what is natural or what is not?) more difficult—few people dare say, and even more have not the words or even the power to analyse what they feel to say it, supposing they dared to. I think that as far as the actual act of buggery, sodomy or what-have-you, is concerned, it happens very, very seldom in the army. Such things are rigidly suppressed for fear of discovery. It would be so hard to conceal. So circumstances governing the expression of desire, not desire itself, are changed.

But the same number of such people exist, probably even more who are unable to express even to themselves desires aroused by living in a world of men. If ever they did rid themselves of their desires, it would be on leave.

One is safe among civilians. There is privacy. The word would not get around. Comradeship is a close dangerous intimacy with a person from whom one must conceal the essential driving forces of one's nature. Instead, there is an 'Act' to be put on for the comrade's benefit—the impersonation of a gay, devil-may-care gamblin', two-gun, whorin', rootin'-tootin' wild blade, or perhaps, more conveniently (since one might meet the bloody comrade on leave), the shy thoughtful quiet bloke who will not fool around with harlots because of High Principles—you see, he is Keeping Himself Unsullied until he meets the One Girl in the World. And other masquerades—seems like maybe I know too much about this racket.

19 February *Sydney*. The sunlight on a wall, the trees and houses scattered on a hill, passing cars, a glimpse of a boy, or the blue harbour full of ships. I really am silly about Sydney. It is my *own* place so much, every jolt of the tram, every yacht in the bays is mine. And all of them are a sort of jubilant celebration at my coming home.

I just can't believe the anxious tension I felt for the dreadful importance I attributed to that stupid Khaki hell I've come from. I suppose in a way, that now (I'm writing in the tram by the way) I'm in a different scene, a different act of the play. This cancels out what happened before. Or (it's more likely) I'm an actor who has left the frantic urgency of the theatre after the play is done, and I'm going home to real life.

On my arrival I went straight to a cocktail party and met Edgar Kaufmann[6], who is quite as delightful as I had expected.

20–23 February He came out to choose a diary, and we had one of those purely Drysdalesque evenings of talk, gin and boogie. I dined with him the night after that, on the eve of his departure to New Guinea.

I met two young artists who are soon having a show—their first—Jesse Martin[7] and Justin O'Brien[8], who have just come back after two years as prisoners of war in Poland. We spent a great part of the day drinking with a sailor we met.

I was greatly surprised to get a note containing £35 from Kaufmann, though I don't really know what it is for, as he has already paid me the price of one diary. Perhaps he wants two.[9] I shall have to write him about it.

I am really staggered by my good fortune in all things that have occurred in this past month. Fortune has conspired to bring this miraculous leave, to make me arrive at the very most exciting hour, to meet so amazingly Kaufmann to arrange thousands of things. Financially too it has turned out so well—I've made in all about £120 in the last four weeks, all of which goes to add to the store I am building up against the peace.

4 March Spent the morning on the beach at Palm Beach[10], lunched there, and returned to Mona Vale[11] for afternoon tea. Mother brought out from some trunk some essays and stories I'd written in my childhood. They were at once pleasing, horrifying, embarrassing and amusing. The discomfort one feels—sometimes because one was such a dreadful, precocious sort of kid, sometimes because they hint at good qualities that have become completely lost in the adult. But despite many important differences, they showed pretty clearly what sort of a person I was

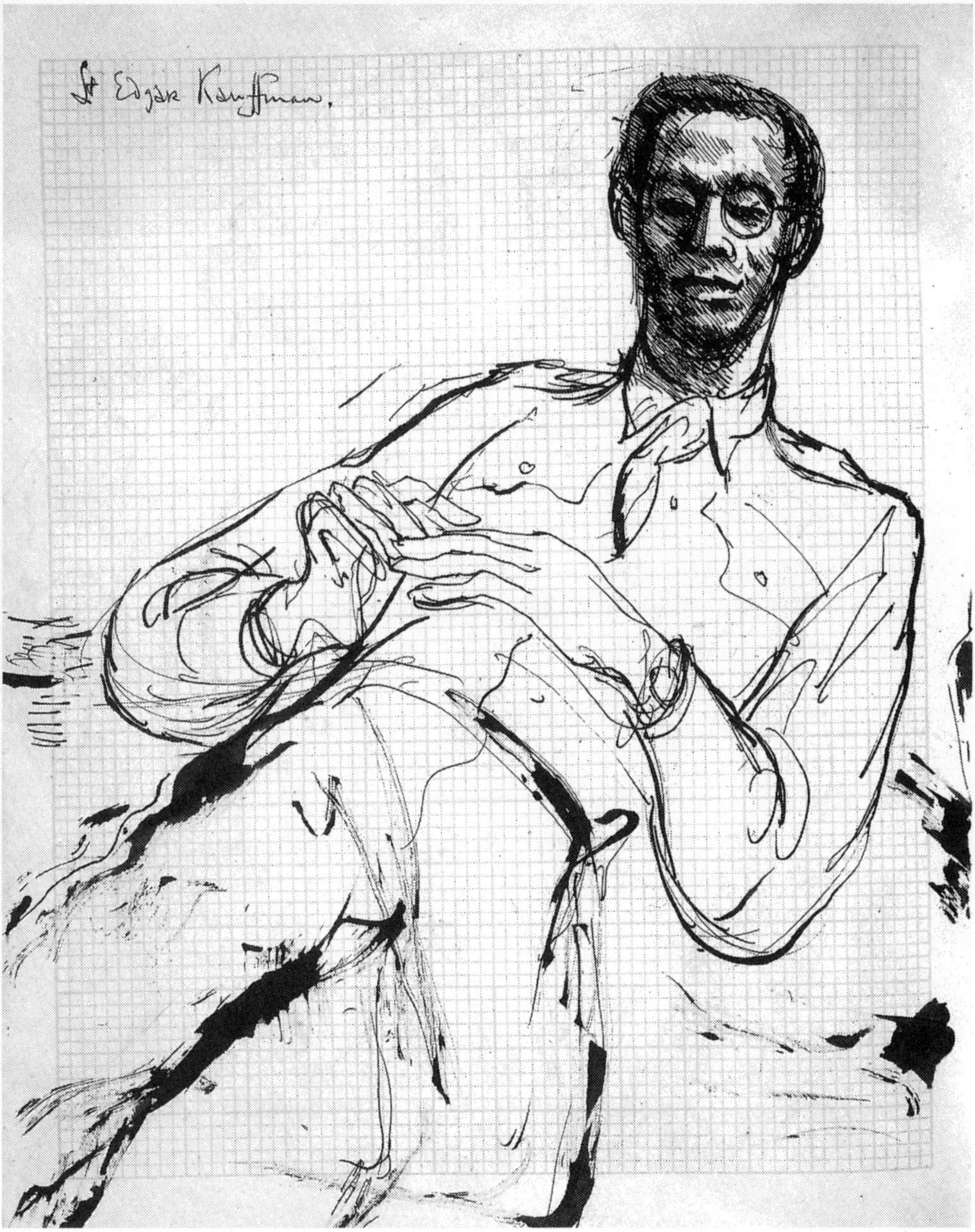

19. 'Lt Edgar Kauffman [sic]' (1944).

going to be—most especially in their reprehensible characteristics—the facility, the tour-de-force mentality, the love of impossible ideas, the cynicism of a dreadful little boy who knew damned well that he was much more intelligent than his schoolmasters.

12 March *Greta.* For the first time in many months, I found myself on a mess parade. I spent those minutes looking at the line of men, and thinking how little I knew of them, wanted or desired of them. Just a lot of noisy characters, existing outside the range of my sympathy or understanding, until I find a need that someone or other of their number can supply. Those that I really like, and who like me, can only satisfy the virtuous side of my character, whilst the people who can attend to my vices (which are after all just as important) are not the sort of people I like or admire at all, neither are they attracted to me. I am most chaste with those I love best; and revolted by those I lust after.

26 March The wireless was turned on, and a man's voice uttered the Holy Trinity of Australian art: 'Dobell, Drysdale, and Donald Friend'. 'He means *me*!' I said. We all felt very famous and happy. There was a lot about Dobell of course, and a lot about the motives for painting, and what was *in* a painting, and what the artist meant. His Message.

That was very funny, though I feel uneasy at laughing, especially when the man was all for us. People will never understand, though it is dreadfully simple. Maybe they'd never buy our pictures if they got to find out. We have no message. Or rather, I haven't. And I don't think the others have. *Everything* is inside the painting. We just paint, and that is all. It is the whole reason. It is the whole motive: the cause and the result. The painting begins and ends in itself. The pictures tell no story. They are things in themselves. You can't really talk about a picture. The picture, if it is good, does all that. I would not paint a picture if I could say it in a conversation, or play it on the piano, or just live it. A picture is good when it is so utterly, independently a thing in itself that it cannot be expressed in any other medium.

30 March I went out to the riverbanks behind Maitland this morning, and saw the lush fields furrowed green with growing things that led up right to the lip of the bank, ceasing only where it sank steeply down to the river. And on the other bank, the town rose, heat-hazed with the sun, and there were old pink-brick walls, formal trees, backyard fences leading to the rear parts of old houses that were more beautiful than the faces they showed to the main street (many have had their original faces hidden by cheap facades of modern tile work and silly attempts at urbanity), and there were spires rising into the blue, towers with clocks, baroque grandiose terrace roofs. The whole place looked lovely, as though (dissatisfaction goes so deep, one feels that whatever is good in front of one's eyes is more deeply related to something better far away) it were all a tranquil picture of some other place, in a distant, unseen country, and very far away.

4 April Oh—'normal men'. They are a sort of race of mathematically controlled lowest-common-denominator-worshipping robots that dwell in the slums of Shangri-la[12]. Give me abnormal people any day. The repressed, the oppressed, the hungry, mad and unhappy. Do you want to hear music?—then listen to the songs the slaves sing, the tragic deep voices of the negroes, the psalms of Jews in exile or the tales told on violins—or any damned instrument—prose, pianoforte, zithers, drums, paints, iambic metres or the art of brilliant conversation—when they are best, most shining, touching, witty, lovely, they are fresh from the heart of a longing for something forbidden by force. Free of law, of tradition, of ethics, morals, religion, of society which does not accept certain behaviour and desires, force of love lost, of a taboo desire discovered.

Those things make the music of our world. *Not* the consciously, securely averagely virtuous droning and bumbling of the all-powerful legend of the Average Man. *I* know, and *you* know, and everybody knows when they look in their secret hearts, that the Monstrous Man-in-the-Street is a legend. None of us exist or feel in tune with that succubus tradition of the Norm. Loud mouths proclaim its edicts, but behind that furious blaring there is a whirring, as of uneasy souls turning, trying to escape, afraid to escape, unbelieving souls, unrecognised, unsung, and pinioned in dungeons by their owners.

Well—I am an abnormal man. I know what I want. I am not ashamed of it, but I am often afraid of the consequences of fearlessness. Thus one man, a rebel, might go into a city full of rebels, yet not dare to utter the password, lest others, rebels themselves, recognise it as a sign of revolt and betray him to the very tyrants they cannot bring themselves to revolt against.

I am drunk now, writing: but I think I am writing the truth. Perhaps that means nothing: I *always* believe I am writing the truth. And I am always right, since *in* myself, *as* myself, *if* I write down what is in my mind, (which I always do) I *am* writing the truth. But only *my* truth. *That* jewel has many facets. Several shine for me; but there are other sides to that jewel, concealed from my eyes.

11 April The ex-railway-ticket-collector Brigadier, to whom a number of startling eccentric and repressive General Routine Orders are attributed, is once more on the only warpath he has ever experienced: that is, the suppression of liberties of everyone his power can reach. These people are crazy. They deliberately cook up unreasonable restrictions in order to enjoy the dispensation of cruel sentences. What is there behind it? What could there be but a personal, sensual, perverted, indirectly sexual sadist delight in driving men to extremes, whipping them, taunting and deliberately provoking them to rebel.

Third week of April *Sydney*. AWL. I was in a practically hysterical state. A talent such as painting can come to mean so much to a man that it will entirely displace the things of normal living. And that if such a man comes under the tyranny of an enforced type of life, such as army life, he will ultimately crack, unless he is provided with an outlet for his natural talents. I am wholly an individual character, incapable of mastering a way of life that does not afford me complete liberty of self-expression.

I was put under arrest. When my time came the ordeal was briefly sudden. 'Fined two pounds.' Then I was marched back to the lines to pack my gear and prepare to go the hospital.

Last week of April *Sydney*. Concord Hospital. The Psychiatric Ward—a species of Krafft-Ebing[13] ballet starred with Somerset Maugham characters. The inmates are mostly nervous shock cases of the less violent sort. War-wrecks verging on the edge of hysteria, very helpless and pitiful.

The Fighting Man. Out he comes like a sausage from the machine. But he is not quite like all the other sausages. Partly because before he entered the Military Sausage Machine he'd already been through several other Super-Mincers: education, family life, employment. Me, I am a cocktail sausage groomed for la Guerre but quite maddened with a lust to be digested with a dry martini. The destiny that formed me omitted to fortify me against the adventures of the hot-dog stand. Brave men and cowards, fools, clever men, and most just ordinary people that I'd really never give a damn about. But nobody, and nothing, has a right to impose that on them. Their hands jittering. Wheeling themselves in wheelchairs or clopping about on crutches like Gothic grotesques.

4 May I managed to get round to seeing the people in the office, and there, after a few fierce arguments and a lot of nonsense, I found quite a sensible sergeant, who said the only way out of returning to Greta was to get the MO to hear the case.

The MO was elderly, Scottish, mule-facedly stubborn, obstructive and conceited: a major, a white-haired old sadist. He listened to what I said, and then remarked, 'There's really no reason at all why you should not go back to Greta. You seem to think that you're someone special. Well, you're not.'

I was horrified and furious. I am convinced I will win out. It is a faith that the righteous must ultimately prevail. I am a painter, quite a good painter. That is my work, and that is the only work I am going to do. No more slavery, nor years of waste, miserable useless toil and bitter idleness, no more foxy evasions. I am done with it.

7 May It's a warm sunny morning, as though it were spring, and the placid sky belies the autumn leaves. Sydney is the loveliest city I've ever seen.

The draft was delayed. I spent the morning in the Mitchell Library looking at the *Desastres* and *Caprichos* of Goya[14]—and found in his work things I had been searching for in my own mind—a crystallisation—for some while. But there yet remains the problem of voicing those feelings in the idiom of my own language. Although Goya expresses those emotions of indignation at a wasteful, useless mad injustice, his work is applicable more to the battlefields and ravaged countries, not to the insanity of boredom and frustration of base wallah's paradises like Greta. For such, perhaps, the best symbols might be found in the etchings of Piranesi[15]—enormous mechanistic prisons built of stone and tyranny.

Last week of May *Chermside, Brisbane*. It's as warm and mild as anything here. The camp is almost in the country, surrounded by fields and trees. Hard work. But I like it here so far. After Greta, everything seems settled. The officers are friendly, non-interfering: one has a job, one does it. No

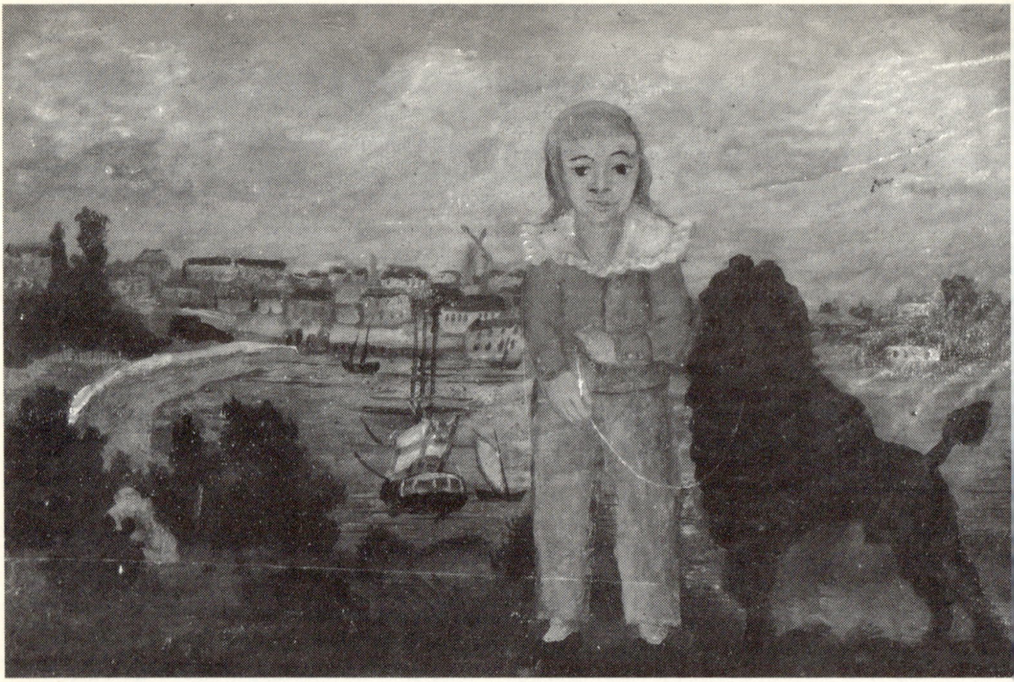

20. Australian primitive hoax: 'Boy with a Poodle, by "Michael Collins"' (1940).

fury, jealousy, persecution, vanities to pander to. We are almost free men. No 'Regimental' business. No futile marching, turning, no useless and difficult ballets to perform.

Last half of June A Sydney newspaper reported a literary hoax. Max Harris[16], a very bogus intellectual in partnership with John Reed[17] (equally bogus, and very rich), runs a quarterly on modern Australian verse of the womb-tomb-pelvic variety. The recently published autumn issue was entirely devoted to a new discovery, a great genius of poetry, one 'Ern Malley'.[18] Suddenly I remembered. Those letters of Harold Stewart's[19]—months ago, asking for details of my Australian Primitive hoax[20], and saying that he and some friends were preparing a colossal literary hoax in Melbourne. I'm certain this is it. Some of the lines seem to me reminiscent of that wordy obscurity that Harold sometimes indulges in as a sort of literary joke. I've written off to him to demand the whole truth.

The *Angry Penguins*[21] shows just how completely Harris and Reed fell for the fake. They devote 35 pages to Malley, and the cover is a ghastly surrealist daub by Nolan[22] (one of Reed's geniuses—he has dozens of 'discoveries') with lines from Malley poems mixed up (it would give too much dignity to use the word 'incorporated') in the design.

The poems are good, damned good. I can imagine Harold and McAuley[23] in ecstasies of malice, bending their minds like bows, each poem an arrow to transfix their victims.

7 July Now something *really* mad has happened. Something spectacular. The Vice Squad raided the Contemporary Group exhibition this morning and after examining *Romantic Landscape* have communicated with the Chief Secretary to the effect that it is an obscene picture.[24] I was so staggered I could only say asinine incoherences. I didn't know whether to be angry or think it was colossally funny. Having the Vice Squad investigate the moral aspect of one's work brings to mind the days when Hitler interested himself in deciding what was Aryan and what was degenerate in German art. German art didn't survive the investigation. I'd hate those Vice Boys to get loose among the Vatican collection. Michelangelo's robust bumps and bulges would lay 'em in the aisles. And the statues! Whacko. Maybe the guide will take the fig leaves off the ancient Greeks for a couple of lire extra.

Perhaps the Vice Boys are upset at having lost another illusion. We are all perfectly aware that the other half of the world clings to a rather sweet theory that underpants were designed to conceal a bunch of violets or some *marrons glacés* which God foisted on to Adam at the whimsical instigation of the Faery Queen[25]. The 'Balls and All' group in *Romantic Landscape* have dispelled this treasured fable, and the Boys, seeing Sex rear its Ugly Head, are justly resentful. They really oughtn't to be allowed into Art Shows or Adult Movies.

21 July Mr Curtin and Mr Forde[26] are about to release 50,000 men from the army for work in industries. Another hint at the change in Australia's role in the war of the Pacific. We will have less and less to do with the actual combat, and progressively more with the production aspect of the war. Actually, our former intensive militarisation was nothing more than a defensive measure against expected invasion: that threat removed, this country will drift back to the rather happy-go-lucky state of affairs that existed until the Japanese took Singapore. And I foresee that with our increasing unimportance will develop as ever a corresponding loud-voicedness.

There's such a list of outworn Virtues that we, as a nation, drag up on every occasion to fling, like a final and convincing argument, in the face of sophisticated Europe: Gallipoli for instance (who cares a damn about that anyway?—it didn't decide anything except a lot of deaths), Kangaroos and Gum trees (one suspects that they were created, not by God or the process of evolution, but by a Dinkum Aussie)—hell, what's the use.

26 August I've been behaving very badly lately—too much drink and sex and general promiscuity. It's no good. Besides, I've a new idea in my head for a picture, and that always makes me impatient of my way of life and shortcomings.

It's no use vowing to change my ways. One might just as well promise to change one's character. I must find a means of modifying them, or substituting my present failings with others that are less exhausting. Not only have I ceased to paint, but I'm becoming rather a dullard all round. I suppose one vitiates in *living* that perceptiveness which gives birth to wit.

Satiation has left me not only without that quality of *yearning* towards things and people that is the beginning of understanding and expression, but also without anything to say to the world except (with sheerly mechanical lust of habit) 'Come to bed'.

First week of September It's really taken this war to give me a sense of nationality. Before, I just didn't have it—except when it was a trifle exotic to say 'I'm an Australian'. I didn't *feel* at all Australian in those days. I usually felt either Polynesian, Malay, Parisian, English or African. Now I feel altogether different. I feel quite intensely Australian. I see everything Australian as being very clearly and beautifully Australian. Even the things I don't like, and the sort of Australian people I just loathe, have a sort of thing about them that couldn't belong anywhere else, even though I wish for no part in it myself. A lot of other people feel the same way. Tas probably always did. His paintings are the most Australian, in the most beautiful sense, that have ever been painted here.

It's easier for me to feel this way now about the country because at this time, with things so mixed up, people become more exaggeratedly themselves. Also, with so many Americans here doing extraordinary things that make such a sharp contrast with the things *we* do, and the way we do them, and how we think about them, and why, Australian things become more intimately and especially Australian.

The Yanks in Brisbane all take it for granted that they'll be gone in two months. Hell, how I'll miss them. The Australians in Brisbane just bore me to tears. They're a tribe of crude dullards. I guess I've changed my mind about being mad about Australia. What I like is Australia in the toils of an American invasion: *that* is what so spices the life here.

9 September Edgar appeared and we had dinner—which developed into a quarrel about something or other—he didn't say what—in which I had offended him. So things got all ballsed up and even now I haven't any idea what it was all about. He's so bloody indirect and oriental in his approach, is so bound by outlandish American tribal codes, subtle, complex and incapable of saying directly what he wants or means.

Me, I am simple and often stupidly dense. I am not competent to deal with or understand these nuances. Additionally it seems that it isn't worth the effort of working it all out. I'll leave it to Edgar and circumstances, and let him severely alone until he makes up his own mind what he's going to do about what. I am oriental in this, that I prefer things to happen, rather than to set in motion a chain of events with my own hand.

I value his friendship, but this I do insist on, that it lasts of its own accord without any patching-up processes on my part. Since he is so damned intricate and indirect about the balance of personal relationships, and since my own understanding is limited and primitive, I'll leave it to him to adjust all those shades of fractions himself. He, not I, is alone capable of perceiving them. Actually, I rather suspect that it's what good old Tas would dub 'half a ton of butterfly shit'—in other words a mechanism to make life exciting by inventing a lot of nonsense.

Third week of September I've spent quite a lot of time lately wandering about the extraordinary ramshackle river's-edge few blocks that constitute the Brisbane Harlem[27]. All that is worst in white people abounds there—a prime example to the 'inferior races'. The eating houses, run by Greeks or Chinese, are notable in that the Whites are in minority and almost without exception the most repulsive, diseased old wrecks.

I met Edgar and we proceeded to the negro quarter. It affected me as always, with a sort of drugged delirium. Edgar enjoyed himself immensely: he is terrifically observant and sees *everything* that is happening. I, on the other hand, go into a sort of a daze of delight and stand among it all, bemused and happy and rather blind. The sight of negroes dancing affects my mind and innards to such a degree that my eyes and ears hardly function except in the most vague way. I see a heavenly generalisation of black and liquid movements that interpret a series of quite ecstatic sounds. Watching negroes, being with them is more lovely than being half-full of liquor. I cannot understand or explain the reasons for this fascination. *Everything* about them—their shapes, their colour, their amazing movements, gives me an emotion and experience more wonderful and intense than anything else in the world—sex included.

Edgar is one of those people to whom, when one has done a painting, one must need immediately take it and show him, to see what he'll say to praise or condemn it. And I find, whenever I do this, his comments and criticisms are so interesting, coming from so fresh and subtle a mind, that they discover for me new and fascinating respects of my own discoveries, extending my experiences to undreamt-of realms.

It is the same with Tas and Donald Murray. They also see beyond what I see, each in their own way, and enable me to perceive in the rough material produced by my explorations, vistas of wonderful and unlimited beauty, strange possibilities and a greater fulfilment of life than I am capable of perceiving without their aid.

So none of my experiences is really complete without the collaboration of these friends of mine.

19 October Brisbane houses are ludicrous architectural ovens, unfit for the climate. There is nowhere in the whole city where one can sit at ease, out of doors, sipping a cool drink and watching the crowds sauntering by. Australians as a race have not even the faintest perception of even the minor details of living pleasantly. To them, the completeness of life is expressed in the possession of a bed, a bath, a lavatory and a cooking-stove. I don't mean that they're Spartan. They're merely stupid human animals with no attitude or knowledge of life.

15 December Painting relieves me enormously of my sense of feeling incapable of dealing adequately with an affair so devoid of anything but infatuated sensuality. I deplore my lack of sense and dignity. I paint all my desire and uneasiness. It is a better sort of world that exists in paintings. A man's follies become cloaked in formal beauty, entirely losing foolishness when, with all the rest of his emotional, intellectual and physical experience, they are transubstantiated into the terms and medium of aesthetic expression.

29 December Amongst the Allies Australia is rather in disgrace with all parties—criticised for taking things easy now the sound of battle has receded from her shores. Quite justified too. I'm thoroughly ashamed of the country, and can rake up no defence for the present mood. Australia and Australians are conceited, self-important, complacent, prejudiced and generally asinine. They approve of no one but themselves. Yet being one of them, I feel involved, attacked, yet would gladly disassociate myself entirely from so boorish and chauvinistic a nation. Somehow it makes me uncomfortable to be lumped in with this handful of tenth-rate white trash scattered over the broad undeveloped acres of the continent. They are less productive, less cultured, less important than the inhabitants of the smallest of the Japanese islands—yet they deem themselves so essential to world affairs as to be given priorities over everyone else. Asses.

1945

January *Sydney*. On leave. I needed a Sign, a Proof, to demonstrate to me that I was actually in Sydney. It appeared on a noticeboard in a park, pointing discreetly towards a sort of pagoda veiled among trees and flowering bushes. It read: 'Ladies Retiring Room. Gentlemen's Convenience.' In Brisbane, you understand, one knows by a powerful stink and a terse notice: MEN. But here in the decadent civilised South, Ladies Retire and Gentlemen Convene. This is no crude province for shitting or pissing.

February Now the most staggering development of all. I'm still in a daze. It's all so sudden and crazy and unlikely, after these years of gun drill, marches, cleaning grease traps and pig tins, being a barman, a gunner, a Permanent Shithouse Scrubber, a wharf labourer, a cloak-and-dagger merchant. Now an official war artist, a captain I suppose.[1]

Still, I was always a gentleman, as they say. Well, this, for one thing, is determined: that I'll paint my own way with no concessions. No 'Official War Art' pictures for me. The things I see and think of as painting have very little to do with War Art—subjects like the crowds of servicemen waiting for pick-ups. The thunder of guns is very, very distant.

26 April Every now and then one pauses to think what a bloody, poor, unsatisfied and unsatisfactory animal one is. After all, a man is limited to four functions of the body that are pleasures—to eat, to speak, to sleep, to make love. And an inordinate importance is given to each of them. Yet none of them, nor all of them combined, constitute happiness, which is so rare a thing that in these days no one knows how it is caused or defined, nor what will ensure its continuance.

Eating's a fool's game. A man who lives to eat is an object of ridicule, a disgusting glutton, a poltroon. Or he who eats merely to live is no more than a brutal animal.

Of speaking we all know that the more we say the more we regret, and the more we listen to others the greater becomes the intolerable burden of our boredom.

Sleeping's a waste of time, an abysmal vacuum of existence, an uneasy absence from intelligent control, or a nightmare: or a horrid lunatic playground of meaningless enigmas and fantasies.

Lovemaking's the worst of the whole lot. Its most unfortunate aspect is that it trespasses into every corner of our life, encroaches on friendships, falsifies the meaning of sheerly intellectual occupations, flavours the sound of music, the sight of fine things.

First week of May Hitler is dead. The Germans in Italy have unconditionally surrendered. Tas, Bon and I had a sort of pre-Peace celebration with some champagne I got in town.

I have received orders to go into town on V-day and make drawings of the shemozzle there. All pubs (the usual wowserish idiocy) will be closed. The general idea seems to be that the government want Victory in Europe to be celebrated like a Methodist funeral.

Everywhere there is tension and excitement and expectancy. The really great part of the struggle is nearly finished. Everywhere in town one sees British sailors and soldiers, and glamorously uniformed marines. The

Australians find the English rather stupid: God knows what *they* think of *us*. They are rather slow on the uptake I will admit, and that is probably the reason why they are not actively disliked as the Americans were. They have not, for one thing, taken all the women by storm, which probably explains our rather patronising tolerance of them. The Yanks made it too patently, tactlessly obvious that they were richer, more amusing, more generous, more sexually potent than we as a race. These things rankled.

Second week of May It's all been the most appalling lousy bloody flop. The most stinking, castrated, joyless idiotic filthy disappointing fiasco. Peace has been declared in Europe. Not the *Peace* that's a flop, yet. But how it happened.

I feel so dead and miserably blue I could weep. Europe all smashed up having to face the years of rebuilding, the dreadful haggard pretence of 'returning to normal'. People meeting, and trying to make it all just like it used to be: but they go down the street to lunch to the place they always used to go in the old days. But there's no place there. Or worse, there's no people there. Anyway, the young ones are all old. The new young ones are different, incomprehensible. The music's different. The old tunes don't signify. All the years we can remember are punctuated with these tunes. They evoke the places, the affairs, the happy and the lousy times. O to blazes with the dreary world and the dreary people and my own dreariness and dreary memories of another world in which I felt young, where people had style and gaiety.

I wish we were in Tahiti. No peace, no war. Nice natives. No Planners; no Communists, Democrats, surrealists, cubists, bullshitists, critics, moralisers, morals: no inhibitions. Lots of people who say 'I love you, I love you'. No pre-war or post-war. No transition into troublesome new ways of living: leisureless, emphatic, organised ways.

The huge headlines read: IT'S ALL OVER IN EUROPE. Boy, I knew that in 1939. All *our* sort of thing. I feel tonight especially as a sort of goodbye forever. After this it looks as though that part of life will be old-fashioned—anachronistic.

I keep thinking that the work I'm doing is far too modern for the Military History people. I've none of that 'journalism' in my work which makes it useful as a record. And after all, they want records, not painting. Good art seldom records anything but itself. Paint celebrates paint. A good picture begins and ends in itself.

Incidentally, quite incidentally, it may depict a place one would like to be, or a person one would want to sleep with.

Last week of May *Lae.*[2] We circled four times over the drome before landing. It was raining blue murder. Hot, sticky, dank sort of rain. We waited about miserably damp until a staff car came for us. Along the roads sauntered American negroes with a sort of loose-limbed gloomy arrogance. And New Guinea natives in blue lap-laps. Everything everywhere seemed to be profusely sprouting and budding and growing and putting forth a peculiarly poisonous rich green. The landscape was untrammelled Gauguin designed without the artistic selection of the Master's hand, lush, and poisonous. One has a sensation of claustrophobia—shut in on all sides by a profusion of vines and grasses and creepers and mad insects and vulgar-voiced birds callously carolling insulting songs.

Second week of June *Labuan.*[3] The town was partly in flames from Jap demolitions. We up-anchored and drove onto the beach at sundown. A frantic loading and packing began. This was all an extremely impressive and beautiful scene. I've had it in my mind ever since—the towering dark form of the LST[4], catching streaks of light occasionally. A sudden torch flashed on deck revealing red-brown bodies milling about in the scramble to load vehicles in the dark. The water, a deep murky olive green, lit up at the bows of the vessel. Men wading, machines covered with men, half-submerged, crawling towards the beach: lights reflecting on the water, smoke, deep grey-blue against the indigo sky, catching the light.

Last week of June Ninety-four drawings to date since I became officially an artist. My main problems have to do with painting and drawing. To express war in terms of good paintings—the enemy's atrocities, our own less frequent but hardly less shameful barbarities. With these in some fashion I find myself exhilarated instead of sickened, absorbed in the translation of actuality into pictorial form: the terror of the night, the Gilbert and Sullivan[5] paraphernalia of high-class ferocity, the drama of it, the surrealist contrasts, the unbelievable wealth of movement, huge destruction, comical relics of peacetime sahibs' existence—how to cram all this into ink lines on a piece of paper?

8 August The Allies have developed an atomic bomb, one of these was dropped on Hiroshima, a city of a quarter-million inhabitants. The city no longer exists. I never thought that this would happen in my lifetime. I suppose it will revolutionise our entire living. It means, I think, that the two nations who possess this power can control the entire world. The full horror of it is that I do not think mankind is yet intelligent enough to use the power rightly.

There was a time, in this war, when British cities were being bombed, that we raised a horrified outcry about 'slaughtering innocent civilians'. In our time we did the same to Germany. The fact that it was necessary made it no less horrible.

Mid-August *Balikpapan.*[6] I drew all the morning: working out subjects to pose my new model for. Nudes—nudes: I can't think of anything else but that superb naked body. So it's more 'shower rooms' and 'soldiers bathing' and the like. The roughs look promising, and I'm pretty sure of success—all one has to do with a figure like that is to delineate it accurately and with style. It needs no changing, no exaggerations. It is a work of art in itself. I think and dream in terms of its flowing streamlined lines, smooth contours, firm rounded forms, a backside smooth as marble and round as twin apples, the belly a classical 'mound of wheat, whose navel is a goblet that wanteth not for wine'[7]—strong legs like pillars, the torso exquisite in simplicity, magnificent in strength. A nice lad too, from what I found out: one of those unelaborate, unpredictable characters, whose unthinking naturalism confounds the most sophisticated. One of those attractive persons of whom it is safer and wiser to think as an *objet d'art*. Or else complications set in, and in no time you're up to the ears in a tangle of desires, frustrations and problems of time, place, inclination and opportunity.

What *is* one's life going to be?—a long dreary succession of infatuations for handsome sailors, urchins, footballers? Reaping nothing but a few rough casual affections, half-contemptuously given moments of sensual pleasure. And then the swift approach of middle age, ridicule and all the rest, the shame and indecency of seeing one's own image caricatured (for of course, one could never see oneself as *that*) in ageing

'Aunties', raddled old pansies. Or the scrofulous despicable menace to youth who gets a few years in jug[8] for perverting adolescents?—or to give it all up and live like an ascetic in a desert, tantalised by visions of golden lads? It seems too late in the day to give it all up. But one can't pretend that the freedom of the Greeks, the Renaissance, and all the other great days when such things were part of the natural order, is anything but dead and forgotten and so far past that no one ever seriously believes that such a love was possible—was not a sort of Period Version of low-comedy jokes about pansies and queens. The subject of the Sonnets[9], and Leonardo[10], and Wilde[11] and Antinous[12] and all the rest are reduced to ridiculous history.

4 September A letter from mother. Four pages of pure, inconsequent nonsensical motherese—she asked 'if I remembered to give Pam a wedding present?'[13]—what the hell could I send the girl from Borneo—an orang-outang?

I think the female mentality is the most silly, uncontrolled and uncontrollable force on earth. I don't see any way in which one could love a woman except in despite of their inherent dilliness. The 'Mystery' of women that man (in novels) finds so unfathomable is contained in the fact that their minds are a species of emotional pecking beak that goes jabbing blindly about seeking the inedible worms of male shortcomings. They're always pecking and pecking over a refuse heap of utter rubbish. God knows why. There are a few exceptions of course.

Mid-October *Sydney*. Everything just as wonderful as ever it was. My first meal consisted of eggs and bacon and champagne. One is conscious all day and every day of the appalling turmoil the world is in—atom bomb wranglings and threatened general strike for a 40-hour week. Peace has released a menace of nearly universal irresponsibility and mischief among the working classes. The city is now without power and half the time—or most of the time—without electricity owing to the strikes. It's the same in America and England. A world worth fighting for?

6 November A reporter came out to interview Tas. A perfect example of the yellow-press-plus-intellectual-hanger-on's attitude to art and painters. Predominantly a talker of utter rubbish about any form of fashionable art. They're all communists or socialists or something. They like modern art—*all* modern art irrespective of whether it's bad or good for the simple reason that they don't know but couldn't risk disliking some artist or poet who was really good but incomprehensible. Hence of course the success of the Ern Malley hoax.

The work an artist produces is all that counts. The rest is his own affair. All this collecting of revealing little facts for morons to read when they've done with the murders, divorces and racing news is an impertinence.

10 November At the Contemporary Art Society's opening all the usual people were there—crowds and crowds of men and women costumed as intellectuals, and in addition an even greater number than usual of willowy attitudinising youths gushing and gesturing. Social gatherings to view modern art nowadays are as great an attraction as The Ballet for aspiring homosexuals.

1 December The studio is in rather a mess. Things everywhere. Yelling children, cups of tea and much mad singing and talking. It has often struck me, when watching with what consciously reverent facial expressions many people 'drink in the ineffable beauty' of a painting—say, for instance, one of Rembrandt's masterpieces—that they would imagine the painter creating it in an exalted, spiritual mood, soothed by soft sound of viols, interrupted only by awestruck earnest and beautiful young men and women who come bearing foods to sustain the great maestro, tiptoeing softly, afraid lest a sound should break the divine thread of inspiration. When what actually occurred, as I imagine, would be a scene more familiar—Rembrandt, greasy and rather smelly, yelling madly for more beer as he dabs at a burgomaster's face, swearing jovially, singing, cracking active lice whilst a rabble of mangy dogs gobble the remnants of a still life and the infants cut up drawings and etchings to make paper toys, the kitchen wench has hysterics and is raped by the baker's boy and downstairs the bailiffs gorge themselves on the joint for Sunday's roast. The net result is a painting like the *Night Watch*.[14]

2 December I lay on a couch and made drawings and drank beer, extremely content until I began to look at books of paintings—ancient Egyptian, Goya, El Greco—and after that I went and looked at my own roughed-in *Bomb Crater*—and could have wept at the hopelessness of painting. In Australia it is so easy to forget that in the world there is Great Art. One becomes a big fish in a little pool with the greatest of ease. Then unexpectedly one goes to sea and meets a whale *or* a school of whales, the smallest of which is infinitely larger than one can ever be oneself. A very discouraging experience.

12 December For me the years that brought experience brought also an intolerable load of spiritual uneasiness. One probes masochistically at all the old wounds, goes over word by word of ancient declarations whose very sincerity becomes yearly more ridiculous, old friends, old lovers and old failures by the dozen. There's only one thing that doesn't succumb to the destroying beastliness of memory, and that's painting. Alone of all the elements my life is made of, it remains sure and secure.

Bon swears I'm *not* an escapist. I think I *am*. I know my desire for foreign places, and my contentment in them and their people, is based on escape from myself. Not from people. But from myself among the familiar people of my own race and class. More race than class actually, since those of the same race but a different class still have the power to make me constrained and uneasy, for fear, not so much of their dumb misunderstanding, but of their understanding and judgement. It's all a sort of guilt complex. Not that one ever really escapes from anything anywhere. One carries the entire world of conscious and unconscious experience within oneself all the time. What one wants is not an exotic race of people, or a distant country, but a person.

1946

5 January One escapes once more into painting, or occasionally dreams of Tahiti. All I want is a sort of partial peace. To eat, to sleep and to paint. To talk with friends and see few people. To be quiet, in a word. I'm in a turmoil of discontent with myself, which makes me poor company for anyone else. But what the turmoil is all about, I don't know myself. The result is a longing for quiet as the only bearable alternative to a complete change.

15 January Extrovertish shallowness is evident in my work. A comparison—absurd on the surface—between the nearly finished *Ned Kelly* and Tas's *Crucifixion*[1] is positively humiliating. Not so much because of the compared qualities of painting itself, but because of the contrast in the psychology of both paintings. Or rather, of the painters who did them. One is a great tragedy superbly expressed. The other (mine) a pleasantly painted giggle.

One is bogged helplessly in the shallows of one's own limitations. One cannot express what one does not genuinely feel. My whole outlook is narrowed to a sort of critical laughter at the rest of the world and an uncomfortably measly laughter at myself. I lack a cause, and so have no effect. Well—clowns all long to play Hamlet.

31 January I only think drearily and longingly of sex and paint. Paint and sex. The two elements through which I can achieve some approach to reality. One yearns for privacy too, but simply as an adjunct to the other two.

2 February One forgets too easily, that *living* is more important (to oneself) than *expressing* life. The fact is, that what I want of life is easier to express than to obtain. Perhaps if I could obtain a permanent and honest assuagement of my desires, I might attain to a profounder expression of life in terms of painting. I'm sure of it. If I am as fortunate when I leave the army as I was before the war, these two things will come to me. One needs freedom and privacy.

To be celibate is to suffer torture, and become warped. To be promiscuous ends in debasement. I have been celibate too long. Now I am on different and equally dangerous ground. Looking back over my last fifteen years I suppose I've had a hundred or so affairs. That's a bit promiscuous I'll admit, except I was really interested in each one when it was happening. All seemed important at the time. They were all crises in my life. Some of these crises lasted many months, some weeks, others days, and some I'll admit had come and gone in a space of hours. But they all were important. Some overlapped. I can't remember the names of more than one in ten. And of a hundred lovers, and about twenty friends, and several thousand pleasant acquaintances, there are not more than a dozen people who have been essential to me personally. An awful thought.

6 February One of the strongest characteristics of Australians—the contempt of culture. I have always held that this contempt came into being in the early days when the hardships that had to be endured eliminated civilised types: those who could survive them and achieve success and prosperity were men of the most brutal type.

Success is always admired. It is logical that successful brutes became an admired type, which led to our present habit of idolising all forms of physical excellence, and conversely, despising the unsuccessful men of learning and culture.

Third week of March Now at last I'm established at Merioola.[2] A very large room, high, and well proportioned. The house is very large and old-fashioned, and a little too populated by people I know.

Loudon Sainthill's[3] room is something to be seen to be believed. The walls are painted a rich mushroom brown, as is the ceiling: the heavily ornamented plaster mouldings that border the tops of the walls are white: the floor carpeted with a yellowish green carpet, the doors white with panels of a green to match the carpet. The fireplace, an elaborate 19th-century affair, draped in sculpted folds of cheesecloth dipped in plaster, and the mantel surmounted by a plaster cast of one of the Elgin-Parthenon bas-reliefs[4]. The furniture is upholstered in light colours, rather 'Vogue Regency'.

There was a cocktail party in the evening. I enjoyed it and got as tight as a tick on rum and cola. But what a parcel of twerps one finds oneself accepting as social equals these days! Notwithstanding which, I genuinely like many of them. All young, beautiful and fascinating: arrogant in the pride of youth and talent, or hopeful of futures glowing with fame and fortune.

23 March I mooched about town a bit, and went to dine at the Cross in the evening—at the Peking Café, still, as in the old days, the haunt of whores and criminals, looking rather like Paris of the Impressionists against the weird murals in garish colours that cover the walls—cobalt skies, vermilion mountains.

There was something exciting about the whole scene of the Cross. Everywhere people moving about among the lights and shadows in search of pleasure and diversion.

Here we are at Peace, already the world is on the brink of many more frightful wars. Politics have wrought as evilly and stupidly as religions ever did, and men are still as credulous and brutal as ever they were.

5 April A major event occurred: I was in my room and heard someone knocking. It was a boy of about 17, dressed in plaster-spattered overalls. But a person of such extraordinary beauty that I just stood, staring. He told me he was doing some casting for the great Piranesi-ruin hall at the back of the house. So I went with him to watch him work, and at each movement he made, and at the frank charm of his manner, I became more enchanted. The boy—Colin Brown—is a student at the Tech[5]. Comes from the country, and talks delightfully with that candid certainty that the things that interest him—hunting, fishing expeditions, exploring in wild mountain glens, botany, bugs, photography—are of equal fascination to his listeners, so that they immediately become so. I do not mean that he is loquacious and arrogant, with that irritating egotism of adolescence. On the contrary—a certain diffidence. He radiates the essence of youth. My God I felt old!—but happy now. Murray said, apropos of this, in sinister tones—'Donald, have you ever read Mann's *Death in Venice?*'[6]

26 April I went to the opening of the Contemporary Society's show: a huge crowd. A great crush of adolescents with very pale faces—'coming artists' I suppose, and a covey of magnificently artistic-looking Beards in very bushy clothes (costume and facial finery, I gather, to be taken as a sort of brazen Declaration of Heterosexuality), many inexplicable old ladies with ear trumpets: what *were* they doing there among Gleeson's[7] surrealist horrors, among the Haxton[8] neo-Byzantines?—perhaps they were incorrigible New-Schoolers, their enthusiasm for modernity untarnished by age?—groups of dullard-artists, solid little packs of bohemians, terrible-looking men, ghastly-looking women. These affairs have begun to acquire a post-war atmosphere. Uniforms are becoming a rarity.

17 May An idea for a picture flew into my mind, on seeing a photograph of an early Greek bronze. A Lapith[9] and a centaur. After lunch I made some tentative sketches of the idea. Nothing much emerged from the pen, but I think I'll yet make something of it. Perhaps two youths. The centaur amorous, one youth half-declining his overtures, a little shy. Colin and the satyr. Colin embarrassed at the centaur's rough embrace. Colin, Colin. Everything I think of turns into Colin.

25 May I regard art as the Puritans regarded religion—a duty, an obsession, a compulsion, a revelation, the only truly good relief from the pressure of one's own evil and the world's, and the only possible expression of one's love and desire and understanding of life.

12 June In Australia there is no abatement of the strikes in all industries, lawlessness and violent crime are rampant, and everyone is disillusioned, discontent and yet acquiescent. Returned soldiers, discharged from the army in thousands, have been cheated of most of what was promised them, or involved in bureaucratic processes of a sort so stupid and discouraging that they've 'given the game away'. Half of the world we knew six years ago has disappeared entirely and the other half is being swiftly destroyed by the present people in power.

30 June Tomorrow morning, at eight-thirty, the experimental atom bomb will be dropped on Bikini.[10] My hope is that something goes wrong, and there is a cataclysm so appalling that it blows up everything—including the fleet of scientific observers. Mankind is not yet sufficiently developed socially to know how to use steam or electricity, let alone atomic power.

2–4 August The weekend constituted the happiest few days I've ever spent anywhere with anyone. The weather was like the best of spring—skylarks sang. And the part of the country we went to, Bass Point[11], was indescribably lovely. In a tiny rocky bay we made camp. There was a spring nearby. Soon we had a great fire going, and so to sleep. Next day was a dream. We moved further up on to the other side of the point to a little landlocked cove facing the sea. It was shut in by steep formations of volcanic rock, very wild, extremely picturesque and lonely. For me it was all a background only for Colin. A joy to watch, all grace and strength and youth. The comfort of the blazing logs at night; lying between the two fires looking up at the stars through trees; the excitement of stalking birds, the triumph of his shooting two of them with his sightless rifle. O the waves, rocks, trees, sky and singing birds, chill dawn, the moon.

Everything was wonderful and beautiful.

20 August A time has come now when there is a certain amount of misery to balance my happiness with Colin. He is not at all in love, nor pretends to be: so my desires beget frustration as often as not, and irritate him. He is young, and I am inconsiderate, and in the face of his honest candour, am jealous of all those women of the future who will see him ardent and ecstatic. The thought is torture. His honesty, his beauty, his affectionate friendliness are all daggers to me at times. My fault, all of it. I think of him with all my love, but I do not think of his feelings at all, only of my own. I wish I could quit myself of this bloody miserable homosexuality that makes a grand tragedy out of friendship.

6 September Still melancholy. Or perhaps, just rather lonely. The worst of being 'queer' is that the usual solution is to find comfort within that Freemasonry, the Sodomite brotherhood of Glorious Buffaloes in their club. A sort of frivolous and yet forbidding neo-Gothic edifice, externally Masonic Temple, internally a sacred cathedral filled with precious voices whispering and hymning (accompanied by the wheeze and squelch of an onanistic organ) the holy names of the Great Pederasts of the Spirit, the holy Bumboys of the arts (Ah Shakespeare—Ah Wilde—Ah Noël Coward[12]), the Sacred Buggers of the flesh (Ah me, Ah me!).

Then the chanted litanies of self-justification—'It is really quite natural especially with intellectuals and artists—think of Leonardo and all the rest of 'em.' My private mumbled prayer, half-excuse and half-manifesto, goes up to the god of Inverts: 'I am *so*. If I resist I am sent mad, if I indulge I am still unhappy. Then grant me as much love as possible, and I'll do my best not to harm anyone.'

2 October One paints out of love and pain and joy and sorrow. The lovely pigment has power to exalt one, but not to hurt one. Painting alchemically transmutes passions and failures into a delight: sorrowing flesh and agony of mind, thwarted love—the whole bloody caboodle—are benign in pigment. Red and black, blue, green and yellow, orange—all of them endlessly and fascinatingly good and beautiful. And to have trafficked all day with them intimately and successfully leaves one with a sense of exhausted wellbeing.

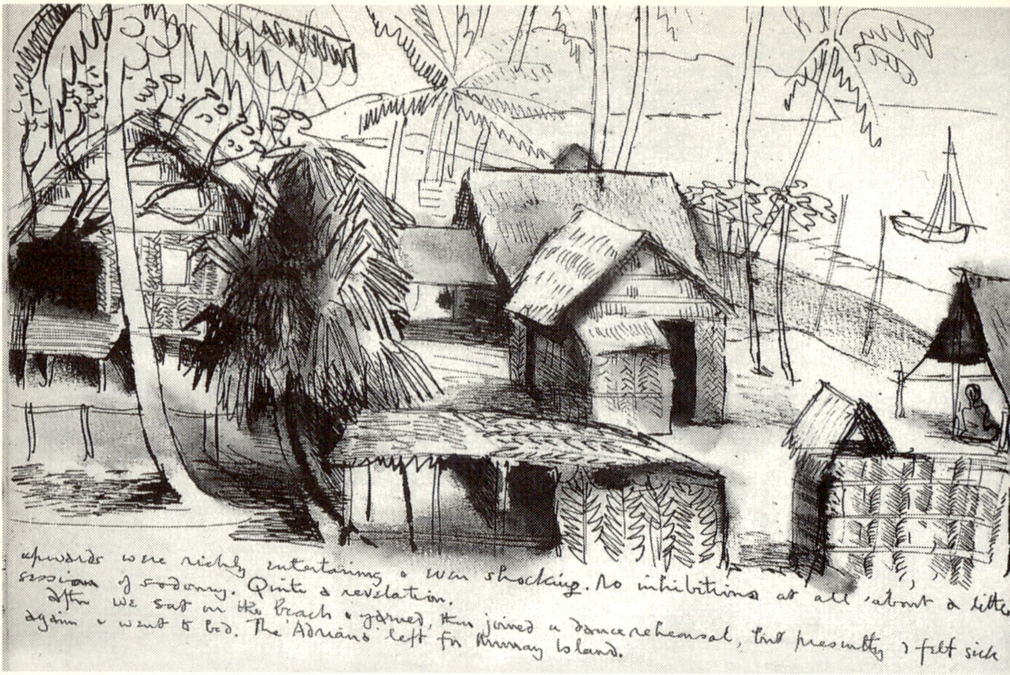

21. Village Scene, Darnley Island (1946).

16 November Still foolish and useless thoughts, regrets and maunderings, souvenirs of moments with Colin keep coming to mind. You've got to get out into the world and run about the face of the earth and find somebody new. A nice simple black boy. But not *too* simple, remember. The snag with Colin was simplicity. A virtue that is apt to distort worldly values. Donald, don't go oozing your saccharine soul sentimentally all over the blameless breasts of the naive heathen—just go to bed with them. They won't mind, you great mug. They *like* you. *They* think you're terrific. They'd enjoy a spot of 'tumble-in-the-hibiscus-bush'. But remember, stupid, none of this Love Stuff. Or if you *must*, don't say it out loud. Love is taboo, if it's queer. So leave it unsaid. People notice and resent words more than actions of that sort.

Last week of November *Cairns*. A different world. The air like warm treacle, and scented with a number of half-familiar odours—molasses, frangipani, mango. We went on a picnic out to the Barron River. Everyone played games, swam, ate, sang, played guitars and enjoyed themselves with utter abandon. Their grace and beauty and friendliness is a sort of feast for me. I watch it dazed. I don't even want to draw it. I feel the same just now to this dark multitude as once I did to Colin. And this also I know is impossible. A glorious abstract, like a wind or the sea, but in the most desirable human shape—brown, affectionately abandoned, but impossible. Or is it?

The sight of physical perfection never ceases to delight me: more than that, when I see a beautiful body, it comes always as a sort of happy surprise. Astonishment and pleasure. Their intense physical energy gives to these people an aura of constant activity. Their beauty is a beauty of energetic movement, like the beauty of a swift stream or a bird in flight. I must sit entranced watching them diving into the water, swimming like frogs or fish, laughing and playing, standing poised to dive, perfectly conscious of and exulting in their strength and grace.

22 December *Darnley.*[13] Gauguin's paintings—if what is true here is true of Tahiti—were an understatement. The colours on his canvases are positively dull beside the glories of this place—and nothing I can write could give an adequate description. Such things as a young diver wearing a yellow flower and a brown and blue butterfly in his hair, dressed in a daffodil sulu[14], idling down the road with his fingers linked with his friend's—a brown character in pastel green with a scarlet flower and a carved comb in his hair.

30 December Young A. and V. were very amusing. We swam and later I made some drawings of them both. About sundown there was a funny scene in the shower. A certain amount of very hilarious and innocently animal horseplay of an erotic nature, which later in the evening, when we went for a walk to the deserted teacher's house, became something of an orgy. There was very little these lads didn't know and enthusiastically practise. It was an eye-opener to me. V's comments on the morals and habits of the girls and boys of the villages from the age of ten upwards were richly entertaining and even shocking. No inhibitions at all about a little session of sodomy. Quite a revelation.

1947

2 January I went with A. up to the eccentric church, built entirely of coral lime, to make some drawings. Later we climbed the hill behind the church to look at the old mission house. The breeze was cool and constant there on the veranda, a contrast to the sweltering still air of the sheltered villages below. So we dallied (and I might confess, dillied—twice) there all afternoon, everything quiet save a creaking door in the empty house, and the sound of the tide in the bay below. A purely Conrad sort of place, the setting for idylls and tragedies, that rambling house, creaking door, tumbledown outhouses, frangipani trees heavily scenting the overgrown garden, the boulder-lined paths (once whitewashed of course). A perfect place to dilly-dally with a charming native boy; lounging on the dilapidated veranda, idly scanning the sea for a sail and not caring a damn if there isn't a boat for months.

Then to shower, and after, virtuously, and, in the light of the afternoon's slap and tickle, comically, to church as the sun sank down. Religion seems to have done more good than harm—softened down the hard Melanesian savagery, imposed a few peculiar and necessary disciplines without inhibiting the native joy in pure sensuality. The tropicalised Victorian Gothic rigors of the London Missionary Society[1] have resulted in nothing but a joyous paganism contrasting with the deathly horrors of their earlier worship. No questions, no answers, none of those torments to offset ecstasies, none of those dreadful principles which build walls to fence off the permissible from the forbidden. Just moonlight and palms, people caressively friendly and in many cases extraordinarily beautiful, nearly all unspoilt. Simple, essentially good and mostly happy.

I suppose there *is* another side to the picture. I *know* there is. The Future. These islands I think are on the brink of ruination. They have been kept remote from the South right up until the war. Now they all, without exception, demand the right to drink liquor. I suppose it is really against my own principles to feel that they should not be given the right to go to hell in their own way. The liberty of the individual etc. But for the life of me I can't see what they want drink for. They are happy as they are. They are the last people on earth to need artificial stimulus, and they don't *know* how to drink. They tear themselves to pieces with it once they begin.

6 January The family all worked in the gardens clearing scrub. I swam. There was an extremely high tide, the water beautifully clear and green, pellucid. A. and I and some of the children played around the dinghies near the beach. A. took his spear and diving-glasses and went for fish. The small children are not shy of me now. They point out to me girls who are willing to oblige a lonely white man. The girls, quite aware of what is being said, shriek wildly, giggle and hide their faces in their hands. All the younger generation from the age of about seven upwards are very eager to get me safely and soundly into bed with one or other of the island belles and are persistent in their offers of help and encouragement. 'When rape is inevitable, relax and enjoy.' But my heart is not in it and I'm *damned* if I will.

10 January *Mer*. We got in at sundown. It was somehow far more exciting than Darnley. As the people themselves say, 'more *native*'. Everything looked more dramatic, more potent, mysterious. The houses clustered and crowded under huge glossy-leaved trees. Lamplight showed up extraordinary groups sitting beating drums, or just sitting. People moved like shadows, swiftly, among the dark trees. A large group of men and women performed, to endless chants, 'sitting-down dances' which are fascinating to watch.

11 February At last I made a drawing of A. The boy was tremendously pleased with it, and kept hugging me and stroking me, and being very proprietary before all the swarm of relatives and friends who jostled around to exclaim over the thing. Later everyone went to the farms to plant, and A. came back to my grass house and spent the whole morning there. He knows not one word of English, but chattered away happily in island language, entertaining himself and me, making love very prettily with an air of playful absorption. I've never known anything remotely like A. in my life before. So assured and delighted at being in love, so innocently knowing in all a lover's ways.

But despite my delight in this boy, and despite all the fascinating things that make a paradise of Murray Island, I am beginning to get restless. Vague plans for a painting in oils, a large painting, are simmering about in my mind. There are passages of paint on the picture quite clear in my vision—I know just how certain parts must be done to get the textures I want, to get the colours (a lot of blue and green). But I'll have to go to Sydney to paint that.

17 February How I wish I could write well, and give a true picture of this lovely remote place, where there seems no echo of the clamour of the machine age, where all values are still human values. Even the war left no mark here. At least, so it seems on the surface. Undoubtedly war has scarred this place in other ways: the whole younger generation of the men of Torres Straits who joined the army came back with new ideas, mostly bad. Those ideas have already begun to alter the style of island life. Discontent in island life, a belief that it is, in comparison with the exciting and glamorous electric-light and merry-go-round civilisation of Thursday Island, a contemptibly primitive existence, make them clamour for all those 'better things'. It is impossible to explain to them what a cold world it is outside, they think of the pubs and picture show at TI. The tradition of their savagery in the olden days gives them no clue to the cold ferocity of civilisation.

19 February The wisdom of the islands deals directly with the struggle to wrest a living from the land and sea. It consists of an intimate knowledge of all natural phenomena—the tides and winds, the habits of fishes, the nature of storms, the lore of the treacherous reefs. They carry in their heads a chart of the whole Straits. It is an encyclopaedia of knowledge so vast I doubt it will ever be written down. There is no need for it to be written, in its present form it has served them well for ages.

It was another calm day, eventless but for A. In these days we have told one another so little in words. Language as a means of communicating has been replaced with signs and smiles and gestures and caresses. Somehow I never realise quite how young he is while he is actually with me. His is the initiative always. The risks he takes of our being caught keep me in a state between fright and admiration. What on *earth* would happen if they found out? What *would* they think, or do?

March *Thursday Island.* A lotus-eating day. I suppose all one's days here are a solid diet of lotus. It is all too warm and wet and idle, too much a matter of blue lagoons and palms, picturesque and affectionate characters with guitars singing the songs the sirens sing, boats painted like bright birds, and seas over which the squalls pass like curtains—decorative effects more than meteorological phenomena. The puritan in me is suggesting that it is all a waste of time, now that I have stored my mind with enough images to paint for a year.

This life I have been leading up here is just not enough. The profound love I have for the natives is an unsatisfactory business. They are essentially physical creatures. The Intellect and the Soul have no part in their existence, and I, who am a sort of half-baked intellectual sensualist, cannot comprehend or enter very deeply into their wholehearted world of the flesh, so for all the love I bear them, for all their love of me, we cannot even communicate much to one another. I probably know more of them than they do of me for the simple reason that I have my intellect with which to consider them, whilst they have only their emotions with which to comprehend me. Yet I love them, which is more than I can say for most of the people I know in Sydney. But I'd better go South and justify my existence to the world. Here I am truly useless. It is not enough to sit down in the tropics and love a tribe of gorgeous primitives, I would never be satisfied with that. I am already satiated with their beauty, have possessed it until it is the whole colour of my sensual mind. Beauty as beauty only (physical, joyous beauty), paint as paint only, the mind limited to pure mind even (supposing I had a mind that could attain so untainted a condition) have ceased to seem complete ways of life. I am going to try to work out some synthesis. All this has a lot to do with painting, of course.

My islanders are about the only thing I have ever seen consistently more beautiful than any art. Watching them in their beauty is an occupation so enthralling that it never occurs to one to regret that this wondrous flesh does not contain a soul and mind equally magnificent, any more than one would desire a racehorse to be capable of composing a set of sonnets. It is only later, when sated, that one knows that saturation point of delight would never be reached if they possessed those other highest qualities of man. My art to paint them then must show not only their beauty, my love of them, but also my desire for other things that do not exist in them.

I know them just a little bit too well. My love of them has not decreased, it has become like married love, whereas before it was the thrilling uncertain yearning of one who has fallen desperately in love on sight, but has not yet learned even the name of the object of his ardours. Their voices, their ways, their colour, the strength and grace of their movements still excite my mind and eye and heart as much as ever, but the quality of the joy I take in them has changed. Now it is the happiness of seeing something familiarly beautiful, each repetition of which is a confirmation that what one once thought wonderful has blessedly retained its wonder, just as over a period of years one can visit an art gallery to see again and again a particular work of art, and each time be confirmed and refreshed by its unfailing loveliness.

14 April *Sydney*. Tas drove me to Merioola. I opened the door of the studio. It was absolutely *crammed* with things. Furniture in every spare foot of space. Extra cupboards, incredible lamps with hand-painted lampshades rioting red leaves—vases, photographs of myself, screens. Chairs had been covered with bright cretonnes with unbelievably dreadful designs. It was all dim and boarding-housish-looking. I felt just sick at heart.

Not only my room. Mother took the whole place in charge, bullied them, organised them, made them have their baths at special hours and so on, imposed on the place a sort of boarding school discipline.

7 May Merioola is just now an ants' nest of cultural and domestic activities—rooms are full of people busily painting and playing gramophones—a walk through the passages is like a tour through the ages of music—Scarlatti[2], Bach, Prokofiev and boogie. Justin O'Brien is working on paintings to send to England. Yossie Rickards[3] daubs day and night—all of the paintings are hotchpotches of borrowed bits from Loudon, Justin, David Strachan[4] and Goya.

9 May My paintings: that state between actuality and fantasy—a plane on which living flesh merges into its inanimate image, ghosts and gods partly materialise into carved idols, fears and desires are visible creatures. Things are what they *seem* because of their associations: *Mana*.[5] Everyday objects haunted with the phantoms of their daily use—landscapes significant because of what happened there, not because of a particular pleasing disposition of hills, trees and sky. It is my world, my countries, not the European world. Nor European beliefs and traditions.

Mid-August I read a newspaper article on the ghost towns left empty after the gold rush of the sixties. Then I began to think there must be lovely old stone houses in that district—the hills behind Bathurst.[6] Tas was equally enthusiastic. A couple of days later we set off. We got to Sofala—a lovely crazy old village. We stayed that night at Hill End. A town character showed us round an old ruined village living in the memory of its former 50,000 inhabitants—and fabulous tales of gold-strikes. Now there are only a handful of rather sordid, jovial mad peasants who live by fossicking and rabbiting.

Those two villages are so different it is hard to know which is the more beautiful. Sofala, I think. Hill End is high on a plateau which just beyond the village drops thousands of feet steeply into the valley of the Turon[7], beyond which rise as steeply again grandiose heavily wooded mountains. Most houses have their quota of fruit trees in blossom, old gnarled and rather neglected. And in the gardens the flowers, the sort that grow in England, iris, daffodil, pansies, violets and so on, are blooming and fresh. The avenue is made up of European trees, many varieties of pine, ash, flowering hawthorn, oriental plane trees, elm, maple and so on.

31 August I stayed out at Tas's and worked on a gouache while Tas, in a frenzy of painting quite unusual with him, worked on the final stages of his picture of the Sofala main street. It is very good.

I should never have looked at Tas's picture. It has made me feel so strongly the inadequacy of my own, which lacks grandeur and discipline, and for all the work that went into it, looks silly and slovenly. The sooner I leave Sydney the better. Here, I don't work enough, or seriously enough. They are right, it seems, the people who say my work is frivolous. Certainly, it lacks depth.

September *Hill End.* Murray and I spent the day exhaustively exploring the town, until at last we found a cottage. It is very small, stands in a couple of acres of ground. It is made of wattle and daub and has four rooms and a well. It's not the ideal, but the nearest thing to what we want.

Got to work on the place, and with picks and shovels borrowed, began working on one of the worst faults of the place, drainage. We lit the fires and the stove to get some of the damp out, and inspected and despaired over, the lavatory, which is 13th-century Flemish in all its horrid attributes.

19 October A telegram from Mother: 'Dad died suddenly. Cremation 10.30 Monday. Try to come.' My reaction was irritation. Why go all the dreary way to Sydney for a cremation? It was hardly likely that the reading of the Will would disclose any benefits for myself, and I disliked taking any part in one of those conventional situations which provide so much material for the writings of dramatists who satirise the bourgeoisie—the Old Family Lawyer, the sons and wives and cousins all sitting around wondering what they'll get, and the fury of those that get nothing. I expect nothing from Dad's estate.

28 October The Will!—it certainly was just as well I didn't go down. I can just imagine what an embarrassing moment it would have been when it came out that the co-heir to the family fortunes was that mysterious creature, my daughter. A situation from a Victorian novel. The Missing Heiress (of whom my father never even saw a photograph). Now how extraordinary it was of dad to leave his money like that. Yet not so odd in a way, when one remembers that all of them, great-grandfather and grandfather, did the same, strung their fortunes out over future generations. I suppose the old man wanted his money to survive him, and to make sure of that willed the capital to his grandchildren.

Last week of December The days have been hot, blue and clear, with the nights drenched in bright moonlight. Such weather as makes one restless, and, entranced with beauty, unhappy—unhappy because, standing on the verandah looking down at the ranks of trees at night, when the moon articulates sharply each leaf contrasted with shadow, and the air is loaded with scent of flowers and the linden blooms, one realises with a pang that the last essential is lacking—there should be someone, immediately, on the instant, someone willing, loving and incredibly beautiful, to pop into bed with.

The youths of the village realise this also with the same poignant uneasiness as I do. They stand in little groups talking and laughing in the shadow of the elms, with lighted cigarettes to show that they're there. They murmur and discuss until bevies of village wenches pass by. Then the louts raise their voices in excitement, and laugh loudly, and when the girls have gone giggling and clutching one another down the road, shout after them, having defeated shyness and found courage too late.

The scent of the linden—much the same scent as Proust's grandmother's lime tea[8] that gave rise to such memorable reminiscences—

must become identified with such summer nights and their desires: the shadowed avenue, the shyness, youth and frustration.

1948

16 January The wicked Wilson's letter arrived and I replied immediately, giving him more details of the vulgar and wretched pile of despised gold for Jennifer that had been left slackly lying about by some ratbag in the colonies. And to make it more irritating, I wrote it with studious inadvertence on the back of such a grocery list—one doz. bananas, two doz. oranges, one pineapple, two doz. eggs, two lb butter, two lb steak—as would drive anyone in starving Britain to distraction. Such a small malicious mind I have; but inventive, for I added to this list of edibles 'six tanned kangaroo hides' to give the whole a colourful antipodean touch, evocative of our boundless forests and the wild strange fauna that inhabit them.

5 February Beyond my personal passions and a Hill End landscape the world is vaguer and remoter than ever. Nearer, tangible and realisable are the bowls of plums, apricots and figs from neighbours' trees, the varied salads from our own garden and the scent and sight of its flowers, and the vista from our door of the avenue of trees in full, rich summery leaf leading to innumerable beautiful landscapes beyond, the house furnished by our own hands, the table loaded with fruits of our own gatherings. It seems so good and so honest. Yet contrasted with the vast and virile evils of the great world, so trivial.

10 March I paint all day until the light fades, trying hard to weld my ideas about light and simpler design into pictures. And I must say that I succeed a little. But the fault, the great fault, the fault that cannot be corrected, lies in myself, the limits of my mind. In paint I can now almost realise my inner vision, but that vision itself has no greatness about it. That is why Tas's pictures are always better than mine. He has a startling and noble perception of what he paints. With the same subjects and a lot of technical proficiency, I turn out things which mean nothing beyond paint itself. Or, when I achieve something, it is an amiable affair, shilly-shallying and rather weak, an echo of the shallow sounds of my character.

Yet what art tells more than mine?—the message of the greatest cannot say more than 'women are beautiful'. 'The sky is blue.' 'The country is lovely in springtime.' 'Behold the muscular grace of men,' 'Holy people'—'Red is a fine colour.' Somewhere in the pigment there lies, amongst these statements, a wonderful abyss, a chasm filled with a great soul, weeping and laughing and shouting and praying. But not in my pictures. In mine there is no chasm, but a sort of rabbit hole from which issues a calm amused voice saying 'Nice weather, isn't it?'

17 April I went to the pictures in the hall next to the pub. At interval the butcher's son, in a pink soft cocoon of alcoholic bliss, was rolling about spouting at random slurred silly talk.

'At least,' he said to me, 'I'm not a poofter. Not a poofter like you are.'

Bystanders giggled, children mostly. Village hostility, veiled. They know nothing of me except that I am not of them. Those books. *Difference*. Artist, speaks differently. Doesn't live like the rabbiters and the fossickers, doesn't trouble to join in their interest in horseracing. So a poofter. Perfectly simple equation. And, as it happens, too near the truth to be tolerated. That is the whole point.

I suppose, according to the best traditions, I should have hit him. It didn't occur to me until after. Cowardice partly, partly indifference, and partly because I don't see what a fight can prove.

4 May A letter from the wicked Wilson—very amiable and interesting. I wrote amiably and interestingly back again. To tell the truth, I was enormously pleased and felt a rush of sentimental feeling about Jennifer and all that. Anyway, I wrote (how delighted I was at the wicked old roué's praise of my drawings!) that I'd send him a batch of drawings in the near future. He is a good judge—and partly for the sake of ambition and advantage. A small show in London wouldn't do me any harm. I'd probably not get much more than a little reputation out of it.

5 May Margaret Olley[1] seems to love the place as much as I do. She and I haven't let up on painting. These days with their stormy skies, the trees raining a golden snow of leaves seem to me more beautiful even than before, which is surprising, for in the past I have always disliked wind and wetness—the intimacy of the cottage provides, whenever we re-enter it from one of our expeditions into the brisk cold, a delicious contrast of warm, white walls, shelves and books and *objets d'art* and mellow fire glow, usually with a large black pot of soup bubbling on the hob. It's a matter of contentment—dull, purring contentment.

5 July *The Apocalypse*[2] is now really complete. It is a mass of research and translation, a store of various sorts of erudition. It contains absolutely nothing of belief in what purports to be the subject—no fear of the Hells, no hope of the Heavens, no credence in the prophesies. It is an exercise in a dozen styles. It is an expression of certain lusts and admirations and its main concerns are with art, imagery, fecundity of invention and a delight in showing just *what* can be done with the medium. The net result is broadly a decoration with a strong literary appeal.

9 August *Sydney*. To the theatre to see the Oliviers' play *The Skin of Our Teeth*[3]. Tas wanted me to wear his tails but I've baulked at it—after we go to supper at Princes[4]. The theatre was a great success—the acting fine, as was the whole production, and the play very amusing, a sort of satirical allegory. After, I felt subdued at Princes. It is a dreary, discreetly lit place where the rich enjoy themselves in a gutlessly disbelieving ritual. I dislike the place—an expensive desert for the souls of the expensive living dead.

The play was the thing. It provided a spectacle of life, for all its artificiality, that was so much more alive than the spectacle presented at Princes.

18 August One thing I am converted to (Lord knows how) during this visit—the unimportance and mediocrity of my oil paintings, on which I'd spent so much thought and work. But my drawings remain good. People on the whole seem to be of the same opinion as myself, except the drawings bore them, except of course the artists, who understand drawing.

23 August *Hill End*. During the night it rained, and when I woke it was snowing gently, a charming sight. The whole village powdered white, the sky that warmish leaden colour scattering down scurries of flakes, and the trees utterly lovely against this new background. I wrote letters by the fire, keeping an eye on the window to watch it.

4 September I am indulging a sort of policy to broaden the range of my artistic reputation. I have again ideas about being famous. Why not? Australian art is a poor sort of thing, and it should be easy. Many things seem almost to conspire in my favour. I am recovering from the fit of pessimism I had in Sydney.

25 September I wrote off to the wicked Wilson and sent him ten more drawings, and told him that the harshness he complained of in my work was partly the result of my environment, and that the only cure was a few seasons in the damp soggy, mildewy mists of England, which would, one hoped, have the effect of blurring the edges of my drawings and generally imbue them with that admired watery fungoid swampiness which seemed to be the most appreciated characteristic of contemporary British draughtsmanship.

October *Melbourne*. So many things happened, one met so many people, and yet so little of it left a good taste. Asked to a party. There were about twenty young men, with few exceptions of that unpleasant Melburnian variety, affected, snobbish, homosexuals with one leg in the ballet and the other in a public lavatory, talking a sort of backslang culled from fashion magazines. In the middle of them all sat a youth of breathtaking beauty. He said not a word and looked shy, hardly glanced around him. I thought he looked horribly out of place and must be wondering what sort of a den of monsters he had got into. Then he suddenly moved and spoke. '*J'ai quinze ans*,' it said, in the most nauseating fluty hermaphroditic voice, and waving a languid lily of a hand. All beauty had vanished. The idol was obviously a male whore. I was terribly shocked.

24 November *Hill End*. I worked all day and finished the stone wall, and then went down to the pub to buy some bottles of burgundy, fell to temptation and extravagantly got also some veritable Benedictine, a young rabbit to fry, and a bottle of dry white wine off the ice, so returning to the cottage where (it was a most beautiful afternoon, the sun sinking in a very clear sky, and smoke rising blue-white from the cottages, and all the trees exuberantly green) I took the gramophone and an armful of Mozart[5] sonatas into the courtyard, and played music, and drank the iced wine and, feeling the greatest pleasure in the circumstance of being here, in such agreement and contentment, in such beautiful surroundings, so well treated by life.

13 December I have finished the Bacchanal.[6] It is good. But looking at it, and at other work of mine I like, I ask myself: 'Is *this* modern art'? It is not. It has profited by certain aspects of modern art, learned a little from this painter and that, but the work itself often seems more appropriate to former centuries. This Bacchanal is like a miniature comment on the work of Poussin.[7] But it is a very pleasant, lighthearted little picture. A boudoir piece.

1949

2 January I spent most of the time working on the little painting of the boys on horses, which was very difficult and at last became dull, until it took an astonishing turn in a way I had never envisioned, yet it retains and fulfils my original intentions for it. In most successful paintings there is a moment when the picture revolts from the artist and begins to make its own demands. Before that moment he has been dictating what he wants from pigment and canvas, but from then on he must attend to the will of the picture itself.

Mr Chifley[1] has announced that for Australia this year we'll be beset with difficulties, and that we might expect an economic 'Recession' because of foreign powers not buying our goods. I suppose we can also expect explanations of just how and in what especial senses Recessions differ from Depressions. I suppose in the former prosperity *recedes* from the public whilst in the latter (even a donkey can see the importance of such a distinction) the lack of money *depresses* the public.

Second and third weeks of January *Sydney*. The art world, its opportunists and its hangers-on and leeches were in a terrible flap about the visit of Sir Kenneth Clark[2], a wealthy connoisseur and collector. He arrived in Sydney with Professor Joe Burke[3] and the British Council threw a cocktail party for him. I had a few words with the great man. He complimented me on a large abstract painting of mine in the Gallery, called *The Market*. It had been away to a show in America and on its return stored in the National Gallery cellars.[4] Hal Missingham, the Director[5], suddenly realised that he had hardly anything modern of any dimensions to show Sir Kenneth, and got out this picture of mine and put it among the 'New Acquisitions' where it made a fine show.

28 January *Hill End.* Murray brought some very good new books—Evelyn Waugh's *The Loved One*[6]—very *good* satire, and an extraordinary first novel by a 23-year-old American, Truman Capote, *Other Voices, Other Rooms*[7], which seems to me to be promise of the sort of new writer one has waited for—Murray says in a few months it will be placed in drawing rooms in eye-catching positions.

I've been painting hard, on a new large oil which so far is very good. I have the highest hopes of it. For one thing, it is 'modern'—breaking away from the traditional sort of things I have been doing, it is lyrical but somehow violent. The subject is the Prodigal Son, and I am so excited with it that I keep rushing into the studio to have another look to see if it is as odd as I remember it.

2 February My mind is dried up and I feel a depression, a staleness about everything. I wish I knew what it was. I am hoping that it is simply the result of living too long in a barren and spiritually arid country, and that Italy, with its rich humanities, its inheritance of civilisation, will restore the lustre that my mind has lost, in the same way that pearls, become dull from not being worn, are soothed back to their erstwhile brilliance by prolonged proximity to living flesh.

I *think* that it is the environment of Australia. Not of Hill End, but of the whole materialistic nation.

4 February The landscape began to go well today. I want to evoke the sensation of that arid, ignorant, brutal, brutish Australian feeling, that half-man-made environment of ruined eroded earth and rock (mined by stupid ignorant men) and its concomitant of rusted tins and old bottles, that anti-human environment that is partly indifferent nature and partly the creation of indifferent, raw, unthinking people. And in the rest of the picture I want an emanation, an expression, of what

I find beautiful and what I am able to make beautiful—the road and the few houses of the town caught in the light of very early morning, painted softly and poetically in contrast to the jagged masses of the foreground.

9 March *Sydney*. I went to the opening of Sid Nolan's exhibition.[8] I had always previously disliked his painting and I still think I was right, but at this show there were four or five works so startling, so strangely moving and in the oddest way beautiful, yet shocking, that I am sure he is something of an artist. I dislike his way of painting—nasty shining paint, and often horrible colour, but he has a vision that in its own way is original as Tas's and equally as forceful. His bad works affect one as unpleasantly as a violent and repulsive action performed by a person who has given some proofs of a noble and intelligent mind—a forceful and perceptive mind.

25–26 March The *Toscana*. The departure went off well. The ship is not bad. The First Class passengers are dull except for two slightly promising ones. The food is superb. There are many Italian passengers who just now are beginning to be gay, have brought out their mandolins and started to sing very jolly songs.

20 April *Colombo*[9]: the air. It had an extraordinary *thick* quality, sticky, impregnated with a smell that was hard to analyse—a compound smell. Smoke?—cinnamon, coconut, mango, decaying vegetation—the smell of people?—food?—sweet cloying smell enticing, suggestive, enervating. We were forever warned of the dangers of robbers and murderers, but disbelieved the warnings, forever being pestered and importuned by shopkeepers and pimps.

29 April *Aden*. The place is the most complete or extraordinary vision of hell imaginable—madly exciting and incredibly beautiful, utterly lacking in any soft spots to alleviate its hard harshness. Even the few gardens exist by miracle among the dry rocks. Too much, too much altogether, the richness of strange designs painted on walls and doors, the unexpected Picassoesque decorations, the innumerable maimed poor children, the utter squalor.

4–5 May *Port Said.*[10] The people were as ugly by day as by night except for children and adolescents who were beautiful. One thing that makes the natives of foreign places fascinating is this—and it is something quite as important as personal beauty—that we suspect them all of being as viciously uncaring as we are guiltily and secretly.

We, all victims and false practitioners of a most hypocritical puritanism, stare greedily at the spectacle of their open naughtiness. We pretend to one another to think it disgusting, but inwardly we are excited and immediately degraded. They, the natives, probably feel little of the intensity of our lust through indulging so often and fecklessly themselves: they do not attach any importance to it—those exhibitions they make are to pander to our fascinated prudery. But two tremendous fears keep us chained to our puritan behaviour—fear of reputation and fear of the pox.

11 May *Portofino Mare.*[11] It's quite extraordinary, the coloured houses clustered round a tiny piazza, the fishing boats and some millionaires' yachts, and villas, bright pink set in gardens on the steep olive-covered slopes. The people are quiet, pleasant and non-pestering, a relief after Naples.

And yet—Naples, its wild colours at night, the pimps, the wonderful children, the vivacity, noise and speed, is much more of a painting-ground for me: that atmosphere of excitement, cheating, vice, laughter—I loved it.

3–4 June *Florence.* It's fantastically beautiful—every house, every street shows something admirable, something one has known about as long as one was conscious of art. This place is the mother of amazing events—the brown Arno flowing by the Ponte Vecchio, the incredible cathedral, Michelangelos standing about grandly in the squares, the Medici chapel, the palaces and castles everywhere, the stone streets and small lanes ingrowing on the ancient culture, faded frescoes in street shrines, stone towers and arches. Passionate political posters proclaim new histories on the old walls. I feel sick and lonely but at last in a place that pours over me the richness of the civilisation I need.

12–13 June Already the paintings of Florence have determined me to undertake a new discipline—the discipline of Cimabue[12] and the

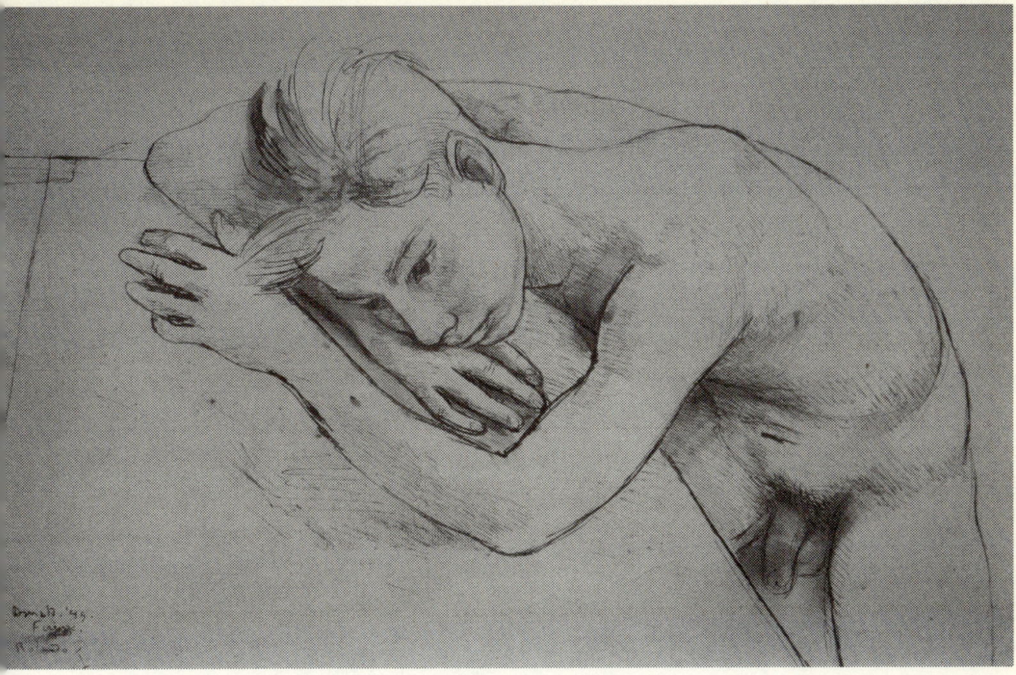

22. *'Firenze. Rolando' (1949).*

primitives, of Uccello[13] and Fra Angelico[14]: their paintings show how wrong the later artists were.

We found a young Yank artist and his wife living in a superb studio. He took us to another superb studio, the atmosphere that is our own life-breath, immediately recognised and treasured. The owner, Aberdeen Goodwin, turned out to be much better than one had a right to expect—young, *negro*, intelligent, charming and amusing. We got on awfully well.

22 June I am working hard and well. This is the second day the model has come. His name is Rolando, a boy of 17 with a good figure. Good humour and the largest member I have ever seen, which waggles when he coughs. I am tremendously pleased about it all—boy, waggles, drawings and every detail of my present life, the good life of an artist.

End of June to mid-July I have done at least a dozen successful drawings of Rolando, some of them so fine, so firm and delicate and strong, that Ingres[15] himself would have envied them. Some I must confess are frankly erotic, as is inevitable when these recent afternoons of drawing have culminated with abandoned lovemaking.

Certain faces recur in the life of the streets that are agelessly familiar—then one recognises someone from the drawings of Michelangelo and Leonardo. Rolando is such a one, and his life and scurrilous adventures that he relates to me (the murder of two German soldiers with a hand grenade at the time of the street fighting, the seduction of himself at the age of 13 by the young wife of a neighbour on the dark stairs of his house) are like tales from the pages of Cellini[16] and Boccaccio. He lives for sensual enjoyment. He thinks we are all a joke. He has no complications, thank God. We are no more nor less than spaghetti to him. I am enchanted. Cupid should be portrayed as an idiot, god of idiots, reigning over a realm devoid of values or sense.

Mid-August to early September *Pallanza, Lago Maggiore*. Neil McEacharn's villa and garden[17] exceed all expectations of magnificence—an ornate 19th-century house, very large, sumptuously furnished with antique furniture, brocade-hung walls, exquisite food and wine, and Neil himself in wonderful form, full of fantastic tales and memories.

All day one lounges about, reads, swims and sunbathes in the swimming pool, wanders through the vast lovely gardens, lives idly and luxuriously, tended by dozens of well-trained servants. It is all delightful, an extravagant dream of luxury such as I have never known before. All bestow on me, along with sensations of pleasure at such deliciousness, a feeling of shame. It is against the grain of that disgusting streak of puritanism in my nature.

Yet I do love luxury, and for Neil especially I have the strangest affection: he disarms that puritan critic within me utterly. The conversation is unbelievable, mostly about sex or royalties. Still, there are numerous moments when I feel a deep uneasiness. Neil is a man of unimaginable wealth and considerable power. The rulers of lands are his most intimate friends, and many of his views of course are theirs also. If one protests at some especial absurdity he grows peppery. What seems to be a fantastic joke, a dream, a satire drama, is after all real life.

One often misses the harsh and terrible beauty of Australia (all rocks, scrub, dry grass, brown trees, vast arid scenes of indifference and hostility) when faced with too much Italian prettiness. What really moves me deeply here are the evidences everywhere of man's nobility and intelligence, so the cities excite me to a greater admiration than these mountains reflected in lakes.

October *London*. I went to the National Gallery, was utterly thrilled and delighted: the pictures are better, in better condition and better displayed than any in Florence—the heavenly Uccello!—and the Piero[18] and numbers of others that have been cleaned recently—Rembrandt's *Flora*[19] utterly and absolutely beyond all belief. Now *that* is painting! Nothing is lovelier. I was delighted. And delighted in London, glad to be here.

I went round streets I used to frequent. Two of the houses I lived in years ago do not exist any more—bombed. London has changed terribly in these last ten years: the people were bad enough then (O God the *stuffiness* of the English!) but now they are eaten away with discontent and defeatism. Life is pretty dreary—the pubs and cafés I know are still there all right, with the same crowd in them, but somehow they have lost their spirit.

I called on the wicked Wilson. Jenny was there, much older, and her sister and a number of children including my own—a charming child who seems to regard me without shyness, and with considerable amusement. Wilson was at his contradictory, mellow best.

'Ah'—he said, speaking of the show of early English watercolours at the Academy[20], 'do you not agree, having seen those pictures, that the best and final things have been said by the English watercolourists? Taste, deliberation, an exquisite sense of values…'

'All excellent qualities in a gentleman,' I mocked him, 'but I fail to see the point of introducing them into art. An artist has no need to be a gentleman, and becomes ridiculous when he pretends to be one. An artist is no more a gentleman than a lawyer, a poet, a dentist, an actor or a doctor. The qualities of great art are sublime, not merely gentlemanly. Most great artists have been dishonourable, rather dirty, immoral, often vulgar, vain, inclined to cheat and lie: they had other qualities of goodness to balance those. But none of these characteristics are those of gentlemen. That is why English art has never been great. Too many talented daubers pretending to be gentlemen. Art reaches beyond the limits of good breeding.'

21 November *Florence*. Heavenly again—moderately warm, sunshine and rain, and the whole city in its autumn colours, with the muddy river running a wild torrent and the trees shedding swathes of golden leaves.

There was an enormous mail awaiting me at the bank. Murray spoke extensively of the garden, the azaleas and iris and wallflowers, our flowering trees, the whole countryside in the Australian spring. Too lovely and desirable, where my heart lies.

8 December *Assisi.* This morning I saw the brown-grey and pink stone town clinging to the steep hill: its colours and shapes those of an exquisite cubist picture—plains of brown and grey flickering in some sort of an exquisite adjustment, patterns of rough textured roofs receding, advancing, seeming to contract and expand, holding within the limits of their varied shapes further design of tubular tiles: every variety of fawn, pink and brown stone wall, juxtaposed intricately at an infinitely varied and delightful play of angles—and beyond us far below the autumn misted Umbrian plains receding dappled with tiny trees, green fields, ploughed fields, fallow in rows, fields in diamond perspectives cut like a harlequin's cloth, but sombre under a wet sky full of clouds, purple clouds—and in the clouds rents and tears through which the sun's light beamed down through the bluish air as tho' through smoke, lighting a snake-like river and wet roads all silver stretching far away.

16 December *Sant'Angelo, Ischia.* The long drive along twisting roads in a *carrozza* through bleached pink and white villages clear in pale sparkling sunlight under a pale pure sky, the air warm, dry, sharp, invigorating—and through hilly country where innumerable farms and vineyards are enclosed in rough pale grey and white stone walls, where grey-green olives stood against strangely cut cliffs of chalky stone and tufa, and behind reared the jumbled crags and precipices of wild mountains, and hills so patterned and textured with terraces of vineyards that the whole hilly background of the landscape at times took on the appearance (what with the whorls of terraces in tiers following the contours forever folding and swelling of the hills) of gigantic fingerprints.

17–25 December It is clear, sunny, fresh—always. Time passes slowly in terms of hours but days have dissolved in an instant. One makes many drawings—all so far of landscape.

One day we climbed the formidable height to Testaccio, a village perched on the very top of a mountain a couple of miles away, to visit Jeff Smart, a South Australian painter.[21]

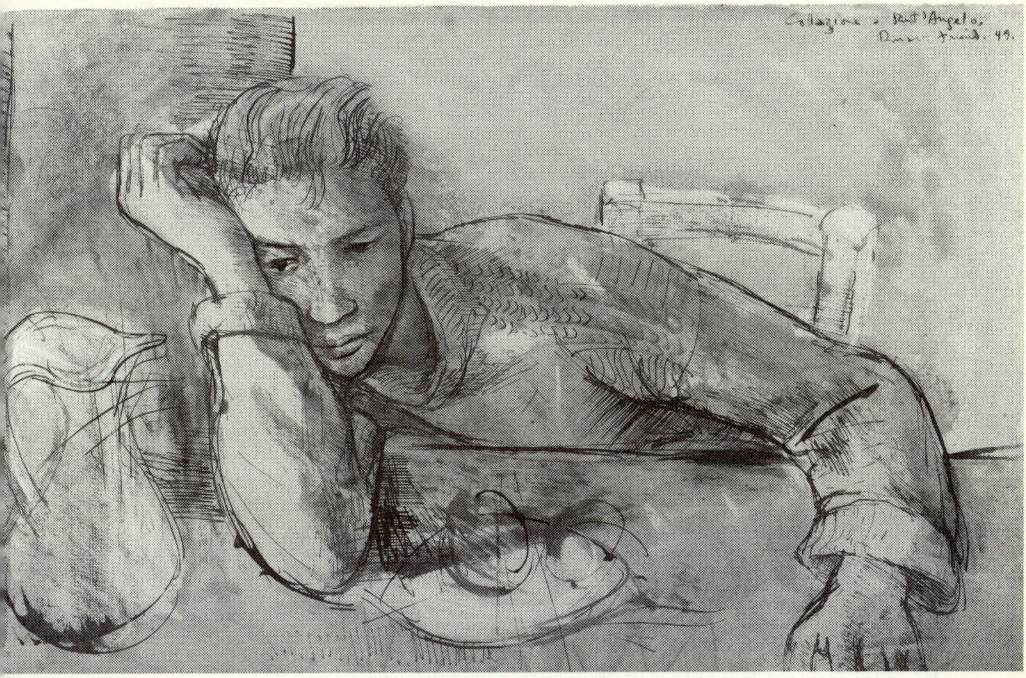

23. *'Colazione a Sant'Angelo';*
also called Attilio *(1949).*

NOTES: 1940s

1940

1. The popular name for the British shipping company Alfred Holt & Co, founded in 1866.
2. The capital of the Western Region of Ghana. The *Nestor* called in here after Lagos before proceeding south.
3. In classical legend, a Trojan prince and the most handsome of the mortals, eyed off by Zeus, who abducted him to serve as cupbearer to the gods and as Zeus's beloved.
4. Painter and stage designer of southeast European origins but born in Germany (1917). He came to Australia in his youth, and Friend first came to know him well about 1934, probably through Dattilo-Rubbo's art school. Cardamatis returned permanently to Europe in 1946.
5. Marlene Dietrich (1901–92), German-born actress and singer, who moved to Hollywood in 1939 and became a US citizen.
6. A scrambled version of *Du Côté de chez Swann*, the title of the first volume (1927) of Marcel Proust's novel *A la recherche du temps perdu* (cf diary entry for September 1942).
7. The subtitle of a symphony written by French composer Hector Berlioz in 1830, entitled *An Episode in the Life of an Artist.*
8. Mock-Latin for 'seduced by suburbia': a pun on *reductio ad absurdum.*
9. Sir John William Ashton (1881–1963), English-born painter, who came to Australia in 1884 and was director-secretary of the AGNSW from 1937 to 1944.
10. The name of a block of flats, one of which Friend's mother acquired for family use in the mid-1930s.
11. Possibly a euphemism for sex.
12. An association of artists formed in NSW in 1939, and in other states in other years. It was designed to promote progressive trends in art and to facilitate regular exhibitions for members.
13. First formed in 1895 as a breakaway group from the Royal Art Society of NSW. It held annual exhibitions from 1895 to 1902, and from 1907 until its demise in the 1940s.
14. A pastoralist dynasty in NSW, whose country seat from the 1830s was Camden Park Estate.
15. A harbourside eastern suburb of Sydney, 3 kilometres from the city centre.
16. Mabel White, former model for Norman Lindsay and at this time for Friend. Possibly, she was also the Miss White whom Friend met and fantasised about in his first drawing classes in Sydney: see diary entries for October and November 1929.

17. Australian painter, teacher and critic (1915–91).
18. A commercial art gallery established in Sydney in 1925, and a regular exhibitor of Friend's work from the early 1940s to the 1960s.
19. Sir George Russell (Tas) Drysdale (1912–81), English-born painter, who came out to Australia when a schoolboy.
20. International newspaper established in 1908 by Mary Baker Eddy, the founder of the Church of Christ, Scientist. Friend was to publish four articles in it: three on African culture (10 July, 23 August, 8 September 1941) and one on songs of the Torres Strait (10 February 1942).
21. A wing of the State Library of NSW named after David Scott Mitchell, collector of Australiana, and opened in 1910.
22. The article was not published but the collage was reproduced in Friend's *Painter's Journal* (1946), p. 65, and is reproduced here: image 20, p. 138.

1941

1. Sergei Rachmaninov (1873–1943), Russian composer, pianist, and conductor, wrote four piano concerti, of which the most popular (and the one probably referred to here) was the No. 2 in C Minor (1900–01).
2. 'The Fall of the House of Usher' (1839) is a horror story by American author Edgar Allan Poe.
3. English author (1818–48).
4. Sir Cecil Beaton (1904–80), English fashion photographer, and stage and film designer.
5. A small coral island on the Great Barrier Reef, 30 kilometres from Cairns.
6. Eponymous hero of Daniel Defoe's novel, published in 1719.
7. An oil painting of 1892.
8. Sir Jacob Epstein (1880–1959), American-born British sculptor.
9. The US naval base in Hawaii, attacked on 7 December 1941.

1942

1. The surrender of the Allied forces (including Britons, Indians and Australians) to the invading Japanese army on 15 February 1942 and the culmination of Japanese intrusion into the Malay Peninsula over the preceding three months.
2. A street in Elizabeth Bay, a harbourside eastern suburb of Sydney.
3. Built in the later 1830s for the then Colonial Secretary, Alexander Macleay. Friend lived in a flat on the top floor.
4. Australian Infantry Forces, in which Friend enlisted as a gunner.
5. A broad thoroughfare in central Sydney, running between George and Macquarie streets.

6. The Hume army camp was situated just outside Albury, a town in NSW near the border with Victoria. Friend's regiment was stationed there till around mid-April 1943.
7. The name given by European settlers to the indigenous inhabitants of southwestern Africa, the Khoikhoi.
8. Elizabeth (Bon, Bonny) Drysdale, née Stephen (1910–1963), first wife of Russell Drysdale. The Stephen family owned property in the Riverina district near Albury.
9. Paul-Marie Verlaine (1844–96), French poet.
10. French novelist (1799–1850).
11. Anglo-Irish novelist (1852–1933), who also studied painting in Paris in the 1870s.
12. Édouard Manet (1832–83), French painter.
13. Sir Ernest Daryl Lindsay (1889–1976), Australian painter, brother of Norman Lindsay (see **1930**, note 15), and Director of the National Gallery of Victoria, 1941–56.
14. A satirical novel of 1930 by Waugh (1903–66), English author.
15. A Northern Beaches suburb of Sydney, 35 kilometres from the city centre.
16. The longest river in Australia, spanning three states: NSW, Victoria and South Australia.
17. A town in northern Victoria, near the border with NSW.
18. A song written in 1825 by German composer Franz Schubert.
19. Johann Sebastian Bach (1685–1750), German composer.
20. Greek mathematician who lived around 300 BC.
21. Characteristic of the teaching method of Socrates (469–339 BC), Athenian philosopher, as enshrined in the works of his chief disciple and explicator, Plato.

1943

1. At 3 Bay View Road, Rose Bay, an eastern suburb 8 kilometres from the city centre.
2. In the style of Aubrey Beardsley (1872–98), English illustrator and author.
3. Elsa Schiaparelli (1890–1973), Italian fashion designer.
4. Robert Gordon Menzies (1894–1978), Prime Minister of Australia, 1939–41, 1949–66. Menzies had retreated to the backbenches in 1943, but was busily reshaping his party into what became the Liberal Party of Australia in 1945.
5. A city on the Hunter River, NSW, 166 kilometres north of Sydney.
6. In the ancient Greek epic *The Iliad*.
7. Sir Thomas Albert Blamey (1884–1951), Chief of Staff in the Australian Infantry Forces in World War I.

8. Princess Imma of Erbach-Schöenberg (1901–47), second wife of Captain Neal McEacharn (1884–1964), Scottish-born art patron and garden designer who came to Australia from Italy during World War II, returning there afterwards (see **1949**, note 17).
9. Jan van Eyck (1390s–1441), Flemish painter.
10. Dutch painter (1399/1400–1464).
11. German-born painter and critic of Swiss nationality (1914–82), who lived in Australia from 1929 to 1958.
12. Greek comic dramatist (c. 450 – c. 386 BC).
13. In the style of William Hogarth (1697–1764), English satirical painter and engraver.
14. John Curtin (1885–1945), Prime Minister of Australia, 1941–45, and leader of the federal Labor Party, 1935–45.
15. Henri Rousseau (1844–1910), French painter, also known as Le Douanier (the customs officer) after his one-time place of employment.
16. The tallest free-standing peak in the world, situated near the town of Gordonvale, an outer suburb of Cairns.
17. Katsushika Hokusai (1760–1849), Japanese artist, best known for his woodblock print series *Thirty-six Views of Mount Fuji.*
18. Main city of the Atherton Tablelands, a fertile tropical plateau located inland from Cairns.
19. Non-commissioned officer, an enlisted member of the armed forces who has been given authority by a commissioned officer.
20. 'The Doctors', the Spanish title of which echoes the picture by Francisco Goya (1746–1828) entitled *El Médico* (*The Doctor*), produced in 1779.
21. Large open space in Sydney, adjoining the Royal Botanic Gardens, and containing a 'Speakers Corner' for public oratory.
22. Australian politician (1897–1981) and, in 1943, the first woman to be elected to the Australian House of Representatives, representing an electorate in her native Tasmania. She was a devout Catholic.
23. Greek god of wine, whose equivalent in Roman mythology was Bacchus.
24. Traditional Irish dance.

1944

1. An army camp at Burleigh Heads, a suburb between Coolangatta and Surfers Paradise on Queensland's Gold Coast.
2. Australian artist (1905–1995), who himself went on to win the Archibald Prize the following year. The prize, administered by the trustees of the AGNSW, was first awarded in 1921 after a bequest from J. F. Archibald, editor of the *Bulletin* (see **1962**, note 9), who died in 1919. It is awarded for

'the best portrait, preferentially of some man or woman distinguished in Art, Letters, Science or Politics'. Cf **1982**, note 3.

3. Nickname for Doménikos Theotokópoulos, Cretan-born artist (1541–1614), who spent the greater part of his career in Spain.
4. The main conflicts between Greece and Persia took place in 490 and 480–79 BC, and there is no historical record of a 'Legion of Lovers'. What could be Friend's source of such a story? About a century after the Persian Wars, Plato, in his *Symposium*, has the character Phaedrus remark: 'if there were only some way of contriving that...an army should be made up of lovers and their loves, they...would overcome the world.' This idea, according to the Roman biographer Plutarch, was an inspiration behind the so-called Sacred Band of Thebes, an elite military contingent of 150 male couples formed in Greece around 378 BC. (See Plutarch's *Life of Pelopidas*, part of his *Parallel Lives*, which dates back to the first century AD and of which there was an English translation in the Loeb Classical Library edition of 1917.)
5. This is probably as much a garbled version of history as Friend's account of the Legion of Lovers. Napoleon Bonaparte (1769–1821), Emperor of France between 1804 and 1814, certainly did not initiate any decriminalisation of homosexuality (or homosexual relations in private), whether in the army or society generally; in France, this process had its origins in the newly drafted criminal code of the National Constituent Assembly in 1791. Napoleon's own Penal Code of 1810 simply did nothing to interfere with this process or with the more tolerant attitudes it reflected.
6. Edgar J. Kaufmann, jr. (as he insisted on spelling it, with the lower-case 'j'), American design scholar and curator (1910–89), who served as a lieutenant and captain with Fifth Army Air Force Intelligence in Australia, New Guinea and the Philippines between 1942 and 1945. Some of the volumes of Friend's diaries were housed at Russell Drysdale's, where Kaufmann visited in September 1943 and first came to admire them. Cf **Introduction**.
7. English-born Australian painter (born 1917).
8. Australian painter and teacher (1917–96).
9. Kaufmann took two of Friend's diaries (vols. IX and XIV in the series *Los Desastres de la Guerra*) back with him to America. These volumes have recently been returned to join most of the other Friend diaries in the collection at the National Library of Australia. Cf **Note on the Edition**, and **Introduction**.
10. The northernmost suburb of Sydney, and one of the most affluent; 40 kilometres from the city centre.
11. Northern Beaches suburb of Sydney, 23 kilometres from the city centre. Friend's mother was living there at the time.
12. A Tibetan monastic utopia invented by English author James Hilton in his

novel *Lost Horizon* (1933). There are no slums in Hilton's Shangri-la; these are an invention of Friend's, signalling his repugnance for what he sees as the idealisation of human 'normality'.

13. Richard Freiherr von Krafft-Ebing (1840–1902), German-born psychiatrist, most famous for his case studies in sexual perversity, *Psychopathia Sexualis* (1886).
14. *Los Caprichos* was a series of etchings produced by Goya in the 1790s after a long bout of illness; *Los Desastres de la Guerra* (*The Disasters of War*) was another series of Goya etchings, produced at the time (c. 1810–13) of the Peninsular War between France and the allied forces of Spain, Portugal and England.
15. Giovanni Battista Piranesi (1720–78), Italian artist famous for his etchings of Rome and of imaginary prisons.
16. Australian poet, critic, publisher and bookseller (1921–95). Cf **1944**, note 21.
17. Australian art editor and patron (1901–81). Cf **1944**, note 21.
18. The pseudonym adopted by Harold Stewart and James McAuley when authoring the hoax poems they submitted to the magazine *Angry Penguins* in 1944. Cf **1944**, notes 19, 21, 23.
19. Australian poet and oriental scholar (1916–95), who spent much of the latter part of his career in Japan following his involvement in the Ern Malley hoax. Cf **1944**, notes 18, 21, 23, and *DFD 1*, pp. 395–99 for the letters between Stewart and Friend leading up to the hoax.
20. See diary entry for November–December 1940, and **1940**, note 22.
21. Australian literary magazine co-founded by Max Harris (see **1944**, note 16), of which there were nine numbers published irregularly between 1940 and 1946. John Reed (see **1944**, note 17) became a co-editor in 1943. The 'Ern Malley' poems (see **1944**, note 18) were published in the autumn issue of 1944.
22. Sir Sidney Nolan (1917–92), Australian painter.
23. James McAuley (1917–76), Australian poet, critic and academic, who collaborated on the Ern Malley poems with Harold Stewart. Cf **1944**, notes 18, 19, 21.
24. This picture of Friend's was in an exhibition that opened at Farmer's Blaxland Galleries in Sydney on 3 July. A complaint about the nudity featured in it prompted the police raid. The complaint was not upheld by the Chief Secretary, and the picture was subsequently purchased by William Dobell.
25. Either a play on colloquial terms for 'homosexual' or an allusion to the female knight of chastity, Britomart, in Edmund Spenser's poem *The Faerie Queene*, Book III (1590).
26. Frank Forde (1890–1983), Minister for the Army from 1941, and briefly Prime Minister of Australia in 1945, on John Curtin's death.

27. Traditionally, the residential area and main cultural stronghold of American blacks living in New York City.

1945

1. The commission was offered to Friend by the Military History Section of Australia's armed forces. He was appointed to the rank of Lieutenant.
2. Town in Papua New Guinea, occupied by the Japanese Army in 1942–43.
3. Part of an archipelago 8 kilometres off the coast of Borneo.
4. The Lend-Lease Sherman Tank, manufactured in America and distributed to the Allied forces under the US government's Lend-Lease Act of 1941.
5. W. S. Gilbert (1836–1911) and Arthur Sullivan (1842–1900), English librettist-and-composer team responsible for a series of comic operas.
6. Port city on the eastern coast of Borneo.
7. Garbled quotation from the Old Testament: Song of Songs, 7:2.
8. Slang for prison.
9. The Sonnets of William Shakespeare, first published in 1609 and dedicated to a 'Mr. W.H.', sometimes presumed to be a beloved of the author's.
10. Leonardo da Vinci (1452–1519), Italian painter, charged with (though finally acquitted of) sodomy in 1476, and the mentor and intimate companion of two youths, 'Salai' and Count Francesco Melzi.
11. Oscar Wilde (1854–1900), Irish-born playwright, imprisoned for homosexual offences in 1895, and the lover of Lord Alfred Douglas.
12. Beautiful Greek youth (c. 110–130) from the Roman province of Bithynia, who became the beloved of the Emperor Hadrian.
13. Pamela Friend, née Walker (born 1923), married to Donald's brother, Terence.
14. Painting by Rembrandt (1642).

1946

1. Friend, *The Apotheosis of Ned Kelly* (1946), reproduced in Barry Pearce's catalogue, *Donald Friend 1915–1989 Retrospective* (AGNSW, Sydney, 1990), p. 57; Drysdale, *The Crucifixion* (1945), reproduced in Lou Klepac, *Russell Drysdale 1912–1981* (revised edition, Sydney, 2009), p. 151, plate 65.
2. A colonial mansion in the Sydney suburb of Woollahra, turned into a boarding house in 1941.
3. Australian artist and stage designer (1918–69), who lived at Merioola with his lover Harry Tatlock Miller before going to live in London. Cf **1950**, note 10.
4. Classical marble sculptures taken from the Parthenon in Athens by Lord Elgin between 1801 and 1805, and displayed in the British Museum, London, from 1817.

5. Sydney Technical College, established in 1878.
6. German author Thomas Mann's novel (1912) about a writer infatuated with a teenage boy.
7. James Gleeson (1915–2008), Australian artist.
8. Elaine Haxton (1909–99), Australian painter and stage designer.
9. Member of a clan from pre-Hellenic Thessaly that, according to legend, engaged in a battle with centaurs at the wedding feast of their leader, Pirithous. The story became a recurrent motif of Greek sculpture and vase painting.
10. Main island of the Bikini Atoll in the Pacific Ocean. Nuclear weapons testing by the US government continued on the atoll till 1958.
11. Shoreline diving location in the Illawarra district of southern NSW.
12. English playwright (1899–1973).
13. Island in the eastern section of the Torres Strait.
14. A type of sarong.

1947

1. A non-denominational Christian organisation with missions in Africa, Asia and the Pacific dating to the late eighteenth century.
2. Domenico Scarlatti (1685–1757), Italian composer.
3. Jocelyn Rickards (1924–2005), Australian costume designer, who was to have a career in British cinema from the 1960s. Cf diary entry for 16 May 1983.
4. Australian artist (1919–70).
5. In Maori lore, a supernatural power associated with people or objects.
6. Regional centre in NSW, 200 kilometres west of Sydney.
7. A major river in NSW.
8. A motif in Proust's novel *A la recherche du temps perdu.*

1948

1. Australian painter (born 1923).
2. A painting by Friend on themes from the Revelation in the New Testament.
3. Written in 1942 by American dramatist Thornton Wilder, and brought to the Australian stage by the visiting husband-and-wife team Laurence Olivier (1907–89) and Vivien Leigh (1913–67).
4. A fashionable French restaurant in Martin Place, Sydney.
5. Wolfgang Amadeus Mozart (1756–91), Austrian composer.
6. Cf **1931**, note 17; diary entries for 24 June 1931 and 8 November 1951.
7. Possibly a reference to *Andrians or The Great Bacchanal with Woman*

Playing a Lute (1628) by French painter Nicolas Poussin (1594–1665), at the Louvre in Paris, which Friend visited in 1937, though Poussin painted or drew other works in this genre.

1949

1. Ben Chifley (1885–1951), Prime Minister of Australia, 1945–49.
2. London-born art historian and broadcaster (1903–83), from a Scottish family.
3. Joseph Burke (1913–92), English-born Professor of Fine Arts at the University of Melbourne from 1947 to 1978.
4. There is no work of this name in the current collection of Friend paintings at the AGNSW, and no record of any public exhibition of Friend's work in America in the 1940s. The reference to such a show may be a confusion of Friend's with the *UNESCO Exposition Internationale d'Art Moderne* at the Musée d'Art Moderne in Paris (November–December 1946) or the *Contemporary Australian Art* show at the Auckland City Art Gallery (June–July 1948), in both of which exhibitions his work had been represented. There is evidence that *The Market* continued to be stored by the AGNSW up to the end of 1956, when it last surfaced in the *Pacific Loan Exhibition of Contemporary Paintings*, on board Orient Line *SS Orcades* and at the AGNSW.
5. Australian artist (1906–94), and Director of the AGNSW from 1945 to 1971.
6. Published in 1948.
7. Published in 1948; by the time of this entry, Capote (1924–84) was twenty-four.
8. At Macquarie Galleries, Sydney.
9. Capital of Sri Lanka, then Ceylon (cf **1936**, note 1).
10. City in northeastern Egypt, near the Suez Canal.
11. Fishing village in the province of Genoa, on the Italian Riviera.
12. Italian painter (c. 1240–1302).
13. Paolo Uccello (1396/97–1475), Italian painter.
14. Italian painter (c. 1390s–1455).
15. Jean Auguste Dominique Ingres (1780–1867), French painter.
16. Benvenuto Cellini (1500–71), Italian sculptor.
17. Giardini Botanici di Villa Taranto, established by McEacharn (see **1943**, note 8) in the 1930s.
18. Piero della Francesca (1410/20–1492), Italian painter.
19. Also known as *Saskia as Flora*, painted in 1635.
20. The Royal Academy of Arts in Burlington House, Piccadilly, a major London gallery (and art school) founded in 1768.
21. Born 1921.

1950s

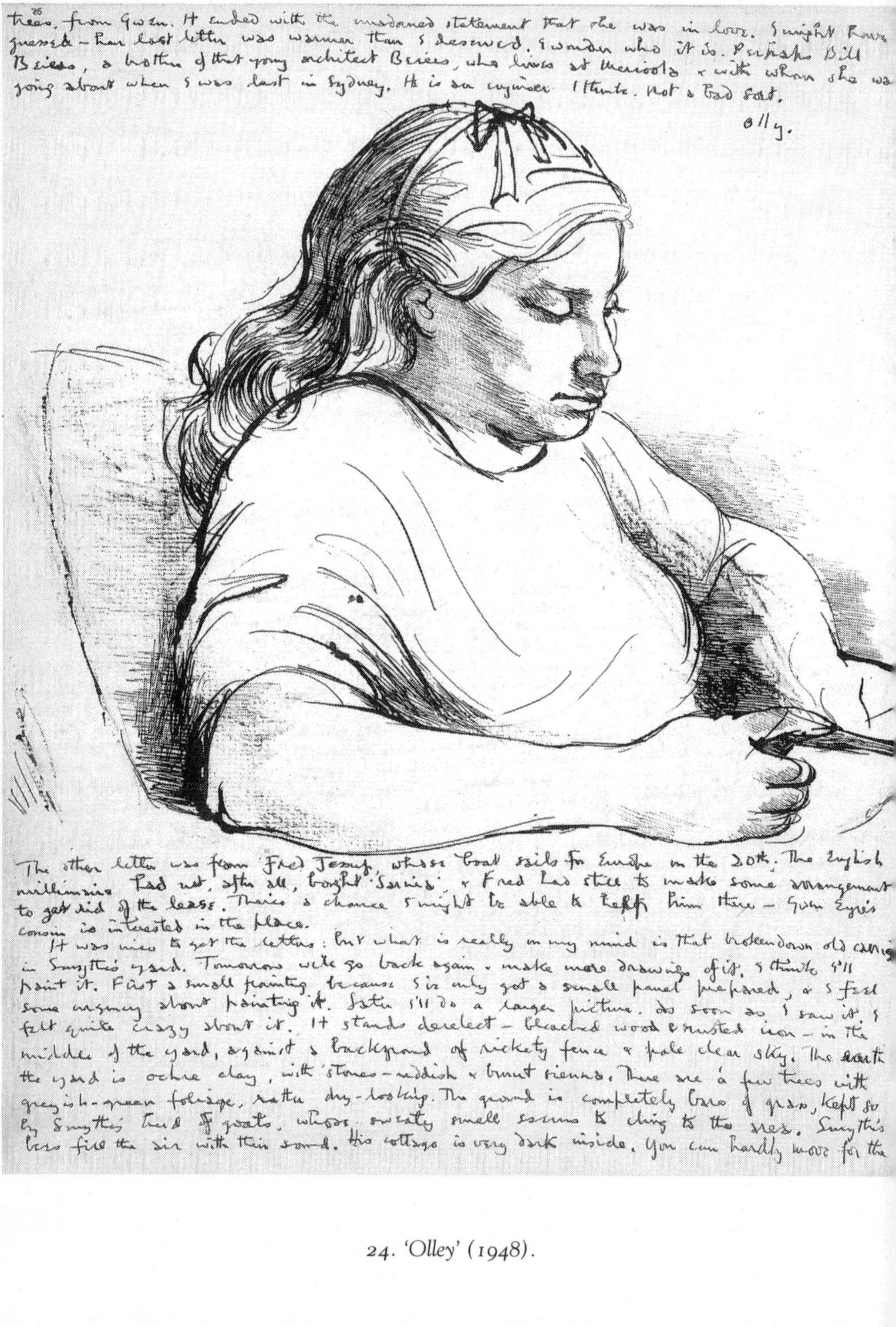

24. 'Olley' (1948).

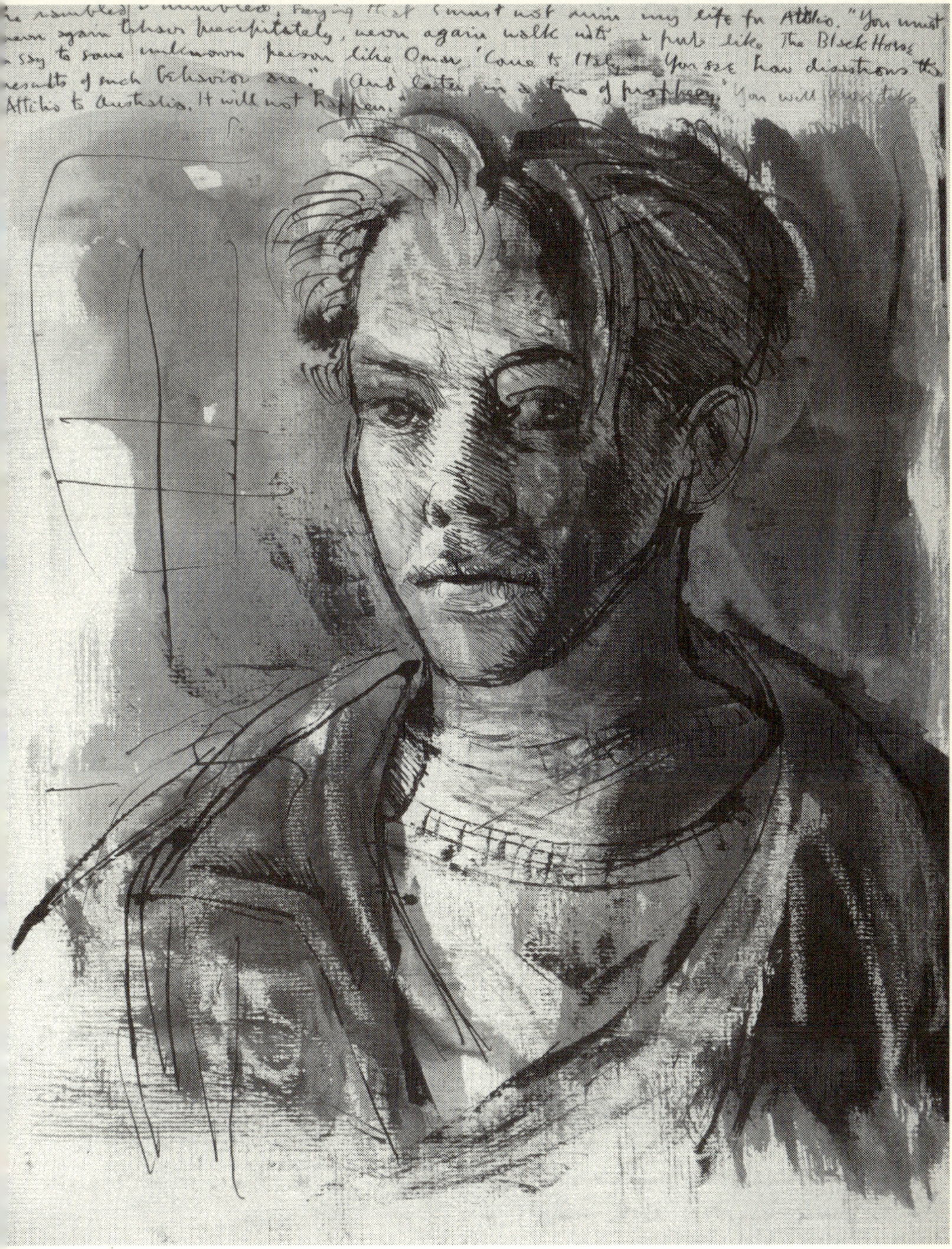

25. *Attilio Guarracino (1950).*

1950

First week of January *Sant'Angelo*. I've have worked most of the time on two successful paintings—a boy in a motley coloured jacket, and an old woman with a fisher-boy. I want to show all these pictures in Australia. I am no longer hungry for a European reputation as a painter. Europe means very little to me. My heart is often in Hill End, and I long for the place, and the peace and quiet and pleasure it always affords me.

Sant'Angelo is a very quiet, practically unpopulated village. The air is crystal clear, the sun shines freshly from the sky on white stone walls, on beach and sea and mountain. It is the setting for an antique idyll. A donkey-boy encourages his beast up a steep path, old peasant women carry baskets on their heads. On the sea the fishing boats rock gently in the glittering path of the sun's reflection.

Jeff Smart arrived for dinner, bringing with him the rascally Attilio[1]. Attilio told us his life story which was funnily sad. When he was still a small boy (he is 18 now) he was sent away to work on a small lugger to dive for coral. For eight months' work Attilio was paid 60,000 lire (about £30) so he decided to take a rowing boat on a misty night out to an American ship and invest his entire pay in cigarettes, which he could sell for three times as much. But he was caught returning by the water police who confiscated the cigarettes and had him put in gaol for a week. Since then nothing good has happened to him, but the satisfactions of a rascal's life.

9 January The American poet Chester Kallman came over from Forio with another writer called Bu and a packet of sandwiches made from a ham sent him by W. H. Auden[2]—despite which, the conversation on the terrazzo was far from literary. God knows how these creatures write poetry: it would seem from their talk that they give themselves day and night without cease to promiscuous sex with the local boys and think of nothing else.

The days pass in painting, very pleasantly: but my work is lousy.

13 January Jeff came down from Testaccio and in the evening we went as invited by Chester. The wicked Attilio was there (for Bu I gathered) and in a long murmured aside told me he was 'desperate' for money and since he had nothing to expect from me at all, I believed his sad story, and was so touched I gave him the only money I had. I knew of Attilio's need of a new pair of shoes as a sort of joke, from both Bu and Jeff, because poor Attilio, without money even for the bus fare, always went afoot to visit his friends, and complained on arriving, exhibiting his worn-out footwear. At that party, it was the lack of shoes that so touched my heart, which resulted in his coming home with me, although I had expressly told him that I gave it for nothing, or for friendship and sympathy, if that is nothing.

I should like to spend a lot of time with Attilio—even perhaps travel with him.

February It seems to me that Jeff, who has been such a good friend and companion, does and says things that appear to be designed to undermine Attilio's relationship with me—he had always been in love with Attilio and was in consequence suffering the tortures of the damned. How much more must one endure in the next few weeks, in the arrangements for our going to Australia.

The history of events for me is always obscured in the fogs of my own thoughts and reactions, so what happens is as much influenced by suspicions, self-taught lies, and my love and jealousies and prejudices, as by the common facts of events, so I often do great injustices to those around me.

March Attilio's passport is not yet ready. For every hour I have had of happiness there have been days of wretchedness.

'If you do not take me with you to Australia, Donald,' he said, 'I will not mind. I will not hate you. I do not love you. When you are miserable I am more miserable than you because I do not love you and will never. I do not want you to love me. I like you. I would like you whenever you want to and find other people to amuse you. Then I will feel free.'

And so on. I think these things over and over again, sometimes admiring the honesty of them, and sometimes despairing over them. There have been moments when I have seen in my actions all the morbid idiocies of behaviour that Proust indulged in with Albertine.[3]

I have been fairly happy but it is not possible to persuade myself any more that I am really alive or really sane. I cannot control the rages of melancholy which descend and devour me, raging like an illness, a fever, so I long to die, wander sometimes the whole day and night about the city desperate and sickened, thinking over and over and over the long senseless catalogue of my thoughts about Attilio.

April All praise to Ganesha, the remover of Obstacles![4]—the Landing Permit has arrived from Australia! Now only remains the passport.

O how is it, and why is it, that so simple, so coarse and stupid a character as I am gets involved in such highly complicated situations—of delicacy and intricacy. I belong to the world of raw meat, rough boys, yet bring with me the absurdities of another standard. All I want is love, sex, money. Work and a quiet place in the country and friends. In other words, Attilio, painting, bank account, Hill End *with* Donald Murray.

That is all I want. I think perhaps I demand too much of life.

1 May The full spring has gloriously arrived: it is hot, the sky is blue, the trees magnificently in leaf.

Aberdeen Goodwin said, 'You'd better begin working again. That is the only thing. I don't think you'll ever be happy in love, Donald. Everybody likes you enormously. But I don't think the sort of boy you like will ever love you. Get back to doing some work.'

So there it is, Ladipo, Colin and now my Attilio. Rather the same pattern, and the same unhappy conclusion.

2–3 May I began writing letters to Pat Jones.[5] I have a crazy idea: Pat, who has always liked me a lot and is now utterly miserable, may be able to alleviate this obsession. I will try to taste the love of women. Sex I think is a habit. Desire is harder to come by as far as women are concerned. Pat is the only person I feel like that about. It might by a miracle be possible to attain a more normal existence. I shall try to be happy in a different way. Work, friends, amusement, and the affection of a woman.

To cheer me up this last night I went to see Josephine Baker[6] sing and dance. She looks very young, wore the most amazing confections of fur and feathers, and seemed utterly alive with a wonderful generous energy.

7 May *London*. I went to see Wilson and my daughter: she was thrilled I'd arrived at last: he the old devil amused himself with appalling talk and his especial brand of slander mixed with drivel and wisdom, but I'm certain that all that conceals a lot of affectionate amiability. Anyhow, I was well entertained.

I had expected to loathe England this time, but it amazes me how much indeed I like these grey-blue streets of London and the idiotic English people, and the green wet lush populated countryside.

19 May I found, and took, a flat at Belsize Park.[7] Not too awful. I rang Pat Jones to come around, bringing with her a bottle of gin and a bottle of rum. We played the gramophone until night came on and peregrinations began. Drank and danced to a wild hot negro orchestra at the Caribbean Club—a crowded floor, boogie-woogie, slim Africans and whores and a rather vicious rabble of spivs, society women and unplaceable characters. Smoking marijuana in the lavatory between dances. It had no effect at all.

June Met Ladipo at Tottenham Court Road Underground Station. He came out of the crowd as I stepped off the escalator, black, grinning, jaunty as ever, brimming over with gladness. 'We have grown old,' he laughed. But he is not much changed, and certainly his way of life hasn't. We straightway dived into the depths of Soho—negro bars, clubs, to the incredible slum flat he lives in. We slept together.

Attilio arrived at last, in a final flurry of confusions, immigration palaver and missed trains. Ladipo is my tower of strength. Attilio and I preserve a sort of armed neutrality of friendship.

I went to see the Redfern Gallery Summer Exhibition.[8] There are three of my drawings, inconspicuously hung—but in a corner one of them is next to a Picasso and below a Pasquin[9], so that is something, and Harry Miller[10], now assistant director of the Redfern, has sold one of the drawings not on show.

3 July Attilio's trouble really is that he's hopelessly bored, without work, and certainly without any sense of gratitude for the little I can do to lighten his boredom. And of course a lot of the time I'm as bored with him as he is with me, sick of his inadequacy as with my own, and sorry for him. Well—he came into my life like his namesake Attila[11], bringing ruin, and leaving a complete loss of civilisation behind, a sort of Dark Age.

For the twentieth time since peace was signed, we are on the verge of another big war: in Korea—Americans, communists—blast them all, swine.[12]

17 July It's been blowing and raining like mad for two days, miserable weather. I've stayed in most of the time, working on drawings. In this week I have completed fourteen drawings, all good. And what is more, despite the fact we've been cooped up with bad weather, lived very happily with Attilio, preserving the illusion of non-attachment and independence on which our possibility of happiness rests, because above all things he dreads my love. And I can't blame him for that: it must remain hidden, and my actions must be cloaked in other motives. Much of the time I am in doubt myself as to what is in my heart, but it needs only half an hour of his absence to dispel any uncertainty on that score.

1–3 August *Lewes*. I am here in this dreary Sussex town alone, depressed and miserable. I decided to come away and leave Attilio to a well-earned holiday from my company. I walked to Glynde[13], getting very wet, trying to walk myself out of this terrible fit of misery, without much success. This countryside I don't like much—all its loveliness is marred by horrible villas and big electric cables, the roads are crowded with cars. I could make no drawings because of the cold driving rain and wind. The only pleasant incident was when I took shelter for a while at Glyndebourne opera house, and heard them rehearsing *Don Giovanni*[14].

Second week of September *London*. It's astonishing how happy life with Attilio *can* be when one lets things slide a bit. One's happiness is almost piercing: it no longer matters that the weather is wet gloomy and cold: work goes ahead: friends seem more delightful than ever, and even his absences inspire neither suspense nor alarm. Jealousy, nearly all of it, just for once in a while, is absent from my heart.

You long streets, you houses full of dullard sleepers, that never know Attilio, know this; that while you sleep and snore he lives, and there is nothing in you that can approximate his beauty. In what little you can know of the orgasm of your greatest ecstasy you cannot attain the power of life of his least glance or gesture. You do not know what life is, because you do not love Attilio.

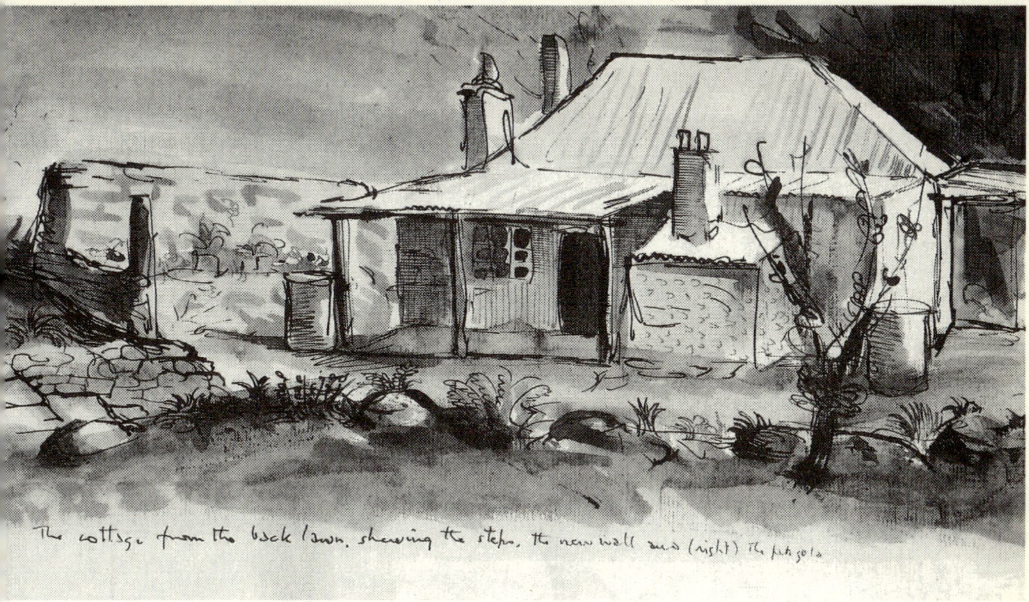

26. 'The cottage [at Hill End] from the back lawn…' (1948).

28 September *Hill End.* Now at last a sort of seething calm, after all those thousands of miles by air. Hill End was small, deeper than ever in its rustic slumber. The cottage seemed terribly small, the rooms unbearably cluttered, an old man's winter quarters, and Murray withdrawn.

Attilio has been playing up. He refuses to work, is amiable and useless and stubborn and is quite plainly planning to leave me as soon as he can. And as ever, I would not be entirely sorry to see him go. I take what I can from the beautiful days, the sun and the garden which is amazingly developed, and the vast bush. Attilio has become a crashing adolescent bore.

November Life has been a series of those crises of happiness and unhappiness, all centred round Attilio, and all tediously alike one to the next. He has been bored at first, and bad-tempered, and I have been quick-tempered and impatient. We started to build the studio. I was careful to break up every day with duck-shooting or rabbit-shooting expeditions, or drives in the car, but he had conceived a hatred and hopelessness of Hill End, yearned for city life, excitements, girls: the little local skirts who dangled their somewhat bulbous rustic charms to tempt him failed to arouse his interest.

So at last there was a grand explosion and I exploded too, worn down and sick to death of his mewling discontent. I packed him off to Sydney, and gave him £10 and told him to go get a job or jump in the bloody harbour.

Some days later I went down myself. Mother had offered me her flat at Kings Cross for the week I would be down for my exhibition at the Macquarie Galleries[15]. The first person I saw on arriving was Attilio. I gave him, perfidiously, a bitter taste of the horrors of city life. He wanted a room of his own first before he got a job. OK. We went room-hunting. Then before him were paraded the sour-faced sallow landladies of the cabbage-smelling brick terraces, demanding appalling rents for ghastly little cells. He saw it all—on foot, tired, wet with the dismal drizzling rain. He saw quite enough to make him regret his rash revolt against our simple country existence, so that hesitantly at first, and in dribs and drabs and hints over a period of three days, he approached me about a return to Hill End.

3 December *Hill End.* I made a couple of drawings in the bush—very satisfactory: the sun is hot brilliant and dry; how different the landscape from Europe, where every stone and tree is humanised, every hill moulded by centuries of tilling, and how hard it is here to show the feeling of these rocks and streams, that in their hostility and indifference seem to refuse obdurately to be an environment for men and their thoughts.

Last half of December I'm rather tired of Attilio at last—the bad manners, the untidiness and dirtiness, the complete lack of comprehension, the boastfulness, adolescent rudeness—no. Nice in bed but—just physical magnificence. Nothing else. He'll make no effort for himself, pesters me and then damns me for whatever I do. This sterile relationship has worn unpleasantly thin.

1951

23 January The painting has gone ahead really well—I have painted most of the hours of daylight, heading off only when my eyes have tired or my brain has numbed and dizzied, and then taken the jeep out to get loads of soil for the garden, or sand and stones for building—but building itself has been neglected. The picture is a life of St John in the form of an ikon, with incidents, presented in squares, but all related to one another by most difficult acrobatics of composition, and I am very pleased with it.

Last week of February *Sydney*. Amazing how lonely one is in a city where one no longer lives: and yet most of the time I am in company of friends. Attilio is always around but I can't quite make him out and am being rather distant. He makes no demands, but his chatter often contains things that cut me to the heart. There is this in his favour, and this to my shame, that he has a loyalty to me in speaking of me and about me that I have not to him. He probably sees me more clearly according to his light than I do him, and in a sort of way is more faithful than I am.

21 March *Hill End*. Attilio coming here. I dread it: Attilio arrives, waves his penis like a magic wand and we're immediately precipitated into a sort of Hill End witches' Sabbath, with the awful local wenches whistling and screaming about, the house in turmoil. However, one should feel some affectionate gladness, even for the fact that he is apparently about to visit all this in Hill End because of a friendship and affection for me that has, however battered and tattered, survived the wreck of our old relationship.

23 March Good Friday. Attilio! He didn't stop talking for hours. I was mostly astonished that there was only the faintest twinge of jealousy and bitterness. I felt I had triumphed: that not only had I ceased to love, but that I felt a nice warmness towards the person who had so strangely and quite deliberately made me squirm and roast and agonise for so long suspended over those fires of his destructive personality.

5 April Murray is an adult accumulation of wasted talent, and his mind has got to be stale and dilettantish with years and indecision. He is a grown man, and is now all that ever he will be. But poor Attilio, cruel, loving, leaning always to a physical destructiveness (as Murray with his soured mind like an ingrown toenail destroys spiritually and intellectually), mercilessly breaks himself on life and people and society. But such comparisons are mean, and meaningless, and betray a paucity of spirit to make them. The plain fact is, both of them are my friends, and both wasters.

8 April Autumn is here, the mellow season, so fresh and ripe and fragrant when everything is coloured in a lively ripe way and the air is keen and bluish with smoke and outdoors is invigorating to the senses, and indoors is more than usually delightful with warmth and comfort, and all the bowls are filled with fruit (my great African sacrificial bowl crowded with squash, persimmons and gourds in lively colours) and jugs and jars cannot hold the flowers bursting with crimson and yellow. Everything is so crisp—the music notes from the gramophone (which has to be heated first by the fire because the oil in the machine is so cold), the cold on my nose and fingers and magpies carolling in the mornings.

Second week of April Newcomers, very 'North Shore', who bought a station, are positively horrified at the primitive goings-on of Hill End. So I, who was born of the land and on the land, who in an early life hated it so and despised it, and escaped, and tasted all the cities and distant parts, and at last was drawn back to earth and common people by a need, cannot help laughing at the spectacle of Sydney suburbanites judging the behaviour of peasantry by the standards upheld at Turramurra[1].

North Shore people don't buy drawings because they want drawings as such, but for the signature, for wedding presents. I long for serious work. I have sent off to Sydney for a large canvas for the Flotta Lauro competition[2], I have already worked out one or two ideas. In the last four days I have completed three drawings and worked on four others. They are fine enough, and good drawings, but lack that 'torture' and longing and especialness that is needed, the essential ingredient of my sort of intimism.

I have lost direction, being out of love, out of friends, and in a state of indifference to the things I suffered and fought for. I await some thought, some invention, to get on with what I have to do.

19 July This evening began a fall of heavy snow, delicious and exciting, changing the landscape into an unlikely gleaming dream. By 10 o'clock the garden was a wonderful fantasy. Attilio and I went out into the curious white night to cut extra firewood to keep up a blaze all night. The garage—ridiculous observation—looked especially fine in a snow scene.

O how moving such a change of colour is, and how utterly lovely everything looks! I have promised myself to go out tomorrow and make snow drawings. So we sat up late by the fire, talking and playing Beethoven piano concertos on the gramophone, and when at last we went to bed it was with a sensation of excitement and expectancy.

15 August I have been somewhat upheld by this idea of freedom from those dominating friends who have relied so much on my presence, person and money, for any number of good and bad motives, and because of course I needed them so urgently. Attilio really has been the best of them all, everything considered: his behaviour and very thoughts demonstrated an integrity lacking in all the others of higher intelligence. His mercy was deeper, his gratitude genuine, and his criticism of my obsessions, on which he based all these, sane and justified. However, his departure seems, for the time being, to be a relief. It seemed lovely to be alone again, and master of oneself.

I started on the big new picture. The painting harks back, after all this time and so many experiments, to the original plan that I began to paint in Florence—the same theme, but with a greatly changed and developed expression of it. Pleasures, youth, pain and death. The group of a skeleton, a boy and a girl: the fountain of Youth, the house containing so many rooms and compartments with people doing various things.

3 September *Sydney*. I won the prize, to the envy, fury and applause of many. So much has been crowded into a few days.

Third week of October *Hill End*. The great Jubilee Week.[3] The garden at its best, with iris, tulips and the may and lilac in flower, and clumps of daisies and sparaxis and grape hyacinths, sweet peas climbing everywhere, and pinks and carnations, anemones and poppies and stocks, and the cloudy-mauve mint bush out in its first glory, and crabapple at its freshest best. In the house I've painted the floors red, and re-whited the walls with calsomine and rearranged the rooms to accommodate the guests, and bought a dozen of claret and burgundy and some good hock, and gin and various supply of groceries, and gone out twice in the Land Rover with an axe, and laid in a good stock of firewood. In all these days I've made only one drawing.

The great climax. We set off to Hawkins Hill for the re-enactment of the discovery of the Beyers-Holtermann nugget.[4] Half of the townsfolk were in costume of the gold-rush days. There was a grand procession through the town with a stagecoach, an ancient automobile, and a float with the Three Beauty Queens crowned and clad in swathes of white stuff.

We lay down afterwards exhausted on the grass in a sunny spot and drank beer and watched the people and the merry-go-rounds. There was a crowd of about 2,000.

8 November The painting has been going on at a great rate, every day, commencing at 8.30 in the morning. The canvas is now covered with hundreds of little bright-coloured active figures busy about innumerable activities, including a rape, a breakfast party, a wrestling match, a wedding, a big game hunt, a bath, a bunch of flowers fresh from the garden, a view of Florence, some centaurs hunting a butterfly, virgins taming a unicorn, Pan amorously instructing a youth in playing of a reed pipe, a gay Bacchanal with four leopards, Silenus[5] drunk on a donkey supported by revellers, and Bacchus in a chariot, all very pretty and lively and full of colour. In a gloomy cave St Anthony[6] sits in full view of these goings-on, more exasperated than tempted, trying to concentrate on the reading of his huge pious book. The whole composition is dominated by the large glowing figures of Death, Youth and a maiden[7].

9–10 December *Possum Point.*[8] Pat Jones's family homestead is a rambling white building sprawling on a hillside that slopes steeply to the river, framed in willows, and alive with trout and very cold even at this time of year, when the sun is a furnace. Inside, the house is richly sumptuous and over-furnished and very comfortable. Most of the two days has been spent in proposing marriage to Pat, and she refusing. Very sensibly I suppose, but a blow to me. In some way it seems my last chance, because I doubt I'll meet again a woman I like as much, and so be condemned to my old sort of stupid life, so aimless and frustrating, with so little hope of love.

Meanwhile, I'm determined to enjoy myself, which is easy to manage in these surroundings. So many things give pleasure. Fresh trout from the stream, and strange flocks of ibis which graze in groups in the paddocks, among the Hereford cattle, and the intense dry prevailing heat, the pale skies hinting of those bushfires which are devastating hundreds of miles of country, far away to the northwest.

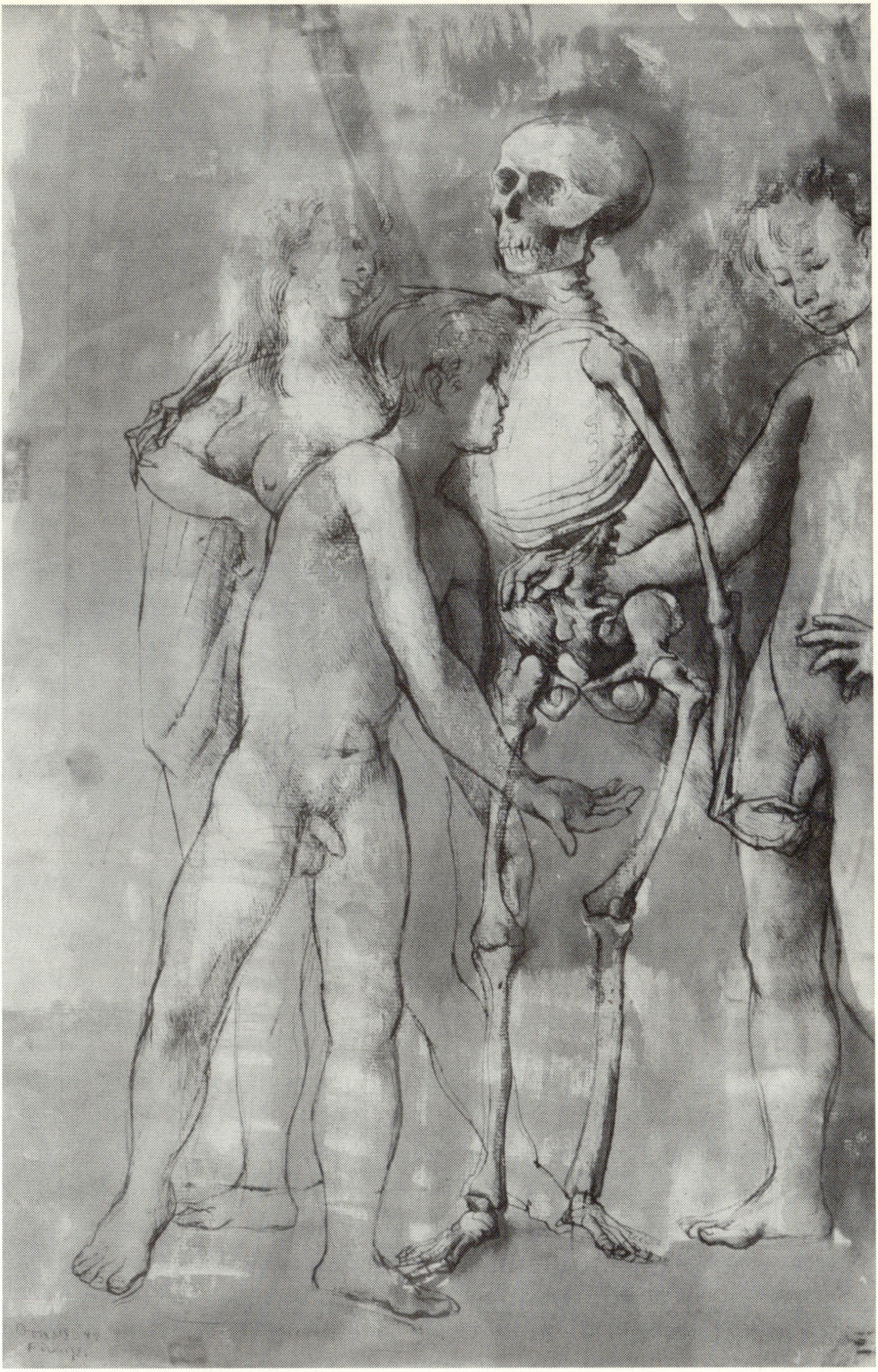

27. *'Youth, Death and the Maiden'* (1949).

26 December *Hill End.* It struck me, sitting here alone and dining off the magnificent cold roast Christmas goose, that in literature this would be termed as a crisis in my life—the end of years connected with my love of Attilio and events that led up to it, and its disillusion, diminution, metamorphosis. But I find that in life itself there are no real crises at all—dramatic events, perhaps, but each event connected and bound up with, and containing seeds of, another dozen other events that even at the moment of the so-called crisis are beckoning all of the actors who participate (as well as a great many others busying themselves offstage) to new scenes and further dramas suggested by the one of the moment.

1952

Mid-January *MV Roma.* The vessel is rather subdued and quiet, and the First Class passengers as yet rather warily wander from one highly decorated lounge to the next. It is all rather like an expensive hotel. The days are consumed in almost inconceivable inactivity. The passengers are mostly old and dull. There is a small smart set who conscientiously try to radiate a cosmopolitan glamour by sitting at the bar in evening clothes, but alas! Their impersonation of international café society is lamentably provincial, producing echoes of Albury and Toorak[1] rather than Paris and New York.

February *Ischia.* Seems to me more beautiful than it was before, probably because I have no Attilio, and so can spend the excitement of my eye on the countryside. Spring is on the way. It is a joy to sit in the pale clear sunlight and gaze at the strange and dreamlike landscape and extraordinary houses, and extraordinary colour of everything.

1 March Something important happened. I was drawing in a vineyard in the hills above Ischia Porto, when two lads saw me, and offered to take me to a part by an old ruined cemetery where there is a fine view of the castle. One of them, Rosario, seemed to take greatly to me.

In the course of the morning I learned what is the usual Ischian autobiography—18 years old, the eldest of his family, father crippled, all out of work, nothing to eat and so on. Now he has adopted me completely, and has, as it were, become a member of the staff, and as we planned it, will come with me always in my travels in Italy.

9–10 March *Assisi.* Two heavenly, terribly expensive days staying in the little hotel over from the St Francis Church. The Giottos[2], when in the morning the sun streamed in the open church doors, were like jewels. I made five drawings and walked endlessly, climbed mountains to see castles, and was very happy with little Rosario.

11–14 March *Florence.* I *am* happy with Rosario, and enchanted with him. His face expresses the whole person—half-innocent, yet savage, a little cunning, and not very intelligent, but extremely affectionate. And young enough to be bossed about a bit. On the whole obedient. And certainly perfect to draw.

20 March to mid-April *Venice.* The place absolutely astonishes me. I had never conceived it possible that there could be gathered together enough men of taste to build such a city. It is a dream, a miracle. I went to the Accademia[3] to see the paintings. The Bellinis[4], Veroneses[5] and Tintorettos[6] leave me quite cold—vulgar overdramatised stuff. But the primitives, the Byzantines and the two glorious Giorgiones[7] and a lovely della Francesca were beyond all belief beautiful.

To Peggy Guggenheim's palace[8], small and beautiful, accompanied by her secretary, a very pale and listless young man with cross-eyes. We went to see her collection—a notable one and well worth seeing if only for the Braque[9] and the Picassos[10].

I find Rosario totally without values except those of Ischia, which by now I've had far more than my share. So I'm not as content as I should be. But he's *very* good at *one* thing, and that is important.

15 April *Athens.* On the whole, I think I dislike it. Mainly because it suggests nothing to paint at all. I've no desire or intention of working here. But the wonders and marvels are fabulous—the Parthenon and the museums. Several of the ikons in the Museum of Byzantine Art touched me in a way that is becoming rarer with the years. But my impressions are confused of Athens itself. It's a bit like Melbourne really—the style of the streets…a Melbourne plus history and minus sanitation.

The Greeks themselves I like. They are very kind and helpful, and so far have not lived up to the dreadful reputation they give themselves for roguing and thieving. The wine, spiced with resin, is very strange. It is pleasant to accommodate oneself to their custom of strolling the streets and dusty gardens eating salted melon seeds and cardamoms, or the sweetmeats made of sesame and honey.

May *Florence*. This is really what I want, to be back again in the studio, with Aberdeen, laughing and changing his mind all day. Rosario is useful, and cooks, markets and keeps the place clean and never stops singing in his terrible ass's bray of a voice those Neapolitan songs that most I detest, but the poor silly boy is happy here.

I have been reading Bernard Berenson's *Italian Painters of the Renaissance*[11]—much of theory and the enjoyment of the spectator, nothing of the artists' purposes. I went to the Uffizi[12] this morning to confront the originals with Berenson's ideas. To round the work off it needs another twelve volumes, two devoted to means and techniques to attain ends, two on the ends the artists had in view, and the rest on the motives which gave rise to those attempts. Cock, cunt and spaghetti I think would cover the field. A bit elemental, but after all spaghetti can be shown to contain religion (Church patronage = money = spaghetti) and the cock and cunt contain social pressure, and provide the painter with the only means of comprehending his fellow beings from within. None, after all, were abstainers, and none were Saints.

I have begun two vastly different projects—a decorative and nonsensical oil painting in the Byzantine manner on a gilded wood panel, and a series of slightly Michelangeloesque cartoons for a deposition from the Cross[13]—all muscles and nudes, and damnably difficult.

13 June *San Gimignano*. A perfect, exquisite, hot day. The countryside was a dream, the sun-drenched fields and hills garlanded with vines hanging between lines of fruit trees, all summer in the richness of their green leaves, and in between the rows of fruit and olives narrow long fields of grain, corn and wheat, the latter all straw-yellow, some already cut and laid in lines of sheaves forming a pattern, some in small stooks waiting to be carted away—the lovely colour of everything! Peasants waking, cutting wheat and spraying vines, misting them over with a spray of turquoise and other groups resting in the shade, with bread and wine, their clothes all colours beautifully faded against the dull pale yellow of wheat fields.

The strange castled town on its hill delighted us. We spent our strength in the hot sun in its streets, climbed down a valley to draw it towering on its hill above us, drew it again from the white dust of a country road, returned to it again madly thirsty to drink cool water from the pump, and to sit and drink coffee and eat piles of ice-cream. That ice-cream is our passion and reward for labour on these expeditions.

Last half of June *Florence*. The urge always to present my thoughts of this place and its associations in drawings is fading. I know that one of the Ischian drawings is better than the tame and proficient Tuscan scenes I have been recently producing, that lack the element of savagery. In the loveliness of Tuscany one finds the dramas of battered antiquity, romantic towers and walls, quaint timeworn statuary and vineclad hills, olives and terraced gardens, all charm and beauty—but not that wilderness, that piling of fierce odd-shaped rocks of Ischia.

18 July At the Etruscan Museum.[14] The exhibition impressed me more deeply than any sculpture show, ancient or modern, I have seen in my life. Sculpture (with some exceptions) does not usually move me—even work by the greatest masters, whilst exciting admiration, does not touch the profound emotions or give me such delight as I have found in paintings nearly every day of my life. But *this* show, from the extraordinary funerary urns cupped with primitive heads and placed in pottery armchairs, to the terracotta heads, the bas-relief marbles, the sublime bronze statuettes, all instinct with amazing vigour and life, all so delightfully defining the terms of their medium in the pure language of art—this show is a revelation.

August *London*. As Rome must have done at the beginning of the Dark Ages, London seems to have settled down cosily among her extensive ruins. In the city around St Paul's[15] gardens grow in the waste of bomb craters and blasted tottering walls. But that great remainder of the city seems cleaner than before, and everyone who can afford it paints their houses for next year's Coronation.

Am at work full-steam. Three large very strange pictures, an absolute break away from the conventional stuff I've been doing in Italy, much more modern, and rather dashingly executed, and in subject utterly fantastic. If they're not original, they're like nothing in contemporary French or English art. I cannot describe them: the *order* of the fantasy is something in the spirit of Chagall[16], but of course owe nothing to Chagall's work. Confidentially, they owe a lot to Catalan Romanesque.[17]

27–29 September *Barcelona.* Seeing the world in an idiotic hurry, à l'American. Yet the little of Barcelona I saw excited me—the taverns with spitted chickens roasting in the street outside, the wide *avenidas* and the gaiety of the people, the prevalence of crippled. I went to mass at the cathedral and after to see the famous and fantastic church of the Sagrada Familia.[18] I know that I'm most likely wrong, and that it is probably appalling, in bad taste, ridiculous etc., etc.—but for me it seemed the only modern church I have ever seen which displays, in its crazy towers and idiotic facade, a great and genuine architecture. I regard it as the work of genius.

I prefer it above all the antiseptic chapels of the French and German schools: this, it seems to me, is a real church, an original church, meant, though uncompleted, to express belief, to worship in, and fashioned in a manner that like the work of earlier church builders, gave voice to the peculiar thoughts of its architect and builders. To me it is most wonderful, striking moving and beautiful, and gives me the same sort of delight I receive from 13th and 14th-century architecture.

Then to the bullfight. Despite my expectations, I was neither horrified nor revolted. It was beautiful, a thing of virile grace and exquisite colour, and skilful—more skilful (because of the peril) than a dancer, and frantically exciting. We saw six bulls killed.

1–2 October *Madrid.* Expensive, glittering and dull. We did see the hermitage of Santa Maria de Florida[19], with frescoes by Goya, painted with crazy verve—great swathes of paint broomed on—the colour very subdued and subtle, and what was a miracle, it was in the rococo manner—cherubs and angels and so on, but its tremendous virility soared infinitely beyond the limits of the style of that epoch. Apart from that, we had begun to regret Barcelona and the gay Catalans. In contrast, these *madrileños* seemed drearily bourgeois.

Ah—but the Prado.[20] One reeled away from the place, positively battered by the impact of those tremendous, magnificent, ill-preserved, horribly lit masterpieces. El Grecos that flamed through black and brown treacle of bad varnish, Goyas that by the miracle of their mastery only managed to overcome the ill-treatment they had received. Velázquez[21] at his superb greatest, and the realisation of a dream that has waited since my student days to be realised—to see the Bosch *Garden of Earthly Delights*[22] that was finer even than merited the long expectation.

12 October *London*. A cold grey Sunday: I found myself by a pub frequented almost exclusively by Africans. I found myself looking at a faintly familiar black face, with four tribal cicatrices on each cheek. The face grinned, came over and greeted me. Then I remembered. Omu. He had lived in Ladipo's home when last I was in London.

Omu and I were friends in an instant, had lunch, went to a Turkish bath. The boy was wide-eyed at the peculiar Gothic Revival underground steamy palace, and the sight, when we entered the first hot room, of innumerable strawberry-pink fat old men sitting around reading newspapers.

13 October Now he is my model. The model I have longed for, the superb, exquisite lithe figure, black as ebony. Omu has that character which young negroes in Europe possess to a great degree, and which I love, the character of the picaresque: their whole lives are of necessity picaresque in those streets and cities, in the sort of contacts they make here, and their negro nature, which allows them to respond with complete freedom to all circumstances and adventures.

Last week of October The Redfern Gallery started hanging my drawings, taking down Sid Nolan's, which had done very badly.[23] They were trivial works: one is surprised at a painter of such power (though his standard has always been very uneven) manufacturing such a spate of slight and meaningless little pictures.

2 November I want some intelligent people to see that I can see and express beautifully a unique and beautiful aspect of life, a most varied, lovely aspect of life, in a way they never saw it before, in a way which is well worth their seeing from yet another viewpoint.

That I want to be the essence of my art: but I am not content till others possess it also by proxy, as they do for instance, when seeing a young girl in the opal iridescence of her beauty, they can cry 'as lovely as a Renoir!'[24] or of a landscape 'Cezanne would have loved it' or of a feast 'Bring more bottles, and louder music, and Breughel[25] will join us.'

14 November Omu has fallen in love with me in a way I do not understand myself: certainly not sexually, for though he plays for hours, laughing and talking and doing everything he can invent to please me, the intense pleasure that he openly and happily takes in this dalliance is unpretendingly a pleasure in *my* pleasure. 'I make you happy, I *must* make you very happy all the time,' he croons, caressing and laughing.

And rolling with negro laughter, put his arm around my neck: 'You are my darling. You are my life and my bread.'

One loses oneself in the childish sweet affection and senseless good humour of this African banter. This is what it is to be loved: after a while one feels chained up with it night and day, succumbing helplessly because it would be too much effort to deny oneself the pleasant dalliance, and give hurt by ceasing to indulge it.

29 November I went to Burlington House[26] to see the exhibition of Dutch Painting, which confirmed in me all that dislike that had been built up for years—boorish carpingly exact pictures of boorish and exact virtues and vices—sleaziness and dirtiness and domesticity—turd-coloured boors in shit-coloured surroundings; drabs keeping pots, peasants pissing: flashy cavaliers flashily painted (by Hals[27]) exuding a false *bonhomie* as a prelude to cardsharping and sordid quarrels, dull women whose stubby hands, kitchen-scarred, are depicted honestly in contrast with their Sunday black churchgoing dress, nasty companies of stuffy burghers posed to catch the 'camera's eyes' each more consciously good citizen than the next: loathsome merchants puffed up with egoism and secure certainty of their own worth, horrid brown landscapes, horrid fat flowers, and horrid over-ripe piles of grapes and lobsters: coarse jests and brutal humours, virtue made unattractive, vice fit only for the vomitorium. Tasteless, inelegant, unwitty art, painted out of the souls and hearts of artists who expressed to perfection their lack of wit, elegance and taste—in so much, they were brilliantly successful.

One great genius only, who, without pretence or artifice presented the whole range of that sordid company in terms so superb, so profound that dullness, dreariness, brownness, turdiness, dirtiness, slovenliness and earthy fleshy baker's-dozen-for-your-money-ness became hallowed in the great depths and heights of the spirit that expressed them.

Rembrandt. All vulgarities are drowned in the profundities of his genius.

1953

1 January Poor Omu. You cannot conceive the starkness of his room. The comparative richness of my life seems to him in contrast a paradise of soft lights, a good fire, easy chairs, silver and china gleaming, food and wine and plenty, and the soothing sound of my voice bleating how hard-up I am. Myriad little common luxuries I take as simple necessity. Yet I have nagged and bored and blamed him because his escape is the limited one he knows, the only one his circumstances, race and education leave open—pubs, drugs and dance halls.

3 January At times one becomes conscious that one has four or five different lives running concurrently. One may be walking in the street, vastly concerned to work out a plan to find somewhere new to live that will be a solution to the opposing themes of friendship, love and career: one is miserable, and conscious of it, when in a flash it is revealed that at the same moment one is almost deliciously happy to note the poses and movements of a group of children playing, and beyond them a facade of Georgian houses interrupted by peculiar patterns of the bare boughs of winter trees. In this same moment one's mind is also going back in time over incidents of the week, remembering conversations, delving into one's bank balance, playing with technical considerations of ink and chalk and a tonal composition to express in a drawing the scene in front of one's eyes, and also running ahead to visits and interviews within the next few hours.

7–8 January Ken Rowell[1] and I have joined forces to find a place for both of us. I have almost despaired during these days: the *dismalness* of people's lives! The stale stink of the houses—the respectable houses—and my surprise in discovering how the English live, or those who live in rooms are expected to live—no cooking facilities, harsh puritanical rules and regulations: those tyrannical burlesque effigies, landladies, towering over all.

14 January Walked round to the Tate Gallery[2] to see an exhibition of Matisse[3]. There were a lot of drawings on show, in themselves of no great worth, but their interest lay mostly in that they were studies for three oil paintings shown, and revealed his method of working, which is almost painstaking: then also, with each of the paintings a whole series of good large photographs showed different stages in the work, and how tremendous alterations were made, a thing one would never guess from the finished canvas, that looked so fresh and free as though it were the result of a couple of hours' inspired work.

4 February Ken has been very busy since John Piper[4] came the other morning, bringing with him the libretto (written by William Plomer[5]) for Benjamin Britten's opera *Gloriana*[6]. There are 400 costumes to design. Piper is a person one likes immediately—a quiet personality, and one recognises immediately an artist who *works*—in contrast to that myriad crew of vaguely celebrated painters who spend most of their time discussing pretentious theories and indulging in intellectual postures.

24 February I feel a surging of ambition again. I haven't produced much to be proud of. More than half my life spent on vanity and amiability. Recently I have devoted more time and ingenuity to, and desired a better sense of success from, cooking. Not that I haven't devoted a few hours each day to painting and drawing, but that the sense of vocation has been lacking, and the feeling of powerfulness that I have in my best days, when my heart beats like mad when I put down a line, and I feel like laughing and singing, and must straightaway show it to someone and boast about it, and during the drawing as it nears completion I am torn with each pen stroke between a sort of dashingness, a wild courage, and a great fear that my hand will fail me and mar the whole thing, until the last line is put in quite frantically and one lays the pen down with enormous relief as a great danger averted.

24 April A very ugly scene with Omu. It began when I told him I was not going to finance his next jaunt. He burst into an appalling rage. He became really frightening, his face thickened and uglied with rage, his eyes seemed to change in colour to a weird reddish brown. He's as dangerous as a panther under all that simplicity. The worst of it is, I ended up laughing as I always do. These situations are superficially so terribly comical. But basically there is nothing very comic about it—it is simply that of the appalling and sad situation of a savage little tribesman in London, and of an artist whose hard work and little genius is set to grind out enough money for the little savage to waste and throw to the winds.

1 May The party took place in a barge moored to the Embankment in Chelsea rented by an Australian girl, who had huge bushes of hair and was dressed, like most of the girls there (they seemed all to be Australians), in very tight trousers. I found myself, to my surprise, to be somewhat a lion. A number of young chaps respectfully clustered round plying me with drinks and gathered up the wisdom from my lips—which gave me a slightly uneasy feeling of being ridiculous. But I scored with John Betjeman, the poet. He leaned at the door being very quizzical and sardonic and not rude but funny about Australians. 'Australians,' he repeated, '*all* Australians. How very odd.' 'Nevertheless,' I told him, 'we are your English Great-Grandfathers.' 'How so?'—'Well, just think of our names—Scott, Johns, Lymburner, Smith, Friend: they were English for over a thousand years, and are Australian for a hundred and fifty. But Betjeman, *Betjeman*? I *ask* you, it isn't even anglicised yet.'[7]

18 May Since the trees have been in leaf, I've been struggling to find means of disciplining the greenness of woods and parks into coloured drawings. Green was never my colour before, but now I feel I am getting somewhere with it. The drawings are almost abstract—large shapes of various greens. I have dealt with the foliage in large veils and swathes, and have learned much from Raoul Dufy's[8] work in the process.

Painting abstract was something of an occupational disease of students, and like cubism provided a most necessary discipline. But I found it too rigid a medium to express what I wanted. There is something narrowly Methodist about it, except in the hands of a great painter, which I need hardly say, I am not. Yet it needs courage to give up depicting unrecognisable objects. I have no pretensions to be modern, especially since it is apparent that one must toe the line to American taste. To conform to the sterility of the American Way of Painting is too much to expect of anyone with a serious interest in art.

2 June The Coronation. A description of events would be quite beyond me—I have not enough scarlet and gold in my vocabulary: suffice it to say, I saw everything very well and made a number of adequate drawings. It was cold and rained a lot. A glimpse of Queen Salote of Tonga[9], vast and vital in her open carriage driving through grey mist of London drizzle. Almost stole the show—wonderful woman. The crowds adored her. The great gold state coach was a fabulous sight.

6 June I went to the dress rehearsal of Britten's *Gloriana* at Covent Garden. The designs, both for scenery and costumes, suffered from an extraordinary lack of historical sense. Strange that, in a man such as Piper who knows a great deal of history and architecture. Also, what is admired as bold and brilliant colour I found to be splashy and tawdry. Odd that I am usually somewhat uncertain about the works of painters—contemporary ones (I can never be sure that they're as third-rate as I think them)—when with the music it is easier to judge in my ignorance. Britten is lauded up as a Great Musician. That well may be, of some of his work. As to *Gloriana*—as much bonging and honking and squawking, so many surprise tings and plonks—I know that Mozart is infinitely, infinitely greater. One may as well stick to such absolute standards in an art of which one is largely ignorant.

30 June Rowlandson[10] and Gillray[11] at the Whitechapel Art Gallery: the former's brilliance displayed in the most complete exhibition of his work I have seen, and here I was equally delighted with the painting as with the subject—those gross, riotous, greedy, quarrelsome, drunken, bawdy, active, merry, lewd, proud, elegant, vicious, amorous, whorish English. As a matter of fact, the traces of those Rowlandson Englishmen and women seem to exist now only in a small area around Whitechapel and Aldgate. I wearied myself tramping the slum streets where the slatterns slumped at their doorsteps, and the streets were rowdy with traffic and children, ragamuffins.

26 July I went to see the exhibition *12 Australian Artists* put on by the Arts Council at New Burlington Galleries[12], and was bitterly disappointed at the three unimportant and mediocre works representing my painting, but thrilled at the startling and strange Sid Nolans. He stole the whole show, and made even Tas's pictures look tame.

16 August I went with Clarice Zander[13] to a house in Chiswick Mall[14]. We had brought a picnic basket and painting materials, and the whole day sat at the edge of the garden where the wall drops straight to the Thames, and chatted and painted. We talked amongst other things of Margaret Olley. My idea is that she is the one person to whom I would be happily married. She is both sensible and sensitive and tender, stubborn and intelligent, proud, simple and complicated. She is not a wasting frippery woman, she works and enjoys, she is gay and serious and independent.

Lord knows if she'd accept me. I know I would be happy with Olley, but it is hard to say how anyone could be happy with me. Can I leave off the private actions and dreams that have been the spring of my life and the fount from which has flowed all my inspiration and understanding? I think I must because that fountain threatens to dry up a bit. The golden youths are not so apt to spirit there, or find their sport spoilt by the leering presence of an ageing satyr. Our Donald is a faun no longer, and must look for a less disreputable, profounder and more lasting haven.

21–23 August *Genoa.* Arrived in the balmy steamy heat. The Italians amuse, over-stimulate and irritate me, and charm me with their humanity and humour in everyday small transactions, and infuriate me by the way they cheat in them. Their crude lusts, gentleness and savagery enchant me, and their terrible corruption moves me more to compassion than disgust, and also to a sort of sulk, wishing that I too were simple enough to be wholeheartedly frank and feckless in my corruption. Such thoughts and regrets as these must be common enough to all confessions of sentimental pederasts.

First half of September *SS Surriento.* The ship took on hundreds of migrants. The lower decks are crowded with a vivacious rabble, who all day cram together, singing, hanging out their washing on the rigging, playing cards, playing mouth organs, the noisy, amusing sperm of a nation:

when I am an old man, these will have changed the face and the fate of my country. As a contrast, the First Class is practically empty—perhaps there are twenty passengers there. We have carried with us the environment of a respectable dreary tearoom: they have brought along the slums of Naples and Athens. The rigging is festooned with strings of washing that seems sordid, obscene and indecent. The children laugh and howl, the adults laugh and howl, all spit, vomit, sing or weep, wherever they happen to be standing, without thought of reticence.

I feel I belong as little where I am as I would down there.

17 September *Colombo*. The steward woke me to say a friend was awaiting me in the saloon. Drove out to Bevis Bawa's[15] estate—Brief, a rubber plantation. The house and garden were like a dream. I can't imagine anything more lovely. The house full of tall rooms, open to the garden, exquisitely furnished, an air of tropical aristocracy, of time and comfort. 'You must come back,' he said, 'come and stay for as long as you like.' There is nothing I'd like to do more.

25 September We have been battered by a great storm since leaving Fremantle. I sat up late drinking whisky with the ship's doctor. Another officer joined us. I was talking of Malaparte's book *La Pelle*.[16]

'Oh, Malaparte,' said the newcomer, 'he stinks. He is an opportunist, a professional martyr and a liar, and a pederast.'

I said, 'That is no criticism of his book. As for being a liar, what are you to expect of an artist?—statistics? Was Dante lying when he described his conversations in hell?[17] You cannot call anything lies which does not deal with scientific truth, or you would have to call all art lies. You would say of Picasso, he paints lies, when he is painting the same lies that Michelangelo did. You do not even try to see beyond the unsatisfactory skin of visible facts. If I told you that time as a dimension had a spiral shape, you would say I was telling lies unless I could lead you by the hand through a dizzy corkscrew tunnel of nights and days.'

3 October *Sydney*. When at last I got through the customs, staggering through the crush of people jammed against the gates of the wharf waiting to see their relatives, carrying on my shoulders the heaviest piece of my baggage because there were no porters—suddenly the suitcase was whisked off my shoulders in the crowd, and there was Attilio. O my dear boy, the core of all my dread, my love, my fear for him!

15 October *Hill End.* The country is looking superb, and the town has everything of that mad quaint character that always delighted me. A pleasant rough and matey sort of code of personal relationships. Something simple, a little stupid, very tolerant of individual eccentricity in people who have been accepted into the community.

Last week of December A quiet Christmas. I'm hard at work on a 'Nativity'. It pleases and surprises me how well it is going, and how closely so far it follows my intentions. I have worked constantly on it, with great energy and pleasure, and have come again on my old feeling for oil pigment.

Good steady soaking rain has saved the garden from ruin, and I have been out in it cultivating the soil, weeding and pruning and pulling out dead plants. Attilio was out most of the time hunting. So we feasted luxuriously on wild black duck, delicious roasted with onions potatoes and apples.

1954

29 January The Queen's imminent visit[1] is extracting the last ounce of social energy from our good citizens, who are wracking their muscles with rehearsed curtseys and ruining husbands by the purchase of tiaras of pearls and diamonds. Sydney is overrun with jealousies and rivalries as to who will be presented. But the main fury of frustrated snobs is directed against those successful ones, the politicians and their wives, who have successfully organised things so far in such a way that the Queen will face for the whole of her visit nothing but solid walls of speechmaking MPs, Premiers, Mayors and councillors. Poor Wretch.

I had an offer from Angus and Robertson to illustrate *Coast to Coast.*[2] The stories are of quite a good standard but they also, as a collection, bring to light a curious fact: not one of them deals with un-sordid subject matter. It is *all* slums, station blacks, wharf workers, dreary cocky farmers. One feels they would be indignant and ashamed, these earnest writers, to mention a ballroom, a satin dress, or a diamond-spangled duchess or any of the other necessaries of stories written last century. They are social cowards, really: one only has to consider Balzac and the ruthlessness with which he mixed good and evil in all his characters from criminals to princes. These modern writers lack realism (though they pretend to be realists) probably because they have little actual contact with the class they write about. Their picture of the outback has become such a cliché, a travestied pastorale that calls to mind the simplicity-loving ladies of Versailles who would totter down to the Hermitage[3] in satin 'shepherdess' costumes to delicately toy with a goat's teat whilst their aristocratic swains played Couperin[4] on the lute.

10 March A great assortment of divertissements. Best of all the book which is wittiest, strangest, deepest, widest and oddest—Sudhindra Ghose's *Vermilion Boat.*[5] Now *there's* a style, and an invention that the modern novel has waited long for—since the *Satyricon* and the *Golden Ass*[6]—a style which can enfold past and present, dream, fancy, fact, satire, folklore, all easily lying together without boundaries.

22 April Oh how I want to escape the wet and the cold, and see that warm friendly North! Already the first robin redbreast has arrived, brisk, friendly, full of a dashing bravura and the self-importance of his tiny magnificence: the honeyeaters that delighted us with a show of elegant nimbleness when they poised in the air with fluttering wings and dipped their needle beaks into the flowers have gone. Only remain from spring and summer innumerable loud-voiced, lecherous and vulgar sparrows, forever shouting and quarrelling in the honeysuckle vine outside my window.

Second and third weeks of June *Brisbane.* David Strachan came up with me. Staying at Olley's. We made several sketching expeditions. To Coochin Coochin[7], a delightful rambling old homestead set in pleasant gardens. To Carmila[8], a spot chosen by Olley in jungle by a stream that I swore was full of crocodiles. A wildly beautiful place of riotous foliage.

Northward again, to Proserpine[9] over a weirdly dreamy plain edged with hazy mountains lost in huge smoky formations of cloud through which burst straight beams of sunlight that contrasted with scudding squalls of rain. At last a truly northern town, set in amongst cane fields and purple mountains: to the stilt-legged fantasy of Queensland architecture is added another odd feature—nearly every house has its own windmill. Above the village they whirl wildly in the wind.

Last week of June *Arcadia, Magnetic Island.* We've taken a little house. A quiet tropic spot where there are not many people, whiling away their time doing very little. The beaches all edged with a riot of trees—palms, mangoes, pines, frangipani and bougainvillea, flamboyance all wildly mingled: behind them rise steep little capes of jungle boulders forested with pine and gum.

I feel restless: bored. That feeling that inevitably prevails on sparsely populated islands—it comes from physical wellbeing conflicting with a narrow environment. There is little in which to expand one's excess energy. And one *belongs* less on an island—one is excluded from the tiny close society of the place, one has no use or place in its life. It is never enough to simply be in a place, admire its many beauties, paint them, and then go home, eat and sleep. Some more intimate contact is needed with the natives, to convey the meaning of the hills and trees, to give those hints of life and usage that insight translates into a sort of inference of usage and living and familiarity. Without that knowledge which one can get only from the inhabitants, one's paintings of the place remain lifeless representations instead of the desired vibrant interpretations.

Last week of August *Port Douglas.*[10] The locals seem to spend a large part of the day talking and drinking, clad in singlets and shorts and sandshoes. In amongst the few shops and houses there grows a luxuriant variety of palms and mangoes and flowering trees and curious pines, tangles of vines and flowering creepers. The buildings, as happens everywhere in the North, seem to have been built in a spirit of laziness and complete indifference to comfort or convenience, and the people who inhabit them are quite evidently devoid of any aesthetic sensibilities whatsoever: the exuberance of nature and the accidental effects produced by decay provide the picturesqueness of their environs: their own conscious contributions to a pleasant life are abominable cooking, slovenliness, lust and senseless excesses of drink and physical violence. And yet there is a distinct fascination about the mildewed damp fungus rotted appearance both of the place and the people, who within the strict limits allowed by their sloth and unintelligence are friendly and extremely obliging.

But how badly they compare with my coloured people in Cairns! They lack utterly the wit, the gusto for enjoyment, the sharp and humane humour, the charming observation and the deep compassion of kindness.

2 September We drove up to the Daintree[11], beautiful in a very sinister way: rolling hills of coarse grass, rotting farmsteads set in clumps of mango and palm against a background of purple hills covered with heavy rainforest that reared their heads to masses of steaming clouds. The road ran by and frequently crossed deep creeks of dark, dark water—wild rushes and lilies grew by the banks, and patches of taro spread their broad leaves to the water's edge where the banks were not overhung by tangles of trees bending and stooping over, dragging their broad leaves in the shadowy stream. The place is lousy with crocodiles.

4 September *Pine Creek.* Olley and I climbed up to my favourite spot, the pool, and swam, and hunted for orchids. Olley was enchanted with the wild ravine, where the huge boulders are crowned, as though by over-ornamented hats of the nineties, by tiaras of strange ferns and exotics, and by trees and palms. I felt glad and proud, after all I had said about the place and its people, that it had been such a perfect day, and everything had lived up to and beyond my descriptions of it. How extraordinarily fine and sweet and pleasing and full of character these people are, what fullness and depth they have in their lives, full of gusto and tenderness and reality. Why I did not come back here long ago I cannot think. This atmosphere and these people, this whole environment is the only one I know that could have cured me of all the ills of heart and soul that so destroyed me during my first trip to Italy and my subsequent return to Australia. Perhaps the peculiar curative and strengthening effect of the life here emanates in part from a sense of continuity such as I do not find in my family down South. There, sure enough, they continue, but in barrenness and folly. With the Sailor family, on the contrary, faults and virtues all have their proper value and are applied to living. There are no trifles in their lives at all. Their motives and actions seem to be conditioned (as great art is) by the simplest essential truths, which by their vast unornamented weight give a classical dignity to what they do in daily life. Their mirth and grief belong to the Greek drama.

7 September The forms of mountains and of forests and fields are comprised of decorative patterns of a curious regularity, the strange designs of large leaves are big enough to register in the general scene, as though in a tapestry or a carpet. These effects I try to translate into terms of art in my pictures, with results at times (it seems it can't be avoided) reminiscent of Gauguin and of Raoul Dufy.

As time goes on I miss books more and more. I don't suppose there are five well-read people in Cairns. Fiction is supplied to the inhabitants in the form of a number of nauseating radio serials (mainly about doctors, doctors' wives, and nursing sisters) and their sole literature are women's weekly magazines. I suppose there is no leisured class whatsoever. It must comprise a source of constant annoyance to the Communists to witness (without being able either to acknowledge or denounce) the phenomena of Culture coming into existence immediately in the vicinity of any group that leads idle, ornamental and useless lives, whilst it seems to flee from communities devoted to hard work, just as it escapes immediately from where puritan Christian endeavour exerts—through means of physical and legal pressure—moral strength on the people. They must draw the conclusion that either art is decadent or earnest political, social or religious projects contain as part of themselves a sort of blight that wipes out the only sure evidence of true civilisation.

Yet the environment of the North of hard-working, hard-drinking illiteracy is a fertile and encouraging field for an artist to work in. He can feel free to paint the cat blue and the mountain crimson, and do so because his picture demands it, not to tickle up that regiment of boobies who in the cities are vociferous in demanding that art must echo the dull rumblings of ordinary minds.

21 October *Brisbane*. To a recital of poems by Dame Sybil Thorndike.[12] The great Sybil boomed and hooted her way, brilliantly, impressively, through Shakespeare, Euripides and lesser poets (the least being three nauseously whimsy feminine coquetries of Edna St Vincent Millay[13], to which the actress imparted an incongruous grandeur) to a triumphant conclusion. Later went to meet her at supper, where idolising young people encircled her, visibly worshipping. Her presence is indeed that of one of the larger, wiser Grecian Goddesses, electric with tragedy, slightly too noble for comedy: grandmotherly, fertile, humane and very, *very* firm. Her questions and comments were like those of Royalty visiting—I mean, completely beside the point. Like Royalty she conferred benevolent interest in those symbolic objects which are a sort of common meeting of our nation, in which we have a measure of proprietary feeling as though we had invented them and made them with our own ingenious labour—the waratah, the jacaranda, the kangaroo, the emu.

November *Hill End.* I was overcome with a furious energy, and did all those chores about the place that give me satisfaction in doing, and seem in some way associated with the joy of private ownership. I've been working hard on several small pictures—Queensland landscapes—with a fair measure of success. The days pass so pleasantly. In the mornings as I paint the sun streams in the windows. Waves of scent from honeysuckle and roses and pinks—the house is gay with great vases of flowers. I am relishing this respite from outside activities, this semi-solitude and complete independence, the joy of living for a while alone in one's pleasant house, the daily occupations that allow so many hours for laziness and work.

In fact, I am happy.

10 December The second picture I began for the Blake Prize[14], *The Baptism*, is now very near complete: a very efficient calm, somewhat dull work with a complicated composition. But the other one, that began as the sacrifice of Jacob or Isaac or whoever it was, suddenly became the underpainting for a picture which so far is nothing but a series of explosions in violent colours, a very 'Miraculous Draught of Fishes'. It is all shocking colours and tonal contrasts defiant impossibilities of perspectives and anatomy, and slabs of paint laid on violently. In fact, it promises to become an exciting picture, and gives every indication of turning my hair white with perplexity, offending all good taste. Certainly, if it continues as well as it promises, it will not 'go with the curtains', nor 'harmonise with the new cushions'.

25 December Christmas Day. The goose was magnificent. I dined at night, in the candlelit courtyard, a slow delicious meal, with iced champagne and an iced rockmelon, and after, coffee and Benedictine, Russian cigarettes.

1955

12 January If I had given the time of my life to London that I have enjoyed in Hill End, I would now be a very celebrated painter. And perhaps I would be happier than I am now when I am happy, suspecting sometimes that this life is a sort of artificial pastorale, that I *persuade* myself of the pleasure I find in living here—I, who was once so well known as a wit, as a brilliant man, whom people thronged to see and speak with, and who is here a sort of mockery for the children, living almost like a leper but for a few souls and intermittent visitors.

20 January The Byzantine Apocalypse is finished. It is rather majestic in its way, despite the fact that the colours—geranium, scarlet, crimson, violet, brilliant yellows and black—are vivid to the point of being garish. Since from past experience I know that it is not wise to paint in subtle and subdued tones for a competitive exhibition, my picture this year[1] is deliberately planned so that the greatest range of contrasts in tone, and colours taken to their ultimate brilliance, will, I hope, 'knock out' other paintings hung near. That may seem—probably it is—a very cynical statement.

1 March I sat down at once to answer Olley's letter[2], which was to say what I now know only too surely about myself, that as a husband I simply couldn't function, and that if Olley and I were of an age when passion is spent, we would be happy together, but as we both now are lively and sensual natures, such a marriage (in view of my own peculiarities) would be a pretence and result in mutual infidelities of a sort that could only result in self-disgust and disgust of one another. I only wish that this were not so.

7 March At last!——the Blake Prize, which I wanted so much to win; they all say round here, 'Well, it's good someone's done something to bring the name of the town up again. Good on you, Don!'—etc. And I am the more pleased because they speak of me as part of the town's reputation and honour; and I am much flattered by their warm participation in my triumph.

Third week of March Overnight in Bathurst on the way to Sydney. I went to Blackdown to see Mrs Brown. That old house (and its amiable, amusing and active hostess) enchants me. I was given a great airy bedroom whose windows looked on to the wide brick-faced verandahs and out into rambling gardens, and I slept in an enormous four-poster bed—the first I ever slept in—and before sleeping in its lofty embrace I had much to savour in that room. One of the windows, Mrs Brown said, was that broken by Mrs Knightly in her desperation to get help from Blackdown after her ride from the homestead where her husband was held up by bushrangers (Boldrewood makes use of this incident in *Robbery Under Arms*, and in the first edition, there is a footnote identifying Blackdown).[3]

8 April *Hill End.* Though I am happy here in the time of gathering cold, my heart really yearns to go back to that spicy illusion, Ceylon. All my old romantic, tempting ideas return again and again—the smell of spice and curry and rotting this and that, the island and its enervating beauty, its lissom people: yearnings midway between erotic and poetic.

Since Omu and I parted in London, I have not done a good drawing. I've made hundreds of drawings—simply to gain records and notes—I have not felt impelled to draw anything of the sort that commands the real essence of my talent. Instead, I've painted: a *very* different thing, for painting as far as I am concerned is a thing of *paint* in itself, whilst drawing is as intimate as this diary.

I will not draw again I know until I meet with such experiences of the passions and mind as Ceylon promises.

2 May *Brisbane.* After arriving in the morning, I went over the river to see Bob Haines[4], whose new house is a masterly expression of Good Taste. The exquisite precision of arrangement produces a sensation that the rugs, china, pictures and furniture are *watching* one with a very critical eye. Almost one would expect a rap at the door to put one's shoes on, so as not to *tread* too much. The pictures on the walls were good but notably sedate—four Sickerts, a Meldrum[5], some John drawings—Rodin[6], a Friend. I inspected the door I am to gild and decorate. It will be quite a job.

13 May *Townsville.* It was pleasing to awake and look from my bed through the French doors on to the verandah beyond to the rose-coloured crags of the Rock, and see the town below it all bathed in light serial colours. The beer garden below the verandah is surrounded by big cages of gorgeous and noisy parrots, and everywhere palms and mangoes and pawpaw trees.

The people rose early and talked in loud clear voices, and radios were turned on very loud.

14 May We passed through Ingham[7] at midday. The town and its buildings presented a typically Australian bush appearance, lining a street in whose centre enormous trees wept dark foliage. The outlandishness in contrast was provided by the thick throng on the pavements and in shops and bars. It was composed almost entirely of Italians, and over a few beers we did not hear a word of English spoken. The difference of manner and spirit in these sprightly vivacious gatherings to the dim subdued peasant mumbling that is the hallmark of Hill End bacchic gaiety is remarkable enough.

We slept at Innisfail.[8] There by the river at night hotels presented an enchanting spectacle, built to a peculiar distinctive design of wood with tiered and ornamental galleries and verandahs, painted white and gaily lit. They looked like romantic Mississippi riverboats, and from each the sound of pianos and singing surged rather rowdily out into the dark warm air of night.

Third week of May *Cairns.* I came on to the Sailors, where I find all as good as ever. Drove out to Pine Creek. Clambered up that fabulous boulder-strewn ravine where the great trees lean over bowed and arched with the weight of stag horns, orchids and ribbon ferns that grow like vegetable cities on their limbs, and up to my enchanted pool, more lovely than ever.

Spent two days painting a small oil of the mosquito-net-draped bed on the verandah—one of those adequate and charming little works that don't mean a great deal but please without causing any great ecstasy. This picture is only one of a series of subjects on the one theme that has interested and attracted me as a peculiar feature of Queensland life—the life on the verandahs. So I shall set out to collect my ideas on these wooden galleries which provide one with both figure compositions and landscape in combination.

4–5 June *Pine Creek.* Saturday night was the big dance. About sixty or seventy Aborigines and half-castes of all ages from Yarrabah Mission[9] came, and their troupe of dancers entered clad in white singlets and red sulus, singing Torres Strait songs and doing the dances they had learned from lugger crews, which they did with much enthusiasm but not very well: nevertheless it was moving to watch and hear, and did not merit the sneers and behind-the-hand remarks of one lot, whose chauvinistic contempt for the poor *savages* (or, for that matter, for any of the coloured races of the world except the population of their own particular island of origin) provides a burlesque commentary on all racial prejudice.

Their usual ugliness and gawkiness, the funny gollywog slack-jointedness that characterises their dancing (which is so opposite to the basic strictness of physical discipline and precise movement of Torres Strait dancing) conveys to me always an impression of the most hopeless tragedy. They seem to comprehend so little of the tag-ends of alien culture that are thrust on them: the debased remnants of their own are ineffectual: they are too weak to live outside their wretched mission without being destroyed by those vices that we make pastimes of, that to them are so fatal. They are cooped up, fed meanly with wretched rations, forced to conform to the most idiotic pious nonsense that the missionaries who control them would not dare to attempt to impose on congregations outside those most un-Christian, cruel concentration camps, the missions.

15 July It is only after a considerable period of intimate knowledge of the life lived in a place that I am able to separate from the great mass of familiar objects used in the daily living of a particular environment, those groups of still-life objects (which are quite apart from strange and exotic things which make the romantic and decorative furniture of a picture, such as a primitive carved idol, a palm, a native mat) that despite their commonplaceness, are clues to the life *outside* the law as that goes to make up much of the force of a picture—thus for North Queensland, on the meal table there should be a bottle of Worcester Sauce[10], tea-pannikins of tin or grey enamel, and an oilcloth cover. Other symbols are the iron bed, the mosquito net, cane-knife, corrugated iron, kerosene lamps.

All of their things are hard for me as an artist to *see*, since they are often either ugly or so commonplace, so everyday, that one's imaginative eye deliberately ignores them. Yet I must force myself to discern them and devise means of introducing them into my pictures, and resist the romantic impulse that would replace enamel platters with carved

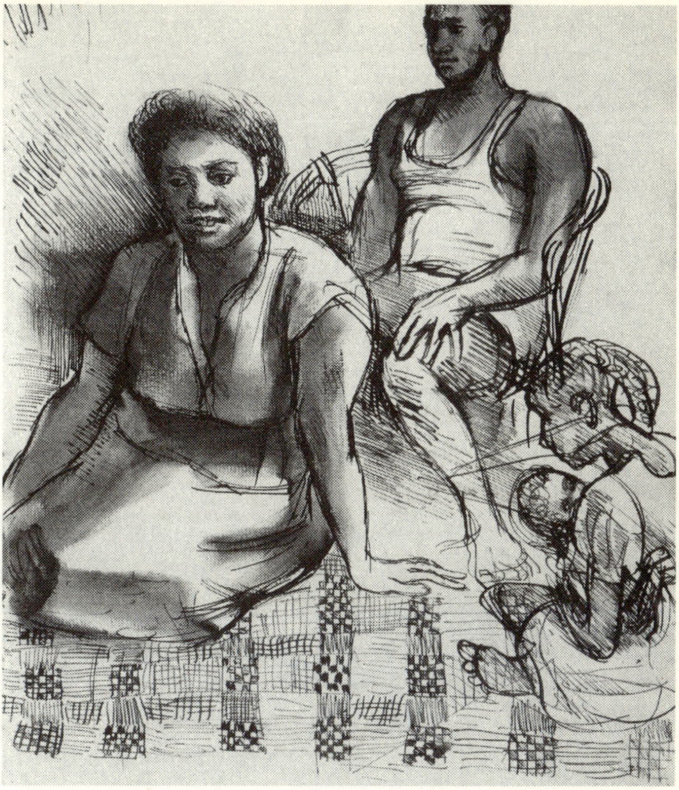

28. Family group at Pine Creek (1955).

calabashes. Not that I propose to attempt to exclude wishful thinking from my pictures, which would be to deny them an important and genuine element of art: but the carved calabash and the tin pannikin may co-exist, and each in its own way help the attainment of complete expression of the subject.

Third and fourth weeks of August *Magnetic Island.* At Nellie Bay, in a tiny cabin made all of windows set among huge boulders on the steep side of the point, where one looks out on the crescent gold sand of the beach, and wooden hills and the brilliant sea, and distantly, in a violet haze, the mainland. An inertia overcomes me. From the tiny hut where I lie all day and read I hear the constant soothing splash of the waves, the sun shines, the tide changes, and I can't raise enough energy to go. But it is in my mind all the time that I should be gone. What for? To meet the inhospitable cold of the South?

29 August – 1 September On the way down I picked up a wandering stockman, an anchorless and rather pathetic young man who seemed to have nothing in the world but himself, and of that he made a gift. So instead of staying at hotels as I would have done had I been alone, we camped at night. He was a smart hand at getting a blazing fire going and grilling steaks. I had lost a bag containing all my blankets, so I slept with him, and to my surprise he turned to me simply and affectionately with an embrace of loneliness and longing, the gesture of his meandering and purposeless life.

October *Hill End.* Since I've been back I've been busy all the time. I painted the outside of the house, worked hard in the garden, and began a large self-portrait with a Queensland landscape background.

The garden a dripping paradise of may and iris, and inside the house, fires and the comfortable sound of the bubbling pot. I finished painting ceilings and stonework, and sat before the fire till late, with music, writing, savouring the real joy of being alone in the white room, a fire of pine cones and a red log, and a great pot of coffee and the last of the cordial Médoc[11], and great vases of the most exquisite flowers, and feeling like a wonderfully comfortable ripe and mellow old man.

Last week of November The supremacy in contemporary art which was won by a group of painters of which I am one is at last being attacked by a new lot. We are about to be outdated, unless we keep true to our own art *and* one jump ahead of these younger ones and new arrivals.

It is of course a reaction against the romanticism of art such as Drysdale's and mine. Yet I find that their revolt is expressed in forms and styles (cubist, abstract, etc.) which were exactly the experiments that we indulged in to announce *our* revolt. However, where we were somewhat noisy, gay and furious, these fellows are trying to topple us off our little thrones with the deadly solemnity of virtuously puritan social reformers.

Well, shall I tremble in my shoes? Not likely. My contempt for fashions in art is such that I can take what I like of the new to delight in. And all I ever have to do, in any case, is to be true to myself and I will produce good work, whether it is in the forefront, in the middle, or lagging behind the developments of the day.

In fashions of creation and appreciation, America has lagged a few years behind Europe, and Australia a few years behind America. So now out here we seem to be about to enter a period of painting something like the non-objective phase that America is just beginning to discard. It *is* rather funny to sit here in rustic retirement, catching occasional faint echoes of that game of musical chairs (or musical beds) which so exercises their passions and wastes their energies in the distant city.

1956

7 January Paul Haefliger and Jean Bellette[1] are at their cottage. I find throughout my pleasure in having them to talk to, also a great weariness in all the disconnected chatter of intellectuals. If you get them one at a time, all right. They are amusing and sensible, but three intellectuals or more together *all* talk *all* the time and listen never, which is distracting and tiring. I need rest.

11 February At night, the first entertainment that Hill End has seen in many months, a travelling Magician and Hypnotist. Two men, with an unbelievably tawdry blonde hag who had a worn but honest face; a hodge-podge routine was shown of con tricks and concertina playing, ending up with fake mesmerism. Very stark and pathetic it seemed. Hill End is hostile to strangers, and takes a view of strolling players that is strictly combative. A great deal of bucolic shouting and jeering. Almost any performer in that bare-brick hall must fight against an inimical setting. I made some sketches, but of the spirit of the evening—the situation in which a community of dolts can bring themselves to refuse to be pleased, regarding the attempt to please them as a species of assault on their right to be bored—such a thing could not be shown in a drawing.

23 March Margaret Olley departed this morning, and such is her character of wisdom, simplicity, sensitiveness and sweetness, I was most sorry to see her go, which I know I would not say of any other woman in the world, especially since bad weather kept us rather cooped up most of the time, and I was more than usually prone to be irritable because of the constant messes and distractions incumbent upon alterations of the house. That is what it is to be a bachelor—to regard all women friends (dearly loved) as menaces to an intricately organised system of knowing where to put one's hands on shirts and socks.

24 May How extraordinary it all seems; how I who once was so wild and wicked, notorious and witty, the life-seeker, hungry for fame, for all that was vivid and restless, desperate for love—here I sit, sipping solitude gratefully as though it were the rarest wine, and living obscurely as I can, feasting only on leisure. How really odd it is.

27 May Village scandals are astir, with burly drunken plain-clothes detectives questioning weeping schoolchildren. There seems to be some injustice that what to country bumpkins seemed a mere romp in the hay will be turned into sordid horrors with unrealistic magistrates and pompous (and vicious) policemen reading from notebooks.

And so quite a few of our normal healthy red-faced peasants may be made into criminals by the law, when all they did was to pay 10/- to root a rustic harlot or two.

I have an unpleasant premonition that yet more evil will come out of this affair. My view is that a very nasty mutation has taken place. The business began as the erotic play of country trollops and strumpets exploiting their animal spirits with a lot of old gnomes and young sprites: then after years (during which these goings-on were looked at with more amusement than horror: it was more like the mating of goats than humans) comes a fresh puritan schoolmaster with suburban ideas on morals. The forbidden games of children are suddenly lifted to a plane on which they are compared with the doings of city debauchees, and engineered into and judged and punished accordingly. And neither judgement nor punishment alleviate the situation: quite the contrary.

24–27 June Attilio here. I paint, Attilio amuses me and himself, we cook, cut wood and live the village life, and the house is warmed by three constant fires.

I am very happy about Attilio. He has at last a serious central purpose in his life, and comes to all his problems in an adult way, and what gives me the greatest pleasure, his affection for me stronger than ever it was, now that at last the whole of his world is seen in its proper perspective.

6 August From Mother, a little note. I can see why extremes of mother-love in these days are almost exclusive to gangsters: their activities are of such a sort that they have a real need of such softening sentiments. But cissies like me have to be chary of being drowned in a maelstrom of treacle.

Most of the day I painted, and in between painting delved vigorously in the garden, where already faint delicious signs of spring—pink knobs on fruit trees, the tips of hyacinths, and a general faint tingly budding—show. These last three days here, white frosts in the morning, mists till 10 a.m., and then mild lovely sunlight, crisp and clear, everything trembly and bright and lovely. On such days I wish I were young again. Yet I seldom regret being alone, knowing how much I would hate the interruption of my idle thoughts and sensations.

So keen the pleasure of standing and looking at the dewy grass, the sky, and thinking, and lazily allowing my mind to take its manifold paths that lead me to place a patch of colour on canvas. And that last act is not the death of my thought but the beginning of a stimulating process.

8–18 August *Sydney*. Caretaker at Tas's house. I'm busy, I'm happy. Every day I've worked in the glorious big studio, sometimes from eight in the morning until the light failed. But there have been also some pleasant excursions into the life of the city, evenings drinking and dining and talking. One evening, Jeff Smart came round with a tech college student, a wild moody boy called John Bell[2], who stays in my mind. He spent a day painting with me in the studio. Now I think about him a lot: a strange boy, 18 years old, faun-like and irresponsible, tender and wayward. I would very easily fall in love. And he? God knows when he'll come again.

28 August to 4 September I'm full of longing, but full also of an utter weariness, of this John Bell. For all my realisation and tender care of who *he* is, there is no echo of recognition for me. To hell with the generation! The best gifts one can make, of extravagant generosity, disguised in the manner I was brought up to do (which is to pretend that such best things are a nothing, a mere gesture of the hand) are accepted or rejected as though they were really trifles. I can't suppose, remembering such rare things in my own youth and how one valued them, that these odd children of today have any glimmer of understanding. Uneducated clots.

If I am not a lonely man, then I know nothing, though Sydney this last visit offered more sheer delight than it has in years (old friends, hope of a new lover, old sights, new acquaintances, the season of the year, a sense of freedom). God I've enjoyed these weeks.

21 September to 3 October The Fairfax party. They are really rather an odd family[3]—the whole arrangements were put into the hands of others and they themselves were rather like guests in their own house. As it was the gathering was a strange one—all the old artist faces, a whole lot of young student girls and, after the theatre, twenty or so of the Katherine Dunham[4] negro dancing boys. There was a tremendous lot of noise and very wild dancing: much drink, mad negroes and negresses whizzing about the place. The chief dancer, a very tall effeminate fellow, wore eight diamond bracelets all down his arm. Jean Bellette swears that at one time during the evening I was making arrangements of flowers in one of the negro's hair. I *do* remember a sort of silly scene in which John Passmore exploded in anger at me and told me to shut up, but that was because of something frivolous I'd said about Rembrandt.

20–21 October *Hill End.* The school festival a great success in every way—the weather was beautiful, the children did their Morris dances[5], there were all the usual things, the tea, the cakes, the lollywater. People came from far and wide.

At night, the Ball: everyone drank a great deal first, and the Sow Pen, as the ladies' lounge at the pub is called, packed with the vivacious 'brittle and brilliant' crew from Sydney, had all the appearance of a Macquarie Galleries sherry opening. The locals looked with fascinated horror at so much outlandish smartness.

7 November A bitchy, brief and upsetting letter from my damned mother. I replied with a shamefully cruel note, cutting off from her for good, that poisonous kindness of hers—the Virtuous Viciousness, the interference. I've really finished with her for good.

13–14 December I came through country I hadn't seen before—a rough mountain road, real bushranger country, and stayed overnight at my brother Harley's place, Rothsay[6]—fine cattle country set in a valley

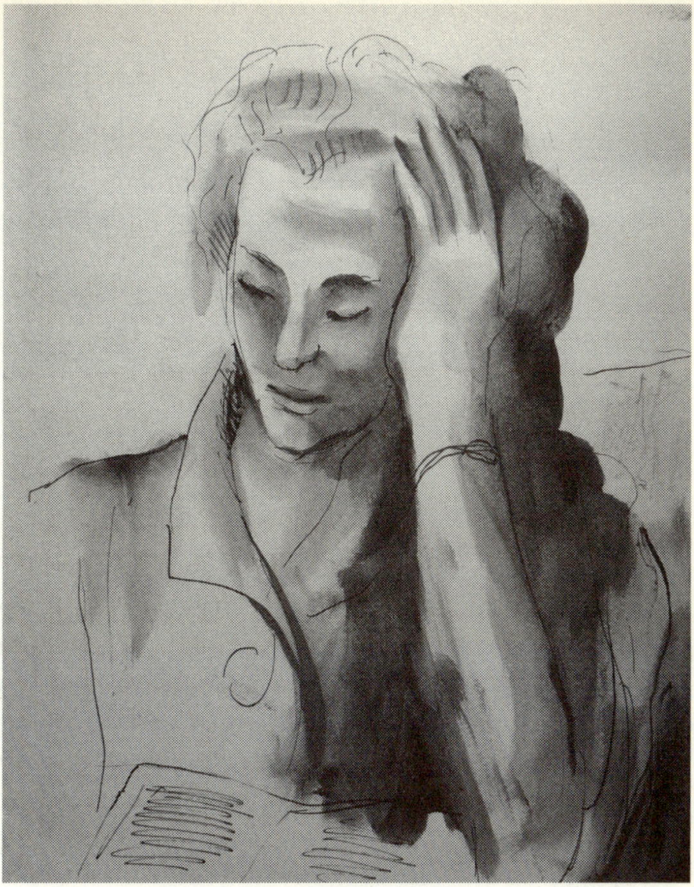

29. *Bon Drysdale* (*1944*).

flanked by scrub covered sandstone hills, rather gloomy looking. There for the first time I met his wife, Janet, a pleasant rather ordinary woman who seems to have livened him up quite a bit. Then on next morning to Tamworth[7], the whole way scorching hot. I found the whole household sweet and welcoming as always. One spends hours just lazing and filling in time on the wide cool verandahs.

1957

5–6 January *Sydney*. Chez Tas. Unable to sleep, I got up and joined Bon in the kitchen where she, also sleepless, was making a cup of tea, and at that hour talked over much of what was on my mind—the main burden being that this trip to Zanzibar was, with shipping complications resultant from the Suez Canal fiasco[1], becoming more and more idiotically expensive. Why not change plans and go instead to Ceylon, which by air will be cheaper, and where I have friends. So it's more or less decided.

25 January *En route to Bentota.*[2] At the airport, towering above everyone, was Bevis Bawa, and as soon as we were through the customs, we got in his car and drove off. That 45 miles to the Brief estate seemed very long, mostly because of the crowding impressions of villages, the bullock carts, the mad wild hazards of traffic, Bevis all the time keeping up his inimitable stream of witty talk and comment. This place is the most beautiful tropical house I have ever seen and with its gardens and fountains and the fantasies of Bevis's invention is truly a sort of paradise. One sinks into a warm strange timelessness, and I have the surest certainty that here I can be happy.

27 January *Southern coast.* Set off for a tour in Bevis's car. Charming scenery all the way. We stopped to call on an American writer called Paul Bowles[3], who lives on a tiny island, situated a mere few yards off the beach. We waded over to visit him and found there an odd assortment of people, Bowles quite likeable but I didn't take much to him (he writes, says Bevis, books that are very difficult and very full of sex). Mad inconvenient octagonal house[4]— all the rooms cut in ugly angles, ghastly furniture, no water for a shower, the lavatory a tiny 'squatter' perched on a rock at the end of a steep twisting path.

4 February *Bentota.* I have got into the habit now of retiring, after breakfast, to a little sort of bungalow-pavilion in the garden, to read and make drawings. To me, curiosity like a magnet draws the garden boys, one of whom I've now made several drawings of. At other times if I pass where he is working amongst the flowers, he smiles ravishingly through a screen of leaves.

In a crazy open-air rococo shower room furnished with stone benches and exotic plants, I make my morning ablutions, sometimes joined by the garden boy for motives of curiosity, or perhaps naughtiness.

23 February I have never come to terms with the shadow that periodically falls over my mind and turns everything to bitterness and frustration: to dispel it I turn—by habit or perhaps instinct—to the illusory warmth to be found in the act of love. But that is not love itself, which I need in my despair. Yet it gives relief for a night from ridiculous phantoms of persecution and conspiracy. I dread, more than anything I can think of, the repetition of an obsessive and passionate love, unreturned in the only satisfactory way, such as I suffered in the days of my madness for Attilio. I tremble to think that in my present state of mind, I perceive echoes and similarities.

In this troubled condition I sought to be cured by a servant's amorous therapy: all night long we lay together, occasionally sleeping. Age 19, intelligent and good-looking. No erotic romantic could desire more of gentle embraces and the casual skill (so young, so young!) of hands that seem to have much humour, a way of making love unblighted by the guilt that infects members of the puritan races and loads their passion with a furtive desperation that turns to bitterness and disillusion when the sun rises next morning.

I am going to be very happy after all.

3 March The women in Ceylon, I've noticed, are commonly extremely beautiful. Gazelle-eyed, satin-skinned, clad in seductive saris of glorious colours, they bring with them a heavy, wearisome languor, and in a trice can transmute a vivacious assembly into something resembling Ladies Night in the Turkish Baths.

19–20 March *Sigiriya.*[5] We drove over towards the rock, the weirdest huge mushroom of stone rising out of jungle that for miles and miles grows over immense ruins, earthworks and moats. The extent of the place—the outer fortifications, temples and suburbs, is staggering. We climbed and scrambled about in these for some hours, and spent more time where excavations are going on in what seems to be a vast water garden. A mysterious maze of vast works, stone walls and huge mounds on which forests of tall trees grow. We idled and strolled for a couple of hours through the ruins, and explored caves which still contained fragments of charming fresco.

23–24 March *Nuwara Eliya.*[6] A tremendous long drive. We stopped for tea. Very much like Bowral, only more pine trees, and a lake and of course a large golf course, and cold dry air, and Englishmen in suits and cloth caps and walking sticks, and people on lawns with jolly jolly voices. Something like my idea of Hell in the tropics.

7 May *Bentota.* The Sinhalese[7] are a very sensitive and emotional race:

their gentleness and courtesy, their smiles and humour and affection, once upset can turn very suddenly to wild rage and murder. Most of the murders are done for love, for debts or to avenge insult. Another side of it is a sort of injury to the soul inflicted by history. The rabid murderous cruelty of the Portuguese, the organised stolid avarice of the Dutch and the infuriating invincible pride and fairness of the British conquerors. But the wondering Sinhalese glance at one another, at long lashes and the lithe grace of their fellow creatures, and the sight begets a smile, and an amorous answering look, and then perhaps a casual caress. They are a very affectionate people.

30 May The political situation here is becoming dangerous. The principal immediate trouble is over the government's language policy—Sinhalese Only, which they are trying to improve hastily and in such a way as to victimise the Tamils, who, a racial minority, are concentrated around Jaffna[8], and are preparing a big campaign of Civil Disobedience to protest against this policy.

29 June This nation's politics are getting madder and more exciting every day—the outbreaks of Nationalism that are like the pimples of political adolescence: every day brings a variety of political scandals. It's all very interesting, but what has it to do with me?

Nothing. My real concern at the moment is an almost feverish delight I take in sitting and sweltering for hours on end staring at crumbling murals and putting down an equivalent of their faded blots and scratches and mutilated figures on full sheets of Waterman's paper[9] while little boys and Buddhist priests breathe down my neck, on a suspicion that one is mad. I must agree, for all this work that pleases me so much is rather fiddling while Rome burns.

24 July *Kalido*[10]—a simple quiet place full of the sound of the sea; it is at the river's mouth, and one looks across at the town, the temple, the mound of the old Dutch fort. I walked along the beach. Quite suddenly I came on a surprising sight. The beach shelved sharply from where I stood, and below me with his back towards me stood a boy laughing at his two friends in the shallow water—a man and a boy of about 16 years. They also had their backs to me. The man was hugging the boy in the water, in a sitting down position. I was filled with envy and amusement, and stood watching this curious and refreshing scene of copulation when the boy on the bank turned and saw me, laughed and said something to the others, who turned in great surprise, but seeing my expression (I suppose of sympathetic interest) smiled. Such an incident gives one an affection for a place.

13 August *Colombo*. A black tie dinner with the Australian High Commissioner[11] was a bore. What I disliked about the evening most was the way these expatriates speak of the nation they are accredited to as 'They'. 'The great tragedy is their lack of education,' says one—by education meaning imported plumbing fitments, cars, industrial equipment, toothpastes and what-have-you. They are dirty and ignorant. They, if only they would, could almost become as wonderful as we are. But 'We', when I glance round the room, are a pretty brash crew of commercial opportunists and professional propagandists of the western way of life, tho' they were all people of ability and, I supposed, goodwill. I thought that, put this party in a roomful of people I like and respect, and what nobodies they would be.

7 October *Bentota*. Bevis's younger brother, Geoffrey Bawa[12], arrived from Europe (where for the last few years he'd been studying architecture)—amusing, cultivated, witty, arrogant, selfish and very good company indeed. There are so few people who really speak one's own language in Ceylon, people to whom explanations are unnecessary, who know from the start the whole background of ideas and experiences that lies behind utterances that to others would need tedious explanations.

10 October I had a letter from Brian Johnstone[13], sending notices of my show—half of it sold on the first day—good write-ups, though as usual the critics complain there's no agony in my work. God, people *are* ghouls!—there's nothing they like to see so much as an artist suffering (though suffering in a painting is liable to make it unsaleable) and resent my light-heartedness. It doesn't seem *right* to them somehow—there ought to be at least a few pictures full of those swirls and whooshes of paint by which a critic may comfortably be assured that the artist has been *suffering*. Fools.

28 October I have been going through one of those protracted periods of self-criticism and dissatisfaction: there is nothing I like about myself, my thoughts and the things I do. I am an age now to look back on my life, and see—at least since the war—that it is a long record of futility and waste of talent. I have built up a history of actions, a system of habits and attitudes that is quite false. I have betrayed myself mostly for the sake of security, and for its sake. I've become a bore. Cowardice and covetousness and sloth have so eroded my original excellence that it is now all rotted away. These days I seize with relief on anything, or any silly part of any thing, that will make me smile, so the praise I give a person or a thing is that it is 'amusing'. 'Amusing' chimes in my talk, tinkles in my work, like a monotonous cracked bell. In company I chatter desperately as any garrulous ass, so as to be thought 'amusing'. While the even worse side of my mind, enquiring, bitter, falsely analytic, looks on and listens disapprovingly. So I have no comfort even in my frivolous diversions.

I am an artist, and should have lived all my life properly as an artist: instead, by admiration sometimes of other people I have striven to emulate them, and thus come to accept and try to live by codes that really have nothing at all to do with me—it is only now, too late, that I have come to realise the hypocrisy of my existence. It is too late, because the lie is such a pervading one, and has reached deeply into my habits and thoughts and the practical ordering of my life, like a cancer that has undermined the whole of my constitution. To begin again now would take more energy and honesty than I have at my disposal.

I am tempted to think that, having taken a stock of the situation, the best thing to do would be to continue skimming the surface, looking at and expressing my observations of life around me with more laughter than understanding.

29 November Out here people are such busy amateurs and dilettantes they have no real respect for the arts at all. They are like our silly society women to whom the best productions of mankind are only of use to flatter their vanity, who would use a Vermeer as a tea tray if it were thought chic.

Like all amateurs they are changeable as the wind and very unbusinesslike, and have only cursory and passing spasms of interest in doing jobs, being much more concerned in being talked about as dashing geniuses, who have *wonderful taste*. My God, I don't think 'good taste' has much to do with the production of any lasting work of art. Taste is the thing needed by the patron and the dilettante. For the rest, I'd leave it to the interior decorators and English watercolourists.

December Colombo is in a ferment. Workers went on strike, so the city was without water, electric light, sanitation and garbage removers. Bombs were thrown and people killed. The stinking streets and drab slums we drove through made me think that if I were poor, I'd certainly be a revolutionary. What right has our class of people to privileges and wealth, if we refuse to be leaders, refuse responsibilities towards the lower classes, and use our powers, our wealth, our privileges, and more, our minds and bodies for aimless indulgences in petty displays of whimsicality?

I have *never* seen anything so inert and flabby as the Ceylon bourgeoisie. At first they impressed me with their White Russian extravagance, and with the very fact that in many ways they represent a class that ceased in Europe 45 years ago, and there was something marvellous in the spectacle of the brontosaurus-like anachronism. If they'd *fight* and show some guts I'd admire them still. But they won't. They know, they see their present position, and are content to fade away in an excess of flabbiness.

Mark you, I am very nearly in the same category myself, or in a worse one. But at least I am a creative artist and have done good work and certainly actively added to the culture of my time. I do not conceal from myself that I am now, by my own standards, a mediocrity, though I hope it will not be generally realised by others. And I do have responsibilities, at least towards my household, which are more than sentimental liabilities. Furthermore, I admit (though only to myself) that the leftists, though only theoretically, ideally and morally, are in the right.

But *actually*, materially, I think they're wrong. It is hardly their fault they are wrong when one considers that no political philosophy in this age can dare to state what all men must know, which is simply that the mass of people of all classes to be ruled by any government, whether it is Democratic, Aristocratic, Fascist or Communist, are stupid, dishonest, weak, greedy and brutish and vain. Their basic instincts, which are those of all living creatures, make them so. Nothing is so unnatural to mankind as those noble graces that political theorists, calling for disinterestness and self-sacrifice, demand as the cornerstone on which to build their edifices.

And if the middle class is flabby and unable to defend itself, perhaps it can be said that the reason is that in their leisure they have absorbed some noble qualities, of delicacy and sentiment, of an instinct for beauty, which have unmanned them, and left them unarmoured against the brutish greed of the more natural masses.

1958

7 January *Bentota.* A letter from Arthur Benjamin. Will arrive by boat. This is the third letter in which he has said 'I think you will recognise me—people tell me I have not changed.' Vanity! I've known Arthur since I was sixteen. Common sense ought to be enough to tell one one's face and figure changes. People are amazing the way they stare every morning in the shaving mirror at bags and wrinkles and yellowing teeth, bald temples and grey hairs, and still persuade themselves their physiognomy shows a static and ageless mask of semi-youth.

11–12 January My Sinhalese teacher told me about a place near here called Uggalkanda—'sugar-cane-rock hill'.[1] A king in ancient times had a palace and buried a treasure of gold bars shaped like sugar sticks. Going to explore them. I don't think anything remains of the palace. Still the mystery of the place appeals to the imagination. One should try to paint what one *expects* of such a place, as well as its reality, for the images stimulated in one's mind by village tales, superimposed on the reality one will find in actually visiting the place, must give some extra quality.

19 February *Kelaniya*[2], with Barbara Sansoni[3]: we had arranged to spend the day with the village potters, teaching them how to make decorative wall tiles. I always find her wonderful company—more so than any woman I've met out here—she has the sort of wit and fantasy I like—she looks marvellous, handsome, Spanish-like with wonderful eyes that flash with amusement or fury as she tells one gloriously funny stories.

We worked all morning and afternoon, with people crowding round and children peering over our shoulders. We may be useful in indicating how their pottery may be applied to different needs and give them a broader market.

4 March *Bentota.* We Anglo-Saxons, even those of us who insist that life must be free and easy and unconventional, actually are horrified when confronted with a nation who act on the assumption that their word has no more value than the air it is breathed out with. So our expectation of consistency is comic and their imitation of an ideal of Western gentlemanliness is comic (especially in view of the shilly-shallying nature of the changing whims and desires which are given voice in Oxford accents that mask Singhalese ethics, the Ceylonese inability to come to terms with anything at all that must be kept to and followed up, such as an appointment, a promise or a bargain).

It is a very bad thing when one is living in a foreign country, when outside events and the incompatibility of one's own temperament persuade one to think of the inhabitants critically as 'They'. I've begun to think too often in 'they' terms, owing entirely to disappointments arising from my naive optimism.

Last week of May The whole island is stirred up again with strikes, riots and violence. Today in Colombo mobs looted and smashed up Tamil shops, and in Polonnaruwa[4] police fired into a mob and killed several people. The strikes continue, and big European factories have been attacked. Two passenger trains have been derailed, and thugs in cars in country parts have held up, robbed and beaten wayfarers.

The government itself now regards this as being more than a racial affair, but instead a large-scale revolutionary plot. The Tamils are stubborn people, who are furthermore fighting for their own language and culture: the anti-racial thing with them is merely incidental. But there is a likelihood that the atrocities they are now perpetrating in reprisal will give rise, unless the government is really firm for once, with further monstrosities here. And my own life will be in danger.

12–14 July *Kandy.*[5] I love staying here. One even does a little work in addition to a number of entertaining things. Anything that happened seemed to supply an occasion to drink a lot of gin in the Queen's Hotel, usually in the company of four or five superannuated rakes left over from colonial days. The cooler, drier air seemed to preserve one from hangovers. We played wonderful music on the gramophone till very late every night. We went out sketching. We found a marvellous-looking boy and took him back to the bungalow and made drawings (*and* ***). He never works, but is always to be seen idling by the road, an enthusiastic spectator of car accidents. A wonderful face, smiling, shy but not at all abashed, an elegant figure. He wore his hair very long, and had numerous tattoos on his arms and hands. His charming smile revealed a gold tooth and he wore a thumbnail very long and sharp.

2 October *Bentota.* Most encouraging news of the success of my Sydney exhibition[6], since I had even resigned myself to its being a flop, thinking that, combined with my absence, new fashions and art movements would have so changed taste and ideas that my own, cut off and uninformed and relying now entirely on myself and environment, would seem to that up-to-date public somewhat provincial and old-fashioned.

My great regret in working here is that one works without hope of informed criticism, which means so much to an artist. So I am much more encouraged by this than by the equally surprising success of the Colombo show. I feel amiably disposed to work again.

The Sydney press criticisms have a familiar flavour for me as my drawings dazzle them against their better judgement. They none of them have digested the fact that the element of wit that so manifestly disturbs them does so because they conceive art as something lacking wit. They know enough to recognise my work as good, and are uncomfortably confused because it *shouldn't* be, because it's often also funny. They're like deeply religious people who are convinced that to *enjoy* church is sacrilegious.

10–13 October *En route to Jaffna.* A fascinating drive through country utterly different from the luxuriant south. Stop at Mannar[7] to look at the ruins. Here the landscape is flat, stark and severe, plains of curious thwarted scrub, tortured cacti and flat-topped thorn trees like inverted pyramids. The town is small, quiet, introverted. Narrow streets of tiny shops, and some delightful old houses. A charming little Dutch fort overlooks resthouse and water. The quietness of Mannar was remarkable after the noisy and busy south and the absence of motor traffic very noticeable, and nothing at night but the sad whining wind.

We came on to Elephant Pass[8], stopping a lot to collect wild plants for the garden—some lilies, jasmine (a thickly white-star flowering, very fragrant variety) and various cacti and succulents and a big bag of orchids.

We soon got through our business with the Bank in Jaffna, wandered about the charming old fort, visited the little museum and a number of Hindu temples.

17–19 October *Medigiriya.*[9] The hoped-for, but incredible (and immoral) *did* happen. At last we got off the beaten track, and followed a bumpy lorry road for twenty miles through jungle to come at last on a complex of ruined temples, and there found, and abstracted, a sandstone torso in two parts for Bevis, and part of a bas-relief for me: sculptures of the twelfth century. The thing really doesn't bear too much thinking about. My own sensations, apart from excitement at possessing a fragment of a second-rate antique, is largely of shame, for without doubt it was an act of vandalism. But Bevis is more fortunate, an amateur in all things, including emotions, so his reaction is more of fright for his own skin if the theft is discovered.

20–21 October *Bentota.* Wonderful to get home at last. I wakened and made everyone work like mad. The garden boy brought a school friend with him, whom I also pressed into service. A *very* black boy, who gave me the most delightful surprise in years, when (I was giving him a small present for working so hard) I caressed his shoulder, and he turned swiftly and embraced me, wrenched off his sarong and ***.

Well, that's not fair—asterisks at such a juncture. The little black boy is an astonishing creature, passionate as no Sinhalese I've ever had to do with, simply burning with sex and hungry for more—in fact, pressed me on to a point of sweating exhaustion, until I felt like the tutor in Petronius[10].

27 November A European ambassador to India came to spend the day. I had three hours solid of the most tedious talk a garrulous and tiresome old pederast can devise—and was amused to note, for God knows how garrulous I am myself, how each of us waited impatiently for the other to finish, or sometimes when we could neither of us wait, and talked loudly in concert neither attending at all to the other. But in that game he won every time. I was busy altering the garden, until some American women arrived. Their breezy open and friendly way, and uncomplicated frankness, was a welcome change from that arid atmosphere given off by sophisticated homosexuals whose vanity seems to drive them to pick and bicker with an awful sort of archness that passes among them for wit. The effect is one of great and restless effort, like provincial women striving to emulate the manner of the metropolis.

20 December Everything I do—such as putting on the roof even—commits me to stay here, to feel settled, to have a home. And I *want* to stay here. I am happy on the whole with these illogical people, for all the contempt I have of them for their lack of all the qualities that make the Yorubas or the Torres Strait Islanders their superiors.

27 December *Dharga Town.*[11] A Muslim wedding feast. A big ugly modern house, the trees in the garden festooned with coloured lamps, a pavilion for music and pavilions for feasting the thousand or more guests. The great musician, a curious, huge, rather sulky Indian, was led into the pavilion. The crowd milled thick around him. The tabala player began drumming, and finally the great man with an air of sad languor produced two pairs of a sort of castanet that were actually simply pieces of glass, and began clicking them. For a little while it seemed a sad disappointment, then one was aware of the most extraordinary and varied variations on the tabala rhythm. He really had something very fine. He sat clicking the things with aloof indifference as though they had utterly nothing at all to do with him—he glanced about, looking vague and uneasy, and then sang a while—it was very odd and fascinating.

Classical Indian music is beyond my understanding. I like to listen, well enough, yet I do not even dimly apprehend what its methods and movements are—I don't know *what* a raga is exactly, nor when the mood is gay or sad or what is being expressed or felt at all. The nearest way I can approach this music is by examining Moghul paintings, which occasionally seem to give me some hint of what it means in terms of a vaguely related and more easily understood art.

29 December *Bentota.* The banks, stores and oil companies are all still on strike. There is expectation of a general strike. Bandaranaike[12] is dithering and saying it will all turn out for the best. The army is standing by, and Colombo is packed with troops. The situation is as dangerous as it was at the beginning of the race riots. There is a great deal of mischief and menace in the air. All is dust and ashes within me, and outside, Ceylon looks lovely, idle, useless and silly—intellectually a rotten stagnant pool, politically a cauldron of boiling poison.

1959

January to February I feel very depressed really. I admit to myself I'm fairly sick of Ceylon. I'd love to go back to Africa, but it's such a long way, and involves so much packing, and changing boats, and arrangements: and I have become greatly attached here to my household, seven in all, hard-working good boys who seem very happy, and whose happiness depends quite a lot on me. And I love the pleasant rich simplicity of this odd bungalow, with the old furniture I have acquired here and there all shining with beeswax, and the polished deep-red floors, and my few books and pictures, favourite china and silver, and the garden with its pools and orchids and frangipani trees where the three small garden boys chatter and play when they should be clipping hibiscus hedges.

Beside these things, the few pleasant friendships I have here are of less account. In Ceylon I think friendship might be defined as 'a competition in egotism'. The one who practises the greater indifference wins.

Of intellectual life I have none at all. It is too hot to think much, and anyway there is utterly no one to communicate with. How one yearns for the sort of talk that exercises one's wits, strikes a few sparks, feeds one's mind with ideas—for the preposterous talk of clowning and invention and camaraderie. The Sinhalese, if ever they possessed intellect, must have dissolved it in charm (like Cleopatra's pearl in wine[1]) a thousand years ago. They are a nice, lazy, smiling undependable lot, and handsome, gentle, obtuse and sinuous in their way, utterly lacking confidence or frankness: never grateful, seldom loyal.

There is no point in going on living like this, pressed for money, ageing, without friends around me and without enjoyment of the things I have, and feeling painfully deprived of the society of the people, talk and books that feed my mind. My daily life is one of physical inertia enlivened when I want it with sexual indulgence. It seems that the only thing that brightens my heart a bit is to see my houseboys cheerful, or to watch the garden boys sweeping leaves dropped by the wintering rubber trees. And *that's* not much compensation for the bitterness of days.

23 March In the company of Geoffrey Bawa I now become automatically a boring garrulous chatterbox. And later wonder why the hell I accept invitations from him that are made only when he wants something for nothing or to help amuse people who are important to him for business reasons but bore him to tears.

But in a way there is some enjoyment in it for me—the spectacle of it all, the superb mixture of good taste and megalomania that is his bungalow, the grand-ducal airs, the cultivated elegant voice and gestures, the sparkle of amused malice in his eyes when he betrays one into saying something more than usually foolish. These things would be quite intolerable perhaps if I had not become aware that Geoffrey makes a great thing of observing with acid irony the silliness of those he patronises and entertains, with the colossal conceit to suppose that he, exclusively, is an object of uncritical splendour. For the rest, one envies him his servants, the products of years of tyrannous selfishness, and his furniture, the products of long-dead craftsmen and (in the fact of his taste in acquiring it) a determined policy of self-aggrandisement founded on an abysmal inferiority complex that originally grew from a desire to be mistaken for an aristocratic Englishman on the strength of possessing blue eyes and yellow hair despite mixed ancestry.

14–16 April The Sinhalese New Year consists of certain customs scattered here and there on a number of days. The dancing started. The costumes were all contrived quite simply and ingeniously with leaves, sarongs and baskets and two small masks. My paints (alas) were used, unsatisfactorily, as make-up. It was rough and weird entertainment: the spectacle was barbaric without splendour, the drumming very loud and *not* very good, yet there was an excitement and some enjoyment in it.

On the whole I was left with a more acute impression than even before that there is no aesthetic that I can comprehend in the Sinhalese simple folk. The dancing is devoid of attempts at grace or beauty. The postures are peculiarly graceless, and they obviously aim to convey at times a ghoulish terror, at other times ribald folk caricature, and at all times grotesquerie. Compared with the dances of any savages or half-civilised people I have seen Sinhalese dancing lacks what is necessary in an art. I think of the Torres Strait, or those slaves liberated from the Japs in Labuan, or a hundred occasions in Africa.

19–30 April *Sigiriya.* I shall paint, or try to: Sigiriya rock, towering far above the jungle like one of those mountains in the world of Hieronymous Bosch. The lake as smooth as glass from the window of our room at Polonnaruwa, dead trees rising like candelabra from the mirror water, ornamented with clusters of cormorants—a pelican like a caricature of a galleon floating solemnly—a canoe very silently moving with fishermen, nude, standing expectantly scanning the still water: a rickety table with rows and rows of bright pink, bright green, bright yellow bottles of warm sticky drinks, attended by an old woman, an old man and boy, in front of the flower—carved pillars and shattered bas-reliefs of a temple. A whimsy bus painted like a carousel full of white-clad pilgrims debouching to bow and pray at a *dagoba*[2].

Second week of May *Colombo.* Shopping at Miller's[3], I saw coming towards me a plump gross-looking figure I thought I recognised. He walked purposely toward me with an expression of self-importance on his pasty face—the sort of face I've seen everywhere I've been in the world, that of a middle-aged intellectual pederast who's letting himself go to seed. A dislikeable, self-indulgent but amusing fellow. He was dressed as I was, in a loose white shirt worn outside his trousers for coolness, giving, on his portly figure, the effect of a smart, holidayish maternity jacket. It was only when he raised a supercilious eyebrow at me that I recognised him—myself, alas, in a mirror.

24 July *Bentota.* Whenever the car has to go to town for market I always go, taking a sketchbook to jot down numerous little nice drawings of whatever goes on in the street, how people walk, talk, squat down, lounge at shops, carry vegetables. All these sketches are immensely useful, provide my pictures with their lively humour and a great variety of the sort of intimate observations that can't be invented. Economical and swift as they are, these sketches are not merely impressions of quaint old characters seen by a foreigner and jotted down: they are done with knowledge and understanding, and the gestures, the figures and costumes I select and define are so expressed that a Sinhalese knows immediately that this man is a *mudalali*[4], that a Tamil, this a sweeper, a Nationalist, a lawyer, a hawker, a moneylender, a bully, clerk or unemployed, by his stance, his gesture, the way he ties his sarong or carries a parcel.

It strikes me that this is passing on useless information to art-buyers who will have no use for it and never know anyway. But it makes the pictures genuine, as now we can immediately guess and make few mistakes about Breughel's, or Rowlandson's, Goya's or Hokusai's wayfarers.

26 July I draw at the wobbly table in the studio by a window looking into the orchid garden. I get tired feet standing long at the table, and go to read—currently D. H. Lawrence's *The Plumed Serpent*.[5] I dislike his puritan soul with its revolt against what he tries to believe in against the avid convictions of his nature: he cannot see himself, and he cannot see himself in other people. And all his mystic *stuff* with 'O mighty Earth Spirit'—and the thous and thees are at times comically Marie Corelli-ish[6], with the conflicts of his back-street soul. So back to the drawing table, and the lies and dishonesties of my own vision.

Now is the time—the rains have eased off—when the pods from the rubber trees explode like bullets and shoot the seeds with a loud *crack* on to the roof: the squirrels rush and scamper, adventure; chasing one another, along the roof beams, and occasionally fall unharmed but dazed on the polished floors, then skid trying to escape from terrifying humans. The garden once again looks rich and varied with huge figured caladium leaves.

1 August 'Power corrupts.'[7] I was idly wondering why that true statement always irritates me. Looking into it I find it is because it is too narrow and exclusive a statement, as though to say that Power alone corrupts. Hate corrupts, property, poverty, heredity, environment and more than anything the experience that matures a man, corrupt. In the wildest wickednesses of my youth I was never so corrupt, corrupted and corrupting as I now am in the kindly, selfish and disillusioned activities of my 44th year.

But still I can say there is no cynicism nor insincerity of intent in my meaningful actions. Duly that I am weary, a little mad, and somewhat blunted in my perceptions and slow in wit. Also I am less grateful than I should be for living as an ageing and unattractive sensualist in a country where the people are sensual and complacent, and have no aesthetic sense such as in another country would make my embraces repulsive.

25 September A man dressed as a Buddhist monk[8] entered the Prime Minister's residence, pulled out a pistol and shot four bullets into Mr Bandaranaike's stomach. The Governor-General[9] has declared a State of Emergency and called up Army Reserves. The surprising thing is that it has not happened long before in a country where murder is so common and many politicians and businessmen keep bands of thugs.

When the radio suddenly left off its customary brassy rock'n'roll inanities and suddenly switched to Chopin, I knew immediately without the announcer telling me that poor old Bandaranaike was dead. For the rest of the morning we had superb music—Beethoven and Mozart, and I thought it would not be too high a price to pay if a Prime Minister were murdered three times a week if one could hear so often concerts of fine music.

1 December Here I am stuck, losing a little willpower every day, in an environment of decaying beauty: the fight against neglect and indifference is a daily one with me. These people are like the Irish—charming, slothful, treacherous and dirty and below the surface, cruel and fanatical. The negroes are an infinitely superior race, true men.

Why all this bad temper?—I am a little lonely. I long for a little mirth, friendship. No one here, least of all my compatriots, speaks my language.

In painting only I have a feeling of communication. And I have been working steadily, with no outstanding results: but if one goes on and on, the chance is, that like the example of a monkey forever tapping a typewriter, one may chance to write one perfect line.

NOTES: 1950s

1950

1. Attilio Guarracino (born 1931), a fisherman in Ischia when Friend first met him.
2. English-born poet (1907–73), formerly a lover of Chester Kallman, American-born poet and translator (1921–75), with whom Auden later collaborated on several opera libretti. Bu Faulkner was another American living in Ischia at the time of Friend's stay on the island.
3. Albertine Simonet, a central character in *A la recherche du temps perdu*, with whom the narrator, Marcel, is infatuated. She is supposedly based on Proust's chauffeur, Alfred Agostinelli, and secretary, Albert Nahmias. (Cf **1968**, note 17.)
4. Hindu god.
5. Patricia Kaiser, née Jones (1924–89), who had first met Friend on the boat that took him to Italy in April 1949. She later married his travelling companion on that voyage, the German-born artist Peter Kaiser.
6. Stage name of Freda Josephine McDonald (1906–75), African-American entertainer who spent most of her career in Europe, becoming a French citizen in 1937.
7. Suburb in northwest London, popular with artists.
8. In Cork Street, Mayfair. Cf **1950**, note 10; **1962**, note 4.
9. Jules Pasquin (1885–1930), French artist.
10. Harry Tatlock Miller (1913–89), Australian writer and critic who had lived at Merioola with his lover Loudon Sainthill when Friend was also living there, and later went to London, where he co-directed the Redfern Gallery. Cf **1946**, note 3; **1962**, note 4.
11. Dreaded warrior (406–453) who took on the Roman Empire when king of the Huns between 434 and his death.
12. War between North and South Korea broke out on 25 June 1950 and lasted till 1953. The USA intervened in the war on the side of the South.
13. Village on the edge of the South Downs.
14. Opera by Mozart (1787).
15. *Exhibition of Drawings*, 22 November – 4 December 1950.

1951

1. Also where Friend's maternal grandmother lived. See **Early to mid-1920s,** note 9.
2. Sponsored by the Italian shipping line of that name, it carried a prize of A£250 and a First Class return trip to Italy for a picture 'Australian in subject or symbolizing Australia'.

3. Celebrating the fiftieth anniversary of the foundation of the Commonwealth of Australia.
4. Discovered at Hill End in 1872 by the German gold-miner and merchant Bernhardt Holtermann and the Polish miner Ludwig Beyers, this remains the largest single mass of gold ever discovered anywhere, measuring 1.5 metres long and weighing almost 290 kilograms.
5. In Greek mythology, a companion and tutor to the god Dionysus (cf. **1943**, note 23).
6. Fernando Martins de Bulhões (c. 1195–1231), an Augustinian canon turned Franciscan preacher and miracle worker, venerated as Anthony of Lisbon (in which city he was born) or Anthony of Padua (where he died). Cf **1964**, note 30.
7. An extension of the theme of youth's vulnerability to death explored in European painting from the late fifteenth century on, and in a poem by German author Matthias Claudius (1740–1815), 'Der Tod und das Mädchen', set to music in a song by Schubert published in 1821. Friend added a youthful male figure to the motifs of this theme in sketches, drawings and paintings from 1949 on; for early examples of his treatment of it, see reproductions in *DFD 3*, pp. viii, xii. Cf diary entry for 16 July 1965 and **1965**, note 15.
8. In southern NSW, on the Tooma River, a tributary of the Murray River (see **1942**, note 16).

1952

1. Prestige suburb of Melbourne, 6 kilometres from the city centre.
2. Series of frescoes attributed to the Italian painter Giotto (1266/67–1337) in the Upper Basilica of St Francis's Church, Assisi.
3. The Accademia di Belle Arti, Venice's premier art gallery.
4. Giovanni Bellini (c. 1430–1516), Italian painter.
5. Paolo Veronese (c. 1528–88), Italian painter.
6. Jacopo Tintoretto (1518–94), Italian painter.
7. Giorgio Barbarelli, also called Giorgio da Castelfranco (c. 1477–1510), Italian painter.
8. Palazzo Venier dei Leoni, the Venetian home and gallery of American art collector and patron Marguerite (Peggy) Guggenheim (1898–1979).
9. *The Clarinet* (1912).
10. *The Poet* (1911) and *On the Beach* (1937).
11. Published 1930. Berenson (1865–1959) was a Lithuanian-born American art historian mainly resident in Florence.
12. Principal art gallery in Florence.
13. A popular scene in fifteenth- and sixteenth-century European painting,

showing the laying to rest or entombment of Christ following his crucifixion.

14. The National Archaeological Museum of Florence, which contains a large collection of Etruscan art and artefacts.
15. The Anglican cathedral of London.
16. Marc Chagall (1897–1959), Russian painter, long resident in France and the USA.
17. Tenth- to twelfth-century style of ecclesiastical art and architecture in Catalonia, Spain, as well as in other regions and countries of the former Roman Empire.
18. Church in Barcelona designed by Antoni Gaudí, construction of which began in 1882 and remains unfinished.
19. Actually, the San Antonio de la Florida Hermitage.
20. Museo Nacional del Prado, chief art gallery of Spain.
21. Diego Rodriguez de Silva Velazquez (1599–1660), Spanish painter.
22. Triptych (1503–04) by the Netherlandish painter Hieronymus Bosch (c. 1450–1516).
23. *Sidney Nolan: Paintings*, 2–25 October; *Donald Friend: Recent Drawings*, 30 October – 22 November.
24. Pierre Auguste Renoir (1841–1919), French painter.
25. Pieter Breughel the Elder (c. 1525/30–1569), Flemish painter.
26. Home to the gallery of the Royal Academy of Arts (see **1949**, note 20).
27. Frans Hals (c. 1580/85–1666), Flemish painter.

1953

1. Kenneth Rowell (1920–99), Australian-born stage designer and painter.
2. London's leading gallery of modern art, opened in 1897 and located in Millbank.
3. French painter (1869–1954).
4. English painter, illustrator, designer and author (1903–92).
5. South African-born author (1903–73).
6. Britten (1913–76) composed this opera about Queen Elizabeth I for the coronation of Elizabeth II. Cf diary entries for 2 and 6 June 1953.
7. The name is of Dutch origin. London-born John Betjeman (1906–84) was appointed poet laureate in 1972.
8. French painter (1877–1953).
9. Salote Mafile'o Pilolevu Tupou III (1900–65), reigned from 1918 to her death.
10. Thomas Rowlandson (1756–1827), English caricaturist and painter.
11. James Gillray (1756/57–1815), English caricaturist and printmaker.

12. Art gallery in New Burlington Place, off Regent Street.
13. Alleyne Clarice Zander (1893–1958), Australian patron of the arts.
14. Fashionable thoroughfare along the River Thames in the London borough of Hounslow.
15. Prosperous Ceylonese landowner, aide-de-camp to three governors of Ceylon, and landscape garden consultant (1909–93). Friend had first met him en route to Italy in 1949.
16. Novel published in 1949 by Italian author Curzio Malaparte (1898–1957).
17. In *Inferno*, the first part of *The Divine Comedy*, which the Italian poet, Dante Alighieri (1265–1321), began composing around 1308.

1954

1. Queen Elizabeth II arrived in Sydney for her two-month Australian tour on 3 February.
2. A series of anthologies of Australian short stories published from 1941 to 1970. Friend illustrated the volume for 1953–54, selected by C. B. Christesen.
3. A house established by Mme de Pompadour in the late 1740s within the grounds of the palace at Versailles.
4. François Couperin (1668–1733), French composer.
5. Published in 1953, the third in a tetralogy of autobiographical novels by Indian author Sudhindra Nath Ghose (1899–1965).
6. Latin novel by North African-born writer Lucius Apuleius Platonicus (c. 123/125 – c. 180).
7. Situated in Boonah, on the outskirts of Brisbane.
8. Town just off the Queensland coast, 835 kilometres north of Brisbane.
9. Coastal town in Queensland, 1070 kilometres north of Brisbane.
10. Coastal town in Queensland, 70 kilometres north of Cairns.
11. Rainforest district, 110 kilometres north of Cairns.
12. Visiting English actress (1882–1976), whom Friend had first seen on her tour of Australia in 1932: see his reminiscences in *DFD 2*, p. 383; *DFD 3*, p. 282.
13. American poet (1892–1950).
14. Annual prize for religious art, first awarded in Australia in 1951, and named after English artist and poet William Blake (1757–1827).

1955

1. *St John and Scenes from the Apocalypse* was the title under which it was entered for the Blake Prize. See **1954**, note 14.
2. A proposal of marriage. See Meg Stewart, *Margaret Olley: Far from a Still Life* (Sydney, 2005), pp. 307–08.

3. Blackdown is a homestead near Bathurst built in 1823. The novel *Robbery Under Arms* was published in book form in 1888. Its putative author was Rolf Boldrewood, a pseudonym for Thomas Alexander Browne (1826–1915). Mrs Brown may have been a descendant of the novelist (the spelling of the family name varied over time). Mrs Knightley was a character in *Robbery Under Arms* based on Caroline Keightley (c. 1840–98), the wife of Henry Keightley (1831–87), who was held hostage by the bushranger Ben Hall on the Keightleys' property, Dunn's Plains, near Bathurst, in 1863.
4. Robert Haines (1910–2005), Director of the Queensland Art Gallery, 1951–60.
5. Max Meldrum (1875–1955), Scottish-born Australian painter.
6. Auguste Rodin (1840–1917), French sculptor.
7. Town 110 kilometres north of Townsville, known for its large Italian community.
8. Coastal town 100 kilometres south of Cairns.
9. A settlement 50 kilometres from Cairns established by the Anglican Church for the local Aboriginal people in 1893 and closed in the 1960s.
10. A liquid condiment first produced in England in the 1830s and later in Australia by local manufacturers.
11. French liqueur, with a famous Art Deco label on the bottle.

1956

1. Australian painter (1908–91). She and Paul Haefliger (see **1943**, note 11) had been married since 1935.
2. Australian painter (born 1938).
3. The Fairfax newspaper dynasty in Sydney dated to the 1830s. Its current head was Warwick Fairfax (1901–87), whose son James (born 1933) became a prominent art collector and close friend of Friend's.
4. Dancer, choreographer and anthropologist (1909–2006), whose African-American dance company was on tour in Australia at this time.
5. A form of English folk dancing that originated in the late fifteenth century.
6. In the Central West Slopes region of NSW, 200 kilometres from Dubbo.
7. City in the New England region of NSW, 420 kilometres north of Sydney, near to where Donald Friend's younger brother, Terence, lived.

1957

1. Zanzibar, off the coast of East Africa, was considerably south of the Suez Canal, but shipping routes there were disrupted after the nationalisation of the canal by the Egyptian government in July 1956 and the international

crisis that followed.

2. Coastal resort town, 60 kilometres south of Colombo and near to the Brief estate (cf diary entry for 17 September 1953).
3. American expatriate novelist and composer (1910–99).
4. The name both of the house and small island is Taprobane (in ancient Greek times a name for Ceylon as a whole). It is situated near the resort town and fishing village of Weligama, 143 kilometres south of Colombo. The house was established in 1927 by an English-educated Frenchman, Count de Mauny. It was purchased by Bowles in 1951, and sold in 1956 to the Irish writer Shaun Mandy, who became a friend of Friend's.
5. The ruins of an ancient fortress and palace, with surrounding gardens, located in the central Matale District of Ceylon.
6. Hill station and resort 180 kilometres northeast of Colombo.
7. The majority ethnic group in Ceylon.
8. Chief city of northern Ceylon, and traditional Tamil stronghold.
9. Superior brand produced by a French manufacturer of fine writing tools.
10. A beach in the vicinity of the Kalo River and the town of Kalutara, 40 kilometres south of Colombo.
11. Alan Eastman (1912–87), who served in Sri Lanka from 1956 to 1959.
12. Ceylonese architect and lawyer (1919–2003). Cf diary entry for 17 September 1953, and **1953**, note 15.
13. Indian-born gallery owner of English origin (1920–88), who founded the Johnstone Gallery in Brisbane with his wife, Marjorie, in 1952.

1958

1. A kilometre from Karantidya estate, in the vicinity of Bentota.
2. Small town just outside the municipal limits of Colombo, to the northeast.
3. Née Douglas, Ceylon-born artist, designer and writer.
4. Historic city (eleventh- to thirteenth-century capital), 215 kilometres northeast of Colombo.
5. Hill-country capital, 115 kilometres northeast of Colombo.
6. At Macquarie Galleries, 24 September – 6 October.
7. Town located on the island of Mannar, just off the northwest coast of Ceylon.
8. Military base, also referred to as the Gateway to Jaffna.
9. Historic city with Buddhist ruins, 40 kilometres north of Polonnaruwa.
10. Eumolpus, a character in Petronius's *Satyricon* (see **1930**, note 16).
11. Suburb of Beruwela, on the southwest coast, 45 kilometres from Colombo.
12. Solomon Bandaranaike (1899–1959), Prime Minister of Ceylon, 1956–59.

1959

1. The eardrop that the Queen of Egypt, around 33 BC, supposedly crushed and sprinkled into her glass in order to impress Marc Antony at a banquet in Alexandria. The anecdote was first publicly recounted in the first century AD by Pliny the Elder, in his *Natural History* (IX. lviii).
2. Sinhalese Buddhist shrine.
3. Department store in Colombo Fort, established in the mid-nineteenth century.
4. Prosperous entrepreneur, often from humble village origins.
5. A novel (1926) with a Mexican setting, by English-born Lawrence (1885–1930).
6. In the highly inflated romantic manner of English novelist Marie Corelli (pseudonym for Mary Mackay, 1855–1924).
7. Common contraction of a quotation from a letter of Lord Acton in 1887: 'Power tends to corrupt and absolute power corrupts absolutely.'
8. Talduwe Somarama (1915–62), of Sinhalese origin.
9. Sir Oliver Goonetilleke (1892–1978) served as Governor-General from 1954 to 1962.

1960s

10th May

I don't really see myself patiently putting up with slobby d[...]
Brian Dunlop for very long, with his dull talk & oafish egoism[...]
Too fine a fellow to take his turn at washing dishes or
doing any of the boring necessities about the place. Attilio &
Yanni & I market, & he does the cooking, she washes up wh[...]
I don't. Alas, she leaves tomorrow. Attilio goes to
Athens on the 25th, & then to Ischia to see his mother. He [...]
return here if I'm here. But I've already half a mind to
go with him & just dump Justin & Dunlop. One has to
choose one's company. I chose Justin, who's well enough at
times. But not Dunlop. No. Not true. He's not too bad, [...]

12th May

all that is not really fair at all to Dunlop, who is not a bad chap & [...]
does his share. Yanni missed the boat to the mainland. Actu[...]
the 'bus from Skyros to the boat caught on fire & the boat was [...]
damaged by heavy seas, so she will wait & go with Attilio [...]
the 15th. He is bound to Italy to visit his mother for a month
before returning here.

16th May

They've gone. I miss them badly, especially of course Attilio: ironic[...]
on the day of their departure two letters came for me, the first
mail I've had since being in Greece. One was from my accoun[...]
to say they'd sent the requested $2000 to Athens for me, & th[...]
they'd paid $15,000 (!!!) income tax, & that I was now
$12000 overdrawn at the bank. Very impressive.
The other was this disastrous letter from Stewart
which awoke a lot of old thoughts I'd imagined dead fo[...]
The irony lies in this: that I would have done nothing to
help, and would have always felt guilty: I am absolv[...]
from all guilt by the case having been heard the day
before (14th May) – the letter had been re-addressed from
Lesbos, opened by the censors of the Military Government
delayed till the 15th. So the poor little bastard is now i[...]
gaol I suppose, where he was bound to go. I think of hi[...]
without fondness, with a sort of fear, seeing the sad prophe[...]
I made to him coming true as he earns the consequence of
his actions. I know now for certain Stewart will become
a habitual criminal incapable of reform; and most lik[...]
from time to time in between gaol sentences he will com[...]
back to haunt me, and try to force his way into my [...]

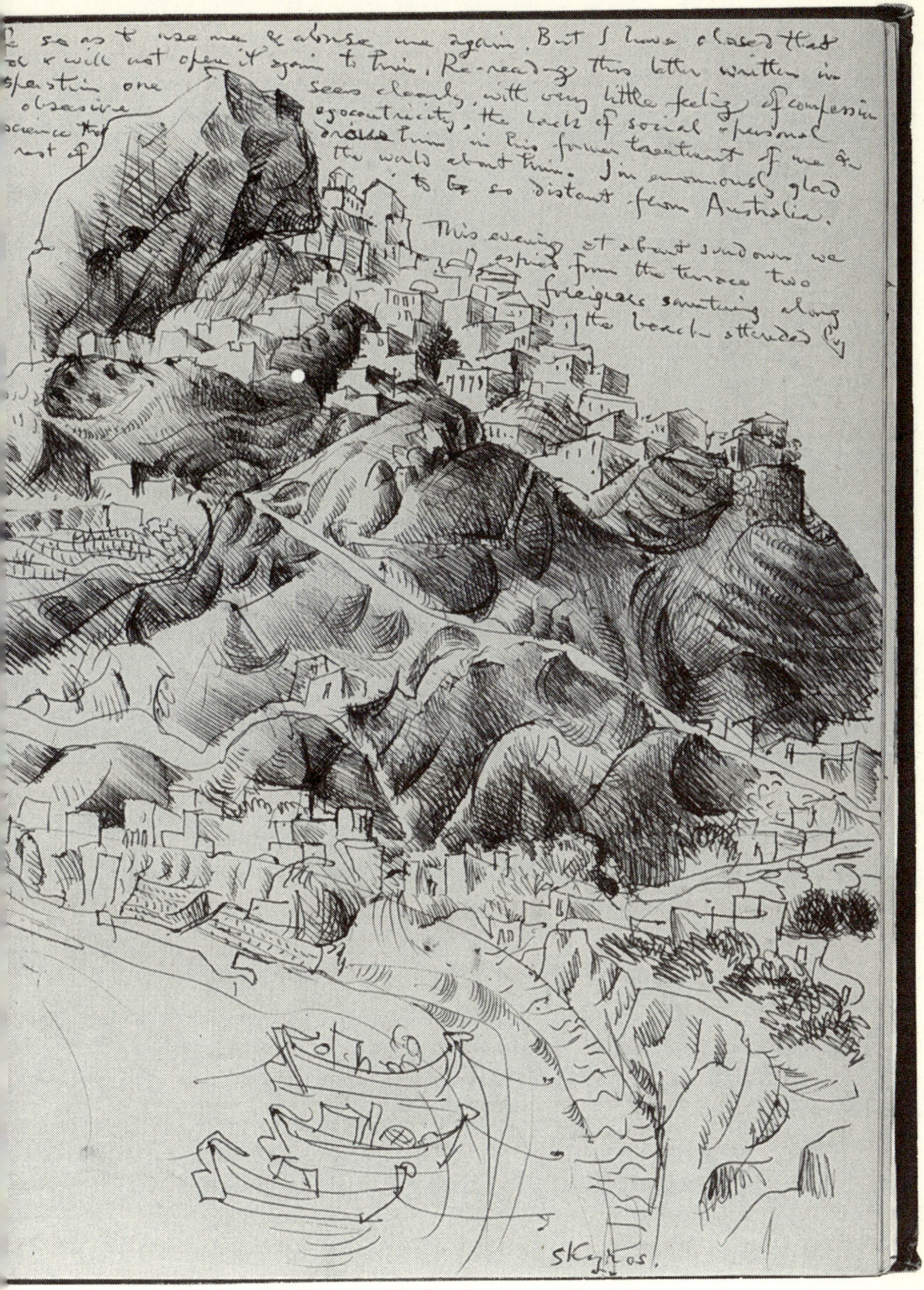

30. *'Skyros'* (1967).

29 March *Bentota*. I think, what I have missed, what I have allowed escape, what I have thrown away—my (once) potential perhaps of greatness. It seems I can feel nothing sincerely any more except regret and irritation. Sad thoughts. I can still I think draw like an angel, but I can't feel like one. My selfishness has narrowed my range. I have little human sympathy left, but more observation than ever, which is no help as the little sharp points I observe are only of failings and follies that lead to a tinny acid laughter, not to important conclusions. I no longer love—am not *tolerant* even.

Alas, I am led to these miserable thoughts by my darling, my beloved gramophone—not by Beethoven and Bach or those European masters who draw from me some illusions of being a reasonable creature still simply because I can still love and be moved by them—but by the ancient negro music of my youth—jazz: Louis Armstrong[1]. There from comes an astonishingly clear apprehension of how once I felt and loved and suffered and in that music with its caring-not-for-tomorrow sensuality, its wonderful invention (its cynicism also) and its negro laughter tender and cruel and real, I recall the loves I loved, and left still loving. I never helped them much when I (in later years) could have—Ladipo, little Omu, Attilio. However much I loved them then and love them still now (vague clouds of remembered emotion) I would not forego a day's comfort for them out of love—only out of guilt perhaps. Yet I often think about them in a sort of anguish now they are gone out of my life, I suppose forever, and wish I could suffer and enjoy as once I did, and see the world a fresh and lovely and painful place because the force of my emotions was set outside myself. Now no more, but still this sort of music evokes those lost irreplaceable feelings.

Is it because now, in my waited-on ease, I know nobody of any positive virtue?—these soft gentle elaborate Sinhalese seem to be no more than pleasing brown shadows on the way to another reincarnation. They mean nothing. Nothing means anything to *them*.

April William Willetts[2], whose book on Chinese art gave me so much pleasure, arrived, being rude and irritable to a harmless clerk at the port on the moment of landing. He has that unpleasant English way of treating the servants as though they didn't exist, and staring at the natives in general as though they were animals who don't quite come up to the specifications and so must, without regret, be condemned.

Evidently I am to pay for car, petrol, drinks, cigarettes *and* his rest-house bills. Rot the damned fellow. One can't help but be wryly amused at his colossal assumptions. *He* has elected to be Grasshopper, and *he* has elected me to be Ant.[3] Damn!—what *is* he? A simple opportunist on the make with archaeology as a gimmick, or another succubus?—but what gets me down is his peculiar ungraciousness to people—a damned middle-class *professional Common Room* nastiness, a finding-fault, a refusal of the niceness around him. These bloody-minded English. It's not that nothing's too good for them, but nothing is good enough. Not even England. The man is impossible. He's not had a shower or bath yet, and consequently it's best to avoid standing downwind from him. My God. Some of these English…a 'French Bath'—that is, a damp handkerchief run over the face and neck, a clean collar, and presto!—the clean-limbed Anglo-Saxon pretending that the reek of body odour emanates from the dirty natives.

First week of May Bryan Robertson[4] showed the keenest interest in my drawings. He has already selected four works in Australia for the big exhibition at the Whitechapel Gallery[5] next year. He was entranced with Ceylon—a gay, witty sympathetic character, full of innate and gentle tact.

This meeting with Bryan, our immediately finding a great spontaneous common flow of ideas, these three days of talking and laughing together, his instant recognition here of all the enchantments that give sustenance to my painting, is I feel one of the important and formative contacts in my life. I feel I have a good friend forever, and what is more, someone who thinks my work is good and who is in a position to give it the little push it needs to place it amongst the best known and respected paintings in England.

12–15 July *Galgamuwa.*[6] I got a sudden fit of wanderlust and went off to explore some little-known sites. It turned out the best trip I've made here yet—simple remote places, simple courteous people. Along unmarked lanes among scrub, searching for a ruin, we met a peasant farmer. On the off-chance I asked him if he ever dug up small statues when cultivating his fields. 'Often,' he said—little animals, monkeys and elephants of baked clay. We gathered a statue—broken in six pieces, an oddity also very primitive, of four little broken figures. All of these fragments struck me as being non-Buddhist. *Perhaps* Hindu. We made a compact with our farmer guide that he would diligently collect all *rupa* (statues), even broken ones, that are found during the year when they work the fields, and we will return and buy them.

23 July *Bentota.* Well, the elections are over. The campaign that led up to them was an epic of shit-slinging on both sides, accusations, righteous denials. The newspapers overplayed their championing of the UNP[7], who won an overwhelming victory. What now? The widow Bandaranaike[8] is to be Prime Minister.

4 August All is harmony in the house. I had a good long talk with N. the driver about my future plans. I *must* have (I told him) someone I could trust utterly and completely. I am getting old. I need a son-servant-friend, and he is my choice. He catches alight with ideas, enthusiasm. His heart shows in his face, he is loyal to his old friends, loyal to me. 'You are like a father to me. I will not leave you so long you are in this country,' he said in the course of this talk.

19 September Suddenly—O, alas—the urgent drive of creation that kept me at work all day, thinking and dreaming all night seems to have popped into nothingness like a burst bubble. My mind goes round and round seeking shapes in paint. Oils. Oils on wood panels with gold-leaf ground.

I notice the extraordinary chasm, too deep ever to be bridged, between Oriental and Western ideas of friendship. Neither Bevis, nor any of the other locals I suppose to be my friends, has lifted so much as a finger to help with the show, as they so easily could. How I envy the wonderfully unruffled *comfort* of this indifference!—no pain, no participation, no directed intelligence, no self-criticism or discipline: just a sort of golden syrup of uninterrupted self-admiration. At last I really think I believe these gutless meandering Easterners, with the dreary enervation they suppose to be culture and civilisation, are a lot of silly savages that deserve to be conquered, given a good dose of salts and put to work. A great pity the English were weakened by history at the wrong moment.

Last week of October Ambition gave me a sharp twinge—a result of seeing Tas's, Nolan's and Dobell's work in full-page colour reproductions in *Time* magazine[9], and various art news from all over about Australian artists and their sudden success in Europe, America etc.

I'm working hard at drawings. My real life is my drawing, my fussiness about the house and the silly objects in it I love. And my servants, and my joy sometimes at seeing friends—in the pleasures, perhaps sordid but here without hangovers of conscience or fear of police, of sex. And reading, and the long hours of fine music on my gramophone every evening.

I wonder whence, in such an unstimulated life, come the urges and ideas for painting. I am so empty and so old already, sick and tired. But for painting, I have a tremendous skill in my hand, and my soul is a bottomless purse, full of—silliness. All that I attribute uncharitably to other people, for one thing alone, my snobbishness, seems to have attained the proportions of almost madness. I catch my mind at work sometimes when it supposes itself unobserved. Surely it's not quite sane.

Friends. Here (or anywhere?) I have so few. N., who is truly as fond of me as I am of him, and is probably, for all of the incomprehension (language, beliefs, modes of living) that makes a great gap between us, my only true Sinhalese friend: and beyond doubt, loyal and gentle and conscientious. Whatever decision I take, he must be the first person to be considered and planned for.

22 December Serious trouble has been brewing for quite a while and now at last is waking up to something very nasty. The cause is Mrs Bandaranaike's government's policies—the new very heavy taxes on the rich, the old Tamil question, the national language (Sinhalese) and the just completed government takeover of schools, which, though reasonable on many counts, imposes several serious injustices that the Catholics are determined to resist.

'All rumours,' said Bevis. We all went for drinks: a Christmas tree decorated with balloons and winking lights, and the gramophone played carols and Christmas songs, whilst in the distance, in the night, the church bells jangled out their alarm. I thought of Australia, and how if any alarm—for bushfire or any trouble, and people for miles rush to help: not here though. They sit about and chat, pretending they don't believe it's any concern of theirs. Those who *do* go, go to loot, or to enjoy a spectacle of havoc.

1961

13 March There come times—sometimes days, or even weeks, when I am happy and Ceylon is enchanting again.

Tonight. The gramophone playing the Goldberg Variations[1], and in the background from the dark garden a concerto of insects: and from the deeper dark beyond, the drums of a devil-dance in the village that I will go to after dinner, partly to store my mind with some images of hell, but mostly because the villager who is giving the dance is a very poor man, and always polite and amiable, and depends on contributions from those who come to pay for the exorcism.

April I've been working intensely and at a great pace nearly every day from early morning until the light fails, on the mural. An elaborate and detailed subject—a sort of architectural fantasy of the walled fort of Galle[2] with the harbour full of sinking ships, the sky in gold leaf. I have finished the big centre gilded panel—it looks so fine, the design of it simple, the details unimaginably complicated.

While I work, the 'calming' radio speeches of Mrs Bandaranaike are present humming in my mind like the sound of mosquitoes—promising a sting from the outside world. While the gramophone, sounding Mozart, hints that nevertheless there is harmony in the Cosmos.

In the garden the tall hedges of huge-leafed plants now produce the Henri Rousseau-like effect of a naively entrancing but not-quite-real jungle as I had planned.

May *Colombo.* The Ceylon–Australia–New Zealand Association[3] people cannot see the uselessness of their stupid exhibition[4] if it is directed only at the rich, and left, or made, incomprehensible to the man in the street. I've seen the ten pictures of our best artists, all hung with great colour, taste and sweat, and my own hung so much more modestly (truly: and *I* did the hanging), I think my pictures, so full of jokes and idiocies and tributes to pleasure and delight, better than any, though less portentous. And less pretentious. And I paint out my life and what I see and feel and know and daydream, but it seems to me my contemporary countrymen are deeply involved in something else entirely which doesn't go so well in paint.

'Gimmicks' like the excellent Nolan *Ned Kelly* picture[5], or competitive like the ghastly Molvig[6] and Lawrence Daws[7] who've painted almost mechanically with only one motive—to kill the next-door picture. I hung both in a 'disgrace corner' where they could cancel one another out. Anyway, the show was a success.

25 June The rather sumptuously got-up Whitechapel Gallery catalogue for the Australian Contemporary Art show[8] came. I regret now having sent anything at all to the damned show which is very evidently preponderantly Abstract Expressionist[9]—splurged anonymous-looking canvases. I can well imagine my work in such company would look anaemic and foolishly refined. Although it is hard to judge from photographs, especially of pictures that seem to rely not at all on drawing, composition and design or tonality for their interest, but on paint surface (and perhaps colour) alone. Uneasily I am aware that it can't *all* be trash, since there are some serious and sincere painters (old dry-as-dust Passmore for example) doing it. Still this sort of work strikes me as a loss of identity. It is puzzling, seeing how alike they all are.

28 September A party at the Art Centre Club. It turned out to be a very rowdy and hilarious evening indeed. The music is something like calypso—it has negro–Portuguese slave ancestry. Very witty and bawdy comments on the life around us are sung in a strange dialect composed of English, Portuguese, Sinhalese and Kaffir. I was in a trance, almost of pleasure to find this, for me, new music. It seemed so un-Sinhalese with its sharp, active satirical wit.

I drank too much, and wanted terribly to dance, but all the ladies—the Ceylonese and Sinhalese sitting in rows like an indigestible batch of scones—would not, but a few of us, Europeans, did. Later I wished I hadn't—post-alcoholic neuroses exaggerated my feeling of having made a fool of myself. But what the hell: God created me a fool and I can do little enough to improve on the job. And I'd lief be a silly middle-aged man enjoying himself like a silly young man—at any rate participating with joy in what is happening, than be one of those sterile creatures who sit and watch and smile absently, more certain of their conventions than their dignity.

29 September Rain, rain, rain! As every day for three weeks, and the garden soggy and overgrown; huge elephant-eared plants trying to march into the bungalow, insatiable in their steamy hothouse greed. Letter to the Skinners in Perth confirming my exhibition there[10] in January '62. I'm to be Perth's artist of the year. Most flattering: a little provincial perhaps—but my vanity is easily sated with a sip of small beer. As Jeff Smart says, in our racket it is a matter of endurance. I want to paint as well as I think I can; which is better than others can. But I don't really wish to be famous for it in the *Time* magazine (despicable) sense. Just let artists respect me, and intelligent people buy me. That's enough.

1 October I've been working hard all day on drawings, feeling a little ashamed that once thought of in my mind they came so quickly and easily to completion. I feel it should take longer, and be harder. But I hear Nolan's prices for his show in Adelaide[11]—watercolours, the smaller of which could take no more than half an hour; and he turns them out in repetition like sausages. I do not envy him anything but the money he makes. Not that he isn't often a brilliant painter.

Last week of November I paint away, slower now, and rather depressed about everything. As a fact, all yesterday, today and tonight, the blackest of black humours. And O how I long to go. I sit and think of ways and means. Crating furniture and books, selling off things, the car, cupboards and chairs, refrigerator. The hell of it. If only I were true enough to myself. I'd give away or burn the bloody lot and go away and make a new start. This place is really destroying me now, and it will destroy my painting too. I *must* go.

A cable from BBC television at Shepherds Bush asking me to telephone London urgently.[12]

2 December *London*. God knows how I managed to get out of Ceylon and on to a plane. Having arrived in England with only 10 shillings I am not to be *paid* for this stupid TV thing, except my expenses.

How London, or such of it as I've seen, has changed. So many new buildings; and everyone dresses differently—the men's styles quite as flamboyant as the women, who now wear their hair piled in top-heavy turbans—a hydrocephalic effect.

And *cold*: I nearly die of shivers in my thin tropical clothes.

3 December We rehearsed, and I met the other people—a very mixed bag from the past of Peter Finch, who is the subject of the program. But the most important people—his first wife[13], Laurence Olivier and Vivien Leigh, and others, are none of them on speaking terms.

One met famous stage people like Dame Edith Evans[14] (wonderful, wonderful): an old pixy-faced lady with a booming 'personality' voice, full of 'mechanical' intimacies and comical 'pointed' looks and gestures that meant no more than she knew, exquisitely expertly, 'how to do it' which subtly she did, with great charm. I felt that acting, the stage and the people in it and on it were to her less than light bulbs and phantasma. To her *we* were actual people.

4 December At last the show, good—or good as such a cheap meaningless transient sentimental rehash of lies could be. *But* its central character, Peter Finch—a real person. Rare, and I sincerely felt looking back on my life, a formative person to me, and now a very full-blown, successful, brilliant, sympathetic, sentimental true adventurer. And O my God how witty and gentle and sweet and chancy a companion!

There was a party at the BBC. Then we went on to Peter Finch's private do—O—Peter's tales. And O, such mass food and wine, and we went on to unlimited champagne, with music and flamenco dancing.

5–6 December I had an energetic and occasionally riotous time—the theatre, 'gay' pubs, even gayer restaurants. Walked the streets for miles and miles, looking at antique shops, crammed with tempting things. I buy etchings by Piranesi and Picasso that I want. They really are very beautiful indeed.

Spent, at the Tate, what was probably the most important two hours for me in the last five years, looking at the new paintings and sculptures. I begin to see that Abstract Expressionism in the hand of artists like

William Scott[15] is a very genuine force. After a while with these pictures, when we went to look at other old favourites so many of them seemed weak and fussy. Van Gogh and most of the Impressionists suffered: Picasso and Braque stood up strongly and beautifully as ever. I began in my mind to change my painting. But I still think Jackson Pollock's[16] a rotten painter. The Tate's Nolan *Woman and Billabong*[17] was merely efficient I thought. But my mind is really full of shapes and colours, all new, that have bubbled up and are brimming over, from that two hours in the gallery.

16 December *Bentota*. I am very depressed. A reaction from England. What *am* I doing wasting my life in this backwater?—my painting begins to die. I have never worked to the full extent of my talent. I just do meaningless pleasant pictures, and I'm tired, bored and discontented with them.

Again I think of going home to Australia. Where would I live?—how find a flat in Sydney?—it's all too depressing and dreary. But I must go. The decay here is irresistible: for five years I have been drawing on inner stimuli, and in the absence of a climate of criticism, have had to rely on my own to assess my painting. Now I am bankrupt of ideas. Also the cost of living has become impossibly high.

23 December Here in the bungalow I paint all day, feeling life for me is meaningless.

And *Christmas*!—bloody Christmas. My table is littered with bright cards from neglected friends. It's amusing to note, nothing from anybody I've ever benefited. The fond wishes are all from people I don't really long ever to see again, nor do they long for me. The others mean something—not much—to me still. It might even be reciprocal. It is not possible to believe there is a single positive human relationship in my life now. How horrid Christmas is, and the realisation it brings to mind to an ageing egomaniac!

1962

1–5 January *Sydney*. I've dined out with all the old friends. (Jeff Smart has been wonderfully kind driving me about to search for a house.) I have been looking a lot at young artists' work—Olsen[1] and so on. They do not really seem to have anything to say in their paintings. But worst of all, in Tas's studio two large mules from his recent show—*awful*. I hope his recent great successes are not going to finish him off as a painter.

6–8 January *Perth*. Joe and Rose Skinner charmingly welcomed me at the airport. The gallery is very good—a really large well-lit room whose walls flatter my paintings.

It was a sweltering hot day for the opening, and there were 400 people in the gallery when Vivien Leigh drove up to make her little speech. She did her part beautifully—brief and gracious and had them all fascinated. TV cameras added to the swelter with their batteries of lights. I was autographing books and catalogues and very much besieged—all very flattering: more pictures sold.

4 February Every day I have largely spent painting, for the most part on gold-leaf pictures, although yesterday, after several frustrated tries, got a numb, dumb shy little Aborigine half-caste from Alawa Camp to pose for me. They seem to me odd, spineless, feckless, tragic people.[2]

7 March *Sydney*. I seem to have entered a period of confusion and irresolution, with no firm idea of what I want, or what is wisest to do. I will *have* to live in this bloody country. I am homesick for order and respect. For Ceylon and my boys and the bungalow. My Australian loved ones, old friends, are so messy and neurotic. Nevertheless I am painting, and if it is not the work of genius it's still a bloody sight better than a lot of the trash I've seen exhibited such as Passmore's later work (the old boy, self-pitying, gabbling about the imminence of death, conceited, touchy and pretentiously solemn).

Last week of March *Adelaide*. Off the plane and straight to a poetry reading in the park bordering a river, where Max Harris and other poets read their works to the ambulating citizens—and then to a champagne party at a great sandstone baronial rich nonsense of a house full of fine pictures and antique furniture. Then Geoffrey Dutton's, Mount Lofty.[3] These are delightful people—really delightful.

Here in the festival environment of several very interesting art exhibitions, I enjoyed most that of Rex Nan Kivell's[4] Australiana collection, but there were several good modern shows. I first saw and was much taken with Clifton Pugh's[5] paintings.

There is a great row blowing up about the big exhibition—part of which is on show here—to go to the Tate Gallery in London. It is a very odd selection, and rather remarkable for the omission of a number of important painters and the inclusion of many nonentities. Bert Tucker[6], that bombastic bearded fake of a painter who energetically contributes to his own importance by styling himself with Nolan and Drysdale as a member of the trio who are world-famous outside Australia, has only one painting in this show and is now organising an interstate newspaper furore about it. (I have as yet none, but trust that Tas will remedy that in his capacity as the newest member of the Art Advisory Council.[7])

14 April *Sydney*. Robert Hughes[8] is a recently made acquaintance, and rather a storm centre. He is very young (about 24) and *very* lively. He paints (*quite* appalling, but anyway quite as good as the other Abstract Expressionists)—studies architecture, writes plays, articles and criticisms on art for the *Bulletin*[9] or the *Nation*[10]. He is a vivid person, virile, restless, energetic, fizzing with ideas, projects, and impatient. He is well-read and *very* quick to learn, and sensitive to the climate of other people's minds. A tremendous lot of people, mostly of his own generation, dislike him with a sort of frustrated anger at his doing all he does. I find him wonderful company—not exactly restful—but enlivening as few of his generation are.

8 May *Bentota*. Home here to find the bungalow as though I had never left it for a day. I felt already the pleasant purposeless indifference of Ceylon like a warm sweet mist all around me. I sip morning tea and wander about the garden, and it all looks lovely, and the place louder with bird song than I remember.

Bevis's chauffeur, looking like a young Tahitian by Gauguin in a red sarong, sweeping leaves from lawn. Murmuring laughter in the kitchen from my cook. I wonder if they see me as a person as I do them. Despite all I feel about them, *and* Ceylon, I have already in my heart deserted them knowing I bloody well must. The future for me is my own sordid ambitions in Australia.

23 May To my peaceful world of silly illusions, after a day of painting villages and wandering in the garden, and reading, and drawing again, and complaining about the frequent showers of rain, and the prevalence of mosquitoes and the indigestibility of omelettes, came, with my income tax papers, a destructive bomb of a letter. I *won't* pay this monstrous imposition. What I have of capital was not much of it earned by me, but others dead and gone, and not made here in Ceylon. So what right have *these* greedy pirates to it? I will set about escaping as quickly as is consistent with completing two mural commissions to get money for packing and sending my furniture, books, china, pictures and various small sculptures.

5 July When the excitement of the packing of possessions subsided I went back to work in the studio, but for the rest of the day and evening there was a series of visitations from the villages around—news travels fast among the simple people. Some of my old favourites, rogues and rascals of servants I'd sacked turned up. Then the big bungalow servants to ask if I would go and have a studio photograph taken with them all.

So the bones are already picked pretty dry. The bungalow looks very stark suddenly.

Last week of July *Perth.* Rose Skinner from the moment of arrival gaily plunged me into dinner engagements etc. Joe had bad news. Tim Drysdale[11] had suicided. So better go over as soon as I can.

It was clear long ago that Tim would destroy himself or engineer his own destruction—having blighted everything else that he could in order to assert himself, I guess that at last he must have somehow recognised himself at a moment when pretences were inadequate. It remains to be seen what effect it will have on Tas and Bon. They are pretty unpredictable in major events. They may even be hugely, sanely relieved (as everyone else will be)—but more likely Bon will be drowning in guilt for things she never did.

15 August *Sydney*. I am buying a tiny little house in Paddington[12]—in Hampden Street by Trumper Park. The smallest house there ever was, but neatly fitted up like a two-storey ship's cabin. Too small for the furniture which is being shipped here from Ceylon. But it will do. I am going to live quietly. Most people seem to have grand and busy ideas, but I want to re-learn how to live alone in this damned busy country full of grief and death and ambition and greed and bogusness (and love and affection too, I must affirm).

4 September To the opening of Johnny Bell's show—so crowded there were fifty or seventy people out in the street who could not cram in. *All* the pictures sold. James Fairfax made the opening speech very nicely.

Johnny's painting owes a tremendous lot to my ideas about drawing. At last I can see *good* work which owes a lot to mine. I don't mean that he plagiarises, but that it gives me tremendous pleasure to see that I have at last contributed to the work of a talented man.

John himself is a wonderful personality. After, Mitty Lee-Brown[13], Chica[14] and I went to his madly beatnik party in Woolloomooloo[15], in a vacant lot, where about 200 mostly very young wild weird people danced and drank and kissed and fought savagely. It was a nightmarish scene among broken buildings, with harsh lights and loud blaring urgent jazz music. Wild girls with veils of hair in their eyes, and superb mad young boys, dancing.

2 December The opening of Tas's exhibition of drawings. All the art-social faces. So much chatter.

I was not impressed by the show. There is, though Tas would not admit it, a sort of resentment (a jealousy) in him towards Sid Nolan. So in a way he does not admit to himself he is competing with Nolan, whom he does not regard very highly as an artist. However, Nolan works hard, whether his painting is good or not.

1963

January This life I live now is an indifferent affair. Most of my positively happy times are when sculpturing in the stable in Mitty Lee-Brown's Jersey Road house.[1] My heart has gone almost out of painting, and I do very little drawing. Australians don't seem interesting to draw—or I can't find a good model.

'Social' life claims some time: the little dinner parties of pretentious people, at which gatherings I figure as a living witness that they are cultured enough to invite me. And I enjoy an hour or so of the occasions, and then grow very weary. Occasionally on a Friday night I go to the George[2], where there is always the spectacle of bohemia (or the 'beatniks'[3], or the 'Push'[4] as the press calls them) and there's talk and a sort of violent disembodied friendliness. The sensational papers have been giving some notice to the pub and its habitués of late, because of a sensational double murder of a scientist and some woman[5]—he was supposed to have been seen drinking there. There have been articles on the 'beat' way of life, with its amorality, or immorality and excesses. They seem to me, these young people, very little different to what my friends and I used to be when we had the youth, energy and inclination to muck up.

3 February Today there was a luncheon party—about fifty people—at the Hungry Horse restaurant, below the gallery of the same name, to start off Bob Hughes's exhibition.[6] I bought a small oil such as will not dwarf the walls of my small house (rest of the pictures are of a fair size). Have also become possessed of a tiny iron maquette for sculpture of Clem Meadmore's[7], who also was there. He is going off to America in a few days. Personally I find his work admirable but undesirable, and I bought it only because I wanted to help: they are blockish, cold things, his works—simulated non-perfectionism, like Mondrian's[8] paintings with deliberate imperfections added. When I look at the angled balance of rectangles of iron sheet welded one piece to another, and hear the intellectuals praising (as Bob Hughes, Daniel Thomas[9] and others do) its wonderful balance of and enclosures of space, I privately think it is really a fashion for dull and boring exercises.

Bob Hughes's work looked well. He has learned a lot about tone and colour in recent months, and the paintings begin to have something like authority.

4 February Another 'typical' day—painting from 7 a.m. till 9 on small 'charming' pieces produced now under pressure for Macquarie Galleries and Rose Skinner, and so I miss most of my pleasure in such things, which is producing at leisure painted half-jesting comments and private jokes. If I have to work like *this* much more, I'll be turning out prefabricated whimsies.

6–7 February Bob Hughes drove me up to a farm near Wyong[10] to visit John Olsen, who is living and painting there away from the rat race of the Sydney art world. Delightful. A simple verandahed bungalow standing on a slope among tall gums. Possums and goannas wander in and out of the house. Olsen is good company and a good host. The pictures he is doing are quite beyond the scope of my appreciation, and I have to take it for granted that they are good. But I cannot somehow quite believe it, yet suppose it must be so.

Last week of February *Brisbane*. To my delight, Brisbane's streets and suburbs, not subject to such changes as Sydney, still retain the same slightly run-down, decayed, easygoing tropical atmosphere that constituted my mental image of it. I stayed with Margaret Olley in her old weatherboard house on stilts—the walls hung with many pictures, the Victorian knick-knacks and vases of flowers, Aborigine bark paintings and Sepik carvings[11]. She was working every day vigorously on a series of large nudes.

June *Sydney*. Johnny Bell comes round quite often: gaunt, thin, half-starved-looking, cat-like, wild, sweet naive simple fellow (he looks so like that Dobell painting Mitty has, *The Irish Youth*)—he moves me. The other night went at his invitation to a wild mad fancy-dress party (I made a mask—a sort of death mask, for the occasion) where all the 'beats', the 'Push' and the riffraff from the younger artists and students' world were gathered, as well as various ones in strange costumes dancing and drinking in a Paddington terrace house.

Second and third weeks of August *Bribie Island.*[12] Olley and I went to visit the legendary hermit, Ian Fairweather[13]. I felt diffident about invading his privacy, but it seems he had written to Olley saying he wanted to meet me.

On the island we found the wallaby track from the roadside that wound among bracken, passing under the natural arch made by a twisted bleached log and then led to a copse of feathery straight trees, whose dappled light and shade help to further the natural camouflage of the two strange and charming huts made of logs and twigs and thatch that the old man lived in.

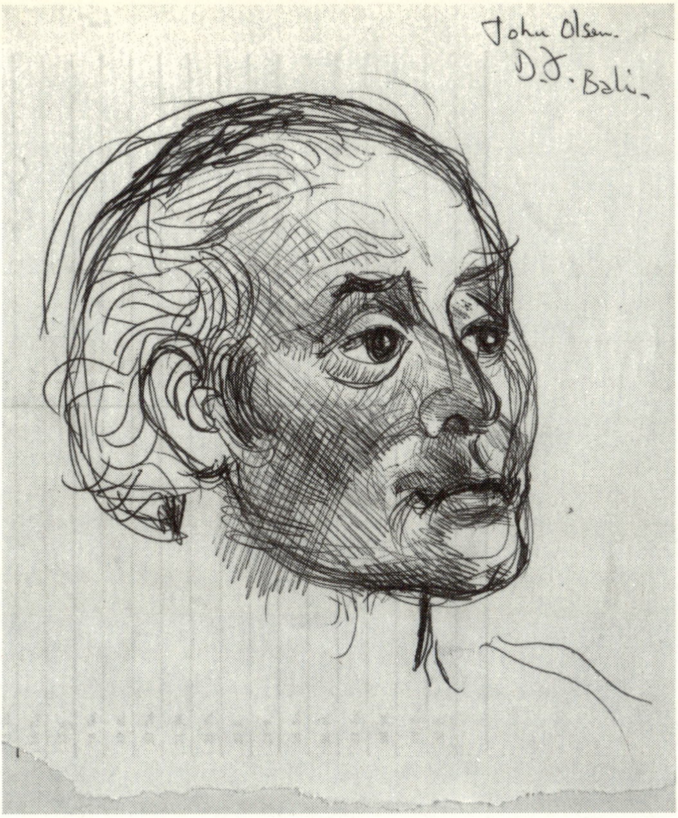

31. *'John Olsen'* (1973).

Fairweather was quietly spoken, tall, thin, battered and bearded. He spoke and acted with an old-fashioned courtesy. He talked not at all of painting, but of his travels, and the looming problem of soon having to find a new place to live, since Bribie Island is quickly becoming a tourist place. I said I might get a hut on Thursday Island. 'I'll come and live there if you do,' Fairweather said. He seemed surprised and amused when I told him of the queues of people who waited up all night to buy his work at the Macquarie Galleries. He lives now in simplicity, solitude and poverty because he cannot bother to change it, or cannot make the necessary effort to cope with the orders of society that hem in his own world like a besieging army.

The huts he has built have a strange beauty of the same order as his paintings: they are very dark inside, and cluttered with books, rustic benches, favourite twisted pieces of driftwood and oddly shaped *objets trouvés*, and many sheets of paper, covered with Chinese calligraphy. Four or five paintings, unfinished, glimmered on the end wall: they are on cheap cardboard, and the paints he uses of cheap powder colours which easily crack and peel off, to the despair of art collectors. He works mostly at night, by the light of kerosene lamps that, I noticed, were hung in dangerous proximity to the thatch.

He talked of his desire to have a little boat to go sailing up the coast in; and of the hardships of his famous drifting raft trip from Darwin to Timor, during which, because of the violent rocking of the craft, he had had to lie half-submerged on his back for days, his eyes tortured by the sun's glare.

'Next time,' he said, 'I must remember to take a pair of sunglasses.'

Mid-September *Sydney*. I like very much going to visit Johnny Bell in his house in Camperdown[14]: it is a very nice house. We drink and talk for hours in the greatest sympathy, and I really love Johnny, to see him there living amongst a few boxes for tables and three chairs that have to be carried upstairs, and from one room to another (because we are always moving from room to room) and his strange and evocative stories. He and Mitty are the only people I see nowadays really to talk to—except for Bob Hughes, who at last is back from Melbourne, and very soon to be leaving for America. Bound, I should bet, for tremendous success. He has somehow about him an aura of the greatest promise: and in addition all the drive and wild nervous energy that is the very ingredient of success in America. I shall miss Bob, and his departure will leave Australia bereft of its best art critic.

Jeff Smart also will be soon leaving for Europe. With him and Hughes gone I shall have only John Bell and Mitty left to talk to (Tas Drysdale I see very seldom now—maybe once in a month).

28–29 September *Canberra*. Except for one important detail, the opening of my exhibition went off very well. Arriving, Mitty and Bill[15] and I—none of whom find Canberra an interesting or sympathetic city—went straight to the exhibition, and found between amusement and horror that I had mistaken the date. The show had been opened days previously. Well-attended, I understand. About eight or nine pictures had sold, which is more than I expected from the town of politicians and civil servants and regimented living.

2 October *Sydney*. Margaret Olley is down for her exhibition, which opened at the Macquarie. Lots of old friends gathered there. It sold moderately well, and the critics were lukewarm and it is ironic that now they have committed themselves so deeply to abstract art that we, the figurative painters, labour under a cloud of disapproval, rebels against the decrees of the tastemakers.

9 October Now here is Bob Hughes—a spiky, nervous, irritable young fellow if ever there was, impatient, bad-tempered, brilliant: and more desperately in need of unreasoning affection than any of the other bright young men I know, and less likely to arouse the affection he needs than most. But I'm very fond of Bob, and dearly like his company. But it's a bloody nuisance when others arrive when he's here—he bristles, becomes obsessively loquacious (and damned good things he says, and soon a sort of bitter attacking tone comes in: I think he loves his few friends jealously so resents the others: he can't forgive absurdities in those who are not included in his small circle of liking and trust).

16 October Bob Hughes's mother fell ill, and died. He came after to see me, and seemed to find comfort here, an escape from the strong Catholic atmosphere of his family, and all the ghoulish occasions and incidents, so full of rending souvenirs of his mother, to whom he was very close.

So much for death. Now for marriage. Mitty picked me up to drive off and be a witness to her marriage to Bill Gordon. After we lunched at the Australian Club[16] in Macquarie Street. I slept all afternoon until it was time for the huge party at Mit's Jersey Road house, which was done as most things she does—in the grand manner: about two hundred guests. Mitty looked very beautiful, vital, electric, and tremendously elegant in a French model. Mitty always has my admiration in the dashing style and taste and energy she brings to any occasion, whether it's the simplest luncheon or an affair of this size.

20–22 November There are times when the decay of the world around one seems suddenly to accelerate: then I bury my head deeper in work. Like an ant trying to build up what is being torn away.

Tas Drysdale returned from business in Canberra and found Bon dead. She had taken a massive dose of tablets. Poor old Tas. I spent the evening with him, he dissolving in seas of grief—rallying himself and talking suddenly, repetitively about geology or a hundred other subjects, and then suddenly plunging again into his loss and misery.

1964

January I sit at home, read interminable detective books, paint a little and despair a lot. Some sort of light I once had has become very much dimmed. Adventures are few and far between. I wash some clothes, and make a little lunch, and read again. Paint?—half a dozen unfinished daubs await the touch of the master's brush in the cramped little upstairs studio.

11–12 February Bob Hughes's energies and inventiveness are in a constant terrific ferment. His wild enjoyment of life and his work, his gusto and wit and the sheer pleasure of his intelligent converse draw series of sparks from one's own mind. He throws himself into all of his many activities with urgency; he enjoys all the gestures of his various roles—the lifted eyebrow, the delighted swoop as he pounces on some phrase; he lunges at ideas. And his good looks—he has a Renaissance head, the features handsomely, definitely sculptured, nervous, impatient, often irresponsible—indicate clearly a lot of his character. He has a fine capacity for friendship, but for those outside the circle of his affections—the very numerous acquaintances among intellectuals—his activities are frequently the cause of rage, fury and exasperation, when his sharp pen happens to pin them down as specimens exhibited in a cultural rogues gallery.

First week of April The air is full of town stinks and most people seem to be tensely performing, rather than living, their lives, and as soon as you come in contact with them their fever contaminates, so in a moment you are yourself smoking and drinking like mad to raise up a protective fog to conceal you a little from their peeking and prodding involvements. I'm back to the old routine of working in hour-and-a-half snatches to avoid involvements, and then saying 'yes' to every damned fool who rings up to invite me to be part of their grisly activities.

9 April Leslie Walford[1] threw a party. I hardly know why I was asked, though there was much to divert me in the sight of so many ambitious-to-be-fashionable upstarts climbing into the giddy heights of interior-decorator-ism, cruising through the rooms which are Leslie's triumph of modish sumptuousness—the gilded mirrors, excellent paintings, marble, marquetry and ormolu are very impressive, and well arranged.

It was an amusing party really, taken as a spectacle. The splendid furniture seemed especially contrived as a setting for those who were ambitious to be Sheridan[2] fops, and each one was carefully dressed as the creature he aspired to be, whilst their actual characters and professions of real everyday life were quite equally and undisguisably apparent—milliners, shop salesmen, decorators, hairdressers and draper's assistants, all attaching themselves as satellites to the stars of their firmament, the 'famous' ones who get their names in the social columns of newspapers several times a week for such difficult attainments as eating in public places in the company of other famous names from overseas.

Yesterday I painted at home all day, and the only visitors, just before I went to bed, were young Martin Sharp and Richard...Neville?—Walsh?—who run a rather scurrilous satirical magazine called *Oz*[3], which is constantly in trouble with police and censors, who are the principal butts for its wit. The wonder is that the magazine continues to exist: I think it is getting an increasing circulation and is improving both in quality and notoriety. They want me to do some caricatures.

10 April Colin Lanceley[4] and Martin Sharp drew up outside in an ancient sports car that one immediately saw had been born a lord but had lived long as a tramp. The works were more than extraordinary: constructions incorporating the works of old pianos, dolls, beads and various junk coloured with gay and optimistic paint—all of a sort of laughing eccentricity. These are for a show in solemn bitch-hearted Melbourne, where I'm sure they'll be awarded wreaths of thorn. Are they any good?—God knows why, but I do think so.

11 April Colin MacInnes[5] suggested luncheon today. He came, a well-spoken tall albino, and after an hour or two's drinking and chatting we went out to Watsons Bay[6], where, buying wine for lunch, we met Bob Hughes and Noeline Brown[7], and joined forces to eat. Very pleasant: and after wandered about Vaucluse House[8] which was subjected to condescending remarks by MacInnes (to my resentment), who then took to making pot-shots at me, which I bore politely enough. So to a long crawl of pubs, flats and houses for some hours, during which this fellow got progressively—God knows why—more snipey, until I began shooting back. Poor Bob, who realised this somewhat late, was in an embarrassing position, since he knew MacInnes quite well. After a silly incident in which MacInnes broke a glass of beer and then shot into the lavatory like a rabbit, I said to Bob 'we scram.' I'm antipathetic to the grand international Kamp[9] type.

12 April In this town either one does nothing at all, or hundreds of fragmented things broken up into little incidents. I painted, slept and read all day at home until evening, when asked over to drinks to meet the PR man for Dame Margot Fonteyn's[10] ballet company. Then one of the dancers came, a very beautiful amiable boy who presently took off all his clothes and leapt and lounged all over the place (wearing nothing but a big jewelled crucifix about his neck on a thick gold chain) with grace and abandonment.

13 April To a reception for Dame Margot Fonteyn and her company of dancers—last night's amiable boy introduced me to the fabulous Nureyev[11]: Sir William Walton[12] came in with Lady Lloyd Jones[13] who was all graciousness and so on and so on.

3 July *Nimmitabel, Bobingah.*[14] Painting continues, and I'm as usual pleased with results—pleased too with the struggles that produce them: some small oil landscapes of this district. Very simple, and rather difficult. No tricks and no pyrotechnics. In these panels I've been at great pains to express the skies, which in this part of the country seem to be vaster than elsewhere, and vary wonderfully in mood and colour, and present many problems to paint. In town somehow all day the sky seems barely to exist until at last one notices it at sundown.

10–12 July This weekend was a great sociable round of visits, luncheons and dinners: we drove down to Bungendore[15] to a dinner party. It was a jovial uproarious and yet very clannish affair and imbued with a sort of virile, slightly out-of-date merriment that often strikes me as veering almost to violence, or at least horseplay—and everyone full of good food and strong drink, faces glowing almost as fiercely as the blazing logs in the fireplace in that great drawing room with its huge noble windows with high cedar panelled shutters closing us warmly in from the wild gale that blew outside: a room that still shows indications of its having been built like the rest of the house, to be defended against the bushrangers. There is *that* feeling even now—that all those in the room were quite accustomed to fight back at the descendants of those same robbers of former days, state members of a Labor parliament who in these days have cut up properties into small blocks for soldier settlement.

These people are all in various ways amusing in a pleasurable way, well mannered, something arrogant with it, and full of charm and goodwill to those they accept. And quite ruthlessly shut off from those they don't.

19 July *Bowral*. I came down to and stayed overnight in a grisly motel. The purpose was to have a look at Retford Park[16], which James Fairfax has bought. The house is being done up by Leslie Walford, and I am to do a mural in the dining room. This is a most important commission to me in a dozen ways. In the first place I want to have a major work on a wall in Australia. Also I like James, and he is a serious patron of painting. I've been working for quite a while on and off in figure drawings and small tempered panels of details for it, to get together a whole bag of ideas I can incorporate in the big work.

Second week of September *Retford Park*. So much is done, and it's so near completion now that I don't know if it's brilliant or bloody awful. This is such an intense and introverted way of living in this huge empty mansion with its banging doors and echoing rooms. I seem almost imprisoned in this room with the painting, the wireless I brought up this time for the companionship of its music, and the fire I keep going day and night, and a jam tin packed with flowers from the garden—daffodils and jonquils and grape hyacinth, and white and rosy camellias.

It's pretty odd to find oneself a fairly celebrated artist at the age of *near* 50, at work at last on the only painting that could be called an important big work in the only country (one can't count poor naive innocent Ceylon!) where I have any celebrity now.

Last week of September *Sydney*. Luncheons, dinners and parties nearly every day: one has not recuperated from one excess of talk, drink, food and tobacco before the next, and I weakly enjoy the vivacious folly-mongers, who fortunately are numerous enough to give some semblance of variety. But there was an evening of fairly good talk at Chica's, where I met (I'd met him many years before, briefly, at Merioola, when he was an unknown journalist) George Johnston[17], author of the very successful *My Brother Jack*[18], and his wife Charmian[19]. We talked mostly of Greece, where they'd lived for the last fifteen years.

Johnston is a garrulous and often funny man, but very longwinded and not a wit: but he is interesting to listen to. I also liked Charmian, who is not pompous but takes herself very seriously, and I think is kind.

10 October I took a small party to a new 'drag' show at Watsons Bay, where Gwen is stage manager.[20] I found my capacity for enjoyment rather tautly stretched to get any kicks out of a mucky ugly and noisy exhibition of dreary imitations of show girls and variety queens by gawky transvestites. It was like a rowdy bad dream. Perhaps I am about to go through one of those souring periodical moods of disillusion that are apt to descend when I find it hard to paint.

31 October Modes of fashion and behaviour in the level of 'society' are no more absurd in their adherence to follow-my-leader asininities than on the bohemian level, whose conformity to established symbols (the beard, the long greasy hair, the worn jeans, the women's uniform look of distraught repletion, etc.) is very much the same thing.

11 November To the Clune Gallery[21] to see their show of modern European. Though there are only three or four of great quality, those—two Rouaults[22], a Miró[23] and a Picasso lithograph—are memorable and marvellous: most especially the Picasso, which is a line design of a merry rape drawn with the most miraculous verve and vigour.

I saw another show at the Macquarie Galleries, of very slight and amusing pastiches by Cedric Flower[24]. There was sherry and a lot of people in smart hats, all rather of a quality with the paintings, which is to say pleasant and pretty vapid.

28–29 November 1 Hampden Street, Paddington. I moved in. Gwen came and helped me, for a very long day's cleaning and scrubbing and organising. And it looked marvellous by the time we'd exhaustedly cleaned ourselves, rang Bill[25] and Lynne[26] and Colin Lanceley and Peter Sculthorpe (musician)[27] to come round and drink a great deal of champagne, so took Gwen to dinner very late, had only time for oysters and then had to dash off to a party which I absolutely *had* to go to, to meet one of the people whose talent has given me great enjoyment all my life since I was a boy, Louis Armstrong.

I was too shy for a long time to go and talk to the great man, but after a long and very amusing conversation with Mrs Armstrong[28], a fabulous negress with deep red hair piled in a turban, I went off to find him, and there he was sitting in the supper room with James Fairfax: and exactly as a person what one felt from his music—that humorous gravelly voice laughing.

We talked about jazz, and he illustrated points by singing terrific crazy phrases. In talking, his tone of voice, thick-honey-like, and his laugh, seemed absolutely part and parcel of his familiar music—very personal and intimate interpretation.

30 December Bilgola[29], to James's cottage perched on the rocky cliff above the sea. The most beautiful hot sunny day. John Olsen was there, and after lunch one of those odd visions occurred when one's environment is suddenly metamorphosed—*explained*—by the work of a particular artist. He and I had been talking about Hieronymous Bosch when we both became simultaneously aware that the party, now somewhat intoxicated, had presented itself in Bosch's terms. From where we sat the other guests appeared as contrasting grotesques in a frieze against a vast backdrop of sea, sky and rocky coastline: some dancing the twist with gawky gestures, some had put on the huge absurd hats of the women, others, replete, reclined idly chewing remaining claws of lobster. They had become before our eyes the crowd of fiends and imps that one finds in the master's *Temptation of St Anthony*[30]. As Olsen said, *these* people capering and posturing in the sun are our patrons. These are the only ones with enough money, leisure and intelligence to enable them to indulge the aesthetic life, yet their lack of understanding of it is almost a total blindness, and they use great and marvellous things only as primpings to conceit. If they could bottle the music of Beethoven they'd use it to scent their armpits.

1965

Mid-January to mid-February *Sydney*. A month during which, quietly, a number of things greatly important to me have been happening, set (for the most part) against a background of much laughter, drinking, dancing and gadding about. Most important of all, a great burst of vigorous work. The drawings pile up: the cream of them set aside for my show[1], and a few of them sold outright for current expenses. Which are very high, as I've become hospitable, and have little caviar and champagne luncheons. For not more than four guests, usually artists.

3 March A dinner party at James Fairfax's—for his mother to meet Patrick White[2]. We faced up to him with some nervousness, as he can be—and is well known for it—devastating. But no one could have been more amusing and pleasant, and in fact the whole party was delightful: there were eight of us to enjoy a superb meal and wonderful wines, and so many entertaining and notable things were said that I've forgotten them all. Patrick White gives me the impression of a man who keeps a tremendous store of power in reserve: a sort of quiet volcano. I don't really like his books, except for *The Tree of Man* and *Riders in the Chariot*.[3]

6 March Changed into jeans and went up to the Windsor Castle pub in Paddington, still so favoured by the art crowd that it was packed to suffocation with polyglots. There are great flocks of hangers-on, very exhibitionist and very young. About sixteen of these were all in one group in the lounge smoking marijuana, the silly little asses. The smell of the smoke is quite distinctive. It says something for Australian naivety that no one else seemed to remark on it.

'Pot' smoking has suddenly become quite widespread amongst the young. I believe there are great paddocks of the stuff growing in the Grafton[4] district, as well as thriving bushes of it in Sydney suburban gardens. One can see this can go on quietly only for a limited period: then there'll be a big newspaper and police noise and scandal and a lot of stuff about sex-mad artists and perverts living in a sea of drugs. My own slight observation of the phenomenon is that the ones fooling around with this stuff are the artists' hangers-on—a gaggle of giggling little queens and jazzy lesbian girls and a few students and no-hopers.

Little coteries of society people come to watch these spirited high-jinks, and there were to be seen also, as more harbingers of its imminent decay, numerous millinery gentlemen who usually frequent the Rex Hilton bar[5]. Some youths in black leather jackets with shoulder-length hair and Christ beards formed a pool of sullen silence in the middle of leotard girls with equally long blonde hair. Everyone's clothes seemed to be white, blue and scarlet and black. Regularly the crash of smashed glasses punctuated the orchestra of hubbub. Heterogeneous couples clung together. Homogeneous couples clung together.

26–27 April About 150 carefully selected ones drank champagne and grinned and chattered at the opening of my show at the Darlinghurst Gallery.[6] Thank God I knew most of them and actually *liked* quite a few. There were enacted, as usual, several comedies, and the whole occasion was one for congratulations all round. We were honoured by the presence of the Governor-General, Lord De L'Isle.[7]

At the restaurant our table was scandalously ribald. Peter Scriven[8] and a Thai boy were with us, and a Japanese boy, a potter and landscape gardener called 'H.O.', bright-eyed and very intelligent. At midnight we walked down to my studio, and at about half-past four in the morning after many more bottles of champagne had been consumed, I sent the last batch of them home, except 'H.O.', who stayed with me.

Success, success, success, etc. It should have a better sweeter sound to the ear. It is the only part of painting that doesn't make me happy.

30 April 'H.O.' and I meet every evening, and will do so until he goes back to Melbourne in a few days. Fortunately he seems to be, from photographs of gardens designed by him, and one or two exquisite pots he showed me, talented as well as intelligent and charming. After having once again accustomed to, and armed against, the sporadic and crude Australian reaction to aesthetic experience, it is a surprise and delight to see him gravely and pleasurably contemplating my treasures. The sudden impact of the idea of civilisation after so much amiable dog-like barbarism takes time to get used to.

Australia is becoming increasingly involved in dangerous little wars in S. E. Asia, with mere token forces that nevertheless are great political commitments. The latest—Australia's sending a silly little force of 800 soldiers to America's war in Vietnam[9]—is the worst and most dangerous, and quite obviously done under heavy pressure from America from purely political (as against military) motives. There are even more photographs of troops and jungles in the newspapers than those I had noticed as a long-term softening up of the popular mind over the last few months.

12 May I have been several times again to see Olsen's exhibition at the Clune Gallery, staying only a few minutes—the force and vivacity and strength of these very lively and gay pictures is at once exhilarating and exhausting. I feel for them, and with them, without understanding them at all.

Lunch at a very good little Italian ristorante I'd discovered in Darlinghurst. There, also lunching, was Olsen. I took the opportunity to speak to him about his tapestry. 'The result is too smooth and professional,' I explained. 'An artist in painting depends on and induces "accidentals" to give liveliness and fascination to his canvas. He invites roughnesses, and often relies on them to give spontaneity. He avoids or conceals perfection and smoothness. A high finish imbues a picture with deadness. The cartoon from your hand is infinitely preferable to the completed tapestry *because* it has all the life of the creator's hand. The tapestry loses because of its marvellous exactitude.'

John got all lit up with this. 'My God, it's the best thing that's been said in weeks about it. *That's* what I want. Yes, by God, you're right'—he burbled on in the greatest delight.

18 May Ian Fairweather's exhibition was nicely timed to coincide with the publication of his book—his translation from the Chinese *The Drunken Buddha.*[10] However I don't really admire the book much—the reproductions are fuzzy and *quite* unlike the original paintings that illustrate the text. The story seems a pleasantly tedious bit of orientalism and Fairweather's English text surprised me by being neither incisive nor poetic nor elegant: in fact it is dull and foot-weary. His prose is apparently inferior to his scholarship.

But the *paintings* at the Macquarie Galleries (a number of them are the book illustrations) are astonishingly good and beautiful. The old boy gets better and better. No great major works, but all intimate and profound and calm and light-hearted.

3 June Rudy Komon[11] reopened his redesigned and now very sparse and elegant gallery. Hundreds of people, champagne, a speech by Harold Holt[12]. I had gone with John Olsen, and later we went to a restaurant where Rudy gave about 30 of us dinner. It was a Swiss place, and the food was fat and dumplingish and indigestible. Later about eight of us came back to my studio and drank and talked. No exact impressions to record except liking Fred Williams[13], the rotund painter from Melbourne whose landscape was the finest picture in Rudy's show.

12–13 June *Hill End*. Pure enchantment: beautiful mild sunlight. The place was packed with tourists—lots and lots of young people from tech and university, very hairy and exaggerated all gathered at the pub, where some had a sort of skiffle band performing in the billiard room. The locals, surprisingly, seemed enchanted with the varied displays of eccentricity.

My new model was there—Stewart Holman[14], whom I like.

The deliciousness of the steaks grilled on the open fire after savourless Sydney cooking!—and the cool pure air. Even the dust (of which there is plenty in the cottage) seemed clean and harmless.

23 June *Sydney*. Work itself is now more than ever synonymous with a world of delight and affection: most of my days are spent with Stewart and pass very cosily. Drawings mount up. Domesticity becomes a pleasant amusement—special dishes are prepared, diverting surprises. Faintly I think wonderingly about 'H.O.' He's long overdue to return and occasionally I wonder if suddenly he's about to walk in—brisk, bird-like, so astonishingly intelligent and charming. *Then* what will happen?

25 June When I came downstairs to answer a knock on the door there was 'H.O.' looking like winter's first robin in his bright red and black pullover, radiating the charming alertness that warms one to him so instantly. He took in the entire situation with a single bright glance: 'I am glad you are so happy.'

I felt guilt at the peculiarly divided nature of my happiness, for my fondness of 'H.O.' is quite undiminished by my relation with Stewart. The two are utterly different, their needs are different.

16 July Drawing Stewart, which resulted in two of my very best drawings—on the 'Youth Death and the Maiden' theme[15], which is particularly suitable to present circumstances, seeing myself in the character of that amorous and ambiguous skeletal character at once yearned-for, hated, accepted, half-mocked and half-feared: my idea of death is something not quite credible, like one's own idea of oneself: a knowledgeable grotesque. As for Youth—more a receiver of gifts than a dispenser of favours.

24 July Stewart asked me out to Mosman[16] to see his studio, and have lunch there. We went down through the very steep and charming bush garden of rocks and native trees and clumps of winter iris and snowdrops in flower, and gums, and fern trees and banksias. Like Gauguin's hut, Stewart's is set romantically amongst these—a tiny place, with a bed and a bunk and shelves and a place for cooking, and his work tables. I find it delightful, and in some ways reminiscent of treasured huts in my days of youth and poverty, where one created as he has, a whole environment of one's obsession with painting expressed by a jug, a lamp, folios and sketchbooks, a guitar, prints of much-loved paintings pinned on the wall, and jars of brushes.

Stewart's pride and delight in all this became mine: we were both very pleased with one another: he cooked a meal of spaghetti with a sauce. We came back here in the afternoon: then 'H.O.' turned up, so drinks talk and music, and I took them out to a long protracted sukiyaki meal at the Cross. The happiest day.

21 August Things have settled down into a comfortable routine enlivened by surprises and felicities: a mutual tolerance, humour, unexpected tenderness. I have almost ceased to work myself, and absorb myself in teaching Stewart some few mysteries of painting, mostly by egging him on and encouraging and criticising. He learns quickly and improves.

Well there it is, dear children, dear apes, dear adults. This day I can walk down the jubilant street with air beneath my weightless feet, and

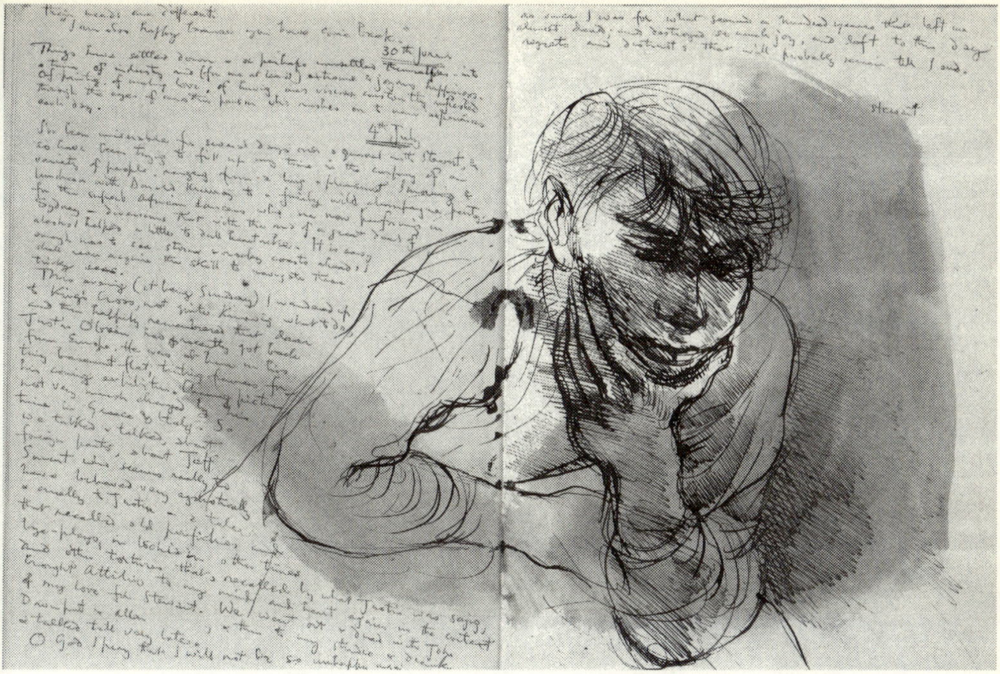

32. Stewart Holman (1965).

tomorrow like sad lead tumble dully down that same dreary lane, and both days (so opposite) lit by the same light, my only sun.

And you all can fucking well laugh. So laugh. But can you love? Are you loved? What good befalls you? Allow me to doubt it, because I *can*. And mine is the only wonderful love in the world I live in, even if it lasts a moment or two. Even more marvellous than that, I am loved. Beat that, all the world. It is new eyes, for to see a new blue, and new red, and new yellow, and all the cubes and curves and squares are new ones, and the sky and the leaves are reborn more beautifully for me through those other delightful young beloved eyes through which I can see, and all sounds and touches are refreshed, and my heart is kept alive with a knife turning slowly in it to remind me that again I am alive, and I could die now happy.

2–13 September *Hill End.* The village was all in a cloud of pink and white fruit blossoms and hazes of very young green leaf. I painted a lot on small oil landscapes, and spent hours each day working in the garden. There seemed little else to do, as Stewart with a borrowed rifle was out most of the time, and in all I saw not much of him, and some of what

I did see I didn't much like—the stubbornness, the babyish selfishness and frequent bad-tempered flashes of brutally oafish ill manners were not endearing, and only very occasionally compensated for by amusing good humour. He hardly worked at all. However, he seemed happy enough when not pointing out my ineptitudes.

18–22 September *Melbourne*. The gallery in Toorak Road is a good one. They hung the pictures and they really do look fine. The show[17] opened very successfully—nineteen pictures sold straight off, a great crowd and many compliments.

Melbourne life is utterly different from Sydney, different clothes, people, streets, houses, way of life. Not much life, *no* bohemia, very bourgeois.

Attilio looks after me like a son. It is really something very wonderful after all these years to see him now, so true to himself as always he was, and to find that I can now love him as dearly as ever I did, but without that passion that wrecked and broke me.

9 November *Sydney*. Stewart came, with an armful of canvases for me to look at. I don't *want* to be a 'Father Image' cliché figure, to be stoned and revolted against for the guilt he feels about betraying me, as so constantly he has done, in word and deed. I want only to love and be (a little bit, and not *all* the time) loved. Stewart to me (it makes me quite furious) is like having won some appallingly demanding and infuriatingly inconvenient thing in a raffle, such as a desert, or an angry crocodile.

22 December Stewart telephones. 'Come to the beach and watch me surfboard-riding.' Glorious weather, all sea and sky and foam, and the beach not crowded for all that it is a holiday period. And I watch with envy and delight these wet bronze figures performing their swift poetic gyrations as they soar through the green water and the foam.

We return here, and I make lunch, and he poses for a while, and then we both collapse in one another's arms, skin still salty from the sea. And presently he sleeps, and his dream wakes him up laughing, still held in my arms, and he talks at length his dream, a comedy in which I figure. And then entertains me with a dozen recent dreams in which I appear sometimes as a comic clownish character, but at others—?

Last week of December *Hill End.* Swimming and fishing and walking and climbing gorges to gather sun-warm ripe figs. We were absolutely soaked in sunlight, our bones almost melted with fatigue.

Selected our bird to cook for New Year's Eve from the hissing and cackling flock. It was all—including the execution and plucking, the advice, the arguments about stuffing, very pleasantly reminiscent of former times here, and so I was moved beyond present happiness by remembrances of the days before youth had quite fled.

Has it yet?—not from my mind anyway. And there are quite a few illusions left still intact and a capacity for loving as great as ever.

The goose was delicious. The wine had reached to just the climax of its excellence. Later we went to the pub for a few drinks with the well-oiled natives who exuded amiability: looked on for a moment at the dance in the hall next door where, unchanged in their rustic custom, the women and children sat all down one side of the room looking gloomily at the almost empty floor, whilst the men in their blue suits huddled on the opposite side, occasionally sallying out to the pub, and all the while a battered piano twanged and thumped a barndance.

1966

3–6 March *Melbourne.* The National Gallery opening of the 'Survey' exhibition of our work (about eight pictures each—Justin O'Brien, Jeff Smart, David Strachan and myself).[1] I dined out with the usual loving gaggle of Melbourne camps (O God the weary-making trillishness of the decorators, the theatre designers and the little old men in suits, from bookshops and the rag trade).

9 March *Sydney.* The heatwave is truly enervating. I couldn't work, but lay instead on the bed in the studio in a sarong, and read Marie Corelli (!) while Stewart, completely a child of the sun, painted all day at some small oil landscapes. His work improves apace from each day to the next.

Brett Whiteley[2] shows some oils (*Christie Murder* series[3]) and lithos at the Hungry Horse. They are extraordinary and very impressive, although, being a very commercial-pop type of young man, each painting contains fashionable and quite meaningless gimmicks, but not enough to wreck the pictures, lovely, limited colours and a draughtsmanship embracing noble forms, *almost* magnificent.

15 March Work, work: and a great deal of worry in my mind about money, and how I will raise enough to pay taxes and some big bills. I am strongly against selling out more capital as the share market is disastrously low, echoing as it does the effects of a long and terrible drought as well as the idiotic involvements we have as a nation entangled ourselves in with the war in Vietnam (a yet-undeclared war, an unwinnable war, a damned silly murderous unjust *American* war bred of American fears, neuroses, greed and hysteria).

26 March Jeff Smart came: he is much the same, why, perhaps, rather *more* so—that is, a little louder of voice, more orotund of phrase, inclined to lecture. His manner struck me as suitable to a drawing room full of women supposing they were listening to a very famous wit. However, what he had to tell of mutual friends in Europe was very entertaining. He showed me photographs of his new work, and his painting is greatly improved, a logical development of all his heartless and inhuman ideas and basic ignorance of his fellow beings in all their aspects except that of being human sacrifices of an antipathetic environment.

1 April At Barry Humphries', the comedian.[4] Barry is one of the rare theatre people who is actually witty, intelligent and non-stagey, but there were so many ham actors there, and journalists and the like, they constituted a tribe, friendly enough tho' notoriously cannibal, with whom one could communicate only by means of well-meaning smiles and pidgin phrases.

3 June I dined with Sandra McGrath.[5] The star guest was Brett Whiteley, small, with a mad little face crowned by a wild medusa-wig of straw hair, talking with tremendous vigour a rapid flow of quick incessant words packed with energy and ideas. I was impressed, and liked him. I can remember utterly nothing that Brett said, but that he talked at one time of certain drugs as being the future salvation by release of the human mind (hashish and LSD), which is not an idea to interest me.

Second half of June Johnny Bell has been coming every morning to draw. And because of this I am beginning to be more free of the obsession of Stewart. Johnny and I took a train up to Newcastle. It was like a mad picnic: railway coffee and scones. We laughed so much. And Newcastle itself was truly strange—friendly, quaint: the gallery was small and pretty and very hospitable, and all the local art-lovers nice in a weird sort of way. Incredible rich women with blonde hair being rival queens of culture bought with intense rivalry.

I am freewheeling my talent down a steep incline, doing a long, bitter, bumpy series of satyric and half-surrealist capriccios, in big notebooks. These are bitter and terrible and degenerate drawings done with hate and disillusionment in my heart, and feelings of great loss, and anger and fury at that loss. The new era I piously pray will be just a little bit less poisonously saddening than the last twelve months of long, unintelligent and unhappy obsession (yet it was fruitful—a whole harvest of the best drawings I've ever made in my life).

16 July This morning Harry Miller[6] rang. Will I join them this evening to see Robert Helpmann's *Elektra*[7]—also will I consider designing sets for a Helpmann ballet? I don't want to do theatre sets.

I did not think all that highly of *Elektra*—for all the talk—'My *dear*, it's so brilliantly sexual—but everything!'—etc. It struck me as a squalling squirming piece of business; a bit of fa-la-la, a bit of incest, a bit of crawling about the floor, some folderol and several ritual murders. Screechy and banging music, arid sets, dreary costumes, and the choreography was a catalogue of agonisingly difficult attitudes.

I much preferred an operetta piece that followed after, all charm and polkas and waltzes and heartbroken clowns, masked beauties and handsome princes.[8]

24 July *Brisbane*. The opening of the show[9] was well ordered and elegant, as usual in Brian Johnstone's beautiful gallery. There is nothing to approach it in Australia—having the wine served downstairs, so that people wander in the dappled light of the tropical garden instead of cramming the rooms makes it so that the pictures are always to be seen.

26 July It is really pretty cold here despite the clear sunlight. Margaret Olley and I go out with sketchbooks drawing the scenery along the banks of the river. It delights one to see in Brisbane how many odd old wooden cottages and curious rickety two-storey boarding houses still go on giving character to the city, jumbled in amongst the brick and cement boxes of later builders. I wander off and explore parks, or walk for miles in the suburbs that draggle out over hills as far as one can go, and find a place to read (or go and decipher the peculiarly different and exciting graffiti scrawled on walls that evoke ideas of a very different and somehow more virile erotic life than exists in the South).

29 July *Bribie Island.* Taking a picnic lunch, to see Ian Fairweather. Looking well in his craggy old way, and charming. We lunched on a long white deserted beach, watched a porpoise, wandered about and in all spent a peaceable day in the open, returning to his strange house of twigs and Kunai grass.

1–9 August *Noosa.*[10] In a little wooden cottage on stilts built right on the beach. There is no sound but the persuasive lulling of the waves breaking in long white lines. Beautiful sun-drenched empty days by the sea—or not empty, full of pleasant purposeless activities—walks along the rocky coast, talking and talking (I already am re-invigorated by Attilio's company that brings with it his zest and energy), swimming, hours of sunbaking, meals, and at night a few drinks at a pub on top of the hill, and early to bed to sleep deeply, and occasionally waking to hear the snoring sea.

The amiable girls (Ailsa Brydon[11] and her friend) cook for us, and wash up, and wash the clothes and do all those tiresome things one is used to doing for oneself, as a matter of course: I suppose they come of a generation—the last probably of its kind—whose mothers trained their daughters in those useful arts without which husbands are not to be caught and they keep on practising them, whilst yet there is hope: also out of the goodness of their simple hearts. But their talk, that betrays all the stilted conventionality of their minds and upbringing, is like chatter from another planet, so utterly strange is their world to mine.

The locals are ugly and gnarled as old sun-bitten saveloys. They are the stubborn living prototypes of Australian ugliness. Everyone seems old. Old old visitors who look anxiously right and left as they shuffle in slippers across the street. Old tourists and old shopkeepers, noses and chins like tomahawks, genuinely antique fishermen, veteran estate agents, old dames in backyards clutter up the scenery as they dodge the pawpaw trees on tottery trips to the outhouses (they're all called *Toilets*). The average age must be 60. Some scampering kids reduce that handicap, chasing a ball along the beach.

17 August *Sydney*. Parties. All different and all the same really. Noise, much drink, Mexican dancers: quite fun. A rabble of Bohemia and those rich 'apes of God'[12] who seem now almost to outnumber us, stock workers who are so interested in the arts they begin to suppose themselves homosexuals, and their wives whose smiling eyes are so weighed down by the weight of their artificial eyelashes that their glances are riveted to that level of our tight denim trousers (paint-smeared) where our talents are best proclaimed. Noise, noise, and with the noise such messily decadent carryings on that we feel ourselves the victims of some sort of takeover.

2–5 September *Hill End*. All it should be. Marvellous, and the people bumbling, mumbling, maliciously intriguing, drunken, stupid and inbred as ever, and the trees just beginning to burst marvellously into bud. Wonderful to sleep again on that hard wooden bed by a fire that flickered and glowed all night, and delightful the clear pure blue dry air so clean and fresh. We went here and there, drove about, walked about, washed for a bit of gold, desultorily sketched, lay on the grass whilst among the plum blossom between us and the sky the bees buzzed and droned: and at night drank at the pub, very Rowlandsonian scenes with the ineffable ghastly locals.

I wonder how on earth I managed to live amongst such people, their goodwill notwithstanding. Yet it was the interest I took in the history of the place, and the book I wrote[13], that resulted in all its present status as (hell) a 'tourist attraction' and a magnet to attract hordes of students and bohemians. And that has now made difficult to attain the rustic peace and calm that one remembers.

2 October *Sydney*. Bill Salmon[14] picked me up to go out and make a television film on a program on art for children he does for the ABC.[15]

My part was to make a pen and wash drawing of Bill whilst talking and answering Bill's questions. We saw the tape run through. This was a narcissist's paradise. The camerawork was sharp and clear. What fascinated me was that *I* looked so fascinating: like a hairy bear, *much* older than I think of myself looking, with a very mobile wrinkled face, very expressive, somewhat grotesque, peering at the drawing, frowning, laughing, being thoughtful as I answered, dissolving into mirth. In fact I gave so spontaneous (to myself as audience) an impression it was as if it was the performance of a highly skilled character actor using face, voice and gesture to extract the best from a good script. I haven't been so pleased with myself in ages.

28 October *Bobingah.* I am rather bogged down in a sort of contentment: the days flow by—I work with Mitty in the garden, we go shopping into Cooma[16], visit a family who own a lot of properties in the district. I can't bring my mind to make even the necessary decision as to which countries of the world I'll spend a month of two in so as to delay my arrival in Greece until spring. Fiji? Samoa? Trinidad? Marrakesh? Or Damascus—and Baghdad (one read, many years ago as an adolescent, so many interesting things about Mesopotamia: ex-colonels from World War I, padres, scoutmasters, who pleading guilty to various lapses in court, habitually asked that the fact they'd seen service in Mesopotamia might be taken into consideration).

Such thoughts. One wonders, is one's personal view of geography *entirely* coloured by sexual fantasies?—I suppose so. The world outside one's own particular location sometimes seems to promise to be one vast sotadic zone.[17] Yet sanitation is also important to him who explores the wilder shores of love. What country has hot and cold running water, proper lavatories, handsome boys, edible food, fine landscapes, magnificent art, an agreeable climate, and yet has not been overrun by the vast predatory ignorant, ugly, vulgar multitudinous horde of tourists?

23 December *Singapore.* In the two hours of waiting for the plane one glimpsed, in the elegant bar and restaurant of the airport, a bubbling energetic vision of a city. I spent that time with Murray Sayle[18], a journalist going to write about the Vietnam war. He was very kind and helpful. We were both feeling the sudden change from Australia.

'Thank God not to be swamped out with Anglo-Saxon faces,' he said.

We felt we were like fascinating characters in a novel—an artist and a war correspondent in the incredible East, observing the many strange and beautiful people floating up and down staircases whilst aeroplanes came and went with their bevies of exotic passengers from every port in the world.

25 December *Sanur, Bali.*[19] I immediately met Wija Wawo-Runtu[20], and was welcomed. He owns the most enchanting house and garden with beach bungalows which he lets. I walked to the nearby village at sundown to see a barong ceremony—like a highly civilised yet rustic, and aesthetically perfect, performance of the same sort as the Ceylon devil dances. It was a delight to sit in amongst the beautiful warm brown people with their heavenly warm sweet smoky smell.

27 December *Ubud.*[21] Here the poor artists live and work as tourist spectacles. They all have shops. The numberless pictures I saw were beyond belief effete and mass-produced. It is not, of course, Art. Nor is the carving, except for here and there an antique piece, full of lively fancy.

28 December *Sanur.* I breakfast on the little verandah of my thatched bungalow in the Gauguinesque garden. Discreet figures already at 8 a.m. are concealed amongst the verdure. Glance at a frangipani and from its leaves materialises a smiling soft-voiced artist with folio and rolls of drawings. I felt light and free and careless, as tho' at last I had thrown off that skin which so long chafed me in Australia.

29 December On the beach in the afternoon. 'Tuan, are you going to swim. Come and I will show you a very good place.' We wandered around a little point which cut us off completely from observation, there being no houses on the beach at that point. 'Tuan, you will teach me how to float?'—I obligingly supported the boy in the small of the back while he lay in the water, then he rolled over and embraced me. 'Tuan, will you come to my house in the village. I live alone with my father. I am sleeping alone all the time. Come with me to my room and we will sleep until I go to work at five this evening. My mother is dead. I have no brother.

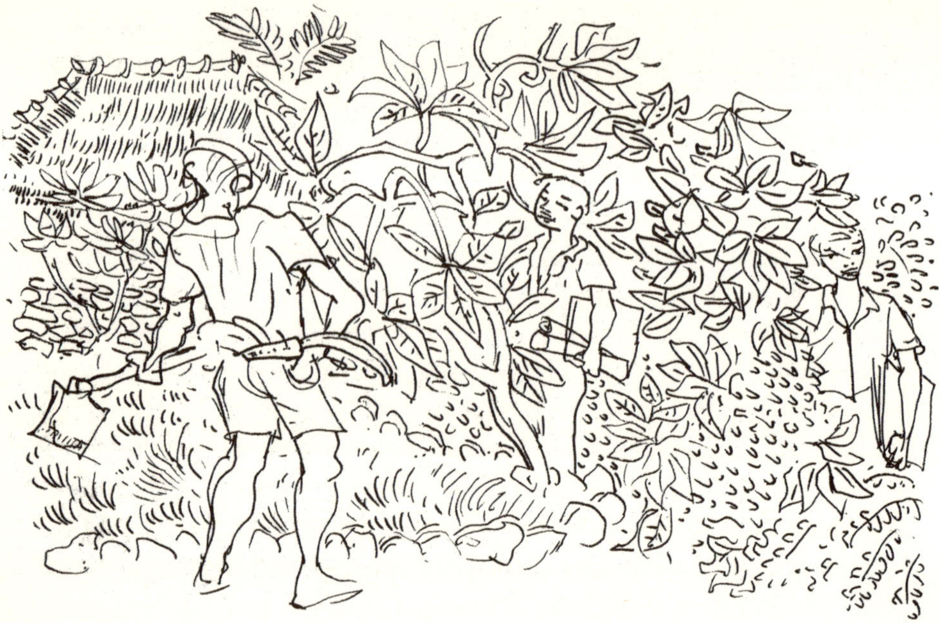

33. *Gauguinesque garden (1966).*

You will be my brother. I love you.'

A very sweet, passionate boy. He made me a present of a little carving of a deer. 'You will always remember me.' A dreadful carving. The warmth and charm of this incident filled my blood with energy. At my age one is more used to demands, so I was very touched. I must whatever happens remember the loveliness and generosity of this Balinese, and the small neat whitewashed room in his house, and the bed on which we lay (it was desperately hot, I was perspiring pints, he warm, brown and dry and smooth-skinned as silk) and how he kept whispering—through the little high-up window came the village sounds of ducks and dogs and chickens and the afternoon calling and chatting of the villagers.

At dinner, to honour the visiting heavy brass, two unbelievably beautiful girls danced to an orchestra of drum, bamboos and flute. The sound of these now still floats over the garden to my bungalow where I lie abed, clad in a sarong, my skin tingling with sunburn and grateful for caresses.

31 December Today, in a hired car I spent the day visiting archaeological sites. The exquisitely graceful badly mutilated 11th-century statue of Durga[22] at Kutri[23] is still haunted by the legend of the beauty of the queen who had it set up. Later we went to the most enchanted steep rice-terraced valley through which a river rushed over rocks, where in grey sculpted cliffs hermitages had been cut, and two shrines faced one another over the gorge, each in the form of arched embrasures containing carved, very simple, architectural forms. It was the most lovely calm place.

Our way took us by slippery narrow paths to a very small shrine whose great feature was a very long, very simple and fine 11th-century Buddhist bas-relief in the manner, it seemed to me, of Paul Gauguin at his best.

1967

2 January Immediately after breakfast I had walked to the Bali Beach Hotel[1], which is a big boring modern many-storeyed air-conditioned nightmare in the style of architecture often blamed on Corbusier[2].

The countryside was excessively green and rich. The earth positively squeezed out of itself hills and mountains gushing with verdure. The three-hour journey (only 60 kilometres) took us on bumpy roads through many villages, finally into hilly country where first appeared signs of Agung's recent eruption—rivers of lava charcoal black in colour flowed flatly over fields, or had clogged river beds. The road through these was of course shocking, and the river crossings were crazy risky affairs, even where temporary bridges had been put up. These desolate areas increased as we came near to Karangasem, where a third of the town had been destroyed[3], sparing the long main street of shops on to which abut the two palaces and various temples.

To see any of these sights entailed much sweat and pushing, clinging to shopfronts and being pressed hither and thither by a very humid multitude.

5 January I worked all day, from eight till five, with Han Snel.[4] It was splendid. We drew the little garden boy, and then Han's brother-in-law. The child is thin and graceful, with huge eyes.

Arie Smit[5] joined us for lunch in one of the pavilions in the garden. Han, who has been working in a very formalised way in oils and pastels, toiled with gusto, despair, fury, in the different technique with inks and tempera that I showed him.

This is the first serious concentrated burst of work after months and months of uninspired idleness. So after all, travel is curative: I have not carried, like a snail, the burden of my frustrations on my back. I am certainly no longer haunted by torturing memories of Stewart.

14 January I idled and read, and tried to learn a little Balinese, a lazy day. After nightfall I got a lift in the truck into town. It was raining torrents. Splashed our way through the downpour along a few streets of mud, ruts and puddles (we had for umbrellas, banana leaves) to a great crowded thatched hall. There, in a moment, the orchestra, a tremendously brilliant gamelan[6], suddenly dashed into a night of wonderful dramatic music. The dancers were also good. The dance illustrated a Ramayana[7] story about Indra[8] and Saraswati[9]—I was enthralled. There is no describing it, nor the spell it casts. I am at loss for words to evoke the marvellous combination of the deft, graceful archaic movements or the now sparkling and vigorous, now languid, then fierce music of the gamelan.

30 January No radio, no newspapers. News from Djakarta even assumes vaguely demonic forms by the time it has been translated and retold and at last comes to my ears. Danger of civil war because President Sukarno[10], stubbornly refusing to retire, might test the weight of his vanity against that of the government and so on. In Bali he is tremendously popular: in fact, everyone I've met who has known him is quite bowled over with him as a personality, even those who dislike his politics.

8 February Wija, Tatie[11], Jimmy Pandy[12] and I sit on the high terrace overlooking the beach, trying to catch a little of the intermittent sea breeze, chatting and playing scrabble. In the water, towards lunchtime, F. and R. appear, making secret signals to me.

F. spent the night with me. He goes about the act of love with a charmingly self-possessed grace—gaily, affectionately and enthusiastically; and in these matters he is very inventive and not at all sentimental, for all the caresses. Clinging and squirming in an embrace he sometimes seizes the radio and holds it to his ear, listening ecstatically to the bat-like squeaks of faint far foreign voices, or to jazz and more static, whispering and crooning to the radio and to me turn by turn.

15 February I asked Wija and Tatie to whom the strip of land on the beach, with some stone wall on it, belonged. It is charming, and the wall would make an enclosed garden. We measured it, sketched out an idea for a two-storey studio pavilion. The price is too ridiculous to resist. Already before I've left Bali I begin to miss it.

19 February *Bombay*. Appalling miles of nightmare architecture of a four-storey sordidness in grey-umber concrete that soured the perceptions with the implications of the life locked within it, and the life locked outside. At the hotel—rather like those big whore-house ones at Darlinghurst, grey cement, thin walls, narrow halls, decrepit lift, and a smell of ancient sweat and cockroaches and cigarette butts and stale piss, we were after all given separate accommodation—I in a tiny servant's room.

One must remember in the East to relent, to acquiesce, to be patient, to match their indifference. Then one gets what one wants (if one hasn't forgotten what it is) and the people become willing to serve you.

Last week of February *Isfahan*. Really a very beautiful and marvellous city. So much tremendous spacious, strong and graceful architecture, and the people handsome and quiet and pleasant. We drove about to admire the elegant ancient bridges, and the quite indescribable mosques. I like the airy sense of space in the architecture here—not only the great buildings, but in a considerable amount of commercial and domestic buildings there is a tall-pillared elegance, with very tall upstairs apartments whose lofty windows look out on and over enclosed gardens of lofty white poplars (leafless now).

3 March *Persepolis*. Quite tremendous—the enormous stone platform on which the palace was built (the stones keyed so exactly it would be hard to insert a knife blade between them) makes a stage for the scattered great carved shafts of the remaining pillars, and monolithic piles of broken carving. The wreckage and all its splendid ghosts, the still visible charred marks from the terrible night when it was burned by Alexander of Macedon[13] rise up all about one in the clear sweet air.

8 March *Istanbul*. Very busy streets, of bustle, activity, liveliness, overwhelming but not chaotic. After the East suddenly it seems to be

Europe and not full of the wasteful curly indirectness of the Orient. Today we wore our feet out on the icy marble of ancient times.

Then the dreadful evidence of an appalling way of life quite shocked me in the Topkapi Palace[14]: the abominable over-richness of the china and glass, then many noble and beautiful costumes, and the same absolutely stunning albums of painting, *then* whole halls of jewelled cups, goblets, rings, swords, pistols, hats, shoes, turbans, clocks, boxes, pots, jugs, bowls, belts. Knives and swords stuck all over with emeralds, diamonds and rubies in confused indigestible profusion—*huge* jewels, tiny gems, immense, actually tennis-ball-sized emeralds, pearls, the dimensions of sparrows' eggs, all set aglitter in abominable sparkling blobs of rich vulgarity, knobs of wealth without signs of aesthetic grace, and such a shocking profusion of it that the mind was lathered into forgetting so many exquisite and fine things one had seen a few courtyards away, an hour previously.

11 March *Athens*. Such an odd sensation to float in from the sky (lonely as a cloud) to a great white and grey city suspended in blue haze and then later to emerge from the cramped limits of the hired room into nocturnal streets surging with people in masks and carnival dress crowding and cramming narrow lanes and broad boulevards, all seeming to be filled with a childish goodwill. Loud, vigorous, vulgar people, music, dancing. The food was awful. *Deafening* loud speakers. What dreadful clothes they wore!—but how true each person to himself—so *full* of himself, brash, and seeming friendly. And what consummate rogues, robbers, liars and cheats they are.

16 March The stupendous collection of ancient Greek art at the museum.[15] At first it was not the masterpieces that moved me, but small intimate pieces that were quite unfamiliar—sexy little primitive bronzes from Olympia—horses, bulls, athletes, goats and a tiny satanic old man displaying a huge penis, a slave in an actor's mask leaping so his bollocks tossed wildly, goddesses in very grandiose hats.

April *Eressos*.[16] Justin O'Brien and I have three rooms—two for sleeping or painting, and a kitchen, in a little house in the village. It is not very comfortable now the cold weather is still here—in fact there are certain acute moments, such as finding the filthy lavatory occupied by a goat—but the house itself is pretty, and scrubbed clean by a stony old woman who owns it, Maria, a talkative octogenarian with no word of English.

It is on the rocky hill above the town, on the land side where there are remains of massive walls, and the ground beneath one's feet is a compound of shards and wildflowers that I most like to walk and sit in the sun and dream. There the feeling of presences is extremely strong. The grass springs fresh from the mouths of bygone warriors and one is always on the point of catching some message it carries from them. One seems to have more company there than in the town.

We have our routines, seldom varied. We work hard till 10 a.m., then shop for our very simple needs. Then work till 12 and lunch. Then work. I often sleep a while in the afternoons. We go walking in the evening. Some days instead of painting in our rooms we take sketchbooks and draw from nature. So far, as the village has remained empty except for 20 or so persons, we have found no models, though occasionally from the upper town descend young labourers of a tantalising beauty, to work on the repairing of the stone houses in preparation for the summer season.

We hired a fisherman's caique to take us up the coast to Sigri[17], where the uncle of one of Justin's former pupils in Australia is mayor. The day was beautiful, the sea a deep violet colour. We rounded a cape and entered a fine big natural harbour where lay the tiny village, white-washed stones and crazy little houses perched on rocks and dominated by a ruined Venetian castle. Nearly everyone we met had sons or families in Australia—it appeared that more than half the village had immigrated.

1–2 May *Skyathos.*[18] Easter. In one of the churches, overcrowded as an antique shop, the candle flames pour out a yellow varnished light, a mellow lambency on stern saintly faces dark against scrolled haloes of silverwork—the shining ikons. Grandly glittering new washed chandeliers are inverted diamond-flowered bouquets hung from dim domed heights.

Brian Dunlop[19], the great friend of Justin's life, is coming with us to Skyros.

May to June *Molos.*[20] We each have a room in a tiny white fisherman's cottage a few yards from the beach. There is a kitchen and a terrace to sit out on under vines, and a beautiful view of bay, beach and the craggy mountain carrying on its slopes the cube shapes of the upper town crowded with an ancient monastery and the ruins of an Acropolis. We have all been working hard. At night we eat at a simple taverna with very good food about a hundred yards away.

Jeff Smart and Baby Jane (Ian Bent)[21] arrive. We were inundated in a deluge of smart chatter and fashionable attitudes: all the gossip of Rome and the international camp—dinner parties, weekends in grand villas, intervals between soup and nuts sauced with the names of cinema directors and princesses. A month of the Smart chatter, after the simplicities of recent times, would drive me to Communism.

I have been up in the town to make sketches of some of the ikons. There are quite a few very good old ones glimmering out from the dark carved wood of the ikonostases of the numerous small churches or chapels.

First half of July *Rome*. The massive beauty of old buildings and tremendous noble trees. The skyline with towers and domes. Decaying palaces, red and umber rising up into darkness. The churches decked with marble angels blowing divine silence through sculpted trumpets. Leisurely watching the strolling crowd silhouetted against the floodlit marbles and their lively streams seemed the best of sybaritic pleasure.

I have rather fallen in love with Rome. I like the wine, the wonderful bread, the good food in the leafy open air on warm nights, and the vivid colour and charming style of the clothes, the vulgar quick little brittle wit of workmen abusing a lorry driver: and the thickness of towering ruined walls, decayed monuments to gross power, the flapping theatricalities of mannerists saints and angels, the rich vulgarity of mind suggested by a superb *Memento Mori* sculpted in precious marble: and alabaster, inlaid with lapis lazuli, as though to say that beyond imminent death lay some territory as sumptuously expensive as the via Veneto[22].

Without Attilio's company all this would have been dust and ashes.

28 July *Sanur*. I am very well content to be here. There are dinner parties accompanied by gamelan music, drives into the hills, swimming in the lucid lagoon water, lying in the sun on clean ivory sand. I can easily forget all those wasted months in other bloody awful places.

31 August *Sangeh.*[23] The famous Monkey Forest is a thickly planted grove of very tall trees, so close together they make an area of green gloom, full of little ugly grey monkeys with appalling manners. They behaved like the most ghastly sort of people—especially the older ones, who were evidently bad-tempered, greedy, over-sexed and thoroughly malicious. They surely needed the refining influences of good homes and a liberal education.

4 October *Sanur.* Movements of tourists, visits of businessmen with an eye on other things than pleasure indicate that Bali is soon to boom as a tourist resort. Alas. Several of them have shown a very sharp interest in the long strip of land on the beach which Wija and I are acquiring piece by piece. Our trouble is lack of money to get more in the little time that remains. I am sure it could be an extremely profitable enterprise, but my fear is that in the course of doubling or trebling our money the dazzling solitary palm-fringed beach will become just another nasty noisy ugly resort.

6 October A lazy day: I painted a little in the morning and lay about in the balmy blue water of the sea, feeling languid from a night of embraces. Lovers here exhaust one only on the physical plane. They give one an emotional holiday from tension. Sex becomes a truce instead of, as in the West, a war of attrition fought on three fronts (the neurotic, the psychotic and the economic).

17 October Everyone delights in dressing up in rich robes, borrowing my krises to play the parts of favourite princes and courtiers, the *dramatis personae* of *Derama*—the Balinese history-based melodramas which are the present craze of the Balinese.

Every village has its Derama group. Their performances last until dawn. The themes can only be compared to the Gothic novel or plays like *The Duchess of Malfi*[24]. The delivery of the lines is intensely dramatic, passionately unreal. The medium has already developed its necessary, favourite and wildly applauded clichés. The populace are mad for it. Men of taste and education despise and dislike it, but without having sat through it. I love it, but wish to hell it didn't last so long.

11 December *Sydney*. Visa and passport business. Had to be fingerprinted at police headquarters for the visa. Too ridiculous. Then lunched with James Fairfax and chatted for hours about people, the art world and current goings-on. This was delightful in the elegant airy rooms full of light from the harbour: water and sky and ships and the islands and points and bays are as much part of the feeling of the house as its beautiful furniture (new acquisitions: a Boucher[25] drawing, a Boyd[26] landscape, a superb Fred Williams).

That evening I made a triumphal appearance at the Windsor Castle. There they all were, much laughter, the confused talk, all very unchanged except moustaches are the new facial feature.

16–17 December *Bobingah*. It was a long journey, because we stopped off and stayed overnight, split up amongst various Gordon[27] homesteads at Bungendore. Bobingah looks superb—the garden magnificent. So strange after months of the tropics, to feel cool, to watch a wild wind tossing the rose bushes, breathing great gusts of the scent of flowers about, to listen as I have all this morning to Vivaldi[28] and Mozart.

The wind has almost blown out of my head the sad and dramatic news that greeted us as we entered one of the Gracious Homes of Bungendore—Gidleigh, an ugly dark house in a sprawling neglected garden with magnificent trees, ruled over by a knife-tongued dowager who greeted us: '*Have* you heard the ghastly thing about Harold?'

'Who?'

'The Prime Minister. He disappeared in rough surf at Portsea. They're sure he's drowned.'[29]

This was agitatedly discussed, as they all knew him.

1968

13 January *Sydney*. Mitty has come down. We go everywhere with a rush and a roar. The noise of the talk is incessant and thunderous. We laugh, we race through the streets in her thundering car, drop in at Natalino's[1] to find James Fairfax and Robin Maugham[2] lunching, and laugh and roar and talk, and dash off again, part for a few hours to catch our breaths, meet and roar again.

I long for a Proustian soundproof room.[3] People in Sydney are extraordinarily kind and hospitable and anxious to entertain one, to the point when I feel that one more drink, one more meal will kill me. I would prefer quiet and intimacy—long silences even—to these gatherings which even in private houses generate the feverish clamour of a public jamboree.

28–29 January *Glenrock, Marulan.*[4] A marvellous weekend—Carole and Peter Muller[5] very good hosts. Such an enchanting house—a house of marvellous meals before log fires, of beeswaxed furniture and Persian rugs, and peacocks dancing on the terrace. The serene proportions of the rooms, the elegant windows piercing a great thickness of wall, and the fine old simple furniture and comfort were a happy contrast to the erratic and irritant temporariness of Sydney houses.

1 February *Sydney.* I have been working on a whole series of ink and watercolour drawings in a large sketchbook, of Double Bay and Darling Point[6]—they are developments of old and new ideas of mine about presenting an intimately known subject in semi-abstract terms in such a way that light, form and shape all equally present, very distortedly, one's reactions to the colour and heat and emotionally familiar personal sensations derived from the water of the bay, the myriad small boats, the beaches on which descend steep slopes of trees and banks of ugly prosperous houses and apartment blocks. It is a very peculiar scene, in that there is in sight not one single beautiful building or even yacht or dinghy. All are intrinsically graceless and ugly and stupid emanations of energetically successful greed. But the light shed on them from on high—as though a god were to gild a congregation of toads—sheds such opal gleams of airy colour, translates all the ungainly architectural ineptitudes from purple brick cubby houses to floating coloured mists of enchanting form, that I am seduced to try again and again to impose my ideas of what it *really* is on paper.

Second and third weeks of February *Gosford*[7], to see Tas Drysdale. A splendid view of forested hills to the waters and islands of the Hawkesbury—but Guilford Bell's[8] creation, though the rooms are grand and well proportioned, struck me as monolithically gloomy. Tas looked as though he's been drinking far too heavily, but was all his old vigorous kindly self,

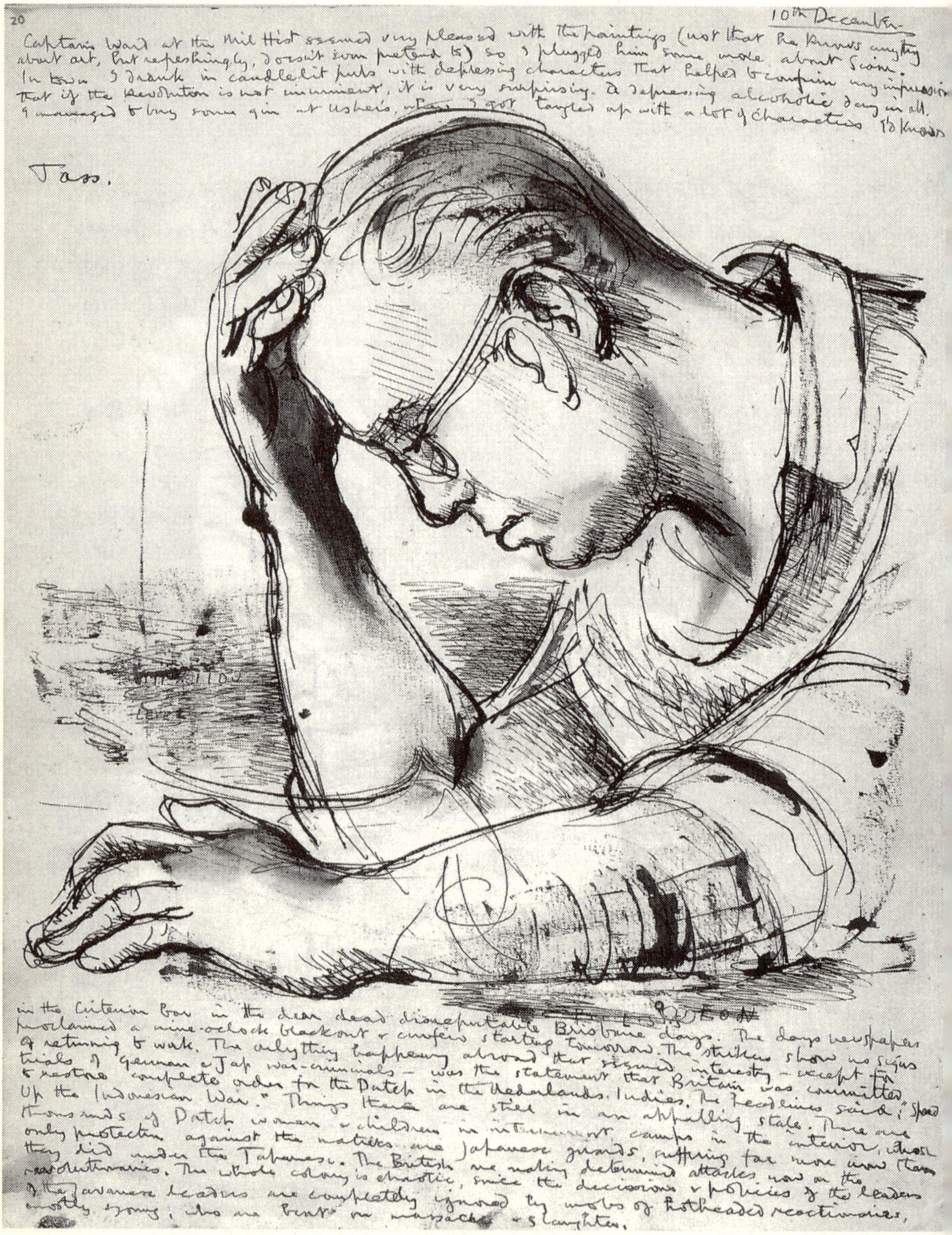

34. 'Tass' [Tas Drysdale] (1945).

and Maisie[9] looked like a Henry Moore[10] statue that Guilford had not decided where to place.

23 February to 8 March *Bali.* A fortnight of ecstasy and unease for me, diving back into all the happiness I find in this place, seeing so many friends, and the ever-entrancing F. and T.—too much. For Mitty frantic ups and downs of temperament, excesses of energy, and all the very occidental obsessions and restlessness that such people drag about with them to all corners of the world in order not to separate themselves from the situations they imagine they are fleeing.

And the house—ah the new house!—soon to be finished. A lot had been done while I was in Australia. It has the oddest beauty, and certainly a rather eccentric one. A couple of dozen workers are busy on it all the time still, and four gardeners putting in trees, lawns, hedges. The servants' lavatory is a sort of thatched pagoda, *very* pretty—the studio is airy and cool and high up, with wonderful views.

Second and third weeks of March The rather mad bearded Russian-English doctor-turned-anthropologist called Polunin[11]—clad in khaki shirt and massively flapping 'Bombay bloomers', hung about with cameras, stethoscopes, binoculars, a tape recorder and a haversack full of books, bottles of aspirin and bars of nourishing chocolate—has his own especial study which is to provide the theme of a book. This is the discovery, by a colleague in New Guinea, of an incurable disease prevalent in certain almost inaccessibly remote cannibalistic tribes. This disease, the sufferers themselves have claimed, is brought on *by eating near relatives*.

I have a private vision of a little circle of hairy head-hunters clad simply in elegantly engraved phallocrypts, sitting round a fire hysterical with laughter at the tales they tell inquisitive white men.

7–8 April We went off antique-hunting—a series of chases and searches, sometimes for porcelain, sometimes for rubies and carved doors, that took us zigzagging about the town and countryside. We found ourselves possessed of four superb doors and a number of other carvings, and on the way back to the jeep through a walled lane guarded by crazy mildewed arches that sprouted ferns and orchids from cracks in the masonry, caught a glimpse of a court in which a pavilion stood in a dried-up lake, an enchanting ruin. Pavilions in various stages of decay stood on the three sides of the empty pool, their carvings half-buried in wasp nests.

As a joke the rajah showed me a carved stick—a sort of shepherd's crook carved with humorous phalluses. Seeing I greatly fancied it, he presented me with it. This fertile crosier brought shouts of delight from the crowds of children who followed us everywhere. They piled the jeep with baskets of fruit, kissed our hands in farewell, and we drove off with the gamelan madly clanging behind us. Hilarious.

Last week of April *Bali*. Sir Robert Helpmann (my how pompous it sounds: but he dearly loves the knighthood, and to please him one calls him Sir Robert once in every half-hour, and Bobby for the remainder) here to listen to music and watch dancers, to select, if it can be done, some for a tour of Australia. We had a fabulous time showing him round.

1 May The day for me to move into the new house at Batujimbar.[12] Tremendous day of offerings and housewarming. The whole morning the gongs and drums dinned away. Shrines had been set up in a dozen places in the garden and numbers of separate offering ceremonies were going on on all sides, whilst on a raised roofed platform an anciently benevolent priest sat amongst the ritual furniture of his ceremonies—flasks of holy water, flowers, incense.

We were dressed in all the gorgeous but uncomfortable finery of the Balinese formal dress, wire jewels, and kris. At altars we were censed: we drank holy water, we were liberally sprinkled, were given flowers. The whole thing was delightful, ceremonial and at the same time gay.

15 June *Ubud*. Stopping at every art shop, studio and curio shop on the way in search of good individual pieces of the standard necessary to include in the Commonwealth Art Advisory Board's collection.[13] So *much* art was a sickening sight—so much skill, so much charm wasted on weak and meaningless gestures. However, after hours of this we had acquired a pile of rough working drawings and a couple of good traditional paintings by painters still living, old men who were trained in the twenties and thirties in the days of Walter Spies'[14] influence and patronage. And found also a number of damned expensive but very fine wood carvings.

17 June *Sanur*. Bidden to an informal reception and dinner for John and Betty Gorton[15] at the Bali Beach Hotel. Toward the close of dinner Betty proposed they should at that moment come to Batujimbar to look at my drawings. So we came. The servants were all asleep, but leapt into action and in a moment drinks were produced and lamps appeared and everyone seemed gay and relaxed. Betty Gorton bought a drawing and offered to take the remaining ones back to Australia for me.

22–23 July Some tourist staying at Sindhu Beach Hotel[16] had given T. a bicycle and a scarlet shirt to procure little boys, so T. had got hold of F. This tale utterly sickened me. And in a year, there will be hundreds coming every week, thousands—all the time like a toothache the thought of F.—the sweet cheat gone[17]—and that whoreson whoremongering pied piper of a tourist.

The Balinese will drop anyone for a novelty or money. They are quite enviably without sentiment. I am positively viciously sentimental. My sentiments about this current adventure of F.'s are of a sort outside the sphere of Balinese emotions—a sort of harrowed and horrified angry pity coupled with a strong frustrated desire for revenge on the boy-stealer. And nasty speculations as to whether, if F. returns, that enchanting wayward lover will have graduated halfway to prostitution.

The rushing rustle of leaves, and again, more evocative of fear and power, a wild surf crashing distantly on the reef, embody somewhere inside themselves an alarming hidden sound of, it seems, voices raised in woe and alarm.

10 September This monthly re-arriving imposition of bureaucratic idiocy, the renewal of my visa, has come up again. At such times as this the full realisation of the black side of Bali, the aspect that has peopled my landscapes with ghouls and bogies, the frightening and very real world of everyday, every-night terrors that haunt the natives of the island—exudes from the beach, the moonlit garden to harmonise with all my black thoughts. The grey-green and scarlet pastorale is not a possibility; the scented prettiness becomes evidently what it really is intended to be—a compliment, a flattery, an offering to delude dark powers.

And why is the island sad and dark and poor?—because behind the vivid festivals, behind the eccentric gods and demons, behind the huge green leaves and scarlet and yellow flowers that conceal the monkeys and the imps and gargoyles and ghosts, there are thousands of concrete offices full of lieutenants and captains and colonels all shining and smiling and neat. The sons of good families. They have neat little round arses like smooth apples. They sit on their arses and smile politely. They are the symbols of power. Very useless, very expensive. Clerks in offices come in army uniform armed with pistols. There is a black market in fountain pens.

Third week of September Australians abroad tend to congregate—horrible little colonies of them unconsciously puffed up with the prestige of living overseas, yet contemptuous of, unable to conform with or enjoy, the customs and manners of their host nation. Who sends them!—why do they come? They are not interested in my painting nor in me. 'I'm from Melbourne, so I'd never heard of you until I got here. Someone said there was an Aussie artist. Nice place you've got. Can't say I go in for art myself.'

They sit their square bums down in the chairs and fill their square mouths with beer.

30 November It is a process quite noticeable to me now, that as I daily get sicker and sicker, and older and older, and hourly more selfish and cranky, and less capable of creative work, that the environment I have created becomes more and more marvellously beautiful and seductive.

Knowing oneself really well does not preclude the acceptance of one's nastiest aspects with approving equanimity.

11 December *Djokjakarta and Solo.*[18] Beggary prevails in Djokjakarta—the maddening monotonous mumbling whine of mendicants followed us from shop to shop, their beseeching falling on our ears like a rain of social guilt for being rich and well fed. We'd spend in a morning enough to keep a hundred of them fed for a month.

Solo is free of beggars. Tall shade-trees line the crowded streets. The traffic is largely of wildly exotic vehicles—four-wheeled, two-horse carriages crammed with passengers and market goods lumbering and creaking bullock wagons, millions and millions of bicycles and a curious hooded bicycle-rickshaw affair, painted brilliantly with bright scenes, flowers, tigers or whatever symbol takes the owner's fancy, that ply as taxis. There are many stolidly, solidly loftily fat-high-pillared buildings, remnant of the colonial Dutch, whose powerful properties lend an aura of logic to the ratbaggery of boutiques and stalls and modern buildings that crowd about them.

Second half of December *Batujimbar*. To be back is a tremendous joy: the people all smiling, singing at their work, the garden, everyone looking so beautiful, effervescing with excitement as the bags of huge parcels were unpacked, bulging with presents. The rains have come!—the garden, green and growing, looks superbly like a Douanier Rousseau.

1969

8 February Little Madé Berata[1] is my great delight, the youngest of the household, who goes seriously about his work, imbues all his acts with an old-fashioned courtesy. Unconscious that I am observing him, he brings in a terracotta brazier of charcoal, adds to it a few grains of incense, notes in what direction the smoke bends, moves the brazier so that it will waft toward me. Then he adds a few more grains of the fine Javanese resin, and as the plume of smoke ascends, with a beautiful very Balinese gesture inbued with absorbed gravity, fills his cupped hands with the smoke and washes his face in its sacred perfume.

14 February There has been a noticeable increase in groups of foreigners coming to Bali to confer with officials, to come and look with great interest at what we have done at Batujimbar. These are groups of bankers, planners and development advisors: they advise governments and huge investment corporations. Their advice really is on how to convert villages, forests and mountains into vast profitable jukebox alleys. 'You can't stop progress,' says Wija when I protest.

'Progress is a word. I'm not talking about progress. I'm talking about the destruction of a civilisation.'

8 March *Singaraja*.[2] Got off to a late start, driving down the beautiful coast, stopping to inspect a number of temples carved superbly in the distinctive Singaraja style that uses spiky, flame-like shapes that endow the figures with vivid energy. And often throughout this morning, battling, as we climbed about these astonishing buildings, with the intense heat and with a terrible hangover, I was miserably affected by the fat tight-clad bums of the younger ones posturing like creatures in advertisements, dragging with them a terrible little red plastic gramophone loaded with the most ghastly popular songs, making a noise that forecast all the hideous affronts that will soon become part of this island's atmosphere with the expected influx of hundreds of thousands of tourists.

Last week of March *Bedulu.*[3] We set out on an expedition over the river past Klungkung.[4] We stopped to examine the carvings in temples. It was a landscape of extraordinary innocent joy, all smiles and richness, peasants singing in the fields, naked children splashing in water channels. So we proceeded cautiously on the narrow track until the road stopped just short of the beach where a great garden of palms and fruit trees sheltered a cluster of buildings. In dead silence, in slow motion, the inhabitants crept out from all about the car. Nightmare people, noseless, deformed, crippled, terrifying creatures such as are embodied in the demons and fiends of the primitive carvings. It was a leper colony.

It was indeed a pretty fine example of what I have attempted to express about the Balinese landscape as a setting for the struggle between opposing forces, the ever-present demonic element haunting the rich warm placid fields and groves.

7 June *Batujimbar*. A party in the bungalow next to me. Go-Go[5] was utterly more dull and noisy and brutal than I thought it could be—actually, I was expecting (half-expecting, quarter-expecting)—shit, what optimism, to *enjoy* it even, just a little bit. But NO. At least six people I like were there. And of those three were infected with the other epidemic—hell, what could be the word for a sort of plaguery conformist crapophilia of dreary if-you're-with-it, you've-got-to-be-with-it. Everyone-says-it's-great-so-it-must-be-great.

So there we were with the lowest common denominator of rowdy ugliness.

I have been so taken up with my detestation of that party that I neglected to mention the one positively pleasant event—Chris Carlisle's[6] arrival earlier in the day, loaded down with purchases made on all our behalfs in Singapore (for me gramophone records—Bartók[7], Berg[8], Couperin, Louis Armstrong, Mozart, etc.) and all sorts of amusing and interesting talk and news. He has now at last resigned from and quite finished with the Diplomatic Service.

1 July Too many days of a restless wind—it makes me nervous. And the enormous cold disc of the moon drives sleep away. And too many people. One has become like one of those Ornamental Hermits, so fashionable in the 18th century, who were lodged in picturesquely contrived grottoes on country estates to be shown off to the goggling curiosos come up from London.

Anyway, everyday at least a couple of hours of work, and in that one loses and finds oneself alternately—oblivious to worries and a heightening of perceptions towards what one selects from visual experience plus the zany visions of translations of experience that are projected like a cinema somewhere inside the skull.

30 July *Semawang.*[9] Roy Grounds and his wife[10] arrived, just in time for the inaugural blessing and performance by full moon of the *ketjak*[11]. Warwick Purser[12] and I for the occasion had dressed with great trouble and discomfort in full Balinese costume—the finest and richest painted batiks, with *songkets*[13] of ancient gold brocades, and the tall batik headdresses of princes. We glittered and dazzled with heavy gold jewellery studded with diamonds, rubies and sapphires. This was very proper for Warwick as patron of the *ketjak*.

It was a great occasion, wildly romantic and dramatically set in the rustic coral temple dwarfed by huge ancient trees. Warwick has cut out all of the comedy and acting interpolations that have been added over the years to make it a musical spectacle for tourists, and reduced it to its original simplicity. The effect is marvellous.

24 September In a few days the Duke and Duchess of Bedford[14] are coming to stay—for about a fortnight—at Tandjung Sari[15]. At the same time Mick Jagger[16] and a party are coming. Jagger is the leader of a popular singing group, a handsome young man notorious in Australia for insulting behaviour and, at parties given for him and his frenzied little group, smashing up the furniture and scrawling obscenities on the walls. He has recently been in Australia making a film about Ned Kelly[17], a part which for some pseudo-historical reason he played in female clothes, to the delight of many and the astonished rage of those to whom our national bandit symbolises more manly behaviour.

2 October Mick Jagger was rather amusing and easy to get on with when he came for drinks here yesterday—very relieved to be out of Australia, where he had fairly solidly been confined in the Bungendore district being pressured by hard-to-get Gordons and Osbornes[18]. Australia impressed him as 'dry bush full of fookin' Osbornes'—all, rather comically in the context of squattocratic history, working as film extras disguised as sundry cattle duffers and bushrangers.

He swims, works composing songs, likes not being a pestered celebrity.

6 October The Bedfords and Mick Jagger turned out to be brilliant guests—he very much the amiable aristocrat with a kindly sort of self-mocking way of talking; the Duchess was vivacious and very funny. They obviously enjoy themselves tremendously in their many wanderings. Mick Jagger had frankly detested his stay in Australia, where a number of unfortunate happenings had added to discomfort. He is not at all the insulting oaf of his reputation based on wild behaviour of three years ago.

Anyway, it was a delightful day. After drinking and chatting for an hour or so at my house (I was so proud of the new extended roof, so exquisitely thatched; soars, tremulous yet airy like a great set of lateen sails, so elegantly patterned, coloured browny, tawny gold ochre like old ivory) we ate in Wija's garden from tables set under clusters of gilded cerise umbrellas.

11 October Mick Jagger is one of the few I shall miss: but I expect we will meet again somewhere—even in Bali, since he's become fond of the place. Last night we were all talking of his making a film here—a semi-surreal one: everyone was inventing fantastic plots for it which in the very elements of strangest unreality were too-true tales of ourselves and people we know.

10 November *Singapore*. Chris and I did a good lot of shopping—numerous department stores are crammed with all the desirable merchandise of the East and West. This city always impresses me only by reason of its tremendous mercantile efficiency. Later ate in the famous street stalls, and went and drank beer and watched the Hogarthian antics of the sailors and transvestites. Their melodramatic, somehow old-fashioned, gestures are a convention the world over—the haughty shrug, the sensuous parody hand-on-hip of Sadie Thompson[19], the petulant pout and long burning smouldering glance that is the almost purely cosmetic (much loaded with mascara) stand-in for boiling passion and desire.

It was raining a drizzly rain: we sat at a table beneath an awning in the middle of the street drinking beer, continually pestered by a succession of grotesque and insistent peddlers selling toys, cheap watches, obscene photographs.

19 November *Batujimbar*. My heart grew lighter as I came nearer to Bali. Everything was so green, the people so handsome. They all looked so gay and smiling and irresponsible that I was a little surprised to find that the servants hadn't all rushed off to make merry in my absence—most of them anyway made me a great welcome at the house, though I was not yet expected for a few days. So there was a great clustering about to unpack and see what presents I'd brought them, and a great lot of laughter and exclaiming over various novelties unheard of in Bali.

23 December I had to go into town to do things long neglected. Wija and I in the car. Jahja—one of his many sons, a bright child who will continue his schooling in Bali—came too, to be entered for his new school, where in the steaming heat brisk nuns in pyramids of crisp clean linen robes coped with his inauguration with admirable kindly and passionless efficiency. They seemed very blessedly sane and real in a town that is a sort of monument to frantic purposeless and wasteful activity directly associated with gormless inertia.

Next we got my passport and at last my long-term visa. It has taken several years to obtain.

NOTES: 1960s

1960

1. African-American jazz trumpeter and singer (1901–71).
2. English art historian and curator (1918–95), whose interests following the publication of his two-volume study *Chinese Art* (1958) shifted to south Indian, Ceylonese and South-East Asian art.
3. An allusion to the fable attributed to Aesop contrasting a diligent ant with an indolent and parasitic grasshopper.
4. English curator and arts manager (1925–2002).
5. Art gallery in the East End of London, of which Bryan Robertson was Director from 1952 to 1968.
6. Village in the Anuradhapura district of north-central Ceylon.
7. United National Party, founded 1946.
8. Sirimavo Bandaranaike (1916–2000) served three terms as Prime Minister: 1960–65, 1970–77, 1994–2000.
9. 10 October 1960, in an article entitled 'Art: Home Sweet Homeland'.

1961

1. A set of compositions for harpsichord by J. S. Bach, first published in 1741.
2. City situated on the southwestern tip of Sri Lanka, 120 kilometres from Colombo. The fort was built by the Dutch in 1663. Images of Friend's mural, *The City of Galle*, are reproduced in Pearce, *Donald Friend 1915–1989 Retrospective*, pp. 88–89.
3. A cultural and philanthropic organisation associated with the Australian High Commission and the New Zealand consulate in Colombo.
4. *Loan Exhibition of Australian Paintings*, which opened in Kuala Lumpur in November 1960, then travelled to New Delhi and Colombo. It originally displayed one work each by 16 artists, among whom Friend was not included.
5. *Ned Kelly, Outlaw*, from the second series of Nolan's paintings figuring the Australian bushranger, produced in London in the 1950s. Cf diary entry for 15 December 1981 and **1981**, note 28.
6. *Ballad of a Dead Stockman*, by Australian painter Jon Molvig (1923–70).
7. *October*. Daws was born in Australia in 1927.
8. *Recent Australian Painting*, London, June–July.
9. The view that art should be nonrepresentational and improvisational, as practised by a group of largely American artists between the end of World War II and the 1960s.

10. The Skinner Galleries, founded by West Australian art dealers Rose and Josiah Skinner in 1958.
11. *Sidney Nolan*, Bonythan Art Gallery, opened 11 September.
12. Having chosen Peter Finch as a subject for the celebrity biography program *This Is Your Life*, the show's producers invited Friend to appear on it among other 'surprise' guests from the actor's past.
13. The ballerina Tamara Tchinarova (real name Rekemchouk), born in Romania in 1919 and married to Finch in Australia in 1943. They divorced in 1958.
14. English actress (1888–1976).
15. Scottish-born painter (1913–89).
16. American painter and leading proponent of Abstract Expressionism (1912–56).
17. Painting of 1957, purchased by the Tate in the same year.

1962

1. John Olsen (born 1928), Australian painter.
2. Alawa people are from Arnhem Land. The camp may have been associated with the Alawa homestead, 220 kilometres east of Perth.
3. In the Adelaide Hills, where Dutton (1922–98), the Australian writer, critic and art patron, had two cottages.
4. New Zealand-born art collector (1898–1977), who co-directed the Redfern Gallery in London with Harry Tatlock Miller (see **1950**, note 10).
5. Australian painter (1924–90).
6. Albert Tucker (1914–99), Australian painter.
7. The Commonwealth Art Advisory Board, the chief government funding and policy body for the visual arts between 1912 and 1973.
8. Australian art critic and historian (born 1938).
9. Weekly Australian news magazine, published in Sydney from 1880 to early 2008.
10. Fortnightly Australian 'journal of opinion', published in Sydney from 1958 to 1972.
11. Born 1940, son of Russell and Bon Drysdale.
12. Inner-eastern Sydney suburb, then popular with artists.
13. Australian painter, born Juanita Lee-Brown in America in 1921.
14. Monica Mary Patricia Edgeworth Somers (1901–83), Australian supporter of artists, and lessee of Merioola at the time Friend had been staying there (see **1946**, note 2).
15. Raffish Sydney suburb, adjacent to Friend's old haunts at Potts Point and Kings Cross.

1963

1. In Woollahra, Sydney.
2. The Royal George Hotel in Sussex Street, Sydney (now called the Slip Inn).
3. Originally, a term for members of the 'Beat generation' in the USA in the 1940s, a loose circle of libertarian writers, artists and musicians; subsequently applied to similar groups around the world.
4. Popular name for the Sydney University Libertarian Society, and more broadly a group of heterodox writers, artists and academics from the late 1940s to the early 1970s.
5. Dr Gilbert Bogle, a physicist with the Commonwealth Scientific and Research Organisation, and Mrs Margaret Chandler, wife of another CSIRO scientist. The cause of their deaths remains uncertain.
6. Hughes was an aspiring painter at the time. The Hungry Horse was in Windsor Street, Paddington.
7. Clement Meadmore (1929–2005), Australian-born sculptor and furniture designer who went to live in New York and later became an American citizen.
8. Piet Mondrian, Dutch painter (1872–1944).
9. Australian art critic and curator (born 1929), and Director of the Art Gallery of South Australia, 1984–90.
10. Town on the Central Coast of NSW, 90 kilometres north of Sydney.
11. The villages along the Sepik River and its tributaries in New Guinea are famous for their art work.
12. Island in Moreton Bay, off the South Queensland coast, near Brisbane.
13. Scottish-born Australian painter (1891–1974).
14. A suburb of Sydney, 3.5 kilometres west of the city centre.
15. Bill Gordon, Australian grazier, and a distant relative of Friend's.
16. Men's club, founded in 1838.

1964

1. Australian interior decorator and social columnist (born 1927).
2. Irish-born comic playwright and poet (1751–1816).
3. Founded in Sydney in 1963, and co-edited at that time by artist and cartoonist Sharp (born 1942), and by Richard Neville and (John) Richard Walsh (both born 1941).
4. Australian painter (born 1938).
5. English-born writer (1914–76; name originally spelt McInnes), who was educated in Australia and returned to England in 1931 but continued to write fiction and non-fiction on Australian themes.
6. Harbourside eastern suburb of Sydney, famous for its fish restaurants.

7. Australian actress (born 1938), then a girlfriend of Hughes's.
8. See **1929**, note 32.
9. Usually spelt 'camp', and defining a sensibility (according to Susan Sontag's 'Notes on Camp', published in this year) that 'converts the serious into the frivolous'—or vice versa. Its customary style of exaggeration and artifice is often, though not exclusively, identified with homosexuals.
10. English ballerina (1919–91), born Margaret Hookham.
11. Rudolf Nureyev (1938–93), Russian-born dancer, who defected from the USSR in 1961, and partnered Fonteyn at the Royal Ballet Company in London as well as on tour with the Australian Ballet.
12. English-born composer (1902–83), who settled in Ischia in 1949, the same year that Friend first visited that island.
13. Hannah Lloyd Jones (1901–82), Australian art patron, philanthropist and socialite, the widow of Sir Charles Lloyd Jones. (Cf **1970**, note 6.)
14. Name and location of the newly acquired property of Mitty Lee-Brown and Bill Gordon, 340 kilometres south-southwest of Sydney.
15. Town in NSW, 265 kilometres southwest of Sydney.
16. In Bowral, built in 1887 for merchant and stockbreeder Sir Samuel Hordern.
17. Australian journalist and novelist (1912–70).
18. Novel, published 1964.
19. Charmian Clift (1923–69), Australian journalist and writer.
20. The main performer was 'Rikki Marshall' (real name Frank McQuirk). Gwen Friend had pursued various avenues of the theatrical profession since the late 1930s.
21. Terry Clune Galleries in Macleay Street, Potts Point, opened in 1957, closed in 1967.
22. Georges Rouault (1871–1958), French painter.
23. Joan Miró (1893–1983), Spanish Catalan painter.
24. Australian painter and designer (1920–2000), whose work leaned to the decorative.
25. Bill McLaughlin (1937–70), Australian accountant and art dealer.
26. Lynne McLaughlin, née Drysdale (born 1938), daughter of Russell and Bon Drysdale. Cf **1977**, note 11.
27. Australian composer (born 1929).
28. Louis Armstrong's fourth wife, Lucille Wilson, a former dancer whom he had married in 1942.
29. Northern Beaches suburb of Sydney, 27 kilometres from city centre.
30. This could refer to the triptych of the subject by Bosch in the Museo Nacional de Arte Antiga in Lisbon (which Friend might have seen in

a reproduction), or to the two single-panel versions of the subject in the Museo del Prado, the originals of which Friend could have seen on his visit to the Prado (see **1952**, note 20). On St Anthony, see **1951**, note 6.

1965

1. Friend could be anticipating here a number of forthcoming shows, including two at the Darlinghurst Galleries, Sydney: *Recent Paintings*, 27 April – 22 May 1965; *Sixty Small Drawings*, 26 April – 22 May 1966.
2. English-born Australian novelist (1912–90), who was to be awarded the Nobel Prize for Literature in 1973.
3. These two novels were published in 1955 and 1961 respectively.
4. Town just off the North Coast of NSW, 600 kilometres from Sydney.
5. In Macleay Street, Potts Point, Sydney.
6. *Recent Paintings*. The drinks occasion was prior to the official opening (see **1965**, note 1).
7. William Philip Sidney, First Viscount De L'Isle (1909–91), the last English-born Governor-General of Australia. Held that office from 1961 to 1965.
8. Australian puppeteer (1930–98).
9. Since 1961 the USA had been committing increasingly large numbers of combat troops to oppose the Communist regime of North Vietnam. Australia's involvement had begun in 1962, with a commitment of thirty men.
10. A twelfth-century fictional work: *Hui t`u Chi-tien chia hua*.
11. Austrian-born journalist and art dealer (1908–82), who arrived in Australia in 1953 and established a gallery in Woollahra in 1958.
12. Australian politician (1908–67), at this time Federal Treasurer; Prime Minister, 1966–67.
13. Australian painter and printmaker (1927–82).
14. Australian student of art at East Sydney Technical College (born c. 1946).
15. For reproductions, see Pearce, *Donald Friend 1915–1989 Retrospective*, p.105; *DFD 3*, p. 598. Cf diary entry for 8 November 1951 and **1951**, note 7.
16. Inner North Shore suburb of Sydney, 5.5 kilometres from the city centre.
17. *Recent Paintings*, Gallery A, 22 September – 15 October.

1966

1. National Gallery of Victoria, 4 March – 25 April 1966.
2. Australian painter (1939–92).
3. A suite of paintings inspired by the crimes of serial murderer John Christie (1898–1953), which were committed in the area near where Whiteley was living in London in 1964.

4. Revisiting Australia, where he was born in 1934. He was based in London from 1959 but made regular tours of his native land with his satiric shows.
5. American-born art critic and writer living in Sydney. The first edition of her study *Brett Whiteley* was published in 1979.
6. Harry M. Miller (born New Zealand, 1934), Australian arts promoter, manager and theatrical producer.
7. A production by Helpmann for the Australian Ballet, with music by Malcolm Arnold and designs by Arthur Boyd (see **1967**, note 26). Originally created for the Royal Ballet, London, in 1963.
8. *The Lady and the Fool*, with choreography by John Cranko and music by Giuseppe Verdi (arranged by Charles Mackerras). Originally created for the Sadlers Wells Theatre Ballet in 1954.
9. *'Barbaric Variations on the Masters' and Drawings*, 26 July – 10 August.
10. Coastal resort town in Queensland, 140 kilometres north of Brisbane.
11. Australian (1931–85), who married Attilio Guarracino in 1973 (see **1950**, note 1.)
12. A phrase for dilettantes and hangers-on in the art world derived from the title of Wyndham Lewis's novel of 1930 (see **1937**, note 29).
13. *Hillendiana* (1956).
14. Australian artist, teacher and broadcaster (born 1928).
15. The Australian Broadcasting Commission (as it was then called) screened this program, episode 23 of *On the In Side*, in 1967.
16. The largest town in the Snowy Mountains, 400 kilometres south of Sydney.
17. 'Sotadic zone' was a term used by Victorian explorer, author and translator Richard Burton (1821–90) to delineate regions in various parts of the world where pederasty was prevalent or generally tolerated. The term is fully explicated in a section on 'Pederasty' in the 'Terminal Essay' to Burton's translation and edition of of *The Arabian Nights* (1885–86), vol. 10. Friend was familiar with this edition from the 1930s. See **1939**, note 24.
18. Australian foreign correspondent, writer and television documentary maker (born 1926).
19. Resort town on the southeastern coast of the island.
20. Dutch-born Indonesian film-maker, architect and landowner (1926–2001).
21. Town in Central Bali, famous for its arts and crafts.
22. Hindu goddess of death.
23. A village 5 kilometres outside Denpasar.

1967

1. Opened 1 November 1966. Now called the Inna Grand Bali Beach.

2. Le Corbusier, professional name of Charles-Édouard Jeanneret-Gris (1887–1965), Swiss-born French architect and pioneer of the so-called International style.
3. The volcano Gunung Agung (Mt Agung), in the district of Karangasem in East Bali, had erupted in February–March 1963.
4. Dutch-born painter (1925–98), who became an Indonesian citizen and lived in Ubud from 1950.
5. Adrianus Wilhelmus Smit (born in Holland, 1916), an Indonesian citizen from 1951.
6. An ensemble of musical instruments characteristic of Bali and Java.
7. Sanskrit epic dating to 750–500 BC.
8. King of the gods in Hindu mythology.
9. Hindu goddess of knowledge, music and the arts.
10. Born Kusno Sosrodihardjo (1901–70). President of Indonesia, 1945–67.
11. Indonesian second wife of Wija Wawo-Runtu (born 1937).
12. Indonesian painter and art dealer (died c. 1975).
13. Alexander III (356–323 BC), king of Macedon from 336 BC to his death, and known as Alexander the Great. His siege and burning of Persepolis (331–330 BC) was part of the Macedonians' long campaign against the Persians.
14. Official residence of the Ottoman sultans from 1465 to 1856; a museum from 1924.
15. National Archaeological Museum, established 1881.
16. Town in the southwest of the island of Lesbos, in the Aegean Sea.
17. Town on the western coast of Lesbos.
18. Town on the island of the same name, in the Aegean Sea.
19. Australian painter (1938–2009).
20. Town on the eastern coast of the island of Skyros, in the Aegean Sea.
21. Australian painter (born 1945).
22. Fashionable street in Rome.
23. Village in southwestern Bali.
24. Play by John Webster, published in 1623, containing several scenes of bloody violence within aristocratic circles.
25. François Boucher (1703–70), French painter.
26. Arthur Boyd (1920–99), Australian painter.
27. A family of graziers in NSW, of whom Bill Gordon (see **1963**, note 15) was a member.
28. Antonio Vivaldi (1685–1741), Italian composer.
29. Portsea is a fashionable seaside resort, 60 kilometres southeast of Melbourne. Holt's body was never recovered.

1968

1. Italian restaurant in Kings Cross.
2. English novelist (1916–81).
3. Proust wrote much of his novel *A la recherche du temps perdu* in the cork-lined bedroom of his apartment in Paris.
4. Town in NSW, 170 kilometres south of Sydney.
5. Carole (born 1936), anthropologist and second wife of Peter (born 1927), architect.
6. An eastern suburb of Sydney, 3 kilometres from the city centre.
7. Town on the Central Coast of NSW, 75 kilometres north of Sydney, near to which Drysdale had purchased a six-hectare farm at the end of 1964, situated on Kilcare Heights, overlooking Brisbane Water in the Bouddi National Park.
8. Australian architect (1912–92).
9. Born Maisie Newbold (1915–2001), Australian student of art at the George Bell School, Melbourne, and, following the death of her first husband, artist Peter Purves Smith (1912–49), a librarian with special interests in children's literature. In 1964 she became Russell Drysdale's second wife.
10. English sculptor (1898–1966).
11. Ivan Polunin (born 1920), English physician, cinematographer, ethnographer and naturalist. Of Russian origin, he has spent most of his career in Singapore.
12. An affluent district and estate in the heart of Sanur.
13. This board (see **1962**, note 7) had commissioned Friend to advise on the collection.
14. Russian-born German painter (1895–1942), who settled in Bali in 1927.
15. John Gorton (1911–2002), Australian Prime Minister, 1968–71, was married to American-born Bettina Gorton, née Brown (1915–83).
16. One of the oldest beachfront hotels in Sanur.
17. *The Sweet Cheat Gone* is the title of the English translation by C. K. Scott Moncrieff (1930) of vol. 6 of Proust's *A la recherche du temps perdu*, entitled in French *Albertine Disparue*. On Albertine, cf diary entry for March 1950 and **1950**, note 3.
18. Cities in Java: Djokjakarta, towards the south of the island; Solo (colloquial name for Surakarta), in the central part.

1969

1. Balinese servant (born c. 1963) in Friend's Batujimbar house, with gardening and 'antique polishing' duties.
2. The old Dutch capital of Bali during the colonial era, situated on the north coast.

3. Village 27 kilometres north of Sanur.
4. Town and district 30 kilometres north of Sanur.
5. Dance craze in bars and clubs, originating in New York in the early 1960s.
6. Christopher Carlisle (born 1937), English former naval officer, and member of the British Diplomatic Service in Singapore.
7. Béla Bartók (1881–1945), Hungarian composer.
8. Alban Berg (1885–1935), Austrian composer.
9. Coastal village 1.5 kilometres from Sanur.
10. Sir Roy Grounds (1905–81), Australian architect, and Alice Grounds, née James (1909–2009), Australian couturier.
11. A form of Balinese music drama, originating in the 1930s.
12. Australian travel company owner (born 1939).
13. Woven textiles in silk or cotton.
14. John Robert Russell (1917–2002), thirteenth Duke of Bedford, and his third wife, Nicole Milinaire, née Schneider (born 1920), a French former television producer.
15. Beachfront hotel in Sanur, recently built by Wija Wawo-Runtu.
16. Sir Mick Jagger (born 1943), English rock musician, songwriter and actor, lead singer and co-founder of The Rolling Stones.
17. *Ned Kelly* (1970), written and directed by Tony Richardson.
18. The Osbornes were a family of graziers, of whom the Gordons (see **1967**, note 27) were neighbours.
19. The central character, an American prostitute, in Somerset Maugham's short story 'Rain', set in Samoa and first published in Maugham's collection *The Trembling of a Leaf* (1921).

1970s

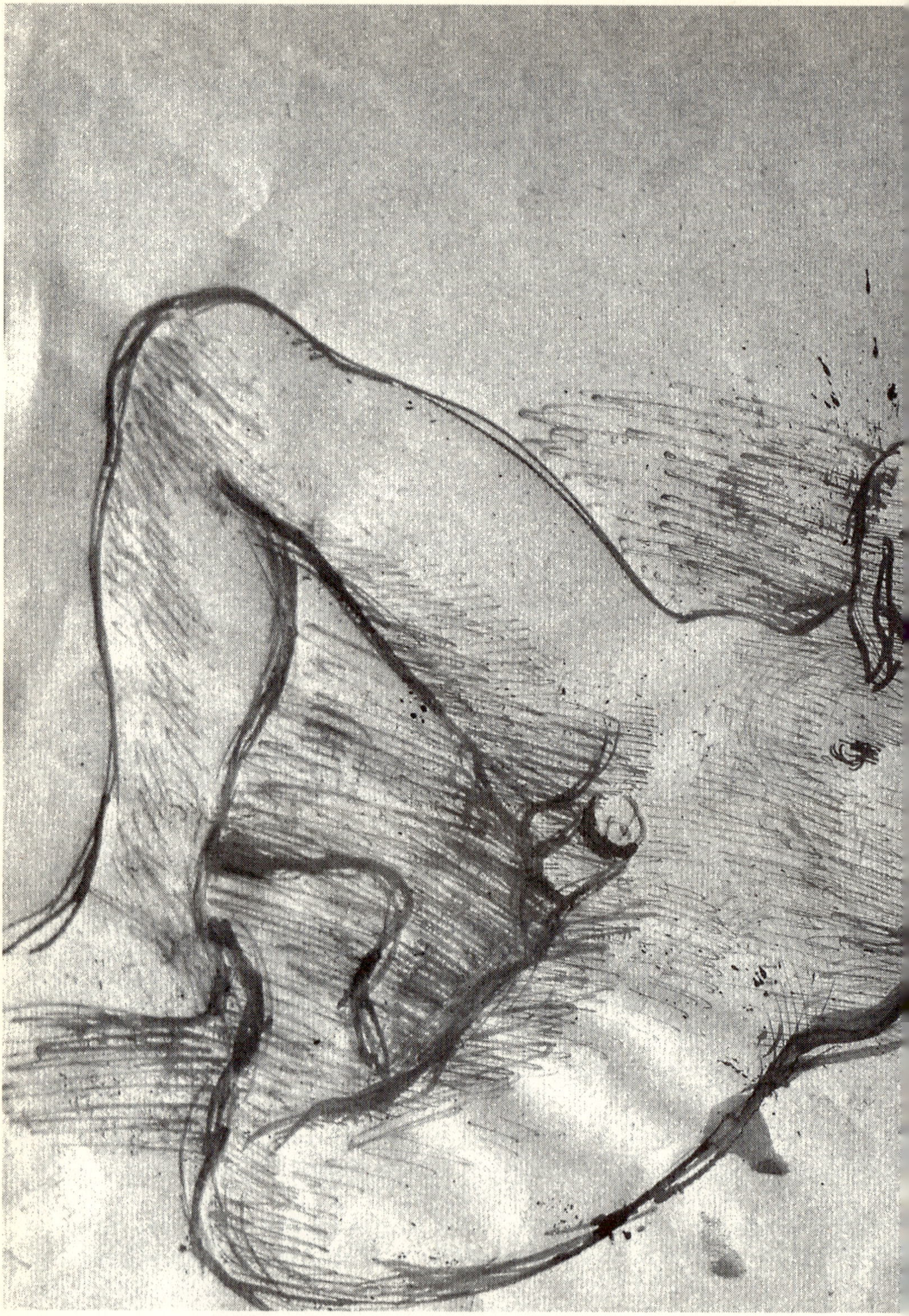

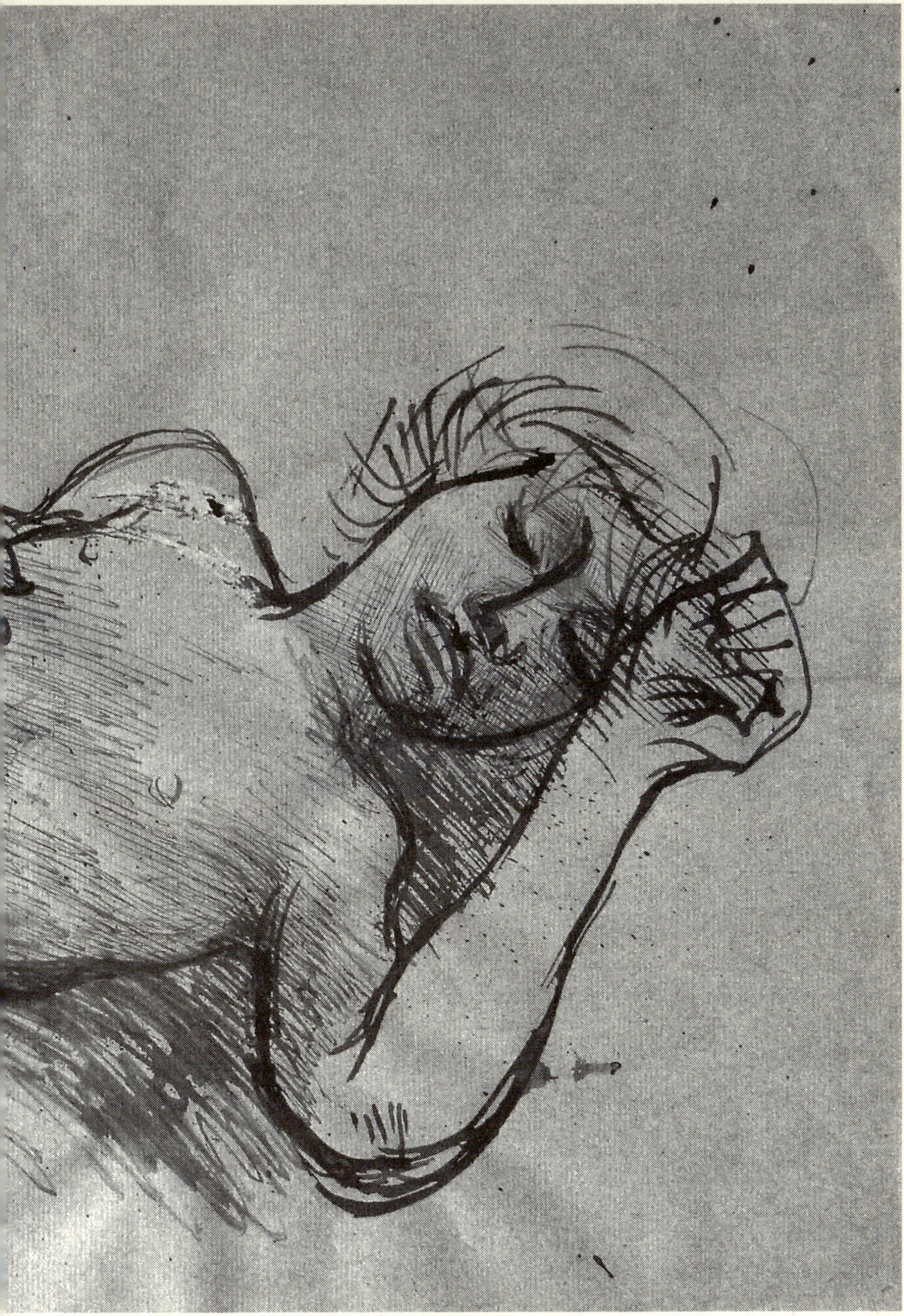

35. *Sleeping youth (1981).*

21 January *Sydney*. St Vincent's Private Hospital.[1] At night, a sleeping pill, and I slept really deeply for the first time in several years: but a sleep haunted with dreams of Bali, and dreams of the houseboys being here in the city with me, and I helpless and they frightened and I was scolding them unfairly as often I do for not being able to do something I wouldn't manage myself. I remember from the dream the unfailing politeness they countered to my unreasonableness, and was ashamed.

6 February My 55th birthday. Here I sit surviving and all around me, crowding out the pill bottles, are vases of roses, sprays of orchids, bouquets of tuberose, carnation, and very lovely they are (the only things in the room or on my balcony or in the vista from my balcony that relieve the astonishing and unrelieved *ugliness* that surrounds one: having become used to Bali it seems that visible Sydney is one vast ocular insult). Most of them come from rival galleries and art dealers.

13 February The gifts of fruit people bring seem to be the ultimate in exotic luxury after two years in Bali, where the few grapes are bitter. Here the punnets of crimson strawberries, velvety peaches, plums with the bloom still on them and firm sweet pears have a Rubensesque[2] effect as though the Garden of Eden had been robbed to supply a banquet for pagan mortals.

My star caller was Betty Gorton. We gossiped, and also talked about the Indonesian collections. I didn't open the book-like parcel Betty brought until she had left. Somehow the joke was a mad surprise—a box of coloured pencils and one of those terrible children's colouring-in books with printed line drawings of camels, kookaburras, Captain Cook[3], fairies, seagulls and kangaroos. Hysterically funny sort of prank it seemed to play on an artist who admittedly is not without a sense of self-importance. I got to work making surreal additions to one of the illustrations showing a policeman, very carefully jazzed it up with lots of bright colours to post off to her.

21 February to 1 March *Glenrock, Marulan*. It's delightful to be back in this beautiful old house, away from the stale air and nervous pressures of town. It is cool, even cold: we have wood fires at night in the book-lined library, and drink sherry to obscure Indian chants or the music of Bach: Peter Muller is deeply interested in oriental music, philosophy, religion, as tiers of volumes on Zen[4] and other mystical belief, and poetry, and architecture of eastern lands, bear witness. Carole, between preparing superb meals, sits at her loom weaving rugs and lengths of woollen cloth. Outside, the peacocks screech at approaching rain, the Hereford herd grazes in rolling pastures. Peter's draughting office is a well set up and lit studio in an old sandstone barn behind the house, and there I've spent a lot of time drawing every day I've been here—a whole series of studies of insects: mosquitoes, praying mantises, beetles—for a big picture I'll get to work on as soon as I can return to Bali. Despite the quiet simplicity and comfort of my stay in this elegant old house and the casual undemanding atmosphere I am still very homesick, and my mind plays with anxieties about this long absence.

13 March *Sydney*. I go to the publishers, Collins, to a scintillating and highly entertaining lunch with Gerald Durrell and his wife[5], then to discuss business about my book. *Then* home here, sleep for two hours, bathe, dress, go out with James to dine with Charles Lloyd Jones[6] and Lord Talbot de Malahide[7]. Dull secrets, aristocratic beast who says *nothing* to contribute to a very good dinner in a house (Rosemount[8]) packed with millions of good, bad and indifferent treasures—millions of rather awful China cottages, dogs, cups, shepherdesses in cabinets and third-rate paintings.

Charles got rid of Malahide and the three of us went on to a drag show. Funny, vulgar, noisy, ultimately boring. Too much to drink (what else to do with all that noise, those lights, ostrich feathers and assorted legs, lips, arms and buttocks?).

My whole idea is now that this life here is a folly, wasteful and tiresome. There is too little time to talk to friends: they have no time to waste on hours that are neither work nor conventional professional 'entertainment'. *I* am tied up in the trade of success. *Me!*

20 March *Bali*. Peter and Carole Muller and I flew here. At Batujimbar—all the houses dressed with banners and umbrellas. As we got out of the car the gamelan exploded showers of music, and all the houseboys dressed for celebration welcomed us: drinks were already set out ready. The house and its garden looked glorious. This was a wonderful homecoming. Later, as dark fell, an *anklung*[9] orchestra took over from the gamelan gong. Guests arrived, and we dined outside in the garden by lamplight and moonlight.

24 March Full moon. A temple festival nearby at Merta Sari[10]—the dark, the lamps, the murmuring crowd so beautiful in their finest raiment, the urgent notes of the gamelan. Eight or nine people went into trance and danced with krises in a wild strange epileptic way, and were led fainting to the temple enclosure. Great drummings and gongings and a sense of excitement, fabulous carvings caught abruptly in a ray of lamplight, the wind from the sea bending the tall white banners. All this was hard to believe in, despite evidence of eyes and ears after the concentrated rowdiness and ugliness and unmeaning activity of Sydney. It seemed somehow very unlikely that Bali would still be where it is and how it is when I returned, for the energetic destructive forces of Western life, I felt, were quite capable of having sought it out and ground it to dust in so short a time.

31 April Barry Humphries (the comedian-satirist, whatever he might be termed) came with his wife[11]. He thinks of coming to Bali to write. Warwick has already snapped him up for a cottage at Ubud, to our ironic amusement. He'll have the village well populated soon. After chatting and having a few drinks we walked down to Tandjung Sari where they had the famous Mengui Topeng[12] performers, who were even more brilliant than usual.

8 May Armand Drouant's[13] amiable partner, now back in Paris, wrote. It all seems very exciting and highly unlikely really—Instant Fame. I would distrust it more, for I have no liking and certainly no trust in the French, if M. Drouant had not said something when he was here that was not only extraordinarily flattering but also, to me, believable about my art—that as a draughtsman he considered I stood as peer and equal with a dozen now living.

Yet, as against the chance of demonstrating this to the eyes of a foreign public sated with conceit about the value of their own culture, the cost of such an exhibition to me would be very great: first, to put aside the cream of my work for one and a half or two years, secondly the burdensome prospect of a visit to Paris where I know no one and can barely speak the language, a damned expensive place. But most serious of all, would the pictures sell?

Also, a reputation cannot be made in a strange country on the strength of a single exhibition. It would have to be followed by others.

9–10 May A free weekend at, of all places, the Bali Beach Hotel. This is our reward for having, at a dinner party there months ago, invented the name of their new sea pavilion bar. As Wija said it was a brief visit to a foreign country, and the utter contrast to how we live in medieval state became a matter of many odd pleasures—air-conditioning (which I loathe, but it's a change), the anonymous mass-produced furniture, the dozens of painted cards announcing various services (with the compliments of the management), and a *telephone*! Room service, steam bath, massage, etc.

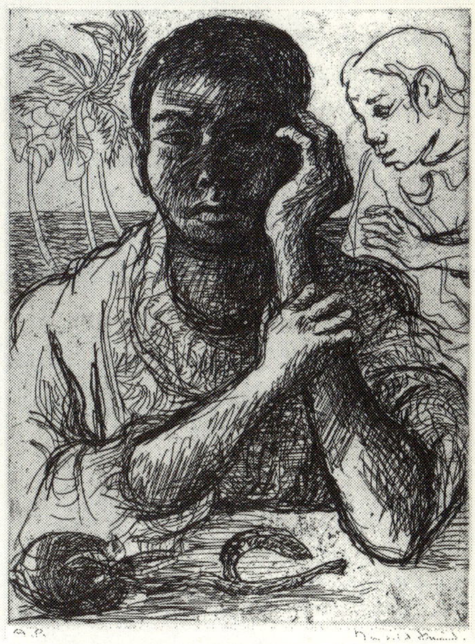

36. *Etching of two males (c. 1970s).*

I sent for my three little house-boys, to treat them. They were utterly thrilled with their first entry into the horrors of the 20th century, terrified of the lift, fascinated to look down from the height of ten storeys to the swimmers in the pool. And the bathroom with *hot water*! But most impressive of all, when I lifted the telephone and ordered them three of the most elaborate ice-creams on the menu.

And with it all, their astonishment and delight, one had to admire the unflappable balance of Balinese manners, for they knew exactly how to behave with all of the accustomed grace and dignity, taking all this pleasure with a charming acceptance. And when I took them over the hotel to see its marvels, they did me honour by their gravity and dignity. They have an innate sense of good style.

10 July This morning the only one of the antique sellers whom I like to the point of trusting interrupted me at work. He was wildly excited. For some weeks now he has been setting up a great project of mine to acquire some bronzes. To begin with, the bronzes only existed as a theory of mine. From a single fragment in the Denpasar museum[14], and from having seen once in farmland on a hill near the lake at Bedugul[15] an old stone Buddha statue, I was certain that in the area there were a number of 10th-century bronzes. He went there, with money I lent him, to scout for them.

In the privacy of the studio he unloaded an extraordinary treasure of 12th-century bronzes from a basket. With a proper sense of drama, first he unwrapped from newspaper eight elegant incense braziers, next an enchanting horse, *very* Balinese, then one after another the gods and goddesses—six of them. In all they form, in a single group, the finest collection of bronzes in Bali in private hands. The museum has nothing so fine. I've been locked up like a miser with them, exulting and re-examining and discovering new marvels. They are an extraordinary mixture of classic and primitive, and quite distinctly so Balinese they could not possibly be mistaken for Javan work.

21 September By now my opinion of the Indonesian character—that of the upper classes especially—is very very low. The intricate intrigues and complicated constructions of lies, delays, bribes and broken words they build about the simplest transactions, and invest straightforward relationships with, defeat themselves. The people they have no need to cheat, who are profitable if collaborated with, become bored or disillusioned, and withdraw.

25 September Today came a note from Wija in Djakarta. He had been seeing some museum and archaeological officials in order to find out what the attitude really is about export of antiquities for national collections. He learned that *all* old stone carvings are to be scrutinised and probably kept in Indonesia for archaeological study, but the bronzes are of less interest. But apart from all this Wija's letter lifted my heart quite a bit simply as a sign of friendship, as a sign that despite recent months he has time to keep a corner for our mutual interests outside the boring, and now alarming, march of business interests.

27 October The sea breezes have dropped, so the kite-flying season is ended, and with it the bands of children and men of all ages setting their kites to the sky, their leaping and applause on the beaches and the paddy fields upcountry—the drama of those huge kites. It takes thirty or forty men to get them into the air, and the ropes are so long that on some days, to wild plaudits and general excitement, they actually pierce the clouds.

21 November The energetic Scheinbergs[16], vociferously and energetically amiable and generous, arrived loaded with presents—a 'Beatles'[17] recording (which I loathe), bottles of gin, books, magazines. The last two days I've been lunching, wining and dining them and conducting them about the island. This morning was Business, Mrs Scheinberg's famous capacious handbag overspilled wads of dollars for paintings.

1971

Last half of January Painting again: half a dozen studies and some landscape with figure pictures.

Tourists keep barging into the house, ignoring 'Keep Out' notices and nowadays are usually given 'brief' treatment. One or two welcome callers. Queen Soraya (of Persia)[1], a very relaxed and pleasant woman, came several times with her handsome Italian lover[2]. A writer, George Hayim[3], a *very* amusing, ebullient and extraordinary man, is exhausting, but well worth the fatigue—very aggressively, openly, a masochistic exhibitionist. He woke us all up—it was as though he divested us of our lethargy and reclothed us as the persons we used to be. For a little while I was transported into my old sense of being, and it made me look with something of revulsion on the routines that have taken over: trying to write, trying to paint: inspecting progress on the (really delightful) buildings I've designed and financed, sure they will be destined to the decaying and degrading processes that Wija spreads about him.

Last week of February *Djakarta.* I drove about seeing some of the half-wrecked and faded glories of the old town—those impressive deep-walled constructions that despite their facades of commercial power and the logic of greed were proportioned also to harmonies of form that belong to their time.

What strange people they are, the Djakartans and the Javanese. Even the upper classes breed like teeming rabbits: all their houses are cluttered with babies and little children. The city swarms for miles and miles. The people I have met almost without exception belong to the nobility.

We all met up at eight in a bar for drinks and went on to a nightclub called Blow Up. A wall of darkness and terrible screaming noise. What *is* it I hate so about the noise they all enjoy, and the ugly silliness of too many people crowded together? Unskilled gawkiness, silly show-off clothes and the vigorous energy of undirected vulgarity—erstwhile aphrodisiacs—provoke me only to weariness.

13 March *Batujimbar*. I have been painting. Trying very hard to break through on paper into several ideas that are unfortunately very vague in my mind, about landscape.

I am sorry to hear, from a visitor, that John Gorton is out. Ironically he had the casting vote when the House was equally divided on a vote of confidence in himself. I have so often asked various sorts of Australians who come to my house *what* has been the cause of Gorton's terrific unpopularity. Various answers—unabating press attacks on him, scandals about his sexual promiscuity, his ruthless tactlessness with members of his own government and his heavy drinking. Also many say simply that contradictorily we Australians despise and suspect our politicians but Gorton's weakness lay in not being enough of a politician. What they mean by *that* I'm not sure: not adroit enough, I suppose.

July Meet these television and film people, Jane and Ian Stocks.[4] We've been very busy indeed with the filming. It's been great fun and well worth doing. They give me great confidence, by the way they set about things, that the result will be something very beautiful, entertaining and seriously interesting.

All the time I've been able to do a little work, and have been flooded with good, bad and indifferent callers—the only one of real interest, Max Harris, the poet: very Rococo and rather pontifical who makes so much play of being a character that one almost forgets he actually is one.

27 August People come and go: most of them leave so little mark, despite all their bustle. Mrs Scheinberg arrived, in admirable form. Came round with a huge suitcase of presents for the children of the house and for me. We are terribly foreign to one another really, but get on terribly well because we both have a rather mad relationship to humanity in general—and we both are determined to enjoy what the world will afford us without in the least compromising our ideals to get it. Her talent for money and admiration for art, and my talent for art and admiration for money meet on grounds that give us both a lot of amusement and pleasure.

12 October *Damn* having to go to bloody Paris. Here everything is very lively. I gave a party—drinks and small food for about fifteen guests. This was to amuse the Duke and Duchess of Bedford. The garden had been converted by the boys into a glowing fantasy with acres of young palm leaf, gilded umbrellas and hundreds of candle-lamps that gently glowed, picking out the eerie faces of a hundred or so *topeng* masks tied among the leaves and branches. Our music was superb, set in different parts of the garden.

20–30 October *En route to Paris.* On the journey I stopped off first in Rome to buy a few cold-weather clothes. Saw quite a bit of Justin O'Brien, now back to his old (pre-Greece) bog-Irish self, and unchanged Jeff Smart. Then to Nice and up to Tourrettes-sur-Loup[5] for a week with Peter and Pat Kaiser[6], a pleasant stay among olive groves—a simple quiet life. We drove about, looked at the Picasso Museum[7] and the Maeght Foundation[8].

November *Paris.* The Exhibition at the Galerie Drouant was a success—that is to say, for an unknown foreign painter it was surprisingly successful—good critiques, and twelve or fourteen pictures sold. The Drouants gave me a marvellous time, and almost killed me with kindness and excesses of wonderful food and wine, made me tremendously welcome in their houses as well as feasting me in famous restaurants (Tour d'Argent[9] etc.). Sybaritic overheated splendours.

Britanny. We stayed with some people who had bought a picture—in their pleasant house, a restored mill near Quimper[10]. I made a lot of drawings and studies in the neighbourhood, fell in love with the numerous stone Calvaries[11]. The drawings turned out very well.

Against all this is the fuss, the excitable *bore* of the French language, and the very considerable cost, all to make a Continental reputation I can do well without: and the *cold.* And the eternal compliments and how'd-ye-dos. The expense worries me, but more than that it is a matter of there being too little time for peaceful work and going about my own life in Bali.

Drouant has the strongest conviction that if I continue to show regularly with him—once very eighteen months—I shall have a very big name internationally. I would quite like that, I'll admit: but with the great name would come also a great rise in the prices of my work—it might be so great that fewer would be sold and I would earn in the long run less than I do now.

London. Bitterly cold and uncomfortable in chilly rooms yet somehow welcomingly familiar. The only warm place was Harrods.[12] Lunched about quite a bit, but really saw very little—it was so ghastly outside (snow etc.), and the way of life there unknowable.

Back to Paris, beginning to feel rather ill. But mornings I spent in Margaret Olley's studio near the Pont Marie[13], drawing the river and houses out of the window.

Nothing except the aspect of Brittany could make me forget Bali and the life here. I don't understand how people put up with the inconveniences of their lives in other countries—they seem only to escape from desperation whilst eating expensive and exquisite food. However, with it all, there was much jollity.

First half of December *Ceylon.* Bevis and Geoffrey Bawa met me at the airport. I stayed at Brief, unchanged in many aspects except that now it is organised to supply Bevis with his only income, from paying garden visitors and tourists and selling flowers and plants. Bevis is utterly the same, but older, iller and poorer, none of which has diminished his kindness nor his casual and fantastic eccentricity.

Geoffrey lives in an incredibly splendid style—his two houses, his office are among the most beautiful houses in the world. We lunched with him at Lunuganga[14] among the peacocks and vistas in a dream of amusing inventive elegance and also at his famous *pied-à-terre* in Colombo.

Colombo—and its government—is otherwise a world centre of pollution and corruption.

1972

1 February *Batujimbar.* The weather is exquisite—*too* lovely, since there's been no rain for nearly three weeks and I've been working, or rather overseeing the putting in of a huge garden in the land next to mine—have taken on four extra gardeners. Driving them hard. They are cheerful, energetic, laugh and sing as they sweat under the sun. And have the force to play gamelan music for a couple of hours for their own pleasure at midday.

There is no one like these people left in the world, and no such enchanting place. A sort of joy in the colour of leaves, of sea and sky, the ever-present sound of music, of laughter. An idle wind to cool the air, birdsong. They gather always in the evening in my bungalow to gossip, to tell me stories: eyes bright as birds in the lamplight, relaxed, happy, amusing, courteous.

16 February I feel very disturbed and restless these days. Part of it is the letdown after I've finished a day's painting, and the exhilaration disperses. And an impatience with the terrible *ordinariness* of the talk of people who come to waste my time. That really upsets me—the Balinese with their determination to chisel and cheat, the tourists with suburban questions. And yet I *long* for company, intelligent company.

So this evening I couldn't bear any more gamelan music. Played old gramophone records, found some serenity in Mozart, and a lot of old sentiments in a disc of Ischian folk songs that evoked a time I can't call youth—I was 34 then—but something that from this distance seems to have been something like it. Full of pain and pleasure of a sort I no longer experience.

10–17 April A week's visit from Mick Jagger. Wija has altered all the furniture and made a sort of opium den effect—suitable I suppose for Jagger and his friends.

Jagger, wife Bianca[1], child and nurse have just left. They were quiet and very pleasant.

21–23 April Just now in Bali the advent of modern times, changes undigested by the government, their inept and inexperienced attempts to control, have given rise to silly laws and regulations and unpleasant undercurrents. Javanese control, an influx of dubious foreign speculators, native resentment expressed in a decay of manners and a sudden bursting forth of the nastiest commercialism, have taken away a lot of the pleasure of life here. A lot of arrogant police interference in private houses. One has become unpleasantly conscious of their spies, *matamata*, stickybeaking about, questioning the servants about what goes on in the household.

My own prestige remains high at all levels, but any man in my position is a target for envy and intrigues, and all Balinese, above all my own household, regard me as an orchard to be robbed of its fruit as frequently as possible.

Last week of April and first week of May *Nice*. Armand Dourant was at the airport. Villa Massony, Villefranche[2] is a largish house in a steep terrace garden. Fabulous views of the bay and town below us. Scent of orange blossom, sound of sports cars tearing along the serpentine roads. Rich yachts at rest in the placid baby-blue water. My room has shuttered French windows onto a balcony, and is furnished with 18th-century provincial pieces and dozens of paintings.

We dined out, fabulous wines and food, with an old odd couple. Everything is rich and established. There's the comfort of repletion. I don't know if I'll endure much of this—the too-deep comfort, the absolutely uncontrollable unreality of high-bourgeois living—and they don't really give a fuck for anything but the next very good meal and wonderful bottle of wine.

The radio is loud, the television, the noises of the household are all loud and energetic. Everything is French to the point of distraction—the ormolu candelabra and gilt porcelain mantlepiece urns are reflected in Louis XVI mirrors[3]. There is a plethora of chandeliers, sconces, brackets, harpsichords, pianos both cottage and grand, cocktail cabinets, exquisite chairs, sofas embroidered with petit-point flowers, and two of the most magnificent Japanese scenes in France. The infantile blue eye of the sky melts into the sea-haze of the horizon, capes covered with lollipop houses embrace the harbour.

This bourgeois living is not geared to painting. The heavy food, the unrelenting amiabilities. But I am being grossly unjust, taking out on these people the discomfort of my own sick body, and blaming them for things that exist, that give me pain, which in reality have nothing at all to do with them.

I showed Drouant the gouaches and oils I'd brought with me. He said, 'You are right. I was mistaken. Your medium is not oils. It was my mistake.' He is right. His mistake has cost me a great deal.

Last half of June *Bali.* I realise that here all I do is carried out in a critical vacuum, and I need informed criticism. It is a great effort to do anything but sit and read novels. I paint—but I don't discover anything new: just now I am repeating old skills. The liveliest part of my days is spent haggling for Balinese bronzes or dining out.

Mid-August Clambering down gorges and up to the ridges where are my favourite Balinese villages—Taro, Blong etc.[4]—cut off from new developments for lack of roads: we walked all day. As before the exertion nearly killed me, filled me at the same time with wellbeing. The air full of singing birds—sacred albino cattle—the villages so clean and swept, so simple. We were welcomed by my friends there. No cars or trucks, no motorbikes, not even bicycles to be seen! It was a heavenly day, perfect for walking. A slight cool breeze kept in motion the bamboo wind instruments that guard the rice fields with funny little tick-tock tunes. And the people all in sarongs or kains, *not*, as now elsewhere, in ridiculous tight trousers.

Batujimbar. An eruption of arrivals—Bob Hughes first. Bob is not at all changed in the eight years or so since I've seen him—all the old ebullience charged with restless intelligence, bursts of friendliness, wit, perception. He obviously enjoys his intense and peripatetic life.

First half of October *Sydney*. I promised to take Madja[5] to Australia to be operated on for his harelip. Madja was thrilled and dazed by everything—enchanted by the poodles and various dogs people have, by the lifts and escalators, the glitzy goods in the shops, the great lofty sterile glass and concrete towers of the city. After a couple of preliminary dental and surgical examinations we took him to hospital. Attilio is wonderful with the boy—talks, and is somehow understood, plays chess, shows him all sorts of things, is playfully, roughly protective. He could not be more perfect.

The Holdsworth Gallery[6] exhibition looks very fine. It starts with a dinner for 150 guests (an artist's easiest work is painting) and once again I shall be a burlesque star.

17 October The child was operated on early this morning. The surgeon rang to say it was done, the hard first part; and it had gone very well. I was greatly relieved: I had slept less than ever in the night for worrying—one takes on a terrible risk with another's life and whole future: any slip, now or later, may bring disaster. One thinks how defenceless Madja is, how trusting. More than that, courageous.

To the Holdsworth Gallery again in the evening. Lots of people eager to ask the great man silly questions. And lots of pictures sold—there are several well-matured ladies of society who have a most peculiar habit by which they are known and not much liked by art dealers. They are very rich and very mean, but like to make a show of splendid extravagance. So they buy pictures and ring up later to cancel the sale. One, after making a tremendous fuss over buying a painting, telephoned an hour later: 'It didn't go with the curtains.'

Last week of October The film, called *Tamu* ('A guest')[7], was a brilliant success. I, for one, was utterly and narcissistically enchanted. It showed exactly what I would have liked to be shown of an individual's understanding (mine) of Bali. It was often moving, and very often extremely funny.

Melbourne. Attilio, Madja and I drove down. My apartment is the loft flat Attilio has made for me above the old stable: made by his own handiwork with loving care and tremendous thoughtfulness. It is perfect and very comfortable and self-contained, with its own conveniences and hot water, and a balcony of iron lace overlooking the garden—begonias, roses, azaleas, rhododendrons blooming beneath a little grove of various trees. Here I can relax. The 'celebrity' aspect of life in Sydney was getting rather unmanageable. In Melbourne I am not much known, and can go about without being stopped and recognised and gibbered at.

I saw for the first time Melbourne's new Art Centre.[8] A forbidding-looking building—a sort of Moloch Temple[9], but adequate. The collection, especially the ornamental section, is superb.

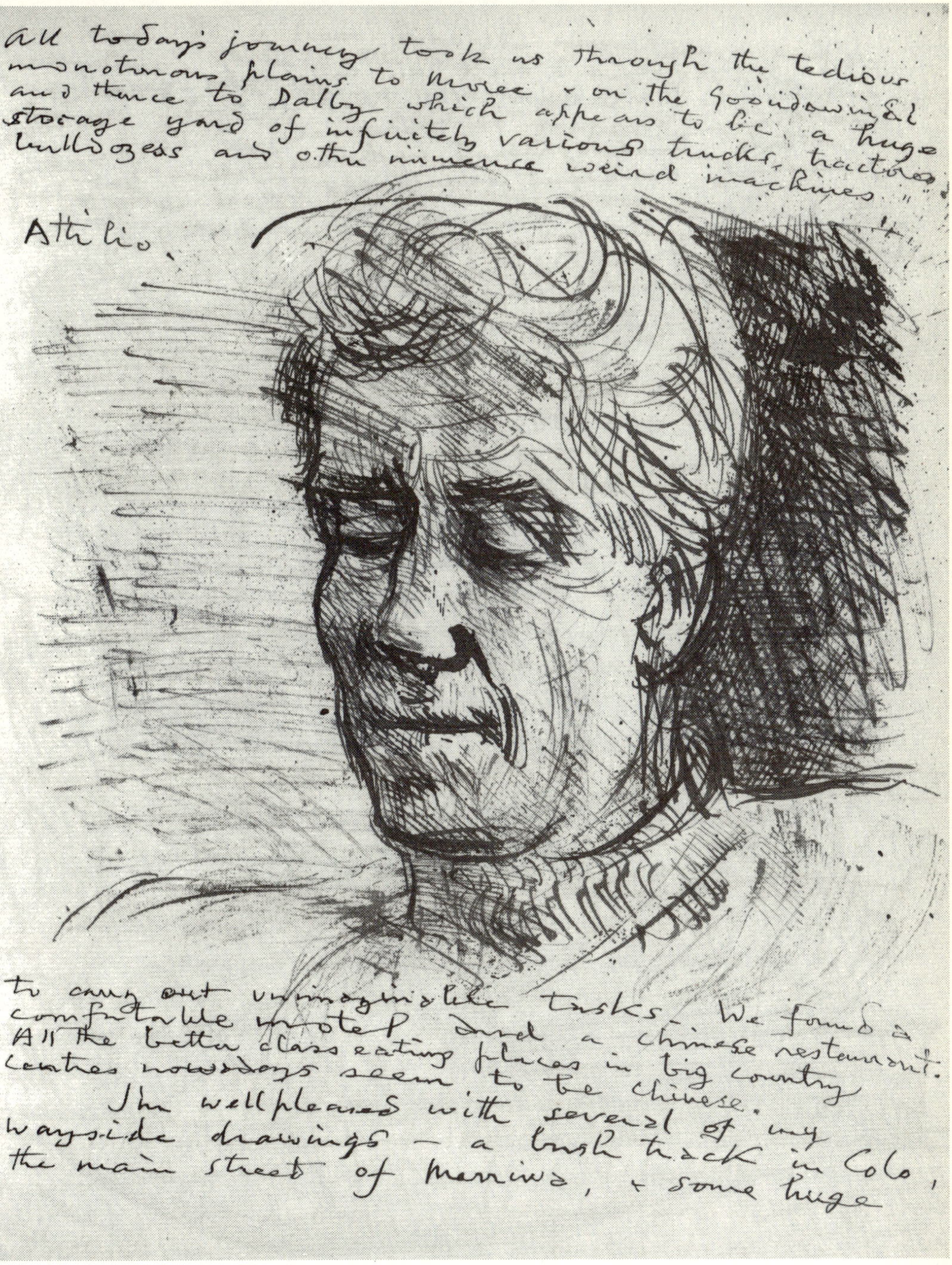

37. 'Attilio' (1982).

6 November Tonight I went to quite a wonderfully Melburnian dinner at Stuart Purves'[10] house. I had forgotten how (in Victoria) people dress very splendidly for dinner—the wives in sumptuous long gowns, special hairdos and the husbands wearing wonderful coats as well as trousers (matching) with rich shirts and ties. Nowadays they wear jewels—rings and bracelets to vie with their elegant wives. I'm afraid my own costume, though sumptuous (and all the rubies and sapphires outshone them all) was perhaps peculiarly simple. The other guests—an Irish too-talkative brilliant lawyer, Frank Galbally[11] and wife—a wildlife television man and wife, the Dowager Purves[12], Stuart and wife. But ah, the star!—John Olsen!!! Marvellous to see him. And so funny, so sweet and genial, so sharp and witty, so full of gusto and gaiety. Joyous Olsen!

The meal was superb—so were the wines. But best, warmest, wildest of all was John's talk, his mad mocking songs and ballads—it was truly good to be in his company again.

18–20 November *Retford Park, Bowral.* It was a harmonious small house party. Attilio, Madja and myself lolled about, strolled green rolling lawns—azaleas and rhododendrons were still out, and the last of the iris. Swathes of roses. James showed ancient films—Laurel and Hardy comedies[13]—at night. We all did absolutely nothing but talk, eat, drink and relax.

21 November *Sydney.* John Passmore was at Mrs Scheinberg's dinner party: he seldom goes out, and Gisella was triumphant at having got him, the bloody pretentious old goat. Still, he has been a fine painter—no one knows if he is one still, since he destroys his work without showing it; which strikes me as a perfect expression of miserly spiritual constipation. The pictures are either too good or the public is not worthy of being shown them, one is given to understand. It well may be so. He had nothing good to say for anyone's art.

The food was dreadfully rich—minced liver in cream: one's plate was piled and placed before one: rich sweet wines. Nothing could be refused, and it was all really poisonous. When we got home I was sick for the rest of the night.

Worse—for my wakefulness was full of bloody John Passmore—the miserly stinginess of the man: a man whose talents had never been given generous rein to gallop off madly, because in the saddle, tight hand on rein, sat this silly pretentious tight-wad. One is reminded of Freud's equation of gold to excrement.[14] Passmore's art is very constipated. Of a good quality nevertheless.

2 December The elections. The Liberal Government which has been in for twenty-odd years was badly defeated: the Prime Minister, McMahon[15], had become very unpopular, even with his own government. So now it's Labor.[16] I did not vote.

16 December A tremendous storm broke up the terrible heat of the day with spectacular displays of lightening against a sky all El Greco contrasts—black pinnacles of cloud, massed purples, edging pools of cool light through which the beams of the late sun shafted like searchlights.

I wish I could think of some scene or incident in this visit to Australia that would sum up my state of mind and being. The whole thing has been very grey on my part—my depression, physical discomfort of debility; my compulsion to carry out obligations. And on the other, Attilio's strength and energy sustaining me; Madja's self-contained and humorous stoicism in the face of pain, and his unquestioning faith in us and our ability to shape his future better.

And then this awful dreary ugly flat[17], trembling and rattling with vibrations of street traffic: its utter, complete lack of any beauty of shape, colour or even admirable craftsmanship. It could be used as a symbol for this country's hopeless material exploitation. It has the character of a very ugly whore demanding big money for unpleasure-giving service. It certainly is a brashly commercial sort of society here.

Last fortnight of December Came into St Luke's Hospital.[18] My room here is comfortable—even pleasant. There is what in Sydney passes for a good view from the window of six or seven skyscrapers and thirty or forty extremely ugly apartment buildings. But one can actually see three *trees*, and in the distance a patch of water with pleasure yachts.

It is a noisy view, because several more skyscrapers are being constructed, which necessitates the use of jackhammers, concrete-mixing machines etc. And then the people in the apartments play radios and television, and below in the streets traffic roars and screeches. Every ten minutes or so nurses and sisters come barging in with thermometers, glasses of orange juice and cheerful medical queries. God how I long for a (forbidden) cigarette.

I awake very early indeed and with many twinges and groans slowly heave one limb after another out of bed—it is an extremely painful process, and would probably be forbidden by the doctor—and get myself into an armchair by the window to watch in quietness the sunrise. The busy cheerful nurses have not at that hour begun their blathering, and there is little motor traffic from the townscape I gaze at.

All is going well. Attilio brings Madja to visit me, who looks absolutely thrilled to see me so spectacularly framed by all the appurtenances of a major illness. His courtesy, the brightness of his eyes, his smile, the way, having greeted me and sat a little to talk, he makes an inspection of everything in the room—these things delight me: and Attilio's guardianship of him. Attilio is in some ways Conrad's Nostromo[19]. His masculinity, his realistic compassion, pride and courage. His spontaneity in action, his saddened pessimism and a sort of tolerant contempt for the upper classes that does not preclude him from liking some of them without being burdened by respect. He really forgives them their selfishness and greed because they are my friends. Whilst people he chooses from his own class inspire no admiration but an affection that seems based more on their weaknesses and failures than on physical or moral qualities.

I do think so much and so often of painting and writing and how I have hardly ever *really* extended myself to the full extent of my talent. There always seemed so many more years in which to do it. Now there are none I can be sure of.

1973

11–12 January *Batujimbar*. The house was chaotic when we arrived. The whole island is like a steam bath, greenly humid: the air is warm and wet on one's skin: the landscape lies languidly inert, bathing, basking, touched by the huge tepid vaporous clouds, the clinging steamy mists.

The quiet is a wonderful boon. For hours at a time now there is no sound but the sea murmuring, the birds singing: distant cheerful Balinese voices. There are huge piles of mail: I've burned most of it without reading it.

20 January Making attempts to paint, without a great deal of success, pictures for Drouant. It is difficult to put down translations of notes and sketches so much later, and so far away from France in such a way as the picture looks freshly spontaneous. I had been trying for burgeoning springtime effects, using gay colours in swirls to make it all reel dizzily, lightheartedly. Houses and trees and people dancing and shimmering like reflections in water. I would rest from those labours when they posed insolvable problems.

Lately my relaxation has been reading memoirs of the 1930s–1950s. Harold Nicolson[1] (dull hypocritical snob), Virginia Woolf[2] (a strain on her friends—bloodless creature), Lytton Strachey[3] (the curate's egg), Carrington[4] (delightful), and now Chips Channon[5]—social-climbing, covetous, intriguing and so self-centredly vain as to conceive his whole acquaintance, and even whole nations, as adjuncts to his own personality, so that in the light of history his judgements of personalities assume extraordinary shapes: in fact, the real value he puts on people depends on whether, as dinner guests, they will enhance his social reputation.

My own interest in these memoirs comes from looking back on my own life, illustrated shadowy by a boxful of blurred snapshots and photographs I found in Australia and brought back here. Here and there these snaps indicate where my own existence touched some of those mentioned in the memoirs.[6]

Second half of February Housewarming drinks next door. It was moonlight. My newly employed nightwatchman, looking very beautiful in his dramatic dark clothes, saw me home after the party. Sat on the bed and massaged me. After a while: 'For fifty thousand rupees you can.'

I laughed. 'One thousand.' After an hour's haggling it was two thousand.

'You will like it so much next time you will pay me,' I said.

A very unimaginative boy, 17 years old, exquisitely built. Someone must have put him up to all this. I was much amused, but his interest was strictly humourless. So much the more surprising, then, the wild abandonment of his actions when he lay naked in my arms.

It is appallingly hot and steamy. Full moon, and a lot of important temple rituals.

I have been working on a series of very strange and perverse erotic drawings with 'writings'—poems of a sort, written into the design.

18 March Spent peacefully painting and drawing for the most part—I have a run of pleasing though not spectacularly original visual ideas, and am drawing with goose quills (Olsen gave me the idea in Sydney last December). I do not have to move from my studio, from where I can see a dozen beautiful things changing their shapes and colours every hour—the beach, the prahus, the fishermen, the garden pavilions embowered in foliage, the gardeners at work, the boys playing bamboo music in the guest *balé*, the plantation, the carved statues set among trees and plants, or those near at hand in the studio itself.

Later, sleepless—it was not yet midnight—wandered into the garden, turned down the lamp in the sea-wall pavilion and sat there in a sort of trance. The moon was near full, in a sky misted with vague clouds, the sea so misted the horizon was lost: but the reef white like the teeth of a vague smile, and to the north rose the volcano's profile, a decorative indigo menace. At my feet sand creamy in the diffused moonlight, and the noisy waves frothy white.

12 April My premonition of a cycle of unpleasantnesses seems to have been right. Today came a summons from one of the many branches of police for me to present myself with my papers. All my plans are thrown into confusion and my peace of mind shattered: one is suddenly poignantly conscious that one is always on 24-hour notice in Indonesia, and quite at the mercy of the corrupt officials of a very weird feudal fascist military pseudo-democracy—officials who derive a cat-like amusement from the helplessness of their victims. They strike terror in my heart when I find myself sitting opposite one of them—so smooth, sharp and impermeable, in a concrete office. They are polite, oily. And greedy. And O may they all rot in hell and let me live in quiet.

Picasso is dead. *That* will panic the art market. The first result I imagine will be a sort of stock exchange crash in the prices of his pictures with people unloading them for fear that his own huge stock will hit the market. Next there will be a 'revolution' of his fame and genius—a scene of jackals tearing it to bits. It will take them some time to balance his nonsense against his great attainments. Armand Drouant when I was in Paris echoed the French fury against Picasso, and belittled him. However much belittled by men who themselves are too inconsiderable to need shrinking, Picasso will remain a giant, dwarfing book-length epitaphs.

25 May America for some time now (weeks) has been much agitated by a tremendous political scandal called Watergate, centering on corrupt practices during and since the election of President Nixon[7], who appears to be as deeply involved as a large part of his White House advisory staff. It is likely to lead to Nixon's impeachment.

The surprising thing is that America seems surprised. I had supposed that this sort of corruption was an accepted norm by a nation whose shining ideals have long been inseparable from the cynical machinations of big business. Their naivety, brutality and greed are the other side of the coin stamped Idealism and Guilt. A weird nation.

Last week of June Geoffrey Bawa arrived. We've inspected the site for the museum and the house in the next block so that each is part of the other's landscape, worked on sketch plans, and got a whole lot quickly agreed on. He is in very good form, and his wit, his immediate grasp of problems and equally immediate creative reaction to them are a pleasant change from dealing with our other associates who turn the codfish glance of impenetrable commercialism on the project.

Second week of July *Bentota.* There are few changes at Lunuganga. The white house set in groves of trees on a strip of rolling land dividing two lakes is itself as lovely and serene as the landscape. The only notable alteration is that, pursuant to a Bandaranaike Government policy that all land must either be productive or confiscated, Geoffrey has terraced and converted to farming a slope of land invisible from the mansion. Pineapples and passionfruit—but also, I noted, a much greater and more profitable plantation of orchids. The last—blatantly inedible burlesques on a Bandaranaike move to avert famine whilst harassing the rich and decorative—very typical of Geoffrey.

14–18 July *Madras.* We were met at the airport, escorted efficiently through customs by a colleague of Geoffrey Bawa's and driven to the hotel—the Connemara[8]: an old hotel which Geoffrey is redesigning. After dark we were threading through broad avenues to markets and narrow crowded lanes that brought us (the vehicle was yet another magnificent Rolls belonging to Geoffrey) to a house in a garden. There is an upper room lined with books. An antiquary and scholar talked delightfully and showed us sculptures and bronzes. How different to deal with a connoisseur who lives by his love and knowledge of fine things. It was the atmosphere I loved. Clever, indirect, sophisticated. At once frank and charming, but full of intrigue, for antique dealing on an international scale here is full of illegalities and pitfalls.

India it seems is full of Rolls Royces, forgotten, lying desolate in the empty elephant stables of Maharajas. There is no sensation quite like driving about in one. This stately conveyance took us out to dine at the Madras Club, of which Geoffrey is a member. A beautiful building. We dined, by moonlight on the terrace, admiring the view and the elegant classic colonnade and cupola of the club[9]. The food itself was like an essay on 'what the Sahibs ate'. It consisted of quite flavourless comestibles, of the neutral sort attributed by the East to the West. 'Blue Funnel Line Soup'.[10]

The air is breathlessly dry and hot—any movement, the flapping crows, the scrambling urchins, momentarily stirs the dust. One thinks, it would need every flapping crow in India, and all its poor children, and all its dust, to mould a symbol for a fraction of the country. And even that symbol would probably be as superficial a summation as the symbol of our Rolls purring through the pressing crowd in a narrow alley at night.

Despite hotel baths and all that, India is so dirty and dusty after a few days one feels as though one's skin was ingrained with filth. And a sort of restless heaviness invades the limbs, and nothing reposes them. Yet I really enjoyed the visit immensely.

27–31 July *Batujimbar*. From the moment of awaking in my own house at last there's been a procession of people, many of whom I could well do without. The most irritating, disillusioning thing about the Balinese is their incapacity for friendship. They have no trust in one another as individuals and as for me, as a foreigner, they trust me by now and like me well enough because I am a source of money. Not one of them comes to this house for any purpose but to sell things or to try and get money out of me. It is really boring to feel that their visit is not complete until they've been paid for it. It makes one feel so dreary. Of my own household I believe Madja is the only one with any love for me. I do not deny that the islanders have many excellent and admirable qualities, but incapacity for friendship makes a terrible hole in the character of a man.

I have been drawing from the nude, much to the resentment—judging by their anguished looks—of my boys: but damn their Balinese prudery. I am firm, dictatorial: reluctantly they divest themselves of sarongs, and more reluctantly of the several layers of underpants beneath. They look martyred, I look thunderous and take up the pen. It's a great strain for all of us, but art must be served.

16 August Among the visitors who keep me from painting was a magazine publisher, and his nephew—a clean fresh healthy youth of 17. 'We come for your help and advice,' he said. 'I publish *Australian Golden Boys* magazine.[11] Male nudes in colour, done with exquisite taste. We're in Bali for three days to do an Asian Nudes number.' He produced a copy of his magazine. I must admit it was rather riveting: the cover showed golden boy Mike in a setting of rocks and trees displaying a dazzling array of anatomical charms. Inside were more of Mike and other youths capering on lonely beaches, laughing under waterfalls, half-aroused and narcissistic. It was hard to keep one's eyes off Mike, comparing the modest youth before me, casually and decently clad, with the sun-dappled animal whose rosy pink-tipped penis waved among the photographs like a magic wand about to turn golden coaches into pumpkins.

'You'll have a hard job getting a Balinese to take off his sarong,' I said. 'I have the greatest difficulty in getting anyone to pose nude.'

Later a boy turned up wanting work. I took him up to the studio and gave him *Golden Boys*. He was fascinated. That book really absorbed him. He made no demur about undressing and I drew nudes for the rest of the day.

12 October The Bedfords are here. The Duchess was really very funny in a way it's hard to describe—something between the Red Duchess in *Alice in Wonderland*[12] and an old vaudeville star who knows all the loudest tricks to raise a hearty laugh from the two and six pennies. The Duke has no chance to put a word in when she is in the brash mood and sat quiet and shy, trying to skewer up a dish of abalones with chopsticks.

23 October The painting continues almost frenetically, and I am greatly pleased with what I am doing. And yet—really, what the devil is it all about? I try to stand outside myself to evaluate what I have done. What is its purpose, what does it add to art or the understanding of anything at all? I have not yet even at my age found out what sort of painter I am, where I belong or what is my direction.

These self-questionings are a very bad symptom—of other disturbances, of some approaching crisis arising from the insecurity of my life here: the fact that all circumstances of my daily life are still in the hands of Wija, along with all the investments I've made here. He plays along his cat-and-mouse game in the same old maddening way. I am becoming deeply depressed at my helplessness, seeking some way to get a grip on what belongs to me.

5–11 November Such of my energies as don't go into painting are spent on visitors. A letter from Jeff Smart and the '*soi-disant* nephew' he speaks of arouse no thrills of ecstatic anticipation. There they all are, these distinguished old things with their desirable ingle-boys[13]. I do not really envy them, nor pretend to know why such associations are not possible for me—I am not attractive enough to attract, nor lustful enough to go to the trouble nowadays, nor willing to put my heart and mind to the service of the heartless and the mindless. It is not sour grapes. The grapes are sickeningly sweet, bursting with juice for all eager harvesters.

Last week of November I've seen quite a bit of Don Dunstan[14], Premier of South Australia—young, good-looking and intelligent. Dunstan is rather a controversial figure because of the innovations he's introduced, changing South Australia from the most conservative to the most lively state, culturally and politically, in the country. Last night when he was here Tim Storrier[15], a young Sydney painter, arrived with a huge package of cheese, fresh butter, gin, jars of homemade marmalade and a magnificent chocolate cake from Lynne McLaughlin.

From a bundle of newspapers I learn the whole Western world faces a winter of power fuel shortage drastically affecting domestic heating, light, factory production and motor vehicles. The financial pages give a picture of great nations rushing towards a chaos of inflation and disastrous shortages. To my simplified understanding it seems that a lot of the harm comes directly from production geared to create merchandise to be wasted (machinery with a life of three years instead of thirty) and appalling wastage of staple foods, wastage of energy, (transport) lighting, electrical power and vast industries whose products are ephemera: deforestation of huge areas of land for newsprint, advertising. Fortunes lavished to sell useless and meretricious things.

7 December The arrangements Chris Carlisle made for his new girlfriend's birthday were a great success. He chartered, at immense cost, a luxurious Chinese junk and invited ten guests to sail on it for the day. The weather cleared to an exquisite morning when we boarded at about 7 a.m. We crossed the straits, following schools of porpoise and cruised up and down the western coast of Nusa Penida[16], drinking iced vin rosé. Nothing could have spoiled the day. We entered a tiny landlocked bay and anchored for lunch ashore. There was a little beach at the entrance to a cliff-sided valley that further in had groves of coconut. Near the beach a rustic temple, and on the sand about a hundred nearly naked inhabitants sat watching us with wide-eyed surprise. A marvellous bunch of gilded lobster had just been served when the rain came down in buckets. Umbrellas and awnings were sent from the junk, but it was chaos, and terribly funny. All in all, a tremendously successful party. Night had fallen when we anchored again in Bali.

24 December A dull day. The morning dutifully painting, and opening Christmas cards from people I hardly know at all, and a few damned callers, complete strangers. Then I was sitting in the sea-wall pavilion looking at a dull sea and overcast sky when Attilio came through the garden, full of all the life-giving affection and loving friendship that lifts one back onto the proper plane of living. Such happiness. And that he should come just now when I was feeling lost and dreary and mundane. He chose the perfect moment to surprise me with his arrival.

1974

Second week of January Jeff Smart arrived. He's very amusing, and entertainingly satirical about the panjandrums of Australia's art world—who are *not* the painters but dealers, critics and civil servants of the national galleries.

1 February Geoffrey Bawa departed after a dynamic concentration on the buildings which instantly showed good results. I worked a lot with him. But today, the day of his departure, I was entirely taken up with a youth with the face of a debauched angel who came to chisel me for money and stayed to pose. A sort of filleted pre-Raphaelite[1] figure which I managed to overlook since he was willing to pose in the nude: and so worked very hard on drawings, which was a great relief to me. However, the 'trimmings' that followed were accompanied by wearisome Indonesian haggling. Serve me right for being an old lecher. Really, life is sometimes quite disgusting, and one is not the least disgusting part of it. He will come to pose tomorrow.

12 March My guest pavilion is now quickly being built. The wood carver has done a superb job restoring the antique pieces, and has now begun a creative work—a teak door for the museum with deeply cut relief panels showing scenes from life at Batujimbar. These are very strange and amusing translations from everyday reality into the eccentricities of demonic folklore. It is a marvellous example of the Balinese mind's ability to relate the phenomena of everyday life to their characteristic prototypes in legend. He is a real artist, as opposed to those fine craftsmen in Bali whose innate artistic sense enables them to master a style and a number of traditional subjects which they repeat without variation. His choice of themes, and the way he has integrated them with traditional imagery is remarkable, and also full of humour. He was delighted when first I told him I wanted a door carved which did not follow a pattern: it was to be a new kind of door carved with designs he himself must invent to symbolise our life at Batujimbar.

16 March The poor wretched Queen of England's visit in non-stop rain. She must have done something awful in a previous existence to reap such a rotten karma.

At dusk I was sitting in the sea-wall pavilion admiring the evening: the sea every pearly variation of grey; the sky sombre with great puffy clouds. The beach, wet still from the day's rain, a warm fawn colour.

11 May In my need for more and more money I've sold a lot of pictures to visitors. My weaknesses combine—a frantic desire to work with a paucity of pictorial ideas—a frantic need for money with an extravagant urge to get rid of it: a lack of policy in dealing with parasites, an inability to refuse pleas for help. And sheer greed of course.

I'm an old painter, with a long-established reputation, ripe to be toppled off my pinnacle. My reputation—the sensuous draughtsman living on this never-never island and producing a stream of skilful decorative unproblematic paintings—provides the best target. The new critics will certainly join the pack.

21 May After lunch my siesta was broken by banging on the door. It was Barbara Tucker, wife of Bert Tucker.[2] The Tuckers were in Bali on a visit along with Clifton Pugh and his wife[3]; all staying at the hotel in Tjampuhan[4], when Pugh was struck down by a bad heart attack and taken to the hospital in Denpasar. Could I go to the hospital and calm Pugh down and cheer him up?

O God, I said, 'There's nothing I'd hate doing more. I loathe sick-bed scenes.' However I half-promised I would go. About sundown I went to the hospital. Pugh was naturally surprised at the visit. Anyway we chatted about the art world, which if one hadn't known about it might be supposed from his view to be something like a shearers' union living in a Labor government paradise after years of Liberal persecution. Labor has just won the elections by a very narrow margin. A good thing, I agree, for the arts in Australia, although there will certainly be a multiplication of 'institutional' men like Pugh buzzing round the honeypot.

24 May I believe Brett Whiteley is in Bali—he came with Bert Tucker and Clifton. He is the only one of them who really interests me—not as a person (I met him once or twice years ago and disliked his snippy incomprehensible talk—he was high on drugs—hard to put up with) but as a painter and draughtsman really remarkably good.

Very late. Very drunk, Wija and I sat talking for hours about everything in our world. Somehow the talk turned to *why* the hell did I choose so deliberately to pretend to be an old old man when I am only 59. I may say, that really physically I am *old*. Impotent. Afraid of foolish activity. And fat and ugly. And slow-thinking. Even my dreams stagger on in slow motion.

6 June *Taro.* The car took us as far as Pudjun near Tegalalang[5], and from there we went on foot down into that steep wildly beautiful ravine of rushing water and dripping ferns. The air is noticeably cooler. The houses all have fine street gates, and over the walls many flowers and shrubs, and great fine trees of lychee and mangosteen. Everything so fresh in the clean morning light—it was by then about 8.30 a.m. and we had entered the courtyard and were given coffee. The grace and dignity and good-heartedness of their welcome: the delicious relief of now being secure for the time being from that determined brand of Balinese politeness which is the inevitable prelude to demands for money. So we relaxed and chatted and joked, and the birds all sang, the pigeons in their cages cooed, roosters crowed, pigs grunted somewhere out of sight. We arranged ourselves then in our finest batiks and went on to Taro proper, about two miles through fields of rice and farms of corn and fruit trees, groves of palm and bamboo to the great temple which was decked in festival splendour. A vast crowd. Those marvellous old pavilions were stacked with ordered rows of thousands of bright-coloured offerings. And everyone according to caste in the robes of their status in the temple. I was taken and given holy water, bathed in incense smoke and blessed and led away again to watch and listen to the two gamelans. Then after an hour or so we set off to climb—O God it nearly killed me—up the mountain on the other side where the car waited to take us home.

17 June *Batujimbar.* Whitlam's[6] policies in Australia will serve as well as any to make the rich get richer. Meanwhile high wages, a 36-hour week and full employment have somehow failed to produce a working class happy in its employment and keen to enrich its free time with the elevated, cultivated and joy-inducing pastimes that were once the exclusive indulgences of the rich. Such as reading poetry whilst sipping a rare wine, diverted occasionally from the intoxicating iambic pentameters by symphonic music or sweet-toned voices discussing philosophy.

Can it be that given equal opportunity the majority will opt for excess of beer, gambling and sloth?—more fun. Or use the free time provided by a 36-hour week working overtime for double wages, thus adding to production costs and contributing further to inflation etc. etc.

5 July Geoffrey Bawa'll be delighted with what's been accomplished. The museum is superb: very severe and classic and beautifully proportioned: the facade, in fact, depends for its beauty entirely on purist lines and volumes of the Balinese canon, and is devoid of ornament.

Second week of July Further additions to the household: a new house-boy, eight or nine years old, thin, shy, an exquisite child, wide-eyed with astonishment at the wonders of the seashore and the eccentric splendours of this house; another nightwatchman, a brilliant pictorial effect, about 24, with the most extraordinary face, rather like Genghis Khan[7], with a very strange sort of *medieval* moustache, dressed for the part in pure Balinese costume with a spectacularly tied headcloth; and a stone sculptor, equally fine, an ancient man—he says he was an adolescent boy when the Dutch conquered Bali, which would make him 85 at least. He speaks no Indonesian at all, is delightfully polite. The younger generation translate some of his quips for my amusement. It is apparent he regards this age with all its changes as a grotesque sideshow arranged for his entertainment. I've employed him to carve the stone bases of the museum pillars—he is one of the few remaining who work in the old style: lively very simple sculptural forms, with none of the lacy over-decorated *tour de force* effects of modern carving.

20 July My boys have been making the preparations for the six-monthly House Shrine festival. My household were all dressed in their finest clothes. Our own gamelan provided the music. Somehow out of the seeming muddle emerged the formal ritual, rising from the drums and gongs and chatter on the prolonged silvery tinkles from the priest's bell: and silent moments, and muttered prayers, and chanted invocations.

As always, this ceremony affects me rather unpleasantly. A feeling of suspense, of queasy expectation. I'm immensely relieved when the time comes for all of us to sit on the mats spread before the priest, to pray, to be chanted over, to wash, drink and be sprinkled with holy water, casting flower offerings god-wards. Then all of a sudden it's over. The oppression lifts. All that remained were the scarlet and blue umbrellas and the decorations at the doorways and gateways, and a prevailing mood of optimism because the gods had been given a fine breakfast and would as a consequence incline to glance benevolently on the house and its people.

16 September All in all a dull period has set in. It probably seems the more so since I am wanting the impulse to start working again. The significant events of such days are that this morning I purchased (at a bargain) a 10th-century stone statue. And yesterday a magnificent Ming pot. But what sort of death-in-life is one leading, wherein the artefacts are so much superior to the people?

It's an ungrateful attitude, quite ignoring my household, their pleasure in work and changing ways and cheerful manners. The naturally flowing stylishness of their small ways is so enchantingly good-hearted and polite. In witnessing them one observes elegantly improvised dramatic encounters, visually exquisite: and hears words spoken by unlettered villagers whose familiarity with their own language has constantly been illuminated by its greatest poetry employed daily in the rituals and entertainments.

24 October I continue to paint. And also now I'm writing some short stories. God, how difficult all this is, working where there are no critics and almost no chance of intelligent literate conversation.

Wija has given up drink. I dined there last night. It was amusing and relaxed. Tatie for once was not commanding the world through the telephone which she so often performs on like a savage African queen who has discovered the novel delights of the water closet.

I find the evenings almost intolerable if I haven't got company, though all day I hide from people.

11 November Every night now there is welcome heavy rain for an hour or so. The moat is full, and lotus in flower: the beautiful breadfruit trees are heavy with great globes weighing down the boughs, and the rich green cloudy flamboyas are topped with fiery vermilion flowers. At some time during the day I get in some work on the big *Black Friday* picture, which is a mad picture, but whether good or not I can't say. It is simply not a picture the public would expect of me.

15 December We were having a drink and gossip yesterday evening, waiting for Wija and Tatie to take them out for dinner, when who should arrive but Gore Vidal[8]. Bob Hughes had sent him. So it was a very good evening, indeed. Vidal has delightful wit. I was very thrilled about it all. He's one of the best novelists alive.

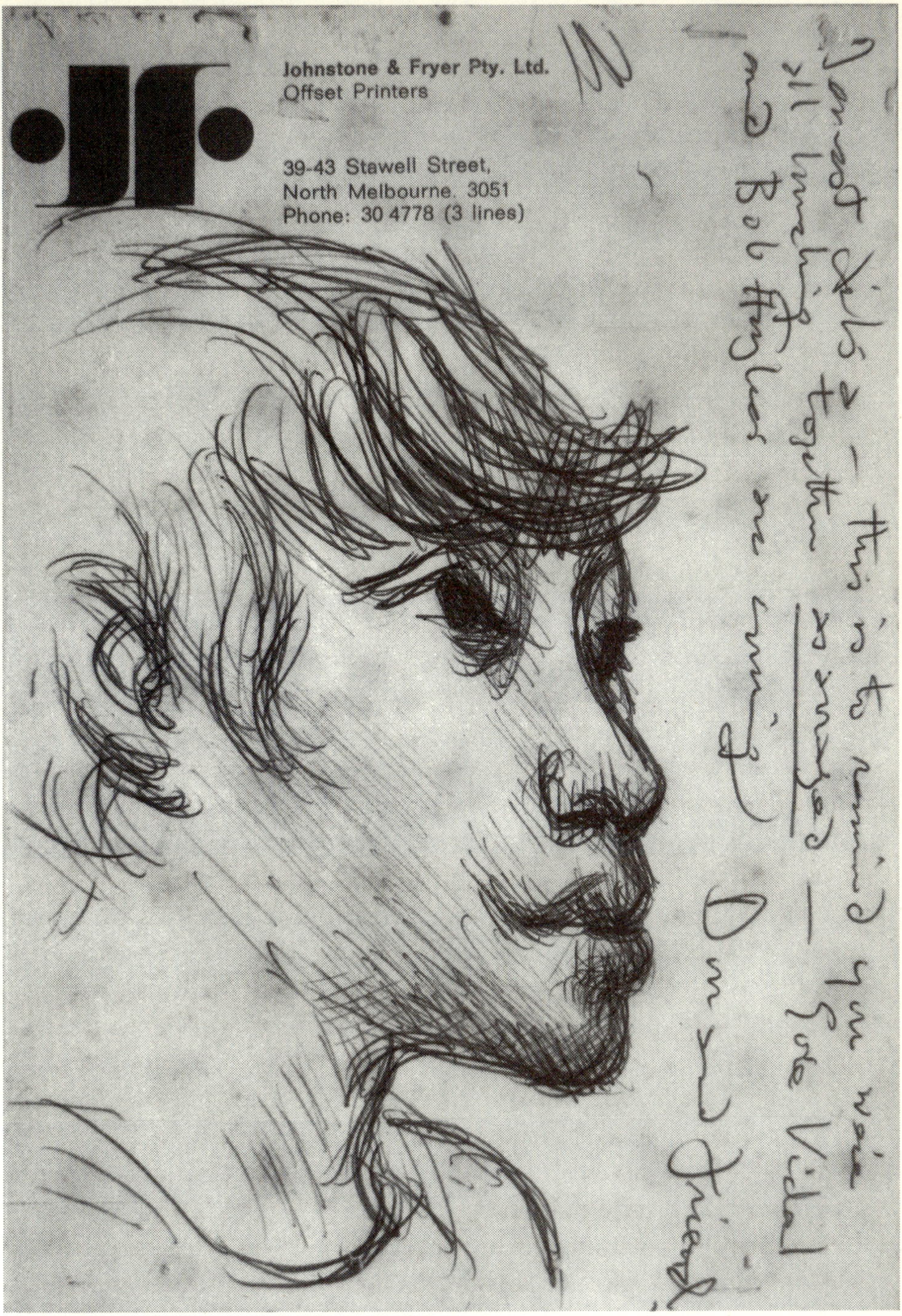

38. Lunch invitation reminder:
'Gore Vidal and Bob Hughes are coming' (1974).

There is—most regrettably—this to be said against the company of wits: after an evening of sheer delight, one can't remember a single one of the good things that were said.

17 December What plague-ridden times we live in, and so disproportionately many of my friends seem to be dying in. Indeed, I am forever thinking I am dying myself nowadays. My real concern would be Madja, the little harelipped boy whom I truly love in a completely objective unsensual way: his quaint devoted trustful sweetness, his sharp bright sparrow's eyes, his swift observation of what is needed. So funny, so lively, so hard-working and modest and gentle. He would lose most, and be least compensated by what I could leave him in dying.

Last week of December Bored to tears reading trivial books, meeting trivial people, having trivial talk. Attilio came soon after Christmas, so now once again I feel the assurance I need. Of course we've so far done nothing but sit talking and talking, and wandering in the garden, and watching the sea. And of course, much time in the museum where the porcelain is his especial interest. We selected a number of pieces—(Soong[9] and Ming for the most part) for his collection in Melbourne. Blue and white is his first interest, which is fairly easy: but now he begins to find the simpler and subtler celadons and white Soong and Ming bowls more to his fancy. And of course I get great pleasure from his appreciation of these things—an appreciation devoid of precocity. A gusto, in fact, all of a piece with his involvement in his work, the personalities in his life, his fishing, house, wife, food, wine—his love of gardens and plants.

1975

14 January Days in the doldrums. No work. I sit and read and see practically nobody—one cannot count as people the tourist gatecrashers who barge in. Rarely, someone turns up who is worthwhile. The other day came two charming Europeans, who for the last ten months have been sailing around the world on a sailing ship they built themselves—a 50-foot craft constructed on the lines of a 17th-century ship. They belonged to that curious masonry which, if it no longer rules the world, at least comprises the essence of what remains of Western civilisation. God. What a claim to make!—but it is curious how recognisable they are: one query reveals one guessed rightly. They are friends and acquaintances of all those 'key people' all over the world. By 'key people' I don't necessarily mean men of power, wealth or birth. I'd be hard-pressed to make a sensible definition. Inevitably they are individuals in whom accidental combinations of talent and character and physical ability enable them to range freely through all conditions of society, and who have a highly selective instinct in recognising their fellows. James Fairfax is such a one, and so is Attilio and (perhaps) Wija. It seems to be a quality that one can lose in the same way as an artist's talent dries up, who else can I think of whom I've known?—Bevis and Geoffrey Bawa, Edgar Kaufmann. Drysdale *once* had it, Lynne has it.

Wherever these persons take up an abode there is a localised expansion of consciousness. Creativity is heightened, the life of those around them improves. They are in a sense 'culture heroes'. Ideas are born. Nothing is quite the same again. The processes are casual and unregulated, and have no end in view (nor profit) except a realisation of the better possibilities of living. To which the arts are essential. And free social converse liberated from bourgeois considerations (business, conformism, etc.)

That's about enough of that. The elite exists.

Second week of February *Melbourne*. Kept fairly busy at Australian Galleries helping with the selection and hanging of the pictures, doing press interviews and a comparatively painless television interview. We attempted at first to do the television interview in the garden but were defeated by a series of ridiculous mechanical mishaps—the leafy glades were constantly rent by incredibly intrusive sounds—the racket of the 20th century: electric trains, roaring lorries, hooting motor cars, aeroplanes whizzing by.

We saw the film before going out to dinner. It was superbly done. I felt immensely pleased. There were very clear shots of pictures in the exhibition—how nude the nudes looked! It is odd the contrast between now and twenty years ago, when the male nude was hardly exhibitable in an art gallery, let alone broadcast. I will confess, those elegantly delineated cocks and bums looked attractively provoking.

23–24 February To the banks of the river near Princes Bridge[1], and made some drawings of rowers in fragile boats on the Yarra. Lovely to look at, the same light flooding sky and water; and all—even the riverbanks, the trees lining them—floating on the flood of light. They are making gay constructions—carousels, a paddlewheel riverboat all blue and yellow and red, for the Moomba Festival[2]. Watery reflections of summer gaiety.

Drove to the public gardens to feed the possums. Walked the windy paths and splendid elm avenues, discreetly floodlit from below so that where they arch over the walks one is in a vault of illuminated layers of leaves, one above the other, forever receding into the night above.

I am happy. I had not felt so during the last months of doubt and fears in Bali.

27 February John Olsen has gone off painting to Lake Eyre[3]. I like especially about his paintings the close cohesion between them and the man himself—they are full of movement, dash, wit, enjoyment. Above all, enjoyment: a delighted devouring of his environment. The other younger painter of great talent, Brett Whiteley, I'm afraid has had it—taken to heroin now, with the stupid conceit it's something he can control. *His* paintings are like wonderful glimpses of the world seen through holes in the death-wish: the tendency toward self-destruction has been an important part of his make-up as an artist for a long time—ten or twelve years at least, since first he was a Wonder Boy. Olsen is obviously the laster—his effervescing reactions in terms of colour and line have a flesh-and-blood vitality which at first glance might appear to disadvantage beside Whiteley's deathly elegance—but they flow from a fountain of generosity, of lavishness.

1 March Went to see Michael Shannon[4], who was one of us sharing the house on Ischia in Testaccio. Now he is white-haired and rather distinguished-looking and lives in a pleasant small old house in Toorak which is furnished with discreet good taste—except there are too many of his feeble dull paintings on the walls. He does not defend them; nor, thank God, demand one's opinion. So they hang about on the walls rather like anaemic kept boys who've been told to make themselves unobtrusive but remain within call in case they were needed to hand around the savouries.

His friends and acquaintances (apart from painters) are like Jeff Smart's, the social and art organisational hierarchy—directors of state galleries, collectors, writers on art and all the parasites on art who can be manipulated into manufacturing a reputation or a 'climate of celebrity'.

5 March *Sydney*. I firmly shut myself away from the noisy commercialism of Mrs Scheinberg's art world: I stayed at home[5] and read, slept, read again and slept again, all day. At night, early to bed after watching, for the first time, colour television. A thing new to Australia. The colour is rather nasty—tomato-sauce red, ochre, orange and purple and a horrid hot brown.

I always wake terribly early, and spend hours waiting for sunrise. Here the tedium of the day's beginning is defeated by the great view from my bedroom windows. The harbour pearly before sunrise. Great ships in silence coming to their anchorage.

12 March Off to the Scheinbergs'—a very odd establishment really, cluttered nightmarishly with the ugliest furniture imaginable, many paintings (some good) and superb Persian rugs. An untidy, chaotic household that has for me something zanily folkloric—the folklore of Marc Chagall. There is even a large goat in the garden. Gisella presides in the kitchen. Nobody helps her, and when her monologue reaches a climax and the goat strains at its tether to chew the azaleas and the children turn up the television one would not be surprised if an angel-winged cow flew slowly, upside down through the room, or an owl appeared, playing a violin.

14 March I think I will not have any more exhibitions. Or not be present at them. The side-shows (and the party at the gallery) are beyond my strength: also they are quite outside my ideas about how life should be lived. The increasing, accelerating, inflating grotesqueness of art dealing and its now unbreakable bonds with commercial advertising used to inspire me with amused contempt. I see, now that I have been deeply involved in it, that I was silly to be amused at all. A vile situation. The real values of an artist's reputation—his *real* reputation: the reputation that arose from appreciation of the qualities of his work—are reduced to rubbish.

Reviewing the results of so many years of work now waiting to be hung at the Holdsworth, I see I have been a painter of very variously interpreted Heavens and Hells. While the Heavens have undeniably been gardens for general, not spiritual, joys, the Hells have been pits of ridicule instead of tortured anguish.

Last week of March *Batujimbar*. A blessed relief to be home. Nothing untoward has happened in my absence. Inevitably the houses have a slight air of neglect. The garden has been well looked after. I'm beginning to feel well again. Lighter, more active. Drawing from the nude. I did three illustrations in a style that veered madly between my own erotics and Blake[6] and Fuseli[7]. A lot of the time I read. I hover between two books—Gore Vidal's colossally dull *Burr*[8] and an excellent biography of Augustus John[9].

First week of April A couple of days with most a charming Chinese-American architect, a man of the most pleasant cultured wit, Mr I. M. Pei[10]. We took to one another immediately. I was greatly charmed when he took up a Ming bowl from the table and translated the poem written on it. He was full of praise for this house, which indeed seems to grow more interesting and beautiful each time one considers it.

24 April A 'lordly guest' (*Tamu Agung*) called in for tea. Ibu Ratna Sari Dewi—better known as Dewi Sukarno: the President's widow.[11] Dewi looked young and attractive as ever, dressed in a fabulous floating cloud of a gown, and tottering with a certain amused difficulty on some new fashion of agonising shoes.

Mid-June to mid-July I have been working consistently, and sold to passers-through enough drawings to fill my empty (almost) bank account. Further to that I've worked on the erotic *Bumbooziana* book of drawings and text.[12] This industriousness suits me well, though I feel very dull in the evenings, and drink too much. Yet I am happy; which is more than a mere absence of misery.

Late July to mid-August A few brief and memorable visits from passers-through: our new Ambassador to Djakarta whom I liked immediately, Woolcott.[13] Very young he seemed for the position. And very intelligent and charming. And then a notable 81-year-old, Buckminster Fuller[14], the inventor of the geodesic dome[15], who took a tremendous interest in the bronze collection. Then quite a lot of people came to buy paintings. Fortunately I have had a sudden rush of ideas, and have worked all and every day.

4 September The jeep I have been waiting for for months arrived. It is indeed a peculiar-looking vehicle and I like it. It is an Australian military vehicle called a 'Pug'. Very strong, very light. It makes an excellent companion to the ancient Chevrolet, which is shaped to a sort of absurd upstanding grasshopper-like dignity—whilst the Pug, though equally high from the ground, is more like a turtle, or a beetle.

18–20 September I decided that, having found it not possible to adopt Madja legally here, to begin now buying land in his own name, so he can grow up a man of property—rice land—which will give authority to back his word when he grows up. Madja thanked me charmingly, remarked that it made him and his family secure for life. I thought of how adult and mature he was, though still a child, in his calm, his pleasure, his gratitude. A Western child would have utterly no conception of the reality or value of such a gift. The Balinese see me as a strange, probably foolish, magical old man, half-demon, half-prince. They're bloody well right in that assessment.

11 November Spent an amusing evening with an engineer for the Hyatt Hotel[16], and over cheese, wine, apple pie and ice-cream we ranged fancy-free through the sparse gossip of the island, which was somewhat overshadowed by the radio news that Whitlam has been dismissed and parliament dissolved by the Governor-General[17] in Australia. Fraser[18] was summoned to head an interim government until elections are held in a month. It happened once before in my memory, in the early thirties during a comparable crisis.[19] The immediate results of this one were infuriated protests of course from Whitlam and union demonstrations—notably one at Sydney Stock Exchange where, expressing hysterical optimism, shares began rising like fountains of joy.

17 December Union labour in Australia had boycotted Indonesian ships and planes in sympathy for the leftist 'Fretilin' Party[20] in Timor, which at last had been invaded by Indonesia. The military situation there seems to have been already resolved and the territory taken by Indonesia. The elections in Australia resulted with a resounding victory for the Liberals. Good. At Batujimbar these world-shaking events have been no more than the trembling of a leaf.

Indeed I've been once more seized with painting ideas—the 'Erotica' and some decorative pieces and nudes of three youths from the hills who, unknown to one another (they are from different villages) come to me as a guru and a lover. Surprising and gratifying after all these years. They have in common great beauty and charm. Each arrives shyly of his own accord, and behaves affectionately and with marvellous politeness. And with much hypocritical shame about posing in the nude. And with even greater displays of reluctance for fun and games until I pretend indifference, whereupon I am charmingly wooed, but it must be stated that in the matter of dalliance they are quite without humour or imagination. It is no more than a function. The sentiments they have for me are aside and apart. They are fond of me—my God, how odd!—for my wisdom.

27 December Attilio and Ailsa arrived, burdened with gifts and desirable house necessities (butter, a leg of lamb), art materials. The treasures of the Occident. We were discussing friends, politics and all when the mail arrived. Santa Claus in the snow on numerous bright cards of good wishes and one cable. A gift from Durga. My mother died. No sorrow for the poor old thing. She must have been 85 or more, and very tired of living. I last saw her—how long ago? Twenty years? Her death is a relief. While she still lived I could not think fondly of the best of what she was many years ago. And could recognise her only in the worst aspects of myself.

1976

6 February My 61st birthday. Some presents—books, biscuits, batik and some charming arrangements of flowers. Wija and Tatie took me to dinner to the new Kulkul Restaurant near here[1]. We dined superbly—really superbly: and there was charming music from two guitars. Part of the place's pleasantness derived from its having no electricity, hence no glaring lights and for the music no amplifiers.

Australian postal workers have boycotted all mail to Indonesia: and now there is a reciprocal ban from here. Stupid Australians are exerting this pressure in sympathy for Portuguese Timor. In actuality *nobody* at the moment knows what is going on there—which parts are subjugated, which are still resisting, because communications are nil, roads few and appalling and the island is in the middle of a heavier than usual rainy season.

27 February I've been working almost every day on nude pen drawings on tinted paper, and am much pleased with them—full sheets of Ingres paper[2] I crumpled, soaked in water and dyed, giving a sort of 'mural' texture, and had the boys flatten with a laundry iron before drawing on them. The model a beautiful figure: firm, well-muscled and flowing. Lovely cock and a bum like twin aubergines.

6 March Elsa Peretti[3] comes and talks. Strange and rather interesting woman, who is, I gather, the chief jewellery designer for Tiffany[4]. For some reason the Balinese think she is a man—though to me she looks enough like a woman, with the sort of elegance that has nothing to do with fashion but comes from an individual fantasy about clothes. She is tall, about 40, wears a battered broad-brimmed sweat-stained felt hat, dark glasses and Thai peasants' wide trousers and blouse—her carriage gives these garments an élan, as though they were the product of one of the great fashion houses.

It is charming to hear again the talk of my own section of the Western world—rarely heard here except from one or two birds of passage. She gave me, to wear as a pendant, a tiny gourd-shaped tear bottle made out of rock crystal. She knows numbers of those world-famous American painters whose work leaves one appalled and uncomprehending (which is, after all, the probable intention of their artefacts), such as Andy Warhol[5].

25 March My niece[6] plans to stay five weeks. She's a nice girl, and if only she can amuse me it will be a pleasure entertaining her. With the young of my race and class, the fault is that they're so *empty*. They've just emerged from the daily indoctrination of years of school. Modern education is geared to produce pampered technicians rather than develop minds and feed them ideas.

Third week of June Rupert Murdoch[7] (press baron) and his pleasant wife have been holidaying here at one of our Batujimbar houses. I regret that, not wishing to seem pushing, I didn't contact him earlier than I did, for when we met we got on very well indeed. The Vice Consul for Indonesia in Sydney, who used to be head of the Immigration Office here, asked if I know Murdoch. He would very much like to meet him and discuss Timor with him, in the hope of getting a better press for Indonesia on the subject. I tried hard. I set up an appointment. But alas, the servant forgot to deliver my note to the Vice Consul—who flew off to Java. And Murdoch went off to Australia.

24 July Cuttings about the *Erotica* show[8] came. So far no critiques, which I expect will combine the Australian talent for 'knocking', with pooh-pooh, not nearly erotic enough, attitude. I dare say the exhibition was fairly mild.

Of course all this publicity is funny, and advantageous. But it's not really a good thing for art and the artist. Art is the excuse for it, but it's not concerned with art standards. It is public sensation and commercial advertisement.

August It is unthinkable. Just the same I'm thinking about it a lot—the idea I may cease to be a painter. It looks to me as if the choice is to go on painting repeating over and over pictures I've done before. I'd continue to make a lot of money—become an old potboiler. My ideas have run dry. There's no more elixir in the cup. Or I can continue painting, very slowly and privately, not exhibiting, for my own pleasure: and paint only when the great irresistible urge comes on, the restless lust for painting.

But how will I live? I have no income to speak of. My holdings in Bali are worth over a million dollars, yet I have no title to them and expect to get no income from them. Actually I expect to be cheated of the lot. I've been giving money away like a madman. I have only a few thousand dollars reserve for myself. Writing, which I enjoy so much, is impractical. Books earn one very little.

First week of September *Lacco Ameno, Ischia.*[9] Attilio's younger brother Mario's house is new and comfortable, right on the hill amongst vineyards above the town's magnificent views. I am dazed by the talk which is amplified by the acoustics of marble floors, and all seem to have voices as strong as their opinions. Possessed of magnificent lungs and vocal cords, and tremendously passionate natures, the Guarracini shout and roar and rumble, all speaking at once with the fullest forces of their natures. The actual subject matter of these conversations is, to the Anglo-Saxon, trivial in the extreme: the flavour of a grape, the best way to cook a fish etc., yet a bystander might suppose it was an angry council of the gods in a mood to vote a war.

How good it is to see on the table at the conclusion of a meal a basket lined with vine leaves full of fresh green figs; and a bowl of pears, peaches and grapes. The fruitful landscape outside visits the table. Just the same I feel I am on the edge of a physical and mental breakdown, and unless I start some sort of cure very soon I won't be able to suffer all the vociferous chaotic goodwill. The tiled simplicity, the arches everywhere, the 'modern' shapes of windows help to send me mad.

A bus fetches me down from the mountain at 9.30 a.m. and deposits me at the baths. They are like a luxurious clinic. I had a bath in radioactive water which was oxygenated, and after was massaged by an amiable gorilla-like personage who gave my belly a reproving whack and remarked 'too much spaghetti'. Then there was a bronchitis treatment—breathing in gusts of steam. Finally, deposited back at the house on the mountain, I felt excessively languid but very well.

The specialist said I must on no account take the baths and massage. Then a blood test for sugar. The grandest of all the specialists, the chest and lungs man, forbade smoking and said no mud baths. I have now a strict diet, may drink wine and whisky, pills and inhalants. Must repose a great deal.

23–28 September *Tuscany*, chez Jeff Smart. His farmhouse[10] is delightful—a typical 17th-century stone two-storeyed Tuscan dwelling, in a garden of trees and vines and cypress and olives. In the fold of hills, with a distant view of a village on a hill. The house has every proper comfort and a huge fireplace, and kelim rugs[11], shelves and shelves of books. He was a kind and amusing host. What I enjoyed most was a motor-trip to Urbino[12], stopping at Sansepolcro[13] to see the della Francescas[14], picnicking in the mountains and going over the wonderful museum in Federico

Montefeltro's palace (*The Flagellation*)[15]. Jeff is a very knowledgeable guide on such occasions.

First week of October *Thailand.* The monsoon is already here. Steamy and wonderfully hot. From my window—the rain-swollen river brown as strong tea: dozens of little ferries. Dozens of brown children swimming near the shore. And in midstream, moving fast in the stony current, boughs and branches swirling along.

We took a taxi and went to the museum. Then I bought silk shirts. A friend who has a travel agency in Bangkok whisked us off to a very good French meal, and after to a series of very noisy but enjoyable gay bars, where in dim lighting many beautiful youths danced together—it was so pleasant and pretty for the spectator. The boys were most polite and charming.

There has been a very dangerous political crisis going on—with student riots protesting at the return of an exiled ex-prime minister. The military coup is now a fact. They hold the radio and have suppressed the newspapers and put on a curfew at midnight. Six hundred students have been arrested and will be tried by military court.

We trailed around the temples and museums, saw rather too many Buddhas, and lunched in a houseboat. Bangkok seemed quiet—a lot of armed police and soldiers about of course. I'd be surprised if many of the people staying at the hotel had an inkling of what has occurred.

12 October *Batujimbar.* An art dealer from Perth came to offer me a commission to do a mural painting for Murdoch University in Western Australia.[16] I had the boys bring a long roll of cartridge paper from which we measured off a piece and I lay in big abstract shapes that will form the foundations of the work. I swooped all over the whole area with widely curving strokes of colour to serve as an underpainting, making a conspiratorial guide for all that must go on top later. Sweeping arcs and spacious rectangles, isogon orbs drawn in with brush in red and black lines and filled in with strong areas of colour. Over these we glue transparent films of rice paper, through which the colour glows in a sort of subtle, milky way; the red and black brush lines are restated. More papers will be glued on later. By this means I get a crusty wrinkled uneven surface like a roughly plastered wall whose surface is coloured schoolboy doggerel that memorably defined the sin of Onan in its churchly precincts. It went

"Oop in belfry Verger stands
A-pullin' pood wi' both 'is 'ands.
Down in vestry parson yells,
'Stop pullin' pood. Pull fookin' bells.'"

This simple and – one must admit – puerile contribution of mine to the discussion was treated with the contempt it merited. Our camp-fire symposium reverted once again to its more habitual plane. The usually timidly silent (but much-liked and respected) photographer, ex-monk, ex-slave Herr Doktor Pfeiffling, ventured some observations to which we hearkened with interested expectancy.

"I have been fortunate enough to witness, over a long period in a professional capacity," he commenced, "Numerous examples of unalloyed conceit – or vanity, or Narcissism, or whatever you choose to call it – posturing in front of my camera lense. The sameness of it all! – you will perhaps out of charity then sympathise with me when I rebel against that soul-less and mechanical device, the camera, and attempt to convert you

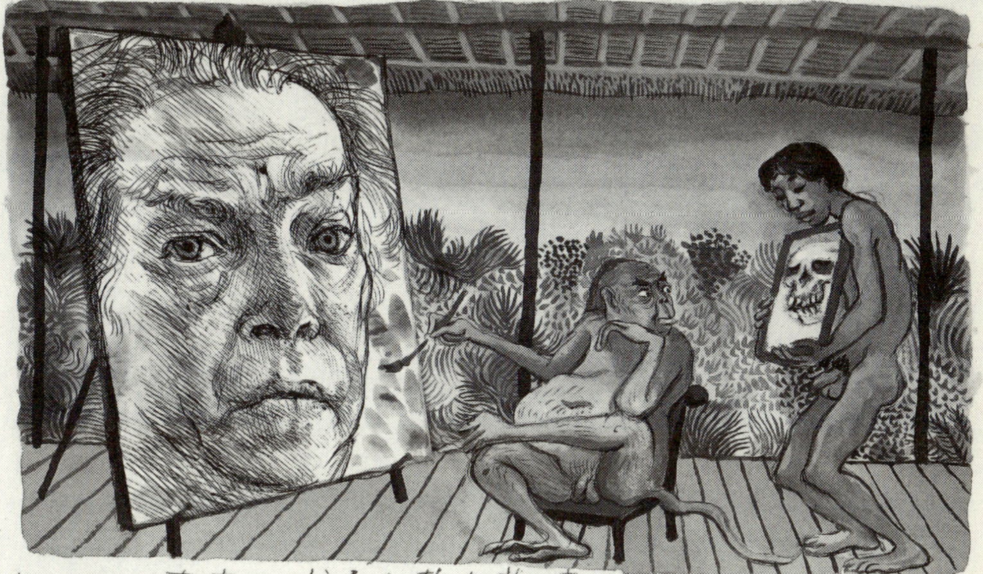

to my contention, which is that the truest and in every way most superior expression of the Narcissistic impulse is exemplified in the art of the self-portrait. A collection of such works will display with unconscious nakedness every shade of self-fascination from bitter disillusion to ardent self-approval – there you may see the infinitely profound warts-and-all depths of Rembrandt; the protestant insanity of Van Gogh, the rough agonies of Michelangelo, of Goya, of Picasso. And of all those others who sought in their mirrored features a reflection of the human predicament. In this context I think of a self-portrait by a very minor Antipodean artist named Fronad Idlien who in a hut in Batu Djimbar depicted himself as a gross ape painting his own cynical likeness from a mirror (held by an able-bodied indigene) which reflects a Death's Head. I'd have liked to have known that man. Probably he'd have liked to have known himself even better. It gives me a curious pleasure to

39. *The artist as self-portraitist* (1975).

as though by accidents of time and nature and divided by spontaneous-looking red and black brush strokes outlining big shapes that are never quite regular, never quite geometrical. Within their boundaries I plan to have very gay surrealist compositions of figures and landscapes which will play variations on the themes of the mural.

Second half of October *Melbourne*. Hawthorn. Attilio and Ailsa are terrifically proud of their house now, and rightly so. By actually reducing its size—demolishing the lean-tos and additions of a former generation—the place has become somehow larger, the rooms spacious and airy, very open into the garden which is just now spring flowers.

There was a total eclipse of the sun. The church bells rang to warn the people. I was in my studio-bedroom in the loft and from there watched the strange change of light—a lurid El Greco light, consume the garden. Then a brief darkness, after which the world about us rapidly emerged from its temporary Hades.

The Cosmic Turtle[17] is not yet officially launched, but the business is reaching a frantic and fervid stage, with advertising directors dashing to telephones, urgent messages, last-minute crises of incredible absurdity. Mouse-like youths scuttled and squeaked about the exhibition room at Myers Emporium[18] hanging the original drawings. I sign copies of the book, of the prints and make radio interviews. News items about the book are beginning to appear in the press. My radio interviews went over well.

Attilio never leaves my side, guards and protects me from upsetting intrusions. Every day since, he has driven me to some spot I've chosen to sketch and I've drawn in the foundations for a series of ink, chalk and pastel townscapes.

First three weeks of November At Myers daily signing books. Making ink and pastel studies of Melbourne and the countryside. What upset me was that several of my paintings are very bad. We'll take a whole lot back to Hawthorn, destroying some and working on others. It's ghastly seeing one's own bad work. Some small comfort can be squeezed out of seeing so much bad work by my peers and equals.

The filthy town air and the vapid and sterile subjects people talk about are a burden. After heatwave, the weather is positively arctic.

24 November Anne and Stuart Purves gave us lunch at Australian Galleries. My twelve pictures hung, looked most handsome. The other guests were Albert Tucker and a younger painter (also critic) Jeffrey Makin[19]. Tucker was amiable, but I think he's a very self-important man: he esteems himself a great founder of the modern movement in Australian painting. It is true that he was alive at the time, and close to such painters as Nolan, and was an artist himself—but his work is all bad. Or perhaps it is not all bad, but none of it is at all to my taste. Like the man, it is opinionated and puritan.

We sitting at the round dining table were somewhat abased beneath a huge and very bad Brett Whiteley picture on to which, wherever some careful painting would have been necessary, the artist had glued colour photographs from magazines. Additional distractions were provided by dead tree branches, a stuffed snake and a stuffed crow protruding very deadly from the picture. It was entertaining to see how hefty hirsute Jeff Makin and the bearded Tucker seemed almost to crouch over their steaks beneath Whiteley's heroin-inspired monstrosity.

The other pictures in the room—it was a small dining room tucked behind the stockroom—were more sympathetic—an Olsen landscape and a very good small Nolan.

27 December *Batujimbar*. Somehow I managed to sidestep all of the ritual and truly fictional goodwill of Christmas. All day and every day I've been painting on the great 'Life on Other Planets' picture[20], which grows more marvellous (in my eyes) as it goes on. That and the discipline of cutting down smoking absorbs all my nervous and mental energy. I go nowhere and see few people. It's a long time since I've been so excited about a painting. The nice thing about it is it will probably take several more months to finish, and take into itself almost any ideas that come to me during that time.

Many of these are restatements of old themes that have been a source of subject time and time again—multitudes of bathers of all colours and sexes in a great pool; somewhat coarse simple jokes such as the 'one-armed trumpet player' which became a visual pun which people are slow to realise; the ape self-portrait; the strange fairies, militant butterflies, zany dancers; the Napoleonic frogs firing off artillery; and innumerable flying machines crowded with passengers; a grotesque dinner party—these and many others, all very spritely and in full movement.

1977

24 January I am painting away every day on the big picture.[1] I have been happy doing this work, feeling it to be important and yet it must be highly priced and is of a size few private houses these days could accommodate. And also the imagery of the subject matter is so outlandish that few of our very rich could stomach it. So in my mind the picture is somewhat unsaleable—which leaves me more free than I would be if money was in the back of my mind.

However, rumours about it are already going about in Australia. A perky little self-made man from Melbourne came and told me he had a half-message from a collector, who is head of the National Gallery board at Canberra, that he was interested in acquiring a major work of mine for the nation. You can imagine how pleased I was. And yet it was better working on something there seemed no chance of selling.

10 February A. is strikingly good-looking, an unusually silent boy and (strange in a Balinese) sad and unsmiling, and like Madja, a good musician. The two of them always play the gamelan for me in the evenings. For each of them it is apparent the music is not merely a pleasant time-filler as for the others, but an outlet for their inner feelings. I am not romanticising: I've long known a good deal about Madja from his trusting confidences to me.

A. would occasionally come long after midnight and sit waiting in the dark on the tiles by my bedside—waiting for me to awake, and then murmuring the problems on his mind. He was one of the really beautiful ones, but thought the darkness of his skin was a curse. About ten years old when he came here, now he is about seventeen. 'I have nothing else. I will work for you until I die.'

'I will probably die first,' I said. 'I want to make sure that when I am no longer here you boys who have been with me for years will not suffer. I will buy you a rice field so that when you marry you will have something to keep your family.'

He sat silent, thinking it over, and then said, 'I would rather use it to build a *pura*—a temple.'

This took me quite aback. A temple!—I did not say 'a temple will not feed you,' but I thought it. As a matter of fact a temple is a source of constant expense for offerings and ceremonies.

'Very well then,' I told him. 'When money comes you shall have your temple. And if there's enough, rice land also. And you will continue to work for me. Your people can work the land, and live off it.'

'I will work for you until I die,' he repeated, looking dark and solemn.

13 February Paul Hamlyn[2] has leased one of our grand houses for his holiday at Batujimbar. He is the multimillionaire English publisher who, as some say, has revolutionised (or, as others say, ruined) Australian publishing, by a series of ruthless takeover moves. He is a very entertaining fellow. Brash and dynamic. He represents just about everything I deplore in commerce. Nevertheless, an amiable character in private. What flatters me is that he, who bandies the names of the great, the famous and the notorious, treats me with deference, as one of them.

Today Hamlyn sent over a note to ask if he could bring David Frost[3] for drinks in the evening at my house. It was a pleasant couple of hours. Frost is a very famous television interviewer who specialises in asking probing questions of famous people. He is good at it, for he is extremely intelligent. He uses sympathy and charm to great effect until the victim is disarmed. Then he moves in to lay all bare with a scalpel. However, this evening he had no such vivisecting in mind. Frost brought out all our best talk. He has the art of making people spark in an agreeable way.

18 February It has become an abiding pleasure to watch Madja develop, to provide, from time to time, the means: or give a nudge, a hint; then watch him take it up and use it. He is growing tall and is now very confident in himself, seeing what confidence I place in him. It is a couple of weeks since I told him that from then on he was to be the manager of the household, which he has taken on with great tact and efficiency. He is discreet; and can be entrusted with confidential money matters.

It makes me feel good, getting those who have looked after me for seven years or more settled one by one. And all done in such a way they get the gift I give—with no governments or other sharks biting lumps out of it.

Of them all it's Madja who is the jewel, closest to me, cleverest, who foresees my needs and attends to them; who in the evening sits to tell me all the news, and his dreams and explains the complications of village customs, and gives shrewd assessments of characters and personalities, and advises how I should act in certain circumstances.

12 March Now we have the famous couturier Hardy Amies[4] staying at Tandjung Sari with Michael White, a charming young Australian known by the Balinese (whose language he speaks well) as Madé Wijaya[5]. He lives on his wits, charm and good looks, and is always to be found where the more interesting people foregather at Kuta, Tjampuhan or Sanur. Amies, 'The Queen's dressmaker', 'adores' Michael. He is a polite, rather prissy old bore of about my age—very much the Englishman of polite society.

After days of idleness I'm beginning to work again both on drawings and writing. It is a relief that my hand has not lost its cunning—at least it does not tremble when holding a pen. I am never a moment now unconscious of my health. Which is to say ill-health, for I was never aware of my health at all most of my life.

19 August There was this afternoon quite a severe earthquake which alarmed us all—the worst I've yet experienced. It continued for some minutes. It is curious how unsettled one feels for some hours after the earth has ceased shuddering. I returned to my siesta but found it hard either to sleep or to read. In fact to do anything other than fidget away the afternoon. There was also, within the lagoon, a strange disturbance of the water, and two great waves—one racing down from the north, the other coming in over the reef—met and wrecked a couple of canoes. Our stout sea wall prevented it from flooding the garden.

Mid-September James Fairfax arrived and is installed in the big pavilion. We went over to Warwick Purser's for drinks and dinner—there was a terrific babble of people there who seemed to be from magazines or travel agencies. Leslie Walford was bubbling over with his nonsense. Listening to Leslie, one receives most absurd impressions about life in Australia, because he confines himself to the doings of a small, rich and fashionable circle whose largely frivolous doings absorb him completely—so the state of the nation appears to depend largely on what Mary F.[6] will wear to the Black and White Ball[7]—all of which nonsense makes better entertainment than the pessimistic grumbling most visitors indulge in about the depressed Australian economy.

Today Warwick bade us to lunch, which was delicious—one of his guests had brought from Sydney fresh asparagus and strawberries—but again more and more people seemed to congregate until I felt dizzy and confused and not at all comfortable.

This claustrophobia is a damned nuisance. What is so odd is that not so many years ago I enjoyed crowded parties and rowdy gatherings: now I break out in a sweat. And it is doubtful whether people believe me. Anyway it doesn't suit them to take notice of it—and why the hell should they since to do so would spoil their own pleasure in entertaining great mobs of friends?

Anxieties made work impossible although I need to try. Once or twice the young artist from Bedulu arrived unannounced. And I made him take off all his clothes while I painted him—although I only did head studies. This seemed to excite him tremendously, and when the sketch was done he'd stand there nude, laughing and make a comic gesture of apology for his body's arousal. Of course I loved that. And without another word we'd make love. He has dispensed now with the bashful delays and coy ploys that used to exasperate me. They were pardonable—one could hardly expect amorous enthusiasm between a youth of 19 for a man of 62, pot-bellied and in poor physical condition. But Balinese attitudes to sex are conditioned by their own values and beliefs.

20 September Anak Agung Raka's[8] wedding day. I didn't go to this morning's ceremonies in Denpasar—I saved myself for the afternoon's procession and the arrival of the bride on a golden palanquin. It was a splendid and beautiful sight, a thousand or more retainers headed by fifty or so with golden lances and banners. In the centre was carried on shoulder poles by many white-clad bearers the great gilded palanquin with a pointed canopy and curtains which is called the *djoli*. They streamed along at a brisk pace, marvellously medieval against a background of rich green rice terraces.

11–14 October We've seen something of my nephew David[9] and his wife Jenny. When David was in England he looked up some cousins in the Cotswolds—the Rudders. Brian Rudder had been making research into the family tree—with one or two rather comical results, as far as the Moses family (my father's—who changed his name) is concerned. We find our first Australian pioneer ancestor was a convict named Uriah Moses[10], transported for life in 1800 for stealing six silk handkerchiefs in London. After serving his sentence he set up a flour mill in Windsor (New South Wales) and married a Miss Annie Primrose who bore him eight children. He died three days after converting to Christianity.

18 October Village talk—the Earth has become too hot. Small earth tremors are fairly frequent. They think there's a big one coming up. With all of this, the island seems still the loveliest place to live. Drought, devils, earthquakes and even a government by stupid Muslims weigh little against the Balinese of a simple sort. My gardeners murmuring and laughing at their work, the loveliness of this garden, the house, the sparkling sea—the whole lot of it. I ought not be old, sick and worried, but happy to be able to look for a while longer at everything I'm bound to lose anyway.

First week of November I plunged into painting with tremendous relief—this long, long time—it must be a month or two months. The first and welcome incursion of this return to work was Lynne's arrival. Lynne née Drysdale, now Clarke.[11] Such old friends belong to a quite different civilisation: it is delightful talking to someone who knows all the terms of reference—she brought one a great parcel of books, all good books I'd never read before. She shares so much of my mind, and friendships and tastes. It is encouraging that there are a number of inhabitants of that world still. Sometimes one goes for months without meeting with them; then one begins to feel isolated. Now I feel I'm suddenly back from the barbaric outlands.

A phone call came from Melbourne. The most incredibly wonderful good news. It was Attilio, ringing to say he had sold the big picture, my masterpiece, to the Commonwealth.[12] The price will be enough to solve my worries for the time being. The news came just when I especially needed more money for Madja's house. It has been a day of good omens; the first durians of the season and, late at night the drought broke with a plenteous downpour of rain.

Last week of November A prehistoric bronze drum, dug from the earth in a coffee plantation in the hills. The farmer wanted a lot of money. The bronze is weird—the tympanum is lost, and about a third of the mantle shattered—but what remains is a tremendous noble ruin. Unwrapped from the mats that protected its transportation by truck over rough mountain roads it stood like a portent on the lawn—an almost menacing presence.

I worked for two days with the boys getting superficial dirt off. On the third day enough of the delicate decorative relief was visible to leave it alone for a while. It is very fragile—the metal is crystallised right through. The patina is spectacular—patches of an almost lapis lazuli blue and turquoise through to olive and almost black.

1978

4 February Attilio and I were bid to a Japanese meal at Warwick and Lisa's tonight. It was a candlelight occasion. I don't much like Japanese food. It's the sort of stuff one has to get down and then make compliments. How I should enjoy sitting down to: three lamb chops (grilled) with mashed potatoes and spinach, or some whiting in breadcrumbs fried in butter, or grilled kidneys and bacon. I should also relish some tender underdone roast beef with utterly conventional roast vegetables including pumpkin and sweet potato. Some of these should taste best on a terrace with a view of rocky coast and ocean. Others, at a marble table in a flower garden. If the weather were bad, in a room with a fire and a big window lashed by rain, where one could see the trees bowing to a bitter wind. Then there'd be a bouillon with sherry to start off, followed by a tender duckling. Green peas. And these meals ought be eaten in a very small company—four people at most. The last is probably the most difficult of all to be sure of.

I'm not homesick. But my health is really deteriorating fast. I think I've not much time left, much work unfinished. It is curious, in this valedictory mood, to think of one's deepest, most necessary friends. Very few, Attilio of course always comes first. Then James, whom I see so rarely. Then I'd count Bevis Bawa but he is so far away. The others who once meant so much are so seldom in my mind and have so small part of my life nowadays that they'd be in a category labelled Retired.

6 February I'm 63. Warwick, Lisa and Attilio arranged a surprise party at the house—a decently small party of people I know and like. It was arranged with great elegance. The rain held off, the whole garden candlelit and the servants superbly dressed—the *genggong*[1] orchestra sat on the verge of the temple pool, and the charming dancers wove the gestures in and out of shadow on the tiny pool island. It was sheer enchantment.

Later, at dinner by the sea wall, the sound of the tide surging half-covered the *tinklet*[2] gamelan music made by my own boys, invisible in the deep shadow of a grove.

Second week of February *Melbourne*. A sky of drizzle. An inexorable dribble of small talk consisting largely of the price of anything mentioned, what it could be bought for five years ago and what it would fetch in another ten. Australian suburban materialism. I was very glad to be here, very weak and iller with exasperation. And these pained reactions, though they have some excuse in the world about me are more truly symptoms of sick mind and body. I make an effort to cut a way through them to realisation of the kindliness offered me.[3]

13 February St Vincent's Private Hospital.[4] The little suite is $200 per day—eight floors up—looking widely over the city shrouded in rain. I brought a parcel of books to wile away the time—a marvellous translation and essays of Li Po and Tu Fu by Arthur Cooper.[5] The poems are extraordinarily moving and they're very 'pictorial'—the imaginative scrolls of landscape unwind among thunderous torrents and pine-clad crags evoke great distances.

The hospital does not deviate from the usual pattern—trolleys rattling along the corridor outside, scampering feet, cheerful little nurses dashing in at 10-minute intervals with meals, thermometers, pills. A television set flickers and miaows on the wall.

19 February Out of hospital—Ah! The garden all sunlit, the marvellous scent of flowers. It is Sunday. We went out and wandered about looking in the window of antique shops. By such means, with an affectionate cunning which I appreciate, Attilio induces me to take some gentle exercise, knowing so well I can never be persuaded to do any if it is not to some purpose—not, that is, the brisk walk to nowhere, the healthful chasing after a ball, etc.

26 February I'm feeling a bit better. We go out in the car and I make sketches. See very few people—I went to a little cocktail party given by John Mockridge[6], an architect friend of Jeff Smart's. A comically Melbourne society occasion—well-dressed dowagers of both sexes. Sundry ageing young gentlemen I seem to remember from years ago when they tossed their golden curls about, the pampered catamites of the snowy-haired old gentlemen who were still (as though all those years had gone in a flash without interrupting the rhythm of their days) rounding their phrases in fluted accents in this charming room opening into a courtyard garden, all bamboos and hanging baskets of petunias; a joy to see.

3 March *Port Fairy.*[7] The two of us drove down—I made sketches on the way. A lovely little place that used to be in the 1890s a whaling station. Many old bluestone cottages, great dark pine trees: a tiny inlet full of fishing boats. The people there were very friendly. There were several good old pubs full of remarkably amiable gnarled ancient characters. I made very rapid sketches to be completed later. It was too cold to draw much on the spot.

24 May *Batujimbar*. There have been heaving rains for two days, and the moon waxing full, very high tides. A slight wind behind the tide brought it singing powerfully into the lagoon, and the waves breaking against the sea walls tumbled them all down. Except for mine, which has held out, though I doubt it can stand another day of battering. Its resistance lies in the planting inside the double wall and the planting on the beach outside it. The network of roots holds all together.

The sea roars angrily on the reef. It swirls and heaves within the lagoon, yellow with the soil it sucks from our land: plants and wreckage float as far as one can see. Smashing against my sea wall it has torn away many of the tough spring plants which have been its protection. I called all my boys as soon as the tide went out to make running repairs and a defence against tonight's tide. We commandeered a lot of bamboo stakes and pig-baskets which were filled with coral rocks and staked into the beach to break the force of the waves of next tide. And to us there on the beach came an ancient priestess of the little temple in our land with a gift of fruit, inviting me to tonight's ceremony. I gave her a sarong.

5 June I've been reading Christopher Sykes' biography of Evelyn Waugh.[8] Chastening experience, for one thinks with gratitude of how much joy his books, re-read so often, still purvey. And then, what a horrid man he turns out to be. Well—one had always known rumours of his brutal rudeness and intolerance, so it wasn't really that which shocked one in Sykes' book.

The horror came from recognising a close and repulsive similarity to the nastier parts of my own character as I have aged. Waugh after 50, with his increasingly absurd conservatism, his chancy temper, vanity, desire to sting rather than delight with his wit. His contrariness and stubbornness. His excessive drinking (well, at least *I* don't drink all that much) and the self-hate that came with recognition of how unlovable he'd become—and how lonely. And then, by 60, his great talent had failed. Inspiration fled. He became prey to hallucinations and a sense of persecution, and at the same time avoided all exercise, kept much to the house, avoided all casual society: became weak and obese. Undoubtedly that all applies to me.

9 June I called in at La Taverna[9] last night and found a whole crowd of newly arrived Australian artists at the bar. Brett Whiteley hasn't changed in appearance at all, although from gossip I expected to see some haggard expiring addict type. He still wears his hair in great frizzy 'orphan Annie' halo but his face now is ruddy and rather coarse. He talked a lot of asinine pseudo-intellectual rubbish as usual. I imagine both his manner of delivering forcefully short zany ecstatic speeches whilst snapping his fingers like castanets and the appearance of that frizzy bee-kip of hair must appeal to the Balinese taste for grotesquery.

Last week of June *Melbourne*. The flight down was damnably cramped and uncomfortable, and there'd been hours of airport delays. However on arrival in Melbourne the Customs, of which we'd been nervous, allowed through without comment all the old jewellery and bronzes we'd smuggled.

I'm very happy to be down here—even the cold is part of cheerfulness. From inside Attilio's well-warmed house one looks out into the

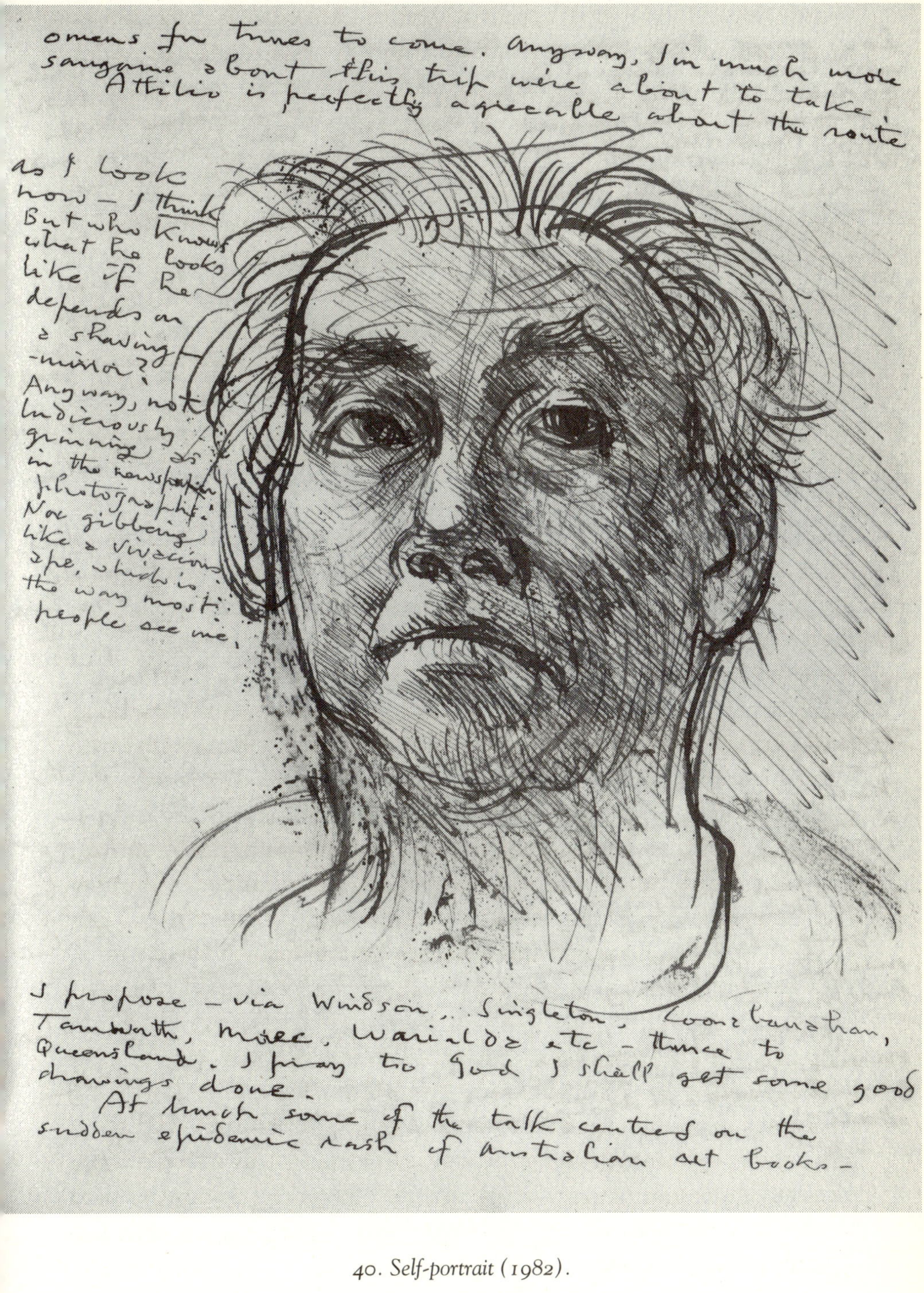

40. *Self-portrait (1982).*

wintry garden—bare silvery trees with patterns of black twigs against the sky—the evergreen leaves doubly richly green: lemons like golden lamps—whirling stars of magnolias. Azaleas. This is the first time it seems in many years I've seen snowdrops, violets and primulas blooming in a garden.

5 July The Realities opening[10] was very well done—the whole exhibition looked most impressive. And Melbourne's social cream, poured into wonderfully tailored suits or gowns and sable coats (it was cold) stalked about impressively looking marvellously like skilfully stuffed sleek animals—seals, penguins, horses. The catering was excellent: delicious satés served by Warwick Purser's Balinese servants who looked very pretty, poor wretches, in their sarongs and brocades. Nearly dying of cold. Smiling and gracefully serving with their usual courtesy they passed shivering among the mink-clad dowagers and the rosy-faced managing directors, society gossip journalists and press photographers.

16 July *Mount Eliza.*[11] To spend the day with Attilio's Greeks. The term is deceptive, for many of the Greeks are not Greek at all, except in some kind of honorary capacity. French, Turkish, Italians. Café owners, publicans, restaurateurs, proprietors of delicatessen shops, sandwich bars. Periodically, tremendous disasters strike this little community who suffer communally because they are inextricably and complicatedly tied together by business partnerships and family relationships. The disasters are all very similar—monstrously so. They are tragedies of money, which are given the full Euripidean[12] treatment—haggard faces, dread of the doorbell: the dread drumbeat footsteps of Nemesis approaching. The Chorus chants its measured strophes of doom. And the audience rocks with laughter, being excusably under the impression that they're watching a comedy.

27 September *Melboume.* Cold, wet and Londonish. Everything for me is running on an even keel, except for occasional rows with Attilio about unnecessary deviousness when dealing on my behalf in the art world, foolish complicated manoeuvres to squeeze a few extra dollars. It's hard to nip this in the bud—he gets furious and shouts and bangs the table and roars he's being insulted.

Yet there is no one else in the world so devoted to me, so partisan in my interest. And this little room above the stable in the back garden where I work and sleep is built entirely of his affection. Every board and brick lovingly worked and put in place with my selfish contentment in mind.

3 October Two days of blustering wind have stripped the peach tree of most its rather vulgar glory, which now lies, drifts of raspberry pink, on the path. But clouds of forget-me-nots float among the green. And iris, clumps of white daisies and blue and purple cinerarias. The cherry tree holds its breath, preparing to burst out fountains of snowy pink.

The wind has dropped. The sky mildly overcast. In Melbourne people talk first of the weather, then of football; and next, money.

November *Batujimbar*. Ah, it's lovely to be back lapped in great tides of warm spicy humid air, a tinge of wood smoke flavoured with incense and mangoes and the smell of wet leaves. The clouds grumbling above with their burden of the coming rainy season.

I've sunk back completely into a life in which work seems the only reality. I work hard, all day, every day, writing and doing illustrations for the 'Codex Bumbooziaticus'.[13] I'm astonished at how good they are—or appear to *me* to be in the absence of anyone who would understand and confirm it. I'm uneasily aware I should be at work on other things: paintings for exhibitions. But I'm damned if I'll potboil.

Sixty-three is no great age. It's disconcerting how freshly, with what wit and invention I think, and how my mind leaps joyously on ideas—while my limbs are weak and heavy with weariness; the least exertion exhausts my whole frame. It's ready for the knacker's yard.

1979

First week of January Days of deep depression and a mind empty of ideas for painting. I avoid seeing people but a few callers, pleasant enough, came. Mick Jagger and various, mostly boring merchants and their wives. The mainstay of my life is Madja—simply his devotion to me in what I'd find a boring job, and a kind of innocent faith and wish to see me well.

First three weeks of February Paul and Helen Hamlyn[1] gave me a birthday supper. Helen—a large overflowing blonde Rubens beauty (one sees her at home with a cornucopia and tribes of plump cherubs, spilling chalices, bunches of grapes and attendant muses) is sweet, affectionate and full of minor importances: well-read, fond of possessions; quite sensible and competent about getting people to do things for her.

Richard Griffin[2] arrived quite unexpectedly—a marvellous guest, which means he entertains himself all day and in the evening we go out or see people for drinks here. Richard had lots of good news—of enthusiasm for my books in England and America. Dick Woolcott called in. He brought the *Playboy* magazine with a long extract and number of colour reproductions from *Bumbooziana*.[3] Good publicity. But O God what an awful vulgar ugly publication it is.

Last week of February *Melbourne*. The usual warm welcome, and the strangeness always of the city's sprawl of suburbs after Bali's remnants of Arcadia. The bookshelves, and above them the glass shelves for bronze and porcelain, are all that can be desired. Attilio and I spent some time arranging them, and hanging on the walls some rare cloths.

Third week of March Attilio and I drove into New South Wales, taking with us the bulk of framed pictures for an exhibition at the Von Bertouch Gallery[4] in Newcastle. It was not in any way an exciting or eventful drive up—Attilio in his dullest utilitarian mood. We drove and drove and stopped only for meals. My hopes had been to get some sketches done. God knows where money is to come from if I don't produce pictures. For Attilio the great purpose of the trip was something he'd put off for years for fear of a disaster—to see his four children in Canberra. We went to a motel in that strange bourgeois city, and that night three of his children came to meet him at the hotel. Attilio seemed pleased but not ecstatic about these reunions—not so bowled over as to entertain the idea of putting up with the dullness of another night in Canberra. So we drove home.

28 March *Melbourne*. Richard Griffin's publishers launching party last night at his new premises—a charming small old house. Lots of people. The guest of honour was old Noel Counihan[5], the painter—Richard is bringing out a book on his (very sincere and tedious) art. A speech was made by that man of many words (as a fellow guest muttered) Prof. Bernard Smith[6]. It was ludicrous to hear him recall the bitter art feuds of the '30s and '40s between Counihan (a Communist) and George Bell[7] and other long-dead painters, the dusty quarrels of those old factions. Most of the people were not older than 40, and looked politely blank. Counihan himself is a mild gentle creature. It is not easy to guess at a connection between him and these old 'Peace or War' social realists' linocuts with their unimaginative symbolism.

16 April *Mt Macedon.*[8] Attilio and I were invited to lunch at the Pursers' weekend house. An old ruinous place they're restoring, weatherboard, with many rooms—dark, quaint and ugly, standing in extensive steep hillside grounds with huge fine old trees, and many tree-ferns, rhododendrons, beeches, oaks and so on. It is a very fashionable sort of stockbroker's rural dream district. A cottage separate from the tottering rambling main house is as yet the only habitable part of the place. It contains the best room of all—the former billiard room. It was a pleasant way to waste a day. The trees blazing with the sudden onslaught of autumn lit the countryside with crimson and gold.

18–19 June *Melbourne*. I'm sort of half-emigrating. I have no more faith in Bali—or rather in *my* ability to stay on and survive there. All this is blameable on myself I realise: the awful dead end my inspiration has arrived at. It is as though living had become a matter of endurance, hoping to be able to put up with it until something either puts an end to it *or* permits me to enter the creative aspects of life.

5 July Since being here the most noteworthy day-to-day events (apart from a series of strikes—railways, all public transport, petrol, telecommunications and dockside workers) have been the extremes of mood that fling Richard Griffin from euphoria to deepest depression. Richard is at his happiest talking about books and writers—as tonight (he came for dinner, and later he and I talked for an hour or so—his delight in finding literary finds in common with me—old books we'd half-forgotten, writers we'd known seldom spoken of now—Arthur Waley[9], Rayner Heppenstall[10] and so on. 'Ten dreary years in this country, as in a desert—and you're the only person I've met who'—etc.).

23 July *Batujimbar*. All's well here. I sink quickly back into oriental lethargy, while Krakatoa[11] threatens to erupt. It often strikes me that my life is a barren empty business compared to that of others. It may be because I expect so much more than I get out of simple events *because* there is no one now whom I have the strength (of character) to *force* to share the potentials of every day—so instead of living brilliantly I am defeated. Obliged to sit glumly through utterly boring vulgar conversations—stupid talk of money and sport and the weather. I have become (my own fault) very cut off from my peers and equals.

Bali is no longer the answer to my needs. It ceases to inspire me, although my fondness for Madja (now very domestic with his wife) remains, and there is the mild pleasure of looking at the handsome natives—this great house full of treasures is a *bore*. The affection and respect I'm held in, while momentarily flattering, leaves me feeling simply unworthy. Because the good people have no inkling of what they are paying homage to.

13 September *Melbourne*. The great historic day—Attilio called several people for lunch with Richard Griffin. Here at the house in Hawthorn. The occasion was to celebrate the arrival, in all its glory, of the first complete bound copy of *Bumbooziana*—the sample copy which Richard will take to Antwerp Book Fair[12] later this month. So Richard very proud lugged in the large and quite superbly bound and printed volume. Nothing of such quality and beauty *has ever before* been published in Australia. With Richard came John Olsen whom I was particularly happy to see and Leonard French[13] who was very entertaining but took up too much of the talk.

Lord Louis Mountbatten[14], whom I believed to be the only great aristocrat who was an equally great man, was murdered in Ireland. I wept. And then wondered if the tears were for Mountbatten or was age and ailment turning me lachrymose?

October I think rather sadly about Bali. I don't see myself *living* there again. And I hate to imagine living *here*, becoming a little more suburban every morning. Melbourne people are desperately ordinary. One politely suffers the most profoundly boring people—rather than suffer nobody at all. Bloody middle-class Melbourne. They have psychic hooks and grapnels to drag one down to their beloved murky level of horrible ordinariness.

7 November I read with some dismay in the newspaper—it seemed unpleasantly apropos—of Al Capp's[15] death at the age of 70 in America. For years, since the 1930s, I enjoyed his comic strips and their richly amusing characters such as L'il Abner etc. He died of emphysema, and the last years of his life he got about in a wheelchair. Well, it's a thought for this day—.

16 December Tas Drysdale spent the whole afternoon with Attilio, Ailsa and me, just yarning and talking and passing the time. It was the first time we'd seen one another in several years—we who were once almost inseparable friends and companions. And really it was delightful simply to talk and joke in that old way as we used to do. And laugh at ourselves and the world, and at the way we've become old and fat and very celebrated and nowadays much inclined to criticise the evil times and decay of manners. And to reassess old associations and remember former friends, and marvel at the ignorance of the new generation, the absurdity of bankrupt talents that nowadays command such fame and praise. We enjoyed ourselves enormously.

Last week of December Our Christmas here was cool and sunny. Ailsa cooked a magnificent goose. Attilio brought up his rarest wines from 1964 from the cellar, and Richard was our guest bringing fine gifts for all of us.

Christmas over, with the world no better for it. The Americans have been disappointed of their hopes of the Ayatollah's fanatics releasing the imprisoned Embassy staff in Tehran[16] and the whole civilised world, and the United Nations solemnly condemns his behaviour as illegal. He is not concerned with legality. An evil man, I suppose—pitting his power against powers of exploitation, avarice (our virtues?).

Bali worries continually at a corner of my mind—not with the alluring voice of a seducer but with some things more like the nagging of a cast-off mistress.

Warwick Purser telephoned from Glenrock—Peter Muller's homestead at Marulan—could I persuade Attilio to drive me up, to stay? It's a long drive. I have a great yearning to be for a few days with people who belong to my own sort of life—or at least, my sort of language—ideas.

The peacocks stalk solemnly and vainly, appearing suddenly perched on unlikely places—an apricot tree, in the head of a 12th-century Hindu stone god in the garden, on a tractor or some such utilitarian agricultural machine. They mewl and wail—a sad and desperate sound. It is wonderfully hot, the whole countryside burnt yellow with drought. I feel very ill, but enjoy immensely the company of these old friends I don't think I'll ever see again in a group. The house was *full* of guests. Good talk, casual country-house atmosphere.

NOTES: 1970s

1970

1. In Victoria Street, Darlinghurst (from 1870). Friend had recently been diagnosed as suffering from incipient prostate trouble, high blood pressure and tuberculosis.
2. In the style of Netherlandish painter Peter Paul Rubens (1577–1640).
3. James Cook (1728–79), English seaman and explorer who mapped the east coast of Australia in 1770, proclaiming it a British possession and naming it New South Wales.
4. A school of Buddhism stressing the importance of meditation in the attainment of enlightenment.
5. Indian-born English naturalist, zookeeper and author (1925–95), and his first wife, English-born Jacquie Durrell, née Wolfenden (born 1929), singer, conservationist and author (professional name Rasen).
6. Australian company director and arts patron (born 1932), son of Sir Charles and Lady Lloyd Jones (see **1964**, note 13).
7. Milo, seventh Baron (1912–73), owner of two properties called Malahide, one in his native Ireland, the other in Tasmania. He was a frequent visitor to Australia between 1952 and his death.
8. Charles Lloyd Jones's Sydney home in Ocean Street, Woollahra.
9. A musical instrument made out of bamboo tubes attached to a bamboo frame.
10. Ancient temple at Semawang (see **1969**, note 9).
11. His second of four wives, Rosalind Humphries, née Tong (born 1937), New Zealand dancer and actress, who settled in Australia and has become a gallery owner, curator and art historian (current surname Hollinrake). Cf **1966**, note 4.
12. Mask dancers from the Sukawati region, 17 kilometres north of Sanur.
13. French art dealer and gallery director (1898–1978).
14. The Bali National Museum in Puputan Square, Denpasar, opened in 1932.
15. Beratan Lake, 60 kilometres north of Sanur.
16. Hungarian-born couple, Albert (1912–2008), businessman and farmer, who emigrated to Australia in 1938, and Gisella (born 1921), who came as a refugee to Australia in 1948 and founded the Holdsworth Gallery in Woollahra in 1969.
17. English rock band of the 1960s.

1971

1. Soraya Esfandiary-Bakhtiari (1932–2001), second wife of Mohammad Reza Pahlavi, last Shah of Iran (divorced 1958).
2. Franco Indovina (1932–72), film director.
3. Writer of Iraqi-Jewish origin, born in China in 1920.
4. Jane Oehr and Ian Stocks, Australian film-makers who completed a documentary about Donald Friend and Bali in 1972 entitled *Tamu–the Guest*. Cf diary entry for last week of October 1972.
5. Village in southeastern France, between Nice and Cannes.
6. See **1950**, note 5.
7. The Musée Picasso at the Château Grimaldi in Antibes, established in 1946.
8. The Fondation Maeght is a modern-art museum located near the village of Saint Paul-de-Vence, in the south of France. It was established in 1964.
9. Restaurant in the Latin Quarter of Paris, with a view overlooking the river Seine and Notre Dame Cathedral.
10. Capital of the Finistère department, Brittany.
11. Sculptured representations of Christ's crucifixion, a feature of the churches of Brittany, most notably that of Saint-Germain in Pleyben, 35 kilometres from Quimper.
12. Fashionable department store in Knightsbridge, the present site of which was opened in 1905.
13. A bridge crossing the river Seine and linking the Île Saint-Louis to the quai de l'Hôtel de Ville. The AGNSW had awarded Olley a three-month residency at the Moya Dyring Studio, Cité Internationale des Arts, on the rue de l'Hôtel de Ville.
14. Geoffrey Bawa's house at Bentota, designed by him.

1972

1. Actress, born Bianca Pérez Morena de Macías, in Nicaragua, 1945. Her marriage to Mick Jagger lasted from 1971 to 1978. (Their daughter, Jade, was born in 1971.) She has subsequently become a prominent human-rights activist.
2. Town on the French Riviera, just east of Nice.
3. In the ornate decorative style characteristic of the age of Louis XVI of France (1754–93), who ruled as monarch from 1774 to 1792.
4. To the north of Sanur, 40 to 50 kilometres.
5. One of the gardeners employed at Friend's house in Batujimbar, subsequently promoted to housekeeper.
6. See **1970**, note 16.

7. See **1971**, note 4.
8. The National Gallery of Victoria in St Kilda Road, designed by Sir Roy Grounds (see **1969**, note 10).
9. As erected for a sacrificial god of that name by King Solomon, according to the Old Testament (1 Kings, 11:7).
10. Australian, born 1946, who became Director of Australian Galleries, Melbourne, in 1969 following the death of his father, Thomas (Tam). Cf **1972**, note 12.
11. Australian-born barrister (1922–2005) of Irish roots, who married Bernadette O'Brien in Melbourne in 1948.
12. Anne Purves (1913–99), co-founder of Australian Galleries with her husband, Tam.
13. Stan Laurel (1890–1965), English-born comic actor, partnered Oliver Hardy (1892–1957), American comic actor, in more than a hundred Hollywood films.
14. An association made by Sigmund Freud (1856–1939), first in a letter of 1897, and developed in his psychoanalytic writings.
15. William (Billy) McMahon (1908–88), Prime Minister of Australia, 1971–72.
16. The Australian Labor Party, under the leadership of Gough Whitlam, was in federal office for the first time since 1949. (Cf **1974**, note 6.)
17. In Ocean Street, Woollahra.
18. In Potts Point.
19. Eponymous Italian hero of Joseph Conrad's novel of 1904.

1973

1. English diplomat, politician, author and diarist (1886–1968).
2. English novelist, critic and diarist (1882–1941).
3. English biographer and essayist (1880–1932).
4. Dora Carrington (1893–1932), English painter and decorative artist.
5. Henry Channon (1897–1958), American-born English Conservative politician, author and diarist.
6. For instance, Carrington had had a youthful affair with Mark Gertler, later Friend's art teacher (see **1937**, note 7), and she had also painted Gertler's portrait. Lytton Strachey and Virginia Woolf were close friends of Duncan Grant, with whom Friend had been acquainted in London (see **1937**, note 28).
7. Richard Nixon (1913–94), President of the USA, 1968–74, and leader of the Republican Party, was shown to have been directly involved in a cover-up of an attempted break-in at the Democratic Party's National Committee headquarters in the Watergate office complex in Washington, D.C. He avoided impeachment by resigning from office.

8. Fashionable hotel in Chennai (formerly Madras).
9. Built originally as a private house by George Moubray, English-born accountant, in the 1780s. The Madras Club moved into it in 1963.
10. Cf diary entry for 20 February 1940 and **1940**, note 1.
11. Gay pornographic magazine produced in Sydney, 1973–74.
12. Friend appears to be conflating here the character of the Duchess in Lewis Carroll's novel *Alice's Adventures in Wonderland* (1865) and the Red Queen in the sequel, *Through the Looking-Glass* (1872).
13. Archaism for catamites or intimate friends.
14. Fijian-born Australian politician, cultural leader and civil-rights champion (1926–99), Premier of South Australia, 1967–68 and 1970–79.
15. Australian painter (born 1949).
16. Island off the southeast coast of Bali.

1974

1. Characteristic of 'primitive' (in a positive sense) painting before the time of Raphael and the High Renaissance, or of its supposed revival by the group of English painters in the mid-nineteenth century who called themselves the Pre-Raphaelite Brotherhood.
2. See **1962**, note 6. Barbara Tucker (neé Bilcock) was Tucker's second wife, whom he married in 1964.
3. See **1962**, note 5. Judith Pugh (neé Ley), born 1945, was Pugh's third wife, whom he married in 1974. She became a gallery director, art historian and author.
4. The former private home of Walter Spies (see **1968**, note 14) on the banks of the river Tjampuhan, near the centre of Ubud.
5. Towns 30 kilometres north of Sanur.
6. Gough Whitlam (born 1916), Prime Minister of Australia, 1972–75.
7. Founder of the Mongol Empire (c. 1162–1227).
8. American essayist, screenwriter and political pundit, as well as novelist, born 1925, and resident at this time in Italy.
9. The ruling dynasty of China, 960–1279.

1975

1. A bridge over the Yarra River in central Melbourne, connecting the thoroughfares of St Kilda Road and Swanston Street.
2. Multicultural community festival, held annually in Melbourne since 1955.
3. Australia's largest lake, 400 kilometres north of Adelaide.
4. Australian painter (1927–93).
5. Friend was staying at James Fairfax's house in Darling Point.

6. See **1954**, note 14.
7. Henry Fuseli (1741–1825), Swiss-born painter whose career was based largely in England.
8. Historical novel (1973) centering on Aaron Burr, third Vice President of the USA, 1801–05.
9. *Augustus John: A Biography*, by Michael Holroyd (1974). Cf diary entry for January–August 1937 and **1937**, note 16.
10. Ieoh Ming Pei (born 1917).
11. Japanese international socialite, born Naoko Nemoto in 1940.
12. A satire on English expeditionary literature of the Victorian and Edwardian periods, *Bumbooziana* was published in 1979. A selection of the working drawings for this book was published in 1978 under the title *Tides of Sensuality*.
13. Richard Woolcott, Australian diplomat and author (born 1927); ambassador to Indonesia, 1975–78.
14. Richard Buckminster Fuller (1895–1983), American architect, designer and author.
15. A spherical shell structure based on a network of circles (geodesics) lying on the surface of a sphere, and used for a variety of buildings. Strictly speaking, its inventor was not Fuller but the German engineer Walther Bauersfeld, in the 1920s. Fuller, in the 1940s and 1950s, developed, popularised and named it.
16. Luxury hotel in Sanur, built in the 1970s and designed in purportedly traditional Balinese style.
17. Sir John Kerr (1914–91), former barrister and judge, who served as Governor-General, 1974–77.
18. Malcolm Fraser (born 1930), Liberal Party leader and Prime Minister of Australia, 1975–83.
19. An allusion to NSW Labor Premier Jack Lang's dismissal from office by the Governor in May 1932; cf **1931**, note 4.
20. Originally a resistance movement that fought for the independence of East Timor from Portuguese and subsequently Indonesian control between 1974 and 1998. The name is an acronym for (in Portuguese) *Frente Revolucionária de Timor-Leste Independente* (Revolutionary Front for an Independent East Timor).

1976

1. At Jalan Danau Tamblingan, Sanur.
2. Handmade, deckle-edged drawing paper from Italy.
3. Jewellery designer (born Italy, 1940), whose career has been based largely in America.

4. Tiffany & Co, leading American jewellery, silverware and design company, established in New York in 1837.
5. American painter, printmaker and film-maker (1928–1987), who became a pioneering figure in the pop art movement.
6. Deborah Friend (born 1954), daughter of Ten and Pam.
7. Media tycoon, born in Australia in 1931, who became an American citizen. He was married at this time to Anna Törv.
8. At the Holdsworth Galleries, Sydney, 12–31 July 1976.
9. Coastal resort town in northwest Ischia, at the foot of Monte Epomeo.
10. Posticcia Nuova, in Pieve a Presciano, 20 kilometres from Arezzo.
11. Hand-woven tapestry-style carpets produced in various parts of the Middle East and Eastern Europe. (More usually spelt 'kilim'.)
12. About 130 kilometres northeast of Pieve a Presciano.
13. The supposed birthplace of della Francesca (cf **1949**, note 14), 40 kilometres northeast of Pieve a Presciano.
14. Most famously, *The Resurrection* (c. 1463–65), in the Pinacoteca Comunale di Sansepolcro.
15. *The Flagellation of Christ* (c. 1455–60) by della Francesca, in the Galleria Nazionale delle Marche in the Palazzo Ducale, Urbino, built by Federico Montefeltro (1422–82), lord of Urbino from 1444.
16. The Murdoch University commission was not confirmed but Friend continued work on the painting; see entries for 27 December 1976 and 24 January 1977, and **1977**, note 1.
17. Subtitled *Batujimbar Bali*, and celebrating various aspects of the local culture with a series of autobiographical essays, fables and drawings.
18. Department store in central Melbourne, established in 1911.
19. Australian painter, born 1943.
20. Finally entitled *The Earth Imagined by Martians* (see **1977**, note 1).

1977

1. *The Earth Imagined by Martians*, watercolour with gold leaf, 197 x 551.2 centimetres (cf diary entries for 12 October and 27 December 1976, and **1976**, notes 16, 20). Images of this work are reproduced in Pearce, *Donald Friend 1915–1989 Retrospective*, pp. 116–17. On its sale, see diary entry for first week of November 1977, and **1977**, note 12.
2. German-born British publisher, businessman and philanthropist (1926–2001).
3. English television satirist and entrepreneur as well as celebrity interviewer (born 1939).
4. Sir Edwin Hardy Amies (1909–2003), English fashion designer.

5. Australian-born landscape architect, author and photographer (born 1953), who settled in Bali.
6. Probably a reference to Polish-born Australian socialite Lady Mary Fairfax, née Wein (born 1922), third wife of Sir Warwick Fairfax (see **1956**, note 3).
7. Fashionable annual social event in Sydney, dating to 1936.
8. Balinese prince and businessman.
9. David Friend (born 1948), son of Ten and Pam.
10. Cf **1929**, note 16, and diary entry for 2 August 1985.
11. Her second marriage, in 1974 (following her first, to Bill McLaughlin, which ended with his death—see **1964**, note 25), was to theatre director, composer and teacher Terry Clarke (born 1935). This marriage lasted till 1986.
12. *The Earth Imagined by Martians* (see **1977**, note 1) was purchased by the Australian National Gallery (now the National Gallery of Australia).

1978

1. Balinese 'jaw harp', part of which is placed in the performer's mouth and plucked with the finger to produce a note.
2. Balinese percussion instrument similar to the marimba but made of bamboo rather than wood.
3. Friend, who was now developing emphysema, had returned to Australia to stay with Attilio and Ailsa Guarracino prior to entering hospital.
4. Catholic-run institution in the inner-Melbourne suburb of Fitzroy.
5. *Li Po and Tu Fu: Poems Selected and Translated with an Introduction and Notes* (Penguin Classics, 1973). Li Po (c.701–62); Tu Fu (712–70); Arthur Cooper (born England, 1916).
6. Australian architect (1916–94).
7. Coastal town in Victoria, 290 kilometres west of Melbourne.
8. *Evelyn Waugh: A Biography* (1975). Sykes (1907–86) was an English biographer and historian.
9. La Taverna Bali Hotel, on the beachfront at Sanur, and one of the earliest hotels in Bali, established in 1971.
10. A party ahead of the official opening of the exhibition *Rare Selected Works of Art from Papua New Guinea, West Irian, Java, Borneo and Bali* at Realities Gallery, Toorak. Friend was one of the private collectors who lent work for the show.
11. Fashionable seaside resort and outer suburb of Melbourne, 45 kilometres east of the city centre.
12. In the style of Euripides (c. 480–406 BC), Greek tragic dramatist.
13. A spin-off from *Bumboozìana*, never published. The manuscript was sold privately in 1984.

1979

1. English former fashion designer and a leading philanthropist (born 1935).
2. English-born publisher (1934–91), whose later career was based in Australia.
3. 'The Eleventh Commandment', in *Australian Playboy*, an imprint (published from February 1979) of the American men's magazine *Playboy*, founded in 1953.
4. Commercial gallery established in 1963.
5. Australian social-realist painter (1913–86).
6. Australian art historian, critic and lecturer (born 1916).
7. Australian painter, teacher and champion of modernism (1878–1966).
8. Town, and prosperous rural retreat, in Victoria, 65 kilometres northwest of Melbourne. It lies partway up the mountain of the same name.
9. English author, scholar and translator of Chinese and Japanese literature (1889–1966). Birth-name Arthur Schloss.
10. English novelist, critic and poet (1911–81).
11. Volcanic island between Java and Sumatra.
12. Held annually in the Belgian city each November.
13. Australian painter and stained-glass artist (born 1928).
14. A member of the British royal family (1900–79), who had served as the last viceroy of colonial India and is assumed to have been killed by the Irish Republican Army in a bomb blast.
15. American cartoonist (1909–79), whose original name was Alfred G. Caplin. The character Li'l Abner Yokum is a simple, good-natured hayseed from a town in Kentucky. The comic strip ran from 1934 to 1979.
16. The capital of Iran was the main focus of serious tensions between the USA and Ayatollah Ruhollah Khomeini (1902–89), the revolutionary leader whose movement had overthrown the previous regime of the Shah in February 1979. The US Embassy hostages were not released till January 1981.

1980s

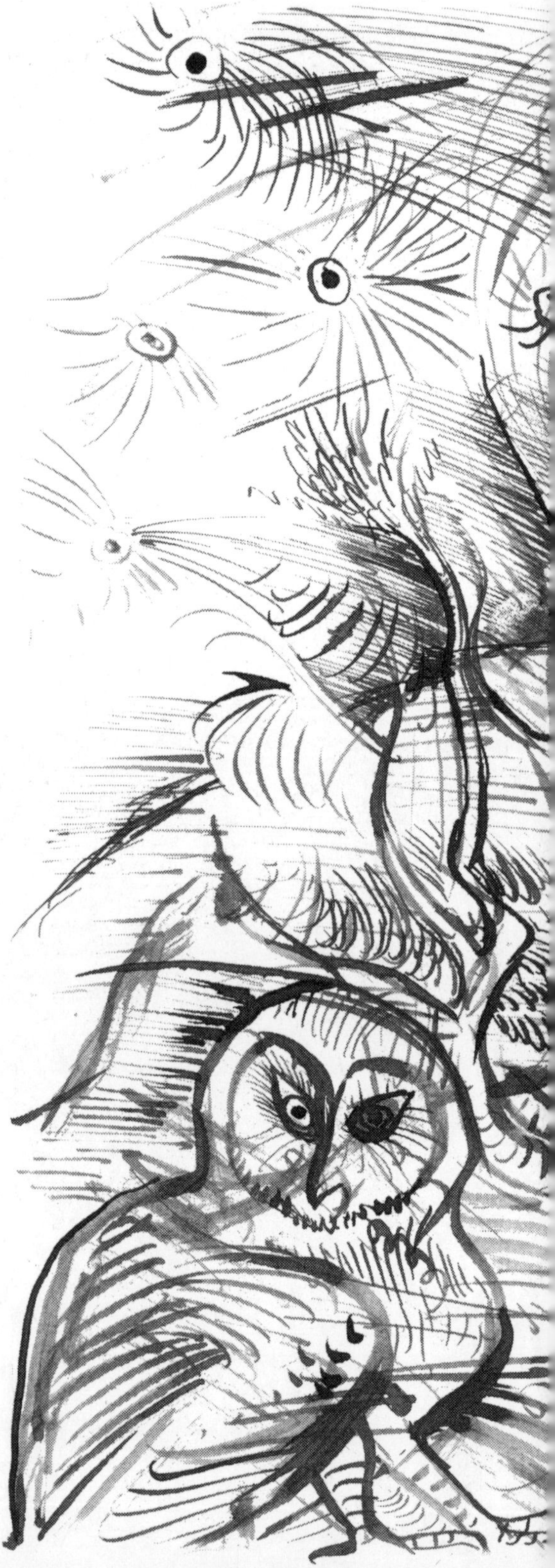

41. Self-portrait with owl (1980).

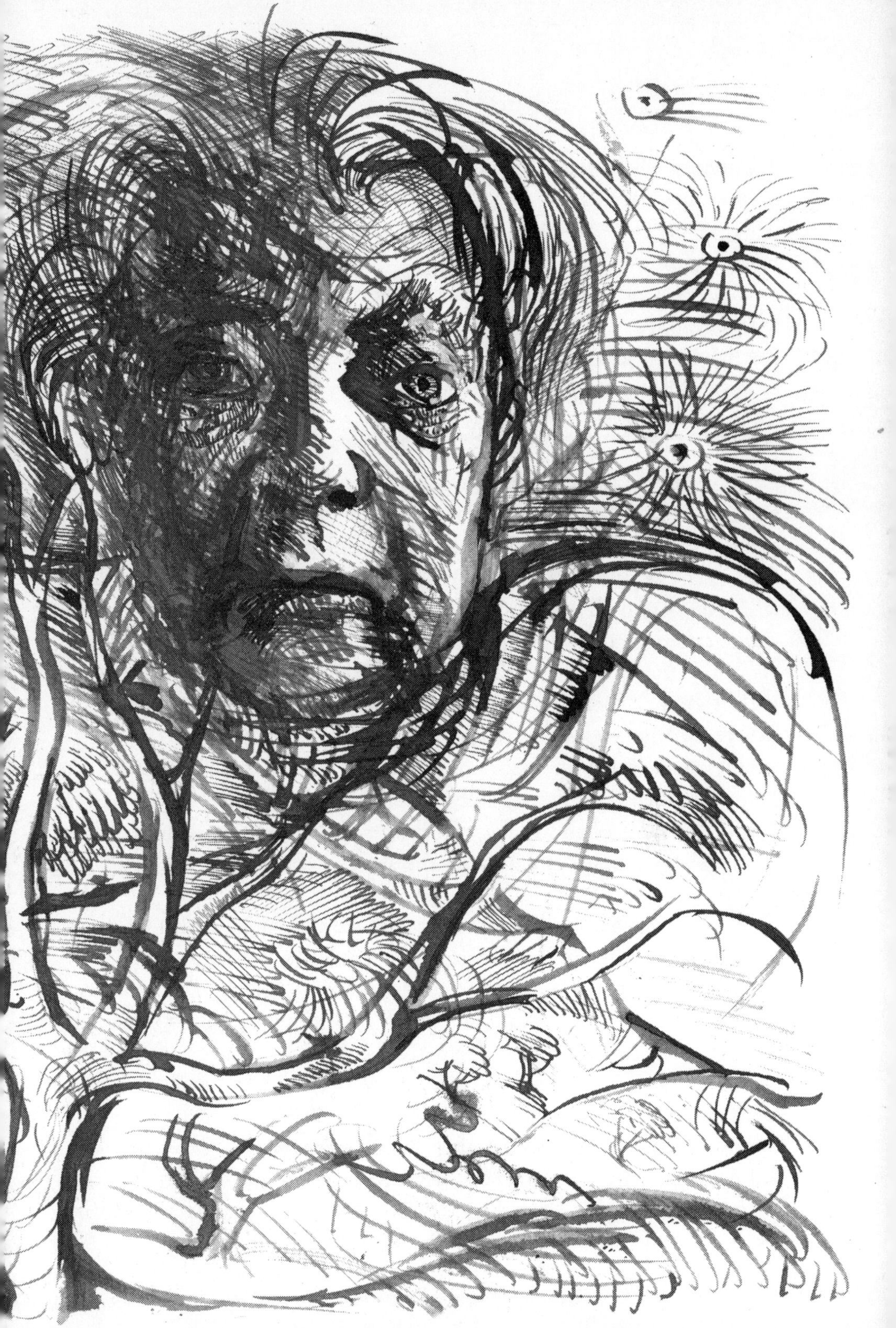

1980

4 January *Melbourne*. I've cut down on smoking and feel somewhat better, but certainly not very well. And I have gone back once more to Rochester's *Sodom*[1], designing sets and costumes as though for a Christmas pantomime.

The greatest nations and many of the small ones are all a-murdering again. And there is no discernible difference between the most savage—the most civilised—ALL are land-hungry, wealth-hungry despoilers and killers. If history has lessons to teach, she has no serious pupils among the rulers of the world.

25 April Lunch at a smart restaurant with Frank Thring[2], the actor to whom I've dedicated *Sodom*. Thring is an actor who never leaves off playing the part of an actor. Tall, fat, completely bald, he dresses in a curious *chic* get-up—all black, with heavy golden chains about his neck with a massive gold pendant, his hand laden with one enormous ring. He was charming and amusing, but not, I thought, a wit. At his best talking about himself (his only subject) and the films and plays he's starred in. He entertained his audience (us and the other diners) delivering his lines in slow, distinct orotund phrases.

He spoke at length about costumes he'd worn in several spectacular films, the weight of the gold embroideries—'I always choose parts where I sit down most of the time, preferably at a banqueting table so I can make sweeping gestures and order the slaves to pour more wine.'

27 April to 5 May *Bali*. The dreaded visit went off surprisingly pleasantly in all aspects, although an underlying melancholy pervaded.

Madja awaited us at the airport—Wija sent my old Chevrolet car (now superbly restored) to take us to Batujimbar, so our progress was distinguished by saluting policemen and waving populace and much laughter. As for Madja, no one could have done more to make this visit memorable for the affection and devotion he displayed.

From the time I entered the house began a series of visits from Balinese friends, old servants etc. came to welcome and farewell me with affection and regrets—for the news had gone all over the island that I was coming back before departing for good.

Sold the house and most of the collection at a great loss—we're being paid for it by instalments. Well, it's over and done with, that part of my life.

June to end of August *Melbourne.* My life, though not entirely uneventful, has been appallingly uninteresting to me, and disillusioning, in everything except my work. The last has been my daily delight, and very fruitful. *The Farce of Sodom* was launched on the world, has sold well, and the exhibition on the 'Return of the Prodigal' theme completed, elegantly framed and sent off to the Holdsworth Gallery[3]. Gisella is very enthusiastic about it.

Mid-September to mid-October St Vincent's Hospital. Here in a room with a view over the city and beyond to the sea. The old ailment, and this time also I'll be operated for umbilical hernia. And so at last have been forced to give up smoking. Also to a large extent, eating and drinking. I am very overweight (12 st. 9lbs). I'm bored of course.

Delayed because on the eve of the day set aside for my operation the surgeon became ill. This very monastic existence is becoming painfully tedious.

The operation having been done was followed by a couple of days of discomfort and immobility. The medicos express great satisfaction at the result. I am horrified. My belly is now like a great swollen overhanging pear.

I feel very depressed about what the rest of my life seems to offer—or what it will be if its course is that charted by good medical opinion. Diet—no sugar, no butter, no wine; very little meat. Lots of vegetables. No smoking. Regular exercise. If those cheerless negatives are the ingredients of a life, it is surely the life of someone who is a stranger to me. When I leave this hospital am I to step into the identity of a senile vegetarian teetotaller who goes for brisk walks in the paltry suburban streets?

If these are the conditions I will accept (there is no *must* about it) and add them to self-disgust and disgust at the world of men and a frivolous sort of guilt at having succumbed to the general money-love of society, how shall I continue to believe myself in so many ways superior to most people? I rather think I will ignore most of the measures recommended to prolong my life, because it is obviously not worth the trouble.

20 October The Liberals won the general election, although by a narrow majority.[4] Malcolm Fraser does not inspire enthusiasm. In fact he's fairly unpopular: he uses none of the personality tricks that endear politicians to the great golden hearts of the rabble.

27 October The party for the opening of John Olsen's exhibition at the Australian Galleries. Attilio and I called in at the gallery in the morning firstly, so as to be able to see the paintings without too many distracting people. During this little session I met Lou Klepac[5], whom I'd long wanted to know. John's exhibition was a distinct advance on his last show—there was much to see that was not merely pleasantly placed blobs, drips and dribbles. There were some lively light-hearted animals—giraffes and monkeys discernible here and there. But I fear that of recent years he has not much of importance to say. As with *most* contemporary Australian painting, the exhibition featured several 'major works'—which is to signify large areas of trivia. Anyone who wishes to identify the most important masterpiece in a collection of contemporary Australian art should seek out a huge and trivial canvas featuring squiggles and blobs.

Late October to early November *Mt Macedon*. A week's stay with the Pursers. Cold, drizzly and damp weather. That house will never be comfortable. However, the time passed well enough, with the usual social luncheons. I even managed to make several landscape sketches. *Gum trees!* At the same time I felt rather ill all the while.

Jeff Smart, looking plump and prosperous, came up with Richard for Warwick's great Sunday luncheon of twenty-six guests. Richard seemed thrilled with Jeff, who was indulging in the profoundly cultured pomposity which is his 'high society' manner. There was a lot of boring chatter about the Melbourne Cup.

4 November In America, the people's disastrous choice for their new President is Reagan[6], an aggressive racist 'conservative' much liked by big business. Wall Street went crazy.

1981

27 February *Brisbane*. Philip Bacon[1] met us at the airport. We drove straight to his gallery. The pictures were excellently displayed, and everything arranged with admirable efficiency. The opening was that same evening, and very well attended.[2] The drawings sold like hot cakes—the oils slowly. I put on the usual necessary grinning and chatting performance for all the grinning and chatting social faces. They were, it seemed to me, in contrast to the dreary restraint of Melburnians, very warm and welcoming. And surely enthusiastic.

After the exhibition there was a dinner party in my honour at a grand restaurant—about twenty guests—the men of a powerful and prosperous description—their sons handsome and already successful in business, and their wives wondrously hung about with large jewels. I was then already exhausted. I simply wanted to sleep after pouring out so much nonsense to please the art-buyers. But there was no escape. The meal, Italian, was rich with cream and avocados and heavy sauces.

24 March *Melbourne.* Lunch at the Australian Galleries with the Purveses, Barry Humphries and wife[3], Jeff Smart and an artist called Senbergs[4] and his wife—Barry and Jeff were both in good form and for a while the conversation went with such verve one was reminded of former times and other places.

I wish I'd settled in Sydney instead of here, although I feel that's an ungrateful thought in view of Ailsa and Attilio's kindness—but oh his dour sourness and her generous dullness. One feels, at meals, we're acting in a dramatised version of *Diary of a Nobody*.[5]

Second week of May An appalling violently hysterical screaming row with Attilio. To an onlooker, the whole thing would appear a wildly funny farce. However it looks as if the outcome will be anything but farcical. I made my peace with Attilio, so calm has descended. Even, unbelievably, a sort of return to the status quo, although I am still going to Sydney to find myself a studio.

Last week of May *Sydney.* After some hunting about, and the sickening feeling one gets from inspecting quite horrible empty dwellings, I've moved out of the Scheinbergs' and into a 'studio apartment' at Bondi Junction[6]—out of the microwave stove and into the frying pan. It's on the 'penthouse' floor of a very modern apartment building full of, I suspect, very dubious residents. My 'apartment' has a glass wall onto a little terrace and a vast staring view to the south of miles of little brick houses with red tile roofs. It comprises one big room, shower, kitchen, stove and refrigerator. It is brand new—a new apartment added on to the roof. My response to it is a feeling almost of terror. It sums up the emptiness and loneliness of an old city-dweller.

How to *cope* with such a life? First I'll have to purchase basic necessities—pots, cups, spoons, pillows and sheets. And a drawing table. But of these practicalities the only purchase I made—it being Saturday afternoon all but the luxury shops had closed—was when we went window-shopping and found in an antique shop a Ching dynasty[7]—*very* late!—blue-and-white brush pot. It was rather expensive but charming in a simple way. So we haggled, and I made up part of the price by doing a sketch of the shop owner. The subject of the design on it had an almost irresistible ironic-comic-philosophic appeal: the 'Three Great Joys'—which were symbolised by a trio of serenely contented and portly gentlemen, chief of whom was a bearded sage holding the peach of longevity. The Joys are Venerable Old Age, Prosperity and Parenthood.

This charming object, already filled with pens and brushes, stands on the tiny dining table in the sparsely furnished studio. There are also two special relics from my past life—a superb small bronze Buddha and a bronze and gold Ganesha, 14th-century Balinese.

9 July Tas Drysdale died. Today I went to the memorial service at All Saints' Church, Woollahra—a concourse of people, many of whom I hadn't seen for years and years. There was lots of social chatter outside the church. A very cold sunny morning. Peter Sculthorpe had composed a piece of cello music for the occasion. This has been a very fatal week for artists of my generation. Graves yawned for several. I have felt the bony finger beckoning *me*—whilst working, appropriately enough, on Totentanz[8] lithographs for Lou Klepac's projected book of the Poems of the Vagrant Poets at the time of the Black Death[9]—my designs populated with merry and ribald skeletons.

I am ill enough to make any hypochondriac happy, yet serene and happy in mind.

29 July Gisella Scheinberg took me to the opera. It is a guilty confession to admit that this is the first time in twenty years I've been to the opera. And of course the first time I'd been inside Utzon's[10] famous opera house. The building, so superbly a series of shapes in its exterior aspect, struck me as resembling a modernistic film set inside—cramped attic-like spaces, all steep and angled, and riddled with steep narrow stairs. Some of the forms were lovely, but generally oppressed with concrete beams above, leaning over one, and confined by an almost gothic and fortress-like concept of space.

The auditorium was small. The work performed, Handel's *Alcina*[11], was most elaborately produced—the sets were good, and full of transformations. Baroque. And elaborate costumes. As theatre the actors in their cloaks and gowns and towers of feathers seemed somewhat petrified by lack of movement or action—it was all very formalised. And the singing provided one's ears with a remarkable richness of very similar soprano voices and a great dearth of arias for the males.

14 August Since his death, I've been thinking more about Drysdale than I have in years, for we'd become distant by more than the geographical space which set our friendship apart. I had never lived away from the constant practice of art, whilst he merely occasionally visited his originally great ability as an artist, in the same way that the source of his inspiration over the last thirty years has been occasional visits to the never-never land of the remote outback, and its inhabitants, the stockmen and Aborigines who peopled his pictures, were in no sense his familiars. He set them down as memories with the aid of photographs.

His influence on my work was considerable. And yet those visionary landscapes of stark and arid vistas, of endless perspectives of leafless trees and grassless acreage, hopeless blacks and scrawny stubbornly enduring lonely station hands and their unfulfilled wives and lives—always still as tree stumps beneath vast hopeless skies threatening permanent drought (there is never a hint that there will ever come a rainy season)—these are dreams of hell really.

In fact his concept of Australian landscape smothered the country like a defoliant—all this was much at variance with his non-painter's life. He loved lush tropical Queensland. Pioneer sugar lands; Cooktown; Cairns. The trees in his Bouddi orchard[12], and at Hill End the gardens of cottages, the grand avenues which set off the gold rush erosions of the scene. He loved gaiety and wild talk and drink, laughter, companionship.

Everything, in fact, that was unlike those superb sad empty pictures he made in which a town was an empty street, a pub was one bored man leaning against a verandah post.

Well, he was, like me, the Aquarian—the escapist who could disappear into other shapes. When the cruel blows of life at last infiltrated his guard and smote him with terrible realities for which he had no visions—the deaths of Tim and Bon—he was quite destroyed. After that he was a mere shell containing a personality. A personality still of kindness and generosity and loyalty to all his friendships, but one which exhibited to us mostly mere tricks of appearance and manners of speaking.

It would seem that his conception of 'reality' was invested in those legends of the outback. He was utterly unarmed and unprepared when tragedy struck at him from within the family, in the city environment of his actual life, and killed two of those within the core of his being, where the 'reality' was quite divorced from the legends that so deeply concerned his inner life.

Tas was adept at self-deception. His ability to swallow whole and digest his own myths was prodigious. Within the space of an hour in his own Sydney home he'd live within those myths, becoming by turn a jackeroo, a Scottish laird, an old hand of the Central Australian wilderness, a London clubman, a jazz pianist. These character parts, and many others were so satisfying that he painted nothing at all for years at a time, so that every time he unwillingly returned to paint a canvas, he had to relearn the mystery. Naturally, that meant going back over old ground. There was no going forward.

26 September Last night Margaret Olley gave a small dinner party in the strange charmingly confused clutter of her studio in Paddington. We sat down to dine at the long Victorian table which just manages to find space for its chairs amongst the clutter of kelim rug-covered sofas, pearl-shell inlaid tabors, carved chests, Melanesian idols, innumerable pots and vases of flowers, paintings, old brocades, statues of Buddha, crucifixes. All treasured loot from her travels in a marvellous jumble, giving a sort of antipodean Old Curiosity Shop[13] effect. All her guests were people I've known and been fond of for years. The meal was simple and delicious, the wine good and the talk animated and amusing with the references of old friendships.

The night turned stormy, and the sound of the wind outside, the rain pattering on the roof, branches from the twig-tangled garden tapping on window panes gave additional comfort—we were like friendly creatures sheltering in a cosy burrow from a storm.

7 October I'm working on drawings from a model who can't stand still. His angelic elfin features are the mask of a restless infantile fiend. He fidgets, complains, whines and tries to haggle for more than the five dollars I pay him. After he's gone I work on, altering and correcting. And completely changing some of them into half-naked Commedia dell'Arte[14] characters—a vagabond troupe rehearsing, masked, the parts of Harlequin, the Captain, the Doctor etc.

Brett Whiteley shows in his studio many large and brilliant brush drawings of nudes. Matisse plus heroin. The studio has many mirrors, and many photographs of himself looking old and haggard and oddly *coarse*. The spectacular nudes have become formalised to give the sensation of the enormous prize-pumpkin clefted rotundity of arse thrust at the viewer, to which is attached a speedily diminishing body and far far distant head—the head like a remote little receding gherkin.

Lou Klepac tells me that Sid Nolan awaits with anguished dread the launching of Patrick White's autobiography[15] which contains a chapter on the Nolans. They used to be close friends, but, as often happens with that bitter self-hating bore Patrick W., the friendship soured to dislike when Cynthia Nolan[16] suicided and Sid quickly remarried Perceval's ex-wife[17]. 'Before Cynthia was *cold in her grave*,' as Patrick W. said in shocked tones. Soft, gentle, charming, weak Sid Nolan could not live without a woman's support. Many women's support perhaps.

And self-loathing Patrick White's way of friendship is comparable to Henry VIII's[18] uxoriousness: the headman's axe is in the next room, newly sharpened, on the chopping block.

For Patrick White and several others of our cultural establishment the brief and stirring period of Whitlam's prime ministership was a time of euphoria. A kind of temporary Camelot. White perhaps was a kind of Merlin. Lancelots, Gawains and Sir Percivals guzzled at the Round Table[19] and jousted in the lists, brawled in the forests. Whitlam's dethronement left Patrick White stranded very abruptly. The towers of Camelot, alas, were an illusion, a mirage. We'll see what he makes of it in his autobiography. We'll all buy it, and hunt for our names in its foreseeably grim paragraphs. He won't have much to say in anybody's favour I think. He'll trounce Sydney society. There'll be little untouched by scorn—except, it may be, the trees in Centennial Park[20] opposite his house, where each morning he walks his dog and glares at the naughty world through icy blue eyes.

Well, well. And how much lesser a mortal am I, whose mild eyes each morning gaze indifferently over the scarlet red tiled roofs to that same park's green pleasances. I am a vegetable. Instead of perambulating I wave my flaccid limp leaves amiably in the direction of the park's noble verdure as an elderly lettuce might do, acknowledging the existence of a tomato plant at the other end of the salad garden.

21 October The printer called in with the remaining *Songs of the Vagabond Scholars* proofs. My lithographs are superb. Also arrived Randolph Stow's[21] translations of the poetry. Literal translations and, I thought, rather *flat*. They contain what I cannot decide are errors of taste or style. I feel, probably unreasonably, that in translating medieval Latin poetry, whether literally or poetically, 'fuck' cannot convey the Latin meaning. In my deep ignorance of Latin I suppose *saltem* is from *saltare* and means to leap. And infers to ravish. And in any case *fuck*, that brief cave-dweller's crude syllable, has been so much over-used during the last several thousand years in the common tongue, that its proper meaning has been lost to contemporary poetry just at the very moment it has become generally accepted as a printed word.

How rarely, I insist, nowadays does the passionate swain plead to his neo-Arcadian shepherdess, 'Give us a fuck, love, before I come in me pants.' Such language belongs to a former and more gracious age. Today the worn out word is used quite indiscriminately—'Oh *fuck*!—if you fuckin' won't give us a fuckin' fuck yer can fuckin' well foot it home on yer fuckin' lonesome to Parra-fuckin-matta. So fuck you!'

'And fuck you too,' replies the spirited wench. 'I'm a respectable girl what's not-fuckin'-likely to waste a fuck on a silly-lookin' fucker like you. So fuck off!'

24–25 October *Bowral.* Retford Park. The weekend was wonderfully easeful. The other guests were all old friends. The garden was in full splendour of rhododendrons and azaleas—irises in bud, aviaries in full squawk of rare parrots, fabled pheasants and several emus which somehow contrived to look *soignée* and antediluvian at the same time. James's additions and improvement have now come to maturity framed by the huge old trees planted about a hundred years ago. I made a drawing—a portrait-drawing of him in a Confederate soldier's[22] cap.

31 October *Sydney*. A ballet dancer came to pose. A fine well-muscled figure topped with one of those slightly-too-big heads furnished with large well-defined features. One suspects that God modelled them in a theatrical mood, and designed them to carry beyond the footlights to the back row of the stalls. That's the trouble with dancers—their whole training is to be very aware of, and to project, their presences. The artist would prefer a passive spectacle on which to impose his own concept, whether it is a nude figure or a landscape or still life he is concerned with.

If only the heavens would open and benevolent Providence reach forth to present me with a big black young negro. A negro without a fuzzy intellectual's beard or an 'Afro' hairdo such as most of them nowadays wear to declare their political affiliations.

13 November A fluffy blonde girl whom Gisella employs as a publicity agent is at it again. She pesters me before exhibitions to 'perform'. And now I won't. I will *not* be interviewed on inane and vulgar commercial television programs. And I'll not lend myself to the stupid stunts she thinks up—they're tricks that must make art appear silly and disreputable. For an example, there's to be a luncheon for the press at the gallery. I must be there to be interviewed. Well and good. But this asinine creature was going to hire *professional clowns* to entertain the press.

'There will be only one clown present,' I told her. '*Myself*.'

I want publicity of course. Publicity with DIGNITY. Oh hell, now I've started laughing. There'll be sighs of relief in the marketplace when I'm safely dead.

8 December *Melbourne*. Attilio and Richard picked me up at the airport—Richard ecstatic on my being again in Melbourne. He went on repetitively, overbearingly loud through a lunch for artists, where Anne and Stuart Purves had invited me—Tim Storrier was there, and Arthur

Boyd (and wife[23]), John Olsen, all in fine form. We murmured in one another's ears while Richard roared happily on. All through the afternoon, and then insisted on staying to dinner at Attilio's. I was by then furious with him.

It was raining when I landed in Melbourne—later in the morning it was hot and sunny until a wild gale arose to blow off roofs, blow down trees and by dinner time the air was still in a cloudy humid sky. A cool night.

10 December The launching of *An Alphabet of Owls*[24] was in a large private house in South Yarra, a comfy fairly run-down house in a largish neglected garden. A crowd of people surged about a table loaded with glasses and bottles of champagne. Three or four artists were there. The women wore sensible dresses with cardigans. They were bookshop people and librarians, middle-aged and a bit dowdy, dangling hand-beaten silver bangles. We chatted away, they drinking champagne and dipping little biscuits in garlic cream-cheese. I abstained, and drank mineral water, feeling weak. Towering above everybody, dressed all in a black Hamlet-Dracula-Batman[25] costume and being monumentally witty, was Frank Thring (a notable contrast to the bookish citizens) sonorously improvising his lines. All the world's a stage.

15 December We drove out to Heide[26], the late John Reed's[27] home, which is now a museum. Fine modern architecture set in a garden of native trees. We went to see Sid Nolan's first Kelly series of paintings.[28] I thought them magnificent.

17–21 December St Vincent's Private Hospital. Time passes—a trance broken by meals, hypodermics and occasional crisp brisk bustling nurses. And sometimes hieratic ikon-like figures of authority in costumes that partake equally of the nunnery and the hospital—medieval costumes melded and modernised.

With a few books for company and only the occasional nurse to give an injection or request a specimen of urine, I am free of the mental irritation and impatience which is hard to avoid outside. I re-read favoured novels: Burgess's *Malayan Trilogy*[29], Joyce Cary's *The Horse's Mouth*[30]. Superb, both of them.

The Patrick White memoirs have made a great impression—his

frankness, etc. For my own part, I thought White's autobiography more readable than most of his writing, but hardly an outstanding work. *Why* is anything of his published long complaints against life considered so wonderful? None of it could be favourably compared with writers such as Anthony Burgess or Lawrence Durrell[31] or several others. *Or* with Randolph Stow, a local product.

29 December I'm oppressed—no, that's not the word, for there's no fear or sorrow to oppress me—progressively more sharply by the conviction I've not much time left for living. I'm utterly *bored* with myself and my life. I'm empty of inspiration, of ideas. Nothing occurs with painting. Yet I'm impatient to have the as yet unpublished books in print. I want all that work done with. I want things tidied up, and then I want to die, swiftly, quietly and painlessly.

1982

11 January *Sydney*. To a party for a kind of bohemian crowd associated with Bali. It's sadly true I resist inside myself going out to the sort of enjoyments that once amused me. I long to go early to bed instead.

The party—about twenty of us—sat at a long table in a restaurant at Kings Cross which seemed crammed with a lively mixture of male whores, 'lost' young people and eccentrics in gaudy costumes. Spangles and bangles prevailed. The talk—shouted above crashing and howling music—was exactly the kind I've missed for so long. The talk of artists and bohemians.

It was all very crazy and refreshing, like those times at the Windsor Castle at Paddington. Indeed, many of us were survivors of the old Paddington crowd. Now, as then, every one of us had a great deal to say, and all of it the greatest nonsense, improvised to impress others rather than to convince ourselves. Nothing could have pleased me more—hours of unleashed exulting in their exuberant verbosity. And not a one of them seemed concerned at all with commerce and the money obsessions and competitiveness of the bourgeois world.

23–25 January Church Point.[1] Staying in a house by the waters of an inlet. One of those weekenders: feebly built. Lots of bush and wild birds—parrots, galahs, kookaburras and magpies. A crowd who now have *all* become involved in film-making—very distracting and really bogus people of the kind one likes to see occasionally in short doses. They all seem to be living parasitically on one another in Palm Beach. They, of course, are on 'pot' and other drugs. Most of them belong to the 'Orange' cult[2], and revere a mystic guru in San Francisco who advocates drugs and sexual promiscuity—essential ingredients, they hold, of the search for the spiritually sublime.

It was an agreeable few days, but a bloody effort. Mosquitoes in droves: an uncomfortable bed in a room—a child's room I suppose, swarming with dolls and toys.

27 January Lou took me to lunch in the Botanical Gardens. We ate overlooking trees and shrubs leading to a pool full of ducks and ornamental birds. The place was rather crowded with holiday-makers quacking less charmingly than the ducks. We went to the art gallery to see exhibited the Archibald, Wynne and Sulman competition pictures.[3] On the whole they were distinctly less awful than last year's efforts. Yet one searches in vain for even a hint of greatness—dullness without distinction flavoured the sincere canvases: drugs and distraction fragmented the shapes of Brett Whiteley's. Lots of wretched talent verging on—or passing over the border to—commercial art. And most canvases showed more than anything else the artists' dilemma—how to paint a true portrait in terms of contemporary art: the usual quasi-solution was an adventure into gimmicks or 'novelties'.

Well. I've no right to denigrate these puny talents nowadays; I'm not an artist at all.

16 February The world news gets worse every day, with American aggression and a massive armaments build-up, and President Reagan making his crude presence felt in all directions from the Arab–Israel world to a massive support of South American military dictatorships against the equally dynamic Communist stirrings. His equally rabid (as far as I can understand) economic policies have upset the world in general.

3 March I was chatting with Gisella at the Holdsworth when a handsome young woman, who was looking at paintings, turned towards us and smiled. 'She is an actress, a film star,' Gisella hissed. 'She lives in North Queensland. A great friend of Margaret Olley.' It was Diane Cilento.[4] I'd not recognised her because she's hardly aged a year since I last saw her in the 1950s. She told us of her farm up in the Daintree country north of Port Douglas, where she grows rare tropical fruits and has introduced durians and mangosteens and rambutans.

Gisella was quite overwhelmed by an unexpected visit from Sid—*Sir* Sid, Nolan, who at this moment is much in every newspaper because of Patrick White's attack on his marriage and his horribly vulgar reply in the form of a nasty painting of White and his friend Manoly[5]. Max Harris in the *Australian* newspaper wrote a fatuous article in which he officially withdrew the ineffable boon of his esteem from Nolan. Which resulted in thousands of dollars' worth of free publicity for individuals who are intensely concerned with cultivating their fame. Nolan contacted Gisella, and booked her gallery for two exhibitions.

There's a great deal more Fame than art in his paintings of the last ten years. It is only when one sees such pictures as the *first* Ned Kelly series and others from the 1950s that one realises what a fascinating artist he's concealed beneath his later work.

Mid-March A Chinese dinner in a restaurant—of all people from Bali. It was heart-warming—news of Madja etc., but significantly no word of Wija until I asked about Batujimbar. Most of it pulled down, all the trees felled, the garden a desolation—the museum a shell, the whole collection of antique doors ripped out and sold, etc. So all that money, greed and vulgarity has had a complete victory.

A letter from of all people Michael White, known as Madé Wijaya. A fragmented, showy and rather hysterical letter, until one comes to the last page where something of sincerity shows through, and one sees how he remembers the few brief years when I was a great man there (however absurd) and made a beautiful place and peopled it and made those people happy. That was truly a considerable achievement. Why am I always yearning for self-approval? Very likely because there are few things I've done worth approving.

A cocktail party in Double Bay with an infinity of champagne and very mixed guests—many 'trendies', smart antique dealers both new and *ancien regime*, a gaggle of Lesbian real estate dealers and publicans, lots of jangly beads and bracelet ladies with Hottentot hair-dos, several quite real people—James Fairfax and two young men who looked like camp pugilists but turned out to be art entrepreneurs from England—and so on. A tremendous sustained noise of yattering, shrieking and babbling competed with recorded pop music. I rather enjoyed it. The place is still in a chaos of being mended, but already on the walls there were some very fine paintings and drawings. Several of mine. And a superb Brett Whiteley drawing. Francis Bacon[6] etc., etc.

Graffiti on the wall of a bus stand reflect Bondi Junction's lower-middle and working-class preoccupations—their chauvinism loud (in this area of very mixed races), the brutal slogans of the mob: 'Export Asians, not uranium'; 'Poofters are criminals'. Well. Vox populi vox…hm. Quite a subject for psychiatrists and sociologists. The authors are adolescents and young men, many unemployed. Mongrel-bred themselves, they resent their Jewish and Mediterranean immigrant neighbours along with Asians and other dark-skinned races. Their attitude to sex, judging by these slogans, excludes women and centres on homosexuality for money with a sort of side slap at politics.

20 April I see a good deal of Lou Klepac: comforting company, very sweet and thoughtful. He finds for me the kind of nibs I use for drawing, which belong I suppose to the 19th century, not made any more since artists don't draw at all or use rubbishy innovations such as felt-pen. We went to the *very* good shop called Artemis to buy sketchbooks, paper and French gouache which I use a lot now.

1 May Fred Williams died. *Not* a great painter (who is?—or was?) but a good one, although his ideas were limited and repetitious. I knew him only well enough to think him a rather uninteresting person.

I went to Rex Irwin's[7] extremely elegant gallery in Paddington, to see a show of crayon drawings of Nolan's, rumoured to have all—about thirty of them—been done in one day. I believe it. Hasty and crude and not good but *very* confident, and certainly a *tour de force* of one day's inventiveness.

This morning I posed again for Judy Cassab[8], who has been painting my portrait. An excellent likeness—but not art. She is a very pleasant woman.

19 May I am at last becoming reconciled to living in Australia, for all that it is a much-diminished style of life which doesn't permit one to have splendid illusions about oneself. I feel somewhat shrunken after Bali, which often invades my mind with nostalgia.

On the other hand, while my self-esteem has been evaporating there are constant encouragements from friends and also from the Press to suppose myself a person of some interest, or even consequence, in the Australian art world. So that although lack of conviction restrains me (rather than modesty) from making any spectacular claims on my own behalf it will not prevent me from pasting in any newspaper paragraphs I find devoted to praising me. Or which mentions me in passing, or criticises me adversely.

It stands to reason, nobody would keep a diary who did not find himself and his world absorbing. As I do. I am aware that the essential ingredient for a fascinating diary is a fascinating life. And that, in my rickety incurable ill-health, bodily feebleness etc., is hardly within my capabilities. A month of fascinating incidents would most certainly kill me. However, there remains the life of the Spirit and that of the Mind: the latter presents no problem at all.

21 May The Falkland Islands[9]: the imperious Mrs Thatcher[10] remains clear-voiced and unbending. The Argentines continue wretchedly, perversely, and wrongly stubborn: there seems no likely solution to their differences but by force of arms. Australian feeling is much against it. There is a general idea based on being very opinionated that *if* there is a war it will spread and spread, and this country will be dragged into it. Years of meat pies, canned beer and televised sport have unfitted us for the realities of the outside world except as a place to go for holidays.

Nowadays, in the playground that fills the forefront of the view from my window, the multicoloured children run faster, leap more wildly, shout more shrilly and dress in warm clothes, for there is a sharp bite in the air. The wind shows its teeth. The flame trees burn with vermilion flowers and the trees in the avenues are changing colour and flying in the wind. Lovely autumn.

31 May Lou Klepac usually comes for a few hours' talk and coffee on Monday evenings. Often he brings me a book. This Monday it was the biography of Ottoline Morell.[11] Fascinating. One experiences quite

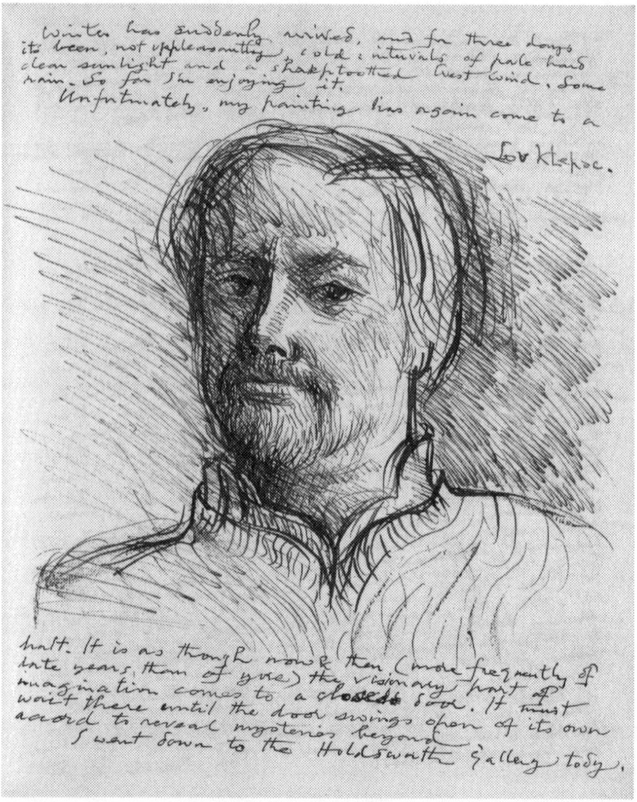

42. *'Lou Klepac'* (1982).

a share of her life, environment and friendships without suffering the anguish which would be unavoidable if they were actually people one knew. Some of them of course I *did* meet when I was a student in London. My teacher, Gertler. But the real influence Lady Ottoline and her friends have had on my life has been from their books and poems and the tales of their doings.

4 June The weather's been wild and cold; yesterday a few flurries of snow fell in the city—the first in twenty years. I stayed home reading.

The war in the Falklands is on the verge of its decisive battle. There's little doubt the British will win, and I'm glad. Sometimes one hears Mrs Thatcher's voice on the radio. Carries on rather like Queen Elizabeth I[12]. Enough to curdle the blood—so cold, clear, authoritative and nauseatingly certain of being morally, legally and even politically in the right: the voice of that sort of English who once ruled the world with such correctness. An especial Heaven has been put aside for them, I understand, and English souls will not be contaminated by the Blessed of lesser breeds. It is a Heaven furnished with chilly marble slabs where neat ranks

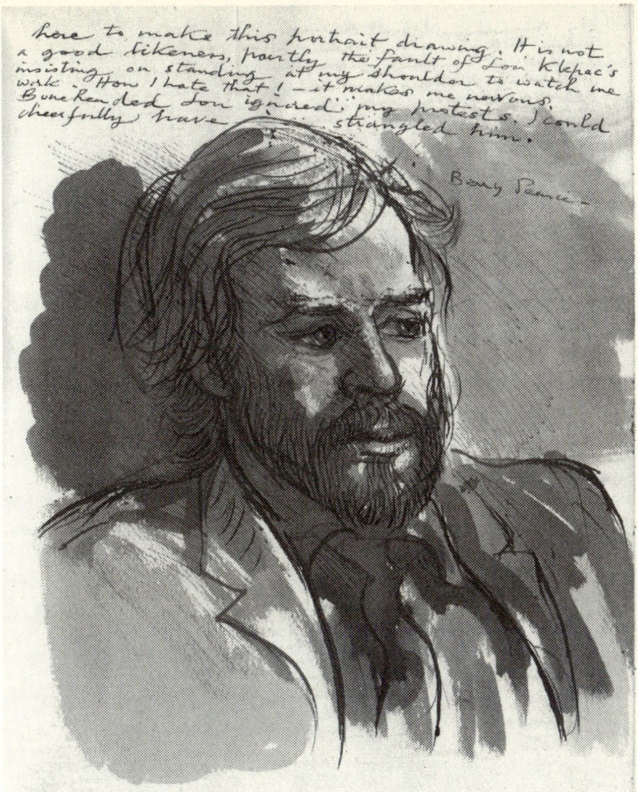

43. *'Barry Pearce'* (*1982*).

of upper-middle-class English souls lie—cool, slippery, silvery-grey in colour, looking (and, the angels complain, smelling) distinctly fishy.

7 June Lou Klepac came in the evening. Our relationship seems a strange one. Friendship it certainly is, but of a kind I've never encountered before, based on long afternoons spent talking mostly about art and incidents and personalities of people I've known in the past, with whom he is concerned as an art historian.

I sometimes think that apart from a perhaps exaggerated admiration for my talents both he and Barry Pearce[13] see me as an absorbing hobby—like philately or collecting rare beetles. And of course there's no denying that even in my present decayed state I am a rare, even a unique, specimen. There are few artists, even those of my own generation, who've led really interesting lives or had much of note to express apart from painting. Consequently their painting has contained a largely humdrum message. I'm referring to Australian artists, who, like Australian shop assistants, travel a lot abroad. And take with them the small-town intellectual backyards of their constricted upbringing, returning thankfully home with news of fellow countrymen living in Paris or wherever... having avoided foreigners.

14 June I've been working on the final drawings and the last pages of volume three of *Ayam 2 Kesayangan*—'The Prodigal Son's Return'.[14] In a way I'm sorry it's finished: leafing back through its pages I'm impressed. Many beautiful drawings. It traces my developments and very varied moods both as artist and writer. I'd not be surprised if one day it was recognised as an important and original work of art.

Lynne and Terry Clarke picked me up in the evening to drive with Colin Lanceley and his wife. They live in a terrace house in Darlinghurst. The house is typical of those old terraces, an iron-lace balcony, folding door to throw the living and dining rooms into one. Fireplaces: we dined by a cosy fire. Much wine, and the food in a huge central bowl we dipped into (no other plates) was a vaguely Spanish dish of rice, fish and vegetables. On the walls a variety of paintings, not at all good: but there were notable exceptions—small etchings by Miro, a good but dislikeable Leger[15], a startlingly good primitive early Australian portrait of an army officer. We were all very jolly and amusing.

17 June The opening of Jeff Smart's retrospective exhibition at New South Wales Art Gallery. Jeff looks well; has put on weight (the erstwhile polished bald egg-shaped head is more pear-shaped. His eyes brilliant, observant and mocking as ever). The paintings looked well. A long progression from early landscapes in South Australia, a developing mastery of paint and an individual manner inevitable to his view of life which selected the subjects and disciplined them to that view.

The show is strong enough to stand as a defiance of everything he hates in contemporary abstract painting. This hatred is very strong in him. He is forever inveighing against its object in conversation, and is to make a public lecture on the subject at the New South Wales Gallery, which will certainly offend many artists and others whose interest is vested in those products. I agree with him of course, but would never put myself in such a public stance; from distaste, or moral cowardice. It may be that Jeff will try to start a movement against that non-representative sort of art which is now firmly entrenched even in the art schools.

Third week of July *Journey to Queensland.* Attilio here. Off on the long drive. We take the route that leads through the northwest, rediscovering places I'd not seen in many years. The country roads curving past the grassy contours of rolling hills, sparsely timbered; a glimpse of a creek's brown waters quiet beneath arches of trees; grey boulders, the stark bleached gestures of fallen branches by clumps of towering eucalypts evoke my visions of this country. In the distance a windmill; beyond it a homestead shelters among pepper trees and oleanders; bush solitudes where seeming silence is compounded of a thousand stirrings of invisible life—insects creaking, whirring. Birds warbling. And other roads twist upwards to pass among the pyramids and spires and craggy bastions of a mountain range. Descending to river and alleys with lonely farms. Deadly holes, with deadly populations leading brutalised lives—but very healthy. Both men and women appear enormous, bulging with strength, fat and loudness. Very jolly, noisy, violently good-hearted. The clamorous mumbles of drinkers in the hotel bar suggests an echo of pioneering rough-and-tumble. Civilisation indeed: with a bed for the night and a beefsteak dedicated to ravenous appetite.

Every day I've made a drawing or two during the progress through Singleton, Merriwa, Coolah, Coonabarabran, Gunnedah, Tamworth. At Warialda we had a drink in the bar unchanged since the thirties. It was crammed with extraordinary drunks—the old, mad, haggard and wizened. The young ones bright-pink-skinned with beery paunches. Wives with babies and young children thronged in with us in a sort of muddle of screaming laughter and Hogarthian gin-alley lurchings. From Warialda we took the Moree road—saw Glendon homestead very grand from a distance. I had no heart to call in. The journey took us through the tedious monotonous plains to Dalby[16], Queensland. We drove from Dalby by roughish little back roads through strange and beautiful country of gentle hills and winding contours and harsh little forgotten towns made of parched wood, corrugated iron and bits of various random chosen material.

It was nearly sundown by the time we'd climbed to a pass through mountains and, descending, beheld the astonishing Glass House Mountains[17]—the range in a profile of marvellous shapes—humps, a perfect pyramid and an erect phallus. We found Lawrence Daws' house about five kilometres out of Beerwah[18]. He gave us a warm welcome. Next day we drove north by back roads to Maryborough[19], making drawings. We spent the night in that charming town rich with the architecture of 1880 tropical prosperity. And on to Hervey Bay[20], a tourist town of holiday flats and caravans, not very interesting at all. I'm overjoyed to be working so consistently. *But*, the actual work on the site of these landscapes, drawings made at great speed and concentration, exhausts me as never before.

Last week of July *Brisbane*. Philip Bacon at his gallery very pleasantly chatted and dealt with clients and introduced us around. We spent several hours in Brisbane's new art gallery. Very fine—lovely architecture, and their collection full of good things well displayed. I was greatly impressed, and glad to see a good work of my own displayed.

3 August *Sydney*. James Fairfax asked me to lunch to meet Bob Hughes and his new wife[21]. It was really a joyous reunion. Bob's new enthusiasm is Australian convicts. He's researching their diaries, letters, personalities and ancient sufferings for a book.[22] I imagine that under the Hughes treatment the history of those poor brutalised wretches will soon be boiling, bubbling and fizzing. It was a lovely warm day. Much harmony—the sunlit verandah: and inside the paintings and lovely furniture, all so fine and all so personal.

20 August I've been working on the landscape drawings from our trip to Queensland, recasting some of them as gouaches and watercolours, or more elaborately finished works. In my own estimation they are well enough in their way. As good as I can make them. But it would be fatal to place them beside nude drawings I made in Bali a few years ago, some of which I've recently seen again, and was myself astonished by their force and beauty. These Australian drawings are forceful, it is true, but their content—the patient passive hostility of the subject (seldom dramatic)—is a laboured extraction of excitement from manically depressing monotonies. Well, I'm not the first to lament our continental drabness, harshness: how the landscape mingles strangeness with sameness!

18 September Tonight at Margaret Olley's, to dine. That crazy studio living room of Olley's, always amazingly cluttered, was now so crammed with still life arrangements of fruit, flowers, innumerable carvings, bits of china, jars of dried flowers, pampas grass, heathen idols that it was not easy to move. Stacked wherever there was space were Olley's new canvases for an exhibition at the Holdsworth. She is a real painter although I fear not one whose work provides extensions of consciousness. Honest work and skill. No exploration of other visions beyond reality, yet there is present in them the warm colouring of her own affectionate constant yet feminine unpretending self.

5 October Holdsworth Gallery. Margaret Olley opening. Who should loom out of the art-loving melée but Jeff Smart, himself a picture of well-tailored social aplomb, dispensing positively ducal greetings left and right. He'd put on weight, and with it an even more suavely important presence. The Proustian attitudinising has become a genuine part of his character, a perfect defence against insecurity. And a useful tool for ambition. The old habit of 'sandwiching' his presence was much in evidence. He'd come on from some other 'do' to Olley's and was already poised to flit off to take in a cocktail party before Gisella's dinner. From thence to grander sandwichings—Canberra, the PM's garden party. Her Majesty's National Gallery inauguration.[23] A list of occasions that curiously mirrored the list I've refused from a silliness equal to Jeff's.

10 October I *do* enjoy memories, but I'm quite sure memoir-writing is *not* for me. My view of life is such as could not be squeezed into shapes acceptable in memoirs, but not true to the constant mutations and shifting perspectives of day-to-day living. *All* changes *all* the time. For example, in youth one's friends (so rare and cherished) often are equally rivals and betrayers: in times of stress allies, supporters, comrades; in times of triumph parasites. In age one leans heavily on them whilst they're busy manipulating one for their own interests. Consequently the best loved and most admired are those seldom seen, flashing in orbit in outer space. Such as James Fairfax and Bob Hughes.

The diary catches the persons and events in flight, as it catches glimpses of oneself—the least satisfactory of all. Is *anyone* reconciled to himself? Or to the inconstancy of events that never stay true to definition. There are no true comedies, no tragedies, but melancholy farces and farcical disasters—the stuff diaries are made of. Memories can emerge only after enormous efforts at tidying up and hiding away the illogical ties. My journal is my only dependable record of a life in which nothing very notable now happens. No use depending on memory. Memory is a compulsive liar when it isn't drowsy with amnesia.

5 November The whole country is gripped in a general Depression now—unemployment, businesses going bust and so on. Sometimes one feels we are on the verge of a popular movement of lawlessness. There *are* small disturbances such as Aborigine riots at Moree[24], and various protest marches. Strikes etc. all over.

A great thing is being made about Abo Land Rights. Whatever the justices and injustices may be of *their* case, I believe it is mainly a cause for white trouble-stirrers motivated by radical politics. Press and radio are full of pro- and anti-Abo news, lectures etc. The principal result seems to be that the public whilst voicing Christian intentions of tolerance towards the Abos are becoming, if not hostile, very fed-up with them.

So much stirring has largely resulted in Aborigines' Rights becoming as boring and aggressive and controversial as Women's Rights. Nevertheless it is really noteworthy how the idea of the wronged blacks has at last burdened the national conscience with a guilt complex of truly American intensity. I say the *idea* very deliberately, for very few Australians have had any contact with Abos either in city slums, country town blacks' camps or in tribal environment, in actuality. Thus their conception of what an Abo is and was comes entirely from propaganda for one view or another. Not from experience.

10 November The *Vagabond Scholars* launching I suppose was a success, in that it was an enjoyable gathering, actually rather distinguished. The Stadia Graphics Gallery[25] is small, simple and elegant in a disciplined sort of way. Peter Sculthorpe (I'd given him and Lou a very good lunch earlier) made an excellent informal speech. I know more of his music than I do Sculthorpe himself: a slight, very pleasant acquaintance. Certainly it is very kind of him to give his time and trouble to launching my work—a thing I myself would do for nobody, in my selfishness. He was a good friend of Tas Drysdale's.

17 November *Melbourne*. Chez Attilio. Today Attilio and I spent an hour in the Art Centre. The oriental collection is still the most distinguished thing they have. Then to a small collection of Rodin bronzes at Georges[26]—which was crammed with sniggering schoolgirls convulsed over a splendidly muscled sculpted prole vigorously masturbating. The other works were weak beside this somehow appalling masterpiece. Appalling, that is to say, in that particular refined and almost absurdly polite ultra-Melburnian environment of Georges' off-white and gilt panelling, pale beige carpeting.

December Nothing happens of notable delight or horror. A pleasant chatty lunch at the Australian Gallery. They're kindly worried about my unproductiveness. Not more than I am. *Nothing* awakens my mind or inspires me. Nothing in my life is inspiring. I read and read. And walk a little for the exercise of it. The weather is hot, cold, clear and cloudy by turns. The terrible drought continues. The Depression (economic) has become a giant, unemployment increases tremendously; and so do strikes and demands for higher wages and nobody seems contented. The more we should admire—envy—the wise wild mother duck with her brood in the Yarra. There is such an arcadian poetry in the spectacle, and it seems so free of human stupidity, greed and brutality that the mind is relieved of tensions and fears.

This house's routines are unaltered—Attilio goes off fishing and returns with a bucket of snapper. Ailsa goes off to work and comes home to cook and I read, mourning for my dead creative talents. Until the miserable ache abated and I got out my oil paints and brushes and began a deceptively simple still life—a newspaper, a white jug and an Annamese[27] flask on one of the caned ebony chairs I bought years ago in Ceylon. It has reached the very perilous almost-finished stage where a few brush strokes can wreck it. Attilio is being by turns angelic, absent playing poker, or present being difficult and stubbornly grumpy. How inconstant people are to any set character we attribute to them!—and how well off the mark are my estimates of them.

A nauseating widespread public attitude to an appalling tragic event which culminated in a woman, Lindy Chamberlain[28], being (probably unjustly) condemned for murder. There could not be a clearer example of what I find sick and loathsome in Australian culture.

1983

1 January Scanning the shelves for a book to wile away boredom I came upon a neatly bound little volume and recognised it as a childhood gift from my mother. My first diary![1] It was diverting for a while to leaf through it reviving old memories until gradually the full horror dawned: I haven't developed *at all*! What seems quaint and even charming in a precocious adolescent is horrifying to find undisciplined and unimproved in oneself approaching one's 68th birthday.

Self-centred, conceited, atrociously snobbish, frivolous, obsessed with aristocratic delusions, adept at self-deceit. None of that's changed. Already I was infatuated with the spectacle of myself as a superior being, a genius destined for fame moving wittily around in a world composed of romantic subject matter, arranged for my own delectation, scathing contempt for the commonplace and ordinarily ugly.

21 January *Sydney*. Christopher Hogwood[2] is in Australia. He took me to lunch, and we talked for hours. He gave me some recordings—Vivaldi, Mozart etc.—and I gave him a copy of *Vagabond Scholars*. He is one of the few people I know who has that attitude to leisurely talk which seems to have been quite lost to the succeeding generation.

2 February James Fairfax told me of a surprise phone call from Malcolm Fraser (the PM). Fraser wished to know if James would be interested to buy a painting by me. One of those decorative gold-leaf ones. Oddly enough, as I was writing this, the radio news announced Mr Fraser's decision to call for a double dissolution of parliament and hold elections on 5 March. At the same time the present leader of the Opposition, Mr Hayden[3], has stood down as leader of the Labor Party to make way for Hawke[4]. Hawke being regarded both as an enemy of business as well as very popular, shares on the Stock Exchange fell. Ah well. I fear that a Labor victory would further exacerbate industrial unrest, thus prolonging this Depression and bringing even greater inflation.

12 February My mind these days yearns to paint, but supplies me with no ideas. I am beginning to wonder if that flow of visual imaginings has dried up forever, like sexual desire and the love of what I see around me.

Last week of February and first week of March A continued absence of creative activity. Nearly all the days given over to reading entertaining useless novels. *Yet*, in just one or two small hours in company of friends a passive hopefulness I may be rescued from my negativism. Lynne Clarke took me to dine at Tony Bilson's[5] Kinsella's restaurant. Marvellous food and wines. Kinsella's, until Tony took it over, was Sydney's best known funeral parlour. The *art nouveau* decorations of the reception room where we dined is an unaltered and rather mad example of that décor.

Another day, lunching at Rex Irwin's gallery I met David Malouf[6], the writer, who was very entertaining.

The elections resulted in a strong Labor win: I'm sorry. I expect even worse times than we've been going through. Hawke's fascinating personality I think won him the victory.

Third week of March *Queensland.* I flew up to Brisbane. An exhibition of twenty works[7] for Philip Bacon. Philip does things in great style: my pictures were well framed and displayed. There was quite a crowd at the opening and thirteen pictures sold. Old friends (unremembered faces) and a few bores. And one strange and lovely surprise, a pleasant looking rather ordinary middle-aged man presented himself. It was Colin. Colin Brown with whom I fell in love so long ago at Merioola, and whose memory has always been sweet.

Laurence Daws drove me to the rough cottage at Beerwah in the Glass House Mountains. I was up by sunrise, watching from a verandah the skyline of strangely shaped mountains form an arabesque across the horizon. And when it was light enough I began drawing. At last I was working again! I was very happy there. We smoked and drank too much.

I was very pleased with the work I did—several landscapes and three interiors looking out on many trees and mountains. And a sketch of the one and only street of Beerwah—palms and great lush trees sprouting devouringly about the ramshackle little shops—the Kozy Boutique, the Supa Market and Marlene's Coiffeur. Laurie made some drawing and oil sketches of me.

Third week of April *Sydney*. Michael White (Madé Wijaya) from Bali came, bringing a letter, the longest I've ever received from any of my Balinese—a very complete expression of affection, gratitude and that deep respect as for an ancestor—for to them I was very truly a *Tuan*. A lord, and more than that—a father as well as a sort of benevolent demon—demigod. The absurdity is not my own self-praise. It is what I was, what I remain in their memory. It makes me happy to read his understanding that I provided a very good life from childhood to young manhood, and gave him affection, sympathy and understanding in these years.

16 May Margaret Olley's dinner to welcome Jocelyn Rickards visiting this country after a 30-year absence was something like a historic occasion. Yossie was a surprise to me: I'd expected a gaunt, smart adept in that malice we all practised with the idea it was wit—instead (I would not have recognised her) she is now *almost* roly-poly. Elegantly plump Rubensesque. Looks young, is calm, amusing. Very likeable and assured. With a truly delightful film-producer husband, Clive Donner.[8] They were both speaking of a project to get a book done on Merioola with lots of Alec Murray's[9] photographs and memories of those of us who lived there. I was rather delighted with Yossie, and with how she now looks: beautifully dressed, not in her former angular sharp smartness, but with a sort of generously flowing simplicity.

Last fortnight of July Disaster, so long held off, struck: and is still pressing me down in pain and weakness and confusion. I am suddenly *very* ill—dying maybe. At Brett Whiteley's incredibly brilliant show of drawings—a chill?—Pneumonic flu? Then days of pain and delirium. The nightmares of these days are peculiarly shot through with fragments of visions of Brett Whiteley's van Gogh drawings. We needn't trouble our minds with the paintings, an uneven gimmicky batch. The landscape drawings, a head, a couple of interiors are among the best seen here in years.

Third week of August I gathered strength for a visit to the Holdsworth—Gisella overflowed welcome. She is so kind, so vulgar, so absolutely the queen of commercialism. We sat in the Gem Room, now settled into an appearance of a half-furnished Katoomba boarding-house sitting room; its walls covered with ill-selected pictures (the ghastly ring-ins making the very few good ones look tawdry)—the dreary bad oriental rugs on the floor with huge price labels. The furniture, cast-off rubbish. At least it was less awful than the Gallery's exhibition room where the most dreadful show of Boyd bronzes[10]—nudes in bras and underpants—was being arranged.

Last week of August to mid-September *Beerwah, Queensland.* With Laurence Daws. It's lovely. It's wonderful. It's coolish, sunny, a bit windy and all the near world lies embraced in the strange gestures of the Glass House Mountains.

Down at the village we attended the annual Charity Sports Meeting! Rustic enough to make one feel decadent!—worldly. Very beautiful horses were on their most formal behaviour in the proud care of equestrians of both sexes dressed like television cowboys and girls. A few—astride blood mares and ladies' hacks—clad in the traditional well-tailored riding outfits. Children everywhere—balloons, ice-creams, hamburgers and a few stalls and sideshows, and most of the countryside's population. Laurie parked the car near where the Fashion Parade was held. The mannequins—local belles bursting with health and wondrous gawky posture—stomped up some steps on the back of a lorry to display frocks of an unselfconscious inelegance.

I made drawings. Here I seem to draw compulsively from a real need, a hunger for it. I am very happy. They are marvellous easy intelligent people. Laurie is an ideal companion for this, since he is painting turn by turn on several large pictures. By a combination of persuasion and nagging he's had me working like the devil on the first big picture I've done in years. It's an interior of the living-room studio with figures, and through doors and windows the horizon's profile of the Glass House Mountains.

We drove to Beaudesert and out a few miles to the St Johns Church, Mundoolun.[11] The occasion was one that had been much gossiped about for months—the marriage of Patrick Hockey[12] (a rich very gay society man—a sort of butterfly in a Rolls Royce: a terribly fashionable painter; an amiable sort of nonsense person) to Margaret de Burgh Persse[13], heiress to a vast fortune and one of the great pioneer cattle stations. It was a most elaborate affair. Three hundred guests had been invited to the ceremony and to the reception afterwards at a marvellous old-style homestead kept up still as it would have been fifty years ago, set in a grand garden embowered in azaleas. The entire event was carried out in a sumptuous extravagant enjoyable style that one would not expect to see in this age. Champagne flowed endlessly, and savouries etc. handed round by numerous servants.

21 November *Melbourne.* I need a medical check, and I'm bored with Sydney. *And* my painting is at a standstill. Attilio met me at the airport.

He is very worried about Ailsa who has not been well and he now knows (although she does not know) has cancer. I went in to town and lunched with the Purveses at the Australian Gallery. A lively gathering with Albert Tucker, younger-looking than ever, pontificating. He speaks as a great man, in measured tones.

December Things go on very much as usual. I read, read, read, and work on a dull watercolour. I'm in that grey pre-Christmas Scrooge[14] mood that descends every year at this time. Hospital has been the usual slow hours of boredom broken into by cheerful interruptions, announcing pills, doses, treatments and quite amazingly saltless meals.

I spent one very strange—in many ways enjoyable but in one sense quite shattering—morning with Richard Griffin at Melbourne Art Gallery, that forbidding Babylonian fortress of a building. Richard wished to view again their recently purchased Rothko[15]. A red colour field painting, which had caused a sensation because of its price. The picture itself continued to shock Richard but privately I thought it rather beautiful but not tremendously stirring. One great room displayed their Blake watercolours and small illustrations. *That* was marvellous. Then there were acres of quite fine but overrated Fred Williams landscapes. Then some vast badly hung overcrowded rooms of their Australian collection. There's a huge room of large contemporary Oz works selected by interstate gallery directors under the title 'Vox Pop'. Ugh. It was *boringly* bad.

Still, these horrors notwithstanding, there would have been enough fine things among the trivia and travesty to leave me happy, had it not been that of my own art there was not a trace. I thought, have I really failed so utterly? I was very downcast. I have been thinking that probably even those who once thought highly of my work have now forgotten, or see it as something quite out of favour and uninteresting.

Attilio's hospitality on this visit left me very much out in the cold. Or so it seemed. His time apart from being necessarily devoted to poor Ailsa was devoted entirely to poker games. I felt like an unwanted poor relation being dutifully received but neglected.

1984

8 January *Sydney*. It's quite a relief to be back in my own room, looking after myself, doing my own cooking and shopping for the things I like. Just now it's tender steaks, plums, nectarines and mangoes.

Second week of February Lou came and took me to the exhibition of 20th-century paintings from the Solomon and Peggy Guggenheim collections.[1] It made for me the best day I've spent, it seems, for years—such pictures!

I think I shall cease keeping a diary. My life is not interesting enough to justify it. The revelations in these pages show a sick old man whose talents decay with his body: whose reactions to daily existence are boredom and self-disgust: who feels for people a weary indifference or outright dislike; whose loving warmth is reserved for very few. A diary such as this reveals the diarist as a very nasty creature—to have such low opinions and reactions to those who befriend him.

First week of March Went with Margaret Olley to inspect the little house she's found for me—No.1 Belmore Place, Paddington, in a little lane just behind the Oxford Street shops. It *looks* all right. Rather quaint: freestanding, with a scrap of garden in front and a battered tin fence surrounding it. A two-storey old house with a tiny wrought-iron balcony: pokey two rooms downstairs and a spacious kitchen. Somewhat primitive shower room and WC in a tiny yard off the kitchen. Upstairs—narrow, steep dangerous stairs—a small front bedroom and a large studio room with very good light. The windows look out on picturesque battered old houses and little lanes. Rather nice.

Mid- to late March and April Things have happened that have quite altered the way I live, and returned me to a much happier state of mind. Moving house was a benevolent cataclysm. Friends were helpful—and especially my sister Gwen, who was positively heroic and came for days, doing odd carpentering jobs, shopping, driving me about to antique shops to buy chairs, chests of drawers, bookshelves—in fact, all the things I was obliged to purchase because Attilio and Ailsa were very reluctant to let me have my sea-chests or any of the other elegances they've had for so long. I cannot forgive that. Buying the sort of thing I like to have around—kelim rugs and all the rest of it—was very costly at a time I was short of money.

First week of July It is uncomfortably cold these days, and this house I like so much is really rather ramshackle. Draughts from under doors, damp and so on. I rise early, chilly, make breakfast, go out to buy the day's necessities in Oxford Street, return home and sometimes paint. Interiors—still life. It goes slowly but well, I think. And dig in the garden. And read for hours. Then sleep nearly all afternoon.

Apart from painting there are few breaks in the routines of daily life. I attend the pub most evenings for an hour or two: a little beer and much tedious talk. Dark falls early. At sundown I walk the chilly hundred yards down Underwood Street to the London Tavern and slowly, gloomily drink several glasses of beer. Sometimes there is someone good to talk to, but usually the company is somewhat beneath me, few artists go there but one or two writers. And an actor or two. Also chumps of loud trendy pop musicians and their hangers-on, youngish yet peculiarly unattractive. Beards, moustaches and long locks, or strange frizzed-up effects prevail among the masculine element. The young girls too often glue their hair in spikes dyed strange orange, green and purple shades. Not *all* of them of course, but enough to make one observe a quite simple hairdo with relief. A *few* conscientiously liberated women frequent the Tavern, emanating an atmosphere of office-girl lesbianism: and a few amateur predators of chains melting into fat or wrinkles who make a point of being 'good sorts' and laughing terribly raucously. But after the days of solitude the company warms the mind a little.

The little Tavern sketches I make there perhaps will in the end form the composition of a larger work I have in mind. Those people I have described are really nothing very significant—their main virtue seems that their quirks and obsessions loom larger than their abilities, and are just enough to elevate them above the ordinary. And my need of bearable company for a couple of hours in the evening is great.

Those of us who used to drink at the Windsor Castle pub in the sixties remember a lost Bohemia of real artists—John Olsen and the rest, now scattered, lost or dead, or living like remote myths, seldom appearing; and when they do almost unrecognisably disguised as distinguished men with white hair and worldly airs.

8 July I attended Olsen's book launching at the Sydney Museum[2]. There in an echoing hall lit from cases dramatically displaying thousands of elegantly grotesque bird, fish, reptile and animal skeletons, a considerable crowd of the elite were gathered to listen to speeches and sip drinks and eye a quite extravagant buffet where chefs and waiters dispensed sandwiches and little hot pastries. Quite a few old art-faces milled around among publishers, anthropologists and ethnologists, art dealers and the like. Photographers bounced about, crouched; flashlights flashed.

And there was Olsen, warmly ebullient. But my feet were aching and frozen on those marble floors. So after talking a while with him and Geoffrey Dutton I sneaked away before the oratory began. I took a taxi and went to lunch with Lynne—her house bright with winter sunlight. Everyone talked endlessly about theatre and films which are not very interesting to me. Nevertheless I liked being there as always.

23 September I attended the launching of the folio of ten lithograph portraits of people prominent in the arts which Lou organised. It was at the Holdsworth Galleries, well attended. He made a speech, brief, pleasant and to the point, introducing the Premier, Neville Wran[3], who launched the folio with his usual competence.

Judy Cassab is a pleasant woman; the lithographs are dull, weak—worse, they are very poor likenesses of a group of people many of whom have remarkable faces—most of them were present. Sir Robert Helpmann, Morris West[4], Lloyd Rees, Peter Sculthorpe, Sutherland[5], Sir Sidney Nolan, Tom Keneally[6], myself.

29–30 September Attilio suddenly arrived from Melbourne for the long weekend. He spent some hours with me discussing our differences and have more or less solved them, although much of what had so infuriated me was left unexplained—nor ever will be explained I think. As for Ailsa, her case is desperate.

We drove out to Vaucluse House, that old site of enchantments that always delights me. The wisteria was still in bloom, and azaleas and camellias: it was an exquisite sunny day with a very chilly wind. There were few people—we spent some time in the beautifully restored old house, now fully furnished with its original furniture. And then on to Watsons Bay where I lavished money on a most delicious luncheon at Doyle's Restaurant[7]—splendid oysters, heavenly chowder of crab, calamari etc. and a good white wine. All sorts of circumstances made it a very happy day.

11 October I continue to be—possibly fatuously—pleased with myself and my painting. The absorption with still life goes on each day, working from 8.30 a.m. with occasional breaks of an hour or two for lunch. The spring days are lovely. The garden blooms like a medieval tapestry. My body's aches and pains, though constant, recede from conscious discomfort in the presence of such simple pleasures.

This morning it was as though midsummer had suddenly arrived unannounced. I made my tortoise progress up the sweltering lane to Oxford Street to buy meat and vegetables at 9.30 a.m. and then to the literary agents Curtis Brown's[8] office to talk over the contracts for *Art in a Classless Society*[9] and *Gunner's Diary*, *Painter's Journal* (in one volume)[10]. Already favourable publicity is appearing in the press. Fame?

23 October All urgencies except painting are put aside. But painting goes on joyfully every day from early morning when I rise with the sun, inspect the wonderfully burgeoning garden, make breakfast and begin work. The still life and Tavern paintings continue to absorb me. During those hours of light the only interruptions I allow are Richard's occasional lunchtime visits. We have a beer and a grill at the Tavern, and much ebullient talk of the melodramas of publishing.

1985

January to mid-February In addition to my regular illnesses I was struck down by some terrible virus sickness and confined to bed, too weak for any activity at all. The ones who did the marketing for me were Lynne Clarke and Gisella—the latter bringing great pots of chicken broth and boiled fowls.

I see nothing to rejoice in being 70. Only a fool would be glad. Aches and pains, irritations, misjudgements and boredoms make up so much of my dreary days of old age. Yet one joy is constant—painting. These last few months I've painted every day except when I've been too ill. Working almost exclusively on big still life watercolours of the things about me. And my happiness is that these works are very alive and exciting, and good as anything I've ever done.

25 March *Melbourne*. The Australian Galleries show's[1] opening. It looked really splendid. To my great delight John Olsen came over from Adelaide to see it: full of his usual wit and energy. We all went to drink coffee whilst he was fitted for clothes at a tailor's. Elegance is the keynote just now. I'm slightly abashed at my shabbiness.

A lot of people came that night to the gallery, and sixteen of the paintings sold. Best of all John Olsen bought one of them—that still life of banksias and a blackened billy. It's something of an honour when a fellow artist of outstanding talent likes one's work enough to buy it.

2 July *Sydney*. My God—Richard! Damnable cancer. It's a despairing affair, loving him so much as a friend. 'They were going to do terrible things. Surgery. I *won't* have it. I'm a coward.'

'You mean you'll just let the cancer take its course?'

'Well, I'm seeing a naturopath. He says garlic is very good for it. So I'll eat lots of garlic.'

A *naturopath*! A garlic diet—I am deeply upset about all this. Actually I sympathise with and understand Richard's lack of faith (if that's what it is) in surgeons. His fear and revulsion, his refusal to submit to indignity.

His faith is in *books*. Also in me, a genius, he believes. That is probably much stronger than a faith in garlic.

But he'll die, poor fellow: and die in pain with all his good nature and affection and love of life. Gentle and defenceless: utterly impractical, choosing garlic and a naturopath rather than a public ward with starched nurses and the surgeons with shining knives.

2 August A call from some sort of cousin whom I've never met and never heard of (nor had he heard of me until recently, he said). He invited me to a family get-together of the descendants of our first forebear—a convict at that—in Australia: Uriah Moses. It will be held at Macquarie Park, which I *suppose* is at Windsor, where the poor wretch's remains lie in the churchyard.[2] There will probably be about 500 descendants, who are invited to bring their own food and wine (a *very* Moses touch, that!). I'll not go of course. It sounds like the sort of sociability I've avoided all my life.

Late August to early September Some really shattering things have happened. A collector of oriental bronzes is wanting to buy my bronze Dong Son[3] dog. I asked Stuart Purves to get on to Attilio and have him

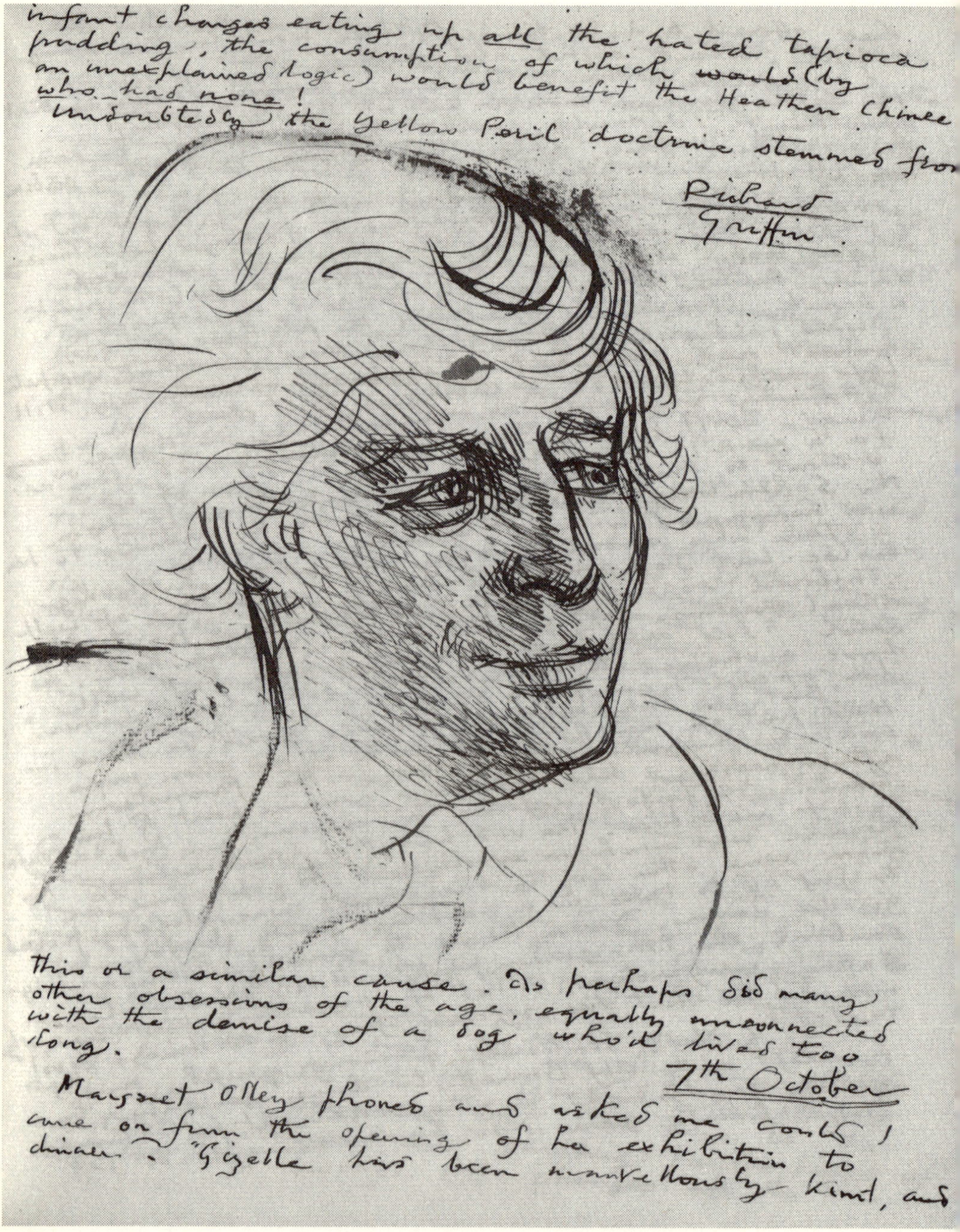

44. 'Richard Griffin' (1982).

pack the dog. Attilio has been grumpy and said he'd send the *entire collection* rather than dribs and drabs, and *would not charge me for storage*. It's too horrifying and disgusting to go on about it. What can I do? Attilio knows there's no room in this poky little house.

I am beginning again to have distressing doubts about my sanity. Of late I've been sicker than ever, and more solitary. Although my paintings seem *to me* to be perfectly sane productions of a clear intelligence, yet happenings like Attilio's behaviour may perhaps be the outcome of some unrecognised aberration of my own failing mind.

Richard says despite much hysteria Attilio seems to be regretting his behaviour which however includes some things beyond recall.

16 September Rather unwillingly, being still sick, I went to Brett Whiteley's new studio—a vast warehouse he's converted into a spectacular place, in Surry Hills[4], which is still a slum district being slowly taken over by the intellectuals. Somehow our visit was not a wild success. There were a lot of unconsidered and inconsiderable small works scattered about his studio and a couple of really superb big drawings laid in with a big full brush. But he himself seemed fidgety and restless.

19 September Dined with Margaret Olley who tomorrow goes to Perth for her exhibition and then off on a protracted tour—down the Nile, on to Turkey. What alarms me for her is the first stop is for four days somewhere in South Africa, at present torn with what amounts to a civil war between whites and blacks, the outcome of many years of shocking injustices.

Last week of September Have been reading, at the slow pace of boredom, Lloyd Rees's autobiography, *Peaks & Valleys*[5]. Prosy, dull, factual, unimaginative yet—one never doubts—sincere and truthful. I'm disappointed, because one can't discern in his words any hint of the poetry, of the serene poetry, of his best landscape paintings. Instead the life he shows us is in total recall of mundane trivia. As a diarist one wonders uneasily if one's daily concerns are equally uninspired.

I met him—and we always exchange a few conventional words since none others are possible with so good and venerated an old creature—on those rare occasions I go to Art Exhibitions. I'm full of respect for that sweet gentle ancient, who usually maunders a bit about what

Roland Wakelin[6] or Norman Lindsay said in the 1920s. His wonderfully distinguished face, glowing beneath a halo of silky, snowy hair, gives an impression even of saintliness. A never-to-be-martyred saint, the patron of middle-class suburban normalcy whose miracle was to perceive and express the innate virtuousness of hills, valleys and streams with nothing untoward to mark the possibility of tears or laughter on the earth.

I have known and liked his work, with its modesty, its real and unassuming qualities, since as a schoolboy I saw his early drawings. His recent paintings don't count. The thin colour washes of oil paint seem formless, amorphous affairs, feebly Turneresque[7]. Nevertheless they are tremendously lauded by the sort who'd applaud, for love of novelty, some pathetic octogenarian dancer sprightly hopping about in *Swan Lake*[8].

9 October I continue painting still life—worked hard to complete one for Richard to take to Melbourne. Richard's reason for the trip is he wants to photograph some of the African drawings Attilio has. He is nervous that Attilio in his present neurotic state will refuse. Of course the pictures are really *mine*, and so is the copyright—etc., etc. How boringly nauseating are the rights and wrongs contingent to a broken friendship.

Late October to early November I'm having my portrait painted for the Archibald Prize by an elderly Russian artist called Vladas Meskenas[9] who talks excitable very broken English louder and faster even than Lou Klepac. He descended on me more-or-less out of the blue. God knows why I've succumbed. Hours of posing wracked every bone in my body, but it was worth it in a way, because two of the big charcoal studies were remarkably good.

1986

February Recently there's been a resurgence of interest in the work of we who survive—men in their nineties now, Lloyd Rees, Desiderius Orban[1] (boring painter, good teacher) and even I, who at the age of 71 am a positively juvenile survivor yet still painting *well* I believe, but too sick and tired to do much else.

June to September My generation of friends and artists are dying off—

not much regretted by me, to whom they've been dead for quite a while anyway, except for Drysdale. Elaborate documentary films are being made about us, and books written. At a luncheon I met Don Bennetts[2], a film-maker, and also Christopher Leonard[3], who has since become a friend. Having shown willing to be part of the scheme, the filming began at my house in Paddington with Bennetts and his film crew.

Stubbornly I clung to my serenity and painted *every* day, even when ill. Went out seldom—once a week perhaps to the London Tavern in the evening. I lived for the most part almost a hermit and saw so little of friends.

First half of October I must *not*, and this is a fierce determination—at least a vague resolve something like an Election Promise—permit myself to allow my journal to fall into neglect again. Yet—what the devil *occurs* in my life beyond the daily struggle to produce deathless masterpieces? Richard visits, concerned about my poor health, ignoring his own stomach cancer (which seems to be under control). He still drives me to despair—so affectionate and impractical. But things are decidedly better for him.

John Olsen made one of his fairly frequent raids on Sydney. Asked me to lunch, along with Chris Leonard, at a notoriously expensive restaurant (a place I dislike). The food was good.

'I've been asked to sound you out if you'd accept the Painters and Sculptors Society's[4] medal, like Lloyd Rees,' he said.

'I'd consider myself much honoured,' I replied, 'so long as I'd not be obliged to attend a banquet!'

Late October More filming—a day of it: much more of this sort of thing will be the end of me. Everything turns into lunches. A deliciously restful lunch of pigeons with Lynne. Then after the filming a Chinese luncheon at the Quay looking over at the splendid Opera House—good food and fairly good company, but too much of it.

These sort of people when they are not actually actively using their abilities in film-making *all* talk at once, loudly, never seeming to listen to one another and I suppose it comes from being born in the television era.

31 December To lunch with James Fairfax. We had a few drinks before lunch on the balcony upstairs with its beautiful view of a wide expanse of the harbour. Grey waters flecked with foam whipped by a brisk wind that rushed with the many yachts: the swift sails arching like hundreds of new moons. Wonderful, wonderful. And we—it seemed to me—a minute group of pleasurably chattering dwarfs with our drinks and social charms. And the guest of honour Harry Tatlock Miller, whom I've not seen for years. Out here on a visit. White-haired now, retired from the Redfern Gallery to live in a cottage in Warwickshire.

This luncheon was an occasion to enjoy very much. A gathering of people who speak the language of my time: a currency of ideas, events and wit casually expressed. The only bad thing was, I was feeling ill and exhausted as I do most of the time. The body is a burden of continued aches and discomforts. To breathe is like physical work.

1987

1 January I do the thousand characterless things that add up to idleness—take upstairs the jug now overflowing with rainwater for painting; add a few strokes to an unfinished watercolour—go downstairs again determined to revive my dying diary with something about the emptiness of my life. Switch on the radio to some classical music. Wash some underclothes and put them out *in the rain* to dry.

There is nothing at all to eat in the house beyond a few peaches, plums, nectarines and a mango. In the sodden weed-infested patch of neglected garden outside the kitchen door one vigorous fruit tree is overloaded with unripe tamarillos.

12–15 January At last, long last, the dead dull weight on my mind has lifted somewhat, and I've been painting, and consequently less distressed. Less weighed with a fear for my sanity. An American negro from Honolulu, Al Irby, poses for me about once a week. A pleasant fellow for company but not much of a model—I use his actual appearance as a sort of departure point for the images brushed on the picture.

Richard comes in about twice a week, does shopping for me which is a boon in this uncomfortable hot humidity. I worry about him for he's looking pretty haggard although as loud and confusing and full of self-induced melodrama. I think this cancer will kill him in a few months. Of all my few friends the maddest and most generous-hearted and illogical. As incapable of either honesty or dishonesty. Incapable also of telling the truth because as he says 'it might upset people'. He spares no time for common sense. His muddles and fictions are never separated from affectionate friendship, love of books, delight in his newly discovered talent as a bookbinder.

February I paint, I read, I listen to music, cook, go to sleep—day after day. Now and then Don Bennetts comes along with Christopher Leonard and I have to go through a few more of the boring discomforts of being filmed. And after that the worse discomfort of another lunch with their unutterably tedious conversation. Nice fellows, but—a different world whose satisfactions are as foreign to me as Libyan politics or American ideals.

The pleasantest circumstance of recent times is the fondness I've come to feel for Al Irby. No good as a model, but he loves gardening and goes at it joyfully and already my little garden has lost its air of weedy neglect. Al is a gentle quietly spoken soul and already a good friend.

In three weeks only one significant event—the publishing of Bob Hughes's long-expected book *The Fatal Shore*. Superbly readable, well researched, and delving particularly into one aspect of our convict past—that of the Irish convicts—which has been noticeably neglected by other conventionally academic historians. Bob's history for me contained many revelations, a great number of them personally applicable to my attitudes and points of view on aspects of Australian life which I now see as belonging to a class quite estranged from mine. I'm tremendously impressed. One senses an extra intensity in numerous passages concerning the suffering Irish that may come from family traditions (the Hugheses are Irish Catholic). Anyway, I wrote him an enthusiastic and appreciative letter.

1 March At long last the meeting with Bob Hughes came to pass. Lynne had arranged it at her house—an intimate party: Bob arrived with some mud crabs. He is more positive and forceful than of yore and so clearly fond of us all as part of his youthful development. The sudden great success of *The Fatal Shore* has imbued him with extra confidence. There was much reminiscing about the old days.

It had been raining and was cool. Scents from the garden—ginger plant in flower and datura wafts through the French windows.

Late March to early April No painting. Idleness. Currently, there's a series of radio broadcasts on Patrick White. Hearing extracts from his writings read aloud I was very impressed—as I'd never been reading those books to myself. Even so there's nothing *enjoyable* about listening in on White's horrible world populated by loathsome people motivated by mutual contempt or dislike. And when, without abandoning his general denigration of humanity, Patrick ventures on 'socially significant' portrayals of the lower orders, the result resembles a *Punch* piece in cockney dialect. In a piece about two derelict women searching through garbage bins the effect is funnily repulsive and unreal. But so lacking the compassionate repulsion that would arise from personal observation one supposes White has never ventured from his own protected environment to *see* his subjects and communicate with them.

18 April Inspired by a cool and very wet Easter I'm delighted to be back painting again. Shoppers in Oxford Street are noticeably mixed, with country people in broad-brimmed hats and riding boots a pleasant contrast to weirdly dyed hair in spikes and comic unisex costumes. So many young men aspire to look authentically female whilst women tend to female impersonation.

Last week of April The diabetes is becoming worse—partly my own fault, since the dozen or so pills I take daily are hardly an antidote to neglect of diet and a passion for ice-cream. I do so greatly need the serenity of days listening to music, reading, contemplating the vagaries that lead to creative invention for painting.

Recently Richard introduced James Whitington[1], who prints and publishes etchings etc. An agreeable youngish man who spent a whole morning chatting, having brought me some etching plates to work on. Reluctantly I've made an attempt. A satirical composition showing Brett Whiteley at work in a studio crowded with his gang of parasites and drug-pushers.

24 May DISASTER, I've somehow injured fingers of my LEFT hand. Perhaps the hand will right itself? I've been trying to work on a plate today, my fingers lack whatever it is that enables them to hold pen or stylus firmly. I write this hoping the exercise will restore to my left hand its former skill. O God my left hand. My life.

25 May What shall I *do*—what *can* I do? There are no friends I can rely on who would be of practical help. My life does not touch theirs at any point now, and in any case they have their own affairs to attend. That goes for Lynne and Olley for whom I am, I dare say, no more than a pleasant memory of times when I was worth knowing. *Now* I am certainly less than interesting. I don't blame them, for I myself never put out for feeble old invalids. Richard of course still comes, brings me novels to read and talks a deal of self-praise and drowns me in senseless lies and still cheats and embezzles all my royalties. He is remarkably like Isherwood's character Mr Norris[2].

28 May I had a rather remarkable visit from a French scientist—a Dr Michael Lefebvre who came by appointment bringing a bottle of Moet. With an art dealer friend, also French. He—Lefebvre—wanted to commission me to design a tapestry. It was to be an official French gift to this nation for the bicentenary, the subject the voyage of La Pérouse[3]. But alas, no. I couldn't face a commission now.

Subsequently I showed him my little etching, not expecting an enthusiastic reaction because really they are not madly exciting or important. However Dr Lefebvre was very definitely interested. He made me a very acceptable and unusual proposition, first explaining that the nature of his art collection comprised the studies and sketches for each work of art. He has offered to buy all the artist's proofs of the etchings and preliminary pen sketches plus a quarter of the completed editions!

2 July A quite unavoidable dinner party after the opening of ancient Lloyd Rees's exhibition. *Twenty* bloody people including politicians and numerous Art-politicians and opportunists wishing to suck a drop of blood from Rees's still-rising fame. Ah for a lamb chop in my own quiet tedious company. The great dinner party started late—in a very grand and elegant mansion facing the Centennial Park. There were numerous fine paintings on the walls, and fine 19th-century furniture and numerous servants so discreet as to be invisible as they filled one's champagne glass.

I was already longing for bed when we trooped in to dine on duckling at 10 o'clock. It went on and on. Presently Lou Klepac made a speech comparing Rees to Turner, the comparison, inspired by the watery vagueness of Rees's late work (the old man is nearly blind). Rees was on his feet before we'd done applauding Klepac. 'Now what was I talking about?' There was some tolerant laughter.

It's bad of me to mock the old man now he's long past his best. Besides, his absurdities today come from encouragement (or pressures applied) by various dealers, publicists, journalists etc. who profit in purse and reputation by pushing the old man into public performances.

12 July 'Genius,' some celebrity once declared, 'is an infinite capacity for taking pains'.[4] And *that* is surely an aspect of it which has been most neglected by the numerous Australian geniuses who litter the road to fashionable reputation. If *I* were asked I'd say that in my own personal experience *Genius is an infinite capacity for self-deception.* And so I suppose looking at proofs of the twenty or so plates I've etched in the last few months. To me they appear excellent.

Yesterday I walked to the polling booths and voted. The general elections don't seem to have thrown up any remarkable leaders in any party. I voted Liberal.[5] A dull lot. The general theme of all parties is the Reduction of Taxes and the nation's regrettable economy. Apart from money matters most politicos strive to move the warm hearts and scintillating intelligences of the Australian public by shouting praise of tennis, football and cricket. After voting I bought a book of Goya's *Tauromaquia.* I'll confess I'd have preferred the *Caprichos* or *Los Proverbios.*[6]

26 July God, what a bore the art dealers' side of the money valuation of art is!—it deeply depresses me. I must guard against becoming quite submerged in the trivia that floods an otherwise empty existence—empty of anything other than creative work. Old age's serenity is the ability to admire without desire. But impotence begets some very erotic dreams. I awake half-smothered by the loving caresses of well-remembered brown boys who now are middle-aged men whose offspring are of an age for loving.

Not for me, alas! Instead I worry about draughts from ill-fitting doors: a leaking hot-water system, damp floors. Tut tut!

10–11 August *Melbourne.* Richard and I flew down together. At Australian Galleries a great crowd smiling non-stop. Many congratulations. It went on and on. Twenty-nine of the forty-five pictures sold on the first night. They looked very fine. The greatest success I've ever had to date.[7]

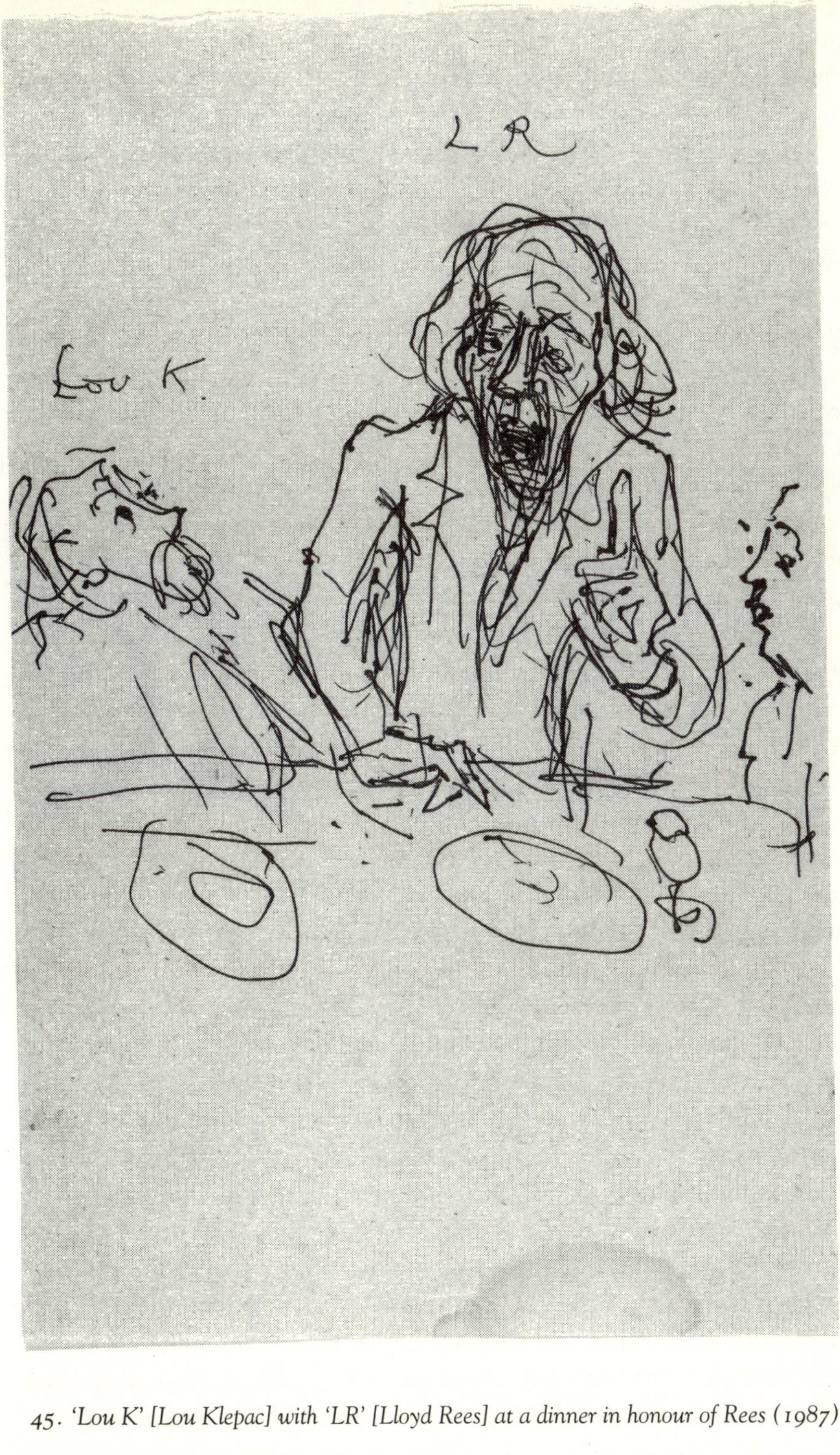

45. *'Lou K' [Lou Klepac] with 'LR' [Lloyd Rees] at a dinner in honour of Rees (1987).*

11–14 August *Sydney*. I'm glad to be back in this draughty damp little Paddington house so quiet and solitary. It's beautifully quiet and serene here: the days are getting warmer. In the garden a hyacinth or two, daffodils, camellias, snowdrops etc., and Al working his war on weeds. I work a little, lazily, on another etching.

September to October These last months have been the most desperate, despairing and painful of my whole life. A lot of illness culminating in a stroke, *left* hand and leg paralysed. I cannot stand or walk without help. But Al Irby, who has become a close friend, looked after me day and night with understanding and compassion, for I could not even piss without assistance.

Rang dear brother Ten, Gwen got us a hire car and chauffeur and Al and I drove to Tamworth—stayed ten days with brother—house full of kindness and affection. Meanwhile dramatic stock market crashes worldwide have ruined money and face us all with possibilities of worldwide depression. The art world has anxiously watched Christie's and Sotheby's[8] auctions of Oz paintings. *Mine* and a few others have risen dramatically in price. So far I am not much affected by the stock market crash.

Helpless, I feel leprous. A disgusting old man smelling of piss.

5 November My thoughts turned to travel. To go with Al on a short explorative trip where I might rent a bungalow and have a few natives to tend me. Chris Leonard suggested Tonga.

I feel dismally depressed. Suspecting already our project of travel is quite beyond range of my capabilities. Yet... *Tonga*!—even the desire, the half-decision to set off for that imagined tropic Arcadia is a wild hope for a life when pleasant follies are not yet totally submerged in the negativity of this dullard process of disease and approaching death.

7 November Geoffrey Bawa called and gave me photographs of the doors I painted for my bungalow at Brief in those old Ceylon days, the doors are now in his splendid Lunuganga house. Seeing them like this after many years gave me immense pleasure. Firstly as evidence of how good an artist I was, even in such frivolous decoration. And secondly to see my work treasured and highly regarded still by a collector and connoisseur of Geoffrey's standing. In addition my feelings are widened by nostalgia and consciousness of long-lasting friendship. The years and the oceans that divide us from friends are of small account compared to today's unpunctualities and silly irritations.

The hours crawl on, nothing to vary them but glimpses through door and window of bright sunlight on bright flowers. I cover pages with hopeful scribbles until hope dies of ennui. No one calls.

Mid-November Over the last few days I've made several attempts at figure drawings. If Chris or James Whitington call, their talk is like those demonic distractions one sees pestering St Anthony in medieval paintings. Bats with frog bodies and lizard-legged saucepans with lids making hats for solemn donkey's heads while saintly Antony pores over a huge holy tome among the rocks and dead trees of desert scenery.

Yet I do irritably relish their company as an alternative to arid solitude.

Having mildly bitched a bit about the harmless proclivities of those who from kindness have given of their time to alleviate my miserable solitude, I've employed my shattered talent in painfully depicting a certain crude sexual allure in a wishful image of a nude primitive Tongan tapa maker who may even turn out to inhabit those islands and exhibit his manly charms for my delectation.

16 November Christopher and James both have to cross the Harbour Bridge to come here in the evening. The bridge nowadays on account of shocking traffic congestion divides rather than links the Northern and Southern halves of Sydney. So *their* convenient time for visiting is most inconvenient to *me*—because diabetes demands punctuality for insulin injections *and* meals. Thus I'm stuck with them. I hate eating while two pairs of eyes follow every spoonful.

30 November Today Chris Leonard called on his return from Canberra. He said Mollison's[9] Retrospective show of 400 Fred Williams paintings was an awful mistake. An indigestible repetitious *oeuvre*. Perhaps he hasn't been dead long enough. His gouache sketches of landscape are very fine, in fact infinitely preferable to the works developed from them. In all, my opinions on this painter would be ill-received in Victoria where he has many rather aggressive admirers. A genius etc. (an abominable third-rate talent, say I). But there is, in Australian art, comical inclination to regard a large canvas as 'a major work'. Size is most important. Fred Williams might well be commended for his acreage.

6 December Disaster!—almost. In the night! I must have had another 'slight' stroke. Rose at 6 a.m. very dizzy and had a bad fall. For ages it seemed I could not move. Fear and dread until finally I crawled to the telephone—Lynne, who came with Terry and got a doctor, made coffee, and somehow got me through the morning until Al came. I'm dying I believe and hope for a sleepy, painless demise with less trouble to friends than I give them now. Truly this is a tiresome tedious last chapter to an interesting and amusing life. It now appears to be an imposition of distress on the few who are fond of me—who once found me very entertaining, if absurd. Now ashamedly am egocentric to the last gasp.

1988

January to April Nothing especially good has happened in all this time. Few pictures painted. Life continues—a weary, often painful thing. So few friends left. Al Irby is the fondest face I see. I've broken at last with Gisella Scheinberg. Our last meeting convinced me that Holdsworth Gallery is no longer suitable for me. It is too big and badly organised. Certainly it will be hard to find another gallery suitable to my present needs since now there are as many bad art shops as ignorant dealers and terrible painters.

6 May Bitterest of all are my thoughts of Attilio, a long past love and friendship—regrets even for my generosity to that thievish ingrate.[1]

June to October Months slide by. Nothing changes much. I draw and paint with a sort of desperation. There is to be a great banquet at the university. The governor will present me with a Medal and speeches.[2] Formal clothes!—O God!—and nearly everything of discomfort. The seat of honour is a bed of nails but I am not ungrateful for this tardy honour, mostly I'm afraid my physical weakness may betray me publicly. Best of all, out of the blue a delightful 14-year-old model so once again I've been drawing from the nude and drawing quite well—allowing for my clumsy right hand.

Al spends most days with me. He has been adding to the pot-plant gardens and courtyard.

Does Age bring Wisdom?—it certainly teaches one to value the trivia which help the hours to pass.

19 December My long list of former friends has shrunk to three: Al and James Fairfax and Barry Pearce. The others are unworthy of the bitterness they generate in my desolate days of solitude.

Soon, soon I *must* die. Goodbye world of lovely colours and amiable nudes. Aloha death, long dull dreamless night. Ah, mortality I *know* you are hiding behind that grey curtain. My soul is transparent. Heliotrope pink but not nearly as invisible.

1989

23 June Let us marry O Kings
Let us marry O Lords
Hold me against the clutch of time
For I am, but a passer-by!!
Be gentle, this bed.
These bones are too old
Remember me, not with hate
Oh the pain in these veins,
How I wish I could die
Yet every fibre in my body screams out to live.
Oh Lord, give me a robe
Remember me thou art your servant
When I die take me to heaven
Hold me, hold me, for I'm falling
Honour all my wishes I beg of thee
Lord, this pen in my hand
For this is my last breath
Please I beg of thee, take me…
O God dear God.
Oh Lord give me a few more days
I beseech thee,
If you do, the pain will be a blessing
Oh my Lord, my body's in great pain
Take me, take me, it's for my best interest.[1]

12 August At peace with everybody. Much affection to Gisella Scheinberg, and other members of the group of society whom I have been so fond of for many years. My happiness about my relations with my brother and other blood relations close to me. And so again goodbye sweet world and goodbye dear friends who have had an awful lot to put up with me for 75 years—and are thought of with peaceful and happy memories now as I shall soon be dead.

And I hope the world will consider itself bloody lucky to be left with most of my best work. I'm at peace with the world, thank God—at least I'm not at war with any particular section. And I wish to express an apology for my lack of proper politeness on this important occasion.

13 August 3 a.m. Coffee Meeting, Lord Rochester's room. I (Rochester) am these days a-weary of my life. I am nowadays in bad health and do not expect to live for long. I have made my last will and testimony and have appointed my brother Terence's children to be the heirs to my possession. I think there is no more to mention, and much love to my sister Gwen. It is a sad matter that I have not a great fortune.

NOTES: 1980s

1980

1. *The Farce of Sodom*, play attributed to Lord Rochester (see **1929**, note 15). In 1980 the Gryphon Press published a limited edition of the play, 'with sets and costumes suitable for theatrical performance by Donald Friend'.
2. Australian stage and screen actor (1926–94), whose most internationally famous role was as Pontius Pilate in the Hollywood epic *Ben Hur* (1959).
3. Taking its title from a parable of Jesus in the New Testament (Luke, 15:11–32), Friend's exhibition of prints, drawings and paintings *Prodigal Son's Return* ran at the Holdsworth Galleries from 6 to 25 September.
4. This was the Liberal Party's third successive election victory since 1975. They lost to the ALP in the following election of 1983.
5. Art historian and publisher (born 1936) of Croatian origins. He emigrated to Australia in 1950.
6. Ronald Reagan (1911–2004), fortieth President of the USA and former film actor.

1981

1. Australian gallery owner and cultural philanthropist (born 1947).
2. Friend's exhibition, *Recent Paintings and Drawings*, ran at Philip Bacon Galleries till 25 March.
3. His third of four wives, Diane Millstead (born 1948), Australian-born painter.
4. Jan Senbergs (born 1939), Latvian-born Australian painter and printmaker.
5. A spoof diary by George and Weedon Grossmith published in 1892, set in genteel London suburbia.
6. Eastern suburb of Sydney, 6 kilometres from the city centre.
7. Ruling dynasty of China, 1644–1912.
8. German for 'dance of death', a popular allegorical theme in late-medieval European art.
9. *Songs of the Vagabond Scholars* (1982), translated by Randolph Stow (see **1981**, note 21) and containing fourteen original lithographs by Friend.
10. Jørn Utzon (1918–2008), Danish architect.
11. A production by Robert Helpmann for the Australian Opera. The opera had its première in London in 1735.
12. See **1968**, note 7.
13. After the title of Charles Dickens' novel of 1841.
14. Form of comic theatre that began in Italy in the mid-sixteenth century and was based on improvised performances of sketches or scenarios.

15. *Flaws in the Glass: A Self-Portrait* (1981).
16. Née Reed (1908–76), Australian-born novelist and travel writer who married Sidney Nolan in 1948.
17. Mary Boyd (born 1926), Australian painter and decorative artist who had married painter John Perceval (1923–2000) in 1944.
18. English monarch (1491–1547), who reigned between 1509 and his death, and married six times, executing two of his wives.
19. Legendary gathering of knights at the court of King Arthur, known as Camelot. Merlin was the wise and wily magician.
20. In Sydney's eastern suburbs, 4 kilometres from the city centre.
21. Australian-born novelist (1935–2010), resident in England from 1966.
22. Member of the Confederate States Army of the South in the American Civil War (1861–65).
23. Yvonne Boyd, née Lennie (born 1920).
24. Illustrated book by Friend, published by Gryphon Books.
25. The title characters, respectively, of Shakespeare's play of around 1599–1601, Bram Stoker's novel of 1897 and Bob Kane's comic strip from 1939.
26. In Bulleen, a suburb of Melbourne, 12 kilometres from the centre.
27. Australian art patron (1901–81), and brother of Cynthia Nolan (cf **1981**, note 16).
28. This first series consisted of 27 paintings on the theme of the bushranger, produced in 1946–47. Cf **1961**, note 5.
29. Alternatively titled *The Long Day Wanes*, by Anthony Burgess, and consisting of *Time for a Tiger* (first published 1956), *The Enemy in the Blanket* (1958) and *Beds in the East* (1959).
30. Published in 1944, and featuring a bohemian painter as the central character.
31. Indian-born English novelist, poet and travel writer (1912–90).

1982

1. Beachside suburb in northern Sydney, 32 kilometres from the centre.
2. Devotees of Bhagwan Shree Rajneesh, born Chandra Mohan Jain (1931–90), an Indian mystic who gained an international following for his spiritual teachings.
3. Entrants for the three major art prizes awarded annually by the AGNSW: the Archibald, for portraiture (see **1944**, note 2); the Wynne, for 'the best landscape painting of Australian scenery in oils or watercolours or for the best example of figure sculpture by Australian artists'; and the Sulman, for 'the best subject/genre painting and/or murals/mural project'.
4. Australian stage and screen actress (born 1933), whose career blossomed in England in the 1950s and 1960s. Returning to Australia in the early 1980s,

she ran a theatre as well as a farm on her Queensland property.

5. Emmanuel George Lascaris (1912–2003), Egyptian-born Greek lover of Patrick White. He lived in Australia from 1948.
6. Irish-born painter (1909–92).
7. Australian art-dealer born in India (1941) of British stock, who established his business in the Sydney suburb of Woollahra in 1976.
8. Portrait painter, born in Austria in 1920, and living in Australia since 1950.
9. An archipelago in the South Atlantic Ocean, 460 kilometres south of the Argentine mainland. The islands are a self-governing Overseas Territory of the United Kingdom but Argentina had long claimed sovereignty of them, and in pursuit of this claim, always rejected by most of the inhabitants, mounted an invasion on 2 April 1982. The British government dispatched an expeditionary force to retake the islands, landing on 21 May. An undeclared war was to follow, which finally ended with surrender of the Argentine forces on 14 June 1982.
10. Margaret Thatcher (born 1925), Prime Minister of the UK from 1979 to 1990 and Leader of the Conservative Party from 1975 to 1990.
11. *Ottoline: The Life of Lady Ottoline Morrell*, by Sandra Jobson Darroch, first published in 1975. Lady Ottoline (1873–1938) was an English aristocrat, society hostess and patron of the arts.
12. English monarch (1533–1603), who reigned from 1558 until her death.
13. Australian curator (born 1944), at the AGNSW from 1978. He curated the Friend retrospective there in 1990 and edited its catalogue (see **1946**, note 1).
14. *Ayam2 Kesayangan* was a projected four-volume illustrated work, the general title of which can be roughly translated as 'Beloved Chickens'. Parts of the manuscript text and several of the drawings found their way into publications under different titles.
15. Fernand Léger (1881–1955), French painter.
16. Town in the Darling Downs, 210 kilometres west of Brisbane.
17. About 70 kilometres northeast of Brisbane.
18. Town on the Sunshine Coast hinterland, 80 kilometres north of Brisbane.
19. Town on the Mary River, 250 kilometres north of Brisbane.
20. Coastal town, 290 kilometres north of Brisbane.
21. Victoria Hughes, née Whistler. The couple had married in 1981.
22. Which was to become *The Fatal Shore* (1987). Cf diary entry for February 1987.
23. The official opening of the National Gallery of Australia in Canberra, by Queen Elizabeth II on 12 October.
24. Near the old Friend family property, Glendon (see diary entry for mid-December 1929). Mounting racial tensions in Moree led on 5 December to the death of an Aboriginal man and the arrest of three white men

on charges of manslaughter. (Two of these were later convicted.)

25. In Paddington. It opened in 1976, specialising in works on paper.
26. Fashionable Collins Street department store that contained an art gallery.
27. Vietnamese ceramic style originating in the thirteenth century.
28. Born Alice Lynne Murchinson in New Zealand in 1948. In October 1982 she was sentenced to life imprisonment for the murder of her young daughter, whom she claimed had been taken by a dingo. In 1986 she was vindicated by newly discovered evidence and set free, all criminal convictions against her finally being quashed in 1988.

1983

1. For 1929.
2. English conductor, harpsichordist and music scholar (born 1941), who has championed the use of period instruments.
3. Bill Hayden (born 1933), leader of the Australian Labor Party, 1977–83, and Governor-General of Australia, 1989–96.
4. Bob Hawke (born 1929), Prime Minister of Australia, 1983–91.
5. Australian chef, restaurateur and food writer (born 1944).
6. Australian novelist and poet (born 1934).
7. *Recent Works*, Philip Bacon Galleries, 16 March – 6 April.
8. English film director (born 1926).
9. Australian-born war photographer (1917–2002), who settled in London from 1948 and became a well-known fashion photographer.
10. Guy Boyd (1923–88), Australian sculptor.
11. In the Gold Coast hinterland, 70 kilometres south of Brisbane. The church dates to about 1905.
12. Australian painter (1948–92).
13. Australian grazier and philanthropist (1941–2004), chatelaine of Nindooinbah, her ancestral property near Beaudesert.
14. The miserly central character of Charles Dickens' novella *A Christmas Carol* (1843).
15. *No. 37 (Red)* (c. 1956), by Mark Rothko (1903–70), Latvian-born American painter.

1984

1. *The Moderns*, from the collection of Peggy Guggenheim in Venice (cf **1952**, note 8) and her uncle Solomon R. Guggenheim (1861–1949) in New York. This exhibition was held at the AGNSW and opened by Robert Hughes on 7 February.

2. The older and alternative name for the Australian Museum, opened on its present site in College Street, Sydney, in 1857.
3. Australian politician (born 1926). Labor Premier of NSW, 1976–86.
4. Australian novelist (1916–99).
5. Dame Joan Sutherland (born 1926), Australian soprano.
6. Australian novelist (born 1935).
7. Beachside restaurant specialising in seafood. It first opened in 1885.
8. Curtis Brown Australia was established in 1967. It was a branch of the literary agency established by American journalist Albert Curtis Brown (1866–1945) in London in 1899 and New York City in 1914.
9. A satirical work of Friend's, published by Richard Griffin in 1985.
10. These two works, extracts from Friend's manuscript war diaries of 1942–45, had been published separately—in 1943 and 1946 respectively.

1985

1. *Recent Watercolours and Drawings*. The show ran till 13 April.
2. Cf **1929**, note 16, and diary entry for 11–14 October 1977. As Friend supposes here, the venue for this event is not to be confused with the Sydney suburb of Macquarie Park.
3. A Bronze Age culture, originally centred in the Red River Valley of northern Vietnam, and spreading in the first millennium BC through most of South-East Asia and into the Indo-Malaya Archipelago, including Bali.
4. Inner-city suburb of Sydney, 2.5 kilometres from the centre.
5. Written in collaboration with Elizabeth Butel, and published by Collins in 1985. Cf **1931**, note 7.
6. New Zealand-born painter (1887–1971), who lived in Australia from 1912.
7. In the style of English painter J. M. W. Turner (1775–1851).
8. A ballet with music by Tchaikovsky, premiered in Moscow in 1877.
9. Sydney-based painter (born 1916). His portrait of Friend won the People's Choice Award in the Archibald Prize competition of 1989.

1986

1. Hungarian-born Australian painter, printmaker and teacher (1884–1986).
2. Australian author and documentary film-maker (born 1937). His film *Donald Friend: The Prodigal Australian* was released in 1990.
3. Australian journalist and curator, who started to research a biography of Friend but never completed the project.
4. The Painters and Sculptors Association of Australia, a Melbourne-based lobby group for professional artists, established in 1984.

1987

1. Australian printmaker and painter (born 1951).
2. Anti-hero of Christopher Isherwood's novel *Mr Norris Changes Trains* (1935).
3. Jean-François De Galaup, Comte de La Pérouse (1741–1788), French navigator who led a significant expeditionary voyage across the Pacific Ocean that took in Norfolk Island and Botany Bay but ended in disaster when his ship was wrecked.
4. Commonly attributed to Scottish essayist, satirist and historian Thomas Carlyle (1795–1881).
5. The Liberals lost this election to the ruling ALP under Bob Hawke.
6. The three series of Goya etchings named here were produced respectively in 1815, 1797–98 and 1815–24. (Cf **1944**, note 14.)
7. The Friend show at Australian Galleries ran from 10 August to 1 September.
8. Christie's art auction house was founded in London in the early 1760s, and an Australian branch was opened in 1969. Sotheby's was founded in London in 1744, and an Australian branch opened in 1982.
9. James Mollison (born 1931), Australian gallery director; at the National Gallery of Australia between 1971 and 1990.

1988

1. There were to be some moves towards a rapprochement (if rather grudging on both sides) when Guarracino visited Friend in Sydney in November. This visit is not recorded in Friend's diary but Guarracino has recounted it in interviews with the editor of this volume, and Barry Pearce noted it in his unpublished diary for the period (see the Guide to Sources CD for this edition, available from Text Publishing).
2. The University of Sydney awarded Friend a medal for services to art.

1989

1. This 'prayer' was dictated to a nurse at Friend's bedside. It is published verbatim here from her handwritten transcript, which was forwarded to Barry Pearce.

ACKNOWLEDGEMENTS

My chief debts are to the Trustees of the Trusts of the Will of the late Donald Friend, and to various institutions and individuals who currently hold, or have recently held, documentary and illustrative material used in this volume: the National Library of Australia; the National Gallery of Australia; the Mitchell Library, State Library of NSW; the Reference Library, AGNSW; the Australian Library of Art, State Library of Queensland; the Queensland Art Gallery; David De Long; Gwen Friend; David Friend; Attilio Guarracino; Lou Klepac; Robin Lucas (on behalf of the late Geoffrey Dutton); Barry Pearce; and Mike Rubbo. Without their generous permission to publish or republish manuscripts, drawings or taped interviews in their possession, this edition could not have got off the ground, nor taken the shape it has. The individuals listed here also gave freely of their time and expertise in answering queries, suggesting leads and generally encouraging the project.

To the staffs of the above institutions—and also those of Fallingwater, Pennsylvania; the School of Design, University of Pennsylvania; the Boston Public Library; the State Library of Victoria; the National Archives of Australia; the Australian Broadcasting Corporation—I am indebted for all manner of assistance and support, often beyond the call of duty. The following deserve my particular thanks in this regard: at the NLA, Maureen Brooks (peerless in her knowledge of the Friend milieu), Margy Burn, Jan Fullerton (Director-General) and Sally Hopman; at the NGA Research Library, Helen Hyland; at the Mitchell Library, Paul Brunton (Senior Curator); at AGNSW, Steven Miller (Archivist); at QAG, Glenn Cooke (Research Curator); at Fallingwater, Justin Gunther (Curator, Buildings and Collections) and Lynda Waggoner (Vice President and Director); at UPenn, John Hinchman (Lecturer, Graduate Program in Historic Preservation) and Suzanne Hyndman; at the NAA (Sydney), Simeon Barlow; and at the ABC, Cathy Bromley (Archives).

For new leads to Friend's student years abroad (1936–38), I am grateful to scholars in the UK—Wendy Baron, Richard Shone, Frances Spalding and Matthew Sturgis—and to the following institutions in London: the National Archives; the National Art Library; the British Library; the Tate Library and Archive (Hyman Kreitman Reading

Rooms); and Claire Harrop and Rob Marche at the Learning Centre, Westminster Kingsway College.

To the editors of the National Library's edition of Friend's diaries, Anne (Anna) Gray, now at the NGA, and Paul Hetherington, now at the University of Canberra, I owe a great debt for their pioneering efforts in clearing through the thickets of the original manuscript, and their subsequent advice and assistance to me on all number of matters.

For indispensable financial and/or institutional support during the course of the project, I wish to thank two departments of the Australian National University—the History Program of the Research School of Social Sciences and the Humanities Research Centre—for electing me to successive fellowships in 2007–08, and the School of Historical Studies, University of Melbourne, for continuing to renew my honorary Senior Research Fellowship there. This project was also assisted by the Commonwealth Government through the Australia Council, which awarded me a grant in 2007. My agent, Mary Cunnane, has been very vigilant in making sure the wolf has been kept from my door during the genesis of this book and in prodding me into action.

The staff at Text Publishing has been exemplary in every respect from the moment I was commissioned to undertake this project. In particular I wish to acknowledge the inspiration and practical advice, in even measure, I've received from publisher Michael Heyward, designer Chong Weng-ho, publicist Jane Novak and editor David Winter.

Editors of other sorts deserve my thanks, either for putting me on the track of Donald Friend in the first place or for granting me space in their publications where I was able to develop some of my ideas about him. These include: the late John Ritchie at the *Australian Dictionary of Biography* (it was when he commissioned me to write the *ADB* entry on one of Friend's earliest companions, Peter Finch, that I first lit on the Friend diaries in manuscript form); Peter Rose at *Australian Book Review*; Jason Steger at the *Age*; Bill Kent, Ros Pesman and Cynthia Troup, who prompted me to contribute an essay on Friend to the book *Australians in Italy*; and Desley Deacon, Penny Russell and Angela Woollacott, who published another version of that essay in their collection *Transnational Lives*.

The list of my friends—or friends of Friend's, including some highly critical ones—who have assisted, counselled, stimulated or challenged me while undertaking this project is all but endless. Several of them I have already mentioned. Others who must be acknowledged are (in alphabetical order): Jane Adamson, Ray Aitchison, Karin Altmann, Chris Andrews, Chantal Babin, Brett Bailey, Ian Baillieu, Marianne Baillieu, Brett Ballard, Paul Baxter, John Bell, Don Bennetts, Ian Biggs, Simon Bishop, Michael Brindley, Ann Brothers, Nicholas Brown, John Buckley, Verona Burgess, Adrian Carton, Chandrabhanu, Janet Chimonyo, Lynne Clarke, Terry Clarke, Carolyn Cliff, Bill Cobbett, Wayne Crothers, Kate Darian-Smith, Jim Davidson, Juan Davila, Michelle de Kretser, Turid de Maré, Paul de Serville, Cheryl Delalande, Dick Denton, Robert Dessaix, Ian Donaldson, Mark Downing, Fraser Fair, Fred Fair, Clive Faro, Kate Fullagar, the late Geoffrey Goldie, Andrew Gosling, Giulia Guiffrè, Grazia Gunn, Richard Haese, Gideon Haigh, David Hansen, Tony Heal, John Heard, Christina Hill, John Hill, Rosalind Hollinrake, Ken Inglis, Bob Iorillo, Shushei Iwamoto, Ben Jones, Nicholas Jose, Fred Kroh, Netta Labb, John Lack, Robert Lee, Madé Madja, Marilyn McBriar, Iain McCalman, Janet McCalman, Brian McFarlane, Geraldine McFarlane, Rosemary Macindoe, Mark McKenna, David McLachlan, Glenys McLaine, John McPhee, Humphrey McQueen, David Marr, Michael Meyler, Ross Moore, Rosanna Morris-Jones, Frank Murphy, Howard Nathan, Kerry Negara, Brenda Niall, Jane Oehr, Philip Olander, Sheridan Palmer, Courtney Pederson, Nicola Pedlingham, Lily Petkovska, Rosemary Piggin, Stuart Piggin, John Rickard, Charles Robb, Claire Roberts, Aldo Radoczy, Carol Radoczy, Charles Rajkovic, Mark Rubbo, Ken Scarlett, Marian Scarlett, Sam Schoenbaum, Maggie Scott, Ann Smith, Barry Smith, Bernard Smith, Graeme Smith, Max Smith, Peter Spearitt, Peter Stansky, Peter Stewart, Lachlan Strahan, Daniel Thomas, John Thompson, David Tredennick, Josie Wadelton, James Whitington, Cynthia Wild, Pam Wild, Lyn Williams, Marguerita Wu, Bob Wyatt, Peter Wyllie Johnston, Eva Wynn, and Francis Zemljak. I regret there is not more space to specify the guidance or hospitality these people have offered me. I am also sorry for any omissions in the list; that these are as inevitable as they are inadvertent is no excuse.

Finally, I must thank my father, who continued after my mother's death to offer me the kind of support that would look like sheer indulgence were it not connected with the kind of intellectual and creative endeavour of which he has been a lifelong champion.

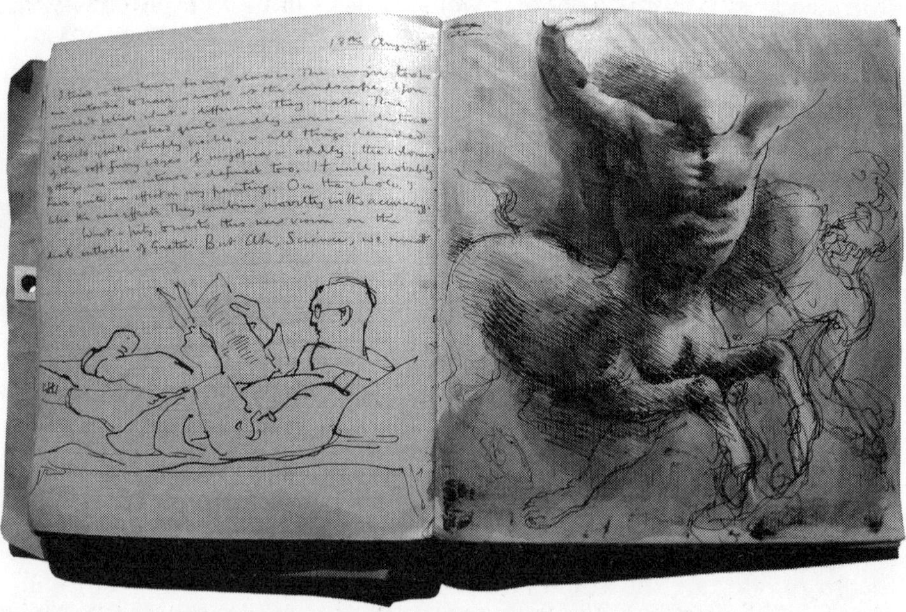

46. *A soldier reading and 'Centaur' (1943).*

LIST OF ILLUSTRATIONS

Titles given by Friend are italicised and in quotation marks. All other titles or parts of titles have been supplied by the editors of this or previously published volumes of Friend's diaries, and are italicised without quotation marks.

The dates in parentheses after the titles refer to the known or likely years of composition.

In the case of illustrations previously reproduced in other publications, the sources cited refer to those publications. In instances where the surrounding text from the original diaries has been reproduced, the manuscript source is also provided. For illustrations reproduced in this volume for the first time, the sources cited are manuscript and picture collections in public or private hands.

The cover illustrations (front, spine and back) are from the recently discovered diaries of 1943 and 1944, NLA MS 5959/52–53, *Los Desastres de la Guerra*, volumes IX and XIV; the diary of 1982–87 (title page), *DFD 4*, p. 535; and a painting at Lunuganga, Sri Lanka.

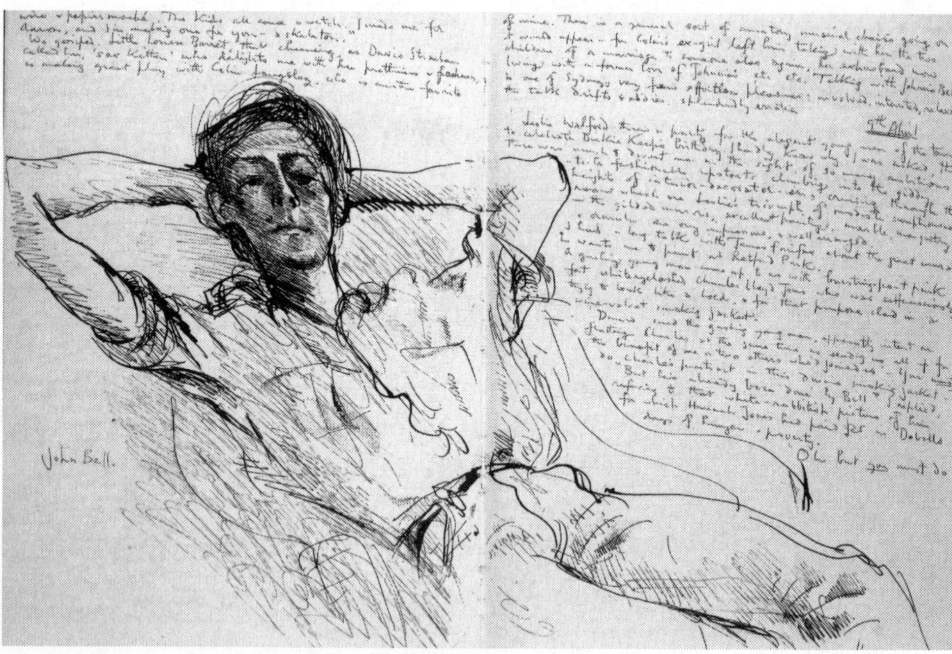

47. *'John Bell'* (1964).

INDEX